HOW TO TUNE AND MODIFY
AUTOMOTIVE ENGINE
MANAGEMENT SYSTEMS

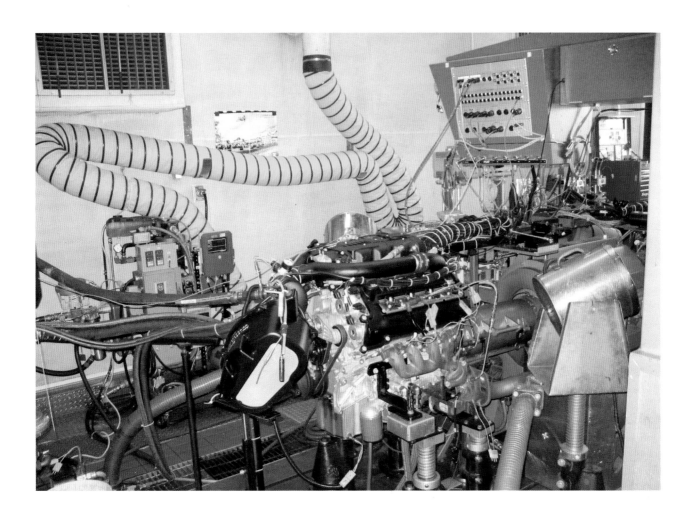

By Jeff Hartman

First published in 2004 as *How to Tune and Modify Engine Management Systems* by Motorbooks, an imprint of Quarto Publishing Group USA Inc., 400 First Avenue North, Suite 400, Minneapolis, MN 55401 USA

Motorbooks titles are also available at discounts in bulk quantity for industrial or sales-promotional use. For details, write to Special Sales Manager at Quarto Publishing Group USA Inc., 400 First Avenue North, Suite 400, Minneapolis, MN 55401 USA.

To find out more about our books, visit us online at www.motorbooks.com.

Library of Congress Cataloging-in-Publication Data

Hartman, Jeff, 1952-
  [How to tune & modify engine management systems]
  How to tune and modify automotive engine management systems - all new edition / Jeff Hartman. — New and Revised.
       pages cm. — (Motorbooks workshop)
   Summary: "How to Tune and Modify Engine Management Systems is Jeff Hartman's follow-up to his best-selling title of the same name. Featuring over 300 photographs and illustrations, this technical manual is a dream for those wishing to upgrade their stock engines"— Provided by publisher.
   ISBN 978-0-7603-4345-6 (pbk.)
  1. Automobiles—Motors—Computer control systems. 2. Automobiles—Performance. 3. Automobiles--Motors—Modification. I. Title.
  TL214.C64H37 2013
  629.25'49--dc23
                                  2013011836

Publisher: Zack Miller
Editor: Jordan Wiklund
Layout: Chris Fayers

Printed in China

10 9 8 7 6 5 4 3

Contents

Introduction 4

CHAPTER 1   Understanding Fuel Delivery . . . 14

CHAPTER 2   Understanding Automotive
             Computers and PROMs   25

CHAPTER 3   Sensors and Sensor Systems. . . 38

CHAPTER 4   Actuators and
             Actuator Systems   56

CHAPTER 5   Hot Rodding EFI Engines 75

CHAPTER 6   Hot Rodding Electronic
             Diesel Engines   92

CHAPTER 7   Recalibrating Factory ECMs   . . 102

CHAPTER 8   Tuning with Piggybacks,
             Interceptors, and Auxiliary
             Components   115

CHAPTER 9   Standalone Programmable
             Engine Management Systems . 129

CHAPTER 10   EMS/EFI Engine Swapping 147

CHAPTER 11   Roll-Your-Own EFI. 159

CHAPTER 12   Installation and
             Start-up Issues. 165

CHAPTER 13   Designing, Modifying, and
             Building Intake Manifolds 171

CHAPTER 14   EMS Tuning 178

CHAPTER 15   EMS Troubleshooting 222

CHAPTER 16   Emissions, OBD-II, and
             CAN Bus 240

CHAPTER 17   Project: Supercharging the
             2010 Camaro SS. 256

CHAPTER 18   Project: Twin-Turbo
             Lexus IS-F. 262

CHAPTER 19   Project: Supercharged
             Jag-Rolet 270

CHAPTER 20   Project: 1970 Dodge
             Challenger B-Block 276

CHAPTER 21   Project: Real-World
             Turbo CRX Si 282

CHAPTER 22   Project: Honda del Sol
             Si Turbo. 294

CHAPTER 23   Project: Turbo-EFI
             Jaguar XKE 4.2 300

CHAPTER 24   Project: Two-staged Forced
             Induction on the MR6 310

CHAPTER 25   Project: Overboosted
             VW Golf 1.8T. 321

CHAPTER 26   Project: Frank-M-Stein:
             M3 Turbo Cabriolet 325

             Appendix 328

             Index. 331

Introduction

This how-to book is designed to communicate the theory and practice of designing, modifying, and tuning performance engine management systems that work. In recent years electronic engine and vehicle management has been among the most interesting, dynamic, and influential fields in automotive engineering. This makes it a moving target for analysis and discussion. Electronic control systems have evolved at light speed compared to everything else on road-going vehicles. This has paved the way for unprecedented levels of reliable, specific power, efficiency, comfort, and safety that would not otherwise be possible.

Simply reconfiguring the internal configuration tables of an electronic engine management system can give the engine an entirely new personality. Changing a few numbers in the memory of an original equipment onboard computer can sometimes unleash 50 or 100 horsepower and release all sorts of possibilities for power increases with VE-improving speed parts and power-adders. But you have to do it right, and that can be a challenge.

THE AUTOMAKERS AND ELECTRONIC FUEL INJECTION AND ENGINE MANAGEMENT

In the case of the car companies, electronic fuel injection arose as a tool that allowed engineers to improve drivability and reliability and to fight the horsepower wars of the 1980s. It also helped them comply with federal legislation that mandated increasingly stiff standards for fuel economy and exhaust emissions. The government forced automakers to warrant for 120,000 miles everything on the engine that could affect exhaust emissions, which was everything related to combustion. In other words, nearly everything. Intelligently and reliably controlling engine air/fuel mixtures within extremely tight tolerances over many miles and adapting as engines slowly wore out became a potent tool that enabled car companies to strike a precarious balance between EPA regulations, the gas-guzzler tax, and performance-conscious consumers who still fondly remembered the acceleration capabilities of 1960s- and 1970s-vintage muscle cars.

Going back further, in the 1950s, engine designers had concentrated on one thing—getting the maximum power, drivability, and reliability from an engine within specific cost constraints. This was the era of the first 1-horsepower-per-cubic-inch motors. By the early 1960s, air pollution in southern California was getting out of control, and engine designers had to start worrying about making clean power. The Clean Air Acts of 1966 and 1971 set increasingly strict state and federal standards for exhaust and evaporative emissions. Engine designers gave it their best shot, which mainly involved add-on emissions-control devices like positive crankcase ventilation (PCV), exhaust gas recirculation (EGR), air pumps, inlet air heaters, vacuum *retard* distributors, and carburetor modifications.

The resulting cars of the 1970s ran cleaner, but horsepower was down and drivability sometimes suffered. Fuel economy worsened just in time for the oil crises of 1973 and 1979. The government responded to the energy crises by passing laws mandating better fuel economy. By the late 1970s car companies

Turbo Chevrolet Corvair engine from the early 1960s. Boost and performance were extremely limited due to mechanical engine management consisting of carburetion and ignition breaker points, with boost pressure limited by exhaust *backpressure*. Later, extremely high-output turbocharged engine output was unleashed with the marriage of efficient turbocharged and electronic fuel injection with digital electronic engine management.

had major new challenges, and they sought some new "magic" that would solve their problems.

The magic—electronic fuel injection—was actually nothing new. The first electronic fuel injection (EFI) had been invented not in Europe, but in 1950s America, by Bendix. The Bendix Electrojector system formed the basis of nearly all modern electronic fuel injection. The Bendix system, originally developed by Bendix Aviation for aircraft use, used modern solenoid-type electronic injectors with an electronic control unit (ECU) originally based on vacuum-tube technology but equipped with transistors for automotive use in 1958.

The original Electrojector system took 40 seconds to warm up before you could start the engine. Sometimes it malfunctioned if you drove under high-tension power lines. In addition to the liabilities of vacuum-tube technology, Bendix didn't have access to modern engine sensors. Solid-state circuitry was in its infancy, and although automotive engineers recognized the potential of electronic fuel injection to do amazing things based on its extreme precision of fuel delivery, the electronics technology to make EFI practical just didn't exist yet. After installing the Electrojector system in 35 Mopar vehicles, Chrysler eventually recalled all and converted to carburetion. Bendix eventually gave up on the Electrojector, secured worldwide patents, and licensed the technology to Bosch.

In the meantime, mechanical fuel injection had been around in various forms since before 1900. Mechanical injection had always been a "toy" used on race cars, foreign cars like the Mercedes, and a tiny handful of high-performance cars in

DI-Motronic

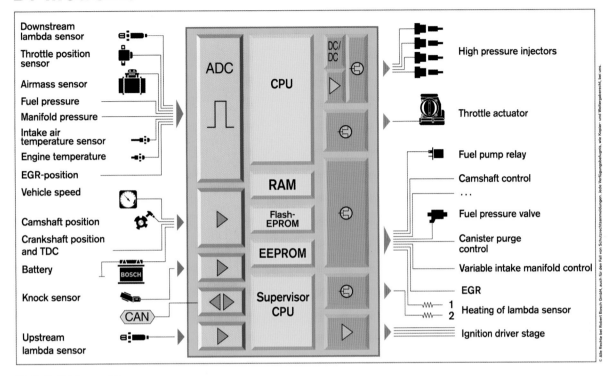

BOSCH 1-K3-10665

Bosch DI-Motronic Gasoline-Direct Injection EMS crunches data from multiple lambda (O_2) sensors, mass airflow (MAF) and manifold absolute pressure (MAP) sensors, the throttle position sensor, and a standard complement of OBD-II Motronic sensors to control high-pressure injectors spraying directly into the cylinders, in some cases over the CAN bus. The system also controlled a fly-by-wire throttle actuator, variable cam timing actuator, electronic fuel pressure regulator, and ignition driver stage. The system could provide homogenous charge mixtures for maximum power at wide-open throttle or a stratified-charge for maximum fuel economy in which a richer mixture in the vicinity of the spark plug lights off a leaner mixture elsewhere. *Bosch*

America, like the Corvette. Mechanical fuel injection avoided certain performance disadvantages of the carburetor, but it was expensive and finicky and not particularly accurate.

In the 1960s, America entered the transistor age. Suddenly electronic devices came alive instantly with no warm up. Solid-state circuitry was fast and consumed minuscule amounts of power compared to the vacuum tube. By the end of the 1960s, engineers had invented the microprocessor, which combined dozens, hundreds, then thousands of transistors on a piece of silicon smaller than a fingernail (each transistor was similar in functionality to a vacuum tube that could be as big as your fist).

Volkswagen introduced the first Bosch electronic fuel-injection systems on its cars in 1968. A trickle of other cars used electronic fuel injection by the mid-1970s. By the 1980s, that trickle became a torrent.

Meanwhile, in the late 1970s, the turbocharger was reborn as a powerful tool for automotive engineers attempting to steer a delicate course between performance, economy, and emissions. Turbochargers could potentially make small engines feel like big engines just in time to teach the guy with a V-8 in the next lane a good lesson about humility both at the gas pump and at the stoplight drags. Unfortunately, the carburetor met its Waterloo when it came up against the turbo. Having been tweaked and modified for nearly a century and a half to reach its modern state of "perfection," the carb was implicated in an impressive series

of failures when teamed up with the turbocharger. Carbureted turbo engines that were manufactured circa 1980—the early Mustang 2.3 turbo, the early Buick 3.8 turbo, the early Maserati Biturbo, the Turbo Trans Am V-8—are infamous. If you wanted a turbocharged hot rod to run efficiently and cleanly—and, more importantly, to behave and stay alive—car companies found out the hard way that electronic fuel injection was the only good solution.

For automakers, the cost disadvantages of fuel injection were outweighed by the potential penalties resulting from non-compliance with emissions and Corporate Average Fuel Economy (CAFE) standards, and the increased sales when offering superior or at least competitive horsepower and drivability.

HOT RODDERS AND FUEL INJECTION

In the 1950s, the performance-racing enthusiast's choices for a fuel system were carburetion or constant mechanical fuel injection. Carbs were inexpensive out of the box, but getting air and fuel distribution and jetting exactly right with one or two carbs mounted on a wet manifold took a wizard—a wizard with a lot of time. By the time you developed a great-performing carb-manifold setup, it might involve multiple carbs and cost as much or more than mechanical injection (which achieved equal air and fuel distribution with identical individual stack-type runners to every cylinder and identical fuel nozzles in every

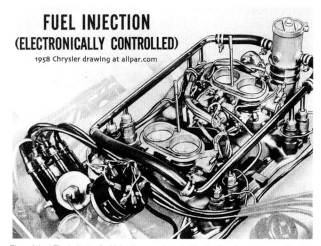

FUEL INJECTION
(ELECTRONICALLY CONTROLLED)
1958 Chrysler drawing at allpar.com

The original Electrojector fuel injection was invented by the American company Bendix in the 1950s. The package was expensive and finicky, and many were converted to carburetion in the days before the cars were collector items. Bendix had already successfully demonstrated pulsed electronic port injection (the Electrojector system), but the pretransistor vacuum tubes had to warm up like an old radio before the car could start, and the whole system could wig out if you drove under high-power lines. A practical system required the solid-state electronics of the 1960s and beyond. Bosch licensed from Bendix the concept of a constant-pressure, electronically controlled, solenoid-actuated, individual-port, periodic-timed fuel injection system and put it into production in some 1960s-vintage VWs. Bosch evolved the original concept, resulting in the newest Motronic engine management systems.

Fuel injection, 1950s-style, meant Chevrolet constant-flow venturi fuel injection. Most Americans' first exposure to Bosch fuel injection on 1970s- and 1980s-vintage VW, Porsche, Ferrari, Mercedes, and other European engines was this K-Jetronic constant-injection system (CIS), which varies fuel pressure based on a mechanical velocity air meter measuring air entering the engine. Although later K-Jetronic systems had add-on electronic trim, the system is not a true electronic engine management system, it is not easy to modify for hot rodding, and more than a few such performance vehicles still on the road have been converted to programmable EMS. *Chrysler*

runner). Assuming the nozzles matched, fuel distribution was guaranteed to be good with constant mechanical injection.

Mechanical fuel injection has been around in various forms since about 1900, and it has always been expensive. Mechanical injection could squirt a lot of fuel into an engine without restricting airflow, and it was not affected by lateral G-forces or the up-and-down pounding of, say, a high-performance boat engine in really rough waters, when fuel is bouncing all over the place in the float chamber of a carb. Racers used Hilborn mechanical injection on virtually every post-war Indy car until 1970.

The trouble is, air and gasoline have dissimilar fluid dynamics, and mechanical injection relied on crude mechanical means for mixture correction across the range of engine speeds, loading, and temperatures. Early mechanical injection was also not accurate enough to provide the precise mixtures required for a really high-output engine that must also be streetable. GM tried Constant Flow mechanical injection in the 1950s and early 1960s in a few Corvettes and Chevrolets, but it turned out to be expensive and finicky. Bosch finally refined a good, streetable, constant mechanical injection (Bosch K-Jetronic) in the 1970s, but as emissions requirements toughened, it quickly evolved into a hybrid system that used add-on electronic controls to fine-tune the air/fuel mixture at idle.

By the late 1970s carburetors had been engineered to a high state of refinement over the course of many decades. However, there were inescapable problems intrinsic to the concept of a self-regulating mechanical fuel-air mixing system that could only be solved by adding a microprocessor or analog computer to target stoichiometric air/fuel mixtures via pulse width-modulated jetting and closed-loop exhaust gas oxygen feedback.

In addition to the accuracy problems and distribution issues intrinsic to cost-effective single-carb wet-manifold induction

systems, by their nature carbs inherently require one or more restrictive venturis to create a low-pressure zone that sucks fuel into the charge air. By definition, this forces tradeoffs between top-end and performance at lower speeds. The carburetor's inability to automatically correct for changes in altitude and ambient temperature is not a problem if the goal is simply decent power at sea level. Distribution and accuracy problems, however, are unacceptable if you care about emissions, economy, or good, clean power at any altitude. Or if you want to run power-adders like turbos, blowers, or nitrous.

Throughout the 1970s, hot rodders and tuners had begun applying turbochargers to engines to achieve large horsepower gains and high levels of specific power for racing. Mainly, of course, 'rodders had to work with carburetors for fueling. They discovered that carbureted fuel systems are problematic when applied to forced induction. Yes, it was possible to produce a lot of power with carbureted turbo systems, but at the cost of drivability, reliability, cold-running, and so forth. Nonetheless, though carbs were a problem, they were a well-understood problem, and besides, what else could you do if you couldn't afford a mechanical injection system more expensive than the engine itself?

Around this same time, car manufacturers began switching to electronic fuel injection. In 1975, GM marketed its first U.S. electronic injection as an option for the 500-ci Cadillac V-8 used in the DeVille and El Dorado. In 1982, Cross-Fire dual throttle body electronic injection arrived on the Corvette. The new EFI would give tuners who wanted to modify late-model cars a whole new set of headaches.

The problem for hot rodders was that there was no easy means to recalibrate or tune the proprietary electronic controllers that managed car manufacturer's EFI systems, and it was difficult to predict whether electronic engine controls would tolerate various performance modifications without recalibration.

Early EFI control logic was not in embodied in software, but was hardwired into the unalterable discrete circuitry of an analog controller, and while early digital fuel-injection controllers were directed by software logic and soft tables of calibration data parameters, these were locked away in a programmable read-only memory (PROM) storage device that was, in many cases, hard-soldered to the main circuit board. In all analog electronic control units and in a fair number of the digital ECUs, changing the tuning data effectively required replacing the ECU. And even when the calibration (tuning) data was located on a removable PROM chip plugged into a socket on the motherboard, the documentation, equipment, and technical expertise needed to create or "blow" new PROMs was not accessible to most hot rodders. While enthusiasts were able, in some cases, to buy a quality replacement PROM calibrated by a professional tuner with tuning parameters customized for high-octane fuel operation or recalibrated to handle specific performance modifications, in those days it was rarely practical for an enthusiast to tune the fuel injection himself. And if you modified the calibration and then made additional volumetric or power-adder modifications to the engine, the new performance PROM was likely to be out of tune—again.

It was only in the late 1980s, as the final factory-carbureted performance vehicles aged and the first aftermarket user-programmable EFI systems became available and the first generation of performance EFI vehicles aged out of warranty and depreciated to the point that it was practical for more people to consider acquiring or modifying them, that large numbers of hot rodders and racers began to take a hard look at the possibilities of EFI for performance and racing vehicles.

In those days, many hot rodders and enthusiasts objected to electronic fuel injection for various reasons:
- Too expensive
- Difficult or impossible to modify
- Illegal in some racing classes
- Too high-tech (that is, complex, finicky, inaccessible, incomprehensible, mysterious, difficult to install and debug)
- Typically required expensive auxiliary electronic equipment for diagnosis, troubleshooting, and tuning
- Regarding the carburetor: "It ain't broke, why fix it?"

Eventually, all these considerations would become much less of a factor, but for a time they put a brake on the hot rodding of newer vehicles. For a time, the sport of hot rodding split into two evolutionary branches centered around 1) familiar, older low-tech specialty vehicles with pushrod V-8 engines—often equipped with carbureted fuel systems—and 2) more efficient newer vehicles with high-tech computer-controlled fuel injection—often powered by smaller engines with multivalve, overhead-cam cylinder heads, some with turbochargers. The advantages of EFI created the critical mass for the 1990s sport-compact performance craze that revitalized hot rodding, but in the early days of EFI there were actually a fair number of engines converted from EFI backward to carburetion.

Knowledgeable racers and hot rodders soon discovered that well-tuned modern programmable EFI systems almost always produce significantly higher horsepower and torque than the same powerplant with carbureted fuel management, especially when the engine is supercharged or turbocharged. This increased performance is within the context of improved drivability, cleaner exhaust emissions, and lower fuel consumption. Early adopter hot rodders discovered there were solid technical reasons behind the superiority of fuel injection and electronic engine management. In fact, there were plenty of carb-to-port EFI conversions of vintage vehicles for the following highly valid reasons:

ADVANTAGES OF INDIVIDUAL-PORT ELECTRONIC FUEL INJECTION

- Injection of fuel against the hot intake valve prevents a situation in which fuel vaporization in a carburetor has the potential to lower intake air temperature below the dew point in cold weather, allowing water vapor to condense and form ice crystals to build up in the carb to the extent that the engine runs poorly or not at all. This problem is so serious on carbureted aircraft engines that they are equipped with a "Carb Heat" control that causes hot air to be injected directly into the carb intake throat.
- Low pressure and high temperatures in fuel lines can cause vapor bubbles to form in the fuel supply system that impede operation; the higher pressures of port EFI systems (30-70 psi) normally eliminates the problem.
- Greater flexibility of dry intake manifold design allows higher inlet airflow rates and consistent cylinder-to-cylinder air/fuel distribution, resulting in more power and torque, and better drivability.
- More efficient higher engine compression ratios possible without detonation.
- Extreme accuracy of fuel delivery by electronic injection at any rpm and load enables the engine to receive air/fuel mixtures at every cylinder that falls within the narrow window of accuracy required to produce superior horsepower and efficiency.
- Computer-controlled air/fuel ratio accuracy enables all-out engines to safely operate much closer to the hairy edge without damage.
- EFI can easily be recalibrated or adapted to future engine modifications as a performance/racing vehicle evolves. When adjustments and changes are required to match new performance upgrades made to an engine, it's often as simple as hitting a few keys on a

Big Block 426-type Hemi with twin Whipple twin-screw supercharges and (out of sight) electronic fuel injection.

PC to change some numbers in the memory of the onboard ECU.

- Electronic engine management with port fuel injection is fully compatible with forced induction, resisting detonation with programmable fuel enrichment and spark-timing retard, enabling huge power increases by providing the precisely correct air/fuel mixture at every cylinder.
- EFI powerplants have no susceptibility to failure or performance degradation in situations of sudden and shifting gravitational and acceleration forces that might disturb the normal behavior of fuel in a carbureted fuel system with float chamber(s).
- Electronic injection automatically corrects for changes in altitude and ambient temperature for increased power and efficiency, and reduced exhaust emissions.
- Solid-state electronics are not susceptible to the mechanical wear and failure possible with carburetors. Tuning parameters stay as you set them, forever, with no need for readjustment to compensate for mechanical wear.

ADVANTAGES OF INDIVIDUAL-CYLINDER DIRECT INJECTION

- Gasoline-DI engines achieve improved fuel economy when operating in ultra-lean burn mode under very light loading or deceleration. In this mode fuel is injected not during the intake stroke but during the latter stage of the compression stroke. G-DI engines are able to combust a stratified charge that is richer near the spark plug but, overall, as lean as 65:1 air/fuel ratio.
- Stratified charge combustion restricts the burn to an island of fuel and air surrounded by mostly pure air, which keeps the flame away from the cylinder walls for reduced heat loss and lowered exhaust emissions.
- No throttling loses on some gasoline direct-injection engines when engine speed and output are controlled by ignition timing and injected fuel mass rather than by throttling engine air intake.
- G-DI engines achieve improved performance in Stoichiometric or Performance Mode by combusting a homogenous mixture achieved by injecting fuel during the intake stroke as pressures as high as 3,000 psi, which improves combustion via improved atomization of fuel molecules and improved air/fuel mixing in the cylinders.
- G-DI engine performance can be further improved in some cases by a second injection of additional fuel late during the power stroke, particularly on turbo-charged powerplants (though problems with exhaust valve erosion from some fuel octanes caused some engine manufacturers to eliminate Fuel Stratified Injection during normal operation).
- The extremely high injection pressure of G-DI systems improves the atomization of injected fuel enough that improved fuel vaporization actually chills the intake air enough to improve density and lower combustion temperatures.
- Compared to the 40-70-psi pressure of multi-port EFI systems, the extremely high rail pressure allows G-DI systems increased flexibility of injection timing and fuel apply rate, which can be tuned via pressure in the common rail and the number of injection events. Combined with twin-cam electronic cam phasing, G-DI

Norwood Performance built this gorgeous custom twin-turbo system for a radically hot rodded Gen-1 Toyota Supra. Under Motec EMS control, with 900 horsepower on tap from 2,954 radically-boosted cubic centimeters, this streetable machine was equally at home as a dragger or a Silver State racer.

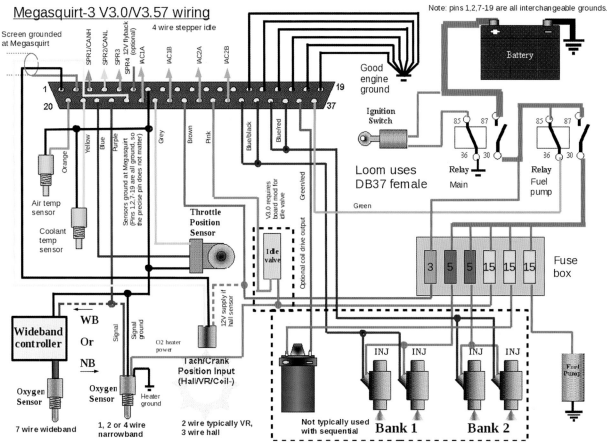

MegaSquirt V3.0/V3.57 wiring showing connections for all required and optional engine sensors and actuators. Note external wideband controller circuit at lower left. Major DI-Motronic components. A powerful digital computer with large non-volatile memory space runs multiple OBD-II monitor software agents with the ability to detect problems such as combustion misfires from minor changes in crankshaft rate of acceleration. New Motronic systems are powerful and complex, but they are table-driven and extremely flexible, which makes modifications a simple programming change—if you've got access for a reflash. In most cases aftermarket hackers have always found a way. *Bosch*

systems can vary valve overlap, injection timing, and ignition timing to heat catalysts lightning-fast on cold start and spool turbochargers much faster by using large valve overlap and retarded fuel and ignition timing to blow some turbo boost through the combustion chamber to supply a combustible mixture in the exhaust.

In the very early 1990s, many new EFI vehicles still utilized factory EFI conversions of formerly carbureted engines (such as the 5.0L Mustang, and the TPI 5.0 or 5.7 Camaro and Corvette). In some cases, such vehicles had separate or quasi-separate distributor-based ignition systems (along with instrumentation and chassis electrical systems that were not integrated with the engine management system). In those days virtually all onboard computer systems, with the exception of idle and light-cruise fuel-air mixture trim and idle speed stabilization algorithms, had no means of detecting if commanded engine management actions were successful. If the computer ordered the opening of a solenoid valve, it had to assume the valve had opened. Many early 1990s aftermarket EFI engine tuning strategies for modified hot rod powerplants worked by inciting the factory computer into providing (more or less) correct fuel enrichment and ignition timing on engines with upgraded volumetric efficiency during high-output operation using mechanical or electrical tricks that might, say, substitute false engine sensor data (such as artificially low engine coolant temperature) that would cause the engine to

run rich during boosted conditions, or by dynamically altering injection fuel pressure with artificial means (such as a variable rate-of-gain fuel pressure regulator) such that the calculated and commanded injection pulse width would deliver more fuel during turbo boost.

A few enterprising companies offered performance PROMs that could easily be swapped into factory engine-management systems such as GM's Tuned Port Injection. These provided alternate tables of rpm and load-based values for fuel-injection pulse width and spark advance that improved power with premium fuel calibrations or provided modified internal fuel and spark tables calibrated specifically for certain packages of hotter cams and other hot rod engine parts. Several standalone programmable aftermarket engine management systems were also available, the most successful of which was the Haltech F3. The F3 was an EFI-only system with an installed base of maybe 2,000 systems that could not manage ignition tasks at all. This was all about to change.

ELECTRONIC ENGINE MANAGEMENT IN THE OBD-II ERA

In the 1980s, independent repair facilities lobbied hard for regulations to force automakers to provide open onboard computer diagnostic interfaces and to document and standardize interface protocols so independent shops servicing multiple

Lee Sicilio's 1969 Dodge Daytona Bonneville Racer, powered by a Keith Black 498-cid Hemi with twin Precision 91mm Pro Mod turbochargers. The engine was controlled by a DIY Autotune Megasquirt MS3X engine management system providing sequential fuel and spark. The MS3 driving was set up to drive eight Pantera IGN-1A coil packs and the fuel injectors were 225 lb/hr Injector Dynamics units with flow capacity of 2800hp on gasoline, and more at increased fuel pressure. The chassis dynamometer used for power testing maxed-out at 1500 wheel horsepower at 6-psi boost, but with an estimated 3000 horsepower on available at higher boost, Sicilio race team was hoping the Charger would eventually smash its way to 310 mph on the salt. In preliminary testing, the car hit 283 mph at the salt running just 8-psi boost. *Scott "Dieselgeek" Clark, Chad Reynolds (Bangshift.com)*

brands did not need expensive and esoteric brand-special scan tools for every make and model of vehicle.

The Clean Air Act of 1990 finally forced automakers to get serious about plans they had been developing since the first serious California air pollution problems in the late 1950s. Standardized onboard vehicle/engine diagnostic capabilities designed to keep engines operating in a clean, efficient, peak state of tune arrived in 1996 (in a few cases as early as 1994). Now that digital computers had conquered the original-equipment automotive world, there existed at last both the possibility of and the necessity for sophisticated electronic self-testing and diagnostic capabilities.

The result was OBD-II (Onboard Diagnostics, Second Generation), a blessing for the typical car buyer, potentially a blessing and a curse for the hot rodder or tuning shop. OBD-II, which was required on new vehicles no later than 1996, implemented a number of interesting capabilities. It defined standards for hardware bus connectivity to onboard computers for scan tools and laptop computers. It defined a handshake for communication between the ECU and diagnostic equipment. It defined an extensive set of standardized malfunctions that the engine management system had to be able to self-detect, and it defined a standardized set of alphanumeric trouble codes. These codes had to be stored by the ECU semi-permanently in nonvolatile memory that would retain its integrity even if the onboard computer lost battery power. OBD-II defined protocols for resetting such codes once a problem had been fixed.

The consequent use of large-scale electrically erasable flash memory to store calibration information and trouble codes was revolutionary because it was now feasible to reflash the device with new calibration or configuration data in the field without PROM. OBD-II thus defined a system that could be used to update the entire parameter-driven engine calibration should a bug be discovered that affected emissions or safety. It also

required automakers to implement countermeasures that made it reasonably difficult to tamper with the calibration without having access to a special password known as the security seed (sometimes referred to as "security by obscurity." At the same time, OBD-II was defining a powerful mechanism that could be used to retune engines without changing any hardware or even so much as a PROM chip. Or even more: it potentially enabled recalibration of an OBD-II computer—or even replacement of the operating software itself!—to handle an alternate engine or important additional engine systems, or even to stop doing OBD-II.

The logic of modern digital engine management systems is highly parameter driven, meaning the software design is complex, modular, universal, and all-encompassing in design. It is also highly conditional in behavior based on the status of a set of internal settings (parameters) stored in tables in memory. Changing such parameters can drastically transform functionality, giving the computer a whole new personality—for example, enabling it to manage an entirely different engine with fewer or more cylinders or one with additional power-adders and so forth.

Before OBD-II, such parameters (where they existed) were stored in read-only memory or programmable read-only memory and could be changed only by physically opening the computer and installing a new ROM or PROM, which sometimes involved soldering and de-soldering and jumpering or cutting the motherboard. It would not be long before clever aftermarketers would reverse-engineer the security seed and sell specialized power-programmer devices designed to connect to the diagnostic port to change parameters like top-speed-limiter or rev-limiter, or even to hack the air/fuel or ignition timing tables on GM OBD-II computers (for off-road use only, of course). When researchers at the University of Washington and University of California examined the security around OBD, they discovered it was possible to gain control over many vehicle components via the OBD-II interface, and they were able to upload new firmware into the engine-control units without proprietary documentation, and concluded that vehicle embedded systems were not designed with security in mind. In fact, there are documented instances of thieves using specialist OBD reprogramming devices to steal cars without the use of a key. The primary causes of this vulnerability lie in the tendency for vehicle manufacturers to extend the OBD-II interface for purposes beyond the original specification, and the lack of authentication and authorization in the OBD specifications, which instead rely largely on "security through obscurity."

OBD-II effectively required implementation of a range of new engine and vehicle sensors to provide additional feedback to the computer so it would know when there was a problem or might be a problem. For example, where the computer might have previously commanded a valve to open to purge the charcoal canister of fuel vapors (and assumed it had, in fact, opened), OBD-II might, for example, require a sensor to measure if, in fact, the valve actually had opened.

OBD-II mandated many new diagnostic capabilities, such as the ability to detect misfires. This required precise and highly accurate crankshaft position sensors and new, more powerful, high-speed microprocessors with the computing power to measure micro-changes in the rate of change in crankshaft speed in real time that indicated healthy combustion versus misfire events. Misfire-detection required the computational ability to correlate a transient misfire to a particular cylinder. Basically, OBD-II required the development of completely new engine management systems.

Since they were developing entirely new engine management hardware and software with a clean-sheet-of-paper approach, automakers and their OEM suppliers such as Bosch took the opportunity to develop powerful new onboard computer hardware and operating software. They made plans to implement an architecture able to handle an impressive range of new vehicle-management capabilities, including fly-by-wire throttle, traction controls, active lateral-instability countermeasures, electronic shifting, Controller Area Network bus (required on all light U.S. market vehicles in 2008 for communication between multiple specialized onboard controllers/computers) , and dozens of other highly specialized and esoteric eMotion control functions.

One such example is a scary-sounding thing GM called "Adaptive Garage Fill Pressure Pulse Time and Garage Shift Pressure Control." And more: Some of the most advanced Motronic engine management systems are equipped with algorithms that deliver directly measured torque-based engine management. Some of the newest BMWs can fire up the engine without a starter motor by identifying the exact engine position, injecting fuel into the appropriately positioned cylinder, and then firing the plug.

The amount of time invested in carefully developing flawless engine calibrations for such vehicles is phenomenal, and can take years, even with complex modeling and simulation tools. The simplest millennium engine management systems used to manage economy subcompacts incorporated months or years of test-and-tune efforts on dynos, test tracks, and highways under all climatic conditions.

Meanwhile, standalone aftermarket programmable engine management systems also increased in power and complexity, with the newest systems from Motec, Electromotive, DFI, and others offering extremely sophisticated software engine modeling and highly flexible and configurable hardware with the capability to control a wide range of complex engines with a wide variety of sensors and actuators, and to keep up with engine management capabilities found on new factory vehicles.

The most powerful aftermarket systems target pro racers and professionals building tunercars for people for whom money is, shall we say, not a problem. Such systems are not cheap. All involve substantial configuration, calibration, and installation efforts to approximate anything close to the observable functionality of a millennium-vintage factory vehicle (much less sophisticated little tricks like Adaptive Garage Fill

Motec ADL3 Dash/Logger communicates with the M800 ECM using a 2-wire CAN bus, which also supports a laptop PC with Motec tuning software and various other sensors and actuators.

Pressure Pulse Time and Garage Shift Pressure Control). Of course, conversion from OEM to programmable aftermarket engine management is not strictly legal for highway use unless the manufacturer or tuner tackles expensive CARB or Federal Test Procedure (FTP) testing in order to prove that their engine management system does not degrade exhaust emissions on one or more specific vehicles in a simulated drive cycle involving a cold start and 20 minutes or so of rolling road exercise during which exhaust is captured in a big plastic bag for subsequent analysis. The FTP procedure was updated in 2008 to include four tests: city driving (FTP-75), highway driving (HWFET), aggressive driving (SFTP US06), and optional air conditioning test (SFTP SC03). In general, the Cold Start CVS-75 Federal Test procedure has been the regimen required to achieve street legality for aftermarket power-adder systems, though Cold 505 can be used, and in the case of diesel-powered vehicles, Hot Start CVS-75 may be applicable.

By the time OBD-II was required on all vehicles sold in the United States in 1996, it had been six years since a carbureted engine had been available on a car or truck in America, and the digital microcomputer was definitely king, both in the onboard ECU (now referred to as the powertrain control module or PCM) managing the engine and in the scan tool or laptop in the hands of the diagnostician or tuner. Powerful laptop computers with graphical Windows or Mac OS interfaces were ubiquitous by 1997, and most people who had been in school since 1982 had at least some degree of training and familiarity with the personal computer. This new generation arrived on the automotive-performance scene entirely comfortable with installing and manipulating user-interface and tuning software on a laptop to recalibrate engine management systems.

Unfortunately, this was only one piece of the puzzle. Ignorant jacking with calibration numbers in the computer of a vehicle with significant engine performance modifications will make a bad situation worse. Tuning an engine well with good diagnostic equipment requires patience, experience, and methodical R&D troubleshooting techniques. Tuning an engine in a car on the street without diagnostic equipment is a risky proposition that is difficult or impossible to do well.

Many casual or inexperienced performance enthusiasts are simply incapable of achieving a good, safe, efficient, drivable tuning calibration from scratch, particularly on high-output engines with power-adders. If such a well-meaning but inexperienced person is lucky, they'll probably end up with an engine that fails to realize the potential of its improved volumetric efficiency. If they're unlucky, they'll end up with a polluting, gas-guzzling slug with marginal drivability or possibly a damaged engine. Even really experienced professionals—genuine wizards—may not have the time to achieve the optimal calibration on a tuner car. What aftermarket supertuner has the days, weeks, months, even years to devote to a calibration task that automakers—forced by government fuel economy and emissions standards and by competitive performance pressures to put in the hard time to get perfect calibrations—can then amortize the effort over tens or hundreds of thousands of vehicles?

One response to the difficulty and complexity of recalibrating factory engine controllers or accurately installing and calibrating standalone aftermarket systems from scratch for excellent performance, drivability, and reliability is the "plug-and-play" strategy, in which sophisticated tuners offer a power-adder package complete with an aftermarket engine management system that plugs into the stock wiring harness (typically with a short adapter harness) in place of the stock ECU, ready to rock 'n' roll.

Just getting all the engine sensors and actuators wired to an aftermarket programmable computer can be a formidable task. It's more akin to buying a motherboard, power supply, disk drive, case, bios, and operating software from Fry's Electronics and building your own Windows system. But it's even worse, because in the case of a programmable engine management system, you'll need to locate subsystems, sensors, and actuators; route wiring; and terminate and crimp wires to connectors that need to work reliably in an environment rife with heat, cold, water, oil, vibration, and various G-forces.

AEM plug-and-play systems provided adapter wiring that was designed to allow a user to remove the stock computer and plug the stock engine wiring harness into an adapter on the programmable computer. Plug-and-play system vendors like AEM, Hondata, Haltech, and most others by now usually provide a starter calibration that will start and run the engine and enable the vehicle to drive without any user intervention to calibrate it. But installation instructions warn users that virtually any significant modifications to the factory engine's volumetric efficiency—that is, performance modifications—would require recalibration to prevent possible engine damage.

Another response to the increased complexity of OBD-II-era original-equipment engine management systems, and the difficulty of reproducing the quality of their factory calibrations, was aftermarket tuners increasingly turning to auxiliary computers or mechanical devices rather than standalone aftermarket engine management systems. Tuners have used variable-rate-of-gain fuel pressure regulators (some even computer-controlled!) and electronic interceptor devices to intercept and modify or augment the actions of fuel injectors or input-output signals from the factory onboard computer to change the behavior of the engine under the relatively limited operating circumstances when power-adders are in action (at wide-open throttle and higher-load operating conditions).

A number of vendors have specialized in supplying programmable "piggyback" computers (in some cases very sophisticated) designed to modify or trim specific designated sectors of the factory air/fuel or spark timing curves—via laptop or, in some cases, dial pots on the processor box—during power-adder operations without affecting the factory tune during non-boosted conditions when the engine is lightly loaded. A related alternative to the interceptor or auxiliary computer is the programmable sensor or actuator that enables tuners to influence the behavior of the main engine management computer by selectively lying to it or by being creatively disobedient.

The complex interactions and constraints of ECM logic, ECM calibration data, ECM anti-tampering or self-protective countermeasures, fuel pump capacity and fuel pressure, injector capacity, duty cycle, electrical limitations, pressure, ignition components, and other such factors have made modifying engines for increased performance challenging, yet potentially rewarding. The tuning of electronic engine management systems has evolved to the point that tuners have managed to achieve stupefying levels of streetable specific power that had previously only been seen in the wild turbo era of Formula One racing.

THE PURPOSE OF THIS BOOK

This book is designed to communicate the theory and practice of designing and redesigning performance engine management

Tuning the Norwood Autocraft Celica Dragger with Motec M 800 engine management prior to drag racing near Dallas, Texas.

systems that work. It's designed to remove the mystery from electronic engine management and fuel injection. It's designed to give you the information you'll need to tune, modify, hack, or install engine management systems and components to unleash "free" power on many stock and modified engines.

This book provides information about how to modify engines in ways that will work with existing engine management systems and how to modify and optimize engine management systems for compatibility with highly modified engines. It's designed to tell you how to design roll-your-own electronic engine management systems and convert engines to the advantages of electronic fuel injection. This book communicates from the ground up what's required to do the job yourself or to knowledgeably subcontract the work—from theory to practical installation details. It supplies the detailed information

you'll need to know about specific fuel injection and engine management control units and related products to tune factory and aftermarket fuel-injection systems properly.

This book is designed to reveal secrets of factory onboard ECMs and PCMs, aftermarket programmable engine management computers, wiring and re-wiring, fuel injectors and pumps, laptop computers, PROMs, engine sensors, electronic boost controllers, chassis dyno tuning and calibration, and much more. This book provides information about what it costs to fuel inject a hot rod using various technologies, including original equipment injection systems. This book will help you decide whether your hot rodding plans might violate government regulations. Finally, this book is designed to document how to make EFI engines more powerful and to make understanding and hacking performance engine management and fuel-injection systems fun.

Chapter 1
Understanding Fuel Delivery

For many older automotive performance enthusiasts and motorcyclists the benchmark for automotive fuel delivery systems is still the carburetor. No electronic fuel system can touch a carburetor in delivering so much performance for so little cost. Many performance carburetors are still sold, priced, at this time of writing, in the $275-$475 range.

Although the emissions carbs installed on new U.S. vehicles in the final years before the demise of automotive carburetion in the mid-1980s were complex devices equipped with extensively convoluted vacuum systems and electromechanical add-ons that enabled carbs to be trimmed for stoichiometric (14.7:1) air/fuel ratios via an electronic controller and feedback from an O_2 sensor, the basic carburetor was still what it always had been: a self-regulating mechanical device that uses mechanical forces to suck fuel into the air stream entering an engine.

Many people have had an easier time understanding carburetors than electronic fuel injection. Perhaps this is because you could take a carb apart with a screwdriver and actually see the air and fuel passages and the mechanical equipment that manages gas and liquid flow to reliably deliver accurate, appropriate, and repeatable mixtures in response to changing engine conditions. If you wanted more fuel with a carburetor, you could remove the main jet and drill it out with a special bit, and you'd get more fuel.

By contrast, for most people, electronic fuel injection is a black box that can only be fully understood by reading complex technical documentation (assuming it's not proprietary). It can only be modified or tuned by changing the internal software or data structures in the onboard engine management computer or with auxiliary add-on mechanical or electronic tricks that typically deceive or even work at cross purposes to the main engine management and fuel systems.

But in reality, EFI systems are simpler than it might at first appear, and many carburetors are actually not simple to understand fully or tune really well. Carbs are intricate and complex devices that have been engineered over the course of many decades to a high state of perfection. Though they are much less expensive than electronic injection systems, carbs are not simple to tune in a major way to a high degree of accuracy. Of course, despite the several-times added cost of electronic injection, carburetors were abandoned by automotive engineers in the mid-1980s precisely because their fuel management capabilities were, in the end, inadequate to meet required new standards for low emissions with high performance and economy.

The basic mechanical principle enabling fuel delivery via carburetion is the Bernoulli effect, which states that air pressure decreases when moving air speeds up to flow around a gentle curve such as an aerodynamic constriction in a tube or curvature of a wing. By designing a smooth constriction or narrowing (venturi) into the inlet of an engine and introducing an atmospheric-pressure fuel bleed into the area of the venturi, the reduced fuel pressure in the venturi will automatically suck fuel into the air.

If an engine always operated at one speed, temperature, and altitude, the job of a carb would be relatively simple, and a simple venturi-based carb would do the job. Indeed, boats, aircraft, and tractors operating over a very limited dynamic range can get away with simpler carburetors. But in order to handle cold starting, transient enrichment, idling, correction for the differential flow characteristics of air and fuel, full throttle enrichment, and emissions concerns in an automotive environ-ment on engines that must accelerate very rapidly and perform well across an extremely wide speed range, street carbs contain a myriad of add-on systems. These systems include choke valves, fast idle cams, accelerator pumps, two-stage power valves, air corrector jets, emulsion tubes, idle jets, booster venturis, and air bleed screws, not to mention the pulse width–modified solenoids mentioned above that pulse open and closed under computer control to regulate fuel flow through the jet(s) of an electronic feedback carb.

Carburetion is an ancient technology, refined by more than 150 years of engineering and tinkering. The engineering context of gasoline carburetion operates within the constraint that liquid

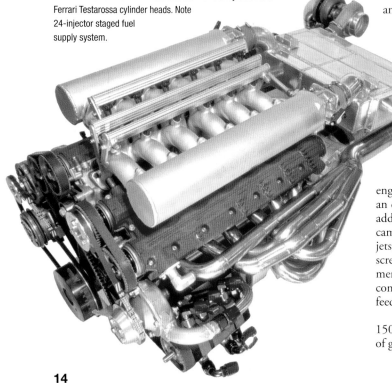

Norwood-Batten 5.0L V12 uses a custom CNC alloy block and Ferrari Testarossa cylinder heads. Note 24-injector staged fuel supply system.

The Edelbrock 3500 kit was the ultimate bolt-on injection conversion package, with everything you'd need to provide air, fuel, ignition, and engine management for a small-block Chevy crate motor: intake manifold/throttle body/injector rail/sensors module, computer and harness, fuel pump and filter, heated O_2 sensor, calibration module, coil driver, and more. Pretty much all you needed was a V-8 long block with a distributor and fuel supply/return lines. *Edelbrock*

gasoline and gaseous air moving though a carburetor or intake system do not necessarily behave the same with increases or decreases in overall flow and pressure, so the tricks required to maintain the proper air/fuel mixture tend to change as rpm and loading change.

Gasoline carburetion is an esoteric, delicate world of countless moving parts and fluids, overlapping fuel/air metering systems (each of which only covers part of the speed and loading range), tiny tubes that introduce air bubbles into fuel bleeds to dilute fuel delivery under certain conditions, and complex interactions among all of the above. A given problem usually has a long list of possible causes that includes everything from the weather to a speck of dirt in a tiny passage, to an incorrectly sized part, to a design flaw.

To truly master carburetion requires a thorough knowledge of fluid mechanics, engine design, and air/fuel theory as well as a great deal of experience and test equipment. Carbs have a lot of parts and systems, and they all do something. Many are interdependent and modify the functioning and actions of each other in complex ways. Fortunately, most people do not try to build a custom carb from parts; they buy something off the shelf targeted loosely for an engine close to what they've got. Off-the-shelf carbs are easy to get running, if only in a suboptimal fashion.

In comparison, a modern electronic fuel-injection system is a thing of marvelous conceptual simplicity that is quite easy to understand. In the end, it only does one basic thing: It turns on and off fuel injectors for a precisely regulated length of time at least once every power stroke. Need more fuel this engine cycle? Open the injectors a little longer. Less fuel? Pulse the injectors a

shorter burst. Pure and simple. Virtually everything else going on in electronic fuel injection has to do with reading the condition of the engine at a given moment, and then doing a little math to compute injection pulse width—before firing those injectors. So let's start by understanding the easy stuff—we'll design a virtual electronic fuel-injection system.

DESIGNING A VIRTUAL FUEL INJECTION SYSTEM

Unlike the carburetor, with EFI, air and fuel are metered entirely separately under computer control, combining only at the last moment in or near the combustion chamber. EFI can define essentially any air/fuel relationship from moment to moment, depending on the status of the engine—or anything else in the world. The relationship between air and fuel in EFI is defined electronically in a computer—and is, therefore, completely flexible. If we wanted, we could change the way our EFI system injects fuel based on the phases of the moon!

So, since anything is possible with EFI, once we've had a chance to discover what an EFI system looks like, we'll take a look at some alternate design choices before getting down to the business of relating specific fuel-injection components to fuel, ignition, and engine theory. The goal is to understand what kind of fuel delivery is ideal under various circumstances and how injection systems go about providing it.

Assume we're starting with a pre-EFI vehicle that was originally equipped with standalone distributor ignition and carburetor but has had the carburetor and intake manifold removed. If we're going to design a fuel-injection system, where shall we start? How about at the beginning, at the fuel tank?

Constant mechanical injection predated electronic fuel injection, and it survives today. Hilborn still provides a large variety of mechanical injection components, though they now also provide stack-throttle body systems like this Ford flathead system that look mechanical but are actually electronic, with all the precision control and enhanced performance of electronic systems. *Hilborn*

Step 1. Get fuel to the engine compartment

The fuel is resting in a tank, ready to make power, often at the end of the vehicle opposite from the engine. Unless we want to put the fuel tank on the roof, we need a pump to move fuel to the engine. Let's put the fuel pump in the fuel tank (which will also help keep the pump cool). We'll drive our roller-vane centrifugal pump with an electric motor so it's not necessarily tied to the speed of the engine. Therefore we'll have available plenty of fuel pressure, any time—say at least 20–40 psi.

Our pump should be sized to continuously move enough fuel at design pressure to satisfy the engine at its highest consumption—maximum horsepower—under full load. We'll run a steel fuel line from the pump to the engine and route a second fuel line from the engine area back to the fuel tank. When the engine isn't using all the fuel we're pumping, excess fuel can be routed back into the fuel tank. That way we don't ever have to turn the pump off when the motor is running—or accelerate pump wear by forcing it to pump against a deadhead of pressure during low fuel consumption—say at idle.

Step 2. Build an intake manifold and throttle

OK, let's move to the engine. Currently, the intake ports are naked holes with no intake manifold installed. Time for some fabrication. We begin by attaching a short pipe (runner) to each intake port that is sized with the same internal diameter as the port itself. We collect these runners in an air chamber (plenum) that has a single circular intake throat bolted to the plenum. We regulate airflow into the plenum chamber (and subsequently into the engine) using a throttle plate (flat, circular plate, completely blocking the circular air-intake throat). This spring-loaded throttle plate is designed to pivot on a shaft and allow more or less air into the motor. A bleed screw allows an adjustable amount of air to bypass the throttle even when the throttle is fully closed so the engine will idle. We decide to name

the chamber containing the throttle plate a throttle body. Now we run a cable from the throttle plate shaft to the accelerator pedal—push down, open the throttle. This will control the speed of the engine and the power output by regulating how much air enters each cylinder in the intake stroke.

Great. We can now regulate air into the engine, and we can get fuel to the engine, but so far we can't yet meter the fuel.

Step 3. Figure out a way to meter fuel

We drill a hole in each intake runner near the intake port, install a miniature fuel valve in each hole aimed straight at the intake valve to inject fuel directly into the port where air is moving fast and swirling as the engine sucks in air. Each injector actually contains a little electromagnetic coil. When energized with direct electrical current from the battery of the car, the energized electromagnet will overcome the force of a tiny spring in the injector that holds closed a miniature check valve. The valve snaps open and allows fuel to spray through a tiny orifice at high pressure in a fine mist until the current is switched off and the valve clicks shut, stopping the fuel flow.

At high engine speeds, each injector must be able to open and close like a frantically buzzing bee—up to 400 times a second! When an injector is open, fuel always flows from it at the same rate per unit of time as long as the fuel supply pressure to the injector remains constant. Therefore, we must meter the amount of fuel going into the engine based on how long we leave the injector open per engine cycle.

Clearly we must carefully select our injectors so that the flow rate matches our engine requirements, keeping in mind the following: Any injector's high flow threshold occurs when it is constantly open, providing an absolute maximum fuel flow. Providing more fuel than this maximum would require either increased fuel pressure, injectors with a larger orifice, or additional injectors. In practice, injectors need a finite amount of time to close and open, and injectors heat up when held open constantly, so an 80 percent duty cycle is a good practical design limit.

On the other hand, when the engine is idling, the same injectors must be able to open and then close quickly enough to inject the tiny amount of fuel required for a good quality idle. In fact, most injectors cannot provide accurate flow below a threshold of 1.3 milliseconds open time because the injector

Electromotive Fuel accessories, including screw-in fuel injector bosses, pressure regulator, D-section injector fuel rail, PWM electronic injector.

is turning off before it has entirely opened, which tends to produce injection pulses that are not entirely consistent. To get less fuel requires changing to smaller injectors or decreasing the fuel pressure. In any case, the correct injectors are ones sized to supply both idle and wide-open throttle requirements (thinking ahead, you may realize that small engines boosted to very high power levels can run into trouble finding injectors that can meet both requirements).

Pushing ahead, we plumb the fuel supply line to each injector, being careful to size and design our fuel manifold, or fuel rail, so that each injector receives steady and equal fuel-supply pressure under all circumstances. We then plumb in the fuel return line through an inline pressure regulator designed to maintain an exact fuel pressure in the fuel rail (loop) in relation to manifold pressure.

This kind of regulator, usually referenced to intake manifold pressure by an air hose, is designed to pinch off fuel flow returning to the tank until fuel pressure builds up at the injectors to a predetermined pressure.

At this point the regulator begins to open and permit sufficient fuel to return to the fuel tank, maintaining a predetermined fuel pressure. Manifold vacuum referenced to the regulator fights the force of the regulator's spring against the fuel diaphragm at idle, lowering fuel pressure anytime manifold pressure is less than atmospheric (and raising it during boosted conditions when manifold pressure increases above atmospheric). As manifold pressure rises with increasing engine loads, vacuum at the regulator drops, and the full force of the regulator spring comes to bear on the diaphragm, raising fuel pressure. The injectors, therefore, always inject against manifold pressure that is fixed in relation to fuel pressure.

At this point, our experimental system is ready to handle the mechanics of air and fuel delivery into the engine: a throttle body and intake manifold to deliver and measure air, and a fuel pump supplying high-pressure fuel to a set of injectors ready to precisely spray fuel into the inlet ports in exactly the correct amount as a function of how long each is opened.

Everything from here on is related to reading and evaluating certain engine vital signs and translating this information into actual engine fuel requirements that can then be used to compute injector open times (pulse width) and pulse the injectors.

Step 4. Turning the injectors on and off
At 10,000 rpm, a port fuel injector must turn on and off at least 167 times a second (and possibly 333 times a second). The on time must be computed accurately to at least a tenth of a thousandth of a second to get the air/fuel mixture just right.

This is a job for a microcomputer. A modern digital microcomputer can perform millions of instructions per second. This speed is so much faster than what is happening in an engine mechanically that the microcomputer can treat the engine, at any given moment, as if it were standing still.

A microcomputer can continuously read the current status of an engine via electromechanical sensors. Based on this information, it can then quickly retrieve from memory reconfigured tables of numbers that provide information about the appropriate injection pulse width at all possible combinations of engine speed and loading. The microcomputer, which maintains a highly precise internal clock, combines sensor and table look-up data with arithmetic computations to schedule injector start or stop times—all before the engine has virtually moved.

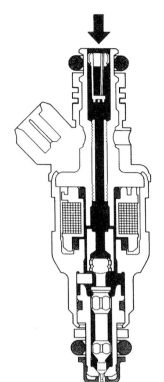

Bosch pintle-type electronic fuel injector. Pressurized fuel enters through the top and flows through the injector until it is stopped by a solenoid-actuated valve about one-third of the way from the bottom. When the injector is energized through electrical connections on the upper left, the centrally located coils magnetically lift the lower armature off its seat. This allows fuel to flow past the valve seat, around the armature body, and spray out the bottom of the injector in the area of the pintle, a tiny pin protruding through the bottom of the injector in the nozzle area used to improve the spray pattern. *Bosch*

Certain vital engine events, such as the crankshaft arriving at a particular position or the internal clock making another tick, can be made to automatically interrupt or alert the microcomputer for action. As engine conditions change, the computer is able to reschedule injector start and stop times on the fly and activate electrical drivers that energize or de-energize the injector electromagnets.

OK, now we have a computer. What sensors do we need to install so the computer can understand what is happening in the engine?

Step 5. Telling the computer what's going on in the engine
What does the computer need to know about the engine? Let's start with engine position, speed, loading, and so on.

First, we'll install an optical triggering device near the camshaft or distributor designed to count teeth on a gear that is missing one or two teeth as a reference point. The cam sensor and gear are set up to send a special electrical signal to the computer each time the crankshaft passes through top dead center compression stroke on the number one cylinder. In between, the crank sensor detects the proximity of gear teeth and passes electrical signals to the microcomputer as teeth fly past. This enables the computer to know the exact position of the engine combustion cycle for each cylinder. The computer uses the toothless reference point (and offsets from it in numbers of teeth) to sequentially schedule timed fuel-injection events for each cylinder coordinated with the time at which each intake valve opens.

Beyond knowing camshaft and crankshaft position and speed, in order to time a sequence of fuel delivery opening and closing events for each of the injectors, our microcomputer must know the number of injectors and cylinders and the displacement and injector flow rate. But most important of all, the microcomputer must know how much air is entering

The MSD fuel pressure regulator is designed to maintain a precise fuel pressure at the injector feeds. Fuel flow enters through the side hose barb, building pressure until it overcomes a spring in the regulator housing, at which point additional fuel bleeds off through the end hose barb for return to the fuel tank. The bolt-type needle fitting on the opposite end can be adjusted to alter the spring preload and raise or lower fuel pressure. Alternately, the optional adjuster-fitting with small hose barb for a manifold pressure reference line raises and lowers fuel pressure as an offset from the basic spring pressure as a function of engine loading. This maintains a fixed relationship between fuel pressure and manifold pressure so fuel is always spraying into the same relative air pressure. *MSD*

the engine at a given moment so it can compute the basic fuel requirement in weight (1/14.7 of the air mass). The microcomputer then determines special modifications to the base fuel requirement (enrichment or enleanment) at the current engine speed and loading and then begins scheduling injector opening and closing times needed to achieve the correct pulse width, providing the correct air/fuel mixture.

To measure air entering the engine, our system might utilize a tiny heated wire located in the inlet air stream just upstream of the throttle body. This wire would measure the cooling effect of incoming air by measuring the electrical current required to keep the wire at a precisely targeted temperature—which will be exactly proportional to the number of air molecules entering the engine at a given moment. This is called air mass. The mass airflow (MAF) sensor's output voltage or frequency will be constantly converted electronically to digital values available to the microcomputer to use in its fuel computations.

Step 6. Startup
How might such a system run? Very likely the engine sputters and coughs a little, but will not start. Eventually we resort to a long shot of starting fluid straight in the throttle body while cranking. The engine struggles to life, coughing and backfiring through the intake manifold and running badly. After a few minutes of warm up it idles great.

After considering the problem, we realize another sensor is required—an engine temperature sensor designed to give the microcomputer information, so we put a temp sensor in the coolant so it can tell when there's a cold-start situation. We know that gasoline doesn't mix well with cold air, that only the lightest fractions of gasoline will vaporize well in the cold. We know that a normal but cold air/fuel mixture will not burn well in a cold engine since much of the injected gasoline has not vaporized or atomized well. The gasoline exists as liquid droplets or threads

of fuel suspended in the air and coating the cold cylinder or manifold walls as dew. In fact, plain liquid fuel doesn't burn; motor fuel must be well mixed with air to burn properly. Once the engine is running, much of the fuel actually vaporizes in the hot cylinders, but during cold cranking, the cylinder walls are stone cold too, and necessary cold-start air/fuel ratio may be in the 1.5:1 to 4:1 range in cold weather!

With a coolant-temperature sensor installed, when the engine is cold the microcomputer knows to inject plenty of extra fuel so that at least some will vaporize well enough to run the engine. The microcomputer gradually diminishes this enrichment as the engine warms up.

The next time the engine is cold, we turn the key and it starts quickly and runs well while warming up.

So we back out of our virtual driveway. . . .

After a few tanks of gas we noticed the car bogged badly on sudden acceleration at lower rpm, got worse than expected fuel economy, and had less than expected power under wide-open throttle. So we're back in the virtual garage installing yet another sensor—a throttle position sensor (TPS)—and reprogramming the computer one more time.

On rapid throttle opening, manifold air pressure increases, but airflow measurement systems can have difficulty keeping up with the rapid changes, and increased pressure slows the rate of fuel vapor. With its new TPS, the computer detects when we are opening the throttle. Now the microcomputer adds transient enrichment to ordinary injection pulse width on throttle opening. The stumble goes away. We also program the computer to create a richer mixture than normal when the throttle is more wide open and to cut the pulse width a little to lean the mixture when we're running with the throttle only partly open.

The fuel economy improves, and the acceleration snaps our necks back. Cool.

Step 7. Naming the system and making it smart
We name our virtual EFI system sequential port injection of fuel (SPIF), and give it one more interesting capability: We give it the ability to learn, and we add some features that make it easier to tune and program.

Locating an oxygen sensor in the exhaust system enables SPIF to deduce the air/fuel ratio of pre-combustion charge mixtures near stoichiometric in the cylinders based on the amount of residual exhaust gas oxygen present following combustion. And we now add code that enables the system to learn from its mistakes and make adjustments to injection times to target proper air/fuel mixtures. This mode of operation, in which the microcomputer is able to evaluate its own performance and make corrections on the fly, is called a closed-loop system, because the results of previous computations (injection pulse width) are fed back as input to future pulse width calculations along with information about the results achieved.

Just for fun, we design the operating firmware on our SPIF microcomputer so we can adjust the behavior of SPIF (reprogram it) something like a video game. We can use a mouse or a few keystrokes to change the height of graphs on the video screen of a Windows laptop computer connected by data cable to our SPIF microcomputer.

Step 8. How did we do?
We still haven't tried to make our virtual EFI system pass emissions, but so far, so good. We've built an electronic fuel-injection system that gets the job done. And our SPIF system is,

Fuel supply for the single-point injection system.
1 Injector, 2 Fuel-pressure regulator, 3 Fuel filter, 4 Electric fuel pump (here as in-tank type), 5 Relay, 6 ECU.

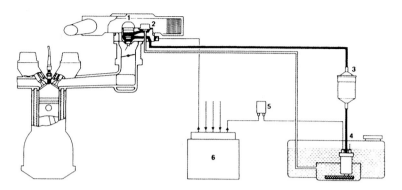

One of the chief advantages of multi-point EFI is the freedom to design dry intake manifolds that only need to handle air rather than air and fuel, which negotiate curves at differently varying engine speeds and therefore require extensive manifold modifications to keep fuel from puddling on runner surfaces and re-entering the air stream at unpredictable intervals.
Jan Norbye

Fuel supply for the multipoint injection system (MPI).
1 Injector(s), 2 Fuel-pressure regulator, 3 Fuel filter, 4 Electric fuel pump (here as in-line type), 5 Relay, 6 ECU, 7 Fuel rail.

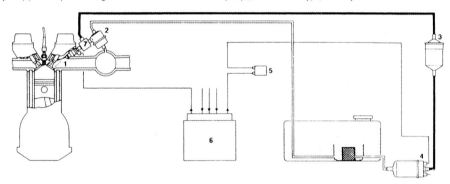

in fact, very similar to some commercial injection systems you'll find on road-going engines from Detroit, Europe, and Japan.

But consider this: SPIF delivers fuel to a set of injectors aimed at the intake ports of an engine. OK, there is a certain amount of programming logic operating behind the scenes to compute pulse width under various circumstances and to make corrections according to exhaust gas feedback. But as we noted before, SPIF really does only one thing to fuel the engine: It opens and closes injectors, sometimes faster, sometimes slower, sometimes longer or shorter, but that's it. At idle—or at part throttle, full throttle during sudden acceleration, even during warm-up—the microcomputer makes its calculations, and the injectors buzz along, opening and closing. That's it.

If we were planning to get into business selling SPIF systems in the real world, we would want to make some modifications to our design for certain marketing and technical reasons, depending on the type of use we anticipated. We'd certainly want to add the ability to control ignition timing, and we might want to add the capability to control idle speed, boost pressure, and other nonfuel engine actuators. Our current version of SPIF is not quite ready for prime time. But it's very close.

Step 9. Revisionist Designs

OK. Our SPIF virtual EFI engine is now running pretty nicely. But before we try to take it to the races or down to the emissions lab, before we install a supercharger or nitrous-oxide injection or other wild stuff like that (which is perfectly compatible with EFI, as we'll see), it might be valuable to re-examine the engineering decisions we made in designing SPIF, and to consider other approaches we could have taken (and that have been taken in the real world) in our fuel-injection system design.

ALTERNATE INJECTION LOCATIONS

SPIF injects fuel into each intake port, directly at the inlet valve, in time with the intake stroke. But we could also have injected the fuel for all cylinders farther upstream in the intake manifold at a single point near the throttle body like a carburetor, which is referred to as throttle body injection (TBI). One disadvantage of TBI is that there is less freedom to optimize intake manifold design for maximum airflow because manifolds must be designed to handle a wet mixture. Another disadvantage is the potential for unequal fuel distribution, which is almost always a factor with TBI systems.

Taking a different approach, we could have injected fuel directly into each cylinder like a diesel engine—also referred to as gasoline direct-injection (G-DI). Injecting fuel directly into a cylinder to achieve some of the advantages of both a diesel and a spark-ignition powerplant requires a fuel pump with extremely high operating pressure capabilities. Under some circumstances the fuel pump may be injected against compression cylinder pressures and in this case fuel must arrive in the cylinders within a very narrow window of time. For these reasons, direct-injection high-pressure mechanical injection pumps have operated at pressures as high as 3,000 psi and thus tend to be noisy and rob power. Injection timing can be critical, since fuel injected during the compression stroke must have time to atomize. This is a small window of opportunity on high speed engines operating near redline—a few thousandths of a second! Nevertheless, mechanical direct-injection systems were used for many years on gasoline-engine Mercedes cars until the 1970s. As the new millennium approached, automakers developed new electronically controlled "common rail" direct-injection gasoline engines (using technologies such as Piezo-electric injectors,

Huge IS550 fuel injector.

which are able to open against direct-injection pressures at high speed with great precision) that offered dramatically improved fuel economy via stratified-charge combustion and improved power compared to the same engines with multi-port injection. Electronic direct-injection control systems are similar to multi-port injection, with the exception that 1) the EMS typically monitors and manages fuel rail pressure, 2) air/fuel ratios can be far leaner (in stratified charge combustion mode), and the voltages required to operate injectors are typically higher (though the injector drivers are typically offloaded from the main EMS computer into an auxiliary controller that has very robust high-voltage electrics).

But as long as we're looking at alternative designs, it is worth noting that with *port* EFI, injection timing is not particularly critical at all. Old Bosch L-Jetronic systems injected half the required fuel from all injectors simultaneously twice per complete engine cycle, meaning that fuel arrived in the intake ports at widely varying crankshaft positions with respect to the four-stroke cycle, meaning some fuel might wait for a time in the intake port until the valve opened, whereas fuel injected in another port during the intake stroke might travel into the cylinder immediately, but for all intents and purposes it didn't much matter. There are some fairly minor fuel consumption and emissions advantages to timed sequential port injection systems like SPIF (at idle and very low speeds; at maximum power rpm, fuel is being injected a large portion of the time whether it's sequential or batch injection), but many EFI systems batch it and perform very well. Batch injection would have enabled us to dispense with the crank sensor, since the microcomputer could easily determine engine speed by counting sparks at the ignition coil (and injection timing is irrelevant to batch injection).

Throttle body injection need not be timed either (although it must use an injection strategy that pulses the injector(s) often enough to provide equal fuel distribution to the various cylinders). With any such single-point injection there is plenty of time on the way to the cylinder for the fuel to atomize. However, as in a single carbureted fueling system, all single-point injection systems must deal with the opposite problem: fuel can separate from air on the long (and usually unequal length) path to the cylinders, wetting the surface of some sections of the intake manifold, which results in uneven and unpredictable mixtures in various cylinders at any given moment.

Single-point systems such as this can suffer from the difficulties of single-carburetor engines in achieving equal air/fuel mixtures in individual cylinders, particularly since getting equal amounts of air to all the cylinders does not always equate to getting equal amounts of air and fuel to each one (fluid mechanics of air and fuel are not the same). Heavier fuel is more likely to gravitate to the outside of a manifold bend, for example, compared to air.

ALTERNATE AIR MEASUREMENT

Another alternate injection design would have us eliminate the hot-wire MAF sensor measuring the amount of air entering the engine. Instead, the microcomputer could do a good job setting pulse width using data from an airflow meter measuring the velocity of air entering the engine, based on air pressure against a spring-loaded flapper valve suspended like a door in the air stream and linked to a linear potentiometer (something like a volume control). Air velocity is not necessarily the same as air mass, but it is when corrected for the temperature of the intake air and atmospheric pressure (two additional easy-to-install electronic sensors). Bosch L-Jetronic systems use velocity air metering.

In fact, an alternate version of SPIF could throw out the entire concept of actually metering air, and indirectly deduce how much air is entering the engine based on less-expensive sensors measuring manifold pressure and engine speed, with corrections for air temperature—which, for a given displacement and engine volumetric efficiency, equates to air mass flow. Although engines always displace the same volume of air in the cylinders, at various throttle positions, speeds, and loading, and with various camshafts, manifolds, and so on, an engine varies in efficiency at pulling in total mass of air.

An engine operating at high vacuum (with the throttle nearly closed) is unable to pull in as much air as the same engine operating at wide-open throttle with higher manifold pressure. The engine is also less efficient on a hot day or at the top of a mountain where the air is thinner. Speed-density injection systems sense engine speed and manifold pressure as well as ambient air temperature to deduce the air mass entering the engine (or skip worrying about VE and just look up injection pulse width in a table for the current combination of engine speed and manifold pressure). This is the same figure supplied by SPIF's MAF sensor but it's arrived at using a different method.

One advantage of speed-density systems is that they do not restrict inlet airflow like velocity air meters (with the pressure drop that exists at the air metering door). Speed-density systems also compensate automatically for any air losses or leaks in the engine's inlet system, which is definitely not true of MAF

Bosch Piezo injector for Gasoline-Direct Injection applications. The injector operates at up to 3,000 psi fuel pressure, using the principle that an electric current causes Piezo-electric disks to expand ever so slightly, but virtually instantaneously. By stacking a large number of disks, the combined expansion is enough to open a LONG fuel injector.

sensors. Speed-density injection systems, without MAF sensors, may allow greater flexibility of inlet air plumbing to the throttle body, particularly on turbocharged engines. On the other hand, speed-density injection systems can have problems at idle if engine vacuum fluctuates and wanders (as it might on engines with high lift, high overlap cams).

Cadillac offered one of the first speed-density EFI systems as an option on its 1976 500-ci motors. Early '80s Ford 5.0 V-8s, all GM TBI V-8s, as well as some TPI (tuned port injection), and many other factory engine management systems have offered speed-density engine management. Virtually all aftermarket standalone engine management systems offer speed-density engine control. Really, it's the default.

Some of the more sophisticated aftermarket systems are capable of using MAF (or even direct-torque load sensing) in the base fuel calculation. After a schizophrenic period some years back when car companies such as Ford and GM skipped back and forth between MAF and MAP load sensing and couldn't seem to decide which they liked better, many of the newest factory engines are equipped with both MAP and MAF sensors, and are capable of providing excellent speed-density engine management if the MAF fails or is disconnected.

VIRTUAL ALTERNATE INJECTORS

It may already have occurred to you that adjusting the on-time of injectors is only one way to regulate how much fuel ends up in the cylinders of an engine. Instead of using injectors that always flow the same amount of fuel per time (like SPIF)—and regulating how long the microcomputer turns them on (pulsewidth)—we could use a set of injectors that spray continuously and vary the pressure to determine how much fuel is forced through the injectors in order to meet engine requirements. Such injectors could be purely mechanical devices, using a spring-loaded check valve to stop fuel from dripping or spraying out the injector until a threshold pressure forces the injector open.

Bosch KE-Jetronic fuel injection used a microcomputer and a set of sensors—including an electromechanical air meter—to vary fuel flow through a set of injectors that flow continuously on CIS. Based on measured airflow, the computer controls a valve regulating fuel pressure exerted against the variable-length slits of a barrel metering valve on the way to continuous port fuel injectors. More fuel through the slits means more fuel out the injectors—on a continual basis.

MECHANICAL INJECTION

If we were using a continuous injection scheme instead of SPIF, we could actually have eliminated the computer entirely—as Bosch did in the original K-Jetronic that pre-dated the Bosch KE-Jetronic. Fuel was regulated to the injectors using entirely mechanical means. A carefully designed velocity air metering flapper valve suspended in the inlet air stream mechanically actuated a fuel control plunger contained in a vertical fuel barrel (something like a piston in a cylinder) such that vertical slit openings in the sides of the fuel barrel were progressively uncovered as the control plunger moved upward, allowing more fuel to flow through the larger unblocked area of the slits and on to the injectors. For a given amount of air entering the engine at any given moment, the fuel metering plunger in K-Jetronic reaches equilibrium at a point where the force of air entering the engine—as transmitted mechanically to the metering plunger—exactly balances fuel pressure tending to force the plunger the opposite direction.

Paxton high-performance port-injection inline fuel pump.

SINGLE-POINT INJECTION

But as discussed earlier, why inject fuel at the ports at all? A single large-capacity injector, pointing straight down at the throttle body, can provide fuel for all the cylinders. This injector could operate continuously and at reasonably low pressures since there would be no need to force fuel through a multi-injector fuel rail at high pressure to ensure accurate fuel delivery and pressure at multiple injector locations.

In fact, we might even decide to operate our single injector at atmospheric pressure. To do this, we could pump fuel into a reservoir near the throttle body, using a float-operated check valve (a miniature version of the valve in a toilet tank) to keep the reservoir full but prevent the fuel pump from overfilling the reservoir. The fuel in the reservoir would then exist at ambient atmospheric pressure. Cleverly using Bernoulli's principle, we could then constrict the inlet air passage slightly above the throttle plate, just above the maximum height of the fuel reservoir, which would create a minor restriction in airflow. Air headed into the engine would speed up as it passes through the restriction, or venturi, and slow down again on the other side.

As we discussed earlier, Bernoulli's principle states that when air speeds up as it flows past a solid surface, it exerts decreased pressure. Presto! We've created a small area that always has lower pressure than atmospheric when the engine is running, with the pressure reduced in proportion to the amount of airflow (the more air entering the engine, the faster the air will rush through the restriction and the greater the pressure drop will be in the restriction compared to atmospheric).

We could then install a tiny injector inside the inlet constriction and run a fuel line to the reservoir. No check valve is needed in the injector anymore as is required on Bosch K-Jet systems. Since the injector is located just above the fuel level in the reservoir, fuel flow will cease flowing the instant pressure rises to atmospheric in the venturi when the engine stops. We could calibrate the flow rate of the passage connecting the injector and reservoir in order to tune the correct air/fuel mixture.

Oh no. We just invented the carburetor. But does it suck or does it blow?

It is, in fact, the higher pressure of the earth's atmosphere that forces fuel out of the float chamber and into the low-pressure area of the venturi. We can conclusively say the carb blows.

ENGINE MANAGEMENT AND THE FOUR CYCLES OF AN ENGINE

In the first cycle of a four stroke engine—intake—the piston is moving down, drawing in air/fuel through the open intake valve. Somewhere near the bottom of the stroke, the intake valve closes. In most cases, the intake valve actually opens a little in advance of the initial downward movement of the piston and doesn't close until a bit after the piston has passed bottom dead center. This allows the incoming air/fuel mixture to continue filling the cylinder due to the inertia of the intake mixture at high inlet velocities as the crankshaft continues its rotation, when the piston has barely begun to accelerate away from bottom dead center.

Particularly in engines designed to operate at high speeds, the valve must stay open a long time in order to make more power as explained above (long-duration cam profile). However, at low speeds, this late closing can allow some of the intake mixture to be pumped out of the combustion chamber back into the intake manifold, particularly at small throttle openings when high vacuum exists in the intake manifold. This pump-back phenomenon means that engines with longer cams have higher manifold pressure (lower vacuum) at lower rpm ranges, even though airflow through the engine is no greater.

A computer sensing engine speed and manifold pressure has no way of distinguishing between a short-cammed engine at a heavier load and a longer-cammed engine operating at a lighter load. Yet very different fueling is required for best power and economy in these two situations.

In the second cycle—compression—the piston moves upward, compressing the mixture. The spark plug fires as the piston nears the top of the stroke, timed in such a way that the maximum cylinder pressure produced by combustion peaks at about 15 degrees after top center in order to deliver best torque. It is necessary to fire the plug while the piston is moving up because it takes time for the fuel-air mixture to burn, and the flame that starts when the plug fires initially exists as a tiny kernel that is expanding relatively slowly.

Combustion is a chain reaction of sorts. Once a few percent of the compressed mixture is burning, the rest of combustion proceeds quickly. Depending on various considerations, spark advance can be anywhere from 5 to more than 50 degrees of crankshaft rotation before top dead center. Normally, engine designers strive to correlate spark advance so that, for all combinations of speed and loading, the engine produces mean best torque (MBT). If the engine begins to knock before MBT is achieved, the engine is considered knock limited.

In the third cycle—power—the piston is pushed down by pressure produced in the cylinder by combustion, typically over 600 psi.

In the final stroke—exhaust—the exhaust valve opens near bottom dead center, and as the piston rises, exhaust gases are pushed out past the exhaust valve. As mentioned earlier, on high-speed engines, there is usually a certain amount of valve overlap, in which the exhaust valve stays open after top center and the intake opens before top center to make use of inertial forces acting on the moving gases. This produces greater volumetric efficiencies at high rpm. At low rpm, particularly with high-manifold vacuum (low pressure), there is some reverse flow comprised of mainly exhaust gases flowing back from the higher-pressure exhaust into the low-pressure intake.

At lower rpm, a cam with more duration and overlap results in higher manifold pressures (less vacuum) but lower airflow through the engine.

In fact, cam specifications have a large effect on spark advance and air/fuel mixture requirements. Other factors affecting mixture and timing include compression ratio, fuel octane rating, and, of course, engine operating conditions

(speed, temperature, and loading). Spark advance requirements tend to increase with speed up to a point. Advance requirements decrease with loading, since dense mixtures produced by the high volumetric efficiencies of wide-open throttle or boosting power-adders like turbocharging burn more quickly. Higher compression also increases the density of the charge mixture and the flame speed. With a big cam, the advance at full throttle can be aggressive and quick. Low VE at low rpm results in slow combustion. Exhaust dilution lowers combustion temperatures and the tendency to knock.

Part throttle advance on big-cam engines can also be aggressive due to these same flame speed reductions resulting from exhaust dilution of the inlet charge due to valve overlap.

Before computer-controlled spark advance, mechanical rotating weights advanced spark with engine speed by exerting centrifugal force against a cam-actuated advance mechanism constrained at lower speeds by the force of mechanical springs. At the same time, light engine loading would independently increase vacuum forces acting against a spring-loaded diaphragm and advance timing under conditions of high vacuum.

Limitations on the complexity of this type of engine-management-by-mechanical-means introduced tradeoffs that meant, practically speaking, that on some engines in order to prevent spark knock under some conditions the spark advance curve might have to be suboptimal at other times. If the engine had a big cam, low idle manifold pressure might mean that there was no good way to achieve required advance at low speeds without over-advancing timing at mid- and high-rpm ranges.

The chemically perfect idle air/fuel mixture by weight in which all air and fuel are consumed occurs with 14.64 parts air and 1 part gasoline. Chemists refer to such a perfect ratio of reactants as stoichiometric. Mixtures with a greater percentage of air are called lean mixtures and occur as higher numbers (14.64 and up with gasoline). Richer mixtures, in which there is an excess of fuel, are represented by smaller numbers. The rich burn limit for a gasoline engine at normal operating temperature is 6.0, the lean burn limit for an EFI engine is above 22. The following table, courtesy of Edelbrock, indicates characteristics of various mixtures. In practice, stoichiometric mixtures are rarely optimal for fueling an engine. Another way of measuring the air/fuel ratio is to consider the ratio of the actual air/fuel ratio to the stoichiometric ratio, also known as lambda. In the case of gasoline, if the actual air/fuel ratio is 14.64, lambda = 1.0.

Air/fuel ratio	Lambda	Comment
6.0	0.41	Rich burn limit (fully warm engine)
9.0	0.61	Black smoke/low power
11.5	0.79	Approximate rich best torque at wide-open throttle
12.2	0.83	Safe best power at wide-open throttle
13.3	0.91	Approximate lean best torque
14.64	1.00	Stoichiometric air/fuel ratio (chemically ideal)
15.5	1.06	Lean cruise
16.5	1.13	Usual best economy
18.0	1.23	Carbureted lean burn limit
22+	1.50+	EEC/EFI Lean Burn Limit

Note: These figures do not indicate anything about the effect of various mixtures on exhaust emissions.

The actual optimal air/fuel mixture requirements of an engine vary as a function of temperature, rpm, and loading. Cold engines require enrichment to counteract the fact that only the lightest fractions of fuel will vaporize at colder temperatures, while the rest exists as globules or drops of fuel that are not mixed well with air. Most of the fuel will be wasted. At temperatures below zero, the air/fuel mixture may be as low as 4 to 1, and at cranking as rich as 1.5 to 1!

Big cams result in gross dilution of air/fuel mixture at idle, which burns slowly and requires a lot of advance and a mixture as rich in some cases as 11.5 to 1 (lambda ≈ 0.79) to counteract the lumpy uneven idle resulting from partial burning in some cycles. Short-cam engines may run at stoichiometric mixtures at idle for cleanest exhaust emissions.

Coming off idle, a big-cam engine may require mixtures nearly as rich as at idle to eliminate surging, starting at 12.5–13.0 (0.85-0.89 lambda) and leaning out with speed or loading. Mild cams will permit 14–15 mixtures in off-idle and slow cruise (0.96-1.0 lambda).

With medium speeds and loading, the bad effects of big cams diminish, resulting in less charge dilution, which will allow the engine to happily burn air/fuel mixtures of 14 to 15 and higher. At the leaner end, additional spark advance is required to counteract slow burning of lean mixtures.

At higher loading with partial throttle, richer mixtures give better power by increasing the likelihood that all air molecules have fuel present to burn. Typical mixtures giving best drivability are in the range of 13.0 to 14.5 (0.89-0.99 lambda), depending on speed and loading.

At wide-open throttle, where the objective is maximum power, all four-cycle gasoline engines require mixtures that fall between lean and rich best torque, in the 11.5 to 13.3 range (0.79-0.91 lambda). Since this best torque mixture spread narrows at higher speeds, a good goal for naturally aspirated engines is 12 to 12.5 (0.82-0.85 lambda), perhaps richer if fuel is being used for cooling in a turbo/supercharged engine.

The main difference between computer-controlled engines and earlier modes of control is that the computer's internal tables of speed and loading can have virtually any desired degree of granularity and can generate spark advance and fueling that are relatively independent of nearby break-points, something that is impossible with mechanical control systems. (Note: Most engine management control algorithms implement mandatory smoothing of fuel and timing matrices by forcing a certain degree of averaging between adjacent breakpoints.)

Bottom line, computer-controlled engines eliminate many of the compromises of mechanical fuel delivery and spark controls. Multi-port injection eliminates problems with handling wet mixtures in the intake manifold that are associated with carbs, resulting in improved cold running, improved throttle response under all conditions, and improved fuel economy without drivability problems.

THEORY OF ELECTRONIC FUEL AND ENGINE MANAGEMENT

All computer-controlled engines basically function using this four-step process:
1. Accumulate data in the ECU from engine sensors.
2. Derive engine status from engine temperature, speed, loading, intake air temperature, and other important parameters.

Lingenfelter Corvette makes use of FAST EMS. Note engine compartment auxiliary fuel tank, which can potentially be used to deliver race gasoline or methanol to a knock-limited engine at very heavy engine loading in a dual-fold EMS.

3. Determine and schedule the next action(s) to control spark timing and fuel delivery.
4. Translate computer output signals into electrical signals that directly control actuators (injectors, coil driver, idle-air bypass control, fuel pump, and so on). Go back to 1.

The microprocessor handling this process executes a program that can be divided into the algorithms that understand sensor input and conditionally compute what to do next based on sensor data and internal calibration tables, and the calibration data acted upon by the conditional logic, which drives the data-dependent conditional logic of the algorithms to execute in particular ways appropriate to a specific engine application.

EFI control systems can be divided into several types, all of which break down fuel and spark event scheduling based on engine speed, but which use different methods to estimate engine loading:
1. Throttle-position (a.k.a. Alpha-N) systems use throttle angle and engine speed to estimate engine loading.
2. Mass airflow systems estimate loading by sensing engine speed and throttle angle and directly measuring air entering the intake manifold.
3. Speed-density systems estimate loading based on rpm and manifold pressure.
4. Some of the newest engine management systems can directly measure engine loading with torque-sensitive strain gauges or even in-cylinder combustion-pressure transducers. Some engine management systems can switch between the type of load measurement system, depending on conditions and/or configuration.

Naturally aspirated race cars often use throttle position and speed to estimate loading. Alpha-N systems are not bothered by a lack of (or fluctuating!) manifold pressure on engines with wild cams. There is no airflow restriction on the inlet. However—particularly on engines with very large throttle areas (such as one butterfly per cylinder)—tiny changes in throttle angle can result in huge changes in engine loading, meaning that the Alpha-N may have resolution problems at small throttle angles.

Many factory vehicles use MAF-based engine control, and MAF metering is available as an option on some aftermarket

Norwood dragger with 250 CID inline-4 MAX-4 DOCH powerplant runs on nitromethane, delivered by staged injection utilizing three electronic injectors per cylinder.

engine management systems. MAF systems measure air mass entering the engine based on the electric power required to hold a hot wire or film at a fixed temperature as intake airflow changes. MAF systems can be restrictive to inlet air, particularly if maximum engine airflow increases due to performance modifications. Designers may find it a challenge to install the MAF sensor in a location where it will be unaffected by reversion pulses in tuned inlet systems.

MAF sensors tend to be slow to respond to very rapid changes in load (sudden wide-open throttle) and therefore require supplemental means of control to manage engines under rapidly changing conditions. Advantages of MAF control include the ability to compensate for reductions in VE as an engine wears over time and the ability to compensate for modest user modifications that increase VE, such as camshaft changes. Note that MAF sensors typically translate airflow into a 0-5 volt signal (in some cases it's a frequency rather than voltage change), meaning that a particular MAF meter will be "pegged" and unable to indicate additional airflow if sensor output voltage reaches 5 volts.

MAF systems automatically correct for altitude and air density changes because these factors affect intake air mass, which affects the cooling of the MAF meter.

Velocity airflow metering uses a spring-actuated door that is forced open by the action of air rushing into the intake through the air meter. A linear potentiometer measures the position of the door, which corresponds to the velocity of intake air. Air velocity must be converted to air mass by factoring in charge air temperature. This system is similar to MAF metering, with the additional disadvantages of additional inlet flow restriction from the air door. Like a MAF meter, a velocity sensor has no

sensitivity to increased airflow beyond the point at which the air door is fully open and "pegged."

Speed-density systems have also been used by car companies for engine control, and virtually all aftermarket standalone EMSs provide speed-density load measurement. These systems may deduce engine airflow with a computation involving a engine speed and manifold pressure, air temperature, and a volumetric efficiency table built for the specific engine and tied to engine displacement and a table of target air/fuel ratios. Alternately, Speed-density systems may use speed, density, and temperature as an index into a look-up fuel table of injection pulse width (or some derivative corresponding to pulse width) at a representative selection of operating points, performing calculations to interpolate fueling and spark for operating points that occur between points on the look-up table grid. Speed-density systems that use fuel pulse width tables are not able to compensate for modifications to the base engine configuration or changes in VE caused by wear over time without recalibration of the fuel tables. Speed-density control systems typically respond quickly to changes in load, offer good resolution at low loading, and do not restrict inlet airflow like air metering systems.

Torque and cylinder-pressure sensing systems are one level closer to the actual functioning of an engine than all of the above systems, in that they know when engine management strategies make more combustion pressure, as opposed to a reliance on more indirect phenomena like exhaust gas oxygen levels, engine speed, or even mass airflow. Rather than focusing on optimizing fuel delivery to chase a particular air/fuel ratio (itself typically a deduction based on exhaust gas oxygen content), such systems have the potential to learn how to make more power, on the fly.

Engine Temp.

Ambient Temp.

Fuel
Injector

Chapter 2
Understanding Automotive Computers and PROMS

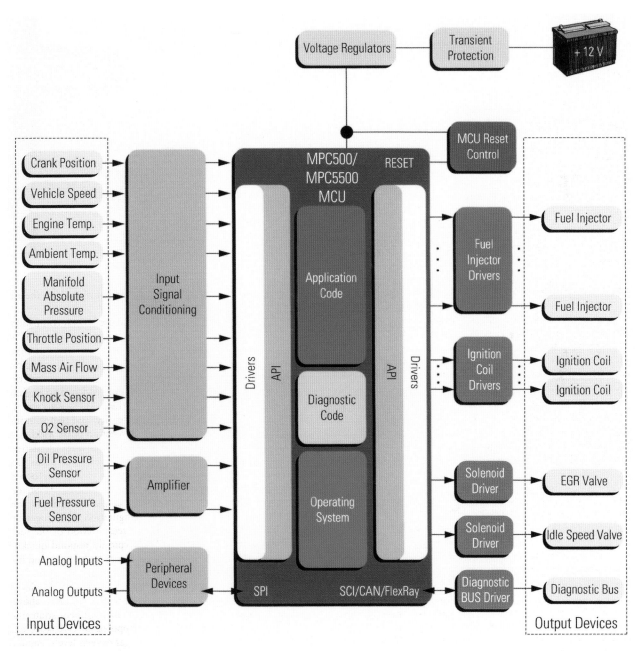

The Motorola MPC500/5500 system diagram illustrates how signals and data from various sensors are conditioned and amplified and then processed by application and operating system logic via application program interface (API) and low-level driver routines. Events are analyzed and evaluated using state-transition logic, then translated into actions via output APIs and actuator driver routines that manage injectors, ignition coil drivers, and various solenoid-driver hardware that in turn manages idle speed, EGR, diagnostics, and other actuators. *Motorola*

Ambient Temp.

Fuel
Injector

AUTOMOTIVE COMPUTERS & PROMs

This Motec M800 consists of a metal enclosure that protects the circuitry and functions as a heat sink to dissipate heat from the power supply and output drivers. This version has three multi-pin connectors on one end. Inside is the processor, memory, and A-to-D input-output circuitry. The controller has no hard drive or other moving parts. Many Engine Control Modules are not designed to survive the harsh heat, vibration, and moisture of an engine compartment. *Motec*

UNDERSTANDING AUTOMOTIVE COMPUTERS AND PROMS

It's time to take a harder look at the demands of real engines and how the logic of engine management systems work to satisfy them. Let's see how a sample engine management computer operates.

A digital microprocessor is essentially an array of microscopic switches and circuits and digital storage locations that have the ability to do a few simple things, such as turn on a voltage to one circuit or memory location if a voltage is present in one (and only one) of two other circuits or memory locations (a capability that allows amplification, rather than just relay-type switching). From this type of extremely basic decision-making ability comes all functionality of modern computers: from the simplest arithmetic to complex algorithms that actually simulate human thought. In the same sense that electrons, protons, and neutrons are combined to make atoms—and atoms combined to make molecules—the basic electronic switching abilities of a digital computer can be combined to perform more complex functions. Arithmetic and logical operations can be combined into a series of steps to solve a problem, like setting the pulse width of a fuel-injection action.

Microcomputers use quartz crystals that resonate at a particular frequency to coordinate internal operations. Microcomputers with very fast crystals and circuitry can perform millions or even billions of instructions per second. Using amplification circuitry, a digital microcomputer has the capability to activate or deactivate external circuits. For example, to turn on an external device like a fuel injector, a microprocessor might perform a calculation, the result of which is that the number "1" is loaded into a special memory location called a register in place of the previous value of "0." This type of register is accessible not only to the microprocessor but to the center lead of a power transistor, which acts like a switch to allow (or not allow) a larger current to flow between the transistor's other two leads, which can be used (perhaps through additional amplification stages of the "driver" circuit) to ground an output wire leading to a coil in a fuel injector whose other end is connected to battery voltage when the ignition is on. Thus, the microprocessor sets a bit in a register that changes the conductivity of a transistor that grounds and energizes an electromagnetic coil that pulls open a needle valve that allows fuel to spray into an engine. Working in the opposite direction, a device outside the computer can input data to the microprocessor as follows: A circuit outside the computer presents a signal from a sensor or other device (such as a nitrous arming switch). Input circuitry converts this to a low power signal that sets one or more bits in a register that represents a binary number, which is accessible to the microprocessor and can be used as the operand in a logical or arithmetic calculation that could, in turn, initiate various actions, depending on the state of the initial input signal.

Random-access memory (RAM) is vital to the operation of a digital computer. Memory once consisted of a grid of tiny magnetic cores comprised of tiny ferrous rings surrounding the intersections of sets of three fine wires. Using the bidirectional principles of magnetic inductance, these cores could be written to or read with electrical current in the same way that an audio recorder writes or reads electrical signals representing music on a magnetic tape.

These days, memory exists in semiconductors—silicon chips containing millions or even billions of circuits representing individual data bits that can be set either on or off, electrically speaking. Depending on whether RAM is static or dynamic, each data bit is stored in a cluster of transistors or in a chargeable capacitor associated with a pair of transistors. Random access memory (RAM) can be written to and read from extremely quickly, but the data is volatile, meaning it is soon lost when the memory is not powered, meaning it is not suitable for storing code and permanent (or semi-permanent) data while the computer is turned off.

Computers use RAM as a high-speed scratchpad to store data used by or generated by a computer program. When the computer is up and running, RAM may be used to store some or all of the programming instructions that direct the arithmetic-logic unit of the computer to manipulate various kinds of data, though the basic machine instructions without which a microprocessor cannot do anything at all (which may be all there is on simple embedded controllers) may reside exclusively on a read-only memory (ROM) chip that essentially cannot be changed. ROM-based instructions, collectively, are often referred to as *firmware*—the term describing a special class of software that is embedded deeply in hardware and therefore relatively fixed due to the difficulty or impossibility of making changes without replacing hardware. A simple program might fetch several data values, perform arithmetic on them, turn on signals of certain durations, turn off the signal, and repeat this cycle again and again. This is the basic functioning of a fuel-injection pulse-width calculation.

Programmable read-only memory (PROM) retains its data when a microcomputer's power supply is turned off. PROM can only be read by the microprocessor, not written to (though PROM, unlike ROM chips, can be removed and "reprogrammed" by a special PROM-burner device using ultraviolet light; still, this can be inconvenient if a PROM chip is soldered to the circuit board rather than plugged into a socket). PROM may contain numbers that represent commands or instructions to the microcomputer, as well as numbers that are simply data. PROM is ideal for storing data that rarely or never changes, such as configuration information (that is, number of cylinders on a purpose-built OEM ECU installed exclusively to manage one type of V-8 engine), or the OEM fuel and timing curves for an engine. The ECU's microcomputer would typically transfer such data into RAM at power-up time for faster access.

The advantage of electrically erasable PROM (EEPROM) is it can be both read from and written to by the microprocessor itself. Byte-addressable EEPROM is relatively slow in access speed and in the past was not practical for storing large amounts

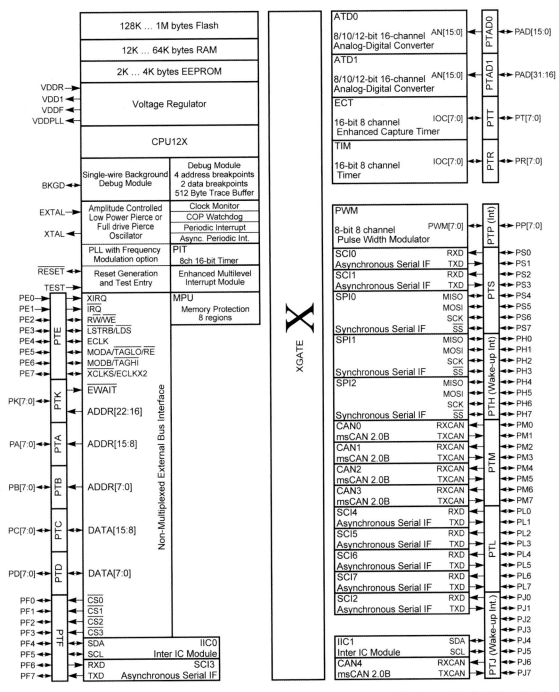

Freescale MC9S12 EPB processor schematic. This is a common chip on modern OE and aftermarket engine control modules, including MegaSquirt. *Copyright of Freescale, Inc. 2013, used by permission.*

of data. Modern engine management computers store all calibration data in *flash memory*, a special class of EEPROM that must be addressed in relatively large blocks. Flash memory is ideal for storing data values that a computer user or program must configure, such as the number of cylinders on an aftermarket programmable engine management computer that is capable of operating engines with 1 to 12 cylinders.

The arithmetic-logic unit (ALU) of a computer performs arithmetic and logical operations and generates the condition codes (status bits) that indicate whether the operation was successful. The ALU performs its operations using its own special high-speed memory called registers. Typically, the ALU loads an instruction that tells it which data to store in its registers, what simple operation to perform on the registers (such as arithmetic shift left, or logical OR, or whatever), and where to store the result of the operation—plus a data bit to indicate the status (success) of the operation. The ALU is a subset of the central processing unit (CPU). The CPU controls the operation of the microcomputer and is usually located in a microprocessor consisting of circuitry and memory located on a single microchip.

Engine Temp.

Ambient Temp.

Fuel
Injector

AUTOMOTIVE COMPUTERS & PROMS

The input/output (I/O) system controls the movement of data between the computer and devices external to the computer with which it must communicate. An engine management computer receives data from sensors via the I/O system that give it information about the engine and its environment. The computer also controls actuators such as fuel injectors that enable it to make things happen in the world via the I/O system. An EMS microcomputer must read data from engine sensors, perform internal processing on this data, and then send data via the I/O system to an injector driver circuit that will activate a solenoid-type injector (actuator) for a precise amount of time.

Analog-to-digital circuitry onboard the microprocessor converts input analog voltages to digital numbers that are meaningful to the computer and useful in computations. Some input data from some external devices is already in digital two-state binary format. Outbound data from a digital computer may be converted to an analog voltage and amplified enough to actuate a physical device such as an injector or an idle air-control motor. Some automotive computers have direct-digital output channels for controlling peripherals like digital boost controllers. The input and output channels, RAM, ROM, A-D circuitry, and the CPU are connected using a data/address bus that enforces a strict protocol defining when a device on the bus may move data to another device so that the bus can be shared by all. Microcomputers managing the engine of all 2008 and newer road-going vehicles and some race cars interface through the I/O system to controller area network (CAN) bus to external diagnostic devices and special-purpose embedded controllers that handle tasks like airbag deployment.

A typical EMS microcomputer contains data and operating instructions that enable the computer to cycle endlessly through a programmatic loop that calculates raw fuel delivery and spark advance for the current engine rpm and loading over and over as long as the engine is running. The computer will modify these with additional enrichments or "enleanments" for cold or hot cranking, after-start operation, warm-up operation, acceleration, and so on. Software routines additionally regulate closed-loop idle and cruise air/fuel calibration. ECUs designed to control ignition events also compute speed and load-based spark advance and knock sensor-controlled ignition retard. An ECU may also contain programming for wastegate control, control of emissions devices such as EGR, and activation of nitrous oxide injection and fuel enrichment.

COMPUTERS AND FUEL INJECTION

It can be a useful exercise to compare modern high-performance aftermarket EFI systems to the Hilborn mechanical injection systems used for decades on all postwar winning Indy cars until about 1970. Hilborn systems are still sometimes used in certain classes of racing because they're relatively cheap and easy to install. A critical thing to understand about fueling an engine is the fact that peak torque occurs at the rpm at which an engine is achieving its best volumetric efficiency (cylinder filling with air). Modern high-speed spark ignition engines usually make more horsepower at engine speeds exceeding this, but only because they are making more power pulses per unit of time. The cylinders are actually not filling as well with air. Therefore, fuel flow as a function of rpm no longer increases as steeply (the elbow in the curve occurs at peak VE).

The problem with such constant-flow mechanical injection systems is that the mechanical fuel pump, driven by the engine, increases in speed with the engine. Assuming a linear increase in

fuel pumped with pump speed (fuel pumped doubles as pump speed doubles), the engine will begin to run rich as rpm increases beyond peak torque and fuel flow continues to increase at a constant rate while airflow into the engine increases more slowly as VE decreases.

Hilborn systems use multiple fuel bypass systems to alter the shape of the fuel curve by returning excess fuel to the fuel tank. The main bypass contains a restrictor (a jet, sometimes referred to as a pill). A secondary bypass returns fuel based on throttle position—through a barrel valve, which serves to send varying amounts of fuel to the injectors based on slits or orifices progressively uncovered in the barrel valve as throttle position changes. A high-speed bypass uses an adjustable-diaphragm regulator to prevent excessive richness at higher rpm when fuel requirements begin to level off.

Mechanical fuel injection of this sort is great at delivering perfect distribution to all cylinders with great atomization. It is easy to understand how changing jets and adjusting regulators will mechanically alter fuel delivered by a mechanical injection system. It's straightforward to optimize peak power using this system, but it's difficult or impossible to optimize the air/fuel mixture at all speeds and engine loading. But who cares? Race cars are always running with 100 percent power or 100 percent braking.

Calibrating EFI requires a strategy that is at once simpler and more complex. EFI fuel mass delivery is rather simple, typically depending exclusively on changes in injection pulse width. On the other hand, the logic that determines injector open time is based on software modeling of engine behavior that can be extremely complex, and the logic path executed in a particular instance can be highly conditional, based on configuration data in scalars or multidimensional matrixes represented to the tuner or programmer as a series of 2D or 3D tables. Optimizing look-up tables that affect the functionality of software logic in a programmable EMS that controls the operation of electronic injectors and ignition timing requires, at the very least, the ability to understand the basic principles of combustion and the ability to understand and operate the graphical interface on a personal computer or interface module connected to the ECU.

To recalibrate or reconfigure the operation of many OEM ECUs—specifically designed to discourage tampering and to protect proprietary logic from easily falling into the hands of competitors—requires engineering skills, because this can be an R&D project. You'll probably need to be able to use relatively complex electronic debugging tools like microprocessor emulators that connect to the ECU circuitry, and you may need to be able to deduce how undocumented, proprietary data structures might be organized. In this case you'll probably need to have the ability to experiment and deduce how such data structures affect the operation of the computer in controlling fueling and everything else in a late-model vehicle: ignition advance, emissions-control devices, turbo wastegates, cooling fans, torque converter lockups, as well as other factors that affect engine power, economy, and exhaust emissions.

This sort of scientific-quality reverse engineering is complex and typically requires bright, experienced engineers or micro-programmers to achieve success. Once the existing OEM ECU operation is well understood, the reverse engineer has to determine the impact of making changes to the internal data tables based on good knowledge and theory and, ultimately, trial and error. This is the sort of thing aftermarket performance calibration designers go through. Of course, the process is

28

Engine Temp.

Ambient Temp.

Fuel Injector

much easier if you can hire an ex-employee of the OEM engine manufacturer (or have a good friend who works for one) who can obtain, through whatever means, access to the OEM ECU documentation (this is sometimes called industrial espionage). By contrast, the builder of an aftermarket ECU has a task that is at once simpler and more complex than reprogramming an OEM ECU. An ECU builder doesn't have the serious, problematic—in some cases virtually impossible—task of hacking or reverse-engineering an existing ECU, but instead must design and debug a real-time microcomputer control system with multiple I/O channels and operating software from scratch (probably after purchase and close study of existing competitive products), and the software has to have the parameterized and table-driven logic required to allow it to manage a wide variety of engines and to work with a wide variety of different sensors and actuators.

The amount of fuel squirting out of an electronic injector is largely determined by the injector open time, which is determined by the length of time the EMS computer maintains a circuit through the actuator's solenoid electromagnet. The EMS computer must vary pulse width on the fly in response to engine status—speed, temperature, and loading; throttle position; air density and temperature; and exhaust-gas oxygen content—which it determines in a fraction of a second via sensors.

Many EMS sensors work on the principle that the resistance of a certain medium to the flow of electricity varies according to mechanical force such as air pressure or energy such as temperature, changing the sensor's output to the computer. Analog-to-digital circuitry (typically embedded in tiny special-purpose microprocessors these days or even located on the main processor chip) converts continuously variable (analog) voltage to a discrete binary number (or a series of numbers over time) that a computer can use in its calculations. Of course, the computer must be programmed with special-purpose logic or table- or parameter-driven logic that allows it to understand the significance of sensor data. Some sensors output a signal that varies in frequency as the parameter being measured varies; a common example is knock sensors and some throttle-position sensors. Other sensors output digital numbers in binary format rather than electrical voltage, which varies in amplitude or frequency.

Computers operating engines execute logical routines over and over again in an endless loop when an engine is operating. EMS computers are what computer scientists call *state machines*. In sequential logic, a state transition table indicates the new state a finite state machine will move into, based on the current state and inputs indicating events that have transpired in the engine. A state table is essentially a truth table in which some of the inputs are the current state, and the outputs include the next state, along with other outputs. One dimension of the state transition table indicates current state, the other dimension indicates possible events, and the cells at the intersections contain the next state if such-and-such event happens, plus any action linked to this state transition.

EMS software determines the current engine state (say, compression stroke cylinder no. 1), examines sensor and internal data to determine what event may have occurred (say, arrived at 22 degrees BTDC), determines from the state transition table the new state (i.e., spark event in progress cylinder no. 1) and associated action (turn on cylinder no. 1 spark), updates the current state and executes the action (no. 1 spark *on*). At this point the loop begins anew.

Many complex and interrelated variables affect the operation of an engine. The ECU control logic may not have a complex

enough engine model to anticipate and process every actual operating condition with infinite granularity, and the engine sensors may not be sophisticated enough to provide "complete" information about what is happening in the engine, so ECUs frequently fail in their goal to achieve "perfect" engine operation. When this happens, there may be many possible causes. Perhaps a sensor is malfunctioning. Perhaps something subtle is going on in the engine that cannot be detected by existing sensors. Perhaps the control logic is not complex enough (smart enough) to anticipate every possible contingency. Perhaps there is a flaw in the system hardware or microcode. Perhaps the computer's actuators or sensors cannot react quickly enough to keep up with engine state changes. Perhaps the combination of engine speed, computer, sensors, and actuators are too slow to keep up with changing conditions, such that by the time the system can react, take action, and produce a certain engine state, conditions have changed so much that now the system can only overreact in a different direction.

We've all seen an engine hunting at idle, unable to achieve a stable operating environment. ECMs that have the speed required to consider the state of all engine sensors in real time to the finest time slice within which anything can change—ECUs coupled with fast sensors and fast engine actuators—allow the EMS to essentially treat the engine as if it is standing still. Under all circumstances, an EMS based on this hardware can reevaluate conditions and make corrections much faster than conditions can materially change.

EMS builders design their systems around a microprocessor. Electronic circuits, especially the microscopic circuits in the microprocessor, tend to be sensitive to heat, which can cause them to fail. The faster the circuitry, the more sensitive it is to heat, which must be dissipated in order to keep the circuitry running without catastrophic failure. Micro-circuitry based on emitter-coupled-logic (ECL), for example, is fast but builds up a lot of heat. The problem is made worse when microprocessor logic is so fast that a few extra inches of distance, even at the speed of light, will slow things down too much. In this case, circuitry must be packed more densely. Unlike the laptop PC used to word-process this book, which is equipped with a multi-speed fan cooling a heat-sink pressed against the microprocessor and designed to operate at "room temperature" (50 to 95 degrees Fahrenheit), most large, high-speed supercomputers have been designed to operate at about 68 degrees Fahrenheit, plus or minus a few degrees. Many large high-performance computers in the past have been water-cooled or even Freon-cooled, but consider the harsh environment of an automobile engine. The engine compartment (where some ECUs are located) may easily heat up to 200 or more degrees on a hot day when the engine is working hard. Even the passenger compartment can easily heat up to temperatures approaching 150 degrees or more with the windows shut on a hot sunny day with a black interior. In the winter in cold climates, the temperature might be well below 0 when the engine first starts. Vibration can be extreme, and the system is subject to high humidity and possibly dust. Offshore boats, aircraft, military combat vehicles, and racing vehicles may operate in still harsher environments. Bottom line, the microprocessor controlling any engine must be very rugged.

The average lifespan of a personal computer is two to four years, but automotive computers must operate flawlessly over the life of a vehicle (which could be measured in decades). To provide a long lifespan and eliminate logic errors due to heat failure and processor errors brought on by computation speeds that vary with temperature, embedded engine management

ECUs have tended to use older microprocessors operating at relatively slow clock speeds, such as the Motorola 6800 and 68000 that were once state-of-the-art devices used as the CPU in high-end workstations and personal computers and that live on as inexpensive chips with decades-old designs relegated to powering controllers installed in consumer applications such as calculators, toasters, and game consoles, or industrial applications such as automotive control systems. Whereas a fast microprocessor such as the hex-core Intel Core i7 Extreme Edition 3960X microprocessor operating at 3.33 GHz could perform *177,730* mips at the time of this writing, aftermarket EMS supplier AEM touted the processing power of its Infinity EMS computer, designed around a 200 MHz, 32-bit microprocessor able to process *400* mips. The microprocessor in AEM's Infinity had eight times the performance of many aftermarket ECUs (some of which still used 16-bit processors), but it was 450 times slower than a state-of-the-art kick-ass multi-core 64-bit processor. The result of using slow, robust processors operating at low-heat slow clock speeds is that some ECUs are at their compute-bound limit handling sequential injection within a granularity of a few ten-thousandths of a second while monitoring and controlling a dozen or so other engine actuators and sensors on a high-revving motorcycle or Indy car engine that redlines in the 10,000- to 20,000-rpm range.

In order for a microprocessor to manage engine-control devices, the ECU contains circuits called latches (something like relays), which respond to a control signal from the microprocessor by turning on, for example, a 12-volt signal with a square wave format to activate injector drivers. Other circuits convert the continuously varying analog voltage signals from sensors and convert them to digital format for the microprocessor. These A/D converters are usually integrated circuits and may in fact be built into the microprocessor itself (the Ford EEC-IV ECU, for example, uses a 10-bit A-D converter on the microprocessor chip itself). The engine management microprocessor contains multiple I/O channels that enable digital data—perhaps from a A/D converter—to be stored directly in the microprocessor's memory.

Injector drivers like the Motorola MC3484 are capable of producing 4 amps of peak current in less than a millisecond (a thousandth of a second) to bang open a fuel injector quickly. After 200 microseconds, the driver drops the current back to 1 amp to hold the injector open. Peak and hold drivers take advantage of the fact that it takes much less current to hold open an injector once the solenoid is initially energized. Peak and hold drivers consume much less power than saturated circuit drivers (that hold continuously at full voltage), yet are able to open the injectors rapidly. The MC3484 uses five leads for power-in, power-out, ground, trigger, and reference voltage. Whenever voltage in the trigger exceeds the reference, the driver will immediately route voltage from power-in to power-out, which can be used to fire an injector.

An operating EMS computer endlessly executes its way through a loop of software instructions that repeatedly sample

GENERATIONS OF OEM AUTOMOTIVE COMPUTERS

Ford's 1980s-vintage EEC-IV, using a proprietary special-purpose microprocessor, was designed specifically for automotive use. It was considered by many experts to be one of the best ECUs of its time. The EEC-IV was built for Ford by Intel, the same company that makes most of the chips for DOS-type PCs. The EEC-IV microprocessor operated at a frequency of 15 to 18 megahertz and was capable of operating at pretty close to real-time speed, evaluating the engine in a feedback loop that took 15 to 40 milliseconds. This ECU was eventually used in all Ford cars, running various subsets of engine management software and 15 to 56K of memory, depending on the complexity of the engine.

GM's Gen III LS1/LS6 Powertrain Control Module for the Corvette 5.7-liter powerplant was based on a 24-megahertz variant of the Motorola 6833x microprocessor. This microcomputer was a GM design purpose built for automotive usage based on the Motorola 68000 architecture. By 2004, the CPU had 19.5K RAM for working storage, with access to 1-mb read-only memory. The PCM maintained twin 16K blocks of RAM that simulate EEPROM with battery backup, which were used to store the learned adaptive and static values. System logic consisted of 112,000 lines of GM Modula source code, which requires nearly 500K of storage in the microcomputer. The fastest engine feedback loops took 6.25 milliseconds. Internal bus speed was limited by the 70-nanosecond speed of the flash device, and the required 1-wait state per memory read, which gave the system an effective internal bus speed of 12 megahertz. The PCM connected to the engine environment with twin 80-pin connectors, an architecture supporting a large number of input (sensor) and output (actuator) devices.

GM's CAN-based E38 and E67 ECMs arrived in 2006 to provide engine management for Corvette LS2 powerplants and many other GM vehicles equipped with a wide variety of engines—in plenty of time to meet a U.S. government mandate that 2008 and newer vehicles sold in the United States support the CAN standard by which embedded controllers on a vehicle communicate with each other and share diagnostic information with scan tools. Originally developed by Bosch and later made into an ISO standard, the controller area network (CAN) bus provided for multiple embedded controllers (upward of 70 in some cases at this time of writing) handling tasks as varied as engine control, transmission control, airbags, antilock braking (ABS), cruise control, electric power steering (EPS), audio systems, windows, doors, mirror adjustment, and battery and recharging systems for hybrid and electric cars to work together to provide vehicle management by broadcasting prioritized small packets onto a fast serial local area network. In a diagnostic role, the CAN bus has essentially become an extension of onboard diagnostics Level 2 (OBD-II), a government-mandated diagnostic protocol that arrived on all road-going U.S. vehicles in 1996 with the goal of improving air quality and keeping independent auto repair shops in business by providing a standardized protocol by which a single generic scan tool could diagnose any 1996 or newer vehicle.

The new GM E38 and E67 controllers were no longer based on an integrated powertrain control module (PCM) architecture that provided both engine and transmission control from the same computer, but rather on separate engine control module (ECM) and transmission control module (TCM) computers that work together by communicating on the CAN bus. The E38 and E67 abandoned the Motorola 68000 processor used in previous LS1 engine controllers in favor of a new architecture based on the Motorola PowerPC, a 40 MHz, 32-bit RISC processor that is assisted in these controllers by the addition of a floating-point math co-processor to improve the speed and accuracy of arithmetic calculations. The E67 is similar to the E38, but has additional input and output lines for handling engines with variable valve timing. Despite being significantly more powerful than previous generations of GM engine controllers, the new ECMs arrived in a radically smaller cast-aluminum package equipped with cooling fins. GM's T43 transmission control module arrived at the same time as the E38 with the capability of communicating on the CAN bus and managing six-speed automatics. The T43 was, for the first time, located inside the valve body of the transmission.

sensors, evaluate their status, make output calculations based in part on internal lookup tables, and activate control devices. If-then-else branching allows the microprocessor to execute various sections of code in the loop, while bypassing others, depending on the truth of certain conditions. Data affecting the operation of the microprocessor comes from internal look-up tables (fuel maps, VE tables, and so on) and sensors. There are various control strategies used to evaluate engine airflow and loading, which, along with rpm, index into internal ECU data structures specifying spark timing, fuel delivery, and so forth.

Some aftermarket ECUs are speed-density systems that calculate the air mass entering the engine (and from this, the fuel requirement) based on minimum and maximum injection pulse width at the idle and maximum torque displacement, temperature, and a volumetric efficiency (VE) table organized according to engine rpm and manifold pressure. Other speed-density aftermarket systems use rpm and manifold pressure to index directly into tables of raw injection pulse width data (often specified as percentages of maximum injection pulse width), which can be equivalent to VE tables corrected for the differing air/fuel ratios desirable at various subsets of engine operating range. Injection pulse width tables can be translated to VE by converting to pulse width, then dividing each number into the derived pulse width for 100 percent VE. Pulse width must subsequently be corrected for actual air and engine temperature when the engine is running.

Some engine management systems such as the Electromotive TEC3 enable a tuner to toggle the user-presentation of the table between injection pulse width numbers, VE-type percentage numbers, and plus or minus offset from 100 percent VE (achievable on performance engine boosted with power-adders or intake and exhaust tuned to take advantage of high-rpm resonation effects).

Many OEM and a few aftermarket engine management systems use airflow meters to measure airflow into the engine directly. Early OEM systems were equipped with velocity airflow meters but the first aftermarket EMS in the U.S. was a actually a mass airflow (MAF) system designed and marketed by a company called Air Sensors that directly measured air mass using a proprietary hot-wire airflow meter. This was a fuel-only EMS that provided no ignition management and was tunable by adjusting a number of external pots on the analog (nondigital) ECU with a screwdriver. High-end modern EMSs are generally capable of reading MAF sensors to measure engine loading, though the tuner may have to calibrate a transfer function table that describes precisely how various MAF voltages or frequencies translate into mass airflow on a particular engine (see the chapters of this book on sensors and calibration).

In addition to speed-density and MAF-based engine management systems, a few aftermarket ECUs such as the analog Holley Pro-Jection system designed exclusively for normally aspirated powerplants have calculated engine airflow solely by modeling engine load based on engine speed and *throttle position*—a type of load-measurement system that is sometimes referred to as *Alpha-N*. Most modern EMSs allow the option to use the output from a throttle position sensor as an indication of engine loading for some or all of the operating range.

Virtually all OEM ECUs and some aftermarket ECUs have the ability to operate in closed-loop feedback mode, which means they can factor in exhaust gas composition as an indication of the trim air/fuel mixture achieved in the last injection event, which can be used to correct the injection pulse width to target AFR. In the past, feedback ECUs exclusively targeted the chemically

Sometimes the computer box itself functions as the user interface. This Carabine ECU from Hilborn was designed for tuners who are more comfortable tuning with a screwdriver than with a laptop. LEDs were used to display information, and the position of the various potentiometers provides information to the internal EMS logic the same way entering numbers from a keyboard defines the operation of the EMS on other systems. This type of user interface is much less flexible and powerful than a laptop but is simpler to tune and can work very well for some applications. *Hilborn*

perfect *stoichiometric* air/fuel ratio at idle and light cruise, but some modern *full authority* engine management systems have used oxygen-pump wideband sensors to measure a wide range of air/fuel ratios at engine loading up to and including maximum loading at full throttle. Many OEM ECUs modify their base fuel calculations semi-permanently as they accumulate data in block learn-type tables indicating what pulse width corrections have been required historically to achieve stoichiometric combustion in a particular engine (with a particular driver, perhaps), and as injectors and other engine parts age or wear out. Disconnecting the battery generally erases this learned behavior, causing the learning process to begin again from scratch.

VOLUMETRIC EFFICIENCY ENRICHMENT

An engine management computer's static memory is loaded during manufacture, initial calibration, or subsequent hacking and modification for hot rodding purposes with tables consisting of numbers that correspond to the volumetric efficiency (VE) of the engine at a representative set of points across the operating range of engine speed and loading. VE is essentially the ratio of the actual cylinder filling that occurs at a certain engine rpm and loading compared to the normally aspirated displacement of the engine at standard temperature and pressure. VE and displacement corrected for air temperature and pressure yields cylinder air mass, i.e., the *weight* of air arriving in the cylinders. When corrected for required target air/fuel ratios in various zones of the operating range, VE table numbers translate directly into inducted air mass and thus the amount of fuel mass (i.e., injection pulse width) required at a given combination of engine speed and loading. In fact, many engine management systems forsake the VE table and target air/fuel ratios concept entirely (or provide the option to do so) in favor of a fuel table of basic injection pulse width values that when corrected for temperature and pressure precisely reflect cylinder fuel mass (much more on this in the chapters of this book about sensors, actuators, and tuning).

An EMS microcomputer determines cylinder air mass on an ongoing basis as the four-stroke cycle proceeds for the various cylinders either by directly reading the data from a mass airflow sensor at the current engine speed or by calculating cylinder air mass based on engine displacement corrected for VE and temperature at the current engine speed and manifold pressure. Given that engine speed and mass airflow are both infinitely variable within the possible range of operation, there is, of course, an infinite number of such values. In reality, a VE table usually contains somewhere between several dozen and a thousand or so representative values logically arranged in rows and columns corresponding to a representative set of rpm and engine-loading combinations. Values for speed-loading combinations that fall in between defined breakpoints must be determined as a weighted average of the closest breakpoints—which is one reason why some newer EMS computers are equipped with accelerator chips that are very efficient at handling floating-point math.

Virtually all newer aftermarket EMS and factory systems store calibration maps in nonvolatile flash memory, which can potentially be overwritten from the ECU's OBD-II diagnostic port if you have the right laptop software, the right connectivity hardware, and the security seed (password) that grants access for calibration changes while the managed engine is running (see Chapter 16 for more information). Older factory engine management systems that were not designed for easy user programmability typically store the engine calibration on a PROM chip (which may unplug from the circuit board fairly easily or may require de-soldering for removal). To make dynamic calibration changes while the engine is running, PROM-based systems typically require a device called an emulator. An emulator plugs into the PROM socket of the OEM injection microcomputer in place of the stock PROM and contains a socket to accept the stock PROM, which is loaded into emulator RAM for testing and modification, and eventually offloaded into a PROM-burner to create a new replacement PROM that can be installed when the emulator connector is removed from the socket. Emulators enable a tuner to modify PROM data interactively on the fly, instantaneously testing the effect of calibration changes on a running powerplant.

How does tuning calibration data get into an EMS computer?

1. In the case of a stock OEM vehicle, the data originates on an identical R&D test engine used to develop the calibration. Engineers or inventors build one set of PROM or flash memory data for a particular engine-vehicle combination and duplicate it over and over for other vehicles of the same configuration during ECU manufacture. This data is then referred to as the engine map or calibration.
2. Virtually all modern standalone aftermarket programmable engine management systems allow digital calibration data developed on one ECU to be copied to a laptop computer by serial data connection and offloaded to other instances of the same model ECU running engines identical or similar to the development engine for fine tuning. Thus, if you have a common variety hot rod engine that is stock or equipped with common modifications, you may find preconfigured maps for your engine available from the EMS manufacturer. For anyone developing a unique engine configuration, it almost always makes sense to start with prefabricated fuel and timing maps from as similar as possible an engine (assuming they were developed by a competent tuner), perform any obvious configuration changes to scale for widely divergent injector sizes and so forth, and then modify the engine management maps by laptop PC while the engine is running. This enables the

tuner to see immediate changes in the way the engine performs in response to the map changes.
3. In the case of a programmable engine management system, the data may be entered one-by-one into the EMS microcomputer's flash memory by someone typing them in individually during the tuning process using the keyboard of a laptop computer connected to the engine management ECU by data link such that changes to data on the laptop are immediately propagated to the ECU's equivalent internal tables. Allowing EMS tables that directly determine engine operation to be calibrated in real time during R&D testing operations while the engine is running means that the effect of changes to fuel, timing, boost, and other factors on engine performance can be evaluated instantly with a load-holding dyno and optimized at all operating points to achieve peak torque, lowest emissions, or best fuel economy.
4. Software running on a laptop computer may partially automate the data entry by allowing a tuner to enter a number of parameters and then copy or interpolate the data to other breakpoints in between using a Fill or Copy feature (as a person might use a ruler to draw a continuous line through several points on a graph).
5. Most programmable engine management systems also allow data entry by manipulating a graphic representation of the table on a laptop with arrow keys or other graphical means that accomplished the same thing. EMS table data may have originated with an identical or similar engine (as would be the case when new cars are manufactured).
6. These days, modeling software on a laptop computer or workstation may have auto-generated the data in ECU tables based on user-specified parameters about the engine and application.
7. Calibration data may also originate in part with the EMS itself, if the ECU has self-learning capabilities that enable the system to "tune itself" with respect to fuel delivery under actually driving or test conditions to achieve specified target air/fuel ratios. Self-tuning (or autotuning)—particularly with respect to spark timing—is made more difficult because most engine sensors are not able to tell the engine management system what is actually happening inside the combustion chamber with respect to the magnitude of peak cylinder pressure engine position at peak pressure. At this time of writing, the *only* way to optimize spark timing is to measure torque output at a certain engine speed and load on a dyno while varying timing until torque is optimal or detonation prevents further advance. Lack of direct combustion data makes self-calibration problematic; however, there are now combustion pressure sensors available that are built into special spark plugs that can provide an engine management computer with direct access to combustion pressure in real time. As well, ion sensing is one of the cheapest and simplest methods for monitoring the combustion event in a spark-ignited engine, and models exist that connect the ionization current to cylinder pressure and temperature. Ion sensors show great promise for engine management.

Let's take a slightly harder look at the context of what is involved in the job of an engine management microcomputer. In particular, air/fuel ratio.

CHECKING OBD-I ECU FOR 5-SPEED OR AUTO CONFIGURATION

THIS APPLIES TO ALL OBD1 P05 / P06 / SOME P07 / P28 / P29 / P30 / P61 / PR4 ECUS.

AUTO

5-SPEED

F.F. SQUAD TECH

This ECU photo was doctored by ff-squad to illustrate how additional components or jumpers can be added to a circuit board to customize an application. Note that the red circled area is stuffed with two additional components in the automatic transmission version of the board versus the five-speed. The circuitry and logic are designed to function differently depending on the presence or absence of these components. *ff–squad*

The stoichiometric air/fuel ratio of gasoline is 14.7 pounds of air to 1 pound of fuel, the ideal ratio for perfect combustion. Under the right conditions, this mixture will combust to release all chemical energy stored in the fuel, leaving no unused oxygen and no unburned hydrocarbons. Stoichiometric combustion produces heat energy, carbon dioxide, and water vapor—nonpolluting and harmless. Theoretically. Under ideal conditions that naturally assume factors such as enough time for combustion to finish completely, perfectly mixed air and fuel, and so on.

But what if the goal were, say, to produce maximum fuel efficiency, especially at part throttle? In the real world of fires burning at high speeds among the swirling mass of air and fuel atoms in the combustion chamber of a piston engine, it is easy to miss a few atoms of fuel or oxygen here and there—particularly when throttle position and engine speed are changing rapidly and the air and fuel will not be perfectly mixed. If you're trying for maximum efficiency, you definitely don't want to waste any unburned fuel by blowing it out the exhaust. So, to make sure every molecule of fuel gets burned, lean out the mixture from stoichiometric (increase the ratio of oxygen to fuel) to improve the likelihood of making use of every last fuel molecule (like inviting extra guys to the dance).

On the other hand, since oxygen is virtually always the scarce component that limits power production, if the goal is maximum power output from an engine, you want to be sure there is enough fuel present in the air/fuel mixture so that every molecule of oxygen that has managed to get drawn or pushed into a cylinder is used in combustion. Therefore, for peak power you should richen the mixture from the stoichiometric ratio with extra fuel to shorten the odds you don't miss using any of the oxygen. (It's a little like inviting extra girls to a dance to improve the odds that every guy will find a partner.)

There is a logical correspondence between volumetric efficiency and enrichment. Engines operate at a higher volumetric efficiency (cylinders fill more completely) when

working harder at wide-open throttle, which is exactly when you want best power. At part throttle and lower speeds, engines operate at a lower volumetric efficiency—just when you want economy. It is a relatively simple matter to construct a microcomputer-based table of engine volumetric efficiency at various engine rpm and loading breakpoints. When running the engine, the EMS microcomputer reads rpm and engine loading from its sensors and uses these to index into the VE table, whose values in various cells correspond rather well to enrichment or enleanment required at a particular rpm and engine load (leaving out acceleration enrichment and cold-start enrichment). When the engine is operating at rpm/load points that fall between set points in the VE table, the computer is able to locate the closest several VE table values and use geometric formulas (typically a running-average linear interpolation) to estimate exact volumetric efficiency and, therefore, mixture adjustment required.

A carburetor approximates this sort of VE-based air/fuel adjustment by sizing the main jet for primary regulation of fuel delivery to the venturi, trimming this fuel flow with air corrector jets and emulsion tubes of precise size to progressively dilute the main jet fuel stream with air in order to limit fuel flow as engine speed and loading increase (fuel flow otherwise increases faster than airflow). A power valve in the carburetor opens under high-manifold pressure (high VE) to allow additional fuel to bypass the main jet and flow directly to the venturi in higher volume. As you can imagine, these physical correction systems in a carb are a blunt instrument compared to the precision of an electronic engine management system.

COLD-START ENRICHMENT

An EMS microcomputer's internal data structures must also contain tables of values defining special enrichment required when a driver starts a cold engine at temperatures where some percentage of the fuel will not vaporize (below about 160 degrees Fahrenheit on a gasoline-fueled engine).

Carburetors provide a simple cold enrichment using a choke plate (located above the venture, it's something like a second throttle), which is designed to physically restrict airflow through the carb. Cold-air activates this choking action based on its effect on a bimetallic spring (thermostat) connected to the choke plate. The closed choke plate increases vacuum in the area of the venturi to create additional pressure differential there compared to atmospheric—thereby forcing additional fuel out of the float chamber and into the inlet air stream at the venturi (producing a vastly enriched air/fuel mixture). Difficulty starting and stalling were common in the pre-EFI days of carbureted fuel systems.

Computer EFI can do much better, because EFI enrichment offsets are normally separated into cold-cranking enrichment, immediate after-start enrichment, and enrichment during warm-up, which are specified independently of each other. The EMS computer adds warm-up enrichment to normal injection pulse width, typically as a percentage. Difficulty starting and stalling are unheard of on properly functioning OEM EFI engines, but this is not always true of aftermarket EFI systems due to the difficulty of testing cold enrichment under actual conditions without expensive climate-control systems or arctic or tropical test sites.

ACCELERATION ENRICHMENT

Sudden throttle opening can deplete the "reservoir" of fuel clinging to engine intake runners downstream of fuel injectors or carburetors, and manifold pressure increases can compound the problem by degrading the capacity of fuel to vaporize as quickly as it does when vacuum is high. Without special "transient" enrichment, the sudden application of throttle—particularly at lower engine speeds—can result in the engine stumbling or bogging. Thus, acceleration enrichment prevents a flat spot on sudden acceleration with parameters that specify a percentage enrichment when the throttle is opening suddenly, followed by the rate of decay in enrichment when the throttle plate stops moving. Many sophisticated modern EMSs allow tuners to specify transient enrichment *tables*, which specify the percentage enrichment when the throttle opens suddenly at a variety of speed-density points. Many EMSs allow transient enrichment based on manifold pressure increases instead of or in addition to throttle position increases, according to rpm or loading. By contrast, many automobile carburetors, such as the Holley four-barrel, provide simple transient enrichment using a diaphragm pump activated by the throttle shaft that squirts raw fuel directly into the throat(s) of the carb while the throttle is opening. The problem is that such systems waste additional fuel into the engine under conditions when transient enrichment is not required, such as on very slow increases in throttle at any rpm, or during sudden increases in throttle at high rpm.

ENRICHMENT SUMMARY

Enrichment values stored in tables in ECU memory include choke enrichments, acceleration enrichments, and volumetric efficiency enrichments (or enleanments). Combined with engine displacement and peak VE, these values together define a fueling map for a certain engine. An EMS microcomputer sums all enrichment values to arrive at a total enrichment for the current fuel-injection event that is represented by G (for the Greek letter *gamma*). The total enrichment (or enleanment) is an offset from the theoretical (stoichiometric) air/fuel ratio based simply on air mass.

EQUATIONS

The following is a representative basic equation used by some VE-type Electromotive EMS microcomputers to compute injection pulse width:

Pulse width = [(MAP voltage ÷ 5) x UAP] + POT
Where
MAP = Manifold absolute pressure
UAP = User-adjustable pulse width, the longest pulse width the engine will ever require
POT = Pulse width offset time at idle

The EMS calculates pulse width by modifying the load percentage of the MAP sensor voltage (0 to 5 volts, correlated to air mass) by the user-adjustable pulse width (UAP), and modifying the result of this calculation by pulse width offset time (POT). UAP is defined as the pulse width required at peak torque (full load) for a given engine displacement with a given injector size and is the longest pulse width the engine will ever require. POT is a modification that corrects pulse width at idle, an additive fudge factor that must be non-zero if the required pulse width at idle varies in any way from linearity between the UAP at full loading and the theoretical zero pulse width at zero loading. Idle, of course, requires more than zero loading, since turning the engine requires overcoming friction and other losses.

The above equation assumes no rpm-dependency for the raw fuel curve derivation since pulse width for an engine with a perfectly flat torque curve will not vary with speed. Therefore, an engine working at 100 percent load would require 100 percent of the pulse width defined by UAP. Note: 100 percent loading is not usuallyt the same as 100 percent VE. An engine operating at 50 percent load would require 50 percent UAP, and so on. In practice, any engine in which the torque curve can be approximated reasonably well with a straight line can be run reasonably well with this simplistic assumption.

The linearity assumption of pulse width versus rpm breaks down on engines that have torque curves that are very nonlinear with respect to engine speed. Two examples are turbocharged engines that cannot make boost at lower rpm ranges and super-high-output racing engines with poor low-end torque.

A VE table, however, allows the EMS microprocessor to make corrections to the basic pulse width calculation at ranges of engine speed and loading where the volumetric efficiency of the engine strays badly from linearity using the following equation:

Pulse width = [(MAP Voltage ÷ 5) x UAP x
(VE Absolute% ÷ 100)] + POT

Keep in mind that in reality, the EMS microprocessor must actually correct MAP values to mass airflow by correcting for temperature (on MAF-based systems this is unnecessary, since the MAF value is already mass airflow). What's more, the EMS computer must always adjust pulse width to include injector turn-on time (ITO) and changes in ITO due to changes in the system battery voltage (BTO) by directly summing ITO and BTO into pulse width.

The EMS computer must also factor in transient enrichment offsets resulting from throttle position changes (TPS), engine coolant temperature (CTS), intake air temperature (IAT), required air/fuel corrections based on exhaust gas oxygen (EGO) sensor feedback, and cold-starting enrichment requirements (SE)—all of which add percentage changes to VE absolute percentage with the exception of battery voltage correction, which adds a specified amount to injection pulse width in response to below-normal battery voltage. Including all enrichment factors, Electromotive's pulse width derivation looks like this:

$$\text{Pulse width} = [(\text{MAP Voltage} \div 5) \times \text{UAP} \times (\text{VE Absolute\%} \div 100) \times \text{TPS\%} \times \text{CTS\%} \times \text{IAT\%} \times \text{EGO\%} \times \text{SE\%}] + \text{POT} + \text{BTO}$$

PROMS

Programmable read-only memory (PROM), electrically erasable programmable read-only memory (EEPROM), and flash memory (block EEPROM) are used to store data and instructions for use by a computer's central processing unit. All microcomputers without a disk drive must have PROM or EEPROM to store the instructions and data they need to begin doing work on power-up, which includes all ECMs running engine management systems.

Historically, due to a lack of sufficient modifiable mass storage, most OEM onboard engine controllers were designed with the software or firmware machine instructions and certain nonconfigurable data parameters permanently stored in read-only memory—meaning that the logic and permanent data could not be modified under any circumstances. That said, the logic could be designed to be data-dependent ("table-driven") in operation, meaning that entire sections of code were executed only conditionally, on the basis of data parameters stored in removable PROM or electrically erasable flash memory that allowed the behavior or logic of the ECM to change depending according to the application.

In the case of aftermarket programmable engine management computers designed to manage many different engines of very different configurations, there must be an easy and straightforward method available to get calibration and configuration data into electrically erasable flash memory. Back when laptops were expensive and many hot rodders were not familiar with personal computers, some early aftermarket systems used a dedicated handheld keypad or LCD device (or even screwdriver-actuated pots!) for configuration and tuning, and this option is still available on a few systems. These days, the user interface on the vast majority of aftermarket programmable EMSs is a Windows PC laptop connected to the ECU with a serial cable that allows the user to customize the EMS data for a large variety of engines. At the time of this writing, a recent development was ECUs able to interface to programmer devices such as laptops or even smartphones *wirelessly* using Bluetooth. Some systems allow access via CAN bus interfaces. Aftermarket engine management systems are typically designed to be extremely data dependent, with embedded software routines using certain data for EFI calibration computations and other data as parameters or switches that customize which logic will be used to manage a particular engine. Based on the value of a certain byte or bit of data, code might (or might not) be executed to handle, for example, computation of additional fuel enrichment when nitrous injection is armed. Modern aftermarket EMS ECMs will behave in many different ways depending on the data in their PROM/EEPROM. In reality, so will modern OEM engine management systems, which allow the same hardware and logic to be used on many or even all new engines, depending on the configuration. The newest factory engine management systems all provide a facility to modify configuration and tuning data using a laptop computer running special-purpose software and hardware interface or a dedicated device that a dealer might use to "flash" new data or even code into the

PIN	SIGNAL / FUNCTION	MCU PIN	CPU 8061	RAM 81C61	EPROM 8763	Notes
29	PWR GND	40,60				
27	VPWR	37,57				Battery +
25	DI		57	22	22	
23	IT		58	21	21	
21	STROBE\		53	20	20	
19	D7		68	10	10	
17	D6		67	11	11	
15	D5		66	12	12	
13	D4		65	13	13	
11	D3		64	14	14	
9	D2		63	15	15	
7	D1		62	16	16	
5	DO		61	17	17	
3	KA5V			7		
1	VREP (+5)	26				
30	PWR GND					
28	VPWR	37,57				Battery +
26	BSO					
24	BS3					
22	TSTSTB				1	1K TO +5 only
20	PROGRAM					
18	RAMDISABLE					
16	EPROMDISABLE				2	10K TO +5 only
14	ERASE					
12	MRESET				9	
10	RESET		3	9		
8	PAUSE		60			1K TO +5 only
6	EXTINT					
4	(High for Access)					IC4-74001 pin 13
2	VCC	25				

```
29  27  25  23  21  19  17  15  13  11  9   7   5   3   1

30  28  26  24  22  20  18  16  14  12  10  8   6   4   2
```

(View facing connector on PCM.)

The Motorola 8061 and other Ford EEC processor components supported extensive diagnostics and control capabilities through special hardware pins that Ford was kind enough to incorporate in a diagnostic connector accessible externally by plugging into the J3 test port in the EEC-IV enclosure. The performance aftermarket used the J3 port extensively to hack into the EEC system and modify calibration and configuration data that affects engine tuning and EMS operation.

EMS. The difference is that factory systems are designed to provide significant barriers to unauthorized "tampering."

It is worth mentioning here that the open-source software (OSS) movement that resulted in the Linux operating system and the Firefox web browser has come to the world of engine management systems in the form of MegaSquirt EMS hardware and software developed by Bruce Bowling and Al Grippo that allows enthusiasts to assemble and customize their own engine management systems. The open-source scheme provides an alternative to the propriety model (in which teams of engineers working at for-profit or governmental organizations develop proprietary computer software that is treated as an industrial or military secret). In the open-source scheme, the source code and certain other rights normally reserved for copyright holders are provided under an open-source license that permits users to study, change, improve and in some cases even distribute the software,

HOT ROD PROM PACKAGES

"Our first level package is the easiest to get started with," wrote TPIS in the early 1990s, "because it involves inexpensive parts and simple techniques. But if you're looking for more muscle, check out Levels II, III, or IV. And when you're ready to blow the doors off everybody in town, look into Level V, which is completely customized to your individual car." In the new millennium, TPIS is still in business and still focused on selling hot rod and replacement parts for performance fuel-injected Chevy V-8s.

The name TPIS is an acronym derived from the company's original name, Tuned Port Injection Specialties, and its original business is hot rod computer and specialty performance parts for the tuned port injection EFI small-block Chevy V-8 used in F-Bodies, Corvettes, and a few other vehicles from 1985 to 1993. The follow-up 1993 to 1997 LT1 Chevy small-block V-8 engine had a different (and somewhat compatible) induction system but was still, in most respects, a traditional small-block Chevy V-8 (which is not true of the newest generation LS-1 powerplants that are entirely new in virtually every way). All TPI V-8s built from 1985 on and some early LT1 powerplants had factory EMS computers with replaceable PROMs.

Arizona Speed and Marine focused on much the same market of fuel-injected Chevy-type V-8 performance. There were so many L98-type engines and vehicles built that there are still many driving around on the streets of America, and many hot rodders are still working with them as raw material. And ASM can still supply custom PROMs for these engines.

What was and is possible with PROM replacement performance packages on performance-oriented Chevy and Ford small-block V-8s?

Aftermarket PROM vendors typically advertised a higher state of tune for targeted stock vehicles and recalibrated fuel and ignition curves for modified vehicles. For people with ongoing performance projects, the upgrade-PROM vendors have sometimes protected the PROM investment by enabling customers to upgrade to another new PROM if they make additional modifications to an engine—for just a small upgrade fee. Most of the companies selling PROMs offer phone consulting to users in order to help them get the combination of parts and PROM right.

Typically, a first stage TPI or LT1 PROM would be designed to work well with a low-restriction air filter, a low-temperature thermostat, a throttle body air foil, MAF screen removal, and modified air filter housing. TPIS claimed a 20-horsepower gain with the above package on a 5.7-liter TPI V-8. This translated into a 0.6-second faster quarter mile with 2 miles per hour faster top end. It is very important to use the right PROM with lower-temperature thermostats (since the ECU could otherwise assume that the car is still warming up) and keep warm-up enrichment activated, which wastes fuel, cuts power, and wears out the cylinders fast from wetting down the cylinder walls.

Stock engine management tuning in the 1980s and early 1990s tended to be very conservative (safe) to protect automakers from warranty claims. Engineers would design an overly rich wide-open-throttle fuel map in order to protect the engine from knocking and thermal stress, and to guard against aging fuel pumps and injectors eventually producing dangerously lean conditions. Typically, stage one PROMs had calibrations affecting wide-open throttle, advancing the timing for premium fuel and improving the mixture (which, in cars like the 5.0-liter Mustang, involves leaning the mixture that is too rich with factory fuel curves). In addition to retuning fuel and ignition curves, a replacement PROM chip might also change the circumstances under which torque converters lock up, eliminating jerkiness in shifting into or out of high gear.

With a few additional minor pieces and a stage two PROM, companies like TPIS and ASM advertised power gains of up to 45 horsepower, cutting a second off the quarter mile.

A third level typically involved low-restriction exhaust (headers, free-flow mufflers, and possibly removal of the catalyst for off-road use), additional MAF modifications, and yet a different PROM.

which is often developed in a public, collaborative manner freely available in that anyone with the necessary programming skills can study the existing source code and develop extensions or modifications that may subsequently be incorporated into the larger software package or made available as "add-ons." MegaSquirt is the registered trademark of a standalone engine management controller platform with operating software that is open for modification exclusively on Bowling and Grippo hardware. The MegaSquirt hardware is also open, in that the schematics are available for troubleshooting and educational purposes for users who want to add optional capabilities, but not for copying or pirating. The product is aimed at the do-it-yourself (DIY) market as some MegaSquirt hardware requires assembly and tuning by the user.

The feasibility of modifying OEM engine management systems varies tremendously. When GM designed its original 1980s-vintage performance multi-port fuel injection, marketed as tuned port injection (TPI), the company was kind enough to design the PROM so it could be swapped easily. GM TPI PROMs plug into a socket that is accessible without even violating the ECU's enclosure. By contrast, Ford's EEC-IV of the same vintage uses a PROM that is soldered in place and not easily replaceable. Fortunately, the EEC-IV ECU includes a multipin diagnostic plug that can be used to load code and data that may be used in place of the code and data in the onboard PROM. Aftermarket entrepreneurs have designed small modules equipped with replacement PROM chips that

plug into the EEC-IV diagnostic port to supersede the onboard EEC-IV PROM.

Older OEM engine management systems were often set up from the factory with PROM calibrations that caused the EMS to behave very conservatively. They were designed to be foolproof and to keep negligent or ignorant operators from hurting their engines with poor driving methods, poor quality gasoline, and poor preventive maintenance. However, for a knowledgeable operator who is willing to take more care, willing to operate a little closer to the edge, to use good gas, to avoid lugging the engine, perhaps to suffer degraded gas mileage or emissions would discover it was often possible to make more power available via a higher state of tune than stock, which could be accomplished by simply substituting a PROM with revised data.

The newest vehicles are equipped with engine management systems that are highly optimized, and it is uncommon to find a naturally aspirated engine-vehicle combination where calibration changes alone can create significant additional power. All onboard diagnostic level II (OBD-II) engines sold in the United States since 1996 are much better than older systems at detecting performance modifications that might adversely affect exhaust emissions.

The good news is that digital EMS logic has always been designed in such a way that the code takes into account many different possible (and configurable) characteristics of a vehicle and engine package in managing the engine. The bad news is that if the operator has made major internal changes to the engine, it

The next level was designed to significantly improve engine breathing with intake porting, larger (and sometimes shorter) runners, higher lift rockers, and a new PROM, yielding as much as 100 horsepower and a 2-second faster quarter. Drivability could still be excellent, with across-the-board performance improvements at all rpm levels.

A stage five PROM package might add ported heads, a hotter cam, and an appropriate PROM, resulting in 130 horsepower over the stock 305 or 350 Chevy TPI motor, with quarter times in the low 12s and 112.5 miles per hour in a 'Vette. These sorts of modifications are designed to work very well with big-displacement 383 or 406 Chevy small-block motors, which need the improved breathing and fuel. TPIS used to advertise that their demonstrator 'Vette achieved almost 23 miles per gallon at speeds as high as 80 to 100 miles per hour, yet turned a 12.1 at 112.5 in the quarter with a stock displacement 350 motor.

With a performance PROM calibration installed, it is essential to treat such a vehicle as the more highly tuned beast that it now is, filling up with the best gasoline around, listening for knock, and giving the vehicle excellent maintenance. It is essential to check with the manufacturer before assuming that any replacement chip would work with a different engine/vehicle combination (for example, installing a high-output Camaro chip in an LG4 or standard 305 V-8 engine).

PROM changes have always required you to know what engine you have. This sometimes requires checking the vehicle identification number (VIN), which contains a code that indicates the type of original engine installed at the factory. If engine changes have been made (or if you think the PROM calibration is nonstandard), check with the manufacturer, and have all internal and external engine documentation available. Most PROM vendors that are still in business (and most probably are) should maintain documentation and serial numbers for all PROMs they've sold. If there is any doubt, they can probably still read your PROM and tell you what you've got years down the line.

PROM Installation

GM TPI PROMs could typically be installed in less than 30 minutes using a small flat head screwdriver, a Phillips screwdriver, a 1/4-inch socket, and sometimes 7- and 10-mm sockets. Locate the ECU (which GM calls an engine control module or ECM), remove the mounting screws, and pull it out for easier access. GM computers have a small cover that allows access to the PROM. Remove it and gently unplug the stock PROM from its socket (it is very easy to bend or break the multiple prongs, especially without a PROM-puller tool). Now carefully plug in the new PROM and reinstall the cover plate. In some cases, you may want to clean the PROM socket with proper solvent.

In the case of Ford EEC-IV vehicles, you'll be adding a power module available from companies like Hypertech, which plugs into the diagnostic port on the EEC-IV computer, superseding the stock chip that stays in place. This procedure requires the same tools as a GM PROM change, plus maybe a 9- or 10-mm Torx bit. Locate and dismount the ECM. Remove the service port cover and side screw from the computer (this is on the end of the computer with the warranty label). The power module plugs into the end of the ECM and includes longer screws that hold it in place using the side screw holes. Reinstall the computer in its place and go have fun.

Some Japanese ECMs require soldering and additional electronics installed by an expert technician before the PROM calibration can be changed. But once these changes are made, a PROM change involves unplugging and removing the ECU, opening it, and swapping in a new PROM chip.

may be mandatory to change the PROM data, the ECU itself, or add auxiliary electronics or mechanical changes to fuel-delivery and ignition components so the engine will operate properly.

In fact, it is essential to understand the operating envelope of the ECU logic and the specific calibration data. Many factory EFI cars are designed with logic and tuning that provide some built-in flexibility with respect to the actual volumetric efficiency of an individual engine. Minor changes to the VE, perhaps a low-restriction air filter, will often work well with an MAF-based EFI system, since the computer has built-in ability to compensate for slight VE changes. But after installing an aftermarket PROM, the EMS might be operating so close to knock limits, suboptimal air/fuel ratios, or other constraints that a change in VE or other engine characteristics could cause it to operate poorly. Without access to system documentation, the tuner has no idea what the envelope looks like and where the system's flexibility ends.

Therefore, it is essential to get good consulting from the people who know, such as factory performance experts at places like the Ford Motorsport Tech Hotline at (800)-FORDTEC, or aftermarket wizards, who have reverse engineered or otherwise acquired internal system knowledge and have tested modified parts and PROMs on dynos and on the street. The whole package must work together or you may end up worse off than you started if you tamper in any way with a factory EFI vehicle, either in PROM or flash changes or in engine modifications.

Many aftermarket entrepreneurs offer packages of replacement calibrations and parts that are designed to work

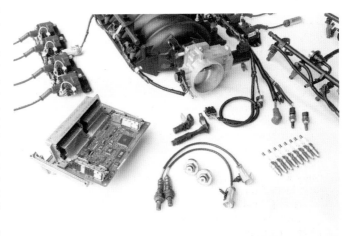

The 2004 Corvette LS1 PCM incorporates 24-megahertz Motorola 6833x processor power and a large 1 MB of ROM. Drivers sink heat directly into a finned aluminum casing capable of surviving in the harsh environment of an engine compartment.

well together on a specific car. An increasing number are approved for legal use on the street, which is nice, considering that all parties concerned—from manufacturer to jobber to user—are potentially liable for any vehicular tampering that might affect emissions.

Chapter 3
Sensors and Sensor Systems

Sensors are the eyes and ears of an engine management ECM. An engine management system makes decisions about fuel injection and ignition events based on data. Such data sometimes exists simply as tables of stored numbers in memory, for example a chart of volumetric efficiencies for a specific engine. This type of data doesn't change unless someone recalibrates or reprograms the ECM. But data may also exist in the form of numbers or values in memory that are more or less constantly being refreshed according to the status of various engine sensors.

Sensors assign an electric voltage or frequency to the status of external systems or events such as a change in the temperature of the cylinder head. A sensor voltage is often converted from an analog physical magnitude to a discrete digital number by A-to-D circuitry (usually now onboard the ECM microprocessor) and made available in random-access memory for processing, exactly like the table data discussed above. Some sensors directly generate digital data ready to be input to the processor. Sensor data heavily affects both which software instructions are executed by the microprocessor as well as the results of the logical routines that are executed.

Let's take a look at how sensors operate and their effect on engine management. A variety of types of sensors may be used for engine management:

- Positional sensors
  - Cam angle
  - Crank angle
  - Throttle position (TPS)
  - Accelerator pedal position (PPS)
- Engine Load sensors
  - Mass airflow (MAF)
  - Vane airflow
  - Manifold absolute pressure (MAP)
  - Torque sensors (strain gauge)
- Air/fuel ratio sensors
  - Narrow-band EGO
  - Wideband UEGO
  - Exhaust gas analyzer
- Temperature sensors
  - Engine coolant
  - Cylinder head
  - Intake air
  - Manifold surface
  - Oil
  - Exhaust gas (EGT)
- Pressure sensors
  - Manifold absolute pressure (MAP)
  - Barometric pressure (Baro)
  - Fuel pressure
  - Cylinder combustion pressure (pressure transducer)
- Air-metering sensors
  - MAF

Temperature sensors change resistance with temperature. The Air Temp sensor is optimized to respond quickly to changes in charge temperature. Coolant or oil temperature sensors have a solid metal bulb designed to be immersed in the fluid being measured. *MSD*

  - Vane airflow
- Knock sensors
- Other
  - Vehicle speed sensor
  - Wheel speed
  - Engine oil
  - Accelerometers
  - Actuator-status sensors (for OBD-II; indicates if the actuator worked as it should have)
  - System voltage (used to model injector performance and coil saturation and dwell time)

POSITION SENSORS
Cam Sync/Crank Angle

Variable reluctor—a.k.a., inductive pickup or magnetic pickup—sensors, along with Hall effect and optical sensors, are used by engine management systems to determine the position of the engine by detecting the proximity of teeth or ridges or magnets on a rotating wheel or shaft. The simplest trigger wheels use a single detectable trigger point on a cam-speed wheel to indicate that cylinder no. 1 is about to begin a new four-stroke cycle. On the other hand, trigger wheels have been built with 360 trigger points that run at cam speed and indicate engine position within 2 degrees of crank rotation, which provides engine position to a high degree of resolution (very useful for misfire detection) at the cost of a more powerful ECU to keep track of trigger events or special-purpose counting hardware that offloads counting from the main microprocessor. Crankshaft trigger wheels sometimes have one trigger point per cylinder, with each point indicating TDC for one cylinder, or more commonly a total of somewhere between 24 and 60 points, with a missing tooth (or sometimes two) indicating a particular crankshaft position follows. The more trigger points, the higher the resolution of engine position and the less time elapsed before the ECU can recalculate engine speed and rate of change. In some cases aftermarket ECUs are designed for a particular trigger wheel and sensor, which must be installed on a carb-to-EFI conversion engine or added to a factory EFI engine in addition to or instead of the stock engine position equipment.

Engine position (CKP) sensors may be located in the distributor, on a camshaft, or on the crankshaft or flywheel. CKP sensors provide the critical function of reporting instantaneous engine speed, and they have been used in the primary circuit of a distributor ignition to fire the coil, to monitor engine rpm, or to time sequential injection or fire individual coils in relation to firing order on a direct coil-on-plug or waste-spark ignition. The location of one or two missing or additional teeth on the trigger wheel of engines with sequential injection or direct-fire engine management systems allows the EMS to synchronize the initial fuel pulse or spark event with the combustion cycle of the no. 1 cylinder. In addition, by analyzing micro changes in acceleration or speed data from the CKP sensors and precise engine position, modern OEM engine management systems can detect and report misfires to the onboard diagnostic system correlated to the particular cylinder with a questionable spark plug, coil, or fuel injector.

Monitoring engine position from the crankshaft is the most accurate method because slop in the timing chain, or timing belt wear and stretch will allow the camshaft and distributor to wander and scatter in relation to crankshaft position, but both have been used to determine engine position. On older engines with adjustable distributors, the distributor could be clocked, or rotated, to adjust ignition (or injection) timing, meaning distributor position was only as accurate as the skills and care of the tuner clocking the distributor. However, determining the exact crankshaft position is ambiguous in terms of the firing order, because crank position by itself says nothing about whether the engine is on the compression or exhaust stroke of a particular cylinder.

Modern engine management systems use a sync-pulse engine position sensor on the camshaft/distributor to alert the EMS to when the number one cylinder is approaching in the firing order. EMSs then use a precision position or reference sensor on the crankshaft to precisely time all other engine spark and injection events.

Variable reluctor magnetic sensors couple a coil of wire with a magnet in an arrangement that is somewhat similar to an electric guitar pickup. In some cases the magnet is inside or next to the coil, and teeth on a rotating steel wheel spinning near the pickup excite electrical pulses in the coil similar to the way vibrating steel strings near a guitar pickup excite electrical frequencies in coils that can be amplified to produce music. In other cases magnets on the spinning wheel excite a current in the variable reluctor sensor each time one of the magnets passes by the sensor. In either case the wheel must be moving to be detected by the VR sensor, which will not deliver a signal from the close proximity of a stopped magnet. Most modern engine management systems are highly configurable as far as the magnitude, timing, and direction ("Rising Edge," "Falling Edge") of changes in the signal from an engine position sensor that the ECU should construe as indicating an engine position event such as the arrival at the sensor of the next tooth on a trigger wheel. Or perhaps the "non-arrival" of a missing tooth or two, which is an indication that the crankshaft has arrived at a particular definite position, which can be used to re-synchronize subsequent events and actions and conclusions for the upcoming

revolution or cycle such that unexpected misfires or rapid changes in engine speed that might cause the ECU to miss a tooth on the trigger wheel cannot cause it to lose track of engine position for more than a fraction of one revolution.

Unlike conventional magnetic sensors (which respond to changes in the magnetic flux as a flying magnet or ferrous tooth passes the sensor, which produces an alternating current output that varies in voltage with speed), the Hall effect principle senses the actual magnetic field strength, and can thus detect nearby metal whether or not it is moving. Hall effect sensors produce a high-quality signal of essentially binary voltage that changes state abruptly from constant maximum voltage to nearly zero and vice versa regardless of rpm. Because of this, Hall effect sensors are sometimes referred to as switches rather than sensors because the on-off square-wave voltage signal they produce is directly usable by digital circuitry without requiring conditioning or interpretation. As such, the sensor determines magnet position regardless of rotational speed and is less sensitive to variations in gap between the sensor and wheel. Timing scatter is greatly reduced, and timing variations with rpm are eliminated.

Hall effect sensors normally have three wires usually for ground, output signal, and reference voltage (from the vehicle's ECU, 5 or 12 volts). Like flying magnet pickups, Hall effect sensors make use of the interaction between a magnet and ferrous metal coming into close proximity. But Hall effect sensors are based on a phenomenon discovered in 1879 by the American scientist Edwin H. Hall. Hall discovered that when an electric current was applied to metal inserted between two magnets, it created a secondary voltage in the metal at a right angle to the applied voltage. In a modern Hall effect sensor, the voltage change occurs in a silicon chip placed at a right angle to a magnetic field.

When a magnet moves into close proximity of the Hall effect sensor (or when a moving metal shutter blade uncovers a magnet located near the sensor), the sensor's output voltage suddenly jumps to full scale. When the magnetic field is removed, the voltage abruptly drops to zero. Additional circuitry conditions the input power that is supplied to the sensor and amplifies the output signal. Auxiliary circuitry can also produce a sensor that outputs 0 volts in the presence of a magnetic field, otherwise full-scale voltage. A notch in a rotating pulley, a rotating gear tooth (or a missing tooth!), or even a rotating magnetic button can serve the same purpose as a shutter blade to disrupt a Hall effect sensor's magnetic window and trigger the switch in an automotive engine management system.

Depending on how its circuitry is designed, a Hall effect sensor may be normally on or off. GM has used crank position sensors that are normally on, producing a steady voltage output when the magnetic window is open or unobstructed. Voltage output drops to near 0 when a blade enters the magnetic window and blocks the field. Ford's distributor-less ignition systems have used profile ignition pickup (PIP) and cylinder identification (CID) Hall effect sensors that work in the opposite manner: When a shutter blade passes through the window, blocking the magnetic field, the Hall effect sensor's internal circuitry switches the output signal from near 0 (off) to maximum voltage (on).

Some engine management systems have used optical engine position sensors that shine a beam of light at a spinning disc. When precisely positioned holes in the disc pass in front of the beam, a phototransistor detects the light and circuitry generates a binary current that allows state-change circuitry in the ECU of an engine management system to deduce engine position.

Magnets flying past a coil induce a voltage spike that a computer can detect and time stamp for use in determining engine position while running. Most engine position sensors use Hall Effect or magnetic sensors (though occasionally you'll find an optical engine position trigger). *MSD*

THROTTLE POSITION
(See Engine Load Sensors)

ACCELERATOR PEDAL POSITION SENSOR

Accelerator Pedal Position Sensors (PPS) are used on engines with ECM-controlled "Drive-By-Wire" electronic throttle control (ETC) systems. The PPS signal may be interpreted by the ECM as a request by the driver that the throttle stepper motor be moved to a particular position (Pedal Follower electronic throttle systems) or as a request for more or less torque (Torque-Based electronic throttle systems) that may be supplied as the ECM sees fit by changing some combination of throttle position, ignition timing, boost pressure, injection pulse width, and other factors. To prevent dangerous unintended acceleration, it is critical to safe operation that the PPS is extremely reliable.

Most acceleration pedal position sensors consist of two potentiometers (variable resistors functionally similar to the volume knob on a stereo) that increase reliability via redundancy. The potentiometers each contain a carbon track connected to a 5V or 12V power supply on one end and ground at the other. A slider mechanically connected to the accelerator pedal tracks across the carbon, picking up voltage that will vary according position of the slider and distance current must travel through the carbon. Typically, each potentiometer receives power from the ECU independently, which means there are usually six ECM-PPS connections.

To further increase reliability, the power supply is usually connected in reverse to the second potentiometer. Thus, the signal voltage of one potentiometer should normally increase in proportion to the decrease of the other, which will not be true in case of a short or interruption in any PPS circuit, allowing the ECM to detect a PPS failure and back off the throttle (which will be closed immediately by a return spring) in favor of a limp-home strategy that limits maximum throttle opening to a very small percentage sufficient that allows the vehicle to be driven slowly. Most ETC systems use a similar dual redundant throttle position sensor (TPS) system to increase the reliability of the ECM's knowledge of actual throttle position.

EXHAUST GAS SENSORS
Oxygen Sensors

The oxygen sensor (also called a lambda or exhaust gas oxygen (EGO) sensor, is critical to modern factory engine management systems because its data enables the ECU to constantly trim or tune the engine on the fly in feedback or closed-loop operation. Because the O_2 sensor is the critical component in the feedback loop used to trim injection pulse width based on exhaust gas oxygen content, an O_2 sensor failure or a problem in the sensor's wiring circuit will prevent the system from going into closed-loop mode, causing a rich-fuel condition and increased emissions (particularly carbon monoxide) and fuel consumption. A bad engine temperature sensor can also prevent the system from going into closed-loop.

The O_2 sensor is mounted in the exhaust manifold or downpipe or in the turbine discharge tube of a turbocharged powerplant to monitor residual (unburned) oxygen in the exhaust. The O_2 sensor tells the ECM if the fuel mixture is burning rich, with a surplus of fuel in the charge mixture (indicated by less exhaust gas oxygen), or lean, with a surplus of oxygen (more exhaust gas oxygen). The ECM reads the sensor's voltage signal and alters the fuel mixture, creating a feedback loop that constantly retrims the fuel mixture.

Oxygen sensors do not actually measure the concentration of oxygen in exhaust gas, but instead measure the difference between the concentration of oxygen in exhaust gas versus air.

The sensor current of zirconia O_2 sensors is carried by oxygen ions that only become available when the sensor is hot enough. When a cold engine is first started, the computer ignores the signal from the O_2 sensor, running open-loop. The default fuel mixture is set to run rich of the chemically correct (stoichiometric) 14.7:1 mixture and stay that way until the system goes into closed-loop and starts reading the O_2 sensor signal to vary the fuel mixture in quest of the stoichiometric mixture. Most late-model O_2 sensors are electrically heated so they will warm up and reach operating temperature (roughly 600 degrees) sooner to reduce emissions. Heated O_2 sensors typically have three or four wires; older single-wire O_2 sensors are not heated.

In closed-loop mode, the EMS can quickly evaluate the effect of changes to engine operating parameters to make corrections on the fly, resulting in improved emissions and fuel economy. The O_2 sensor operation is so important that some technicians routinely replace the O_2 sensor before attempting to go any further with tuning since they figure an O_2 sensor is not terribly expensive and O_2-sensor-oriented problems can be so confusing and waste so much time. The computer leans the mixture when a lack of oxygen indicates a rich mixture and richens the mixture when a relative presence of oxygen indicates a lean mixture.

The O_2 sensor used in many vehicles is a voltage-generating sensor that can be thought of as a sort of "air battery." In the lead-acid battery used to start a car, an acid medium induces a current flow between two dissimilar metals, freeing energy stored in the acid. The chemical composition of the medium changes as the battery discharges, affecting the output or voltage of the battery. One could, therefore, deduce the chemical composition of the acid (state of charge) based on the output voltage of the battery. In a similar way, the tip of a standard zirconium oxygen sensor has a zirconium ceramic bulb coated with porous platinum on the inside and on the outside. The coated inside and outside serve as the electrodes of the air battery. The bulb contains two

Flying magnets install in a rotating trigger wheel to induce a signal in a crank or cam position sensor.

platinum electrodes and is vented through the sensor housing to the outside atmosphere. When the bulb is exposed to hot exhaust, the difference in oxygen levels across the bulb creates a voltage.

The zirconium-dioxide element in the tip of an O_2 sensor thus produces an electrical voltage that varies according to the difference in oxygen content between the atmosphere and the exhaust gases. The sensor can generate as much as approximately 0.9 volts when the fuel mixture is rich. When the mixture is lean, the sensor's output voltage can drop to as low as 0.1 volts. When the air/fuel mixture is chemically balanced (about 14.7:1) prior to combustion, the exhaust gas oxygen sensor will generate around 0.45 volts.

In a lean mixture, there is a surplus of oxygen (not enough fuel for all oxygen molecules to participate in combustion); the opposite is true of a rich mixture. The higher the concentration of unburned oxygen, the less differential there is in the zirconium element of the sensor and the lower the voltage output of the sensor. The sensor's output varies continuously from a lean value of 0.1 volts to a rich value of 0.9 volts, with the perfect 14.7 stoichiometric air/fuel mixture producing a sensor voltage in the middle. By design, the sensor bounces from rich to lean every few seconds, but an average of 0.5 volts indicates a correct stoichiometric mixture.

When the engine is running in closed-loop, with the ECM chasing the stoichiometric air/fuel mixture, a full-functioning O_2 sensor will produce a voltage signal that is constantly changing back and forth from rich to lean. The transition rate is configured in the EMS data tables according to the ability of the various fueling systems to execute a fuel trim action, stabilize, and get meaningful feedback. The rate is slowest on engines with feedback carburetors, typically one per second at 2,500 rpm. Engines with throttle-body injection are somewhat faster (two or three times per second at 2,500 rpm), while engines with multi-port injection are the fastest (five to seven times per second at 2,500 rpm).

Post-1994–96 late-model vehicles equipped with OBD-II are equipped with multiple oxygen sensors, with an oxygen sensor located on each exhaust manifold and an additional oxygen sensor mounted behind each catalytic converter to monitor cat operating efficiency. An LS1 Corvette equipped with dual cats thus has four oxygen sensors. A Toyota Avalon with the 1MZ-FE V-6 and single cat has three O_2 sensors. A 2003 Honda VTEC four-cylinder has two O_2 sensors. The OBD-II system compares the O_2 sensor readings before and after the cat, and may set a malfunction indicator lamp (MIL) code if there is no significant change in exhaust gas oxygen readings to indicate the converter is functional.

WIDEBAND UEGO SENSOR

In 1994, Bosch introduced a variation of the standard zirconium O_2 sensor called the Universal Exhaust Gas Oxygen (UEGO) or "wideband" O_2 sensor. It is a five- to six-wire sensor that makes use of a Nernst cell and provides the ability to measure air/fuel ratios far from the stoichiometric ratio, especially under heavy loading when stoichiometric air/fuel ratios are not feasible and air/fuel ratios in the range of 0.78–0.88 lambda are mandatory to optimize torque and eliminate detonation. The wideband sensor provides a vital tool in meeting increasing requirements for better fuel economy, lower emissions, and better performance. Most UEGO sensors are still built by Bosch or NTK.

Initially, the Nernst-cell wideband sensor (and required controller circuitry) was prohibitively expensive for dedicated use on individual engine management systems. Bosch's solution was the LSM 11, a "pseudo wideband," four-wire, narrow-band O_2 sensor with the ability to detect minute amounts of exhaust gas oxygen. According to Bosch, "Where the standard sensors . . . are 'narrow band' or 'two-step' sensors that purely cycle when the lambda value of 1 is achieved, the LSM 11 sensor has a . . . flatter operating curve than a standard sensor, allowing it to measure lambda values of between ~ 0.80 and ~ 1.60" (gasoline air/fuel ratios between about 11.8 and 23.5). Motec has supplied LSM sensors with some M8, M48, and M4 engine management systems, and the LSM has been supplied as well on some Autronic EMSs.

The Bosch UEGO sensor was designed to deal with the problem that as engine air/fuel mixture moves further away from the stoichiometric ratio, changes in exhaust gas oxygen content can be extremely subtle or nonexistent. Moving quickly in the rich direction from the stoichiometric ratio, there is little or no oxygen in the exhaust. Beyond this, additional richness simply adds more unburned fuel to the exhaust gases, hardly affecting the oxygen content.

It is actually something of a misnomer to call the wideband sensor an "O_2 sensor," since rich mixtures are not really detected according to exhaust gas oxygen because there is *very* little free exhaust gas oxygen below about 0.9 lambda, and therefore no good way to distinguish between, say, air-gasoline mixtures of 13:1 and 11:1. Instead, air/fuel ratio is measured according to how much oxygen must be pumped into a reaction chamber to convert excess hydrocarbons and carbon monoxide into water and CO_2.

A wideband sensor looks like a narrow-band sensor, but the sensor has a five-wire connector (really six, but two of the elements can share a connection) and is composed of a Nernst "reference cell" and an oxygen ion "pump cell," plus a sophisticated heating circuit. UEGO sensors typically contain wires connected to the resistive heating element (two wires), the zirconia sensor, the pump, a calibration resistor, and common. Basically, a narrow-band zirconia sensor is used to measure the oxygen concentration within a small reaction chamber, and a bi-directional oxygen-pump cell transports oxygen ions to or from the surface of this small chamber as required to maintain a stoichiometric ratio in the chamber. The pump cell current required to achieve a stoichiometric mixture in the Nernst cell thus provides an indication of air/fuel ratio.

Wideband UEGO sensors require a controller to run the pump cell and correlate pump activity with zirconia sensor readings and to control sophisticated heater circuitry essential to UEGO accuracy. Wideband controller circuitry is built into all air/fuel ratio meters and some ECUs that support

SENSORS

O$_2$ sensor cutaway. A standard O$_2$ sensor is essentially an "air battery" in which exhaust gases act as an electrolyte that affects the voltage output of the sensor based on oxygen content in the same way the specific gravity of the liquid in a lead-acid car battery affects voltage. Given a sensor voltage, an EMS can correlate the exhaust gas oxygen content to the likely air/fuel ratio that would have resulted in this amount of residual oxygen. *Bosch*

UEGO sensors, but it is more common for ECUs to require an external controller supplied in a kit with the wideband UEGO sensor itself.

The reference cell consists of a standard planar zirconia element, and the pump cell consists of an electrochemical gas pump or diffusion chamber wherein the control circuitry always attempts to maintain a perfect stoichiometric air/fuel ratio by controlling the pump cell current and flow of oxygen ions. A feedback loop in the control circuitry manages the pump current to keep the output of the electrochemical Nernst cell constant. The pump current is a direct indication of excess exhaust gas oxygen concentration. It indicates if the engine air/fuel ratio is lean of the stoichiometric ratio or if excess hydrocarbons and carbon monoxide are present, or if the air/fuel ratio is rich of the stoichiometric ratio, or the amount of oxygen that must be transported by pump current to react with them and convert to water and CO$_2$. Not only can a UEGO measure air/fuel ratios far from the stoichiometric ratio in either direction, but the design eliminates the rich-lean cycling inherent in standard zirconia sensors, allowing an EMS to adjust lambda and spark timing much more frequently.

UEGOs are useful tools for dyno tuning under heavy load, and wideband sensors have been used on OE control systems for stratified direct-injection engines and diesel engines that must meet EURO and ULEV emission limits. Many aftermarket engine management systems now incorporate wideband UEGO sensors (WBO$_2$) that are potentially capable of delivering accurate air/fuel ratio results all the way from lambda = .55 to lambda = 2.0. Wideband O$_2$ sensors provide the possibility of an EMS giving full authority fuel delivery correction with target air/fuel ratios far beyond the usual range of narrow-band sensors, but even when the wideband sensor is not integrated with the EMS, sensor readings are a powerful tool for tuners calibrating an engine.

The wideband sensor consists of a dual inner layer referred to as "reference call" and "pump call". The wideband controller AFR sensor circuitry always tries to keep a perfect air/fuel ratio inside a special monitoring chamber (a.k.a., diffusion chamber or pump-cell circuit) by way of controlling its current.

As such, if the engine air/fuel mixture goes lean, the pump-cell circuit voltage goes low and the controller immediately regulates the current going through it to maintain a stoichiometric ratio inside the diffusion chamber by maintaining a set voltage value. At this point, the pump cell discharges excess oxygen through the diffusion gap using current created in the pump-cell circuit.

On the other hand, if the air/fuel mixture goes rich, the pump-cell circuit voltage rapidly goes high and the controller immediately reverses the current polarity to trim the pump-cell circuit voltage to its set stable value. The pump cell moves oxygen into the monitoring chamber via reversed current in the controller's AFR pump-cell circuit. The current in the pump-cell circuit is thus proportional to the oxygen concentration or deficiency in the exhaust gas such that it serves as an index of the air/fuel ratio. The wideband controller constantly monitors and adjusts the pump-cell current circuitry in quest of a set voltage. The sensors are current devices lacking a cycling voltage waveform.

Due to manufacturing tolerances, the electrical output of wideband UEGO sensors must be calibrated at the time of manufacture via laser trimming of a resistor element that's then incorporated in the connector, or the UEGO must go through a free-air calibration phase to work accurately.

Exhaust pressure and temperature can degrade the ability of the heating circuit to maintain a precision temperature in the wideband. The magnitude of the difference between current air/fuel and stoichiometric ratios will affect the required pump cell current, which must be continuously corrected on the fly in the interest of wideband accuracy.

Existing air/fuel ratio mixture diagnostic equipment makes use of UEGO sensors that offer fast operation over a wide range of mixtures. The original problem for production EMS use was the expense of the sensor. A problem for some ECMs with reading wideband air/fuel ratio sensors is that the wideband sensors typically return a voltage between 0 and 5; whereas, a narrow-band sensor usually returns a 0-to-1- or 1.5-volt signal, such that employing a wideband sensor may require conditioning resistor-divider circuitry to function on some ECUs.

Exhaust pressure can and will affect wideband O$_2$ sensor readings, with most UEGO sensors rated to deliver reasonably accurate results between 0.8- and 1.3-bar exhaust pressure, with error increasing if pressure exceeds the normal range. What's more, pressure sensitivity increases as air/fuel ratio moves further from the stoichiometric ratio in either direction such that the sensor reports increasingly exaggerated air/fuel ratio results in both lean and rich directions when exhaust pressure is high. Some turbo systems produce shockingly high exhaust backpressure, and to avoid catastrophic inaccuracy at higher engine loading, UEGO sensors should ideally be installed downstream of the turbine on turbocharged applications. If this is not possible, fuel enrichment should include an extra safety margin to compensate for inaccurately rich (or lean) sensor readings when the UEGO is pressurized.

Depending on specifications, the body of some wideband air/fuel ratio sensors may need to be protected from excessive heat from turbochargers or high EGTs, which normally involves carefully locating the sensor bung and installation of a heat sink or heat shield between the sensor body. However, if the sensor is installed downstream of a turbine or some distance from exhaust ports, it may be necessary to correct air/fuel ratio results for transport delay to correctly correlate air/fuel ratio results with the engine conditions that produced them. Most EMSs that support wideband sensors provide a facility to configure delay.

Vee-type engines may have difficulty sharing a single wideband air/fuel ratio sensor, particularly when the engine is equipped with isolated exhaust systems for each bank of cylinders. Some sophisticated advanced aftermarket EMSs do support dual wideband sensors with independent air/fuel ratio correction for individual cylinder banks, in which case the cost

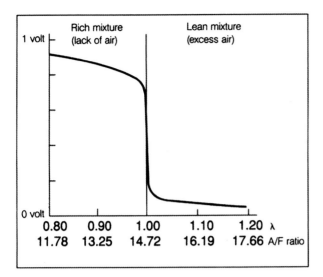

	Rich mixture (lack of air)		Lean mixture (excess air)		
0.80	0.90	1.00	1.10	1.20	λ
11.78	13.25	14.72	16.19	17.66	A/F ratio

O_2 sensor voltage graph. Standard (non-wideband) O_2 sensors are extremely precise in the vicinity of the stoichiometric 14.7 air/fuel ratio. ECMs operating in closed loop mode are constantly trimming injection pulsewidth to chases stoich mixtures at idle and light cruise, causing AFR to fluctuate back and forth very near to 14.7.

of dual wideband sensors may not be significant compared to the overall investment in the EMS and engine, but the more common solution is to install a single wideband sensor in one of the Vee banks and consider reported results to be representative of both cylinder banks—or to install 18x1.5-millimeter O_2 sensor bungs in both exhaust systems and move the sensor to test alternate cylinder banks (plugging the bung that is not in use).

In some cases, highly accurate narrow-band O_2 sensors without an oxygen ion pump cell have been used as "wideband" O_2 sensors. An example is the Bosch LSM11 sensor used by Motec on the M48 ECU used in some of the project vehicles in this book.

TITANIA O_2 SENSORS

Some late-model vehicles use O_2 sensors with Titania elements that operate effectively at lower temperatures. They do not operate relative to outside air as zirconium sensors do, so there are no reference vents to become blocked. Titania O_2 sensors are rare on OE engines and even more rare on aftermarket engine management systems. Due to the lower operating temperatures, Titania O_2 sensors warm up in as little as 15 seconds and allow the system to begin closed-loop (feedback) operation almost immediately. They don't cool below operating temperature at idle, and they can be located farther downstream from the engine or used with turbochargers, which bleed off a lot of heat from the exhaust gases.

Titania O_2 sensors do not generate a voltage like zirconium sensors; rather, they change resistance dramatically as the mixture changes from rich to lean. The change is not gradual. The mixture changes from low resistance of less than 1,000 ohms when the mixture is rich, to high resistance of more than 20,000 ohms when the mixture goes lean. Therefore, the ECU supplies a 1-volt reference signal that passes through the titania sensor and is then evaluated by the ECU.

The effect of the sensor is such that at rich mixture (and low resistance) the computer reads back at nearly 1 volt. As the resistance dramatically increases with the change to lean

mixture, the voltage switches suddenly to 0.1 volt. This type of sensor is therefore binary: the sensor tells the ECU that the mixture is either too rich or too lean—and not how much. But a clever ECU can make educated guesses as to the actual mixture based on pulse width changes required to flip rich or flip lean. However, the titania sensors are obviously not well suited to closed-loop operation at nonstoichiometric ratio mixtures (such as wide-open throttle in turbocharged vehicles when 14.7 is dangerously lean).

LIMITATIONS OF O_2 SENSORS

Most O_2 sensors will not function until their temperature reaches 600 degrees. This means the sensor is not available immediately on startup when the rich mixtures required to start and sustain a cold engine produce the most pollution. Virtually all oxygen sensors on 1995-plus engines now contain heating elements to help the sensor reach operating temperature sooner and to keep the sensor from cooling off too much at idle..

Tetraethyl lead will rapidly kill a conventional platinum/ceramic O_2 sensor. Lucas, Bosch, and others have introduced sensors that resist lead contamination for tuning or monitoring racing engines. Special Bosch O_2 sensors for European use with leaded fuel are able to tolerate up to 0.4 grams of lead per liter, which is a lot. O_2 sensors can also become clogged with carbon or fail prematurely due to poisoning from solvents used in some RTV silicone sealing compounds.

An O_2 sensor normally lasts 30,000 to 50,000 miles, and UEGOs can last as much as 100,000 miles. As the sensor ages, drivability problems can result because the sensor loses its ability to react as quickly to changes in exhaust gas oxygen. This results in improper mixtures that produce loss of power, rough idle, poor gas mileage, and high emissions.

The computer's ability to correctly deduce air/fuel ratios based on exhaust-gas oxygen can be adversely affected by air leaks in the inlet or exhaust manifold (which will cyclically cause exhaust to pulse out of the exhaust system and air to pulse into the exhaust system, which can skew O_2 sensor readings lean), by malfunctioning injectors, or even by a misfiring spark plug, resulting in huge amounts of oxygen from unburned charge mixtures being released into the exhaust. One or more cylinders misfiring or running significantly leaner or richer than the rest can fool the O_2 sensor and computer about the overall air/fuel ratio, which can cause the computer to make incorrect closed-loop adjustments (or a human tuner to perform inaccurate calibrations). If leaks pollute the exhaust with oxygen, the EMS may richen mixtures to compensate for what it thinks is a lean mixture, which may lead to additional problems if plugs foul and misfire, polluting the exhaust with additional oxygen and leading to further erroneous enrichment, and so on. A weak ignition system that leads to misfires will create false lean readings from an O_2 sensor. The problem should be corrected by increasing exhaust energy or narrowing the sparkplug gap to prevent the spark kernel from being blown out before robust ignition commences.

Cam timing can create O_2 sensor problems when increased cam duration used to create power results in overlap that sends unburned charge and air straight through into the exhaust, resulting in adverse effects similar to exhaust leaks that get in the way of EGO mixture control. As you'd expect, the effect diminishes at higher engine rpm and loading when there is less overlap time and resonation effects ram more charge into the cylinders rather than out the exhaust valve.

AEM's Universal Exhaust Gas Oxygen (UEGO) sensor and controller measure air/fuel ratio over a wide range compared to ordinary O_2 sensors, which are essentially just rich-lean indicators in the vicinity of 14.7:1, the chemically ideal air/fuel ratio for combustion. An oxygen sensor is basically a type of battery that generates a varying voltage depending on the amount of oxygen in exhaust gases (from which it is possible to deduce what the air/fuel ratio may have been). By re-normalizing such sensors to non-stoichiometric mixtures across the bandwidth with the addition of a Nernst pump cell, wideband AFR/UEGO sensors can accurately measure rich mixtures approaching 10:1 or less, or lean mixtures in the 17–20:1 range. *AEM*

Most narrow-band O_2 sensors are only accurate plus or minus approximately one air/fuel ratio from the stoichiometric ratio, which is why most narrow-band O_2 sensors are unsuitable for any task beyond targeting lambda = 1.0 at idle and light cruise on engines with mild cams.

Ordinary narrow-band oxygen sensors produce a saw-tooth voltage change that can be useful to the ECM in the 1- to 2-millisecond time range with clever computer algorithms. However, as the ECM makes injection pulse width corrections, the pulse width and actual air/fuel mixture tend to "hunt," varying around the stoichiometric mixture in a wave pattern as sensor voltage changes markedly in the neighborhood of lambda = 1.0.

Emissions compliance is so critical that original equipment (OE) engine management systems tend to believe the O_2 sensor before any other sensor (though they also monitor the sensor output for implausible electrical activity indicating failure or partial failure, and will set a malfunction indicator light [check engine soon] in the case of a suspected failure). An OEM ECU is constantly making judgments about the accuracy of various sensors and actually builds a correction table for each sensor in memory in an attempt to maintain the best possible functioning. When the battery is disconnected, the correction factors are reset to 1 and reevaluated subsequently as the engine runs. This enables the system to function reasonably well in spite of aging equipment and manufacturing tolerances.

If hot rodders or tuners attempt to tamper with sensor data in order to defeat performance limitations of an engine management system (for example, increasing maximum boost and richening peak-load air/fuel ratio), the EMS may work against them on newer systems by correcting suspect sensor data in an attempt to bring the system back to EPA-legal calibration. It is not uncommon on the newest systems for some types of modifications to air/fuel ratio, manifold pressure, fuel pressure, timing, or acceleration to be defeated with EMS countermeasures—perhaps not immediately but in a short distance or time.

TEMPERATURE SENSORS
Coolant or Cylinder Head Temperature

Piston engines operate most efficiently within a narrow temperature band, and it is critical that the engine management system have a good handle on engine temperature to deliver efficient operation. If the engine is too cold, fuel entering the engine will not atomize well. If the engine is too hot, there is a risk of hotspots in the combustion chamber causing engine damage from detonation or preignition, or from thermal expansion or distortion warping critical internal engine sealing surfaces. Target engine temperature depends on the application, with most liquid-cooled, late-model factory engines thermostatically controlled to run at about 200 degrees Fahrenheit coolant temperature to optimize combustion and emissions. A drop to 180 degrees Fahrenheit could cool combustion enough to allow a few degrees of timing advance on knock-limited engines sufficient to increase horsepower, but it is critical that cooler temperatures not prevent termination of warm-up enrichment when the engine reaches the new normal temperature.

The coolant or engine temperature sensor has been called the master sensor because the ECU uses engine temperature data along with data from the oxygen sensor in the decision to go into closed-loop mode to dynamically control the air/fuel mixture.

The coolant temperature sensor is used by the ECU to deduce the operating temperature of the engine and therefore the applicability of cold operation enrichment. Engine temperature may also determine the following:

- When the ECM is willing to enter closed-loop operation (not while the engine is stone cold, but as soon as possible as it warms up in order to monitor and keep emissions low)
- Fast idle (only while cold or when the air conditioning compressor is active)
- Spark advance and retard: Spark advance is often limited for emissions purposes until the engine reaches normal operating temperature.
- EGR flow is blocked while the engine is cold to improve cold drivability.
- Canister purge does not occur until the engine is warm to improve cold drivability.
- Energizing the electric heater grid under the carburetor on older engines to improve early fuel evaporation when the engine is cold.
- Operation of the throttle kicker idle speed when the engine is cold.

- Transmission torque converter clutch lockup after a cold start.
- Operation of the electric cooling fan (if a separate fan thermostat isn't used) when a certain temperature is reached.

On water-cooled engines, the main temperature sensor usually protrudes into the coolant water jacket through the head or intake manifold. Thermistor-type variable-resistance sensors accurately and predictably change resistance with temperature, modifying a 5-volt reference signal (VRef) from the ECU that is then returned to the ECU and evaluated to determine engine temperature. Most of these are the negative temperature coefficient type, which means the sensor's resistance decreases as the temperature goes up. An NTC sensor's resistance is high when cold and typically drops 300 ohms for every degree rise in temperature. Obviously, a CTS sensor must be located where it accurately reflects the actual engine temperature, rather than a spurious hot or cold spot in the cooling system, so it is important that the sensor is not located in a gas bubble where the temperature or thermal transfer coefficient is different from that of the coolant itself. Cylinder head temperature sensors that measure the temperature of the casting rather than the coolant avoid such problems, but the cylinder head is likely to be 7.5 to15 degrees hotter than the coolant. At the very least, the sensor reading must be proportional to the real engine temperature.

Some vehicles also use switch-type coolant temperature sensors that open or close at a certain temperature in a binary fashion like a thermostat—either on or off—to control the operation of something like an electric cooling fan. The switch-type sensor may be designed to remain closed within a certain temperature range (say between 55 and 235 degrees Fahrenheit) or to open only when the engine is warm (above 125 degrees Fahrenheit). Switch-type coolant sensors can be found on older GM T-car minimum function systems, Ford MCU, and Chrysler lean burn systems.

A faulty coolant temperature sensor or circuit can cause a variety of symptoms, given the sensor's global effect on so many engine functions. Symptoms might include stalling when cold from wrong mixture, retarded timing or slow idle speed, poor cold idle from wrong mixture, lack of heated inlet air or early fuel evaporation (EFE) enhancement, stumble or hesitation from lack of EFE or too early EGR, poor gas mileage due to extended cold mixture enrichment, lack of open-loop operation, and failure to activate full spark advance when warm.

Modern ECUs often incorporate "limp-home" operations strategies in which the ECU will disregard sensor data that it decides is suspect. In the 1970s, ECUs could be fooled into providing fuel enrichment during turbo or blower boost operation by grounding out temperature sensors to make the ECU think the engine requires cold-running enrichment. Today, a CTS sensor suddenly indicating cold temperatures may cause the ECU to disregard the sensor data and default to 70 degrees Celsius as the computer's trouble strategy takes effect. Modern tuners/hackers have had to develop alternate means.

INTAKE AIR TEMPERATURE

Most engine management systems measure the temperature of intake air in order to correct for changes in its density. Colder air is denser than hot air, meaning cold air contains more molecules of air per volume and air temperature is critical to the ability of speed-density engine management systems to accurately estimate cylinder air mass at a given manifold pressure. As well, Bosch L-Jetronic and many other older EFI systems used a pressure vane air meter to measure the velocity of air entering the engine, In this case, converting vane pressure to mass airflow required correcting for altitude and air temperature. Besides temperature-based air density changes, hotter air temperature increases the burn rate of charge mixtures in the combustion chambers, which changes optimal spark advance. Colder inlet temperature allows more spark advance without detonation, which could be used to increase horsepower. The heat of compression from turbos or blowers (even after intercooling, in most cases) will usually mandate reduced spark advance to avoid detonation.

The air temperature sensor is a thermistor sensor like the coolant sensor. The difference is that the lower density of intake air versus engine coolant allows an IAT sensor to be unshielded without damage, providing quicker response to changing conditions, such as sudden engine loading on a forced-induction engine increasing air temperature entering the intake ports from 75 to 100 degrees to more than 300 degrees on some

Tech Edge Do-It-Yourself Wideband Kit, populated by user with discrete components. Wideband AFR sensors require calibration and very sophisticated control circuitry to function accurately under all achievable temperatures and pressures.

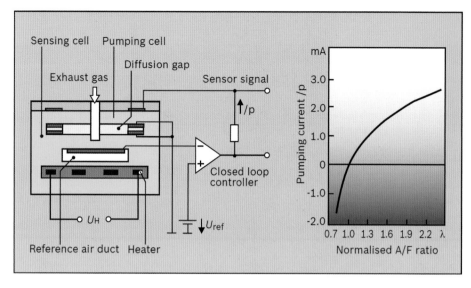

Bosch LSU 4 Wideband AFR sensor schematic. Wideband AFR sensors make use of a standard O₂ sensor and a Nernst pumping cell. Most wideband sensors are made by Bosch or NGK.

nonintercooled applications. Placing the sensor after the blower or turbocharger and intercooler in a position where it will not be rendered inaccurate by heat transfer to or from the mounting surface is critical. Many aftermarket and factory speed-density EFI systems also measure inlet air temperature and use this reading for various corrections to fuel, ignition, and other engine management calculations.

Intake air temperature (IAT) sensors are similar to coolant sensors, with the exception that they are designed and made with materials intended to minimize heat soak from the surface in which they are mounted. So far as possible, IATs react quickly to measure the temperature of the air moving past the sensors on a moment-by-moment basis (for example, as a turbocharger spools and immediately heats the air, then de-spools and passes cold air again). Testing procedures are identical to thermistor-type coolant sensors.

Some engine management systems have deployed multiple IAT sensors in different locations, and in an effort to model cylinder intake temperature, some speed-density EMSs have added manifold surface temperature sensors which can be combined with intake air velocity estimations to determine air temperature increase as charge blows past the hot metal of the manifold.

Beyond using IAT sensors to modify engine timing and trim air/fuel mixtures, additional IAT sensors before and after an intercooler can be very useful to monitor and datalog intercooler efficiency under various conditions, with potential actions including activating intercooler fans and warning alarms.

OIL TEMPERATURE

Some OEM and aftermarket engine management systems have the ability to monitor oil temperature via sensors that are virtually identical to coolant temperature sensors. Some aftermarket engine management systems can be set up to turn on oil cooler fans and pumps to control oil temperature, and beyond that provide an alarm to the driver or initiate limp-home strategies or even engine shutdown.

It is a mystery why virtually no street engine management systems are set up to provide audible warnings or limp-home/shutdown actions. Like high coolant temperatures, high oil temperatures definitely call for backing off the throttle or stopping the engine *now* before the engine is damaged.

Acceptable temperature range for 10W-40 synthetic oil is 180 to 240 degrees Fahrenheit, according to Redline Synthetic Oil. A narrower range of 200 to 220 degrees is ideal for best performance. Maximum safe oil temperature is 300 degrees. Even the best mineral-based oils will encounter durability problems at 250 degrees or higher, above which synthetic oil is mandatory.

EXHAUST GAS TEMPERATURE

Peak exhaust gas temperature (EGT) occurs when an engine is burning a stoichiometric air/fuel ratio (air/fuel ratio), 14.68:1 on gasoline engines. However, best engine performance at wide-open throttle occurs at air/fuel ratios between 11.5 and 13.0, at which point EGTs will be considerably cooler. Retarding timing without making other changes will raise EGT, because the mixture is still burning later in the burn cycle or even while the exhaust gases are in the exhaust ports.

EGT begins to drop at air/fuel ratios above 15:1, so it is critical to know on which side of peak EGT you are operating. On piston engines, EGT readings of 1,300–1,500 are common at the maximum power mixture, but this can vary considerably, depending on the engine. Combustion temperature is much hotter in the combustion chamber than EGT measurements in the exhaust ports, which will already have cooled.

EGTs above 1,550 are cause for concern, though some racers like Bob Norwood have successfully run temperatures measured in the 1,800–1,900 degree range during land speed record trials at Bonneville. No matter what the EGT, you should monitor air/fuel ratio with a wideband AFR sensor to see if the engine is running at a sensible air/fuel ratio. If you subtly tune from an air/fuel ratio known to be sub-optimally rich by leaning until you make peak power subject to EGT remaining safe, there should be a range between rich and lean best torque where power stays the same.

On less radical engines, you can sometimes feel a lean-of-peak condition as the mixture gets harder to ignite and power begins to fall. Once the air/fuel ratio gets close to 17 to 1 at WOT, the engine will typically start to misfire. The answer is to tune for peak power, keeping an eye on EGT. When power is falling on a boosted engine with a climbing EGT, stop immediately.

Most tuners always recommend to begin the programming or jetting process from a known very-rich initial setting, carefully leaning until torque falls off slightly, then richen the mixture to the point of maximum torque and note the EGT at this setting for future use. Keep in mind that this can be a tricky business unless you do it on an individual cylinder basis. Bob Norwood points out that radical engines working hard on an engine dyno almost always make more and more power as you lean from an excessively rich direction, making the most power right before the leanest, hottest cylinders burn down.

Exhaust gas temperature is useful as a benchmark for establishing which tuning parameters made maximum torque at wide-open throttle on a particular engine application. EGT gauges are widely used to set mixtures on specific aircraft engines used for steady-state high-power applications where operation has been studied and documented in advance.

Once optimal EGT is established for a particular application on a dyno, a tuner can establish a similar air/fuel ratio any time, the way airplane pilots lean an engine at altitude for peak power or peak fuel economy using EGT. Of course, it is really the air/fuel ratio that is important, not the EGT. Most engines will make maximum power at a gasoline air/fuel ratio between 11.8 and 13.0 to 1.0, but EGT may vary from 1,250 to 1,800 degrees Fahrenheit, depending on a variety of factors.

Keep in mind that a target EGT is valid only on the same engine configuration used on the test dyno. Ignition timing, cam or piston changes, or headers may change the optimal EGT. For example, changing compression ratio to a higher static setting with no other changes will lower EGT at the same air/fuel ratio, while retarding ignition timing will usually raise EGT at the same air/fuel ratio.

Be aware that altitude, barometric pressure, and ambient air temperature may affect this optimal temperature to some degree.

Exhaust gas temperature (EGT) sensors are commonly used in piston-engine aircraft to manually trim the air/fuel mixture. They are also frequently used as input to engine management systems on race engines (usually to measure turbine inlet temperature). EGT gauges like this are vital to manually guarding against damage, particularly when hot rodding diesel engines, since burning more of the air surplus with richer mixtures *increases* EGT. Some ECMs are capable of directly reading EGT sensors, which are typically installed at each exhaust port or header or at the turbine inlet for datalogging and readout on engine dynamometers. Healthy EGT can vary a lot, but high or rapidly rising EGT is a very good indication of looming trouble and engine damage. *AEM*

Wankel engines typically have higher EGTs than comparable piston engines due to their lower thermal efficiencies, with 1,800 degrees Fahrenheit a common optimal peak EGT. The trouble is, while one engine may make best power at 1,375 degrees, a similar engine might be happier at 1,525. But tuning purely on EGT without a frame of reference is just a waste of the money you spend on the EGT instrumentation. You need dyno torque and wideband air/fuel ratio data because you should be tuning EGT for whatever temperature produces mean or lean best torque (MBT or LBT).

Which is better, an EGT gauge or an air/fuel ratio meter? Once again, standard narrow-band O_2 sensors are useless (or even dangerous) for peak-power tuning, though they will warn of a grossly lean condition when the air/fuel ratio passes the stoichiometric ratio in a lean direction (an air/fuel ratio way too lean for peak power, in serious danger of knocking). Wideband/UEGO sensors combined with standalone lab-quality meters are expensive but accurate and useful, and they are essentially required somewhere in a responsible tuning regime (unless your EMS will directly read the wideband sensor). EGT gauges have the advantage of working with leaded fuel (which will kill oxygen sensors of any type, some faster than others), and they will warn you of dangerously hot combustion.

PRESSURE SENSORS
Manifold Pressure
(See Engine Load Sensors)

Barometric Pressure
Baro or BP or BAP (barometric absolute pressure) sensors are nearly identical to MAP sensors but are referenced to the atmosphere to measure ambient air density, which allows an ECU to distinguish between manifold pressure changes due to changes in engine loading versus manifold pressure changes due to changes in altitude, which may require changes in calculated load and spark advance. Frequently, the combination of a DPS (differential pressure sensor) and BP is used to determine absolute pressure in the manifold. These two functions have occasionally been combined in one sensor, as in the BMAP, once used by Ford in EEC-III and early EEC-IV systems. Some aftermarket ECUs have built-in barometric pressure sensors. Others require an auxiliary external 1-bar MAP sensor vented to the atmosphere to provide altitude and weather correction.

Fuel Pressure Sensors
The fuel rail pressure (FRP) sensor is similar in concept to a 5-bar or 10-bar MAP sensor and can be used by an EMS to provide fuel pressure compensation with changes to injection pulse width. Fuel pressure sensors are less common because they are not required on return-loop fuel systems, which use a mechanical regulator referenced to manifold pressure to provide a fixed ratio of fuel to manifold pressure at the injector discharge. The FRP sensor is used on returnless fuel systems where fuel pressure regulation is performed by varying the duty cycle of a special fuel pump. Returnless fuel systems eliminate the need for a return line and remove a certain amount of fuel heating and evaporative emissions due to fuel splashing back into the tank upon return. To control a variable-output fuel pump, the ECU needs to know how much pressure drop exists across the injector discharge. Like MAP sensors, FRP sensors are exposed to fuel pressure on one side of the diaphragm, but to manifold pressure on the other side rather than atmospheric, thus providing a

"difference" or delta reading. Thus, 44-psi absolute fuel rail pressure–supplying injectors delivering fuel into a manifold pressurized by a turbocharger to 15 psi would report a delta of 39 psi.

Diesel and direct-injection-gasoline system pressure sensors require the ability to operate at hundreds or even thousands of psi.

Combustion Pressure Sensors

By placing a small reference port in the head gasket or a spark plug, combustion pressure can be measured throughout the combustion cycle in real time, which can be used to detect detonation pressure spikes directly (rather than listening for indirect evidence of knock in the form of sounds coming from the engine). Combustion pressure sensors (also called in-cylinder pressure transducers) can also be used in feedback mode by an EMS to trim fuel and spark timing to directly optimize power production. Such sensors tend to be expensive, and, obviously, require fast controllers to condition the signal from a combustion pressure sensor for datalogging or analysis for feedback usage in a high-speed engine. This involves sophisticated engineering typically found at OEM car builders or advanced race teams and in the EMSs they use.

Engine Load Sensors

Engine load sensors provide a measurement of how hard a powerplant is working at a particular speed by providing a measurement or estimation of engine airflow or torque, which can be used to calculate fuel and timing requirements.

Throttle Position Sensors

The throttle position sensor (TPS) may be used to detect when an engine is at idle or full throttle, when to provide transient fuel enrichment for sudden acceleration (via rate of change in throttle angle), or to determine engine loading.

TPS sensors are variable resistors, also known as potentiometers, that change resistance as a shaft is physically turned in a way that's functionally similar to the operation of a volume control knob on a stereo system. When installed on the throttle shaft of a carb or throttle body, a TPS indicates the position of the throttle via the specific voltage output. By evaluating the change of throttle position over time, an EMS can determine the rate of throttle opening or closure, allowing it to determine whether the driver is attempting to accelerate, decelerate, idle, or cruise at steady state, and whether the driver is trying to change states. Some older fuel-injections systems such as the Lucas/Bosch EFI on early Jaguar V-12s also incorporate throttle microswitches, or nose switches, that indicate idle (closed throttle) or wide-open throttle (WOT). The TPS may be installed directly on the throttle shaft on the outside of the throttle body or carburetor (inside or outside the throttle housing), or in some cases on an auxiliary shaft linked to the throttle shaft with a belt, chain, or rod that may or may turn at a 1-1 drive ratio.

The TPS is typically a rotary three-wire, variable potentiometer that changes resistance as the throttle opens and closes by increasing or decreasing the electrical path through a set of resistors according to position. The ECU provides the TPS with a voltage reference signal (VRef), usually 5 volts, and a ground. As the position of the throttle changes, the corresponding change in the TPS's internal resistance alters an output voltage signal that returns to the ECU via the third wire. Therefore, the

MAP Sensor Voltage and kPa Relationship

Load Percentage	MAP Voltage	1-Bar kPa	2-Bar kPa	3-Bar kPa
0	0.00	10	8.8	3.6
5	0.25	15	18	17
10	0.50	20	28	33
15	0.75	24	38	48
20	1.00	29	48	64
25	1.25	34	58	80
30	1.50	39	68	96
35	1.75	43	78	111
40	2.00	48	88	127
45	2.25	53	98	143
50	2.50	58	108	159
55	2.75	62	118	174
60	3.00	67	128	190
65	3.25	72	138	206
70	3.50	77	148	222
75	3.75	81	158	237
80	4.00	86	168	253
85	4.25	91	178	269
90	4.50	96	188	285
95	4.75	100	198	300
100	5.00	105	208	315

computer receives a variable voltage signal that changes in direct proportion to the throttle position. Most TPS sensors provide 0.5 to 1.0 volts at idle with the throttle closed, with 4.5 to 5 volts indicating wide-open throttle. On engine management systems with special idle or full-throttle fueling spark tables and adjustable throttle stops, it is important to correctly calibrate the threshold between closed throttle and part throttle so that the computer uses the correct table when the driver's foot is off the accelerator pedal or at full throttle, particularly if you adjust the throttle stop to prevent stalling or increase idle speed. The TPS transfer functions on many EMSs are nonlinear, with more resolution provided at small throttle angles where fixed increases in throttle angle have a much greater effect on airflow than they do when the throttle is more open.

On virtually all modern emissions-controlled passenger cars, the TPS is used to initiate transient fuel enrichment on sudden throttle opening, like the accelerator pump on a carb, in order to prevent bog from rapid depletion of injected liquid fuel ("Tau") on manifold walls that temporarily leans the air/fuel ratio when the fuel puddle contribution to the air/fuel mixture is reduced or eliminated.

Some normally aspirated aftermarket street EFI systems and certain racing EFI systems combine throttle position data with engine speed sensing to estimate engine loading, and thus air entering the engine—with which the ECU can calculate fuel and timing requirements. Throttle-position engine management systems are also known as Alpha-N systems, with alpha representing throttle angle and N representing the number of power pulses per unit of time. Alpha-N systems make use of the fact that a big throttle angle for a given engine speed implies higher manifold pressure, higher engine loading, and, therefore, more air entering the engine. Throttle-position engine management systems tend to be very responsive and therefore good for racing, and they work well for high-output naturally aspirated engines with fluctuating, turbulent manifold pressure that could confuse a MAF or MAP system. However, Alpha-N systems have no ability to automatically correct for changes in engine VE unrelated to throttle angle. This makes load estimate based solely on throttle angle entirely unsuitable for turbocharging applications where a given throttle angle and engine speed cannot distinguish between a wide range of possible engine loading and mass airflow.

Exact TPS calibration is critical on throttle position (Alpha-N) load-sensing engine management systems. The system specification requires a specific voltage signal that tells the computer that the throttle is closed. Today, many modern aftermarket engine management systems allow calibrating the TPS with software by manually instructing the EMS when the throttle is closed and then when it's wide open so the system can correlate specific sensor electrical outputs with these states. Alternately, at closed throttle, loosen the TPS and rotate while watching TPS resistance with an ohmmeter. At the correct voltage, the tuner would tighten down the TPS mounting screws. On some speed-density or MAF-based systems the TPS does not require calibration, since it is only used to detect changes in throttle position, for transient enrichment—not absolute position.

Some ECUs require a linear potentiometer TPS, which is more expensive than a nonlinear potentiometer TPS (where resistance in the TPS might, for example, change output rapidly with initial increments of change in throttle angle and less the farther the TPS moves toward wide open). Today, many aftermarket ECUs can correctly interpret nonlinear TPS data. (A mathematical function corrects the nonlinear voltage from the TPS to accurate specific throttle angles for use in fuel-injection pulse width calculations.)

A faulty TPS can cause drivability problems that include hunting or erratic idle, hesitation, stalling, detonation, failure of torque converter lockup, hard starting, intermittent check engine (MIL) light during driving, poor fuel economy, and generally poor engine performance.

If the TPS attachment screws are loose, the TPS could produce an unstable signal as if the throttle were opening and closing, causing an unstable idle and intermittent hesitation. This condition probably won't set a trouble code.

On older applications with adjustable TPS, the initial adjustment is very important. If not set correctly to specifications, it can have an adverse effect on the fuel mixture, particularly on engines with Alpha-N engine management systems.

A shorted TPS produces an output signal equivalent to the high voltage of constant wide-open throttle. On OE systems this will typically result in a set malfunction indicator light and cause the fuel mixture to run excessively rich.

If the TPS is open, the computer may assume the throttle is closed and stationary, and the resulting fuel mixture may be too lean and a malfunction code that corresponds to a low-voltage TPS may be set. With an inability to detect sudden throttle openings, the engine will bog and stumble during acceleration, particularly from lower rpm. Dead spots in the TPS (which are a common condition) can cause flat spots in engine performance that only occur at certain throttle positions.

Manifold Pressure Sensors (MAP)

MAP sensors are critical to the functioning of speed-density engine management systems. MAP sensors are equipped with a diaphragm affected by gas pressure that acts on a strain gauge to deliver a voltage corresponding to absolute pressure (pressure above a perfect vacuum) in the intake manifold. Manifold pressure corrected for temperature equals density. By knowing the engine-pumping efficiency at a given speed-

A mass airflow sensor is designed to provide frequency or voltage readout corresponding to the weight or mass of air moving through the sensor, from which deriving the appropriate raw fuel injection pulse width is relatively simple. MAF sensors typically measure the amount of current required to keep a wire or film heated to a predetermined temperature. The cooling effect of inlet air is exactly proportionate to its mass or number of molecules. Since the MAF sensor actually only samples a tiny proportion of the air passing through it, it is critical that the air be conditioned to eliminate turbulence. This special-purpose aftermarket Z06 Corvette MAF from Nitrous Express incorporates nitrous oxide injection and supplemental fuel delivery orifices. *Nitrous Express*

density breakpoint and multiplying it by the air density in the manifold and the engine displacement, an ECU can deduce mass airflow into the engine (and use it to calculate fuel-injection pulse width and ignition timing. Manifold absolute pressure is low when intake manifold vacuum is highest (during deceleration or idle). Pressure is high when vacuum is low (at wide-open throttle on a normally aspirated engine or when manifold pressure is forced above atmospheric pressure by a turbo or blower under boost conditions).

A speed-density engine management system lacking a mass airflow sensor can deduce engine airflow and loading by using rpm and manifold absolute pressure to index into a volumetric efficiency (VE) table explicitly calibrated in detail with pumping efficiency data for the particular engine, and combine this with engine displacement and air temperature data to estimate air flow. Airflow plus engine speed indicates engine loading. A VE table and target air/fuel ratios table can be used with injector flow data to lean the mixture and advance spark timing under low loading conditions for best fuel economy. Under high loading/high manifold pressure and high VE, an EMS under control of the two tables will typically enrich the fuel mixture to produce best power while simultaneously retarding spark timing to prevent knocking (like a carb power valve and vacuum/boost advance/retard unit on a conventional distributor).

Speed-density engine management systems (without airflow sensors) are highly sensitive to faulty MAP problems. If the MAP sensor is defective or out of calibration, severe drivability and performance problems will occur. Such engine management systems are especially dependent on the MAP sensor's signal because the ECU needs it (along with engine rpm, throttle position, and ambient air temperature) to calculate airflow. Engines that estimate engine load using input from Mass Air

Flow and Throttle-Position sensors do not need MAP sensors, though turbocharged engines often have both MAP and MAF sensors (which provides a certain degree of redundancy).

A MAP sensor is referenced to inlet manifold pressure by direct mounting on a manifold port or using a vacuum hose or pipe connected to a manifold port if the sensor is mounted remotely. A pressure-sensitive electronic circuit in the sensor generates an electrical signal that varies with air density. The sensor is not influenced by ambient atmospheric pressure like a DPS/VAC sensor (which reads the *difference* between manifold and atmospheric pressure and is therefore affected by altitude and weather). MAP sensor is pre-calibrated to measure absolute pressure regardless of these factors.

A pressure-sensitive ceramic or silicon element and electronic circuitry inside the MAP sensor generate a signal that changes voltage with changes in manifold pressure. Most MAP sensors have a ground terminal, a voltage reference (VRef) supply (typically a 5-volt signal provided by the ECU), and an output terminal for returning data (voltage or frequency) to the ECU.

As engine manifold pressure changes, so does the MAP sensor's output. Typical MAP sensor output voltage might be 1.25 volts at idle and just under 5 volts at wide-open throttle. Voltage reads low when vacuum is high and increases as vacuum drops or moves into boosted territory on forced-induction engines, depending on the range of the sensor. On naturally aspirated engines with 1-bar MAP sensors, output generally changes about 0.7 to 1.0 volts for every 5 inches of change pressure from full vacuum to full atmospheric pressure (100–105 kPa). On boosted engines with 2- or 3-bar MAP sensors, the same 1–5 volt range must represent two or three atmospheres of change in pressure, with a corresponding decrease in accuracy and sensitivity in the normally aspirated range of operation.

Some Ford MAP sensors have been designed to produce a digital frequency signal rather than an analog DC voltage. Ford-type MAP sensors output a square-wave signal that increases in frequency as vacuum drops. A typical reading at idle might be 95 hertz (cycles per second) when vacuum is high, and 150 hertz at wide-open throttle when vacuum is low.

The MAP sensor on a Speed-Density EMS is critical to correct engine system functioning, since any accuracy problems will immediately affect both spark timing and fuel mixtures (though OEM Speed-Density systems will detect loss of correlation between TPS and MAP signals and attempt limp-mode operation using TPS data to estimate engine airflow like an Alpha-N system). A defective MAP sensor or wiring problems in the circuit connecting the map sensor to the ECU or air leaks in the manifold or in plumbing connecting the MAP sensor to the manifold can result in the MAP sensor delivering bad data. Bad MAP data can cause drivability problems such as detonation from lean mixture and excessively advanced spark, or power loss and poor economy due to retarded spark and over-rich mixture. Note: Knock sensors can sometimes mask problems with lean mixture and advanced spark by retarding spark timing under detonation.

Velocity Air Meters

Velocity or vane airflow (VAF) sensors provide an indication of engine airflow by measuring the force of air rushing into an engine against a spring-loaded door in an air tunnel. A linear potentiometer linked to the shaft of the air door measures the angle of opening and sends an electrical signal to the ECU that changes as the door opens more or less as air velocity changes. After making certain corrections, the ECU can estimate airflow

into the engine based on VAF position. The problem is that the force against the door is a function of two variables—weight of the air and speed of the air—and the ECU cannot distinguish, for a given door angle, whether the air is less dense but traveling faster or whether the air is more dense (heavier) but traveling a bit slower. Therefore, air velocity must be corrected for air density using temperature and barometric pressure to reflect air mass entering the engine per unit of time. Velocity air meters are commonly found on many older Bosch L-Jetronic and other factory EFI systems, though VAFs have been superseded by mass airflow sensors, which have many advantages and are less restrictive to engine VE. Velocity air meters can be rather restrictive, especially when engines have been modified for significantly greater airflow than stock. Velocity meters have the additional liability that once the door is fully open ("pegged"), there is no way for the sensor to measure further increases in airflow.

VAF sensors were used mostly on European imports equipped with Bosch L-Jetronic fuel injection, Japanese imports equipped with Nippondenso multi-port electronic fuel injection, and Ford vehicles equipped with Bosch multi-port EFI (those include Escort/Lynx, Turbo Thunderbird, Mustang with the 2.3-liter turbo engine, and Ford Probe with the 2.2-liter engine).

Because VAF sensors can be restrictive and run out of measurement upside on the high end of airflow, they are virtually never used with custom aftermarket engine management systems, and factory VAFs are often replaced with speed-density or MAF conversions on hot rod engines, though some programmable engine management systems like Motec can be configured to use VAF data for estimating engine loading.

A vane airflow sensor is located upstream of the throttle. The flap has a wiper arm that rotates against a sealed potentiometer (variable resistor), allowing the sensor's resistance and output voltage to change according to airflow—similar to the action of a throttle position sensor. The greater the airflow, the farther the flap is forced open (at least until it is fully open, at which point it cannot measure further increases in airflow). This changes the potentiometer's resistance and the resulting voltage return signal to the computer. Thus, a vane airflow sensor measures airflow directly, enabling the computer to calculate how much air is entering the engine independently of throttle opening or intake vacuum. The computer uses this information to determine injection pulse width for the target fuel mixture.

With the L-Jetronic-type vane airflow meter, adjustment is accomplished by tightening the spring tension. One notch is approximately equal to a 2 percent change in fuel mixture. For example, if you change to 20 percent larger injectors, you would tighten the spring by 10 notches. A sealed idle-mixture screw is located on the airflow sensor. This controls the amount of air that bypasses the flap, and, therefore, the air/fuel ratio at idle. Verify fuel mixture by checking with a wideband meter to verify that the air/fuel ratio is correct and adjust if necessary.

Some older VAF sensors contains a safety switch for the electric fuel pump relay, which is designed to stop the fuel pump if the engine is stopped (in case of an accident). Airflow into the engine allows the pump to be active.

EMSs using VAF sensors cannot tolerate air leaks. A vacuum leak downstream of the VAF sensor allows un-metered air to enter the engine, which can lean out the fuel mixture and cause a variety of drivability problems. Closed-loop oxygen sensor systems can compensate for small air leaks at idle once the engine warms up and goes into closed-loop, but large air leaks will cause large problems.

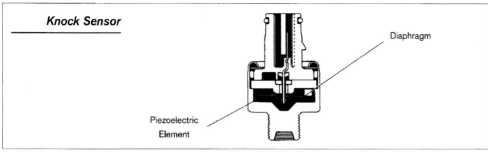

Knock Sensor

Diaphragm

Piezoelectric Element

The vibrations from spark knock excite a piezoelectric element in the knock sensor. The voltage or frequency output of the sensor is highest during knock, though other engine noises can also generate knock sensor output. It is up to the EMS to decide what threshold constitutes genuine knock, requiring countermeasures. *Toyota*

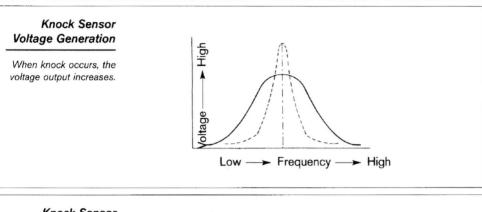

Knock Sensor Voltage Generation

When knock occurs, the voltage output increases.

Voltage — High

Low → Frequency → High

Knock Sensor

Ignition   Strong   Ignition   Weak

KNK Signal   Time →

Voltage

Vane airflow sensors are vulnerable to dirt. Unfiltered air passing through a torn or poor-fitting air filter may allow dirt to build up on the flap shaft, causing the flap to bind or stick. Backfiring in the intake manifold can force the flap backward violently, bending or breaking it. Some VAF sensors have a backfire valve built into the flap to protect the flap in case of a backfire by venting the explosion, though the valve itself can become a source of trouble if it leaks. Some vane airflow sensors are sealed units, preset at the factory with nothing that can be replaced or adjusted except the idle-mixture screw, which should ideally be adjusted to lambda = 1.0, using a wideband air/fuel ratio meter or to proper carbon monoxide readings with an exhaust gas analyzer.

Factory turbo engines always install vane airflow meters upstream of the turbocharger because it can be difficult to get an accurate reading out of a VAF sensor that's under pressure. Turbo conversion engines with vane airflow sensors must deal with the fact that the vane sensor can be very restrictive when the engine airflow increases dramatically. Another problem is that a vane sensor designed to meter stock airflow will probably be wide open on a turbo conversion engine with greatly enhanced airflow long before engine airflow peaks. Ideally, vane airflow systems on turbo and blower conversions should be converted to speed-density or MAF metering using aftermarket engine management systems.

Mass Airflow Sensors

The easiest way to ensure accurate fuel delivery is to base fuel calculations on accurate airflow information, and the ideal way to do this is not by deducing air mass from air velocity or manifold pressure with air temperature and engine speed data, but by directly measuring air mass entering the engine.

MAF sensors are located inline in the air ducting between the air cleaner and throttle body where the sensor can measure all air that is being drawn into the engine and react almost instantly to changes in throttle position and engine load that impact airflow into the engine.

There are two varieties of MAF sensors: hot-wire and hot-film. Unlike vane airflow (VAF) sensors, MAF sensors have no moving parts. They use a heated sensing element to measure airflow. In some hot-wire MAFs, a platinum wire is heated 212 degrees Fahrenheit above the inlet air temperature. In some hot-film MAFs, a foil grid is heated to 167 degrees Fahrenheit. As air flows past the sensing element, it has a cooling effect on the element proportional to the air mass flowing over it, which increases the current required by control circuitry to keep the sensing element at a constant temperature. The cooling effect varies directly with the temperature, density, and humidity of the incoming air, inherently providing temperature compensation. The electrical current change is proportional to the weight or mass of the air entering the powerplant. Since fixed-size increases

Garret turbo speed sensor kit. It can be extremely useful to datalog turbine/compressor speed to optimize engine tuning and to evaluate anti-lag engine management strategies that intentionally burn some fuel in the exhaust system upstream or even *in* the turbine housing to radically accelerate compressor spooling. The extreme speeds of turbochargers operating at up to 300,000 rpms can make speed sensor design and signal interpretation a challenge. Some speed sensors require auxiliary signal-processing and conditioning electronics to function well under all conditions.

in airflow at the low end represent a much greater percentage airflow increase than they do at higher airflows (where it takes a relatively large airflow increase to affect a given temperature change), the transfer function that maps MAF output voltage or frequency to airflow ends up looking like an exponential curve, with more resolution available at lower flow rates to accurately meter airflow at light cruise and especially idle.

Both voltage- and frequency-based MAFs have been built. Hot-wire Bosch MAF sensors, found on some import cars with LH-Jetronic fuel injection dating back to 1979 as well as 1985–89 GM TPI V-8 engines, generate an analog voltage signal that varies from 0 to 5 volts. Output at idle is usually 0.4 to 0.8 volts increasing to 4.5 to 5.0 volts at full throttle. Ford MAFs have also generated a 0-5 volt signal. Hot-film MAFs were introduced by AC Rochester in 1984 on the Buick turbo 3.8-liter V-6 and used on Chevrolet 2.8-liter engines and GM 3.0- and 3.8-liter V-6 engines. The early GM MAF produced a square-wave variable-frequency output with frequency ranging from 32–150 hertz, with 32 hertz being typical for idle and 150 hertz for full throttle. In 1990, GM switched most performance engines to speed-density fuel-injection systems, except for the Buick 3.3- and 3.8-liter, which was switched to a Hitachi MAF. In 1994, the MAF sensor returned (though the speed-density MAP sensor remained) on GM LT1 performance V-8s and continued in the same configuration on the LS1 in 1998 and later models. Modern GM MAFs deliver a 0-12,000 Hz wave.

Clean aerodynamics are necessary to maintain a smooth flow of air over the MAF wire or film to maintain proportionality to total flow through the air intake and avoid any aerodynamic forces or turbulence in the tunnel that would mean a disproportionate amount of air missed the wire or film. Modified engines with cold-air or high-flow intakes are subject to radiator fan blast or wind forces that can interfere with MAF functioning. Consequently, there can be a tradeoff between accurate air measurement at low speed and restriction at high speed.

Engines run with a steady airflow at or below about one-third of full throttle, where all pressure drop from atmosphere to cylinder is produced by the throttle plate, a realm that accounts for 50 percent of all driving in which all air meters perform equally well. In the remaining throttle range, the air pulses wildly from actual reverse flow caused by valve overlap, pneumatic hammer, and acoustic resonance up to a maximum of four times the swept volume of each cylinder, at which point

the intake stroke happens in one-half a crank revolution and the piston is moving at two times average piston speed.

If any part of the intake system limits maximum flow, there is a potential for performance improvement. Most factory MAF sensors are designed to be slightly smaller than the rest of the induction system to improve accuracy by controlling air velocity through the MAF. Because of multiple screens and poor fluidics design, some production factory MAF sensors have had pressure drops in the order of 12 to 24 inches of water. This reduces maximum horsepower by 5 to 7 percent due to the drop in engine VE, and it's made worse by altitude, which reduces efficiency by 0.7 percent per thousand feet. Aftermarket performance specialists have in some cases utilized patented aerodynamics to deliver accurate high-flow MAF units that outperform factory sensors.

In other cases, enthusiasts and tuning shops have gutted some or all of the flow screens from factory MAFs in an effort to remove an airflow bottleneck. The problem is that removing screens can disturb laminar flow through the sensing element and alter the percentage of air that contacts the sensing element versus total airflow through the MAF at some or all mass airflows, which usually lowers the MAF output compared to real mass airflow, at a worst case in a nonlinear fashion, usually with increased inaccuracy at low-rpm airflow.

Tuners working to increase the horsepower of MAF-equipped engines run into another problem when they increase engine airflow significantly beyond stock. Factory MAFs are normally sized to spread MAF output range across the anticipated airflow range of the engine to deliver the highest possible granularity of resolution. Extensive engine modifications that result in dramatically increased engine airflow can result in a situation where the MAF reaches its maximum output below the maximum airflow of the engine, which effectively "pegs" the MAF sensor, leaving it unable to meter the highest airflow of the powerplant. In this situation there is no choice but to install an aftermarket MAF sensor with extended range, and recalibrate relevant EMS tables (MAF transfer function) so they translate MAF output into increased flow rates. Or convert it to speed-density engine management. Air filter design and location have a similar potential to disturb MAF functioning if the blast from fans or road air causes uneven flow through the MAF. Avoid any changes in the diameter of intake ducting leading to or from the MAF to avoid sudden changes in air velocity that introduce tumbling into the air stream with injurious effects on laminar flow through the MAF sensor. Strive to have a straight, constant-diameter length of tubing at least double the diameter in length ahead of the MAF, and keep any flow-straightening laminar flow screens in place to function as intended to smooth airflow by reducing clocking and velocity effects. Not only is there a high probability that removing a flow screen will decrease MAF metering accuracy, but power improvement from removing the screen is usually negligible to the point that it cannot be measured within the statistical accuracy of most chassis dynamometers. In fact, if there are signs of erratic MAF output versus manifold pressure on an engine with a modified MAF or modified intake plumbing, you may want to try improving laminar flow through the MAF by *installing* a flow screen or straight ducting upstream of the MAF.

Changes to induction plumbing upstream or downstream of the MAF sensor should be undertaken with great care, given the potential for uneven flow through the MAF to disturb the relationship between total mass airflow through the MAF and airflow over the MAF sensing element that must be representative of total intake airflow for the MAF to function as intended. It is critical to maintain laminar (smooth) airflow across the MAF sensing element. The chief culprit in disturbing laminar flow is commonly a bend in intake ducting immediately ahead of the MAF sensor, which will bias airflow toward the outside radius of the bend such that a MAF sensing element in this area will over-report airflow. The opposite is true if the element happens to be located in the inside radius of the bend. If the MAF must be located near a bend in the intake plumbing, it should be clocked so the sensing element is located halfway between the outside and inside radius of the bend.

Beware of turbo or supercharger conversions on engines with MAF sensors. In theory you can install a MAF sensor either upstream or downstream of a turbo or centrifugal supercharger, but turbulence downstream of a turbo or blower can interfere with laminar airflow through the MAF. Another problem to avoid is blow-off valves that recycle blow-off air into the induction system upstream of the MAF, which could result in over-rich air/fuel ratios if the MAF over-reports airflow due to measuring some airflow more than once when blow-off air is recycled back into the induction system upstream of the MAF or by over-reporting airflow because some air is dumped overboard by a blow-off valve downstream of the MAF.

Karman-Vortex-Type Mass Airflow Sensors

Another type of mass airflow sensor that has been used on some Japanese vehicles is the Karman-Vortex (K-V) airflow sensor. The advantage of using this type of sensor instead of a VAF sensor is that it causes less restriction. It is also simpler and more reliable than MAF sensors, where contamination of the heated wire or filament can cause problems. The K-V sensor responds more quickly to changes in airflow than other types of mass airflow sensors, which helps the EMS do a better job managing the air/fuel mixture.

A K-V sensor measures the amount of turbulence behind a small object placed in the incoming airstream to generate an airflow signal. The principle is that as air flows past a stationary object, it creates turbulence or vortexes (swirling eddies of air) behind the object similar to the wake created by a passing boat. The greater the airflow, the greater the turbulence. Turbulence can be measured electronically by sending light or sound waves through the air to detect the changes in pressure,

Two MAP sensors, the smaller designed for installation directly in the intake manifold , the larger designed with a barb for a MAP reference line from the intake.

or by measuring the frequency of the pressure changes (air turbulence). This allows the sensor to generate a signal that is proportional to airflow.

Karman-Vortex airflow sensors were used on 1987 and later Supra turbos, some Lexus engines (all except the ES 250 and 300), and some 1983 to 1990 Mitsubishis. The sensor has a five-pin connector and an integral air-temperature sensor. A light-emitting diode (LED), mirror, and photo receptor are used to count the pressure changes in these applications. The mirror mounts on the end of a weak leaf spring placed straddling a hole leading directly to the vortex generator area. When a vortex forms, the drop in pressure wiggles the spring, which causes reflected light from the LED to flicker as it is picked up by the photo receptor. This generates an on-and-off digital signal that varies in frequency in proportion to airflow. When airflow is low at idle, the signal frequency is low (30 hertz or so), but as airflow increases, the frequency of the signal increases to 160 hertz or higher.

Early Mitsubishi applications use ultrasonics to detect the pressure changes associated with changes in airflow. A small tone generator sends a fixed ultrasonic tone through the vortex to a microphone. With increasing turbulence and a higher number of vortices, the tone is increasingly disrupted before it reaches the microphone. The sensor's electronics then translate the amount of tone distortion into a frequency signal that indicates airflow. Early units contain an integral air-temperature sensor while later ones also contain an integral barometric-pressure sensor. In 1991, Mitsubishi changed to a redesigned Karman-Vortex sensor that replaces the ultrasonic generator with a sensor that measures fluctuations in air pressure directly.

Torque Sensors

Torque sensors measure the strain on an input shaft or axle to provide a snapshot of the force being applied to the rotating shaft. They are useful in any area that requires the monitoring or control of a rotating shaft, where indirect means are either unavailable or inadequate. An example is the Torductor, a noncontact sensor without moving parts. This type of sensor is actually part of the load-carrying shaft, so that the measured torque is the actual transmitted torque. A high-output signal provides integrity against electrical or magnetic interference from the surroundings, with the advantages of high accuracy with high overload capacity and fast response.

Increasing demands on performance and fuel efficiency stress the need for precise control of the combustion process. Torque sensors measure the actual mechanical output of the engine. This gives the EMS direct insight into the operation of the engine and a measure independent of wear and other uncertainties of engine components and fuel.

Some sensors are capable of measuring not only overall torque, but subtle changes in torque during individual combustion events. This makes a torque sensor capable of engine diagnostics such as misfire detection and control of cylinder balance. This measurement can also be used to calibrate engine output and to alert the driver to engine trouble at an early stage.

Torque sensors are sometimes used to provide control in power-steering systems designed to optimize feel and performance (by only working when they're really needed), and in gear-shifting applications to monitor and control transients and oscillations due to backlash and wheel slip. A torque sensor can be an excellent tool to optimize manual gearshifts, and controlling torque with closed-loop methods can help eliminate the need for over-design of transmission components.

The surface of a shaft under torque will experience compression and tension. Displacement sensors may be optical via toothed wheels or magnetic via a variable coupling. Strain gauges or magnetostrictive coupling strips can also be used. One example involves placing two finely slotted concentric rings on either side of the angular deformation zone of a shaft that will twist when torque is applied, and measuring the overall electrical effect on a current of specified frequency as the slots in the two rings no longer precisely overlap due to torque on the shaft.

There are now some interesting new products like the Wheel Torque Sensor (Leboy Products, Troy, Michigan) designed to bolt to the brake drum or spindle of a vehicle, or in place of the wheel itself. The sensor uses a slip ring or rotary transformer to connect the torque sensor to an instrument or EMS in the vehicle. The Wheel Torque Sensor is a strain-gauge-based device that has been used by General Motors' truck division for on-road brake development testing.

Knock Sensors

Knock sensors output a small electrical signal corresponding to the resonant vibration frequency of engine detonation. Knock sensors are essentially a microphone with a bandpass filter to eliminate frequencies not associated with detonation. Upon receiving a knock signal, the ECU will temporarily retard ignition timing to prevent the condition as a countermeasure to prevent engine damage from explosive knock. The ECU will also typically advance the maximum spark timing to take advantage of higher octane fuels and higher altitudes when there is reduced tendency to knock. In some cases, the ECU will correlate knock to specific cylinders and retard only the cylinder(s) currently knocking.

The optimal ignition timing under load for a high-compression engine can be quite close to the point where engine knock occurs. However, running so close to the point of knock means that knock will almost certainly occur on one or more cylinders at certain times during the engine operating cycle. Since knock may occur at a different moment in each individual cylinder, the ECU uses a knock-control processor and engine position data to pinpoint the actual cylinder or cylinders that are knocking.

The knock sensor (or sensors) typically mounts on the engine block to take advantage of the fact that sound travels about 15 times faster through aluminum or iron than air, but is sometimes located on the head(s) or intake manifold. The device consists of a piezoelectric crystal measuring element that responds to engine noise oscillations. This signal is converted into a voltage signal (analog) that is proportional to the level of knock and transmitted to the ECU for processing. The knock frequency from the sensor is usually between 6 kilohertz and 15 kilohertz, and most detonation occurs in the 10-12 kHz range.

A sophisticated modern ECM analyzes the noise from each individual cylinder and sets a threshold noise level for the cylinder based upon the average noise over a predetermined period. If the noise level exceeds the reference level, the ECM initiates knock-control countermeasures.

Normal timing occurs at the optimal ignition point, but once knock is identified the knock-control processor retards the ignition in steps. After knocking ceases, the timing gets re-advanced, but if or when knock returns, the ECU retards it once more. The process is one of ebb and flow, and the knock sensor and EMS monitor the engine continuously to allow for optimum performance.

For example, Bosch's Motronic KCP (knock-control processor) was designed to analyze the noise from each individual cylinder and set a reference noise level for that cylinder based upon the average of the last 16 phases. If the noise level exceeds the reference level by a certain amount, the KCP will identify the presence of engine knock and retard the ignition timing for that cylinder or cylinders by a set number of degrees.

Approximately two seconds after knock ceases (20 to 120 knock-free combustion cycles) the timing gets advanced in 0.75-degree increments until normal timing is achieved or knock returns. This process occurs continuously in an effort to keep all cylinders at their optimum timing.

If the knock-control system develops a fault, the ignition timing typically defaults to a setting several degrees retarded from normal as a safety precaution, which will probably lead to a reduction in engine performance. Turbocharged engines, which are significantly more susceptible to damage from spark knock without a functional knock sensor on line, usually implement additional anti-knock, anti-performance countermeasures such as severe timing retard, low-boost turbo wastegate control, severe rev-limiting, and disabling variable intake systems and performance valve timing to lower VE. In all cases, the EMS will turn on the check engine light.

If a fault exists in the Motronic KCP, ignition timing is then retarded 10.5 degrees by the ECU (which provides an additional incentive to solve the problem, since this will severely affect performance). The Motronic ECU also limits revs to no more than 4,000 rpm.

When dealing with engine-control systems not equipped with knock-sensing systems, some calibrators have found it useful to install add-on individual-cylinder auxiliary knock-detection and retard systems to protect the engine from damage during calibration or to determine the detonation threshold for the various cylinders of a specific engine. Unfortunately, other engine sounds can sometimes mimic detonation, including valvetrain, piston, and exhaust components, or contact between any part of the engine and the chassis, which may be transmitted to the knock sensor, leading to false-positive knock detection. In fact, if you are wondering if a knock-control system is functioning properly, monitor spark advance with a timing light and tap the block with a hammer and note whether or not the EMS temporarily retards timing. False-positive detonation can present a serious problem on a vehicle equipped with a factory knock-control system if you modify any of the above engine components. Some aftermarket engine management systems permit adjustment of the sensitivity of knock detection, and some tuners have undertaken countermeasures against false-positives by decreasing the sensitivity of the knock sensor by, for example, wrapping Teflon tape around the sensor threads where it screws into the block. In cases where valvetrain or piston noise cannot

GM MAF sensors, new and old. The newer version of the sensor shown on the left is designed to improve air flow by offering less restriction to charge air. *GM*

be remedied, it may be possible and necessary to entirely disable the knock detection and control system after implementing a conservative air/fuel ratio and spark timing strategy designed to prevent engine damage on an unprotected engine.

OTHER SENSORS
Vehicle Speed Sensor

The vehicle speed sensor (VSS) controls many vehicle and engine systems. In fact, the VSS is much more than a digital version of the speedometer cable. Using the VSS to generate digital speedometer readings is a relatively recent application for the VSS. Before powering a digital dashboard, the VSS was used to regulate the cruise control and control transmission shifts.

1. Vehicle speed is part of overall engine operating strategies on OBD-II systems.
2. The VSS is a factor in operation of the idle air control valve and canister-purge.
3. Automatic transmission control logic needs VSS data to provide optimal performance and mileage. In an electronically shifted transmission, VSS data—not hydraulic pressure in the valve body—is used to determine shift points.
4. Torque converter lockup clutch operation is controlled by the VSS.
5. VSS signals may be a factor used by the EMS to determine whether to run electric cooling fans.
6. Vehicle speed data is a critical factor used to operate variable steering and intelligent suspension and handling equipment.
7. VSS signals are a critical factor controlling ABS, disabling the system below a certain speed so the wheels can come to a complete stop.
8. The VSS is used to limit top speed on some vehicles via electronic throttle or fuel regulation.

The VSS is a counting, rather than a measuring sensor. The VSS typically counts revolutions of the transmission output shaft. The higher the count that the VSS sees, the higher its output signal, which is typically a square-wave pulse transmitted

to the EMS. The ECM is programmed to compare the count, or signal, received from the VSS against its internal clock to determine vehicle speed on an ongoing basis. Below a threshold speed of 3 to 5 miles per hour, VSS data becomes insignificant and the EMS will ignore it.

At least two types of VSS have been used:

1. The optical VSS is located inside the speedometer. It uses a light-emitting diode (LED) and a two-blade, mirrored reflector to generate a signal. When the vehicle is moving, the speedometer cable turns the two-bladed mirror. The mirror rotates through the LED light beam, breaking the beam twice for each revolution. Each time the mirror interrupts the LED beam, light is momentarily reflected to a photocell. Whenever light hits the photocell, it generates a discrete electrical signal pulse. The faster the mirror rotates, the more electrical pulses that are generated per unit of time. The EMS transforms the number of pulses from the photocell per time to an electronic measurement of vehicle speed (based on configuration data regarding tire size, final drive ratio, and so forth).

2. A permanent-magnet VSS mounts on the transmission/transaxle case in the speedometer cable opening, in series with the speedometer cable or replacing it entirely. A permanent magnet rotates past a coil in the sensor to generate a pulsating voltage correlated to vehicle speed. The pulsating signal from a VSS creates an alternating-current (AC) voltage. At one time, VSS circuitry used an external buffer module to convert VSS output into a digital output that could input to the EMS computer. Newer systems convert the VSS signal in the ECM.

If the VSS fails, a lack of signal from the VSS to the computer should trigger a trouble code in the EMS. Obvious signs that the VSS has failed include a digital speedometer that's not working, a dead cruise control, and rough and erratic automatic-transmission shifting. Other problems may include rough idling and poor fuel economy. A more difficult problem is a VSS that works but sends out an incorrect signal, which may still cause a code to be set—for example, if the VSS signal tells the computer the vehicle is traveling at a high rate of speed, but throttle position and MAP voltage tell the computer that the engine is running barely above idle. On a vehicle using the VSS as a speed-limiting safety device, a defective sensor could incorrectly indicate a too-fast condition, shutting down fuel flow at the wrong time. Symptoms could be a random or intermittent sudden loss of power and poor performance.

Typical OBD-II codes for a malfunctioning VSS include:
P0500 Vehicle Speed Sensor Malfunction
P0501 Vehicle Speed Sensor Range/Performance
P0502 Vehicle Speed Sensor Low Input
P0503 Vehicle Speed Sensor Intermittent/Erratic/High
P0716 Vehicle Speed Sensor Circuit Input Intermittent
P0718 Vehicle Speed Sensor Input Circuit Input low

Chapter 4
Actuators and Actuator Systems

Actuators are electromechanical devices that enable an EMS to make things happen in the world. In the realm of EFI, these include such devices as fuel injectors, boost controllers, and idle air control valves. Most but not all actuators are directly controlled by the ECU.

EMS actuators include the following:

- Fuel delivery: electronic fuel injectors, electric fuel pumps, variable duty-cycle fuel pumps, fuel pressure regulators (FPR), and dual-fuel switching systems
- Air delivery: throttle angle controls, IAC stepper motors (idle speed control), boost controls, electronic wastegate controls, supercharger boost bleeds, and supercharger clutches
- Nitrous delivery: single- and multi-stage solenoids and pulse-modulated solenoid
- Temperature control: radiator fans and engine compartment fans
- Ignition and spark delivery: ignition amplifiers and coil drivers
- Knock control: water- and alcohol-injection solenoids and boost timing retard
- Cam phasing and valve-lift controls
- Variable intake: plenum volume, runner length and secondary runner actuators (i.e., TVIS)
- Emissions controls (exhaust gas recirculation, air injection, and so on)

ECU/relay assembly illustrates that many actuators, such as nitrous solenoids, are triggered by 12-volt relays. In the case of progressive nitrous, electromechanical relays are too slow, so high-power transistor drivers must be used, either internal to the ECM, or in an external module. A transistor is, itself, a type of relay, in which a low-power lead changes the conductance of the pathway between the other two leads, which can be used as a decision switch or a power amplifier.

- Transmission controllers and auxiliary onboard computers
- Information delivery: dash displays, diagnostics, and telemmetry

FUEL DELIVERY
Electronic Fuel Injectors

Imagine a nozzle on the end of a hose on a windy day: Squeeze the spring-loaded handle on the nozzle and water sprays out into the air. Release the handle and the spring closes the valve and the flow of water spray stops. The higher the pressure and the longer you squeeze, the more water comes out. If you imagine several nozzles on the same length of hose pointing in different directions, you are visualizing the situation in a port fuel-injected engine.

Unlike most mechanical injection systems, which spray fuel constantly when the engine is running and regulate fuel delivery by varying the pressure, electronic fuel injectors use a timed-injection architecture, opening and closing with extreme rapidity at least once per combustion cycle to a resolution as high as a 10,000th of a second in order to precisely spray gasoline into the charge air rushing through the intake manifold—or, in the case of direct-injection engines, directly into the combustion chambers. For a given size injection orifice and pressure drop through the injector, the amount of fuel delivered by electronic fuel injection is dependent on the length of time the injector is open.

The goal of EFI is always to deliver the charge mixture in a precisely targeted air/fuel ratio optimized to generate maximum cylinder pressure per injected fuel mass in order to efficiently push against the piston and cause the engine to get work done, ideally with the highest possible efficiency and the least possible air pollution. Injected fuel enters the charge air in pulses, but by the time fuel and air are in the cylinder and compressed, the fuel must be mixed with air as evenly as possible and fully vaporized, with at least some of the mixing and vaporization occurring inside the hot cylinders. An injection pressure of 30 psi above intake manifold pressure will shear fuel into a fine mist of fuel droplets of very small size with a lot of surface area that evaporate well and burn quickly. The larger the pressure drop through the injectors, the better the atomization. Modern gasoline direct-injection engines inject fuel with a rail pressure as high as 2,900 psi, and some modern diesel engines inject fuel at pressures as high as 25,000 psi.

To inject fuel into the air in precisely timed pulses, electronic injector nozzles contain tiny electrically controlled valves actuated by electromagnetic or Piezoelectric circuitry that is powerful enough to overcome the force of a spring and fuel rail pressure to push the injection valve open in less than a millisecond. As the valve begins to open, pressure in the supply

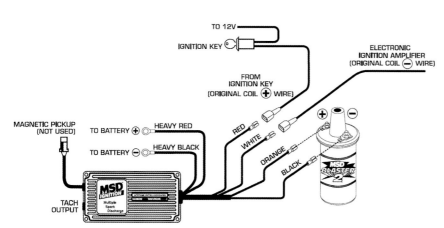

Classic MSD 6a connections. The 6a delivers a spark voltage increase at higher rpm using capacitive-discharge system, and improves ignition at lower engine rpm by delivering multiple sparks. The 6a can be triggered directly by some ECMs, or triggered by an ignition amplifier triggered by the ECM. *MSD*

line causes fuel to begin spraying through a tiny metering orifice to mist out into the charge air in a precise pattern in the intake manifold or combustion chamber. The instant an injector is de-energized, the pressure of fuel and a spring immediately begin to force the injector closed, which is even quicker than opening time but requiring a tiny, but finite amount of time. Port fuel injectors are normally aimed directly at the hot intake valve to enhance vaporization, and direct injectors are aimed toward a recess in the piston crown that forms a partial pre-chamber around the spark plug when the piston is at top dead center to form a stratified-charge for lean-burn operations when it is advantageous to have a locally richer air/fuel mixture in the immediate vicinity of the spark plug to kindle combustion.

Robert Bosch GmbH, based in Europe, long ago licensed the rights from Bendix to build the "Electrojector" pulsed EFI system invented in the United States in the 1950s. Bosch has built more than 150 million electronic injectors and currently dominates the market. Several other companies, including Lucas, Rochester, and Siemens, design and manufacture large numbers of electronic injectors.

ELECTRONIC INJECTOR ARCHITECTURE

The electronic fuel injectors installed in a port-injection architecture—a.k.a., *indirect injection*—consist of a housing, a fuel supply inlet, and two-wire electrical connector, and a valve assembly that consists of valve itself and a solenoid armature. The housing contains the solenoid winding and electrical connections. A helical spring assisted by fuel pressure forces the valve against its seat in the valve assembly when the injector is not energized, blocking fuel from passing through the injector. When the ECM energizes the solenoid windings in a port-injector, the valve lifts by approximately 0.102 inches, and pressurized fuel is forced through the valve body and sprays from the injector.

Direct-injection Piezoelectric injectors are similar in concept to port injectors, but instead of an electromagnetic coil pulling a needle valve off its seat, a 4-inch stack of some 200 0.02-inch thick Piezoelectric sheets in the injector energized by 140 volts of electricity expands a maximum of 0.004 inches to lever a needle valve off its seat to inject fuel—with much greater speed than an electromagnetic injector and against much high pressure. Depending on the voltage applied to the Piezoelectric circuit, the stack can push open the valve less than the maximum, which is useful for increasing the precision of injected fuel mass at idle when the injection interval might otherwise be too short for repeatable results. Direct fuel-injection costs more than port

injection systems because the injectors are exposed to more heat and pressure, mandating more costly materials, and because the high pressure and more complex operating algorithms require higher-precision electronic management systems and the addition of an expensive high-pressure mechanical fuel pump.

According to Bosch, injectors are designed with the following goals in mind:
1. Precise fuel metering at all operating points
2. Accurate flow at narrow pulse widths, with deviation from linearity within specified tolerances
3. Broad dynamic flow range
4. Good fuel distribution and atomization
5. Valve leak tightness
6. Corrosion resistance to water, sour gas, and ethanol mixtures
7. Reliability
8. Low noise
9. Ethanol injection: heated injector technology

Port injectors can be divided into the following metering categories:
1. Annular orifice metering, which uses a pintle to optimize the atomization via a conical-shaped spray pattern and which meters fuel by the size of the gap between the pintle and the valve body.
2. Single-hole metering in which fuel spray is injected directly from the drilled passage in the valve body downstream of the needle valve (atomization is not as good as with a pintle design, at worst case producing a "pencil beam").
3. Multi-hole metering (C-version) that forces fuel through a stationary drilled plate located at the end of the valve body orifice, downstream from the needle valve. This design, which normally includes four precisely spaced and aligned holes, results in a good conical spray pattern.
4. Multi-hole metering for multi-valve engines is similar to 3, but aligns the metering holes so a separate spray of fuel hits each intake valve.
5. Disc metering uses a drilled disc that moves off a flat seat with the armature. Claimed benefits include resistance to deposit buildup and clogging so no cleaning is ever required, wider dynamic range for improved idle, quieter operation, lighter weight that improves response, and operation with alternative fuels like natural gas, propane, methanol, and ethanol. Atomization quality may be similar to single-hole metering.

The Bosch pintle-type injector is the earliest design but is still widely used. The valve housing in this type of injector

ACTUATOR SYSTEMS

narrows to form a seat upon which a tapered needle comes to rest when the injector is closed, choking off fuel flow. Bosch improves the spray pattern by extending the needle valve assembly into a beveled pintle assembly that protrudes out of the end of the injector through a plastic chimney. An electromagnetic solenoid lifts the spring-loaded pintle off its seat to release fuel. Bosch injector pintles and seats are always the same size. Bosch regulates flow by varying the size of the bore after the seat. Problems with the pintle design reportedly include increased chance of clogging in the small orifice area, slower response time because of the heavier armatures used to lift the pintle, and reduced service life.

In some cases, injectors will use a ball valve to seal the metering orifice. This allows the use of a lighter armature to improve response time compared to older pintle types. There is also reportedly less wear and a longer service life. The orifice can be designed with multiple openings, which allows a wider spray pattern and higher fuel delivery.

The disc-type injector eliminates the armature so the solenoid acts directly on the flat disc through the core of the injector body. The valve assembly in a disc-type injector consists of the armature attached to a disc with six tiny holes drilled around the outside. In a closed position, the disc rests on a seat, the center of the disc covering a hole in the middle of the seat that prevents any fuel from passing through the injector. When the armature is pulled open as the injector energizes, fuel passes through the six outer holes, through the hole in the seat, and sprays out of the injector. The flow of a Lucas disc injector is determined by the size of the six holes drilled in the disc. This arrangement is even lighter than the ball-type for a faster response time. This disc and seat design also results in less deposit buildup at the orifice and longer service life.

Injectors vary in the time it takes to open and close. Larger injectors are built with heavier moving assemblies that are a little more sluggish due to higher inertia. To compensate, they are typically designed with more powerful low-resistance windings that require peak-and-hold circuitry to power them open quickly. The Lucas Disc injectors are lighter, according to fuel system expert Russ Collins, which enables disc-type injectors to operate down to 0.8, 0.9, or 1.0 milliseconds. Most pintle injectors are limited to a minimum 1.3 to 2.0 milliseconds.

Some performance experts recommend when upgrading injectors for higher flow to switch from traditional pintle-type injectors to ball or disc-type valves.

Injector Fuel Flow

Injector flow is rated in pounds per hour at a given pressure, or in cubic centimeters per minute at pressure—either static (injector open continuously) or pulsed at a certain duty cycle. The amount of fuel that actually enters an engine from an injector depends on several variables.

(1) The first is the size of the valve or orifice in the injector through which fuel must flow. Most electronic injectors are rated in pounds of fuel per hour that will flow at a certain pressure if held wide open. The electrically actuated valves in injectors with larger orifices tend to require larger, heavier parts with more inertia, and, thus, stronger closing springs. An injector's maximum size is practically limited by the increasing weight of the injector's moving parts. Larger weights have more resistance to moving quickly and require increasing power to activate them quickly. This follows the physical laws concerning momentum, which describe the resistance of stationary objects to movement and the resistance of moving objects to stopping.

When it's time for a fuel injector to open, under onboard computer command, injector drivers in the ECU energize an electromagnetic coil in the injector and cause it to lift a spring-loaded armature off its seat and allowing fuel to spray from the injector for a precisely timed interval. Many high-flow aftermarket fuel injectors are designed for peak-and-hold driver circuitry, which energizes the low-resistance coils with a peak-voltage spike designed to bang the injector open very quickly, after which a lesser voltage with hold it open.

Higher flowing injectors can get expensive. As injector size increases, each opening event has a greater effect on the hydraulics of the fuel supply system, implying larger fuel pumps, fuel rails, fuel line size, and higher pressures. And the larger an injector is, the higher the minimum flow possible—limited on the lower end, by the amount of fuel that will flow in a millisecond or two at a given pressure. This is particularly important on engines with a high dynamic range, such as small, high-output turbocharged engines with few cylinders, where the amount of fuel required at maximum horsepower is high in comparison to that required at idle. In certain cases, where higher-flow fuel injectors are not available in a certain configuration, it may be possible to have some types of factory fuel injectors modified to increase the flow rate, usually up to about a 50 percent increase.

(2) A second factor affecting injector fuel delivery is fuel pressure in the supply line delivering fuel to the injectors. The lower the pressure, the less fuel sprays out of an open injector per unit of time, effectively limited on the low end by a pressure below which repeatability suffers (most port injectors are never operated below about 28-psi gauge pressure). On the high end, fuel delivery begins to suffer from diminishing returns as pressure increases and is absolutely constrained when the injector's internal electromagnet can no longer overcome fuel pressure to open or when the internal injector spring pressure cannot consistently overcome the pressure of fuel rushing through the injector valve under high pressure and the injectors cannot close. Many experts have recommend 72.5 psi as a maximum fuel pressure for most port fuel injectors.

On many port-injected engines, the dynamic range of the injectors is increased by increasing the fuel pressure commensurate with load, usually by regulators referenced to intake manifold pressure. On some large displacement engines or smaller engines with large dynamic range, it may become necessary to use multiple smaller injectors that are staged.

Electronic injectors in newer gasoline direct-injection (GDI) systems that deliver fuel directly into the cylinders typically operate at a pressure between 25 and 200 bar (368–2,940 psi), pressure required to accomplish injection in some cases in a short time near the end of the compression stroke against the pressure of compression in ultra-lean burn mode, during the intake stroke in high-output or stoichiometric mode, or against combustion pressure in the case of a second injection used to increase power on boosted engines by adding fuel as the pistons are descending on the power stroke.

There are a number of factors that can make it difficult for an EMS to deliver perfectly consistent fuel pressure. In the first place, there is always a tendency for port injector fuel supply pressure to drop slightly after the initial burst of fuel spray when the pressure differential is highest, which delivers a split second of higher than normal injection pressure that introduces a small amount of nonlinearity that in some cases can be significant enough to make a difference at small injection pulse widths. Resonance and hammering in the injector rail can produce pressure waves and pressure drop at some of the injectors under certain circumstances, particularly if the combined injector flow rate is relatively large compared to the flow capacity of the fuel rail. Even if fuel rail pressure remains constant, uncompensated changes in manifold pressure would affect the *pressure drop* through the injectors, with a significant effect on injected fuel mass. Thus, most modern EMSs are designed with fuel pressure regulators (FPRs) referenced to manifold pressure to increase or decrease fuel pressure in 1:1 correspondence with changes in manifold pressure to maintain a constant pressure drop through the injectors so that injector flow is not degraded. An example would be during turbo boost by injectors spraying against a head of pressure in the intake manifold. Any problem that interferes with accurate reference manifold pressure (such as pressure influenced by pulsing in a single manifold runner) arriving in a timely manner at the regulator housing can cause injected fuel mass to diverge from what was intended.

(3) The third main factor determining injected fuel mass is the total amount of time an injector is open—or partly open—per combustion event. The longer an injector is open, the more fuel mass sprays out, which will max out at a point when the injector is open all the time. Even though injectors are rated by the amount of fuel mass they flow at a 100 percent duty cycle, this is not realistic. Since energizing injector windings causes heat buildup, if operated much above an 80 percent duty cycle, some injectors could begin to fibrillate or overheat, which could eventually cause them to lose consistency or even fail completely.

There are a number of problems with treating injector flow as a pure function of fuel mass per time.

Theoretically, there is no lower limit to the length of time an injector could be opened, but practically, injectors do have a lower limit. This occurs at a point (usually somewhere between 1 and 2 thousandths of a second) when the injector is open so briefly that random factors that tend to cause injector open time and fuel flow to vary slightly each time the injector fires become significant in comparison to the planned duration of open time. The consistency of the open event begins to suffer, and you will not get a clean, repeatable spray pattern. This situation becomes even more unstable when injector open time is so short that the injector never has time to open all the way before the injector driver de-energizes the injector and the spring begins to close the injection valve.

Coils come in all shapes and sizes, but they all do essentially the same thing, which is to transform a low primary voltage pulse from the ECM or ignition amplifier to a high-power pulse that will leap a spark plug gap and start a fuel fire in a cylinder. Since coils *multiply* the primary (input) signal, ignition amplifiers or igniters can greatly increase the output of a coil. Depending to the igniter/coil driver characteristics, a coil may be induced to deliver one, or a rapid-fire series of multiple sparks, useful for improved combustion at low rpm. *MSD*

At short pulse widths there is a tendency for an electronic injector's spring-pressure-inertia architecture to overshoot the ECU's commanded pulse width. Some engine management systems model injector flow rate with separate flow rates for the longer pulse widths typical of cruise/power versus the shorter pulse widths of idle/starting, with a changeover point that must be established, usually in the range of 1 to 3 milliseconds, such that the effect is seen only at idle and very light loading. Some ECUs model short-pulse width behavior by assuming the static flow rate of the injectors remains fixed but applying a small time compensation at short pulse widths that becomes less ascendant as pulse width increases. Since injector lag or "dead time" has a greater effect on fuel mass delivery at short pulse widths, most EMSs depend exclusively on this method to compensate for short pulse width fueling errors, particularly since the dead time characteristic is often easier to establish than the crossover point between separate high- and low-flow injector flow slopes.

A factor affecting the linearity of fuel mass injected per time is the fact that no injector can open or close instantly, meaning injected fuel mass is *nonlinear* during the transition period when injectors are *partly* open or closed. Opening and closing delays determine the length of the period when fuel delivery is nonlinear and reduce the length of time an injector is wide open. Injector *closing* delay depends on fuel pressure, spring force, and the inertia of the injector valve. Injector *opening* delay is influenced by these same factors plus the available driver voltage and the design of the electromagnetic coil in the injector. This means it takes electronic injectors longer to open than close. The difference between the greater opening delay and the lesser closing delay is referred to as injector *offset*. Offset reduces the effective fuel flow of any length injection pulse. The above factors combine to produce an injected fuel mass that is not an absolute function of injector open time, meaning the basic fuel mass calculation must be corrected in the final injection pulse width calculation to avoid error according to the exact design

Coil-On-Plug assembly from 2005 2.4L GM Ecotec inline-four. It is now common for igniter circuitry to be built into individual coils. *GM*

of the installed injectors. Note that one of the advantages of direct injection is that using voltage to expand a Piezoelectric stack to open a direct injector is generally quicker than using electromagnetic force to open a port injector.

In the real world, fuel mass flow from an electronic injector is never a perfect linear function of commanded injection pulse width due to minor fluctuations in fuel pressure and injector opening and closing performance that will be amplified in the case of large fuel injectors operating at very short injection pulse width at idle and light cruise. Any nonlinearity in fuel mass delivery becomes increasingly significant in percentage terms as commanded pulse width *decreases*. Boosted engines with fewer cylinders, high specific power, and large dynamic range equipped with one injector per cylinder will require relatively high-flow injectors to meet fuel requirements at max torque within the time available in the four-stroke cycle, but such injectors will then require a short injection pulse width to idle on such an engine. This may require operating in the nonlinear range of injector flow. In the worst case, the commanded pulse is so short there is no longer time for injectors to open all the way before it is time to close, in which case the injectors are at least partially closed 100 percent of the time. This will obliterate linearity of fuel delivery and interfere with repeatability.

Combined injector opening and closing time is typically 0.2 to 0.4 millisecond for low impedance port injectors, and 0.4 to 0.8 millisecond for OEM-type high-impedance port injectors. In the case of a calculated pulse width of 14 milliseconds under heavy load, if the injector offset is 0.8 millisecond, only about 5 percent of the driver circuit's energizing pulse would be consumed getting the pintle valve open, but if the calculated pulse width at idle is 1.5 milliseconds, more than 53 percent of the pulse would be spent opening the pintle. In some cases injection pulse width may be too short for perfectly repeatable fuel mass delivery and steady air/fuel ratio. Where injectors large enough to provide sufficient fuel for maximum power simply cannot open for a short enough period, the engine will require multiple injectors per cylinder and an EMS capable of staging them.

As electromagnetic devices, the opening time of electromagnetic fuel injectors is heavily influenced by system voltage, which has a significant effect on opening performance. Increased voltage through the injector coil increases the strength of the magnetic field and allows an injector to open faster,

which reduces the delay time to full-open and allows fuel to begin flowing into the intake ports sooner. Since the system voltage of an automotive electrical system changes according to the amount of charge in the battery, the power output of the alternator, and the load on the electrical system, it could be as low as 0 volts in the case of a drained battery or as high as 17 volts if a faulty regulator is causing overcharging. All modern EMSs have a voltage compensation table that models the effect of voltage changes on injector performance, and, if possible, a generic table reflecting the fact that all fuel injectors tend to change performance with voltage in a similar way should be calibrated precisely for the installed fuel injectors.

Fortunately, modern EMSs provide configurability of installed characteristics affecting injector flow across the plausible range of fuel pressure and injector-driver voltage so that the ECU can correctly and precisely model injector fuel delivery to correct the injection pulse width calculation for electrical and hydraulic dwell time to arrive at a corrected pulse width that will deliver the target fuel mass from the installed fuel injectors. On VE-based EMSs, it is critically important to specify injector characteristics correctly to avoid creating an erroneous VE table or delivering incorrect air/fuel ratios.

All of the above factors have to be considered when you are selecting injectors for an engine that has been modified in some way versus an engine for which factory engineers have already determined injector requirements.

Injector Flow Rate Calculations

The following formula is designed to allow high-performance-oriented tuners to determine which injector (flow rate) they will need for a specific engine based on horsepower output:

Flow rate = (HP x BSFC) ÷ (#Injectors x Maxcycle)

where

Flow rate = pounds per hour of gasoline (at rated or specified pressure)
HP = projected flywheel horsepower of the engine
BSFC = brake-specific fuel consumption in LB/horsepower-hour (0.55 if turbo, 0.45 NA)
#Injectors = the number of injectors
Maxcycle = maximum duty cycle of the injector
Example: 5.7-liter V-8
Flow = (240 HP x 0.65 BSFC) ÷ (8 cylinders x 0.8)
Flow = 24.37 lb/hr injectors required

The Lucas 5207011 injector, rated at 23.92 pounds per hour is close.

Unfortunately, to get an accurate answer out of the equation for a specific engine, you need to put accurate numbers in, which requires a dynamometer with full instrumentation.

In the case of a 530-ci stroker version of a Cadillac 8.2L V-8 with turbocharging that outputs 800 horsepower:

Flow = (800 x 0.55) ÷ (8 x 0.8) = 68.75 lb/hr injectors

Injectors this big can be expensive and might not idle well on some engines. In this case, a designer might decide to use two smaller injectors per cylinder, staged so that only one injector per cylinder is operating at idle with the other gradually phasing in as engine loading and rpm increase.

Gasoline contains a certain amount of chemical energy that is released when it is burned (oxidized). If all the energy in gasoline could be converted to work, a gallon of gas could make 45 horsepower for one hour. Internal-combustion engines are notoriously inefficient, so the actual horsepower you can expect to make from a certain injector is significantly less than theoretical.

An inline fuel pump operates under computer control to pressurize the injector fuel rail. Typically the ECM turns on the pump for a few seconds when the key goes on, and again while cranking, and after starting only *as long as the engine is running* (to prevent pumping after a crash). Usually the pump is energized by a computer-controlled relay, though pump output can also be altered by managing voltage to the pump under ECM control, or in some cases under the control of an external voltage controller with its own sensors and microprocessor, like the Kenne Bell Boost-a-Pump control. *MSD*

The following formula is a revision of the above equation rearranged to yield the maximum engine horsepower that a given type of injector can make at a specified fuel pressure:

Horsepower = (Flow rate x #Injectors x Maxcycle) ÷ BSFC

Assume we're using 20 lb/hr injectors on a six cylinder engine.

Horsepower = (20 lb/hr x 6 x 0.8) ÷ 0.55 ≈ 175

Injector Pressure Changes

Altering fuel pressure is a good and inexpensive way to increase fuel flow or increase the dynamic range of any fuel injector, which is why this is done on many original equipment injection systems. The normal method is to reference the fuel pressure regulator to manifold vacuum. As manifold pressure rises and falls with increasing and decreasing engine loading, it is used to increase or decrease the force of a preload spring located in the fuel-pressure regulator pressing against the regulator's diaphragm, which dynamically changes the pressure pumped fuel must reach before it can force its way through the regulator. The result of referencing the fuel pressure regulator to manifold pressure is that fuel pressure is lowered at idle (high vacuum, i.e., low-manifold pressure) and raised at wide-open throttle (WOT) when there is high-manifold pressure (low-manifold vacuum). For example, fuel system pressure that was 39 psi at WOT (101.4 kPa, zero vacuum, 1.0 bar) would be reduced to 28 psi at idle on an engine with 22 in-Hg vacuum gauge pressure (26.6 kPa). Note that because fuel pressure is higher when manifold pressure is higher, and lower when fuel pressure is lower—in a 1-1 correspondence—the net effect is that a fixed-length injection pulse delivers the same amount of fuel under all circumstances. On the other hand, were fuel pressure not referenced to MAP, fuel mass injected per time would *decrease* as manifold pressure increased, lowering the maximum fuel mass injected per time under heavy load. And if fuel pressure were set high to provide maximum fuel flow at high-manifold pressure under heavy load, the fuel pressure would be just as high at idle with low-manifold pressure, which would increase the minimum fuel that could be injected at idle. In fact, some older fuel pressure regulators are not manifold vacuum-referenced, and but have an adjustable bolt or screw that can be turned to increase or decrease regulator spring pressure against the diaphragm to alter base fuel pressure at ambient MAP pressure (which is also true of some FPRs that are referenced). As we'll see shortly, for a given pressure drop through the injector, the static flow rate of a fuel injector is directly proportional to changes in system pressure.

In the case of a turbo/supercharged engine, 15-psi boost against a manifold pressure-referenced regulator would raise the system fuel pressure 15-psi above fuel pressure at zero vacuum (assuming the fuel pump has the capacity to provide the fuel!). Fuel pressure on a forced-induction version of the engine would vary from 28 psi at idle, to 39 psi at ambient MAP pressure, to 54 psi at 15-psi turbo boost. Referencing the regulator can provide a tremendous difference in the amount of fuel that can be injected into the engine at a given injection pulse width. The long and short of it is that referenced regulators enable larger injectors to idle better, and smaller injectors to produce more high-end power.

The following formula calculates the effect of changed fuel pressure on injector flow:

Statflow2 = [SQR (SysP2 ÷ SysP1)] x Statflow1
SQR = square root of (the value in parentheses)
SysP2 = proposed new system pressure (psi)
SysP1 = specified pressure for the injector's rated flow (psi)
STATFLOW1 = rated static (nonpulsed) injector flow rate
STATFLOW2 = calculated new static flow rate

For example, let's say a certain Bosch injector on a 4.2-liter Jaguar inline-6 is rated at roughly 20 pounds per hour at 39 psi. At 25 psi:

[SQR (25 ÷ 39)] x 20 = 16 lb/hr at 25 psi! (a 20 percent difference)

On the other hand, consider the same injector at 55 psi:

[SQR (55 ÷ 39)] x 20 = 23.75 lb/hr at 55 psi (a 19 percent difference)

Keep in mind that some fuel pressure increase is required just to keep even with increases in manifold pressure. To actually increase fuel delivery relative to increases in MAP, *the fuel pressure increase must be above and beyond any manifold pressure increase.*

Therefore, simply by changing fuel pressure based on manifold pressure, the maximum flow of the injector is changed 40 percent! Most experts suggest 70 psi as a maximum system pressure, particularly if the ECU is not programmable. This is because very high pressures begin to affect the ability of the injector's internal spring to force the injector closed against fuel pressure flowing through it and may also affect the ability of the armature and windings to open the injector. As a consequence, the opening time, closing time, or repeatability of flow during the open event can change and become unpredictable. Furthermore, as mentioned previously, flow gains with increased system pressure offer diminishing returns. MSD Fuel Management discovered the following effects when varying the pressure of 72 and 96 pound-per-hour (*at 43.5 psi*) injectors using 85 percent duty cycle:

Fuel Pressure	72 Pulsed Flow (lb/hr)	96 Pulsed Flow (lb/hr)
30	56	72
40	64	84
50	71	93
60	76	101
70	76	106

The ability of an injector to realize high flow rates depends upon the ability of the fuel pump and plumbing to supply enough fuel. As the fuel pressure increases, most electric pumps are constrained to supplying progressively lower volumes of fuel. Positive-displacement pumps that permit zero backflow will maintain flow as long as the pump motor has sufficient

Grimmspeed's MazdaSpeed 6 PWM boost controller. Note 3-port design, with 1) intake port piping in manifold pressure reference, 2) output port delivering conditioned manifold pressure limited by the action of the boost control solenoid's internal PWM valve operating at various duty-cycles under ECM or piggyback control, and 3) ambient bleed port used to discharge air to the atmosphere. *Grimspeed*

horsepower to drive the pump. In addition, it is worth pointing out that a fuel pump can be limited in its ability to supply fuel by the hydraulics of supply line size, filter restrictions, restrictions posed by bends and turns in the supply line, and restrictions and pressure differentials in the fuel rail. The ability of the pump to supply fuel will also be affected by the voltage available from the vehicle's electrical system.

VRG Fuel Pressure Regulators

Since increasing fuel pressure in a 1-1 correspondence with manifold pressure only increases fuel flow per injection pulse width relative to what it would otherwise have been without pressure correction, increasing fuel flow in absolute terms requires the variable rate of gain (VRG) fuel pressure regulator, a.k.a. fuel management unit (FMU). Mechanical FMUs are inline FPRs that are adjustable in terms of both the threshold of onset and the rate of gain, which makes them especially useful when adding turbocharging to engines with factory stock fuel-injection systems, where the ideal situation would be to maintain stock injection characteristics under low load conditions, and only increasing the fuel injected per squirt to provide fuel mixture enrichment during bursts of turbo boost that increase the volumetric efficiency of the powerplant.

A typical rate of gain would be to raise fuel pressure roughly 7 pounds per pound of turbo boost, which automatically forces the injectors to provide more fuel even with no changes to injection pulse width. Mechanical FMUs are installed downstream of the stock-type FPR, usually with the threshold set above 100 kPa, such that under naturally aspirated conditions, the VRG regulator is dormant and fuel rail pressure is managed by the stock FPR. Given the fact that most injectors do not function well above 70 to 100 pounds of fuel pressure, starting with nominal WOT fuel pressure of 40 psi, an FMU could provide an increase in fueling for maximum turbo boost in the 4.3- to 8.6-psi range.

FMUs work well to increase fuel delivery when manifold pressure is above the range of a stock 105-kPa MAP sensor on a speed-density engine that has been converted to turbocharging. The stock MAP sensor on the NA engine is likely to have a 1-bar sensor that is essentially blind to pressure much above atmospheric (although it may have just enough range to detect abnormal positive manifold pressure and activate a fuel cut!). In most cases, a speed-density EMS will continue to provide fueling for 100 kPa manifold pressure when positive pressure builds in the manifold, leaving it to an FMU to increase the volume of each injection pulse to provide necessary fueling increases under boost conditions.

Electronic fuel pressure regulators are an essential part of gasoline direct-injection systems, in which an electronically actuated bypass maintains fuel rail pressure under ECU control based on feedback from a rail pressure sensor. There are now also fast-response aftermarket electronic pressure regulators that operate in the 25- to 90-psi range and can coordinate with variable duty-cycle pumps to provide cooler fuel on port EFI systems. Such devices offer great potential to work with piggyback computers and feedback from wideband air/fuel ratio sensors to alter rail fuel pressure on the fly to provide accurate fuel increases for engines with turbo or supercharger conversions.

Injector Electrical Characteristics

Another factor to consider when selecting fuel injectors has to do with the electrical power requirements of the injector, which must be compatible with the power supply and switching capabilities of the electronic control unit (ECU) that drives them. In addition, the fuel-injection system power requirements must fall within the constraints of the electrical output of the vehicle's battery and charging system.

Most car people intuitively understand fuel supply systems. They understand what pressure (pounds per square inch) means, they understand the concept of flow in pounds or cubic centimeters per minute. They understand discussions of injectors as valves, and they understand fuel line size and resistance to flow and supply restrictions and so forth. Electrical properties affecting fuel injectors and ECUs are similar to plumbing concepts, but the terms used to describe them are different. Voltage is used to describe electrical "pressure," as psi is used to describe fuel pressure. Amperage is used to describe electron flow, as pounds-per-hour describes fuel flow. Resistance in ohms describes how easily current flows through something like a wire or coil, which is similar in concept to the varying resistance to the flow of water through a small pipe versus a large pipe. Ohm's law states that:

Current = Electromotive Force ÷ Resistance

or . . .

Amperes = Voltage ÷ Ohms

Since injectors are activated by electromagnetic force, each injector contains a magnetic coil with a particular resistance to the flow of electricity through it. This is also referred to as its impedance, which is rated in ohms. A coil of wire rated at 16 ohms has much greater resistance to current flow than a coil of wire rated at 2 ohms. Many port fuel injectors are rated at roughly 16 ohms resistance, but some are rated at 2 ohms or lower. A 16-ohm coil will allow much less current to flow through it for a given voltage than a 2-ohm coil.

Very large port injectors and throttle-body injectors (usually huge in comparison to port injectors) typically require more current to produce enough magnetic force to operate the injector quickly and reliably. These large injectors require powerful springs to force the injector armature and needles closed against the large volume of fuel flowing through them, which adds to the electromotive force required to open them. This can be achieved by lowering the resistance of the windings of the injector coil to flow more current and by designing the ECU injector driver circuits so that they can safely provide sufficient current to drive the low-impedance injectors. ECUs designed to drive low-impedance injectors effortlessly provide the lower current needed to drive high-impedance injectors. But factory ECUs designed to drive a port-injection system may encounter a problem if you want to change to large, low-impedance injectors.

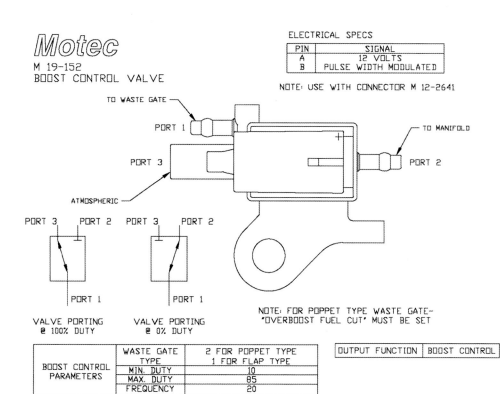

Motec
M 19-152
BOOST CONTROL VALVE

TO WASTE GATE

PORT 1

TO MANIFOLD

PORT 3

PORT 2

ATMOSPHERIC

ELECTRICAL SPECS

PIN	SIGNAL
A	12 VOLTS
B	PULSE WIDTH MODULATED

NOTE: USE WITH CONNECTOR M 12-2641

PORT 3 PORT 2   PORT 3 PORT 2

PORT 1   PORT 1

VALVE PORTING   VALVE PORTING
@ 100% DUTY   @ 0% DUTY

NOTE: FOR POPPET TYPE WASTE GATE-
"OVERBOOST FUEL CUT" MUST BE SET

BOOST CONTROL PARAMETERS	WASTE GATE TYPE	2 FOR POPPET TYPE 1 FOR FLAP TYPE
	MIN. DUTY	10
	MAX. DUTY	85
	FREQUENCY	20

OUTPUT FUNCTION	BOOST CONTROL

Essentially a controlled leak under pulse width–modulated computer control, a PWM boost control valve flutters the valve open and closed at high speed to vary the amount of air that bleeds through the valve to produce a target pressure on the downstream side. Such a valve is typically used to control a Deltagate-type wastegate by feeding a percentage of pressure to the Deltagate port to fight pressure tending to open the wastegate at the standard port, or to directly limit boost pressure to the standard port (i.e., to lie about manifold pressure). Motec EMSs have the capability to configure whether the boost control valve being open increases boost/manifold pressure or closed increases pressure. *Motec*

Let's say your modified V-6 turbo needs larger injectors because the injectors are already running close to the limit in duty cycle (meaning they're on most of the time at high loading). You will discover that many of the high-flow injectors readily available are low-resistance units. If it's a factory-stock ECU, the transistors and integrated circuits in the driver section of an ECU could blow out trying to regulate the higher electrical draw of a low-resistance injector. Virtually all modern aftermarket ECUs can drive low-resistance injectors. Since most electrical circuits are often over-designed to some extent, a stock OEM powertrain control module may work fine for a time, but with a shortened life—or it could melt down quickly, particularly with 2-ohm injectors. It is essential to match injector resistance to the capabilities of the ECU driving them.

Most high-flow, low-resistance injectors are designed for peak-and-hold drivers, which conserve power circuitry by supplying a higher peak current to bang open the big injectors quickly, then reduce power to the lesser state required to hold the injectors open, which simultaneously reduces thermal loading through the injector windings.

Direct-injection engine-management systems amplify the power of injectors to open quickly at up to 200-bar fuel pressure (while minimizing the current required from an ECU to energize ultra-high-pressure injectors in less than a millisecond) by operating at 4 to10 times the voltage of a standard 13.9-volt vehicle electrical system. Driver circuits operating with 60 to 140 volts energize injectors with a typical resistance of 800 milliohms, i.e., 0.8 ohms. A Bosch Motorsport 90-volt HDEV 5.2 injection valve with 0.8-ohm resistance requires pick-up current of 9.6A and hold current of 3.0A supplied by a dedicated power stage unit.

Injector Physical Layout
The final factor to consider in injector selection has to do with the physical layout of the injector, which must be compatible with the fuel supply plumbing. The layout must also permit the injector to mate properly with the bosses on the intake manifold or throttle body or cylinder head. Some port injectors are supplied by an O-ringed side feed, others an O-ringed top feed, while others present a top-feed hose-barb fitting. Still others are designed for supply via banjo bolt. The injector's metering or spray pattern must also be compatible with the application, in terms of single-hole metering, annular orifice metering, multi-hole metering, and multi-hole metering with two sprays.

Bosch Motorsport direct-injection valves are 3.42 inches long, with a top-feed O-ring connection, bottom combustion seal, and a 4- to 7-hole configuration with high spray variability concerning spray angle and spray shape.

FUEL SUPPLY SYSTEMS: PUMPS, FUEL LINES, REGULATORS, DUAL-FUEL, AND HYBRID MECHANICAL-ELECTRONIC

Fuel-injection systems require a reliable and stable fuel supply. In the absence of a sufficient fuel supply at the expected pressure, the most precisely calculated injection pulse width will not provide accurate fuel mass delivery.

Many port-injection systems run a return-type fuel supply system where an electrically driven roller-cell or peripheral fuel pump located in or near the fuel tank moves fuel through a one-way loop to an inline injector rail on the intake manifold pressurized by an inline regulator downstream of the injectors that maintains upstream pressure by restricting fuel flow through the regulator to the extent required to maintain pressure as dictated by the preload delivered by a spring against the regulator diaphragm, allowing excess fuel not needed to fuel the engine to travel back to the fuel tank through a dedicated return line. Most modern pinch-type regulators are referenced to manifold pressure such that rail pressure varies according to manifold pressure to maintain a constant pressure drop through the fuel injectors. Some vehicles such as the LS1 Camaro use a short pump-regulator loop near or in the fuel tank that maintains pressure to a one-way fuel line that branches off the loop upstream of the regulator like a cul-de-sac to deliver fuel to an injector rail located at the end of the line on the intake manifold. The advantage of this type of system is that less fuel is exposed to the heat of the engine compartment, but it is usually not feasible to reference the pressure regulator to manifold pressure, meaning the system runs at a constant pressure that requires pulse width changes to compensate for a varying pressure drop as manifold pressure changes. Yet another type of fuel system is the true "returnless" system, where there is no pressure regulator at all. In this case the ECU regulates pressure to the fuel injectors by sensing feedback from a pressure sensor in the injector rail (which may also be referenced to manifold pressure to indicate pressure drop or "delta") at the end of a one-way fuel line and uses this feedback to regulate the duty cycle of a special electrical fuel pump that may deliver as little as 10 percent of the maximum fuel flow at idle. This type of system not only subjects the fuel to less thermal loading from the engine compartment, but enables the ECU to increase the effective size of the fuel injectors by increasing fuel pressure relative to manifold pressure so that a given injection pulse width delivers more fuel mass. Such returnless systems have sophisticated fuel delivery models that use multiple tables that define fuel pump flow on the basis of fuel pressure, manifold pressure, engine demand, and available electrical system voltage.

Modern gasoline direct-injection fuel systems are similar to diesel systems, consisting of a low-pressure supply pump in the fuel tank that transports fuel from the tank to a cam-driven high-pressure fuel pump pushing fuel into a robust common rail that feeds special electronic valves in the cylinder head that inject fuel directly into the combustion chambers. Modern gasoline direct-injection pumps consist of a mechanical, cam-actuated reciprocating plunger that rams slugs of fuel into the rail at up to 200 atmospheres of pressure, plus a built-in electronically controlled bypass-valve pressure regulator that bleeds off pressure under ECU control to the degree required to achieve target injection pressure. Aftermarket tuners have been able to manipulate some factory-stock direct-injection ECUs into delivering additional fuel for enhanced turbo boost increases on vehicles like the BMW 335i by inserting an interceptor circuit into the fuel rail pressure sensor circuit that underreports rail fuel pressure (and manifold pressure as well, in most cases), causing the ECU to command the regulator to bypass less fuel to increasing fuel pressure.

Any automotive fuel pump must be capable of providing adequate fuel at the conditions of highest demand, which is wide-open throttle (WOT) at max-horsepower rpm with maximum manifold pressure and maximum fuel rail pressure. Fuel pumps are rated to provide a certain fuel flow at a certain pressure. Be aware, however, that there can be bottlenecks in the fuel line, the fuel filter, and the fuel rail that result in pressure losses between the fuel pump and the fuel injectors that result in a higher head of pressure at the pump discharge than at the fuel pressure regulator. Also be aware that a standard electric port-injection fuel pump's ability to deliver a certain volume of fuel declines when it's forced to supply increased fuel pressure within the common 25- to 90-psi pressure range of most port injection systems.

A fuel pressure regulator must have adequate capacity to supply the highest engine fuel requirements at the required pressure, and loop-type regulators need the capacity to bleed off sufficient excess fuel through a return line back to the fuel tank under the conditions of lowest engine fuel requirements in order to prevent undesirable pressure creep at idle. Port EFI regulators are equipped with a diaphragm spring that regulates fuel pressure upstream or downstream of the regulator, depending on the type. Inline regulators of the type used on some carbureted engines throttle the amount of fuel that can get through the regulator to limit pressure *downstream* of the regulator to the configured limit that prevents excessive pressure from overwhelming the float needle in the carb. The fuel-loop regulators used with most port EFI systems prevent fuel from passing through the regulator until pressure reaches a threshold *upstream* of the regulator, at which point the diaphragm will allow fuel to bleed through the regulator and return to the fuel tank and to the extent required maintain the target pressure in the fuel rail.

In addition to a pressure-regulating diaphragm spring, some regulators are equipped with an adjustable bolt that varies preload against the diaphragm spring to increase or decrease fuel pressure at ambient manifold pressure. Some sophisticated regulators now have an electrically actuated plunger that can dynamically increase or decrease fuel pressure under electronic control. Most modern regulators have a vacuum-boost reference port designed to employ manifold pressure to vary fuel pressure to keep it consistent with the pressure of the intake manifold into which the injectors are spraying. It is actually possible to have all four mechanisms in a single regulator.

To a worst-case scenario of inadequate fuel supply leading to low injector rail pressure and engine-damaging lean air/fuel ratios, it is critical to verify that a fuel pump, regulator, fuel filter, and fuel supply plumbing are capable of delivering enough fuel at the required pressure to match the horsepower of the engine. It is important to have components with performance specs that are up to the job, but it is also important to verify that the system works. You can check the actual maximum fuel delivery capacity of a fuel supply system with the engine stopped by artificially supplying a target manifold vacuum/pressure reference to the regulator, energizing the fuel pump, and collecting the fuel that would normally return to the fuel tank in a safe container of known volume over a fixed period of time (such as 30 seconds or a minute). This will yield the maximum amount of fuel available from the pump at the system pressure to feed fuel through the injectors into the engine without producing a pressure drop in the fuel rail. This method takes into account any restrictions in the fuel supply plumbing that may affect the advertised fuel delivery of a known new fuel pump. It can also tell you the capacity of an unknown pump or a used pump that may have suffered inefficiencies due to wear.

Some newer vehicles are equipped with deadhead fuel supply systems. They have no fuel pressure regulator, no fuel return line, and a variable duty-cycle electric fuel pump that operates under ECU control. ECUs controlling an EMS with deadhead fuel supply control fuel pressure by monitoring data from a fuel rail pressure sensor and varying the fuel pump duty cycle to increase or decrease fuel pressure. Such systems typically

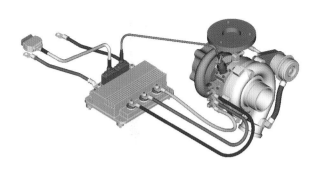

Experimental electrically-assisted turbocharger offers improved spooling under EMS control when exhaust energy is low at low rpm and light engine loading. To be practical, the device requires higher than normal automotive voltage. *Garrett*

do not attempt to maintain an exact fuel pressure like a pressure-regulated system, but instead provide pulse width compensation according to measured fuel pressure and MAP, which is similar to battery-voltage compensation.

The following fuel supply formula can be worked backward or forward. You can start with a known engine power and efficiency specification and calculate a minimum fuel pump capacity that will provide adequate fueling. Or you can start with pump data and calculate the maximum horsepower and efficiency of the engine it can fuel. Let's say you have a 300-horsepower engine

FLOW = Horsepower x BSFC

Assuming this is a turbocharged engine, most experts suggest using 0.55 as BSFC (brake specific fuel consumption in pounds per horsepower-hour).

Therefore:

FLOW = 300 x 0.55
FLOW = 165 lb/hr

Convert pounds to gallons by dividing 165 by 6 (slightly more than 6 pounds per gallon of gasoline). The answer is 27.5 gallons. Therefore, the fuel pump must supply 27.5 gallons per hour at the rated pressure of the injectors, which comes out to slightly under half a gallon of fuel per minute. Doing a little math, we can figure that at full throttle this engine requires a quart of fuel every 33 seconds. It is clear that any pump that could fill a container through the outlet of the regulator at the required pressure in less than 33 seconds will do the job. The calculation looks like this:

27.5 gallons per hour divided by 3,600 (seconds in an hour) equals 0.00763888 gallons per second of fuel required. Dividing 1 (gallon) by 0.0076388 tells how many times this volume goes into 1 gallon, or looked at another way, how many seconds of this flow it takes to make a gallon (130.9090909). Dividing this figure by 4 (quarts in a gallon) yields the number of seconds of this flow it takes to fill a quart container (convert this to metric on your own).

MSD Fuel Management has offered a roller-vane electric fuel pump for port fuel injection designed to deliver 43 gallons per hour (282 pounds per hour) at 40 psi and 12 volts of power, which would be adequate for the 300-horsepower engine discussed above. Many normally aspirated engines have used fuel-injection systems designed to run at roughly 40 psi under full load, meaning 0 vacuum or approximately 100 kPa. But suppose you turbocharge this engine to 10 pounds of boost, referenced to the fuel pressure regulator, raising fuel pressure by

10 psi? It is critical to understand that this pump will deliver less fuel at 50 pounds of fuel rail pressure than it would at 40 psi (50 psi is what a nominally 40 psi manifold pressure-referenced regulator will produce in the fuel rail at 10 pounds of boost).

How much horsepower can the MSD pump support? At 40 psi with 12 volts of power, the MSD pump will flow 282 pounds per hour.

Horsepower = Flowrate ÷ BSFC

Assuming a BSFC of 0.55 (turbocharged engine), the equation becomes:

Horsepower = 282 ÷ 0.55 = 512

The pump can support 512 horsepower at 40 psi.

But suppose a pump could only deliver 200 lb/hr at 50 psi?

Horsepower = 200 ÷ 0.55 = 364

Just when you need it most (under boost) the pump is only good for 363, not 512 horsepower!

There is no simple formula to compute what happens to pump fuel flow capacity with increased pressure, since this depends on various factors, including the horsepower of the pump motor and the type of pump. You have to either measure fuel flow at the target pressure or get this information from the manufacturer.

Many fuel rails are equipped with a connection allowing attachment of a fuel pressure gauge, and if there isn't one, adding one should be a simple matter for a competent fabricator. This allows a mechanic or EFI designer to observe the fuel pressure while operating the vehicle. In fact, today some ECUs can monitor fuel pressure through a sensor on the fuel rail and then display it on the engine data page (or sound an alarm or activate a check light if pressure varies more than a specified amount). Clearly, unless yours is a deadhead fuel supply system, the pressure should remain constant under all conditions or, if the regulator is referenced to manifold pressure, vary in exact correspondence with manifold pressure.

The performance of an electric motor varies with changes in voltage. Experiments by MSD Fuel Management showed that at 40 psi and 12 volts, a particular MSD electric pump flowed 220 pounds per hour. At 13.5 volts, the flow increased to 340 pounds per hour.

The voltage delivered to a fuel pump will be a function of the capacity of the battery and charging and regulating system and other applications drawing electrical power such as headlights, possibly limited by the resistance of the wiring connecting the pump to the battery and alternator. You will get the most power to the pump by running a heavy-gauge low-resistance wire directly from the battery to the pump and switching this wire with a low-resistance relay controlled by the ECU. Beware: Some original-equipment fuel supply systems are equipped with a relay-switched fuel supply designed to prevent an excess fuel flow bottleneck through the regulator from increasing rail pressure under conditions of low demand by delivering power to the pump using a resistor-equipped wire so that it supplies less fuel at idle and light cruise. At higher demand, the ECU switches the relay so that the system now supplies power to the pump through an ordinary low-resistance wire. If you rework the electrical supply to the fuel pump, make sure you are not inadvertently using a high-resistance connection that might dramatically reduce pumping capacity.

IGNITION SYSTEMS TO CHARGE THE COILS

While most early factory and aftermarket digital engine management systems were fuel-only EFI controllers rather than full-service engine management systems, virtually all modern aftermarket EMSs have the ability to connect to and manage a variety of factory and aftermarket ignition systems. In a few cases, EMS vendors bundle a complete multi-coil direct-fire ignition system into the package.

Extremely precise spark timing is critical to engine performance. In some cases a degree or two of spark advance or retard can significantly increase torque or improve drivability. In some cases a difference of a degree or two can damage the engine from detonation or preignition.

The great thing about digital ignition control is that it permits a tuner to dynamically modify spark timing while running the engine or vehicle on a load-holding dyno to search for the optimal timing that provides maximum torque at all speed-density breakpoints. As well, EMS ignition control can usually be configured to provide special spark timing optimized for cranking, cold engine temperature, unusually hot intake air temperature, nitrous injection, fuel octane or composition, and other factors.

Dynamic spark advance adjustment under actual operating conditions to achieve best performance is a capability that existed in the early days of automobiles when an operated spark control in the cockpit permitted (and required!) the operator to adjust timing on the fly while striving to improve drivability, maximize torque, eliminate detonation to compensate for large variability in gasoline specs, and produce easier cranking (with an actual hand crank, in the early days!) via retarded ignition timing. The task of manually adjusting timing on the fly was less demanding than you might think in the early days because automotive engines, like those in farm tractors, operated within a narrow rpm range at very slow speeds by modern standards. The Model T Ford, for example, achieved peak power at just 1,600 rpm. Dynamic timing adjustment under operator control began to go extinct beginning in the 1920s when the first electromechanical automatic spark advance systems began appearing on a few cars. For four decades following World War II, spark advance was a deterministic automatic function under electromechanical controls. The only user involvement in spark timing occurred at tune-up time, when the mechanic used a timing light to verify that initial advance at idle speed with vacuum advance (if any) deactivated was where it should be. Although the rate of increase in rpm-based spark advance in this type of system can be changed by swapping the strong or weak spring in the auto-advance mechanism for others with different force in the days when distributor-points ignitions were common, not only could it be difficult or impossible to find alternative auto-advance springs, virtually no hot rodders had access to the expensive dynamometer test equipment required to determine if timing changes were beneficial or detrimental to performance at various engine speeds.

Pre-electronic distributor-based ignitions cycle power on and off to a single spark coil with a set of spring-loaded breaker points that are periodically opened by cam-type raised bumps on the distributor shaft, one per cylinder. The spark coil charges from the primary low-voltage side while the points are closed and abruptly discharges through the high-voltage side each time the breaker points open briefly to interrupt primary current flow. Because engine speed varies, breaker points open and close for a period that can only be expressed in crank degrees, meaning that coil charging time—a.k.a., *dwell*—i.e., the percentage of time the points are closed, is all over the place on this type of ignition. Depending on the size of the gap when the points are wide open (adjusted with a feeler gauge), eight-cylinder dwell angle representing the percentage of time the points are closed could theoretically vary from 0 to 45 degrees of a cam revolution, six-cylinder dwell time from 0 to 60 degrees, and four-cylinder dwell from 0 to 90 degrees. A minimal points gap results in longer coil charging time, but affects degradation of the points surface. Points gap affects dwell angle, which affects spark timing, which in turn mandates setting static timing at tune-up time by clocking the distributor after setting the points gap (usually after installing new points). Measured in real time, dwell on a single-coil V-8 engine turning at 6,000 rpm can thus vary from almost nothing to the length of time it takes the engine to turn 45 degrees. At this speed, 1 rpm takes 1/6,000th of a *minute*, which is 0.01 or 1/100th of a second. A cam revolution therefore takes 1/50th of a second or 0.02 seconds. Since 45 degrees is one-eighth of a cam revolution, available time for charging a single V-8 coil at 6,000 rpm is $0.02 \div 8 = 0.0025$ seconds, i.e., 2.5 milliseconds. Maximum operational single-coil V-8 dwell time could be as long as $1 \div 275 = 0.003636$ minutes or 0.2181 seconds = 218 milliseconds while cranking at 275 rpm. If the ignition is left on when the engine is stopped at a position where the breaker points are closed, however, dwell time is essentially infinite, which could easily result in coil damage from overheating. For this reason, points ignitions are normally equipped with a ballast resistor wired in series with the coil to limit primary current flow via heat-induced resistance that increases rapidly above the normal duty cycle of the ignition.

Each time the primary coil circuit is grounded, charged, and de-grounded such that the electromagnetic field in the coil collapses, the high-voltage side of the coil emits a brief (***?), high-voltage spike in the range of 20,000 to 60,000 or more volts that travels to the center terminal of the distributor cap and through a rotary brush to the center of a distributor-resident rotary switch known as a rotor. The voltage spike travels through the rotor to an outboard copper electrode that is elongated such that some portion of the electrode is adjacent to a certain plug wire terminal on the distributor cap throughout the possible range of rotor position during which a spark for that particular cylinder might be generated. The distributor cap itself is designed such that when the distributor is correctly clocked, the appropriate plug terminals for the next combustion event in the firing order are within close proximity as the rotor sweeps by. As the rotor turns, voltage spikes leap the gap to adjacent plug wire terminals and travel through the plug wire to the center electrode of the spark plugs and leap the gap to the ground strap, producing a 100,000-degree Fahrenheit spark channel that ignites the air/fuel mixture in the cylinder.

Early transistor ignition systems were identical to ignitions with breaker points with the exception that points—which wore out relatively quickly—were replaced by a transistorized switching circuit timed by an optical or magnetic sensor in the distributor. Whether a coil is switched by points or transistors, static spark timing on this type of ignition is set using a timing light by loosening a pinch bolt that allows a tuner to adjust the clocking of the distributor—complete with mounting plate containing the points or sensor—relative to the distributor shaft until timing marks on the crank pulley line up correctly with a pointer. The distributor shaft itself must be clocked in relation to camshaft position when the distributor is initially installed in the engine by making sure the rotor is oriented per specification as the helical gear on the bottom of the distributor shaft mates with the opposing cam gear.

Aqua-mist HFS-3 water-alcohol injection systems brought modern electronic controls to charge cooling. Water or water and alcohol injection can be extremely effective as a supplemental anti-knock countermeasure in difficult circumstances where premium street gasoline is less than 93 octane (in California, for example) and detonation is a serious problem. *Aquamist*

Predigital distributor ignitions provide rpm-based spark advance according to centrifugal force acting on a set of spring-loaded rotating flyweights that dynamically re-clock the upper section of the distributor shaft as speed increases to change the phasing of the rotor and trigger points relative to the crank. The downside of a centrifugal advance system is that it limits the engine to a rather simplistic linear rate of rpm-based spark advance increase based on the strength of a spring—or in some cases a set of springs in which a weaker spring defines spark advance "curve" (slope) for the lowest portion of the rpm range, with a stronger spring coming into play to define an alternate advance slope for faster engine speeds. There is a fixed amount of maximum increase in spark advance that arrives when the flyweights reach the limit of their travel, at which point no additional rpm-based advance is possible unless you re-clock the entire distributor, which advances timing across the board at all engine speeds.

Many pre-electronic or transistor-ignition distributors are also equipped with a vacuum advance system that acts as a load-based independent variable affecting spark advance and retard. Vacuum-advance canisters use a pressure-actuated diaphragm to rotate a plate in the distributor that re-clocks the orientation of the points or sensor in relation to the distributor body to increase spark advance at high vacuum when lower manifold absolute pressure delivers a less-dense slower-burning charge mixture to the cylinders.

Spark timing defined by a weighted centrifugal advance and a vacuum advance canister is unlikely to be optimal at all combinations of engine speed and loading, but the system worked well enough that it persisted for decades until digital engine management with spark timing control began to arrive on factory automobiles in the 1980s.

Most modern EMSs use dual sensors on the crank and cam to provide precise engine position with respect to both crank rotation (360 degrees) and the four-stroke cycle (one cam revolution or 720 degrees of crank rotation). A single cam-speed sensor can do the job if a slight reduction in timing precision resulting from the cam drive system is acceptable (or if the cam is gear-driven). A single crank sensor can do the job if the ignition system is a distributorless direct-fire system in which pairs of cylinders 360 degrees out of phase fire at the same time every engine revolution on both intake and exhaust stroke, either with the ECU triggering individual wasted-fire coils with twin high-tension leads leading to sets of correctly phased cylinders or coil-on-plug (V-8) coils wired in pairs like a wasted-spark system.

With precise engine position information available on an ongoing basis as engine position sensors interrupt the ECU with the arrival of the next trigger point, the ECU calculates engine speed and rate of acceleration on an ongoing basis and calculates the ideal timing of the next spark event starting with the entry in a lookup table of optimum spark advance data indexed by engine speed and loading. Table-based spark advance for the current engine speed and load may require compensation for engine temperature, air intake temperatures, exhaust gas temperature, exhaust gas oxygen, or detected detonation. After determining final spark timing for the next cylinder and the dwell time required to charge the coil to produce the spark event, the ECU launches coil charging at the calculated time by switching on a primary voltage to the coil (or in some cases to an auxiliary ignition amplifier driving the coil), and subsequently triggers the actual spark event at the correct time by grounding the coil with a switching circuit.

Sparks from a single coil may be distributed by the EMS sequentially to the various spark plugs one at a time by way of a distributor, as described above, or sent exclusively to a single spark plug on a multi-coil direct-fire system equipped with one coil per cylinder (or in some case per *pair* of cylinders 360 degrees out of phase that receive spark on both the intake or exhaust stroke as the coil fires every revolution). Multiple coil systems are usually triggered by wiring that connects the ECU directly to each coil, but in some cases the ECU sends a synchronized stream of spark pulses for all cylinders over a single wire to an electronic switch that sequentially de-multiplexes individual pulses and allocates them to wires leading to the correct coils. The advantage of direct-fire coil-on-plug ignition systems is that 1) there is much more time between ignition events to charge coils that need only deliver spark to a single cylinder, and 2) no requirement for long, potentially problematic high-voltage wiring between coil(s) and spark plug(s).

Direct-port Fogger V8 nitrous kit from NOS. Like any traditional self-pressurized nitrous system, the mass flow of nitrous actually delivered to the engine will be a complex function affected by temperature, refrigeration effects, pressure drop, liquid nitrous thermal expansion, and other factors. Engine Management Systems often provide a range of nitrous injection controls, with the simplest providing ECM triggering of a single stage of nitrous, more complex systems providing pulsewidth-modulated nitrous solenoid control and supplemental fuel for nitrous provided as an offset to the base fuel injection calculation and delivered through the primary fuel injectors. *NOS*

In some cases, ECUs contain driver circuitry capable of directly charging coils for a configurable dwell time and as well as firing each at the correct time by switching off ground. Switching circuitry typically uses an insulated-gate bipolar power transistor referred to as an IGBT. Having armed a relay that delivers continuous +12V battery power to the positive side of a spark coil, the ECU grounds the negative side of the coil when it is time to begin charging the coil and drops ground when it is time to deliver a spark. Where an ECU is not equipped to directly charge the coil(s), it will require an external coil-driver module containing IGBT circuitry. Some coil-driver modules can control the dwell time, but others cannot.

If the coil-driver is a *dumb* module, the ECU must manage dwell to charge the coil(s) for the appropriate time. In some cases, the ECU turns on a signal to the module at spark delivery time minus the required dwell time to command the coil-driver module initiate coil charging, holding the signal high until it's time for the module to launch the spark event, signified by the ECU dropping the signal. Alternately, the ECU may control dwell by *grounding* a wire connected to the coil-driver module that implicitly commands the start of coil charging, and then interrupts grounding to command the spark event. In either case, the ECU must be configured to know the proper protocol for managing the coil-driver module and the proper dwell time for the coil(s).

So-called *smart* coil-driver modules contain a circuit designed to regulate dwell time and may simply require a digital square wave signal from the ECU that tells the coil-driver it is time to fire the coil, signified by the signal from the ECU changing state from on to off (or vice-versa, depending on the requirements of the coil driver module). Some "smart" coil-driver modules actually aren't very smart, charging the coil for a fixed dwell time. This type of module must be paired with a coil design that will fully charge in the available time. Some coils contain a built-in IGBT circuit in the coil casing that manages dwell internally.

Because 13.9-volt current direct from automotive batteries and alternators is not powerful enough to leap a spark plug gap, virtually all modern ignition systems on engines with battery or alternator electrical systems are equipped with spark coils containing specialized transformers that provide an essential step in delivering output voltage in the 20,000 to 60,000-plus-volt range that's required to leap the 0.020- to 0.050-inch spark plug gap.

Many ignition coils operate according to a principle called *inductive discharge*. A coil-driver circuit supplies positive battery voltage to one end of the primary coil and grounds the other. Current charges the coil over the course of a few thousandths of a second until the magnetic field is fully saturated at full power and unable to absorb more energy. When the coil-driver circuit disconnects the negative side of the coil from ground, the electromagnetic field around the primary coil collapses, causing stored energy in the field to produce a small voltage spike on the primary side that's transformed into an enormous voltage spike in the high-tension side of the coil willing and able to leap tall spark plug gaps with a single bound.

In this type of ignition a spark coil increases the voltage from the vehicle electrical system to a level capable of firing a spark plug using two coils of wire located in close proximity, wherein voltage transformation is directly proportional to the ratio of wire turns in the primary versus secondary coil. The low-voltage or primary coil in an automotive spark coil typically consists of 100 to 200 turns of wire wrapped around an iron core, with the current flowing through the primary coil as controlled by an ECU, ignition module, or coil-resident IGBT. The secondary or high-voltage coil has tens of thousands of turns of wire wrapped around the same iron core. If the primary coil consists of 140 turns of wire and the secondary coil has 40,000 turns, working as a transformer the device has the ability to multiply voltage by $40,000 \div 140 \approx 287$ times; 13.9 volts of electricity from the electrical system transforms to 3,971 volts. This is not enough to fire a spark plug. An ignition coil, however, has the ability to store energy in the electromagnetic field over a finite period called dwell time, during which the coil charges to a maximum energy and levels off. When the magnetic field collapses, there is a small voltage spike in the primary coil. Transformed to a high voltage, the resulting secondary-side spike can easily be 10 times the voltage you'd expect just from the transformer function alone.

Inductive discharge effectiveness depends on sufficient dwell (charging) time to fully saturate the magnetic field of the spark coil. In the case of an antique canister-type coil installed on a 1950s automotive engine, coil charging time could take more than 15 milliseconds. Modern coils may saturate in as little as 2 to 4 milliseconds, but that may still not be enough under some circumstances. Insufficient dwell time is not a problem on modern distributorless coil-on-plug ignition systems with a separate coil for every cylinder that could theoretically charge for as long as 360 degrees of dwell (though running excessive dwell or using coils designed for V-8 direct-fire ignitions as the sole coil in a distributor application could and would overheat many such coils designed, assuming there'd be plenty of time to cool between charging events). In the case of a single-coil firing a high-rpm engine with a lot of cylinders, if there is insufficient time for full worst-case coil charging, the system will be unable to generate a full-strength spark at higher speeds. In the past, some high-revving V-8 and V-12 engines have been built with twin distributors and coils, each running half the cylinders. Doing this doubles the available dwell time for coil charging.

A solution to limited dwell time that eliminates the need for lightning-fast spark coils, dual distributors, or multi-coil direct-fire systems is adding a capacitor-discharge ignition (CDI) module upstream of the primary side of the spark coil. Instead of depending on the magnetic field surrounding the primary windings of the spark coil to store the energy needed to induce a voltage spike in the secondary windings, CDI ignitions store energy by charging a capacitor. Inside the CDI module, a transformer initially raises battery and alternator voltage from 12 volts to 400 to 600 volts. Electric current flows out of the transformer to a circuit that charges the capacitor, while a rectifier prevents capacitor discharge. Upon receipt of a command signal, a triggering circuit halts the operation of the charging circuit, which permits the capacitor to discharge rapidly to the primary side of the spark coil, which transforms the 400- to 600-volt capacitor discharge to 40,000 volts at the secondary high-voltage terminal. When the triggering signal stops, the charging circuit reconnects to charge the capacitor. Because capacitors charge significantly faster than a spark coil, CDI ignitions can deliver a full-power spark at much higher rpm than a simple inductive ignition that runs out of dwell time. A secondary advantage of CDI is that charge buildup in a capacitor is unaffected by current leakage through spark plugs fouled with carbon deposits as may happen during the slower charging of an inductive coil ignition. The short, intense spark of a CDI system provides less time during the spark event itself for current drainage through plug deposits. CDI modules thus offer the advantages of fast voltage rise time to carbon-fouled spark plugs (whether from oil leakage or rich fuel mixtures), high energy throughout the rpm range for faster starting, improved power and economy, and reduced exhaust emissions. In order to compensate for the short duration of a single CDI-generated spark, which may be too brief for reliable ignition during cranking and low-speed operation, CDI ignition modules like the ubiquitous MSD 6A deliver a rapid-fire sequence of multiple sparks during lower rpm operation (hence the name MSD—multiple spark discharge).

The first practical solid-state CDI ignition modules came on the market during the 1960s, and CDI modules soon became mandatory for distributor-based performance and race engines. This is no longer true. With the advent of digital engine management systems with coil-on-plug (V-8) direct-fire ignition in which dwell time is no longer a factor, pure inductive discharge ignitions made a comeback, and there are now inductive ignitions that are more powerful than traditional CDI systems.

KNOCK CONTROLLERS

If an EMS does not have the ability to retard timing on the basis of feedback from a knock sensor, there are external knock-control systems like the J&S Safeguard, which provide individual-cylinder knock detection and ignition retard by monitoring its own auxiliary knock sensor and one or more igniter signals and then correlating detonation with the ignition of particular cylinders and then retarding the timing of only the cylinder(s) actually knocking. In some cases, the knock-control smarts are built into a high energy dwell-control ignition module designed for a single-coil distributor ignition. Interceptor-type multi-channel knock controllers for direct-fire ignition systems control install between the ECU and the ignition system and drive ignition modules or smart coils with internal igniters. Yet

another multi-channel knock-control architecture connects directly to multiple coil negative signals without interrupting the existing stock direct-fire ignition. In each case, the knock-control aspect of the device is invisible to the ECM, which must be configured to treat the knock-controller as some common variety of coil, igniter, or ignition module.

AIR DELIVERY
Electronic Throttle

Until the advent of electronic throttle control (ETC), a cable connected the accelerator pedal to the throttle blade, such that the driver's foot directly controlled throttle angle. Engine management systems monitored the throttle position sensor and the ECU factored in throttle angle as one of many considerations in the calculus of engine control. Electronic throttles eliminate the need for a cable, because the throttle is actuated by an electric stepper motor managed by a dedicated throttle controller unit under ECM control. Stepper motors contains multiple electromagnets arranged in a circle around a toothed gear that work in sequence using electromagnetic force to move the gear to a particular commanded location within the resolution of the stepper motor. The ECM determines driver intent based on the output from a TPS-like pedal position sensor (PPS) located on the accelerator and sends commands for changes in throttle position to the throttle controller, which executes electromagnetic control algorithms that move the stepper motor and throttle to a new position. Dual-redundant TPSs on the throttle shaft provides feedback regarding actual throttle position to the ECU so the ECU can adjust throttle position to improve drivability, idle quality, and tip-in throttle response. Removing the throttle from direct driver control allows the EMS to manipulate final throttle position to improve drivability, control idle speed, implement traction control logic, and improve fuel economy and exhaust emission with minor corrections for poor driver throttle technique.

Electronic throttles are the bane of performance tuners working with stock factory ECMs that have not been hacked because ETC systems enable computers to back off the throttle if the maximum airflow rate is too high or if the slew rate (vector representing the maximum rate of change of a signal) of a sensor indicates the engine or vehicle is accelerating out of the stock envelope. An example is where someone has added a turbocharger to the engine. ETC is ideal for automakers seeking to avoid expensive (and fraudulent) warranty claims resulting from the installation of warranty-voiding power-adders that damage the engine (followed by de-installation and presentation of the vehicle to a dealer for free repair). Too much air, too much performance, the ECU pushes back on the throttle and goes into limp mode.

With direct throttle control in the hands of a computer, and no cables or external springs capable of closing the throttle or forcing the throttle cable to retract when the driver lets off the gas, it is critical that the stepper motor remain under control at all times to eliminate the possibility of engine damage or even an ETC-induced crash from unintended acceleration. Computer-controlled throttle systems require fail-safe countermeasures against potentially catastrophic failures such as a throttle butterfly that's stuck open or unintended throttle operation at partial load.

It is essential that the ECU know the correct throttle position data at all times or, in case of failure, that throttle position is questionable, so ETC designs improve the reliability of throttle position information by providing redundancy in the form of a second TPS. The secondary TPS output signal typically has a different range or slope than the primary sensor, which improves the ability of the ECU to verify throttle position with high accuracy and allows it to perform a plausibility check between the two sensors. Any discrepancy between the two throttle position sensors triggers a malfunction code and will probably lead to ECU throttle control algorithms entering a fail-safe limp mode in which throttle position is limited to the minimal range that will move the vehicle (less than 20 percent throttle is typical), a state that persists until the system can be reset.

The EMS's automatic last line of defense against the consequences of a catastrophic throttle control failure is an EMS table that specifies maximum airflow rates for representative breakpoints of commanded throttle position and engine rpm. Airflow that exceeds the maximum causes the ECU to conclude that there is a serious problem with the ETC system and enter limp mode. EMS countermeasures against excessive airflow are robust, given the potentially lethal consequences of a stuck or out-of-control throttle, and potentially include not only limiting throttle angle but extremely aggressive timing retard that limits power at any airflow to a fraction of normal. Consequently, turbo or supercharger conversions are nearly impossible on ETC engines unless you reprogram the maximum airflow table to allow higher flow rates under heavy load without entering limp mode. Simple enough if you have access to the connectively hardware and security seed that allow table access and modification via laptop computer, otherwise impossible. The ideal maximum allowable airflow rate at any given combination of rpm and loading should be low enough to protect against the consequences of ETC failure but high enough to prevent unintended limp mode. Twenty percent above expected maximum flow should accomplish both, but new maximum airflow table values must ultimately be confirmed for specific combinations of stock and hot rod parts and levels of boost in actual rigorous testing. Keep in mind that eliminating maximum airflow thresholds entirely could expose the tuner to ruinous liability in the event of ETC-related crash or engine damage, as could faulty maximum airflow values that fail to halt a stuck ETC throttle runaway that results in injury or loss of life.

The two main classes of EMS electronic throttle control strategies are commonly referred to as "pedal-follower" and torque-based.

Pedal-follower throttle control is rather simple. The EMS straightforwardly translates PPS sensor input into throttle position in a way that is equivalent to what would happen if a cable connected the accelerator to the throttle blade. Exceptions to this 1:1 correspondence of pedal position to throttle position occur during

- Idle, during which the electronic throttle assumes the functionality of idle air control (IAC) throttle-bypass hardware to maintain or increase idle speed after cold start or when the A/C compressor is running by allowing the ECU to make small corrections to throttle angle that raise or lower idle rpm.
- Deceleration or sudden throttle closing, to prevent the engine from stalling, similar to an IAC.
- Throttle tip-in, to smooth driveline lash and eliminate "clunk."
- Automatic transmission upshifts, when the ECU may briefly reduce torque to improve longevity of clutches and smooth the transition into the next gear.

- Poor traction, when the ECU may push back the throttle to control wheel slip.

Torque-based throttle control is more complex. The EMS interprets pedal position not as a demand for a certain throttle position but as a demand for *torque*, which gives the ECU some flexibility in deciding how to deliver the requested torque. Parameters under the control of some ECUs that can affect engine torque output include throttle position, spark advance, air/fuel ratio, cam phasing and lift, intake plenum configuration, turbo or supercharger boost, nitrous injection, exotic tricks like actuating a hinged upper block surface to vary the compression ratio, and a nearly infinite range of combinations of the above. Torque-based engine management requires that the ECU have access to multiple tables that model the engine's torque output under all possible operating conditions, allowing the EMS to calculate and recalculate exact torque output on an ongoing basis. The EMS processes torque demands from the driver via the accelerator pedal position (to, say, maintain or increase vehicle speed) exactly the same as torque demands that are not directly under driver control, such as incremental torque needed when the ECU turns on an A/C compressor.

Torque-based ETC is dependent on an accurate model of torque the engine can deliver under various conditions in the form of a table that lists engine torque output as a function of the various combinations of engine load and rpm (torque being a derivative of airflow, timing, and air/fuel ratio). To find predicted engine airflow (loading), the EMS combines the torque table with a second table unique to the engine configuration that models airflow (loading) as a function of effective throttle area (a derivative of throttle butterfly angle). As you'd expect, any modifications to the intake manifold, camshaft profile, throttle diameter, exhaust backpressure, or intake manifold pressure that affect engine airflow can require changes to the airflow and throttle area table to avoid triggering EMS malfunction codes.

Torque-based ETC calibration is a final stage in EMS calibration that comes after everything else in the calibration is perfect. The procedure is to manually command the electronic throttle to a particular position with the engine or vehicle on a load-holding dyno and populate the reference ETC tables with actual values obtained in steady-state conditions for load versus rpm and torque versus load and rpm. When the contents of the ETC tables are specified, it is possible to build a transfer table that maps a torque request in the form of incoming data from the pedal position sensor into desired engine outputs. Feedback from MAF or MAP sensors is then used by the EMS throttle control logic to verify that actual engine loading matches predicted loading to protect against any error conditions that could result in unintended or undesirable acceleration.

By definition, any hot rodding modifications that increase power change the relationship between throttle position and engine power, which will often be seen as a fault by a torque-based EMS. Since as little as 5 percent extra airflow may trigger limp mode in some EMSs, the solution is to modify the ETC tables to match the increased power the engine is now making, though it may also be possible in some cases to reconfigure the EMS ETC strategy from torque-based to pedal-follower.

Note that many transmission-control strategies depend on engine torque at the input shaft. ETC vehicles with automatic transmissions usually integrate engine and transmission torque control strategies, modeling not just engine torque output but

GM electronic throttle used on 2005 3.9L LZ8 V6s. Electronic Throttle Control is now common on many OE engine applications, but some standalone aftermarket systems provide this capability as well. The simplest "Pedal-Follower" systems translate accelerator pedal position directly into a specified throttle position, but more sophisticated Torque-Bases schemes interpret pedal position as a request for torque, which may be achieved by changing throttle position, but may also be achieved with changes to spark timing, air/fuel ratio, boost pressure, and so forth. *GM*

wheel torque as well. In this case, accelerator pedal position will be interpreted as a *wheel* torque request needed to achieve a certain vehicle speed or rate of acceleration, and the EMS can convert calculated engine torque output into delivered wheel torque based on gear selector position and torque convertor status. When the EMS controls an electronic throttle and automatic transmission, a happy situation exists where the EMS can simultaneously optimize engine and transmission parameters to supply the requested wheel torque while maximizing fuel economy with earlier upshifts and convertor lockup at lighter load. If the requested wheel torque is not obtainable within the reserve available in the current gear at or less than wide-open throttle, the ECU can multiply wheel torque by downshifting into a lower gear. When it comes to delivering elegantly smooth gear changes with minimal noise, vibration, and harshness, ETC with auto transmission allows the EMS to manage wheel torque so that it remains the same throughout the process of moving from one gear to the next.

IDLE AIR CONTROL
Engine idle speed affects idle quality, idle emissions, charging output, engine cooling, and the automatic transmission—so precise idle speed is important. Before electronic idle speed stabilization, tuners adjusted idle speed using an adjustment screw on the carburetor or throttle linkage to set minimum throttle opening. Thermostatically controlled fast-idle cams increased idle speed during cold-start and warm-up condition, but once set, an adjustment screw had no intrinsic way to compensate for changes in engine load at idle. Turning on the air conditioning or activating high-consumption electrical accessories could lug down the engine, as could maneuvers like parallel parking that increase loading on the power steering pump.

Modern engine management systems maintain idle speed within a preconfigured optimal rpm range, regardless of engine temperature or parasitic loads, but at very low airflow rates it may not be feasible to control idle speed with sufficient accuracy and resolution using the main throttle. The answer is a small auxiliary "throttle" installed in parallel with the main throttle that controls engine speed within a much narrower range than the main throttle to a higher degree of accuracy and has the ability to control idle stabilization and deceleration. This has come to be known as IAC, which originally referred to GM's Idle Air Control system. An IAC valve is opened and closed by an electrical stepper motor that regulates a small air circuit by moving a plunger to cover a variable portion of the entrance to an alternate air path that allows more or less intake air to bypass the throttle. Increasing the volume of bypass air (or vice-versa) raises or lowers idle speed exactly like moving the throttle slightly. Alternatively, some IAC values use a pulse width–modulated (PWM) solenoid to control bypass air by regulating duty cycle.

The IAC valve is controlled by the ECM, which typically has a transfer table that associates various command positions of the IAC valve with actual airflow through the bypass circuit. The IAC control circuit of the ECU has a variable output with which it commands the flow rate of the IAC valve, which is used to control coarser aspects of the idle control strategy, the finer of which may be controlled using variable spark advance, which has the advantage of faster response due to availability as soon as the next engine cycle while the IAC valve maybe still be moving.

The ECM monitors idle speed when the throttle position sensor or throttle switch signals that the throttle is closed (or very nearly closed). If idle speed is out of range of the target spec, the computer commands the IAC valve to either increase or decrease the bypass airflow. Target idle speed will typically be modified according to sensor inputs from the coolant sensor, brake switch, and vehicle speed sensor. Idle speed may also be increased when the air conditioning compressor is engaged, the alternator is charging above a certain voltage, the automatic transmission is in gear, or when power steering loads are high.

BOOST CONTROLLERS
On forced-induction engines, the throttle is not the only way to control load. Under some circumstances it is possible to vary engine load at a fixed throttle setting by dynamically changing the amount of boost pressure, which delivers engine loading directly proportional to the amount of positive manifold pressure at any given operating breakpoint.

Supercharger boost is limited by the compressor speed delivered by the ratio of the blower drive system (and internal up-gearing in the case of centrifugal superchargers), but many OE supercharging systems include a pressure-actuated bypass valve that can recirculate some or all charge air around the compressor to lower or eliminate boost, with reference pressure to the actuator managed a pulse width–modulated valve under EMS control.

Turbocharger boost is controlled by an exhaust bypass valve upstream of the turbocharger (controlled by reference manifold pressure) that dumps excess exhaust energy when boost rises enough to overcome a diaphragm spring in the wastegate actuator. Boost pressure on many modern turbocharging systems is managed above a minimum level by the EMS using a PWM valve to limit reference pressure seen at the primary wastegate actuator port, or by using a PWM valve to deliver a fraction of boost pressure to a secondary reference port on the backside of a dual-ported wastegate actuator that offsets some of the force of full reference pressure on the primary reference port.

Turbo boost controllers thus use pulse width–modulation (PWM) techniques to either 1), under-report boost pressure that the wastegate actuator sees such that it will allow a turbocharger to build more boost pressure in the intake than it otherwise could (essentially lying to the wastegate under ECU control), or 2), to build offsetting pressure that renders the wastegate diaphragm less effective, thus raising boost. The boost control solenoid contains a needle valve that can open and close very fast, much like a fuel injector. By varying the digital control frequency to the solenoid, the solenoid valve can be commanded to be open a certain percentage of the time, known as a duty cycle. This effectively alters the flow rate of air pressure through the valve, changing the rate at which air bleeds out of a T in the manifold pressure reference line to the wastegate. This effectively changes the air pressure as seen by the wastegate actuator diaphragm.

The wastegate control solenoid can be commanded to run at a variety of frequencies in various gears, engine speeds, or according to various other factors in a deterministic open-loop mode. Or—by monitoring manifold pressure in a closed-loop feedback loop—the engine management system can monitor the efficacy of PWM changes in the boost control solenoid bleed rate at altering boost pressure in the intake manifold, increasing or decreasing the bleed rate to target a particular maximum boost.

The basic algorithm sometimes involves the EMS "learning" how fast the turbocharger can spool and how fast boost pressure increases. Armed with this knowledge, as long as boost pressure is below a predetermined allowable ceiling, the EMS will hold the wastegate completely closed until full boost pressure has been achieved rather than allowing manifold pressure to incrementally crack it open, as is the usual case.

CAM CONTROLS
Cam Phasing and Valve-Lift Control

Although a few tuners have modified the basic operating equipment of variable valve systems, this type of activity involves expertise on the level of sophisticated engine design and construction. For the vast majority of tuners, the actuator system itself is a given, and what might be considered for modification is the EMS control portion (though this likely involves duplicating the factory control strategy exactly when an aftermarket programmable EMS gets installed for other reasons).

The earliest variable valve systems from Honda, Porsche, and others were essentially binary. The valvetrain was in either high-rpm or low-rpm mode. Under certain conditions, the ECU triggers a solenoid valve that supplies pressurized engine oil to a spring-loaded plunger that pushes against the camshaft drive in such a way as to increase the length of chain or belt between the intake and exhaust sprocket to advance the intake cam relative to the exhaust cam.

In the case of Honda's original VTEC system, an early pioneer in variable-cam technology, the EMS opens (or closes) a valve that pushes into place a set of pins that lock a complement of cam followers into place for all cylinders such that an alternate more radical set of high-lift and longer-duration cam lobes comes into play to actuate the valves at higher rpm, which improves power. Honda's three-stage VTEC system is similar to the two-stage system, except that the EMS controls *two* binary valves, one to begin opening the second intake valve on a four-valve combustion chamber, the other to switch the intake cams to a more radical profile for both valves. So the EMS simply opens the two electrical switches at various combinations of engine rpm and loading, and the factory hydraulics do the rest.

The other main approach to variable valve timing involves variable cam phasing. The simplest cam-phasing

systems from Honda, Toyota, and GM followed BMW's pioneering VANOS system in using a single set of cam lobes to actuate valves but allowing the EMS to dynamically change the indexing of the cams relative to the crankshaft in such a way as to amplify ram tuning effects across a wider speed range than would otherwise be possible, improving the overall efficiency of the powerplant. Because this type of system provides a linear range of cam phasing with a lot of granularity rather than simply a "low" or "high" speed configuration, engine performance can be optimized over a wider rpm range than a binary system like Honda's original VTEC. Engines with twin overhead camshafts allow the possibility of phasing the intake and exhaust cams independently with respect not only to crankshaft position but each other. The EMS can adjust the position of the two cams to increase exhaust duration so as to provide increased exhaust gas recirculation, to increase cylinder pressure by modifying intake cam timing, and to increase intake-exhaust cam overlap exclusively at high rpm so as to increase the ram-tuning effect for more power without paying the low-end cost of undesirable EGR flow and loss of compression and torque. In some cases OE variable cam timing systems have improved starting under extremely cold conditions by increasing overlap to reduce cranking compression effort and transfer heat more quickly into the intake manifold from hot exand haust.

When it arrived, Honda's i-VTEC (intelligent VTEC) systems was exactly like earlier DOHC VTEC systems with the addition of infinitely variable (within a certain range) intake cam phasing, the main purpose of which is to vary valve overlap to optimize midrange torque and smooth over torque dips that tend to occur when the VTEC system is switching between the low-rpm and high-rpm cam lobes.

The VTC (Variable Timing Control) portion of the Honda system uses a spring-loaded intermediate hydraulic piston sliding on a helical gear between the intake camshaft and the cam sprocket. When the intermediate piston moves sideways along the helical splines, it is forced to rotate slightly, changing the phasing of the cam relative to the sprocket (and, of course, the exhaust cam and crankshaft). This is similar to the VarioCam system used on newer liquid-cooled Porsche powerplants. When the cam phaser is commanded back to zero degrees, a spring forces it back to the default position.

Phasing control is simple on a binary system (advanced or retarded only), but when the cam phasing must be infinitely variable within its authority range, a control valve directs the flow of pressurized oil to either side of the phaser piston depending on the duty cycle of the PWM input. Such systems require cam phasing measurement feedback based on interrupt pulses from the crank ref and cam sync sensors. The response of the PWM valve to varying system voltage, oil pressure, oil temperature, and oil viscosity requires highly sophisticated algorithms for accurate repeatable control.

One of the latest variable valve control systems is a BMW design providing continuously variable valve *lift*. The system uses a special solenoid-actuated cam to increase or decrease the degree to which cam lift translates into actual valve lift, such that anywhere from 0 to 100 percent of the cam lobe's lift is applied to the valves. Obviously, continuously variable lift combined with continuously variable phasing has enormous performance potential. A variable-lift system like BMW's has the potential to eliminate the need for a throttle by allowing the intake valves themselves to limit airflow into the cylinders.

GM Variable Intake Manifold Tuning Valve. Variable intake configuration may increase cylinder filling by altering plenum volume, runner length, or runner cross-section under EMS control to optimize engine torque as rpm changes. *GM*

VARIABLE INTAKE SYSTEMS

Automotive engineers and racers have long recognized the potential to optimize intake manifold design to take advantage of intake charge inertia and resonation effects that improve performance in certain subsets of the rpm range. Longer runners increase charge inertia for improved cylinder-filling at low and moderate engine speeds, while shorter runners improve the ram tuning effect at higher speeds. The problem is that this is a zero-sum game: Optimizing torque at one speed tends to degrade it at others. But dynamically changing the intake system with the use of throttle-type butterflies can direct all intake air through alternate flow paths of differing length and area, bring additional intake runners into play, or add to the volume of the manifold plenum. Variable intakes can thus simultaneously improve specific power and low-end efficiency for improved performance across a broader rpm range than would otherwise be possible (and allow a smaller displacement engine to do the work of a larger one). Variable intake systems were less practical in the days of pre-electronic engine controls, and when gasoline was cheap. The easiest pathway to plenty of torque at all engine speeds was simply installing a huge V-8 engine.

Electronic engine management changed the game, allowing EMS-controlled electro-pneumatic actuated variable intake control as a complex function of throttle position, rpm, or the input from any other engine sensors. Runner-control variable intake systems in the 1990s included secondary intake runner control systems as found on GM's 32-valve ZR1 Corvette and Toyota's Yamaha-head turbocharged 3S-GTE MR2 with TVIS. Both systems go beyond providing alternative flow pathways of different lengths in the unitary stream of air between the throttle and intake plenum. Both engines are equipped with four-valve heads and intake manifolds with dual primary and secondary runners per cylinder directing air separately between the intake plenum and individual intake valves. Throttle-type butterflies close off the secondary intake runners at lower rpm, restricting the intake flow path to a single primary intake runner per cylinder, accelerating air to a high intake velocity with a lot of inertia for improved cylinder filling at lower engine speeds. At higher engine rpm and loading, the secondary-runner butterflies open to double the intake runner area for increased airflow and horsepower. Charge motion systems provide what is essentially binary functionality: the secondary runners are designed to be fully open or fully closed according to solenoid-actuated pneumatic pressure switched under computer control. Conceptually similar port-flap charge motion control systems restrict flow across individual runners at lower speeds to divert high-velocity airflow toward *one side* of the intake port in order to improve the mixing of charge air after it enters the cylinders. Poorly designed intake runner butterflies—like a wide-open throttle—may function as a bottleneck to runner airflow at wide-open throttle compared to plain runners, but hot rodders who remove runner control systems in a quest for more high-end power almost always find there is a noticeable decrease in low-end torque and little or nothing gained in peak horsepower unless the intake runners themselves are a significant bottleneck on a boosted powerplant.

The variable plenum systems arriving in the 1990s on engines like Toyota's 1MZ-FE were designed to provide a similar benefit to intake runner control systems. An electrically controlled solenoid uses manifold pressure to open a set of butterflies in the intake plenum at high engine speeds and loading, thereby providing full plenum volume for improved runner airflow. At lower rpm, the butterflies close to divide the plenum into halves whose reduced volume effectively elongates the intake runners of each cylinder such that inertial effects extend through the walled-off plenum halves and all the way to the throttle body for improved low-speed cylinder filling. Porsche's Vario-ram is similar in concept.

From an engine management system perspective, variable intake systems are binary—in either low-speed or high-speed configuration—with electro-pneumatic switching operations easily accomplished with general-purpose output drivers that are either on or off.

NITROUS INJECTION

A nitrous solenoid is a valve similar in concept to a giant electronic fuel injector. In many cases, the nitrous solenoid remains open constantly when activated. Many modern engine management systems have the capability to monitor the status of a triggering signal from the arming switch of a nitrous system, and under specified conditions, provide a large power boost by opening one or more nitrous injection solenoids and supplemental fuel solenoids that provide a large increase in the fuel and oxidizer arriving in the cylinders. Nitrous systems with hardware that injects auxiliary fuel into the intake system are known as wet nitrous systems. Some engine management systems have software subroutines that allow the ECU to make the complex calculations that enable the EMS itself to provide supplemental fuel for the nitrous to burn as an offset to the normal unboosted fuel calculation, thus eliminating the need for auxiliary nitrous fuel delivery hardware. This type of system is known as a dry nitrous system.

The tricky thing about fueling nitrous boost through the fuel injectors this way is that engine airflow and nitrous flow occur on different scales. Ordinary pulse width-modulated fuel injection calculates a timed amount of fuel to inject per *engine cycle* to match the calculated mass of air ingested per cycle at the current rpm and engine load. Nitrous injection, though, is purely a function of time, which means that the faster the engine turns, the *less* nitrous will be injected each engine cycle, which is opposite of normal increases in mass airflow that occur per cycle as engine speed increases from idle in the direction of peak torque. Nitrous flow per cycle is also completely unaffected by throttle position or variables independent or semi-independent of engine speed that affect mass airflow such as turbochargers

Haltech's iQ3 is a programmable LCD dash display and warning light system that communicates information to the driver, usually while racing. In this case, the LCD display is showing vehicle speed, engine rpm, lambda (air/fuel ratio), manifold Absolute pressure in millibar. *Haltech*

with electronic boost controllers. The result is that any offset made by the ECU to the nonboosted fuel calculation to fuel nitrous injection is unrelated to the magnitude of the nonboosted injection pulse width, except that the nonboosted component of combustion may affect the need for supplemental fuel during nitrous injection as an anti-detonation countermeasure.

Some ECUs have the ability to provide a pulse width-modulated signal to a nitrous solenoid that provides proportional nitrous control, such that instead of simply activating or deactivating full nitrous boost, the ECU is able to modulate the flow rate of nitrous by rapidly pulsing the solenoid on and off to achieve a particular duty cycle. Proportional nitrous control enables nitrous injection to be feathered in rather than to arrive as a massive hit. It allows the possibility of varying levels of nitrous boost. It also complicates the fuel calculation if supplemental nitrous fuel is to be delivered through by the fuel injectors. Depending on the magnitude of the nitrous power boost, it is quite likely that fuel injectors and the fuel supply system could require upgrading in order to deliver enough fuel for the combined power boost.

TEMPERATURE CONTROL

Radiator fans, engine compartment fans, intercooler fans and water-spray systems, and oil-coolers and fans involve relay-controlled on-off functionality with feedback control based on temperature sensor input.

Many aftermarket engine management systems provide fan-control that takes hysterisis into account by providing differing configurable temperatures for fan on and fan off,

depending on whether the associated temperature sensor reaches a certain potentially triggering temperature with the fan currently on or off.

WATER INJECTION

Water injection systems mist water or water mixed with alcohol into the charge air during boosted operations to fight detonation by cooling combustion with the powerful heat of vaporization. The fluid injection system consists of a fluid reservoir, plumbing, a pressurizing pump, and one or more injection nozzles (which might be simple continuous windshield water-type nozzles, or more sophisticated PWM fuel-injector-type valves). The control system that might be as simple as a manifold pressure switch connected to a relay to switch on the flow when boost exceeds the threshold of the switch. Higher-quality standalone systems have a more sophisticated control system consisting of a microprocessor to monitor captive manifold pressure, reservoir level, and optionally air or engine temperature sensors. Rather than injecting fluid with a simple continuous-injection nozzle, such systems may have the ability to trigger a PWM fluid injector similar to a fuel injector when trigger conditions are satisfied.

Virtually all sophisticated engine management systems have the ability to turn on a relay connected to a fluid injection system when configurable engine conditions are true,

If a boosted engine depends on water injection to avoid detonation, it is advisable that there be a fail-safe capability that will protect the engine from damage in case anything goes wrong with the water injection system. Ideally there should be sensors there to tell the EMS when the water injection system is functioning properly (which would not be the case, for example, if the water injection reservoir runs out of fluid or if the injection nozzle is plugged).

TRANSMISSION CONTROL

All modern OEM ECUs provide automatic transmission control and many aftermarket ECUs provide programmable control over torque converter lockup, activating lockup based on rpm, manifold pressure, and throttle position.

INFORMATION DELIVERY

All OEM EMSs provide a check engine light that turns on to indicate a problem with the engine or its EMS, and can be forced into a diagnostic mode in which it will flash out a list of specific trouble codes indicating what the EMS thinks is wrong. A few aftermarket systems have a check light, though most don't, given the powerful laptop-based user interface virtually all provide. Some engine management systems can drive a dash display, usually called something like dash-logger, which is a (somewhat) general-purpose display that can act as a combination gauge or warning alarm and one-way interface to the driver. Some advanced aftermarket EMSs can deliver data to the CAN bus or to a telemetry system that transmits information via FM transmitter or cellular line.

Chapter 5
Hot Rodding EFI Engines

Making power is simple the way dieting is simple: if you want to lose weight, the secret is to eat less and exercise more. If you want to make more power, the secret is to put more air and fuel in an engine and light it off at the right time. Of course, the devil is in the details.

The name of the game in increasing power is removing bottlenecks. Bottlenecks come in various forms: air bottlenecks, fuel bottlenecks, and control system bottlenecks. Some power bottlenecks are generic to any piston engine, while others are specific to various types of electronic fuel-injection and engine management systems.

In general, well-designed modern original equipment factory EFI systems will have balanced components, without unusual bottlenecks in any particular area. However, as soon as you begin modifying components of a performance engine, the bottlenecks will begin to shift around—at first subtly, then more dramatically with basic breathing improvements like head-porting and cam changes.

Modern normally aspirated piston engines are ultimately limited in the amount of torque and horsepower by the amount of air they can draw into the cylinders per displacement, that is,

Supercharged GM LS3 being calibrated on Whipple's load-holding engine dynamometer. To optimize performance at all points, it is necessary to optimize air/fuel ratio across the board with conservative ignition timing, and then optimize spark timing with a "spark hook" test. The calibrator sets the dyno to hold the engine at a particular rpm, and adjusts spark advance at each breakpoint of engine loading available in the ECM's timing table until the read-out indicates maximum torque, at which point torque begins to drop or "hook." Many engines with forced induction running on street gasoline are knock-limited to sub-optimal spark timing by the need to avoid detonation, and could make more power with high octane fuel. *Whipple*

engine volumetric efficiency. It is conceivable there could be minor performance improvements possible via engine management recalibration alone if the engine would always be using super-premium fuel. Even this is dubious, since modern performance engines rely on knock sensor strategies—not sub-optimal default tuning—to protect the engine from bad gasoline. Any engine that would benefit much from more timing and better fuel is already set up to seize the day when good fuel is there.

In modern engines, almost no free power is available from EMS calibration changes. In fact, the EMS on a vehicle like the C5+ Corvette is so well balanced that it is unlikely that any external bolt-on performance parts will individually make any power (with the exception of turbo blowers, nitrous, high-powered alternate fuel, or large displacement increases). The exhaust system, the air cleaner, the air inlet—the easy things—are simply not a restriction anymore on a modern factory performance engine. If any bolt-on part would help much, it's already in the dealer showroom—for the power or the fuel economy to avoid a gas-guzzler surcharge. If you find a bolt-on part for your new Porsche that makes power or torque or both in some rpm range, it probably takes it away in other ranges in a way most people would find unacceptable (a tuned air intake with resonation box being one such example).

Bottom line: today, unless you're talking serious power-adders, the real power increases these days come from packages of breathing parts that almost definitely include hotter cams and maybe high-flow heads, or a big displacement increase via bore and stroke changes to make much more power and torque. It is amazing how much some people with late-model Vipers or 'Vettes will pay today for performance exhaust systems that can't do any good.

However, for reasons of emissions, drivability, and warranty, some older original-equipment EFI systems may have air, fuel, or control bottlenecks that can be removed by the performance enthusiast or racer, and some of these have external breathing parts that are suboptimal. But don't expect to set the world on fire.

But factory turbocharged cars are a different story. And a much more interesting one, because they are often rather easy to overboost, and an *overboosted* turbo engine can breathe so well that many internal and external factors then do become a bottleneck. At stock power levels, forced-induction engines are almost never limited in performance by volumetric efficiency considerations but rather by artificial boost-control devices designed to prevent detonation and/or protect engine components unable to withstand the severe mechanical or thermal loading of full overboost without damage. Careful hot rodding can typically unleash a lot of power and torque on a factory turbo-EFI engine and (to a lesser extent, usually) on a supercharged EFI powerplant.

Whether normally aspirated or forced induction, traditional methods of improving engine pumping efficiency with balanced improvements to the valvetrain, cylinder head,

and intake/exhaust systems or the addition of power-adders work well with fuel-injected vehicles with electronic engine controls if done properly. Of course, any improvements in VE require commensurate increases in fuel-delivery capacity, as well as appropriate spark timing.

EFI POWERPLANT CONSTRAINTS
Air
1. Throttle body (and fly by-wire throttle body)
2. Airflow meter (VAF, MAF)
3. Air intake ram tube
4. Air cleaner
5. Intake manifold temperature (cold vs coolant-heated or exhaust cross-over)
6. Intake manifold
7. Exhaust (headers, pipe[s], cat, muffler, tailpipe)
8. Displacement (bore and stroke)
9. Cams and VE (including variable valve lift and cam phasing)
10. Head-porting
11. Engine change
12. Cold-air intakes

Fuel
1. Injector (size, duty cycle, pressure limitations)
2. Staged injectors
3. Fuel pump (flow @ pressure, voltage, and so on)
4. Fuel lines and filters
5. Fuel rails (rail pressure pulses, flow constraints)
6. Injector geometry
7. Fuel pressure
8. Fuel pressure regulators

Controls
1. Speed/density vs MAF vs Alpha-N (vs combustion pressure or torque)
2. Recalibration versus auxiliary computer versus standalone aftermarket versus programmable sensor issues
3. Variable rate of gain fuel pressure regulators (fuel management units), mechanical or electronic
4. Cam changes
5. EMS blind sports
6. Knock control
7. Water injection
8. Injection duty cycle
9. Emissions
10. Limp-home strategies
11. Boost limits
12. OBD-II and flash-PROM ECUs
13. Traction controls
14. Electronic (fly by-wire) throttles
15. Engine mathematical model and complexity
16. Anti-tampering countermeasures

Power-Adders
1. Forced induction (turbos, blowers)
2. Boost control
3. Bypass/blow-off valves
4. High-powered fuels
5. Nitrous (proportional, fueling through primary injectors, and so on)
6. Blower-clutch control

INJECTION SYSTEM AIRFLOW BOTTLENECKS
Throttle body: A throttle body should have enough capacity to provide sufficient airflow at peak power without producing a significant pressure drop (bottleneck) through the throttle area. A throttle that is too small for a normally aspirated powerplant will kill horsepower. The situation is a little trickier on a boosted engine, because a given amount of air might be forced into the engine through a larger throttle body at a lower boost pressure, or—assuming the compressor has some excess capacity—might be forced through a smaller throttle body with less CFM capacity with a higher boost pressure.

So why not just install a huge throttle body guaranteed to have more capacity than the engine can use? Throttle bodies that are much too big for an engine lose their authority way below full throttle, because once the engine is fully loaded, it simply cannot ingest more air (think of driving up a long, steep hill below peak power rpm). Part and full throttle may deliver exactly the same power. Conversely, at lower throttle settings, an oversized throttle body can be twitchy and over responsive, with a tiny bit of additional throttle producing a large airflow increase in a way that hurts drivability.

The way to match a throttle body with an engine is to compute the engine airflow and throttle body airflow separately to make sure the throttle body CFM exceeds that of the engine. The way to do this is to compute engine airflow at an assumed volumetric efficiency, or, even better, to compute current airflow based on the horsepower produced on a dynamometer. Throttle body airflow will be available from the manufacturer—in the case of a new aftermarket throttle body—or can be calculated. If you have drivability problems from a twitchy throttle, progressive units that accelerate or decelerate the number of degrees of throttle-shaft rotation with increasing accelerator percentage have been used on some engines.

Many engines now have fly by-wire electronic throttles that are driven by a computer-controlled electric stepper motor under electronic-accelerator directives rather than by a cable connected to the accelerator. Such throttle-control systems are very effective for traction-control systems. They can smooth out poor driving habits that waste fuel, and they can prevent people from hurting an engine by driving it too hard when cold.

In some cases, performance tuners have eliminated the electronic throttle in favor of an older-style cable-actuated throttle body when switching to an aftermarket EMS. If the throttle size is a constraint, there is no reason why companies like RC Engineering—with the ability to machine larger openings in a throttle to accommodate a bigger throttle plate in a traditional throttle—couldn't increase the flow potential of an electronically controlled throttle if it becomes a restriction (though this could seriously impact the calibration of some engine management systems, in some cases requiring recalibration).

Air meters: The air metering section of the injection system, located upstream of the throttle body, can become a bottleneck to higher horsepower on modified engine by restricting airflow into the engine, thus reducing volumetric efficiency. EFI systems that are designed to measure airflow directly usually estimate mass airflow (MAF) by considering the cooling effect of intake air on a hot wire or film suspended in an orifice of fixed size through which all inlet air must flow.

In the case of older velocity airflow meters, the pressure of inlet air against a spring-loaded door suspended in the inlet air stream produces the air velocity reading. If there is a significant pressure drop through the airflow sensor, then the cylinders will

Vortech 6.5-7.5 psi blower kit for the 2010-2011 Camaro SS was designed with V-3 Si-trim centrifugal supercharger, air-air intercooling system, supercharger driver system, and air intake. Standard power increase is 47 percent. Tuner kits with V-7 YSi supercharger support up to 1200 horsepower. Vortech's kit illustrates the scope of what's required to hot rod a modern EFI engine. Note upgrade fuel injectors and connectors, with EMS changes handled by reflashing the ECM with a new calibration optimized for supercharging. *Vortech*

not fill as well with air, which will lower power output. OK, why not use a gigantic airflow meter? The problem is that the larger the airflow meter, the less sensitive it is to small variations in airflow because smaller orifices magnify changes in air velocity that make it easier for the sensor to get accurate readings. Big sensors with lazy airflow through them can also have problems with turbulence that affect the readings. (It is critical under all circumstances that a MAF be positioned where the air cleaner, sharp bends in the intake ram pipe, and the throttle body do not interfere with smooth airflow through the MAF). Many MAF meters are equipped with aerodynamic grids designed to straighten airflow before it contacts the metering element; removal is not advisable, since this can affect the MAF air-vs-signal transfer function and render the meter inaccurate over some or all of the operating range.

There are several ways to eliminate MAF or VAF airflow restrictions. The first is with a high-flow aftermarket performance MAF. High-flow MAFs are available for many performance engines equipped with OE MAF sensors, and some of them can be adjusted or programmed to optimize operation on different engines, or to compensate for larger injectors. Some engines with OE VAF meters can be converted to a higher-flow MAF meter (a newer, superior technology that requires no correction for air temperature and is not subject to problems from manifold and intake shock waves fibrillating the mechanism).

The second way to eliminate air-meter restrictions is to eliminate the airflow sensor with an aftermarket metering device that combines data from add-on MAP and air temp sensors with engine speed and a complex table of internal translation numbers to calculate airflow for a specific vehicle in the proper electrical format that exactly simulates the output of an airflow meter, but without the airflow restriction of the air meter. An old HKS device called the vane pressure convertor (VPC) eliminated Toyota's VAF meter.

Another path to eliminating intake restriction from a MAF meter is to junk the factory EMS. Converting to an aftermarket speed-density EMS that measures manifold absolute pressure (MAP) and air temperature, calculates engine speed, and then deduces airflow or engine loading based on this data without requiring an airflow metering device enables a tuner to eliminate the metering system bottleneck. Virtually all aftermarket engine management systems permit use of speed-density engine controls as the default engine load sensing, though some allow MAF or other types of load sensing. Several of the project vehicles in this book involve such modifications.

The main disadvantages of replacing the stock fuel-injection system are that it may not be legal (for emissions reasons) and that the replacement may not preserve all the capabilities of the original EMS.

Custom Porsche 968 turbo conversion from Norwood Performance represents the apex of radical club-race/outlaw street performance. Using sophisticated Motec engine management, high-boost turbocharging, and super-duty internal parts, the engine made over 600 horsepower at the wheels.

Air cleaner and cold-air intake: It is critical that an air cleaner should clean the air well and flow enough air that the filter is not a bottleneck that hurts engine VE. Dust or other foreign contaminants in charge air will dramatically accelerate engine wear. The only excuse for ever running any engine with open stacks or other unfiltered air intake is if it is a competition engine with severe-to-impossible space constraints.

Virtually all modern factory EFI systems use cold-air intake systems that breathe air that is 100 percent isolated from hot engine compartment air, which is very important because colder air is denser and will noticeably increase power. The air cleaner should not introduce undesirable turbulence to intake air that interferes with a MAF sensor. The air cleaner system should insulate intake air from heat soak by hot engine components.

Intake ram tube: An intake tube of the proper length can improve throttle response and actually make power on some engines. Air moving through a long tube has momentum and inertia that can help get air in the engine when you suddenly open the throttle (a very large inline air cleaner or resonator can interfere with this). You can tune an intake ram tube on some engines to provide pressure-wave tuning benefits at some engine speeds—exactly like tuning the length of intake runners in the manifold and cylinder head (see the chapter on intake manifold construction in this book).

Intake manifold: Freedom of intake manifold design is one of the great things about multi-port electronic fuel injection. Dry manifolds can be optimized to deliver air into an engine without the compromises required to manage a wet mixture of fuel and air. Mixture distribution is almost never an issue with port EFI, and there is no need to choose between a single, centrally located carburetor and the expense and difficulty of mounting individual carbs or carb throats on each runner for

perfect distribution (like a motorcycle). Dry intake manifolds do not require power-robbing coolant- or exhaust-heating chambers that help wet manifolds keep fuel vaporized in cold temperatures on carbureted and throttle body injection engines but hurt VE by heating up the intake air. Some port-EFI throttle bodies are heated by engine coolant to prevent ice from forming in cold weather with a low dewpoint, but the intake manifold itself should not need heating on a dry manifold. This is something to keep in mind if you are converting a wet-manifold to port EFI

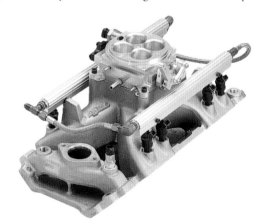

With a small-block Chevy V-8, you've got a lot of hot rodding options. This turnkey EFI intake from Accel provides a high-flow single-plane intake with injector bosses cast in, injectors, fuel rails, water temp sensor, four-barrel Holley bolt-pattern throttle body, TPS, and idle air control stepper motor. This package could be used to convert a stock throttle body injection system to port injection, as the basis of an EFI conversion (with aftermarket or GM EMS), or to upgrade the airflow of a long-runner TPI setup (along with a PROM upgrade). *Accel*

Mass Air Meter Sizing	
Meter Diameter	Max HP
55mm	320
70mm	380
80mm	485
75 mm Bullet	600
87mm Bullet	650
77mm Pro M	700
80mm Pro M	800
83mm Pro M	900
92mm Pro M	1000
117mm Pro M	1500

Kraftwerks Honda S2000 system uses air-cooled intercooling, which can increase the *effective* thermal efficiency of a Rotrex centrifugal supercharger from a maximum of 75-80 percent into the 80-90 percent range for increased power and cooler combustion. The key to reliable performance is good engine management, including sufficient fuel. Note upgrade fuel injectors. The S2000 used an OBD-II engine that was reflash-able via Flash Pro to a supercharger calibration that added fuel and removed timing during supercharger boost. *Kraftwerks*

by installing injector bosses. Carb-type V-8 intake manifolds will not require the exhaust-heating cross-over passages cast into the manifolds on many engines, and these could be blanked off to help improve engine VE on an EFI conversion.

Some intake manifolds on four-valve/cylinder engines are equipped with staged runner systems that close off half the runners at low rpm with auxiliary throttle butterflies in half the ports that are designated secondary runners. These systems improve cylinder filling by maintaining very high port velocities in the primary runners to improve cylinder filling at low engine speeds, while opening the secondaries under computer control as airflow increases with high rpm and power settings to prevent the intake from becoming a bottleneck.

It was common hot rodding practice on engines like the 16-valve Twin Cam MR2 Turbo to remove the staged intake system (Toyota Variable Intake System or TVIS) and siamese the two intake ports for each cylinder by band sawing the manifold open and cutting/grinding out the wall between each pair of runners. This will hurt low-end performance but contribute to power gains at high levels of boost and airflow. I built a custom-welded stroker crankshaft MR2 project to improve low-end torque when the TVIS was removed for the big peak power. This type of radical intake surgery affects both runner tuning and flow.

Some dry intake manifolds are equipped with variable-plenum intake manifolds, which is similar to Porsche's Varioram, in which a giant butterfly can open at higher flow to convert a dual-plane intake into a single-plane intake. The "MR6" project in this book used a 3.0-liter Toyota 1MZ V-6 with such a system. The Toyota system is equipped with a vacuum-operated diaphragm that closes the plenum butterfly at high vacuum, while opening it at higher manifold pressure or under boost. This vacuum-operated system does not necessarily require computer control to function effectively to improve low-end torque and high-end power.

Intake manifold design is so important to drivability, torque, and power that this book contains a whole chapter about it. If you are lucky to have an engine commonly hot rodded (a small-block Chevy V-8, Honda four, Ford 5.0, and so on), there will be off-the-shelf aftermarket performance intake manifolds available to change the torque and power curves on the engine. Airflow rules and tradeoffs with dry EFI intakes are identical to those of carbureted manifolds. Long narrow runners produce great low-end torque and tuning effects at lower rpm. Short, wider runners flow better and produce tuning effects at higher engine speeds. Variable-intake systems attempt to get the best of both.

If you fabricate a custom sheet-metal manifold or heavily modify a factory or aftermarket manifold, you should always have a cylinder head shop test it on a flow bench (before and after) to make sure there are no problems or inconsistencies that should be corrected, and to make sure you haven't done something that is performance-negative.

Injector placement and aim in a custom EFI manifold is important. If at all possible, fuel injectors should aim at the base of the intake valve where the stem joins the cup (or between the two intake valves on a four- or five-valve engine). Increased distance from a port injector to the valve(s) can aid in fuel atomization and vaporization, and injectors have been successfully aimed straight down the throats of intake runners from across the plenum. Beware of resonation effects and "standoff" causing fuel to reverse-flow out of the intake runners back into the plenum and migrate from port injectors closest to the throttle body through the plenum in the direction of runners farther from the throttle body.

The EFI intake manifold may be an issue if you are interested in supercharging. Traditional Roots-type positive-displacement superchargers are usually bolted directly to a vestigial intake manifold on American performance V-8s, with one or two four-barrel carbs bolting directly on top of the blower, with the wet mixture helping to cool the supercharger rotors enough to maintain proper clearance. Today it is common practice on modern four-valve four- and six-cylinder EFI engines to develop supercharger conversions that utilize a special intake manifold casting in which the casting doubles as the blower housing and a compact modern Eaton supercharger rotor assembly essentially replaces the plenum section of the OEM manifold.

Building a custom blower conversion for an EFI engine for which none is available is a difficult engineering job that requires a thorough understanding of supercharger flow versus speed characteristics and extensive fabrication capabilities (if not the ability to build casting mold bucks) that include the ability to make a belt-drive system work with the stock crank pulley and accessories. The alternative is a centrifugal supercharger of

In a magazine article I called this thing "Psycho Nitrous Vette." The owner called his 2006 Z06 Vette "Rice Killer," and this was the only angle most drivers were going to see it from. The main strategy was a huge 428-inch stroker and incredible amounts of nitrous injection. This Dual-tank Nitrous Express system was designed to deliver 350 horsepower on top of the stroker powerplant's all-motor capabilities.

With a 600-horse hot rod 428 cid Z06 motor and a 3-stage 350 nitrous shot, "Rice Killer" was good for 863 rwhp at 7,000 on the streets of Dallas, TX, an estimated 915 hp at the crankshaft. Engine Management consisted of GM E38, recalibrated with HPE custom hot rod/nitrous tuning. Plus a 3-stage Nitrous Express multi-port fogger nitrous injection system. Yee-haw!

the type that looks something like a big alternator and requires dealing with blower drive-belt issues but would rarely require changes to the EFI engine's intake manifold.

Exhaust: Traditional performance exhaust flow principles still apply to computer-controlled port EFI engines. However, many electronic engine management systems require O_2 sensors to function in closed-loop mode in order to optimize economy and drivability at idle and light cruise, and O_2 sensors don't work well until they're hot. OBD-II factory EMSs may have as many as four or five O_2 sensors in the exhaust headers and after the catalytic convertor(s). Any modifications that steal heat from the exhaust (such as a turbo conversion) can render unheated O_2 sensors inoperative. And cats with too much flow may not stay hot enough at idle to "light off" and do their job. Really, all O_2 sensors should be heated these days. Some highly effective turbo conversions for new engines mount the turbocharger downstream of the cat. Engine management tuning strategies can use retarded timing at idle to put more heat in a cat and O_2 sensor.

Some cat-back exhaust systems have made some power on otherwise stock engines (particularly on over-boosted turbo engines), but the greatest value of such systems is as part of a balanced package of performance upgrades that free up bottlenecks all across the engine's pumping system in a coordinated fashion from intake through cylinder heads and camshaft through exhaust.

Displacement: Hot rodders used to say there's no substitute for cubic inches. That's not strictly true, but it is true that displacement is essentially always a good thing in terms of street performance. How does adding bore or stroke affect the EMS on a powerplant with electronic fuel injection? In terms of percentages, without extremely radical monster-motor procedures, except in the case of V-12 engines with huge bore and stroke increases, it is difficult to add more than 10 or 20 percent more displacement, particularly on engines with fewer cylinders. Think of GM 350 V-8s bored and stroked to 383, 396, or 421—increases of 9.4, 13.1, and 20.1 percent. Without commensurate cam and head breathing upgrades, peak power is unlikely to increase as much as the displacement

because breathing is likely to be suboptimal for the larger displacement.

Engine control systems with MAF sensors will often handle 5 to 15 percent more airflow without complaining, and closed-loop O_2-sensor-based feedback will certainly trim idle and light-cruise operations for stoichiometric air/fuel ratio with no trouble. Engine control systems with speed-density engine management will probably require fuel pressure increases as a countermeasure against lean mixtures at peak power (which will require interceptor/piggyback electronics on direct-injection engines, where fuel pressure is managed by the EMS computer). Dyno testing with a wideband air/fuel-ratio meter and an adjustable fuel pressure regulator should enable a tuner to optimize the fuel pressure for best power on standard port injection engines.

Cams, Heads, and VE: Changing the camshaft and cylinder head airflow specs changes the volumetric efficiency of an engine because the purpose of such changes is to increase engine breathing—in at least some range of operation—and that's what volumetric efficiency is. But on traditional engines lacking variable valve timing/lift controls, there is usually a cost to a cam change. If you make engine breathing better in one part of the operating range, you typically make airflow worse somewhere else. As long as the airflow changes are not so extreme as to move airflow out of the bounds of what is acceptable airflow with the stock calibration (and within the authority of the airflow sensor, on engines so equipped), a MAF-based engine-control system should provide good timing and fuel control. A MAP-sensor-based system will not be able to compensate for these cam-change or head-porting VE changes without recalibration.

Engine changes: If you can get an EMS to work with changed displacement and even changed cams and breathing, why not with a foreign engine in a complete engine swap situation? For example, is it feasible to swap in a Ford 460 big-block in place of a Ford 5.0 V-8 and use the stock EMS, or, say, replace a Chevy 5.7-liter V-8 with a Chevy 7.4-liter big-block? Or maybe replace a Honda 1.6 VTEC with a 2.3 VTEC? The simplest situation would be if you swapped out an engine with MAF controls to a much bigger powerplant with similar

volumetric efficiency, retaining the MAF system, changing fuel delivery with a combination of larger injectors and fuel pressure regulation such that pulse widths for the old engine size worked well for the changed engine size. For example, if you changed a Ford 5.0L/302-cid to a 7.5L/460-cid engine (which is 152 percent larger), you could change out the stock 19-pounds-per-hour injectors to 30-pounds-per-hour injectors and lower fuel rail pressure slightly to reduce the injector flow to 28.8-pounds-per-hour. This should get fuel delivery very close. Now, if you replaced the stock MAF sensor with an aftermarket programmable MAF and adjusted it for across-the-board underreporting of airflow so the new engine's airflow looked to the EMS like the old engine's airflow, you could potentially tune fuel pressure on a dyno with a wideband air/fuel-ratio meter to optimize horsepower at peak-power rpm and then let the closed-loop system trim idle and light cruise for perfect air/fuel ratios. Another solution to keeping the MAF and EMS calibration in sync would be to build a MAF bypass tube to bypass a percentage of air equal to the increase in displacement. On the other hand, if you had complete programmatic access to the EMS internal tables on an engine with OBD-II engine controls, you could install a MAF large enough to measure maximum airflow on the big-displacement engine and calibrate the EMS with a new MAF transfer table that remapped MAF sensor output to airflow values in the internal EMS tables that worked with the data in the stock fuel table(s).

The situation with a speed-density EMS would be at once simpler and more complex. All the EMS knows about is manifold pressure—not airflow—so the radically changed airflow of a large displacement change would be invisible to the EMS. Assuming the volumetric efficiency curves of the two engines were close, simply adjusting fuel injector size and pressure would get the replacement engine running, and then you could trim fuel pressure as above to optimize high-end power, leaving it to the closed-loop feedback system to get air/fuel ratios perfect at idle and light cruise (assuming stoichiometric mixtures would work).

But what about performance at power levels too high for closed-loop, but below peak power? Good luck. If drivability were acceptable, a dyno and wideband air/fuel-ratio meter would reveal the details of how good or bad the existing calibration was for the new engine. I would not go down this path unless it was possible to retune the engine with a custom calibration (hacking the EMS with a tuning program like LS2-edit) or using an interceptor box. Clearly, big VE changes would not work well on the above speed-density situation without recalibration or interceptor, but, of course, on engines like the small-block pushrod Ford and Chevy V-8s, the factory built both MAF and speed-density controls, so you might be able to convert over to MAF control if necessary and to use the first strategy.

INJECTION SYSTEM FUEL BOTTLENECKS

In general, getting more fuel into an engine is way less of a challenge than providing more air. This is mostly because the engine requires 15 times the air by weight (and much more by volume), and normally aspirated engines depend on air being pushed in by atmospheric pressure alone. However, internal-combustion engines do require a certain amount of fuel per horsepower (exactly how much varies somewhat according to the brake specific fuel consumption of the engine), which is related to the efficiency of the combustion chamber, how much fuel needs to be wasted cooling off combustion, the quality of

the state of tune, the internal friction of the engine, and power wasted turning a supercharger or wasted in reduced exhaust pumping efficiencies related to driving a turbocharger turbine.

Injector capacity: Injectors need to be small enough to provide a good engine idle at minimum achievable pulse width (never less than about 0.8 milliseconds, often as much as 2 milliseconds). Yet injectors need to be large enough to provide sufficient fuel for peak power at a fuel pressure that is within the limits of the injector's ability to open and close against the pressure (figure 70–110 psi max; see the section on injectors in the chapter on actuators) and at a duty cycle (percentage of time open) between about 10 and 80 percent.

It is easy to find higher-flow injectors that will install in place of the stock injectors on most factory engines. It is a different matter to recalibrate the control system to adjust the opening time and pressure so the upgrade injectors provide the right amount of fuel. Injectors must be electrically compatible with the ECU firing them. If the dynamic range required of injectors on a small engine with few cylinders that's capable of extremely high power is beyond what's possible (even with dynamic pressure changes), the solution may require multiple staged injectors per cylinder, with one injector operating at idle and a second (possibly of higher flow) coming into play as the engine requires more fuel.

Fuel pumps: The high-pressure port-EFI electric fuel pump (and its plumbing!) must be up to the job of moving sufficient fuel to maintain the required fuel pressure (which may vary according to engine speed and loading). Fuel pumps vary in capacity and are capable of less volume as pressure increases. If your fuel pump will not pass muster, there may be a higher-flow in-tank unit available, or you'll need to supplement the stock in-tank unit with an auxiliary inline pump (usually operating in series).

Auxiliary fuel pumps can be activated by the factory EMS as needed (for example, to boost pressure) via a relay from the primary fuel pump power supply activated by a simple boost-

Powerhouse modified a normally aspirated Toyota Supra to make more than 700 horsepower with a massive turbo conversion that includes huge fuel injectors and aftermarket engine management. Hot rodders loved Gen 2 twin-turbo inline-6 Supra Turbos, because the car was capable of 320 street horsepower like the 300ZX Twin Turbo, but the injectors, fuel supply, turbo, and other components were capable of supporting much more power (unlike the Nissan). All it takes to unleash really big power is tweaking the engine management system.

HOT RODDING CHEVY'S TPI

Chevrolet's L98 Tuned Port Injection engine was the last traditional small-block Chevy V-8, of which there were about 60 million built since the mid-1950s. TPI will fit on any traditional small-block Chevy, which gives it importance even though the last TPI engine was built in 1993. TPI will also fit many TBI truck motors built in the 1990s and a few in some big vans built beyond 2000. It is, therefore, still important. The Jag-rolet project in this book involved swapping a TPI engine into a late-model Jaguar sedan, and hot rodding the power with a centrifugal supercharger and other significant performance modifications.

Chevy designed Tuned Port Injection for a 305-ci engine that would be driven on the street. Design goals included responsive acceleration with an automatic transmission in a heavy car under average driving conditions (which means low to medium rpm), plus good fuel economy and emissions (which implies tall gears). As it should with these goals, the TPI system makes great low-end torque that dies out rapidly above 4,000 rpm. This is a situation that left hot rodders and racers looking for ways to make more power at higher rpm on a TPI-injected Chevy.

It's important to keep in mind that torque is what makes a car fun to drive. Horsepower is a measure of how much work an engine can do at a certain speed, such as lifting a weight of a certain size. Torque measures the moment of a force, that is, its tendency to produce torsion and rotation around an axis. In other words, twisting force—the kind of force that causes a car to leap forward when you nail the gas because of the instantaneous rotational force of the engine's crankshaft. Torque is critical to an engine's ability to accelerate.

Peak torque usually occurs at the engine's point of highest volumetric efficiency. Both race and street engines need to accelerate well from a variety of speeds; therefore, good torque over a broad range is important, not just peak torque. High horsepower achieved at high engine speeds over a narrow range (above the peak torque where the cylinders are no longer filling as well, just more often) tends to produce cars that aren't flexible or fun to drive—you have to drive it like you're mad at it to get any performance.

Tuned-runner port injection is great at making torque, but there are trade-offs, just as there are with intake manifolds designed for carburetors. Port EFI manifolds do not have to deal with keeping fuel suspended properly in air as wet air carburetors or throttle body injection manifolds must do, which gives designers more flexibility with runner length, geography, and cross section—that is, the ability to tune the intake for the best torque curve for a given application.

However, it is a fact that intake runner length and cross section (as well as exhaust port/header length and cross section) do affect the torque curve of an engine. Longer, narrower runners accelerate air to high velocities with high momentum that produces higher air pressure at the intake valve. If the engine is turning slowly, time is not a critical factor in cylinder filling and VE is higher with longer, narrower runners. At higher rpm, time is critical. There is not time for a long column of air to accelerate and enter the cylinder to fill it well. The narrow cross section of a runner implies less volume and more pressure drop at high rpm. Again, less cylinder filling.

If the motor is stock, and always will be, it is hard to beat the GM TPI system, which works well up to 4,600 rpm. Stock TPI manifolds negate the effect of better heads and cams and headers for higher-rpm power. If the motor is not stock or you need power above 4,600 rpm, the stock TPI manifold will have to be modified with larger runners and a larger throttle body or a complete new manifold. You'll need an aftermarket ECU or a modified PROM for the stock GM computer that is matched to the new engine modifications. With a new intake system, the heads will become the flow bottleneck. As always, every part of the complete system must be designed to work well together or some unexpected bottleneck can negate the effect of other expensive modified parts. A mild stock 305 engine is well matched to the stock TPI system.

But let's say you've improved the cam a little, and installed headers, perhaps even upgraded to a crate 350 HO motor with somewhat better cam and heads, designed to make roughly 350 horsepower. It's easy to install larger runners and a matching larger throttle body. Typically, the TPIS runners are 0.190 inches in diameter larger than stock and 0.325 inches longer, which adds considerably higher rpm torque and power from 3,000 rpm up—in one test 75 lb-ft over stock across the board from 3,700 rpm on up to redline!

Runners are available not only in larger sizes, but with adjacent ports siamesed so a cylinder can share two runners for better breathing at rpm (which hurts lower rpm power and torque). Serious hot rodders may decide to extrude hone the manifold base to match the flow capabilities of the new runners and higher cfm throttle body—or switch to a large manifold base like the TPIS Big Mouth, with its round 1.750 entry sizes and 1.960/1.200 exits.

A serious big-displacement Chevy small-block motor with a good 240-degree duration 0.550–0.600 cam and compression over 10:1, with some seriously ported good high-rpm aftermarket aluminum heads will require a complete new manifold to really take advantage of this configuration's ability to make high-rpm power. Accel, TPIS, and other such manifolds, designed with considerably shorter and fatter runners and much higher-volume plenums. The Accel SuperRam runners were more than 3 inches shorter than the stock TPI (4.125 versus 7.250) incorporating D-section geometry of 1.878 x 1.970 (versus stock 1.470 round runner). The one-piece TPIS Mini-Ram was a serious high-rpm manifold with still shorter runners (3.5 inch) and huge 2.600 x 1.350 entry, tapering to 1.960 x 1.200 exits.

Properly sized carburetion can make virtually as much maximum horsepower as port EFI. Unfortunately, by sizing the venturis in such a way that they are not restrictive on a hot motor at high rpm, the carburetor would provide terrible low- and midrange power and torque. Good, big-runner TPIS manifolds, even short-ram EFI manifolds, and stock TPI will all be making 100 lb-ft more torque at 2,500 rpm compared to a higher-rpm carb and manifold, which is power you can feel as well as measure.

pressure switch. Alternately, many aftermarket ECUs can activate an auxiliary fuel pump at a certain manifold pressure or MAF setting in much the same way that ECUs turn on cooling fans at a certain configurable threshold temperature and then off at a second user-configurable pressure.

Devices such as the Kenne Bell Boost-a-Pump can widen the dynamic range of a fuel pump by varying power supply voltage with increasing manifold pressure. This is similar to the action of an OEM "deadhead" (returnless) fuel supply system that controls fuel pump voltage in stages or continuously with

the main ECU to target approximate required fuel pressure according to data from a fuel rail pressure sender, then trimming injection pulse width to precisely fine-tune the fuel delivery.

Fuel pressure regulator: On loop-type fuel supply systems, a pressure regulator determines how much fuel sprays out of an injector per length of pulse by pinching off the flow of fuel returning to the tank to the degree required to target a certain fuel pressure at the injector manifold/fuel rail. Some pressure regulators allow adjustment by turning a jam bolt that varies the preload against the diaphragm spring in the fuel pressure

Quatro valvole 3.0–3.5-liter Ferrari V-8s make good hot rodding material, says Bob Norwood, who liked the combination of high compression and turbocharging on a small-displacement four-valve powerplant to keep the torque up until the turbo kicks in. It is a rather simple matter to remove the K-Jet mechanical injectors and open up the bosses for electronic injectors. In its day, there were people who tried to hot rod the K-Jet system, but an EFI conversion is much better equipped to handle power-adders like turbocharging.

This C3 'Vette uses twin turbos without intercooling to rack up the boost. Fuel cooling via rich mixtures is a viable trick to fight detonation.

regulator. And most regulators dynamically raise and power fuel pressure according to a manifold pressure reference line that supplies vacuum or boost pressure to augment or retard the action of the diaphragm spring.

Adjusting injection pressure can be a highly effective way of tuning the final air/fuel ratio under open-loop conditions. Fuel management units (FMUs), also known as variable-rate-of-gain fuel pressure regulators, take this principle one step further by increasing fuel pressure as a *multiple* of boost pressure increases (in one big step, in the case of some nitrous FMUs). Electronic FMUs go beyond this by varying pressure under programmable electronic control according to configurable graphs in the control unit.

Be aware that "deadhead" factory engine management systems may adjust injection pulse width to compensate for rail pressure, defeating efforts to tune air/fuel ratio via fuel pressure changes. EMS closed-loop mixture-control strategies will similarly trim pulse width to achieve certain target levels of residual exhaust gas oxygen at idle and light cruise (or at higher power levels in some full-authority engines equipped with wideband air/fuel ratio sensors).

CONTROL SYSTEM BOTTLENECKS

Basic control strategies: If an engine uses an EMS with MAF sensor load sensing, then additional air entering the engine at a given speed will automatically call for more fuel, and most stock EFI systems can deliver some additional fuel for a given speed. For example, older Mustang 5.0L MAF systems and the GM TPI system could deliver a small percentage of extra fuel for heavier-breathing engines—about 10 or 15 percent. This is enough for minor modifications like small cam changes, air filter changes, and so on, but not enough to support fueling for significant turbo or blower boost.

The situation is more complicated if the EFI system is not programmable and uses a speed-density or Alpha-N control strategy. Changing cams may alter the manifold pressure for a given engine speed and loading, causing the ECU to be confused or wrong about how much air the engine is consuming and therefore injecting the wrong amount of fuel. Alpha-N control systems that determine engine load purely from engine speed and throttle position similarly have even less ability to compensate for modifications that affect engine volumetric efficiency, including—notably—the variable effects of a turbocharger on engine VE.

Throttle-position control strategies are great for engines with big cams that have difficulty idling smoothly due to fluctuating manifold pressure (which can cause MAP or MAF systems to hunt—as the ECU chases it own tail with a wandering load signal). Throttle-position load-sensing strategies cannot work well with turbochargers, which can produce huge VE changes while throttle and engine speed remain steady. Note that some sophisticated aftermarket engine management systems can switch from Alpha-N to MAP sensing when a turbo begins making boost.

An engine management system's blindness to hot rodding–induced changes in engine volumetric efficiency can cause

John Carmack's boosted Ferrari F50 used a 60-valve high-compression 4.7L V-12 and twin-turbo conversion to make some serious horsepower at medium boost pressure. In a gutsy move aimed at achieving emissions legality and avoiding detonation problems, Bob Norwood converted the car over to E80 fuel, a blend of ethanol and gasoline that has high octane, good intercooling capabilities, and a clean burn.

As legions of hot rodders have discovered, the relatively low horsepower per cylinder (15 hp! and up) of the low-deck pushrod Ford Windsor V8 makes the 4.2-5.0L engine excellent raw material for supercharging. Shown here with a simple but effective Paxton Novi blower kit, non-intercooled. Still the one. *Paxton*

Another simple trick to more EFI 5.0L Ford Windsor horsepower is nitrous injection. This Edelbrock nitrous spacer plate installs between the upper and lower EFI intake manifold of 1986+ Ford pushrod V-8s, providing direct-port capability without having to drill the stock intake manifold. You're always going to want to pull timing when the nitrous kicks in. With aftermarket standalone EMS, it's an offset to the base timing maps when nitrous is spraying. With stock EMS,. You'll want to boost-timing retard device as the perfect complement to stock engine management. *Edelbrock*

problems with speed-density controls, but sometimes blindness is a blessing. Whereas a MAF-sensed system's awareness of airflow increases can be good in the case of moderate airflow increases within the authority of the MAF and EMS to manage, this awareness can also produce incompatibilities with EMS modification strategies such as VRG fuel pressure regulators if both attempt to increase fueling in certain operating ranges. And airflow awareness can also alert a factory EMS to levels of overboost that trigger limp-home countermeasures that disregard sensor values and attempt to protect the engine with limp-mode engine management procedures that kill performance—particularly on an EMS with OBD-II capabilities. In such cases, a speed-density MAP system may have an easier time tolerating a power-adder than MAF systems.

The solutions to the above problems include the typical array of PROM recalibrations, interceptors, and piggyback ECUs, aftermarket standalone EMSs (which might take over all or just some functions from the main ECU), programmable sensors and actuators, additional injector controllers, and so forth—some of which will not be legal for street use.

EMS blind spots: Knock sensors are essentially sensitive crystal microphones, and many OEM knock sensors are matched to detect specific resonant vibrations that are highly correlated with spark knock on the particular engine they are protecting. Unfortunately, engine modifications—particularly valvetrain items or other components that affect other parts—can sometimes produce vibrations and resonation that can appear to be a knock to the engine-control system. Some aftermarket knock sensor controllers have a sensitivity or tuning adjustment that can be used to help filter out vibrations unrelated to actual knock.

Keep in mind, true detection of actual spark knock requires in-cylinder pressure transducers that detect the steep pressure spikes characteristic of genuine detonation. These are expensive but obtainable and can be found integrated into special spark plugs. A second-best method of detecting genuine knock involves carefully monitoring micro-changes in crankshaft acceleration and deceleration to detect signs of explosive

combustion. This typically requires high processing speed and highly accurate engine-position sensing of the sort used to detect misfires for OBD-II.

Some aftermarket knock-control systems are capable of associating detonation with specific cylinders and launching knock-control countermeasures such as spark timing retard exclusively for the cylinders actually knocking, allowing other cylinders to remain at peak efficiency—simultaneously protecting the engine but maintaining higher power levels. Some aftermarket EMSs can trigger water or water-alcohol injection at higher levels of boost as an effective anti-detonation preventative measure or in response to an indication of detonation from a knock sensor. Keep in mind that the volume of water required for knock control is small, which makes port water injection impractical. Single-point injection can result in poor water distribution through EFI-type dry intake manifolds.

Some modern aftermarket ECUs warn tuners when the basic calibration reaches 100 percent duty cycle driving fuel injectors (which means the injectors are open constantly and the air/fuel ratio is at least temporarily out of control).

Many fuel experts agree that it is not a good idea to run pintle-type injectors at more than 80 percent duty cycle. This is because at higher duty cycles injectors may not have enough time to close all the way, and thus can fibrillate somewhere around 85 percent duty cycle (see the section on fuel injections in the actuator chapter of this book for much more information), with fuel flow becoming less predictable and even diminishing in fuel flow in a dip around 85 percent until the injector goes static and fuel flow reaches maximum.

Obviously, the ECU is blind as to whether an individual injectors is open or not or fluttering somewhere in the middle (or even whether it is stuck completely open or stuck closed). The ECU usually has no way of knowing whether the installed injector can accurately carry out commands to open for short intervals (say, shorter than the injector's combined open and closing time) to idle well on small, high-power engines. That said, engines are run every day with injectors at 100 percent duty for short periods without adverse consequences. Although injection pulse width cannot increase when the injectors peg at 100 percent duty, but if the engine is equipped with a fuel management unit, keep in mind that an FMU will continue to increase the amount of fuel injected as long as boost

Powerhaus 968 turbo was designed to duplicate the "968 Turbo" Porsche coulda-shoulda-woulda built but never did, so of course it had to use Motronic controls. Powerhaus techs sorted through the 944T, 968, and Motronic parts bin to put together a slick package of turbo conversion parts for the 968 that followed the Porsche design philosophy. They then worked with Autothority to build a calibration for the 3.0-liter powerplant good for 400–500 horsepower with excellent streetability. Adapting the 944 Turbo's brain box to handle the larger 968 engine size and four-valve 968 breathing was a lot easier than attempting to retain the 968's normally aspirated Motronic ECM. Powerhaus' 968 Turbo package required some "special" parts—like the reworked Porsche manifold, throttlebody, and MAF sensor.

pressure increases by pumping up the fuel pressure to the wide-open fuel injectors.

Lack of complexity in the EMS's engine model and limited processor speed can cause blind spots. An EMS with insufficient resolution in the speed or loading tables may in effect be unable to distinguish between subtly different operating conditions that ideally require different engine management strategies. Does the EMS have the brains to correlate knock sensor data with detonation in specific cylinders to target countermeasures at the cylinders that need them and not the others? How much time—or how many degrees of crankshaft movement—does it take before the EMS can reexamine the state of engine sensors and execute new actions to affect what is happening in the powerplant?

Limp-home strategies: When an engine management system decides it has detected a serious problem such as a failed MAF, MAP, or TPS sensor, high levels of overboost, uncontrollable knock (or total lack of a knock sensor signal), or serious overheating (or lack of oil pressure!), the engine management strategy becomes one of keeping the engine operating in a way least likely to cause engine damage.

Engines equipped with MAP *and* MAF sensors can be run with excellent performance with one or the other having failed, and some turbo engines (like VW's 20-valve 1.8T) will tolerate more overboost without going into limp-home mode with one or the other disconnected (the MAF, in the case of the 1.8T). However, uncontrolled overboost, knock, or overheating is so dangerous to the health of an engine that the EMS will immediately do anything and everything it can think of to avoid engine damage.

Limp-home tactics may include the following:

- Turning on the check engine light (so the driver can help out)
- Defaulting questionable or failed sensors to "reasonable" safe values to keep sensors that have failed in exotic ways from instigating insanely dangerous engine management strategies
- Retarding timing the maximum amount to prevent or kill possible knock and limit performance while keeping the engine running
- Attempting to cool off combustion with rich air/fuel mixtures, radiator fans running at high speed, and so on
- Killing knock or preignition and limiting performance by injecting tons of fuel into the engine
- Limiting turbo boost to the maximum degree possible (for example, via dual-diaphragm wastegate)
- Closing secondary intake runners to limit intake airflow to minimize volumetric efficiency and performance
- Entering "camel mode," (in the case of some GM V-8s) in which coolant loss or overheating triggers the EMS to run on only four cylinders by switching off fuel and spark to four cylinders on alternate banks at intervals that optimize the ability of intake air to cool the resting bank to the maximum extent possible before the operating bank can be damaged by excessive heat
- Using rev-limiter-type fuel or ignition cut to limit engine speed below normal redline
- Kill the engine entirely

Naturally, you don't want any of this to happen just because the ECU is unhappy you have installed a turbo kit or pumped

85

up the boost too much on a powerplant that is otherwise fully capable of making serious power.

Overboosting: What is overboost and how does a factory EMS work to prevent it? Most turbocharged engines are equipped with calibrations that provide a good state of tune to the maximum all-out boost capacity of the turbocharger in case the wastegate system fails, and the fuel injectors will be sized such that the compressor chokes before the fuel injectors run out of capacity. It makes sense to provide plausible engine fuel and ignition mapping to the limits of the factory fuel injectors, which would typically be sized sufficiently large to provide optimal fuel to the airflow/boost limits of the stock turbocharger even though the wastegate should normally prevent the engine from boosting so high. This is because the engine can overboost if the wastegate manifold-pressure reference line is cut (melted, crushed, disconnected, and so on), and a "safe" calibration—even in forbidden overboost territory—is one more countermeasure designed to help avoid engine damage from lean mixtures if the engine does overboost if fuel cut strategies fail.

The first line of defense against overboost is typically the wastegate setting, which will bleed off exhaust gas pressure upstream of the turbocharger turbine inlet to limit turbo boost to safe "normal" levels, say 9 psi. The second line of defense will be a fuel cut when overboost reaches levels that could damage the engine if it were fueled with regular unleaded gasoline, say 12 psi. The last line of defense would be anti-knock/limp-home countermeasures described elsewhere in this book, which implement performance-killing timing retard and over-fueling (while there is still enough fuel capacity to produce excessively rich combustion-fooling mixtures) and limp-home breathing limitations (secondary ports close, and so on).

The fuel-cut tactic is implemented when airflow or MAP sensor data signals reach levels defined as overboost in the EMS configuration. This implies that every time the ECU looks at the current MAF/VAF or MAP data, it checks to see if airflow or boost exceeds the overboost threshold to see if the system should supply normal fueling or cut fuel as defined in a configurable (internal) parameter defining overboost. If the EMS detects overboost, it will set the overboost flag, which can only be cleared by turning off the engine (or, in some cases, by removing power from the ECU by temporarily removing a fuse or a battery terminal).

Outlaw tuners working with factory ECUs on overboosted turbo engines or turbo or supercharger conversions of normally aspirated powerplants typically work to disable the fuel cut using several possible methods:

1. Manual or electronic air bleeds and pressure regulators installed between the wastegate actuator diaphragm and the manifold pressure reference source enable a tuner to "lie" to the wastegate, causing the wastegate's mechanical controls to raise boost pressure (assuming the turbo compressor has the airflow capacity)—whether or not the factory EMS has any control over wastegate operation. Alternately, electronic PWM controllers dictate the duty cycle of an electronic valve to directly modulate manifold reference pressure (or by controlling the duty cycle of a valve controlling leakage through a bleed orifice in the reference line) in order to limit pressure seen at the wastegate, thus raising boost by delaying wastegate opening. Some factory and standalone aftermarket EMSs (like the Motec system used on several projects in this book) have this capability, controlled via internal tables that define target boost under a defined (and sometimes complex) set of conditions via PWM boost control solenoid. Pulse width–modulated solenoids flutter an electromagnetic valve open and closed at varying frequencies to limit airflow and pressure through the valve to produce a desired flow and pressure.

2. Electronic voltage clamp devices typically use variable-compressor (or resistor) circuits that truncate or transform the MAP or MAF signal on its way to the ECU, minimizing the signal to make sure the factory ECU never sees overboost when it happens. However, this tactic also means that during overboost, the factory ECU is calculating fuel and timing as if the engine were making less boost than it actually is. Not only is a voltage-clamped engine overboosting, it is being under-fueled. This mandates an auxiliary method of providing fuel enrichment during overboost to prevent engine damage via lean mixtures or too much spark advance.

3. Check valves can prevent positive manifold pressure from reaching a factory engine management system's MAP sensor. This is useful for systems like the factory Honda engine-control system used on two project vehicles in this book, which has the ability to measure almost 9-psi positive boost pressure despite the fact that the Honda engines being controlled with this ECU are universally normally aspirated factor stock. Unfortunately, Honda ECMs abhor boost and will complain and limp at anything over a pound or two of positive boost pressure. A one-way check valve and bleed allows negative manifold pressure (vacuum) up to atmospheric to reach the sensor. If the reference line from the intake manifold begins pushing positive boost pressure in the other direction on a turbo or blower conversion, the valve closes so the maximum pressure ever seen on the MAP sensor is atmospheric. The bleed is there to prevent vacuum or boost from being trapped in the reference line between the check valve and MAP sensor.

4. A disconnected MAF sensor is sufficient to prevent some ECUs from noticing overboost (for example, some VW 1.8Ts).

Increasing turbo boost and fueling enrichment: With a factory turbocharged vehicle, it is often a simple matter to increase the power output by increasing the maximum boost—which is possible if there is a way to raise the pressure at which the wastegate opens to stop any further increases in turbo boost pressure. A turbocharger increases torque about 8 percent per pound of turbo boost. An MR2 project produced massively increased power and torque at 16-psi boost versus the stock 7- to 9-psi maximum. Piggyback PWM electronic boost controllers (used on several projects in this book) provide a programmable method by which a tuner can overboost an engine to make more power.

A boost or valve controller fools the stock turbo wastegate by underreporting manifold pressure to the wastegate under electronic control. Equivalent mechanical means of increasing boost include mini regulators that restrict manifold pressure to the stock wastegate, adjustable pressure bleeds that leak boost pressure to prevent full manifold pressure from arriving at the wastegate actuator, increasing the diaphragm spring pressure of certain stock wastegates, and installing replacement wastegates or larger turbochargers. Many or even most factory turbochargers have excess airflow capacity that can be used with the above wastegate tricks.

When TRD developed a supercharger kit for the Scion tC engine space constraints were daunting. The intake manifold is behind the engine. The accessories are squeezed between the engine and the frame on the passenger side of the engine, leaving little space for a supercharger. The solution was a remotely-mounted centrifugal blower with a long drive shaft, and a tight 90-degree bend on the supercharger air inlet ducted to a relocated MAF sensor. Note the production version of the kit provides a molded air intake behind the blower. Basically a pretty simple kit, as these things go, though they don't scrimp on upgrade fuel injectors and a reflashed Toyota for supercharged engine management. According to rumors, despite being part of the Toyota family, TRD was initially forced to the expediency of hiring a Denso engineer to get them into the ECM, at which point Toyota—one of the least hot rod–friendly of all car companies, decided to provide supercharging calibrations for TRD supercharging packages for Toyota V6 and V8 trucks. The TRD calibration must be installed by a Toyota dealer as part of the TIS reflash system. *TRD*

Fuel bottlenecks: Methanol and ethanol (alcohols) have very high octane and better specific energy than gasoline and can be delivered by electronic injectors. The main engine management issue has to do with the large volume of fuel required in the case of E100 or neat methanol, since stoichiometric air/fuel ratios (9:1 and 6:1 for ethanol and methanol) are much lower for alcohols than gasoline, due to the fact that alcohols are partially oxygenated hydrocarbons. Alcohol fuels tend to be expensive, and you burn a lot because of the lower air/fuel ratios. But specific power is higher than gasoline because a given weight of air can burn more alcohol (remember, it's already partially oxygenated), and air tends to be scarce in a piston engine.

Nitromethane, which can actually combust as a mono-propellant in the complete absence of oxygen (the molecular structure is rearranged into more stabile forms, liberating heat), requires fuel in such copious quantities even when burned with oxygen that even gigantic 1,600 cc/min electronic injectors used for methanol injection are far too small for nitromethane, which requires multiple injectors or cylinders. IRL racers are currently running 98-percent ethanol and 2 percent gasoline, but in the past Indy cars have used mixtures of mostly methanol with nitro as a power-adder.

Nitro*propane* can be mixed with gasoline (nitromethane cannot), and a gasoline-nitropropane mixture might be electronically injected. However, nitropropane is too rare, expensive, and unavailable to be practical as an automotive fuel except under unusual circumstances in odd competition classes.

Methanol is a harsh compound that is corrosive to ordinary gasoline fuel components, which typically must be upgraded to stainless steel pipes and other components. Nevertheless, it is common practice to purge the fuel supply systems of methanol-fueled race cars after a race to protect injectors and other delicate components from being damaged. Neat methanol burns with a clear, invisible flame. It is a cold-blooded fuel that can be difficult to start in cold weather, requiring a gasoline mixture to fire up. Despite these disadvantages, methanol is a great racing fuel because it makes more power than gasoline, it has an extremely high octane rating, and it burns with a cool, smooth, even combustion that is easy on piston engines. A happy combination of electronic engine management, methanol, and high-performance turbochargers has enabled tiny 1.8-liter inline-4 engines to run at power levels above 900 horsepower in drag racing. Interestingly, O_2 sensors and wideband O_2 sensors work fine with alternate fuels like alcohols, because even though the target air/fuel ratios may be greatly different than gasoline, the target exhaust gas oxygen is quite similar.

Propane and natural gas, by the way, are not "high-powered" fuels, in that they make less power per pound of air combusted than gasoline, alcohols, or nitro fuels/ However, propane and natural gas are very clean burning (meaning they're street legal with almost no emissions devices), and they have extremely high octane ratings, so they are capable of making a lot of power with an adequately large turbocharger.

Since they're gases, propane and natural gas mix well with air. Older propane *carbs* (gas mixers, really) and intake manifolds do not have to deal with liquid-gas problems like gasoline-fuel engines, but the latest trick is *liquid* propane injection using special high-pressure port injectors that easily open against several hundred psi rail pressure (at 100 degrees Fahrenheit, the vapor pressure of propane is 177 psi).

Propane is commonly used as a power-adder for turbo-diesel engines (by combusting some of the air surplus). And for this purpose, electronic solenoids similar to nitrous-oxide solenoids have typically provided the required on-off constant-flow functionality required, though the relatively new PWM electronic injectors mentioned can be used to inject liquid propane into a diesel in a more sophisticated strategy that provides proportional propane injection.

Street diesel engines are now universally managed with computers, which control turbo boost, fuel pressure, and even electronic diesel throttles and multiple (pilot) injection events per engine cycle that help reduce emissions and noise.

Nitrous injection maintains its longtime reputation as an easy and effective power-adder on the most modern OBD-II engines, the only real downside being the limited life of a tankful of nitrous and the fact that it can cost $100 to fill a 20-pound tank that will provide two or three minutes of full-throttle boost.

ENGINE DESIGN CONSIDERATIONS AND THE JOB OF EFI ENGINE MANAGEMENT

Spark timing and advance have a large impact on the efficiency and exhaust emissions of an engine. As an engine turns faster, the spark plug must fire earlier in the compression stroke in degrees before top dead center (BTDC) in order to allow time for the mixture to ignite, achieve a high burn rate, and build maximum cylinder pressure by the time the piston is positioned to produce best torque at roughly 15 degrees past top dead center. Rpm does not affect the time required to burn the charge mixture for a given air/fuel ratio, but the time required for combustion takes place over more degrees of crankshaft rotation at higher engine speeds, which requires that the spark be further advanced in degrees BTDC. Rpm spark advance was accomplished in the days of mechanical engine management using a centrifugal advance mechanism in the distributor that phased the distributor cam that pushed open breaker points in relation to the distributor shaft by action of a set of spring-loaded rotating weights such that the points were pushed open further in advance of TDC (in crankshaft degrees) as rpm increased.

Another second (independent) factor affecting optimal spark timing is the need to modify ignition timing to account for the effect of engine loading combustion speed. This is due to the effect of throttle position on cylinder filling and corresponding variations in the optimal air/fuel mixture and the effect of MAP on cylinder pressure during the ignition and burn process. A denser combustion mixture burns more quickly, and a leaner mixture requires more time to burn (two independent variables). In the days of mechanical engine management, manifold-pressure advance/retard was handled using a spring-loaded vacuum canister attached to a metal rod that progressively retarded spark advance with increased manifold pressure by rotating the points breaker plate, making vacuum advance independent of centrifugal advance. Many carburetors have special ports for timing spark that deliver full manifold pressure reference at all speeds except idle, at which time the port source is covered by the throttle plate. Referencing a distributor vacuum advance canister to this special port did not produce any vacuum advance at idle (but did produce a surge of advance [and power] as the throttle opened).

Some engines have been designed with suboptimal spark advance as an anti-emissions strategy. One tactic was to retard ignition timing at idle, in some cases locking out vacuum advance in lower gears or during normal operating temperature while allowing more advance if the engine was cold or overheating.

Another hot rod Honda S2000, this one with the Comptech supercharger package. The fact that all post-1996 U.S. market vehicles had to have OBD-II capabilities, and given that the possibility of an emissions-related recall is a lot less expensive if you've got reflash capability, the U.S. government effectively established the infrastructure for late-model EFI hot rodding via stock ECM reflash.

Since oxides of nitrogen are formed when free nitrogen combines with oxygen at high temperature and pressure, retarding spark reduces NOx emissions by lowering peak combustion temperature and pressure at the expense of increased EGT. This strategy also reduces hydrocarbon emissions. But retarded-spark combustion is less efficient, lowering fuel economy and increasing thermal loading of engine coolant as heat energy escapes through the cylinder walls into the cooling jacket. The cooling system is stressed as it struggles to remove the greater waste heat during retarded spark conditions. Fuel economy is hurt since some of the fuel is still burning as it blows out the exhaust valve, necessitating richer idle and off-idle AFR to get decent off-idle performance. If the mixture becomes too lean, higher combustion temperatures will defeat the purpose of ignition retard, producing more NOx. Combustion inefficiency under such conditions also requires the throttle to be held open farther for a reasonable idle speed, which, combined with the

higher operating temperatures, could lead to dieseling with carbureted engines where fuel delivery did not require electricity (not a problem on fuel-injected engines that immediately terminate injection when the key is switched off). By removing pollutants from exhaust gas, three-way catalysts tend to allow more ignition advance at idle and part throttle.

Valve timing has a large effect on the speeds at which an engine develops its best power and torque. Adding more lift and intake and exhaust valve opening overlap allows the engine to breathe more efficiently at high speeds. However, the engine may be hard to start, idle poorly, bog on off-idle acceleration, and produce poor low-speed torque.

This occurs for several reasons. At low speeds, increased valve overlap allows some exhaust gases still in the cylinder at higher than atmospheric pressure to rush into the intake manifold, diluting the inlet charge exactly like EGR. This dilution continues to occur until rpm increases to the point

HOT RODDING FORD'S MPI

The Ford 221/260/289/302 arrived on the scene in the early 1960s, and, like the small-block Chevy, the Ford Windsor was built in enormous numbers. The MPI 5.0 is the system Ford used on 1985–93 Mustangs and some Explorers and trucks into the later 1990s. The MPI 5.0, like Chevy's TPI system, will retrofit to older Windsor V-8s.

In order to get the pushrod 5.0-liter Ford V-8 air metering to work properly in low-range airflow, Ford restricted the high end, which created a market niche for companies like Professional Flow Tech, which built performance MAF meters. The Pro-M MAF line uses patented aerodynamics that used resonation effects to get excellent metering at low airflow while handling 1,000 or more cfm on the high end. This translates to a bolt-on 15–20 horsepower on the 5.0-liter engine. The Pro-M 77 was assigned to work on any MAF EEC-IV engine, including the Mustang, the Supercoupe, and the SHO Taurus. Professional Flow Tech designed a system for Ford speed-density EFI trucks that converted the system to Mustang high-output programming, including a high-performance MAF.

Many of the same principles that apply still to GM TPI also apply to the Ford 5.0 system, which was designed to make good low-end and midrange torque. And, like the TPI systems, many parts are available to pump your 5.0: high-performance upper- and lower-intake manifold pairs and iron and aluminum heads, which will increase the breathing of a 5.0. Other common mods on Mustang 5.0s include cams; high-flow mass air kits; Pro-M 77-mm complete conversion kits (with wiring, computer, and 77-mm sensor); SVO complete mass air conversions; 65- and 75-mm throttle bodies; 24- and 30-pound injectors; adjustable pressure regulators; the Crane Interceptor; shorty headers; cat back exhaust systems; and high-volume fuel pumps. There are still turbocharger and supercharger kits for the Mustang, some of which are even street legal in California. Most of these kits use add-on fuel pressure regulators that massively increase fuel pressure under boost to provide adequate fueling and enrichment.

The problem in modifying Ford 5.0 engines is that maximum horsepower is limited by the stock injection components: The 19 pound per hour stock injectors can make 300 horsepower at 45 psi. The stock fuel pump will supply sufficient fuel for 300 horsepower at 45 psi, and the stock MAF meter will supply air (and voltage signal to the EEC-IV) for about 310 horsepower. The limit with stock EFI components is roughly 300 horsepower. Any strategy to increase power levels above this must address these limitations.

EEC-IV PROMs are not replaceable, but there are systems that use a performance module inserted between the EEC-IV and the wiring harness to alter the performance of the OEM computer, while other devices reprogram the EEC-IV by plugging into the diagnostic port.

---

where the overlap interval is so short in time that reverse pulsing becomes insignificant. The charge dilution of reversion tends to make an engine idle badly.

Valve overlap also hurts idle and low-speed performance by lowering manifold vacuum, which can cause problems on engines with carbs or throttle body injection. Since the lower atmospheric pressure of high vacuum tends to keep gasoline vaporized better, racing cams with low vacuum may have distribution problems on engines with wet intake manifolds and a wandering air/fuel mixture. This, again, may require an overall richer mixture to keep the motor from stalling. Changed or wandering vacuum will affect OEM speed-density fuel-injection systems but would have less effect on MAF-sensed engine management unless excessive pulsing and turbulence interferes with the MAF's ability to accurately read airflow.

Intake air temperature affects fuel injection because colder air is denser than hotter air, colder air inhibits fuel vaporization, and colder intake air lowers combustion temperature. Engine management systems virtually always have sensors to read the temperature of inlet air and adjust the pulse width of injection to compensate. Engines make noticeably more power on a cold day because the cold, dense air charges the cylinders with more molecules of air. Carburetors, unfortunately, have no ability to self-compensate for air density changes, the only means of compensation being mixture screws and jet changes (one size per 40-degree temperature change).

As you'd expect, racing automotive engine designers always endeavor to keep inlet air as cold as possible, and modern street cars universally make use of cold air inlets, since each 11 degrees Fahrenheit of air temperature increase reduces air density 1 percent. On the other hand, gasoline does not vaporize well in cold air. In fact, oil companies change gasoline formulation in cold weather to increase vapor pressure. In the days of carbureted engines, this could cause a rash of vapor lock in sudden winter warm spells. Vapor lock, however, is rare on injected engines, though it is not unheard of to get vapor bubbles in the fuel supply system, particularly if there is pressure drop caused by a bottleneck.

EFI cold-start fuel enrichment systems are designed to produce a rich enough mixture to run the vehicle even when much of the fuel exists as drops of nonflammable liquid fuel suspended in the air or clinging to the intake manifold runner walls rather than burnable vapor mixed with air. Most air pollution is produced by cold vehicles burning cranking mixtures as rich as 3 or 4:1 (even 1:1 during cranking!). Electronic fuel-injection systems sense coolant temperature in order to provide cold start enrichments (cranking, after start, and warm-up). Port EFI systems usually inject fuel straight at the heated intake valve and into the swirling, turbulent high-velocity air in that vicinity, which greatly improves atomization and vaporization. EFI does not normally need the exhaust gas heating that carbs require to provide acceptable cold-start operation. EFI manifolds may use coolant heating to increase vaporization at idle in very cold weather.

Air density varies with temperature, altitude, and weather conditions. Hot air, with greater molecular motion, is less dense for a given pressure. Air at higher elevations is less dense, as is air with higher relative humidity. Air is less dense in warm weather, but air that is heated for any reason on the way into the engine becomes less dense and will affect the injection pulse width required to achieve the correct air/fuel ratio. Intake system layout can have a great effect on the volumetric efficiency of the engine by affecting the density of the air the engine is breathing.

Air cleaners that ingest hot engine-compartment air will reduce the engine's output and should be modified to breathe fresh, cold air from outside. Intake manifolds that heat the air will deliver less dense air into the cylinders, although a properly designed heated intake manifold will quickly be cooled by intake air at high speed and can improve distribution at part throttle and idle when hot.

High compression ratios squash the inlet air/fuel mixture into a more compact, dense mass, resulting in a faster burn rate.

BEGi's twin-screw supercharging system really cranked up the power on the BMW 318 inline-4. Note the BEGi Variable-Rate-of-Gain fuel pressure regulator (next to the air cleaner). This type of Fuel Management Unit installs downstream of the OE fuel pressure regulator, and pinches off fuel return flow during boost to increase fuel pressure as a multiple of boost pressure to deliver correct fueling. Not all FMUs are user-adjustable, but BEGi's allows you to adjust both the onset pressure threshold (anywhere from slight vacuum to several pounds of boost pressure) and the rate of gain from about 4-7 psi per pound increase in boost pressure. Stock engine management is unaffected during non-boosted operations. Because increased power requires fuel and higher fuel pressure reduces fuel pump flow capacity, it is common to upgrade the fuel supply system when using an FMU.

Turbochargers and superchargers produce effective compression ratios far above the nominal compression ratio by pumping additional mixture into the cylinder under pressure. Either way, the result is a denser mass of air and fuel molecules that burn faster and produce more pressure against the piston. High peak pressures produce more heat and tend to produce more NOx pollutants.

Lower static compression ratios (typical of many forced-induction engines) raise the fuel requirements at idle because there is more clearance volume in the combustion chamber that dilutes the intake charge. Because fuel is still burning longer as the piston descends, lower compression ratios raise the exhaust temperature and increase stress on the cooling system.

Until 1970, high-performance cars often had compression ratios of up to 11 or 12 :1, safely accommodated with the vintage gasolines readily available in those days with octane as high as 100 ((R+M)/2). By 1972, most engines were running compression ratios with 8 to 8.5:1 compression ratios. In the 1980s, 1990s,

and beyond, street compression ratios in computer-controlled fuel-injected vehicles were in the 9.5 to 11.0:1 range based on fuel injection's ability to support higher compression ratios without detonation coupled with precise air/fuel control and catalysts that are able to keep emissions low.

Higher compression ratios (or effective compression ratios) demand higher octane fuel and other anti-knock countermeasures to prevent detonation, which at worst case can shatter pistons and rings. Prior to 1984–1995, many high-octane gasolines contained the additive tetra-ethyl lead to slow down gasoline's tendency to explode as combustion pressures and temperatures rise. Environmental concerns caused Congress to outlaw leaded street gasoline by the end of 1995, completing an 11-year phase-out in favor of unleaded gasoline requirements in street cars. Precisely controlled mixtures in all cylinders via port fuel injection are a key tactic in avoiding lean cylinders with increased tendency to knock.

Chapter 6
Hot Rodding Electronic Diesel Engines

Diesel powerplants are a special case for engine management because compression-ignition combustion is so different from that of a spark-ignition engine. In fact, the most problematic aspects of spark-ignition turbo engine management are not even a factor with turbocharged diesels. This includes detonation boost limits, precise air-fuel ratio control, narrow rich and lean flammability limits, air famines or shortages, overboosting issues, and so forth. Exhaust emissions are as much or more of an issue for modern diesels as gasoline engines, but diesel engines emit a different mix of exhaust gases and particles and require different emissions control strategies. Turbocharging improves all aspects of diesel performance, which is why all U.S.-market diesel vehicles built since 1998 are now turbodiesels.

It gets even better when you focus on diesel *hot rodding*. Compared to gasoline engines, the mechanical systems of light truck diesel powerplants that currently comprise most of the noncommercial road-going diesel fleet in the United States are typically much less of a constraint when it comes to boosting performance. Diesel engines routinely tolerate substantial power enhancements and manifold boost pressure increases that would be considered radical on spark-ignition engines. Diesel powerplants—with or without turbochargers—are compatible with nitrous or propane-injection power-adder systems.

Diesel powerplants are unique compared to the vast majority of spark-ignition engines in that every diesel vehicle manufactured since 1994 for the American market is already turbocharged. When done right, turbocharging a diesel powerplant not only adds power but also makes the engine run cleaner than stock, which is the most important reason why new U.S. diesels are turbocharged.

The newest American diesel engines are now universally equipped with sophisticated electronic fuel injection that is similar in concept to the port-EFI found on all 1987 and newer gasoline-fueled American cars—except for the fact that diesel injection sprays fuel directly into the combustion chamber at pressures that may exceed 24,000 psi, which is roughly 500 times higher than ordinary gasoline port-EFI fuel pressure. Diesel injection pressure is now so high that careless mechanics have had diesel fuel injected subcutaneously into their flesh when they pulled a diesel injector out of the head and cranked the engine to verify operation. In fact, 25,000 psi approaches the pressure required to cut metal with water. Such pressure will get the fuel into a cylinder *very* fast, with incredibly good atomization (which is the whole idea). Electronic diesel control (EDC) has facilitated diesel engines with unprecedented levels of power and low exhaust emissions, but the electronic injection systems suitable for operating at such extreme pressures do not come cheap: The diesel injection system and electronic controls now constitute 30 to 40 percent of the cost of a modern diesel powerplant.

Edge hot rod diesel pickups at the drag races. With the arrival of modern common-rail diesel injection systems in the early years of the new millennium, electronic tricks alone can easily add 50-100 horsepower to most full-size U.S.-market light trucks with Duramax, Cummins, or Powerstroke engines via additional fuel and overboosting to maintain the air surplus needed to cool down combustion. For maximum power while retaining factory reliability under heavy loading, other VE-improving parts and transmission upgrades will be required. *Edge Products*

The good news for performance enthusiasts is that the widespread deployment of turbochargers and electronic diesel control (EDC) in the 1990s to boost clean power and precisely manage pre-injection, injection timing, fuel pressure, rate of injection, and boost pressure on modern road-going diesels has provided unprecedented opportunities to easily hot rod diesel engines to unprecedented or even radical levels of power and torque.

DIESEL AND TURBO-DIESEL ENGINE MANAGEMENT

From both factory-engineering and aftermarket-hot rodding points of view, there are major benefits to the powerful but expensive common-rail electronic diesel injection and control systems that became universal on all late-model U.S.-market diesel powerplants in the early years of the 21st century. Common-rail diesel injection systems are superior to other systems because they permit the use of ultra-high injection pressure at any engine speed and provide the ability to "shape" fuel delivery over time during a particular injection cycle using pulsewidth-modulation (PWM) techniques capable of delivering multiple injection events to each cylinder during the compression and power stroke that effectively vary the amplitude of the injection fuel flow *over time* as a series of micro-bursts separated by as little a 7/10,000th of a second. Not all electronic diesel control systems use common-rail technology, but all do use PWM electronic injectors to provide precise injection management under computer control.

Previous mechanical-diesel injection systems were much less accurate. Mechanical diesel injection systems deterministically regulate engine speed and power via changes in fuel injection quantity, which varies as a simple function of (1) *pressure from the fuel pump,* which increases with engine rpm on such systems until the fuel pressure regulator prevents any further increase, and (2) *fuel throttle position*, which determines the length of time fuel can flow to individual injectors. Fuel injection to each cylinder on mechanical diesel systems occurs in a single pulse, which tends to be sub-optimally rich at start-of-injection and sub-optimally lean toward the end-of-the-injection event, producing undesirable noise early in combustion and sooty exhaust later on, due to sub-optimal burn efficiency. Vintage mechanical diesel injection systems required (mechanical) governing systems to prevent seriously over-speeding an engine when it was lightly loaded.

Like mechanical diesel injection systems, common-rail EDC systems throttle fuel delivery as a function of two variables: (1) Under computer control, common-rail systems precisely modulate *fuel pressure* independently of engine rpm to a common fuel plenum or "rail," which simultaneously feeds all the fuel injectors. (2) Common-rail systems then sequentially modulate the length of time injectors stay open to fuel individual cylinders. Normal common rail fuel pressure typically varies from 280 bar (4,000 psi) to 1,600 bar (24,000 psi), though when the electronic controller commands it, some systems are capable of delivering even higher pressures extreme enough to potentially damage injection components.

Benefits of EDC/common-rail systems include:

- Computer management of (1) diesel injection, (2) PWM wastegate controller, and (3) other actuators based on electronic sensor input data crunched on by software logic driven by internal tables of calibration data, providing the capability to implement highly complex engine management strategies tailored to react precisely to subtle changes in engine status for low emissions and excellent fuel economy.
- EDC thus provides the potential for tuners and hot rodders to modify parameters like fuel delivery, injection timing, and boost pressure in order to unleash more power by uploading calibration changes from a laptop computer to the electronic control unit's flash memory or PROM, or by installing intercepting piggyback microcomputers that modify input or output signals to the EDC system to create a false "virtual-reality" bubble around it that changes engine management in the desired ways for increased performance.
- PWM injection techniques can reduce direct-injection combustion noise to spark-ignition levels with a tiny "pilot injection" of fuel just ahead of the main injection event, making less-efficient, indirect-injection diesel powerplant designs obsolete for controlling noise, and making diesel engines more acceptable for applications where low noise, vibration, and harshness are critical.
- Common-rail systems can deliver ultra-high-pressure direct injection at any engine rpm, which reduces fuel consumption 30 percent and increases power 40 percent over indirect injection—mainly via smaller micro fuel droplet size and more uniform in-chamber fuel distribution.
- PWM post-injections can be used to reduce soot emissions.
- PWM injection techniques can also be used to spool a turbocharger more quickly via momentary increased exhaust gas temperatures from fuel enrichment.

Banks race truck on the chassis dyno. For road racing, this hot rod Duramax engine must maintain extreme levels of power on an ongoing, sometimes continuous basis. Electronic diesel engines require dyno calibrating, too, and the ECM manages diesel injection pressure, injection timing, injection pulsewidth, and boost pressure. *Banks Power*

- Common-rail EDC controls make it relatively simple to adapt diesel engine management to large increases in boost from larger turbochargers.

HOT RODDING TURBODIESELS

There are several strategies for dramatically increasing the performance of a diesel powerplant and all are feasible for use on diesel and turbodiesel trucks, cars, tractors, and industrial equipment to increase torque when the engine is under load. These include

1. Installing propane injection
2. Over-fueling (and frequently overboosting) the engine
3. Installing a turbo conversion package if the engine is an (older) normal-charged diesel
4. Installing nitrous oxide injection on a rich-running diesel or along with some variety of over-fueling or auxiliary fuel strategy.

Any of these can seriously amp up a diesel's power and torque.

Propane Injection

The old-fashioned way to hot rod mechanical-injection diesels is to regulate a controlled flow of gaseous propane into the inlet airstream using a propane carb or "mixer." Whether or not a diesel engine is turbocharged, propane injection provides a way of burning up some of the air surplus of typical diesel combustion without producing black smoke. Propane injection can make a lot of power if there is sufficient surplus air. If there is not surplus air, propane injection will do nothing good at all.

Propane is useful as an auxiliary fuel for boosting diesel combustion energy because it has the highest auto-ignition temperature of any common motor fuel (1,004 degrees Fahrenheit, versus 851 degrees for methanol, 495 degrees for gasoline, and 410 degrees for diesel fuel itself). When injected sparsely into the air stream to produce a weak air-fuel mixture that's less than 10 percent propane (and thus beyond lean *continued on page 96*

continued on page 96

THE SCOPE OF DIESEL VS. SPARK-IGNITION HOT RODDING

Unlike a spark-ignition engine, where the maximum energy potential of a particular combustion event is determined the instant the intake valve closes to trap a certain amount of charge air in the combustion chamber, the energy resulting from a modern diesel combustion is rarely limited by either the volumetric efficiency of the engine or the requirement for a particular air-fuel ratio.

Spark-ignition powerplants must be charged with a homogenous mixture that is within the rather narrow range of air-fuel ratios that will sustain an excellent, high-speed flame front. Getting the air-fuel ratio and mixture distribution perfect for a spark-ignition engine is not trivial, especially during transitional performance as the throttle opens and closes to adjust engine speed and power output by modifying the volumetric efficiency of the intake-stroke airflow. Once a certain amount of charge mixture is trapped in a cylinder of a spark-ignition engine, it is compressed by piston movement and subsequently lit off with an electrical spark delivered at one location in the combustion chamber (OK, a few engines have more than one spark plug per cylinder). At this point, a three-dimensional flame front burns away from the plug in all directions through the compressed charge gases, similar to a fire burning its way through a field of dry grass on a still day. Unfortunately, the high effective compression ratios that produce high thermal and volumetric efficiency in a super-high-output spark-ignition engine (maximum of about 15:1 on methanol or racing gasoline) are effective precisely because they produce hotter, denser charge mixtures. As combustion proceeds in a high-performance spark-ignition engine, the trick is always to keep large pockets of unburned air-fuel mixture from exploding all at once if temperature and pressure skyrocket to levels that exceed the auto-ignition threshold of the fuel. High-octane fuels are specifically designed to resist compression ignition, which produces extreme spikes of pressure and severe shock waves in a spark-ignition engine that can damage mechanical engine components if significant pockets of charge mixture suddenly pre-ignite or detonate.

Diesel engines, on the other hand, ingest pure air and intentionally heat it with ultra-high static compression ratios in the range of 15 to 25:1 to temperatures hot enough to effortlessly auto-ignite diesel fuel, which is formulated specifically with a high cetane rating to ensure fast auto-ignition at low temperatures. Such high compression ratios have the happy side effect of delivering superior thermal efficiency to that of spark-ignition gasoline engines. Diesel combustion commences immediately with start of injection as a jet of extreme-pressure fuel bursts into the combustion chamber at up to 24,000 psi, crashing into the burning-hot compressed air and immediately shearing into microscopic droplets that burst into flames almost instantly. Unlike spark-ignition combustion, there is no diesel flame front as such: Individual diesel molecules spontaneously burst into flames wherever they encounter high-temperature free oxygen as they streak through the combustion chamber at tremendous speed. In diesel combustion, there is no widespread flame front but instead a micro "flame front" around the periphery of each tiny diesel droplet, with the vaporous boundary layer of fuel burning progressively and peeling off like the skin of an onion as droplets blow through the combustion chamber and are gradually reduced by flames.

Since diesels ingest pure air on the intake stroke and diesel fuel burns as fast as it is injected into the combustion chamber at the top of the compression stroke, there is normally no possibility of large air-fuel detonations of the type that can damage spark ignition engines. "Diesel knock" actually can occur in the case of early injection timing or an inappropriately high volume of propane injection.

That said, it does take a finite time for diesel fuel molecules to heat up to the auto-ignition temperature and combust, and this tiny delay is longer at the beginning of injection when the cylinder is relatively cool and the air charge has mostly been heated by compression. Because the injection event itself and subsequent combustion take a finite time to unfold, start-of-injection must begin in time for cylinder pressure to rise and peak at about 14 degrees after top dead center in the power stroke—exactly like a spark-ignition engine. In the real world, early diesel combustion may tend to lag slightly and then proceed ferociously as the cylinder heats, which produces the characteristic noisy diesel "clatter" but is not true detonation.

In the past, to reduce combustion noise (when it was an issue, particularly on diesel automobiles) some normal-charged diesel cars and light trucks were equipped with indirect-injection diesel powerplants. Indirect-injection engines inject the fuel into a special pre-chamber partially walled off from the main combustion chamber, from which the burning combustion gases blow into the main chamber, resulting in quieter operation at the expense of some reduced power and fuel efficiency. With the arrival and flexibility of "common-rail" electronic diesel injection, engineers discovered that a tiny "pilot injection" of fuel immediately before the main injection pulse will preheat and condition the combustion chamber in a way that modulates the otherwise noisy pressure spike of combustion that inevitably otherwise occurs with regular direct injection, particularly at idle, resulting in direct-injection diesel engines that are now virtually as quiet as gasoline powerplants.

As discussed elsewhere, the correct air-fuel ratio is extremely critical in spark-ignition engines, where a wave of combustion must travel through the spark-ignition charge mixture at tremendous speed, burning, heating, and igniting successive fuel as it proceeds. For full-power combustion, and as an anti-knock countermeasure, particularly when turbocharged, conventional gasoline-fueled piston engines require an air-fuel ratio that stays within about 7 percent of the mean best torque (MBT) air-fuel ratio of 12.4:1 (0.85 lambda). Too much boost pressure and too little fuel will quickly detonate a spark-ignition engine to death.

Not so diesels. The chemically perfect stoichiometric air-fuel ratio for diesel combustion is roughly the same as gasoline's (15:1), but with no requirement to sustain a continuous flame front in compression-ignition combustion, diesel powerplants will operate cleaner, cooler, and better with large air surpluses, typically idling with air-fuel ratios as lean as 60-1. Ultimately, diesel lean flammability limits are approximately .3 percent of the charge air by volume. On the rich side, although diesel fuel actually oxidizes with an air-fuel mass ratio nearly identical to the ratio of gasoline (15:1 versus gasoline's 14.65:1), there are various operative factors that virtually mandate modern turbo-diesel engines run with a large air-surplus all the time. Although the rich flammability limit of diesel combustion is a tremendous 10 percent of charge air by volume (again, no need for an efficient flame front), air-diesel ratios richer than 22-25:1 (about a 50 percent air surplus) produce undesirably high combustion temperatures, soot, smoke, and poor fuel economy and are almost never used in turbocharged diesels except in some classes of tractor-pulling largely for the entertainment value of a dramatic plume of thick black smoke blasting out the exhaust when the engine is really working. Normal-charged diesels designed for operation at sea level are usually tuned to deliver about 18:1 air-fuel ratios for full power without smoking, but must be de-fueled to lower power at sea level if they will be operated above 1,000 feet elevation to keep them from smoking at altitude. And diesel smoke is bad: Besides polluting the atmosphere, diesel smoke works its way past rings to increase the rate of oil contamination, which slowly neutralizes oil critical additives and causes the engine to wear faster.

As diesel engine research and development proceeded in the early years of the automotive age, it quickly became obvious that the large air-fuel-ratio flexibility of compression-ignition combustion completely removed the need for an air throttle butterfly of the type that was required on all spark-ignition engines to regulate engine speed and loading through changes to engine volumetric efficiency. True, the earliest diesel engines used highly compressed air to force diesel fuel into the cylinders, and were relatively constant speed devices that were too heavy and large to be suitable for anything other than stationary use or as ship engines (requiring, as they did, huge heavy injection pumps, complete with powerful air compressors and storage tanks). But by the time Bosch developed a mechanical high-pressure diesel injection pump in 1927 that was durable, compact, and lightweight enough for trucks, buses, and heavy aircraft, it was already clear that engine rpm and power delivery for lighter road-going vehicles with "high-speed" diesel engines could easily be regulated simply by throttling the quantity of injected fuel. Subsequent fuel pump size reductions facilitated the first practical diesel cars of the mid-1930s.

For the next 60 years or so, the air-fuel ratio and combustion pressure flexibility of compression-ignition allowed diesel engines to get by entirely with crude mechanical engine management that had little or no ability to adapt as temperature, altitude, or other environmental and engine conditions changed. These vintage diesel engines required no electricity whatsoever once the engine was running, and—fitted with an inlet air snorkel—these engines could, and actually did, run underwater. To optimize the power from a particular displacement engine, older normal-charged mechanical diesel powerplants had to be fueled as rich as possible (usually about 18:1 AFR) up to the point on the lean side of stoichiometric combustion at which the engine began emitting "excessive" amounts of visible smoke (plus a little lean margin to prevent extreme smoking if the vehicle moved to higher altitudes). As air-fuel ratios richen, normal-charged diesels reach the smoke limit and 1,300-degree maximum exhaust gas temperature at about the same time. In the old days, power junkies who weren't too fastidious about dumping black smoke out of the exhaust stacks of their diesel truck onto cars following them up a long hill could and did tweak the injection pump richer to make power—at the cost of questionable peak EGT.

Running a diesel engine of any vintage rich of stoichiometric is not normally feasible due to the massive amounts of smoke generated, but fattening up diesel injection from lean mixtures in the direction of stoichiometric combustion will definitely make power (and eventually smoke). Again, richer mixtures also have the unfortunate side effect of *raising* EGT, a fact that is counter-intuitive to most spark-ignition hot rodders. In the case of diesels, since an increasing proportion of charge air is involved in combustion as you add fuel to make power (and heat), there's less surplus air available to moderate combustion temperatures, something that is analogous to using exhaust gas recirculation to cool combustion on gasoline-fueled engines. Of course, horsepower is God, and in the younger America of the 20th century, smoking diesels were a common sight until various government agencies began cracking down on diesel air pollution.

People began working to turbocharge compression-ignition engines within a few years of Rudolf Diesel successfully demonstrating the first workable prototype compression-ignition powerplant in 1897. Turbocharger inventor Alfred Buchi focused his early efforts exclusively on building a practical turbodiesel (which, of course, required a practical turbocharger first). In the early days of the automotive age, diesel combustion had the tremendous advantage for primitive early turbos (equipped with turbines constrained by the markedly inferior metallurgy of the time) that compression-ignition combustion produces exhaust gas temperatures hundreds of degrees cooler than gasoline-fueled spark-ignition powerplants. Not only are diesel engines easier on turbochargers, but turbochargers return the favor: If there is a turbocharger installed on a diesel powerplant, it is simple to pack plenty of surplus air into the cylinders in order to (1) banish the smoking that would otherwise occur when air starts to get scarce, (2) *lower EGT,* and (3) potentially make power.

Diesel engines are more efficient than gasoline-fueled spark ignition powerplants for a number of reasons:

Diesels run high static compression ratios, and the forced induction of a turbocharger makes the *effective* compression ratio even higher, which results in improved thermal efficiency on any four-cycle engine.

Compared to many gasoline-fueled truck engines, modern diesel powerplants gain pumping efficiencies from the use of four-valve combustion chambers that have become ubiquitous on all late-model U.S.-market diesels (cost-justified by the fact that a four-valve layout allows the fuel injectors to be located centrally above the combustion chamber, which improves combustion and emissions).

Diesels have better pumping efficiency compared to spark-ignition engines on the intake stroke because diesels do not require a throttle, so there is never any manifold vacuum in a diesel engine and minimal pumping losses on the intake stroke.

The lack of a throttle means there is no engine braking when you let off the throttle, but it also means there's nothing in the way to stall a turbocharger compressor or impede it from stuffing the cylinders full of boost, so it's easier for a diesel to run more boost more of the time.

If a diesel engine is turbocharged (and all newer ones in the United States are), the engine gets a free ride during the intake stroke when positive turbo boost pressure helps push down the pistons on the intake stroke, with the turbine reclaiming waste energy from hot exhaust gases and putting it back into the crankshaft. Note that diesel engines tend to have *lower* exhaust energy than spark-ignition engines due to lower EGT, which typically necessitates smaller turbine nozzles to recover the required energy to drive the turbocharger's compressor.

Because diesels normally run a large air surplus, have no critical air-fuel ratio, and do not have to sustain a flame front like a spark-ignition engine, fuel injection can continue far into the power stroke, which can *massively* increase torque by delivering more piston downforce as the crankpin moves sideways to give the rod increasing leverage converting cylinder pressure into torque in the crankshaft.

Blowing all exhaust through a certain turbine nozzle area represents the majority of pumping losses in a modern turbodiesel, but since 80 percent of the energy to drive a turbine comes from waste exhaust heat rather than exhaust pressure, exhaust backpressure on a well-designed turbo system can be surprisingly low (under ideal circumstances lower than intake manifold pressure). Many turbodiesels are now equipped with efficient variable turbine geometry (VTG) turbochargers, which are installed to harness the comparatively weak exhaust energy of a diesel engine at low rpm for rapid spooling to reduce emissions by maintaining a good air surplus on sudden application of throttle, yet adapt to minimize pumping efficiency losses through the turbine when the engine is operating at higher rpm and engine loading.

Unlike spark-ignition engines, which throttle the engine air supply and therefore compress only a partial charge of air except during full-throttle operations, diesel engines are always compressing a high-VE charge of air. Not only are diesel engines compressing a dense charge under all circumstances, but compression-ignition combustion requires and permits very high compression ratios that can heat charge air to temperatures as high as 1,400 degrees. Turbo-diesel combustion thus requires a high level of force to compress a certain density of charge. Fortunately, the compression event also provides almost as much bonus "rebound" during the power stroke—a little like compressing a spring to "charge" it with potential energy that is then recovered when the spring exerts force to expand. Of course, the rebound energy is in addition to the energy from combustion.

Even the fastest-turning modern "high-speed" diesel powerplants are severely limited in operating range compared to state-of-the-art four-stroke spark-ignition powerplants (which currently redline at engine speeds of nearly 20,000 rpm in 2.4L Formula One racers and nearly as high on high-tech street motorcycles like the Yamaha YZF-R6). Diesels have a narrower operating range than most modern gasoline powerplants, with

THE SCOPE OF DIESEL VS. SPARK-IGNITION HOT RODDING, continued

the peak torque of many diesels arriving in the 1,750–2,000 rpm range. Most diesels redline below 4,000 rpm, with fast-turning experimental diesels running at an engine rpm of less than about 5,500 rpm. In fact, watching a super-high-output turbodiesel vehicle make a chassis dyno pull can be a bit like watching an Olympic weightlifter making a "snatch" power lift: Diesel torque rips from negligible to humongous so quickly and in such a narrow rpm range that it seems over before it's even started. The narrow powerband is why big-rig diesels have so many gears.

But why are diesels so rpm-limited? The reduced diesel redline results from a combination of two factors: (1) heavy reciprocating parts and (2) innate time constraints imposed on diesel injection and combustion that require the entire fuel portion of the charge to be injected directly into the cylinders and burned to peak pressure within a maximum of about 44 crankshaft degrees versus the constant 720 degrees available for injection on a port-injected four-stroke spark-ignition powerplant. At 6,000 rpm, the diesel injection window shrinks to less than 1.2 milliseconds or 12/10,000ths of a second—which is one reason you never see 6,000-rpm diesels, and why you do see 24,000-psi injection these days on "high-speed" diesels. With respect to engine speed, turbocharging has the beneficial effect of increasing the burn rate of diesel combustion. In some cases this can require that start-of-injection timing be delayed during high boost to optimize torque, exactly as ignition is on a turbocharged spark-ignition engine (only less so, since turbocharging will *greatly* speed up the flame front of spark-ignition combustion). Depending on *many* factors, optimal diesel injection start timing can vary from 0 degrees BTDC to as

much as 24 to 26 degrees BTDC in some racing diesel powerplants.

The fact that diesel powerplants are already rpm-limited, enables them to be designed with a long stroke to increase torque. The advantage of designing engines with a greater proportion of displacement provided by stroke is that a long stroke provides greater *leverage* against the crankshaft, exactly like using a longer torque wrench to tighten a bolt. Engines with a longer stroke than bore are referred to as undersquare, and undersquare gasoline powerplants were common in the early automotive age when all powerplants had a relatively low maximum speed.

Diesel fuel itself has about 10 percent more BTUs of energy per gallon than gasoline (which has more energy per gallon than all other common motor fuels, including simpler hydrocarbons like methane, natural gas, or propane, and partially oxygenated fuels such as nitromethane, nitropropane, methyl alcohol, ethyl alcohol, and ethers). It is important that diesel fuel stay reasonably cool until injection, because having *liquid* rather than vaporized fuel flowing through injectors is critical to enabling diesel injectors to live in the intense heat of the combustion chamber. As one might expect of the larger, heavier 15- or 16-carbon molecules in diesel, the fuel is less volatile than gasoline (with 7 to 8 carbon atoms), which, in turn, is less volatile than lighter hydrocarbons in fuels like propane or methane whose 1 to 3 carbon molecules make them a gas at room temperature. Unfortunately, only fuel vapor can react with oxygen to support combustion. The need for fuel *vapor* is one reason for the increasing prevalence of 20,000+ psi almost-metal-cutting common-rail injection pressure, which does a great job of shearing liquid fuel into a finely atomized mist of microscopic hydrocarbon droplets.

continued from page 93

flammability limits), propane will ignite only as a secondary consequence of the primary diesel injection.

Overboosting Factory Turbodiesels

It is debatable whether this section should even be called "Overboosting." As discussed earlier, unless a diesel powerplant is smoking badly, increasing boost by itself does not add any power whatsoever. Diesels overboosted this way will run just fine and make less smoke, though the turbocharger may have its life shortened if it is working hard to make boost to no good effect, and the increased exhaust backpressure could *subtract* power and raise combustion temperatures.

On the other hand, over*fueling* a modern turbodiesel engine with no other changes *will* burn up some of the typical diesel's large emissions-related air surplus and make more power, though exhaust gas temperatures will increase with richer-than-normal air-fuel ratios, and if the air-fuel ratio gets rich enough the engine will begin smoking. Fuel delivery can be cranked up on mechanical diesel engines by recalibrating the fuel pump pressure upward, and EDC common-rail systems can be recalibrated in a conceptually similar way to get more fuel in a diesel. If a stock normal-charged diesel engine were running a 25:1 air-fuel ratio and making 100 horsepower, you could probably overfuel it to 105 to 110 horsepower without burning up pistons and rings right away or producing embarrassing amounts of black smoke, though overfueling would definitely shorten the life of the engine in the long run (or in the short run under heavy load for extended periods without a pyrometer to watch EGT and back out of the power if necessary).

High power increases can be safe under some circumstances, the safest of all being a lightly loaded street vehicle on a flat road on a cool day that will only accelerate in bursts for brief periods,

but the American Society of Agricultural Engineers once held an academic conference about "overpowering" diesel farm tractors, which develop high engine loading over extended periods when doing hard work like plowing where additional power is useful. Proceedings revealed the following with respect to over-fueling normal-charged tractors in the 70- to 100-horsepower range:

- Forty percent more fuel used per acre or per job and only 20 percent more power output in return.
- Higher engine temperature everywhere. Combustion area, pistons, valves, rings, and gaskets damaged.
- Engine block and head, cracks, leakage, injector pump, injector maintenance costs.
- Cooling systems: 26 percent higher engine temperatures equal higher maintenance costs.
- Crankcase: 10 percent increase in temperature equals a further deterioration of oil and lower efficiency.
- Extra strain on transmission and final drive will shorten gear, bearing, and shaft life.

Meanwhile, if the hypothetical 100-hp diesel engine were turbocharged, results would vary depending on whether or not the additional power and combustion temperatures could generate more turbo boost, but it is likely that with no other changes the overfueled 100-hp turbodiesel would outdo the 100-hp normal-charged diesel by eliminating black smoke under all circumstances (including high elevation). If the stock turbocharger on the hypothetical 100-hp turbodiesel had the typical headroom of modern road-going vehicles for a 50 to 100 percent boost pressure increase, then fuel and boost increases with no other changes to intake, exhaust, or compressor would almost definitely allow a 30 to 50 percent power increase, upgrading power into the 130- to 150-horsepower range without causing sudden death.

Overfueling a turbodiesel engine to richer air-fuel mixtures can definitely be hazardous to the health of the powerplant due to hotter combustion temperatures and heavier thermal and mechanical loading on various engine and transmission systems—which is one reason why many vendors selling equipment to get fuel in a diesel typically provide multiple staged solutions of increasing power, expense, or risk. It's why most diesel performance vendors *really* want you to install and monitor an EGT gauge, so you take on the responsibility to back out of the throttle if combustion temperatures are going wild. Since you do not want to fry your beloved diesel (and surely you do not want to blow smoke at cars following you up a long hill—do you, you anti-social bastard?), the *ideal solution to hot rodding a turbodiesel is to commensurately increase both fuel* and *boost pressure.* This will help keep combustion temperatures down, even if there is still considerable thermal stress on engine systems from the higher levels of power. The good news is that modern factory turbodiesels typically have excess capacity in both injection and turbocharging systems—or upgrade diesel injectors and turbochargers are available if you decide to get more radical.

The engine management calibration data that drives the software logic on a modern common-rail EDC diesel has the ability to modify fueling to make power by (1) raising fuel pressure (to maximum safe limits—and in some cases beyond), (2) increasing injection pulsewidth (as long as the resulting injection event will still complete while the combustion chamber is still small enough to harvest any significant power; some common-rail systems do as many as five discrete injections per power stroke), (3) advancing (or retarding) the start of injection timing, (4) accommodating larger fuel injectors to increase the fuel flow per time to target levels under conditions of greatest demand by pulling fuel under other circumstances with pressure or pulsewidth changes, or (5) some combination of the above.

In practice, modifying the actual EDC calibration requires hacking into the electronic control unit's calibration data stored in flash memory or PROM and knowing which numbers to change in order to modify EDC operation, which is not trivial. Reverse-engineering an engine control system is a job for experienced engineers and pro-tuners, and even so, depending on expertise, some hackers may only gain access to a subset of engine control parameters. As is the case with OBD-II spark ignition engines, late-model diesel controllers can be recalibrated by reflashing all or some of the calibration data in controller flash memory.

In the case of older electronic diesels, sophisticated interceptor control units may be able to accomplish most or all of the above, and there are piggyback control units available through the aftermarket that plug in between the stock EDC controller and the stock wiring harness and are designed to trick electronic diesel control (EDC) systems into "overfueling" the engine, typically by intercepting and underreporting common-rail fuel pressure sensor data when more fuel is required such that the EDC system commands higher pressure from the fuel pump.

If you are recalibrating or manipulating the stock EDC system to modify diesel fueling, you'll probably also have the ability to increase maximum boost pressure simply that manage the data in EMS speed-density boost tables that manage an electronic wastegate valve controller. Diesel engines, like gasoline powerplants, typically build in excess capacity to the turbocharger's compressor section and combine this with a high-energy turbine nozzle to create a turbo system that build boost rapidly, with a wastegate coming into play to prevent overboost as engine rpm increases under heavy loading. Particularly on heavy vehicles, good low-rpm boost produces dramatically better low-end torque for improved drivability, and these days diesel

EFIlive's Flash Scan V2 system makes it possible for turbo diesel performance enthusiasts to calibrate the engine (usually by loading prefabricated performance calibrations designed to optimize the engine for a certain type of drive), and drivers may also modify automatic transmission performance to improve the speed and aggressiveness of the shifts. *EFIlive*

turbocharging systems also need to maintain large air surpluses to eliminate or minimize smoking on sudden acceleration, making it even more critical on modern emissions-controlled diesel powerplants that the turbocharger is highly responsive, spooling quickly to make boost on sudden acceleration. Fortunately, unlike turbocharged gasoline engines, which are usually found in high-performance cars where wide dynamic engine range is important and thrilling acceleration in the mid-upper rpm range is critical, there's really no tradeoff for diesels in sacrificing high-end performance in order to size turbochargers for great low-end, because diesels simply don't have much "high-end" in any case. By gas-turbo standards, factory turbodiesels already run a ton of boost, but overfueling to radically increase torque requires more. Fortunately, achieving this can be as simple as using an interceptor or recalibrated factory EDS to direct the operation of a PWM electro-pneumatic wastegate controller or variable turbine geometry controller to let the stock turbocharger go a little more wild.

continued on page 100

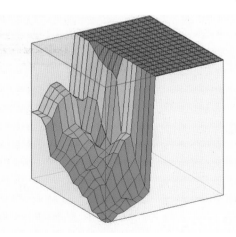

EFIlive Cummins turbo diesel common rail pressure map. Target injection pressure may vary as a function of engine speed and throttle position, or even available boost pressure, but lacking a throttle, manifold pressure is not available as a measurement of engine loading. *EFIlive*

10 COMMON RAIL COMPONENTS (BOSCH)

Engine control unit and high-pressure fuel-injection components
16 High-pressure pump
23 Engine control unit (master)
24 Engine control unit (slave)
25 Fuel rail
26 Fuel-rail pressure sensor
27 Injector
28 Glow plug
29 Diesel engine (01)
M Torque

A Sensors and setpoint generators
1 Accelerator-pedal sensor
2 Clutch switch
3 Brake switches (2)
4 Operator unit for cruise control
5 Glow plug/starter switch ("ignition switch")
6 Vehicle-speed sensor
7 Crankshaft speed sensor (inductive)
8 Engine-temperature sensor (in coolant system)
9 Intake-air temperature sensor
10 Charge-air pressure sensor
11 Hot-film air-mass flow sensor (intake air)

B Interfaces
12 Instrument cluster with signal output for fuel consumption, engine speed, etc.
13 Air-conditioning compressor with control
14 Diagnosis interface
15 Glow plug control unit
CAN Controller Area Network (vehicle's serial data bus)

C Fuel supply system (low-pressure system)
17 Fuel tilter with overflow valve
18 Fuel tank with filter and electric fuel pump
19 Fuel level sensor

D Additive system
20 Additive metering unit
21 Additive control unit
22 Additive tank

E Air-intake system
30 Exhaust-gas recirculation cooler
31 Charge-air pressure actuator
32 Turbocharger (in this case with variable turbine geometry)
33 Control flap
34 Exhaust-gas recirculation actuator
35 Vacuum pump

F Emission control systems
36 Exhaust temperature sensor
37 Oxidation catalytic converter
38 Particulate filter
39 Differential-pressure sensor
40 Exhaust heater
41 NO_x sensor
42 Broadband oxygen sensor Type LSU
43 NO_x accumulator-type catalytic converter
44 Two-point oxygen sensor Type LSF
45 Catalyzed soot filter Type CSF

HOT RODDING DIESEL ENGINES

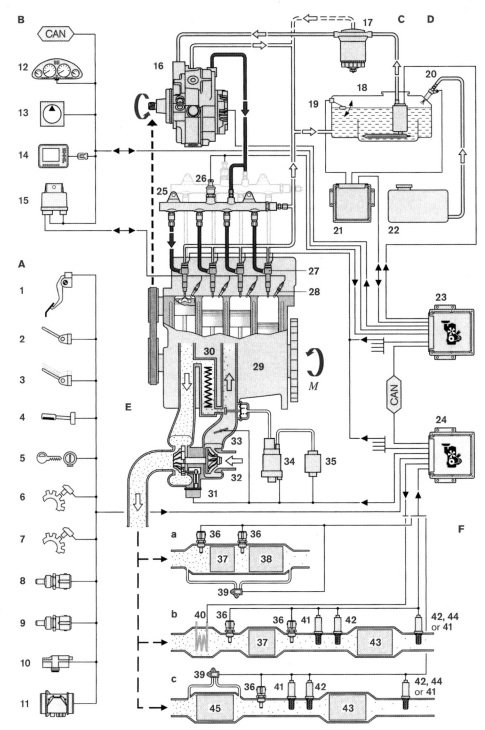

Factory diesel engines run conservatively lean because lean means clean, and lean means cool and safe combustion temperatures. This has provided a twilight zone of sorts in which enterprising entrepreneurs have milked the margin between the conservative factory injection pressures and increased amounts of increased power available when injection pressures are limited only by max safe EGT or legal black smoke.

"The Therminator," originally developed by Diesel Dynamics of Las Vegas and later sold under a different name by Edge Products, is an interceptor power module for Ford Powerstroke and Dodge Cummins turbodiesels that demonstrates the reliable power that is achievable when hot rodding pre-common-rail EDC turbocharged diesel powerplants without replacing major intake, exhaust, or turbo components.

When the Therminator arrived, the competition was so-called power chips (a.k.a., power-PROMs). A typical aftermarket PROM-with-microprocessor power-upgrade module plugs into the diagnostic port of the computer on a pre-common-rail Ford Powerstroke to substitute its own recalibrated table of injection pressures for the factory-original injection pressure table stored in the stock engine-management computer. Factory engine management computer algorithms monitor the injection control pressure sensor on a continuous basis and calibrate diesel injection to deliver target pressures according to the factory internal tables unless superseded by a "diagnostic" aftermarket PROM calibration.

Unfortunately, without any feedback on actual internal engine combustion conditions, a power-chip module's deterministic approach to diesel hot rodding pushes blindly closer to the ragged edge of engine damage. The power-chip calibration, therefore, must still retain *some* margin of error and cannot be fully optimized for extremely rapid power ramp-ups or maximum safe peak-power. And even so, for reasonable safety, PROM upgrades require add-on gauge packages so the driver can monitor actual engine conditions. The driver must be paying attention and get out of the throttle if EGT starts to go nuts.

Diesel Dynamics' Therminator did not simply redirect the computer to target higher-power injection pressures. Instead, the Therminator was designed as an *interceptor* device that could lie subtly to the Powerstroke computer in real time to understate injection control pressure. Based on feedback from the Therminator's own fast exhaust gas temperature sensor (pyrometer), the Therminator could force the EDC system to inadvertently drive injection pressures upward toward the ragged edge of safety, extracting every last safe horsepower from a 1999 or newer (pre-common-rail) Ford Powerstroke. The unit was capable of achieving almost 50 percent more optimized peak horsepower and torque while continuously monitoring exhaust gas temperature (EGT) and stock powerstroke engine sensor data.

What can you do with another 100 horsepower on a heavy truck with big custom wheels and tires? You can accelerate from 0 to 60 in 8.23 seconds instead of 9.17 in a 2001 F350 Dually truck with oversize tires. You can roll from 0 to 1/4 mile in 16.79 seconds instead of 18.29, with a top-end speed of 88 versus 81. How about when you add an 8,500-pound trailer to the back? Then you can climb a 7 percent grade hill outside of Las Vegas, Nevada, at 69 mph in the F350, whereas the stock 2001 Ford Powerstroke could only make 47 on the same hill. You can pass other vehicles with the F350 in 12.54 seconds instead of 17.21, starting from 50, with a limiting speed of 70 mph. With a Therminator in place on a Powerstroke, torque arrives with a massive lunge. Put the pedal to the metal and torque increases by 148 lb-ft between 2,000 rpm and 3,000 rpm over stock. Power similarly increases by 87 horsepower to almost 290 horsepower.

In addition to power increases, Therminator customers claimed a fuel economy improvement of 1 to 3 miles per gallon in normal driving, though Diesel Dynamics co-owner Lawrence Bolton only claimed a 1 mpg improvement and qualified this by adding, "Not if you go berserk. Not if you floor it all the time."

Compared to other PROM-only solutions, dyno charts showed the Therminator offered a flatter, broader torque curve, resulting from EGT feedback algorithms that permit more aggressive fueling strategies while automatically preventing "too much power" from hurting the engine. The Therminator could ramp up power more rapidly due to the lack of excessive-EGT worries.

The Therminator was user-installable in less than an hour, though Diesel Dynamics claimed to have installed a system in nine minutes in a record-setting effort. Here is the sequence:

- Begin by drilling a 3/16-inch hole in the exhaust tube between the driver's-side exhaust manifold and the turbocharger, close to the manifold where the Therminator's exhaust gas temperature probe will see maximum heat. Thread a washer-gasket onto the EGT probe, and insert the probe into the new hole. A clamping mechanism holds the EGT probe firmly in place and prevents any leaks. Tighten the clamp. Now plug in the EGT thermocouple to the Therminator's wiring harness.

- The Therminator's "brain-box" mounts with Velcro tape to the Ford Power Distribution Center (a glorified fusebox near the firewall in front of the driver next to the inner fender well).

- Unplug the stock Powerstroke injection control pressure sensor (ICP) located near the front of the engine on the driver's side. Plug the sensor into the Therminator harness, and then attach the Therminator's harness to the stock ICP harness.

- All Powerstroke diesels have used fly-by-wire fuel "throttle" actuation in place of a cable since 1993, with a potentiometer-type sensor connected directly to the accelerator pedal used to control diesel injection via the ECM. Route the correct lead from the Therminator harness through the firewall into the passenger compartment. Connect the Therminator lead to one wire of the stock harness connector at the TPS sensor.

- As above, connect the Therminator to the manifold absolute pressure (MAP) sensor located next to the firewall at the right-rear of the engine.

- Rock 'n' roll.

The Therminator's interceptor approach had several advantages over PROM-swapping related to installation. Unlike a PROM installation, there was no need to carefully scrape the lacquer coating from connections on the diagnostic port, which had to provide excellent connections for every prong on the chip (or the engine would not even start). The interceptor approach was less risky; if a power PROM is installed or removed while there was accidentally battery power to the stock ECM, the ECM would probably be damaged.

Unlike chip modules, which typically require a calibration code for installation and must be sold by the year and model of truck, the Therminator was designed to work on all 1999 and newer pre-common-rail Ford Powerstroke. One design goal was to prevent trouble with dealer mechanics wanting to replace the Powerstroke computer when the truck went into the dealer for servicing, due to nefarious trouble codes activated by power-chip modules, or when dealer diagnostic equipment detected a "ROM error" on a vehicle that has had a chip module installed. The Therminator intercepted control pressure data and fudged it a bit, with updates 256 times per second. Though it was theoretically possible for a radically modified Powerstroke engine with a Therminator installed to push engine sensors far enough out of range that the stock computer would set a trouble code, this was apparently rare, even if the Therminator was enhanced with major modifications to injectors, turbocharger, and exhaust. Should a Therminator unit fail, you'd know it right away, because power and torque would return to stock.

BANKS' COMMON-RAIL HOT RODDING TRICKS

At the time of this writing, Six-Gun, Speed-Loader, and Power-PDA performance upgrade packages from turbocharging specialists Gale Banks Engineering were typical of what is possible when you hot rod U.S.-market light trucks and motorhomes in a conservative way with an emphasis on maintaining factory reliability. Banks once built gasoline-engine turbo packages and kits for automotive and marine applications and still sells a generic twin-turbo small-block V-8 Chevy kit and a complete turnkey twin-turbo engine for classic hot rod applications on exempt vehicles, but more recently the company focused new development almost exclusively on diesel performance. When hot rodding light truck diesels from Ford, Dodge, and GM for "Sport" applications, 100–160 horsepower was the typical range for horsepower increases with EDC behavior modifications and a full package of bolt-on tricks. If the application was towing, the range was 50–100 horsepower.

Upgrade Dodge Cummins diesel injectors provide a larger volume of injected fuel for increased power and torque. Stochiometric combustion in a diesel powerplant is a bit over 15:1, but diesel engines will tolerate a wide range of air/fuel ratios, and combustion runs *cooler* when there is a large air surplus. *Edge Products*

continued from page 97

These days, the newest trick in late-model super-duty common-rail factory diesel powerplants is twin staged turbochargers, with a smaller variable geometry turbine (VGT) turbo fed previously boosted air by a larger conventional Stage 1 turbo. The small Stage 2 variable area turbine is driven with fresh hot exhaust gases direct from the exhaust headers, and boost is available virtually from idle under EDC control, with essentially no lag. Partially depleted exhaust gases flow from the Stage 2 turbine exducer to the Stage 1 turbine inducer, spooling up the larger Stage 1 compressor upstream of Stage 2 as power and airflow increase. When the Stage 1 compressor begins working at higher boost, it contributes to high maximum torque and power by precompressing charge air for the Stage 2 compressor, which multiplies boost pressure to high levels. The turbine nozzle gradually increased to maximum area for least exhaust restriction.

Diesel Calibration

Diesel tuning for peak power and efficiency can be more complicated in some respects than tuning a spark-ignition engine. Even though air-fuel ratios, detonation constraints, and overboosting are not a factor in avoiding engine damage in diesel engines the way they are on turbocharged gasoline powerplants, fuel economy and torque are even more critical to the economic viability of most light truck and commercial diesel applications. Achieving low exhaust emissions has become so critical to the future of compression-ignition as a viable method of combustion and so difficult to achieve that the U.S. government mandated

exotic new diesel fuels with virtually no sulfur content to permit the use of exhaust catalysts starting in 2007. Radically expensive electronic diesel control (EDC) engine management systems that now comprise 40 percent of the cost of a diesel powerplant are the order of the day.

Injection timing in particular is critically important. Early injection causes combustion pressure to peak too early, causing power loss and possible engine damage. Late injection can result in burned exhaust valves and fried turbines if combustion continues into the exhaust system (which causes EGT to REALLY skyrocket). In either case, thermal loading goes up and power goes down. Factory EDC systems are precisely calibrated to advance injection timing with engine speed and turbo boost to maximize torque and minimize combustion temperatures (EGT). Since combustion commences everywhere at once in the combustion chamber of a diesel as fuel blasts into the chamber and atomizes, the improved combustion speed from turbo-boosted charge density is less of a factor on a diesel powerplant than it is on a spark-ignition engine.

Diesel engineers and tuners typically work on an engine dyno to build a comprehensive performance map for an engine, which determines parameters across the board for (1) rpm, (2) torque, (3) intake manifold pressure, (4) exhaust manifold (back) pressure, (5) EGT, (6) BSFC (fuel consumption), (7) smoke level, (8) start-of-injection timing, and (9) weather conditions (ambient temperature and barometric pressure). The typical procedure would be to increase fuel injection under full load to achieve maximum torque until the engine is smoking visibly and then vary injection timing to find maximum torque and reduce fuel consumption. At this point engineers work at partial loads

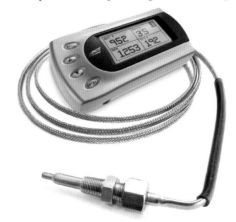

Edge products Exhaust Gas Temperature gauge allows a careful diesel hot rodder to back off the gas pedal if combustion is getting too hot before there's engine damage. Some diesel performance piggybacks incorporate EGT feedback into the algorithms that determine how much power the piggyback will instigate with increased fueling and boost.

STOCK TURBODIESEL PERFORMANCE

Dodge (Cummins) 5.9L/6.7L	325 hp @ 2,900	610 lb-ft @ 1,600
Ford 6.0L (&7.3)	325 hp @ 3,300	570 lb-ft @ 2,000, 32-valve
GM 6.6L	300/360 hp @ 3,000–3,200	520 lb-ft @ 1,800

Banks' Six-Gun system consists of an interceptor module capable of increasing power via overfueling and overboosting by making EDC changes to injection pulsewidth, fuel pressure, and injection timing, and maximum permitted boost. Performance is user-selectable from six or seven "levels."

On 6.6L GM trucks, advertised power increases are up to 155 horsepower and 385 lb-ft—typically in combination with VE-improving upgrades to the intercooler system, wastegate actuator, air-intake, exhaust system, turbine housing, and muffler. How much of this is really essential to achieve the maximum power and torque is unknown, since Banks advertises only "up-to" results, and a user-selectable six-position switch chooses the maximum permitted power.

Varying the "level" and auxiliary performance equipment can move turbodiesel bottlenecks around in interesting ways that are quite different from the bottlenecks typical of a turbocharged gasoline powerplant. For example, if you crank up the fuel and boost, retaining the stock intercooler might produce a bottleneck, but not because there is not enough air mass getting in the engine or because the engine starts to detonate (as might be the consequence of a too-small intercooler on a gasoline powerplant), but because the diesel engine is running richer (smaller air surplus), which causes EGT to skyrocket.

The Speed-Loader is essentially a closed-loop module that is especially useful for increasing performance in heavy-duty towing and climbing applications because the Six-Gun system modulates or "de-rates" maximum power and torque by pulling fuel (sometimes referred to as "back-down") to prevent engine damage based on data from to its own turbine-inlet temperature (TIT) EGT pyrometer. Other auto-protect features monitor and protect against slippage in the torque converter lockup clutch and transmission from increased torque and prevent turbocharger overspeeding at higher altitudes.

Injection Control Pressure sensors provide feedback to an electronic diesel ECM that can be used in a closed loop mode to maintain pressure according to the rail pressure map. *Diesel Power Magazine*

of 25, 50, and 75 percent of maximum torque (electronically, or by advancing the fuel pump lever on mechanical diesels) to establish the limits of the EGT curve.

In the old days, following initial dyno testing, engineers would optimize the injection system of vintage mechanical-diesel turbo-conversion powerplants by removing the injection pump so it could be recalibrated on a test stand by a diesel injection specialist, who would optimize the injection timing and *torque backup* characteristics. Automotive, agricultural, and construction equipment diesel powerplants are usually fueled so that torque *increases* as engine speed decreases from the maximum, which is known as *torque backup*—expressed as a *percentage* of torque at maximum engine speed. Twenty-five percent torque backup is typical, and this gives diesel engines excellent lugging power. On the dyno, increases in EGT without an increase in power are a probable indication of over-retarded injection timing. No non-race hot rod diesel powerplant should ever have the injection timing advanced beyond the factory setting; too much advance can cause overpressure in the combustion chamber and power loss. Way too much advance could actually cause diesel knock—actual detonation!—if injection started before the heat of compression had reached auto-ignition temperature for the cetane rating of the fuel.

Automotive and light truck diesel owners can assume that the factory EDC calibration is already optimized to put the peak brake-specific fuel consumption (BSFC) island at factory maximum boost pressure so that it occurs at normal highway speed (which is largely a function of proper gearing). However, changing the turbine nozzle size *can* move the peak efficiency island of the diesel combustion map to a somewhat higher or lower engine rpm.

On direct-injection diesel engines, engineers strive to select a turbocharger and state of diesel tune where EGT is high enough to increase turbine efficiency sufficient to achieve enhanced clearance-volume-scavenging at heavier loads resulting from intake manifold pressure that is higher than backpressure in the exhaust manifold, a desirable phenomenon known as crossover. Crossover allows residual exhaust gases in the clearance volume to be pushed out the exhaust by fresh intake charge air during the brief valve overlap period when both the intake and exhaust valves are partially open. This crossover scavenging effect cannot be significant on an indirect-injection diesel powerplant because the pre-chamber is too shrouded for effective flow-through, but it is an important goal for direct-injection powerplants.

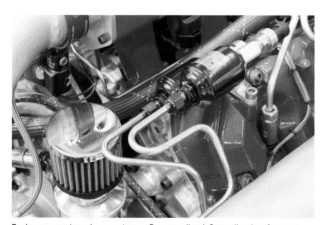

Banks pressure transducer system on Duramax diesel. Some diesel performance schemes have increased power with piggyback interceptors that increase rail pressure by mis-reporting the signal from a rail pressure transducer. *Banks Power*

HOT RODDING DIESEL ENGINES

101

Chapter 7

Recalibrating Factory ECMs

Edelbrock eForce supercharged Mustang provides a supercharger calibration via reflashed stock ECM. *Edelbrock*

Edelbrock eForce tuner from Diablosport allows supercharger conversion installers to reflash the Ford ECM.

Virtually all digital engine management systems use table-driven software designed to be flexible so the basic software logic is capable of running a variety of different engine applications. It is the calibration tables and configuration parameters—the data—that give the EMS a substantial portion of its personality for managing a particular engine application.

This book has several projects in which we recalibrated the stock factory EMS as a tactic in a major performance increase.

Keep in mind that all engine management systems—even aftermarket programmable systems—have an overall hardware and software architecture that is specialized enough to limit the flexibility to manage some types of engines. This is especially true of mass-produced OEM systems, where cost is important. As an example, EMS hardware and software might have the ability to run either speed-density or MAF-based engine management, or both, or neither (in the case of some Alpha-N bike computers). Modern ECUs—with greater processing power and more memory space for code and data—tend to have greater flexibility to handle unusual engines, sensors, and actuators, but there are almost always limits in what can be done with parameterized (conditional) code versus extending or replacing entire software algorithms with new logic. Which is why there has been some movement toward providing open-source capability in the case of at least one aftermarket engine management system (MegaSquirt), which gives purchasers of EMS hardware the option to gain access to the OE source code for modifications and extensions. Obviously that's not going to happen in the case of factory engine management systems.

In some cases, the ECM software architecture only provides the ability to *enrich* fuel delivery above the raw, air-meter-based fuel calculation, versus the ability to enlean fuel delivery (which is admittedly not usually as important for hot rodders looking to increase boost and horsepower). Some important basic operating considerations such as the number of cylinders, which are typically configurable on an aftermarket programmable EMS, have often been fixed in the OEM system logic. But they might not be if—as is increasingly the case—a particular manufacturer decides it is simpler and cheaper to maintain a single software architecture across the entire landscape of the company's vehicle and engine platforms.

There are many examples of software logic that limits the recalibration flexibility of the EMS. And it is not usually practical or cost-effective to modify the software architecture, that is, to change the actual machine instructions that the onboard computer executes, though, again, MegaSquirt is a counter-example. In most cases, the only choice is switching to a different ECU hardware architecture.

EFIlive's Flash Scan connectivity. On one side the scanner device connects to a vehicle's OBD-II port within easy reach of the driver's seat. The Flash Scan device can operate independently, or in conjunction with a Windows PC. Note that Flash Scan can also connect to a dynamometer or wideband AFR sensor.

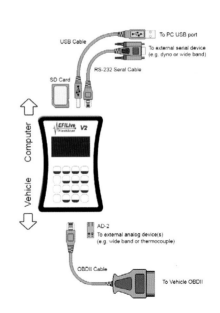

Hondata provides various packages of hardware and software that convert certain stock Honda ECMs to user-programmability, and offers reflash capability on applicable OBD-II engines. In the case of older pre-OBD-II engines like the 1995 Honda del Sol project in this book, the trick is to socket the motherboard for an auxiliary PROM, add two jumper resisters, and attach a Hondata datalogger/interface box to the Honda ECU. With the PROM calibrator data in a PROM-emulator box plugged into the PROM socket, tuning is completely interactive from a laptop PC. The alternative is an iterative process of logging acceleration air/fuel data, making changes offline to the calibration, and then burning a replacement PROM for immediate installation and retest. The "Hondalogger" box allows a tuner to datalog the complement of stock Honda and modified sensors during test runs, including, optionally, wideband O_2 data. Note the 9-pin serial connector for laptop PC user interface and connections to Honda ECM. Datalogging is the true path to good optimized recalibration of any engine. *Hondata*

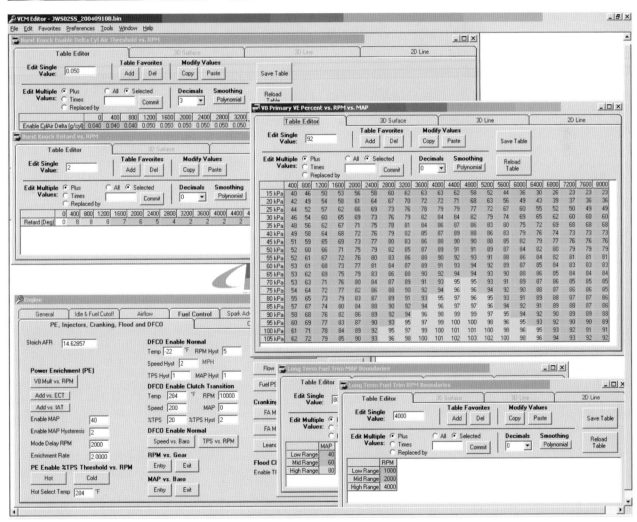

LS1edit screen in use to configure the Volumetric Efficiency table as a function of rpm and MAP.

Factory engine management systems have utilized a variety of hardware architectures that affect the difficulty of modifying the factory calibration.

THE MANY LEVELS OF PROM HACKING

For pre-OBD-II factory engine management systems (all '93 or earlier ECUs, and the vast majority of '94 and '95), the simplest kind of hacking is to buy an off-the-shelf performance chip or module from one of the many suppliers and install it in your car's computer. Such a solution should plug and play (though it may not if your application is at all nonstandard). More likely, the problem is that it will add little or no performance, producing reduced fuel economy and resistance to knock in favor of really minor power gains at or above the stock redline.

Except in the case of turbocharged engines, there is typically little "free" power available from a simple chip change on a factory EMS. But hope springs eternal, and firms like Superchips, Hypertech, Jet, and others make a nice living selling chips and upgrade modules.

A second option is to buy a custom-made chip or module from an expert designed specifically for your engine and its performance modifications. Since it may take a few iterations to get it right, if you are remote from the expert, you may need to install the modifications and then run the vehicle on a chassis dynamometer with a coupled wideband air/fuel-ratio sensor and send the dyno/air/fuel ratio chart back to the expert to be analyzed and optimized—and possibly repeat the procedure more than once. ASM, Autothority, Active Autowerke, and others sell custom chips and calibrations.

Yet another option is to acquire a calibrator software package that can modify or edit the calibration in PROM or flash memory in your factory EMS. This is sophisticated software that intimately understands the calibration data structures of your engine application and provides an intuitive, user-friendly human interface. (The package usually includes hardware you'll need to attach a laptop computer to the ECM to offload the calibration data to a personal computer and replace it with the new calibration when the tuning is complete).

You'll probably need a communications cable, PROM burner, emulator, OBD-II diagnostic link, or other equipment. In some cases, it may be necessary to extract the motherboard from the ECU and remove or install components using advanced soldering techniques. As always, if you are recalibrating fuel, timing, or VE tables rather than configuration paraments, the tuning process itself will be a typical iterative session of science plus trial and error, with all the standard risks and pitfalls of dyno and road tuning. Calibration software-hardware packages are available from companies such as Hondata, ZDyne, Techtom/Technosquare, Bonneville Motor Werks (Motronic Editor), Carputing (LS1edit/LS2edit), HPTuners (GM vehicles), EFILive, SCT (Ford), Shiftmaster (EEC-Tuner), and others.

A significant increase in difficulty involves using general-purpose low-level PROM-hacking software to display the hex data from selected PROM or flash memory addresses, in order to modify the data to alter the behavior and tuning of the EMS. This is true hacking—though you may not be entirely on your own, since there may be documentation available from similar ECMs that have been successfully hacked that will be at least partially applicable to your application.

For example, no one may have documented the memory locations of critical EMS tables and parameters in ROM for your application, but someone may know roughly what the tables should look like. You can probably get some help from the person who wrote the PROM editing software or other enthusiasts who love hacking car computers and are working on other related projects with the same editing package. Programs like LS1edit, EEC-Tuner, FreeScan, Tunercat, Winbin, and Winhex are able to edit entire ROM images (as well, in many cases, as automatically finding calibration tables on known applications for display and modification).

The next step beyond this level of hacking can only be described as reverse engineering, which is done by the guys who write the software used by the hackers. Some are car guys who got started in ECU hacking as obsessed hobbyists who had serious day-job computer or electrical engineering skills. They may have begun the hacking process by dumping all ROMs or other non-volatile ECU-resident memory on a factory EMS into a workstation, and then exhaustively working to separate code from data by processing the ROM data with a disassembler that attempts to convert machine instructions back into assembly language source code, tagging the target addresses of instructions that move data out of the code address space (presumably into calibration tables), working with logic probes to observe how memory addresses change when you diddle various sensors, and so forth.

"I'm going to simulate this using some standard hardware," wrote Jim Conforti some years back when the Motronic Editor was barely a gleam in his eye. "Run the speed signal through a PLL (with div. by 3 in the feedback) setup to provide a 3x freq . . . count this in a counter, while comparing it to some latched values (dwell and spark) in 8-bit identity comparators . . . the comps output to a flip-flop which through an igniter fires the coil . . . a third comparator will provide the reset signal to the counter . . . all the CPU will need do is look at inputs, go to a MAP or three, and output two values to the latched comparator registers . . . the hardware does the timing for me."

Gulp.

Fortunately for car guys who are not super-geeks, there are people out there who love to hack car computers and who post the results on the Internet for free or a reasonable fee for the goodies needed to delve deeply into the knickers of your onboard computer.

The original ECUs from the late 1960s and 1970s were analog computers that did not have separate hardware and software instructions like a modern digital computer but whose logic was instead purely rooted in the hardware circuitry that simply processed varying input voltage signals to generate output signals of varying magnitude and duration. Such an analog computer is permanently deterministic (unless you rip out and change discrete components, which is not going to happen, given the alternative of a standalone digital aftermarket ECU that would cost less).

The only realistic way to modify the behavior of an analog ECM is to add external equipment to modify the signals to and from the sensors and actuators to selectively lie to the computer about engine/sensor status or selectively disobey commands to external actuators. The project Jaguar XKE in this book was originally carbureted but was later run by an analog Bosch L-Jetronic EFI system with an additional injector controller, (and later converted to aftermarket programmable digital engine management). The Cadillac 500-ci engine in the GMC motorhome project in this book was also initially run by a GM factory analog computer.

The earliest digital engine management systems typically used read-only memory (ROM or PROM) to store the logic (executable instructions), and a programmable read-only memory (PROM or EPROM) chip to store calibration tables and parameters. This enabled carmakers to manufacture a computer box with one or two circuit boards that could be given a personality for a particular type of engine application depending on the PROM data.

In some cases—where flexibility was not important or cost was critical—manufacturers soldered the PROM onto the circuit board. In other cases, the circuit board was socketed so a PROM specific to a particular engine could be inserted into the board without requiring soldering. So, for example, if the ECU on a particular vehicle had to be replaced, the original PROM calibration could easily be moved to the new computer

AEM Plug-and-Play ECM connects to OE wiring harness. Note that only three of four ECM connectors are usd in this application.

box so the dealer parts inventory system would not need to stock different ECUs for every application.

GM was kind enough to locate the socketed PROM of first-generation digital ECMs in such a way that the PROM was accessible externally without even opening the computer box on early GM digital computers in 1980s-vintage cars like the TPI Corvette and F-body.

If a PROM is soldered to the circuit board, modifying the calibration requires desoldering the old PROM and replacing it with a socket into which a new PROM chip with the modified calibration can be plugged—or swapping the computer box for a different unit with the required calibration preinstalled.

In some cases, manufacturers have gone out of their way to make it especially difficult and expensive to modify the calibration, though in most cases the strategy is "security through obscurity." For example, in some cases the processor and PROM are designed so the EMS will not function without the original PROM chip in place. In this case, more expensive solutions are required to substitute a new calibration for the original factory PROM data. For example, in the case of recalibrating the Toyota computer in a Gen-II MR2, we were forced to install a special miniature daughterboard (TechTOM's ROMboard) on the factory motherboard in place of the original PROM. The ROMboard installation procedure was to desolder the stock Toyota PROM, socket the circuit board where the original PROM had been, install the original PROM into a socket in the small (ROMboard) daughter-card, and then install a second aftermarket PROM into the daughterboard with the modified calibration. A special processor on the daughterboard repeatedly instructs the stock Toyota computer on a regular basis to run in diagnostic mode, causing the main Toyota processor to read modified calibration data from a specific alternate memory address on the auxiliary PROM.

In order to make changes to a PROM-based calibration while the EMS is running an engine, you'll need an emulator, which is a fast microprocessor device with a cable/connector made to plug into the PROM socket of an ECM or other microcomputer in place of the PROM. A PROM socket in the emulator accepts the PROM that is to be emulated, and the emulator subsequently stores the PROM data in the emulator's Random Access Memory (RAM) where it can be manipulated via laptop-based user-interface software.

Hondata, which markets a package of hardware and software that converts a wide variety of pre-OBD-II Honda

ECUs to full programmability with datalogging capabilities (including the project del Sol turbo conversion in this book), embeds specific emulator commands in the Hondata ROMeditor graphical calibrator interface software in a pull-down menu that include functions such as: REALTIME UPDATE, INCREASE CURRENT CELL, DECREASE CURRENT CELL, GOTO CURRENT CELL, DOWNLOAD CURRENT TABLE, DOWNLOAD WHOLE ROM, and REBOOT ECU.

An emulator will greatly speed up the process of testing new changes to the PROM-based calibration. Without an emulator, every time you want to try out a change to the calibration, you must burn a new PROM and install it in the ECU (though some EPROMs—erasable PROMs—can be reused multiple times). Unfortunately, extracting and reinstalling a PROM always risks damaging the device by bending prongs or torquing the processor itself (though knowing what you're doing and having experience and a specialized extraction tool greatly reduces the risk of damage). When you arrive at the final calibration, the emulator must dump the PROM image to a PROM burner to blow a new PROM for installation in the ECU in place of the emulator. Relatively inexpensive PROM burners could be found online in the $100 to $200 range at this time of writing.

Not all emulators are the same. They vary in both speed and flexibility in the types of PROM devices they can emulate. Really fast emulators can be expensive, but expensive emulators are better at keeping up with the high demands of feeding data to the ECU in real time without stumbling while simultaneously interfacing with a tuner making calibration changes from a laptop.

Starting about 1994, many automakers began moving to powertrain control modules (PCM), which are controller modules with some automatic transmission control capabilities. GM released vehicles with transmission control provided by the same controller hardware as the engine control module as well as on a separate unit. The CAN bus provided increased flexibility for elegant multi-processor cooperation starting in the 2005–2008 timeframe. PCMs use electrically erasable flash PROM to store calibration data. This architecture became standard on the OBD-II computers found on all 1996 and later U.S.-market vehicles, which are universally equipped with flash memory, a form of electrically erasable EEPROM suitable for storing significant amounts of code and data. Flash memory acts like ordinary PROM or EPROM, except that the microprocessor itself can write to the memory device in complete blocks to modify its data (no special PROM burner required).

Since it can be problematic for technicians to install PROM chips without damaging the chip or the circuit board, flash-based ECUs have introduced a welcome reliability and ease to the process of upgrading the calibration of a PCM or giving a generic replacement computer box its personality. Flash ECM greatly simplify the inventory of PROMs of ECMs replacement and warranty parts infrastructure. Flash memory can be read from as many times as required, but can only be rewritten a finite number of times before it wears out (usually in the range of 100,000 to 1 million-write operations).

OBD-II defines a protocol by which a standards-based diagnostic device can handshake with a 1996 and later OBD-II EMS to move data of various kinds back and forth between the PCM and the diagnostic device. OBD-II defines a standard 16-pin data link connector, with some pins rigorously defined and others reserved for future or proprietary use. Note that U.S. government-mandated implementation of the controller

The 993 twin turbo was the last air-cooled flat-six power-meister from Porsche, good for 400 horsepower. But—as with most turbo cars—there was more available with calibration changes and increased boost. High-boost chips for turbocharged cars running Motronic EMS are available from several sources.

Factory recalibration is not always such a chore. Here's a stock 993 Motronic ECU. Note the three large chips along the edge of the board next to the ECU enclosure.

This is the chip, ready for installation.

area network CAN bus by 2008 on all light vehicles sold in the United States established a prioritized scheme by which multiple onboard computers could communicate in order to work together to manage all onboard electronic systems in a coordinated fashion—from the engine to the transmission to the airbags to electronic stability control and much more.

OBD-II defines several different electronic protocols of varying speed and complexity that can be used to communicate between the EMS controller(s) and a diagnostic device. A typical OBD-II communications message from the tool to the EMS consists of a header byte, a byte identifying the originating processor, a byte defining the destination processor, a command (code) byte, data bytes, and a final checksum byte.

For example, the hex message C4 10 F1 23 FF 06 8D from Scan Tool 10 to PCM device F1 REQUESTS DATA (hex 23 command) from memory address FF06, with a final checksum byte 8D. The PCM will then respond with a message such as C4 F1 10 63 FF 06 56 4E 41 41 92, which says the destination device is the scan tool, the originator is the PCM, message type is a RESPONSE TO DATA REQUEST (hex 63), that the address being dumped is FF06, that the data contained at this address is 56 4E 41 41, followed by a checksum byte of 92.

The basic OBD-II standards are rigorously specified so that a basic diagnostic device will work with any OBD-II vehicle, but OBD-II connector and wiring definition and electrical specification, and the link-layer protocol, were defined in a robust fashion that permitted car companies to use undefined connector wires and an open-ended link protocol to implement a rich superset of diagnostic and support capabilities that go far beyond the basic diagnostic purpose of OBD-II.

OBD-II communication protocols can be used to retrieve diagnostic data, but carmakers like GM have extended the interface to allow it to be used to offload some or all of the PCM's calibration data for analysis and to enable engineers or techs to modify and *replace* all or some of the calibration data in ECU flash memory, or even to replace (*reflash*) the operating system of the PCM itself (with the exception of code equivalent to the boot loader and BIOS on a PC that performs input-output from nonvolatile memory or a network to load operating software and start the microcomputer running). OBD-II messaging can be used by the PCM to request a password. After granting what is essentially *superuser* privilege, the PCM/ECM can initiate certain actions, such as supplying, uploading, and overwriting calibration data or blocks of code. This sort of proprietary procedure is not a standard OBD-II procedure, but it is permitted within the standard, and standard communication and messaging protocols provide the mechanism. Many car companies have extended the basic OBD-II protocol to include such operations.

Aftermarket firms have been able to reverse-engineer many proprietary messaging protocols and internal calibration data structures that are extensions of OBD-II and develop software tools that handshake with the PCM and display the PCM calibration data in an organized tabular or graphical format for examination and modification. With the help of a 16-pin OBD-II datalink connector and laptop-based communications card, PC-based software programs such as EFILive are able to offload, modify, and replace the factory calibration data on cars like the C6 Corvette—while the engine is running. This is exactly analogous to calibrating a PROM-based system with a laptop and fast emulator.

Some of the data and code used by a flash memory-based OBD-II system may be built into the microprocessor itself,

Chip installation is all thumbs, very carefully. This is a simple procedure compared with what's required on many Japanese computers, but is more involved than pre-1994 GM PROM computers, which provide access without even opening the enclosure! OBD-II systems, of course, allow reflashing the EEPROM using a communications cable and laptop PC or diagnostic box.

though there are commercially available—but in some cases, hard to find—adapters that enable hackers to access and modify such microprocessor-based data. This kind of hacking is not for the faint of heart.

It is one thing to have the access required to physically change a PROM or to modify a flash memory with a hex editor or calibrator software; it is another thing to have detailed knowledge of the internal data structures sufficient to modify the calibration in ways that make the car run better. In pre-OBD-II days, some automakers had very poor standards for organizing the data structures of their onboard computers, swapping the order of internal data structures (calibration tables and scalars)

The early-1990s-vintage Mitsubishi 3000GT VR4 is an all-wheel-drive car with an SOHC twin-turbo transverse V-6 powerplant good for 320 crankshaft horsepower. The turbos are small, but there are two of them, and there is definitely more power available from the stock engine—if you can get into the calibration. I took the computer to Tadashi Nagata to photograph Techtom programmability upgrades to the factory ECM that unlock the door to recalibration. This upgrade involves much more than simply unplugging and swapping out a chip.

in PROM for no apparent reason on otherwise nearly identical engine applications on identical size PROM chips. Not to mention the chaos of inexorable increases in PROM chip size as EMS software engineers required more and more space for increasingly complex engine modeling software and data. GM, for example, used several different sizes of PROM throughout the life of the PROM-based computers that ran 5.0-liter and 5.7-liter tuned port injection and (early) LT1 small-block V-8s. What's more, even when the PROM was physically identical, even when the data structures were conceptually similar between different engine applications, the exact locations of the fuel table, spark timing table, and other data often varied from application to application.

At the lowest level, it is critically important that a hacker know precisely the manufacturer, engine, vehicle, and year (and in some cases the VIN) before modifying PROM or flash memory. In the past, some calibration software was targeted to work exclusively on one particular vehicle or engine application. These days, PCM/ECM hacking software (in this case, let's call it calibration software) is typically flexible and powerful enough to calibrate multiple years and models of vehicles in a way that is relatively transparent to the user. The user interface can thus automatically find, display, and label various data structures in ways that are appropriate to the purpose of the particular structure, making it much easier for the tuner to understand and modify. Commercially available calibration programs are now typically smart enough to recognize when there is a mismatch in data locations if the tuner misidentifies the PROM engine application, or if the exact vehicle has not already been reverse engineered, and most calibration software has built-in checks designed to prevent users from damaging a calibration or rendering a PCM inoperable by modifying it with hacking and calibration software that is not fully compatible with the PCM hardware, operating system, or calibration structure. But PCMs are a moving target that change continually, and checks may fail. Thus, many hacking and calibration packages have "recovery" features that automatically enable fallback to the previous (known-good) state if reflashing or modification fails. However, it is sometimes possible to damage the data, firmware, or software of a PCM in ways that are not recoverable without desoldering and replacing one or more hardware memory components on the PCM with a noncorrupted chip.

Meanwhile, with the advent of OBD-II and the CAN bus, engineers at the car companies have undertaken major efforts to standardize and modularize the operating software, data structures, and engine modeling structures of engine management systems, which makes it easier to develop, maintain, and adapt engine management systems for new engine platforms and to add capabilities. Modular engine management systems had the unintended consequence of allowing aftermarket tuning-programming-editing tools to be leveraged across a wider range of vehicles and engines without major changes.

There are hacking tools available that are not so much designed to tune an engine as to facilitate hacking or reverse engineering data structures using engineering-class scientific methods. General-purpose computer-science programs like WinHex will display the contents of any file in hexadecimal format: Each byte is displayed as one of the 256 hex numbers between 00 and FF (counting as: 1, 2, 3, 4, 5, 6, 7, 8, 9, A, B, C, D, E, F, 10, 11, 12, 13, 14, 15, 16, 17, 18, 19, 1A, et al.). Some hacking tools also have the ability to display data in graphical format so that a tuner can search out the telltale sawtooth-like

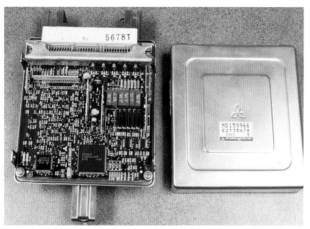

Above: Here's the Mitsubishi ECM with cover removed. Note the large square processor/memory chip near the edge of the circuit board. Right: With the motherboard removed from its enclosure, Nagata first employs a special desoldering tool to simultaneously melt solder and fasten all the multiple pins to the motherboard.

appearance of fuel and timing tables, display the hex contents of any location in the map, and modify individual bytes of data by typing in replacement hex data. This sort of hacking, however, is not for the timid, it's more for the sophisticated professional tuner who can leverage the R&D investment by hacking a particular PROM calibration to sell for profit.

Calibration-hacking software like Winbin, TunerPRO, TunerCAT, CarBYTES, TurboEDIT, uberdata, CROME, csb118r2, and Diacom provide a visual user interface for PROM-based GM systems that displays the contents of a GM PROM in graphical format for modification. Many of these came out of the DIY-EFI (do-it-yourself) movement that sprung up in the early years of the new millennium in which online forums enabled hobbyist tuners to share information about factory engine management system data structures and how to hack into the systems, and many of them require proprietary or general-purpose OBD-II scan tools for 1996 and newer engines, and special-purpose hardware to hack into earlier EMSs. Over the years, many of these tuning hackers have evolved barebones tuning hacks into sophisticated user-friendly software packages, and some of the hobbyists are now full-time entrepreneurs in the business of selling tuning software and hardware packages.

Some calibration-hacking software is actually quite sophisticated and user-friendly, though some systems may also have a powerful set of primitive, low-level capabilities. You tell the Windows-based program the make and model of your vehicle, and it finds the tables and parameters and displays them in graphical or tabular format and provides the user-specific turnkey-type modification procedures.

Companies like Hypertech and Superchips have commonly marketed specialized "turnkey" retail tuning and datalogging tools based on proprietary hand-held "programmer" devices designed to work on a particular type of engine or vehicle, and can typically only be used to modify one vehicle at a time (or a limited number of vehicles). Such packages enable the user to raise stock speed and rpm limits, modify auto transmission shift points and firmness, modify fan control parameters, and replace the stock calibration with prefabricated calibrations advertised to improve fuel economy, power, torque, drivability, or towing performance. In the case of turbodiesel engines with

electronic fuel injection, the gains can be very real and dramatic, in general at the cost of higher thermal and mechanical loading that eats into the "idiot-proof" factory safety margin designed to minimize warranty claims. Diesel hot rodding devices often require more out of the user than factory EMSs, which usually means installation and monitoring of exhaust gas temperature gauges—coupled with a driving technique that keeps EGT from rising to dangerous levels. With programmer device tools, the stock calibration must be offloaded and stored in the programmer, and the programmer tool cannot be used to work on another engine unless the original stock calibration has been returned to the PCM it came from before—thus requiring a separate programmer for each every modified vehicle. All turnkey programmer devices consist of proprietary hardware. Such programmer modules typically restrict modification capabilities in an effort to keep would-be tuners who are more in the class of shade-tree mechanics from getting into trouble and damaging the engine. Powerful hacking tools that will modify any of a class of engine management systems—repeatedly—are marketed to pro tuners, and they are typically not cheap. As always, it is critical that nonstock calibrations be matched with the appropriate engine configuration (usually one is identical to that of the engine the calibration was developed upon).

Of course, when you gain access to view and modify internal EMS tables, the trick is still to modify (tune!) them in ways that make sense (and this is no less trivial to accomplish than it would be calibrating a standalone aftermarket engine management system). LS1edit, for example, is loaded with warnings that require the user to explicitly acknowledge that they understand that this or that type of hack could actually damage the engine or transmission permanently, or that interrupting the process, say, of updating the PCM could render it inoperable. In any case, this is the point at which hacking becomes tuning, with its own art and science.

OEM ENGINE MANAGEMENT SYSTEMS
GM

General Motors entered the digital age with certain Cadillac models in 1980, but the first true performance engine management systems were delivered shortly thereafter on

The chip is free.

A special tool simultaneously heats and vacuums out any remaining solder from the pinholes in the printed circuit board.

Here Nagata solders a special socket into the motherboard in place of the chip. This type of socket enables installing a chip or daughterboard without requiring solder.

The de-soldered Mitsubishi chip will have to be soldered onto this Techtom ROMboard (daughterboard), which is already equipped with a diagnostic processor that will redirect Mitsubishi memory access to twin auxiliary PROMs that will be located on the daughterboard.

Corvette and Camaro-Firebird 5.0 and 5.7-liter V-8s in the form of Tuned Port Injection on L98 Chevrolet small-block V-8s. All 1985–93 Chevrolet and Pontiac V-8s are equipped with PROM-based TPI or TBI engine management systems on which the PROMs can be changed without even opening the computer box.

The performance precursor of TPI, Crossfire Injection, a twin-throttle-body injection system similar in concept to the subsequent single-throttle TBI system found on Chevrolet trucks and low-performance car V-8s in the 80s and 90s, arrived on the final C3 Corvettes and continued on in the new 1984 C4 'Vette. Crossfire injection is a PROM-based system of little performance consequence beyond historical interest. The same multi-port PROM-based EMS electronics were used on the first 1992–93 LT1s, which thereafter were switched to a new flash/EEPROM-based system (which also introduced sequential fuel injection). Throughout the life of these systems there were engineering changes that took the EMS gently away from full compatibility with the traditional small-block Chevy long block, though all pre-LS1 components can be made to work on older V-8s with minor modifications and most are not a problem at all.

The original high-energy ignition (HEI) with add-on EST electronic module was eventually integrated completely into the main processor and became the entirely nonadjustable Opti-spark delivered on the first LT1s. The original MAF-based air metering system was abandoned in favor of a MAP-sensed speed-density system in 1990 and later C4 'Vettes and F-body cars (but later returned on the 1994 LT1 that was equipped with both MAP and MAF).

All PROM-based GM systems are very capable of recalibration for almost any reasonable purpose, up to and including turbocharging and supercharging. If so inclined, you can downgrade 1996 and later LT1 PCMs to a pre-OBD-II 1994 EEPROM ECM (for off-road use only). Aftermarket suppliers have offered wiring, MPI intake and fuel rail, and a replacement PROM required to convert a TBI EMS to multi-port injection.

Like all closed-loop GM engine management systems, TPI and later systems may attempt to undo certain main fuel table calibration parameters by correcting the air/fuel ratio to 14.7:1 in closed-loop mode, and building up block-learn tables of semi-permanent correction factors that the system then folds into the main fuel calculation.

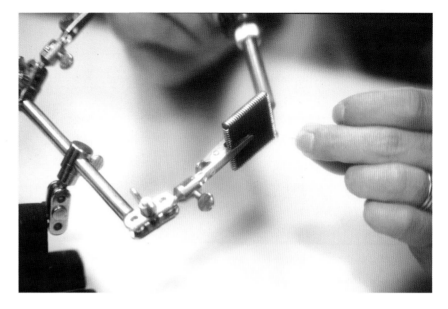

Right: Priming the Mitsubishi chip for installation. Below right: The Techtom daughterboard now plugs into the socketed Mitsubishi ECM motherboard (note two additional PROM sockets on the ROMboard).

Flash memory arrived on GM EMS controllers in the (OBD-I) 1994 LT1 F-body powertrain control module (PCM). The controller was equipped with 128KB of flash memory and two 16-bit Motorola 68xxx-series processors. It actually used two separate computer boards, which GM referred to as the Event and Time processors, each with its flash memory and microprocessor. The 1994–95 LT1 Corvettes used essentially the same PCM, with an auxiliary chip providing OBD-II-type communications.

GM 1994–95 LT1/LT4 flash EMS must be programmed with a dedicated programmer module or the right communications cable/hardware interface combined with laptop software such as LT1edit from Carputing. LT1edit is a powerful calibration editor designed to work with all LT1 engines (16188051 or 16181333 computer, complete with name upgrade from electronic control module to powertrain control module) in any vehicle in the 1994 or 1995 model years (some very early cars might require an upgrade to PROM revision level C).

GM's flash-based EMS architecture allows editor software to change the main fuel and spark tables and provides an extremely powerful set of other functions, including disabling traction control, MAF-metering, crank AIR, vehicle antitheft, and charcoal canister purge. You can select an alternate decel fuel cut and modify the EMS to use just one knock sensor. You can set several idle speed and IAC parameters, define EGR functionality, and disable diagnostic tests for various DTC codes. You can turn on cylinder balance tests.

With flash EMS architecture, you can adjust a target air/fuel ratio table, battery voltage injection compensation, define WOT, power enrichment versus temperature and rpm, and modify a 0–7,000 rpm VE table. You can modify the calibration curve for MAF sensor voltage versus airflow, which tells the PCM the correspondence between sensor voltage and grams per second airflow. You can also define the conditions for closed-loop mode, and you can adjust the cylinder size in cubic inches and the injector flow rate per injector. You can set a variety of spark advance table parameters, including rates of retard and advance in case of knock detection and several other knock-related parameters. There are a variety of automatic transmission parameters affecting shift points and harshness. Finally, you can adjust gear-tire scaling, rev limiting, maximum speed, and several cooling fan parameters.

The 1996/1997 F-Body LT1 PCM with OBD-II was similar in architecture to its predecessor, but featured a faster 68xxx series processor and 192KB of flash memory. The 1996 LT4 Corvettes included a removable knock-control module that allowed more aggressive spark advance and improved power, which made it a transplant favorite for LT1 engines. The difference between LT1 and LT4 controllers was exclusively the calibration.

GM's 1996 and later OBD-II performance engine management systems provided the new ability to detect and pinpoint individual-cylinder misfires, and were equipped with a full complement of emissions equipment including four O_2 sensors, EGR, and air pump. The LS1 engine, which appeared in 1997 'Vettes and 1998 F-bodies, arrived with direct-fire ignition, and in 1998 the familiar fuel loop was gone in favor of a supply line only to the injectors from a vestigial loop and regulator in the tank used to bleed off excessive pressure, which can make fuel pressure modifications much more difficult. LT1 engines from 1996 and later can be downgraded to OBD-I electronics for off-road applications.

The Gen III LS1 engine arrived in 1997 with a new single-board PCM designed around a faster Motorola 68000

FACTORY VERSUS AFTERMARKET CONTROLLERS

Engineer Dave Darge of Powertrain Electronics had the following to say about GM powertrain electronics in the era of the final pre-CAN controllers:

"GM OEM controllers are capable of performing on almost all engine applications. This includes throttle body injection (dual and single), port fuel injection (1 to 8 high-impedance injectors), with GM auxiliary injector driver 12 low-impedance injectors, batch fire or sequential, single-coil or coil-on-plug, and electronic transmission control. All of the GM controllers offer an OBD-I type of diagnostics with a port for a scanner. The last time I compared functions for a customer quote to a leading aftermarket controller the GM unit offered 56 additional features compared to the aftermarket unit. The customer decided the GM controller is the best for reliability and functionality. At this time the GM controller is far above the capabilities of any aftermarket controller except when triggering a nitrous system or handling functions like multiple rpm limiters.

"In fact, I cannot name any function limits that are beyond the scope of GM parameters or tables up to 9,000 rpm. On the contrary I see the GM controller as having more features and controllability than any aftermarket engine controller. Yes, there are times when the OEM-designed functions and diagnostics are hard to discern and cause problems that are difficult to determine. With several hours on a simulator the solution can usually be found.

"As you can see I am Pro-GM OEM when recommending an engine controller for any application. At times, I use two GM controllers on one engine when it is required. Most aftermarket engine controllers do not have the versatility of the GM controllers or the reliability and in most cases are not able to control the injectors precisely for dynamic situations (accel fuel enrichment and decel enleanment). An engine is a dynamic power source and the controller must be able to follow in all situations."

series processor with 512KB flash memory, which continued through 1998. The EMS now included a crank position sensor and direct-fire coil-on-plug ignition, a more sophisticated user interface, and familiar short- and long-term fuel trim minus the individual-cylinder fuel trim available on LT1s. While LT1 controllers were equipped with 128 connector pins spread over four connectors, the new LSx controller increased to 160 pins in two connectors.

The 1999 and 2000 GM controllers arrived in a more compact package. Harness connectors were interchangeable but simply swapping in the new controller had the potential to damage the controller due to changes in the pin assignments. Internally, the new controller ran a Motorola 68000 with increased clock speed. The MAF table range was extended for 1999 from 11,250

Hz to 12,000, with load tables commensurately increased from a maximum of 1.0 gram/cylinder in 1998 to 1.2 gram/cylinder in 1999. The increases allowed the controller to manage larger engines.

Although externally identical, 2001–2003 LS1 PCMs were equipped with a faster version of the Motorola 68000 chip and changes to internal data structures that had the potential to interfere with backward compatibility on 1999–2000 powerplants. Software changes provided advanced spark control influenced by ECT, IAT, and air/fuel ratio.

Editing the 1997 to 2002 LS1 is similar in concept to recalibrating the LT1, and the EMS control logic is similar to what is used on pushrod-V-8 Vortech truck powerplants. The LS1 system is more extensive and powerful than the LT1, in effect a

Nagata fires up a Windows PC running MightyMAP, a PROM hex editor for producing recalibrated (re-mapped) automotive PROMs for Japanese engine management systems with Techtom modifications. The PC is connected to a PROM-burner device. After editing the PROM image with MightyMAP, Nagata offloads the recalibrated data to twin PROMs of a common type designed to plug into the ROMboard.

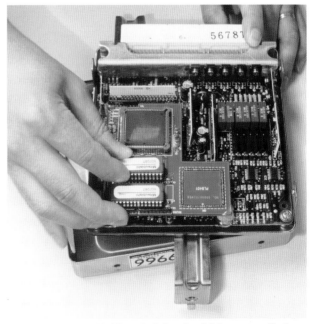

Installing the recalibrated PROMs on the Techtom board. Subsequent recalibration is now a simple matter of a PROM change, and with an emulator plugged into the ROMboard in place of the auxiliary PROM(s), calibration changes could even be made on the fly with the engine running using a laptop PC to modify PROM image(s) stored in the emulator.

FACTORY ECMs

superset of LT1 PCM's capabilities. GM allows some of the LS1 fuel parameters and tables to be modified, these include MAF calibration, injector flow rate, VE table modification, closed-loop enable temp, fuel pressure versus voltage compensation, injector offset, fuel air multiplier, stoic ratio, cylinder size, max allowed enrichment, and power enrichment.

Trucks from 2003-2007, and 2004-2007 Vettes and GTOs, received EMS controllers with a faster 68000 microprocessor and flash memory doubled from 512KB to 1MB. Multiple-brand controller hardware/flash memory sourcing forced changes in tuning/diagnostic tools. This hardware is considered the apex of pre-CAN controllers, making it optimal for LS1 engine swapping.

In 2005, GM began phasing in controller area network (CAN) protocols mandated for 2008 and newer vehicles, beginning with the Gen IV LS2 and truck LH6 engines. The new compact E40 module (ECM) employed smaller harness connectors and a faster version of the MC68xxx processor with faster flash memory, with transmission management transferred to a separate T42 transmission control module (TCM), a flash-based controller with 1MB autonomous memory. Transmission control migrated to a new stand-alone transmission control module (TCM) named T42, which allowed greater flexibility integrating Gen IV powertrains into various vehicle platforms. The E40 was now equipped with 185 I/O pins, 25 more than previous engine controllers.

In 2006, GM introduced a new controller architecture based on the Motorola PowerPC (Performance Enhancement With Enhanced RISC) microprocessor, a reduced instruction set computing (RISC) design developed in 1991 by an alliance of Apple, IBM, and Motorola that was used in the Apple Macintosh PC from 1994 to 2006 and many game consoles. RISC machines make use of the concept that a microprocessor can execute individual instructions faster when the set of instructions is limited. Of course, a particular algorithm may require additional instructions when some specialized instructions are not available. In any case, the new controllers were equipped with 2MB flash memory and, for the first time, floating-point math coprocessors that improved engine management accuracy by enabling calculations to proceed quickly with accurate fractions that minimize round-off error until the equation is complete and mapped into the accuracy of the device being controlled. The E38 and E67 controllers used a 32-bit PowerPC RISC processor operating at 40 MHz and were similar in appearance to the E40. The E38 actually had fewer I/O pins than the E40 (total of 153), though the 202-pin E67 featured additional I/O pins for variable valve timing and lift applications. The companion T43 TCM with 49 I/O pins arrived in 2006 with the ability to manage six-speed automatic transmission and was designed to be installed inside the transmission, within the valve body.

BOSCH ENGINE MANAGEMENT SYSTEMS (BMW, FERRARI, MERCEDES, PORSCHE, VOLKSWAGEN, AND OTHER VINTAGE EUROPEAN AND JAPANESE VEHICLES)

Bosch licensed the original Electrojector EFI system from the American company Bendix in the 1950s and introduced commercial electronic injection in the late 1960s in the form of the D-Jetronic system ("D" stands for *Druck*, the German word for *pressure*. The system evolved into the much more common L-Jetronic system of the 1970s and 1980s, components of which were found in the 1983+ tuned port injection, GM's first digital port-EFI system. L-Jet was a fuel-only EFI system, which depended on an entirely separate traditional solid-state ignition to light the fires.

Automakers as varied as Nissan and Jaguar used L-Jet systems on vehicles such as the 280Z and the XJ6. Bosch L-Jetronic injection was modern in most respects except for the ECU, which used analog electronics ("L" stands for *Luft*, the German word for *air*). Bosch K-Jetronic fuel injection is an old-style constant mechanical injection system (not EFI), with the addition of mechanical air metering and—in later KE-Jetronic systems—O_2-sensor-based closed-loop electronic fuel pressure trim to target stoichiometric air/fuel ratios at idle and light cruise. Early L-Jetronic systems used a velocity air meter, later LH-Jetronic systems used mass airflow metering. L-Jet systems are fuel-only, requiring separate independent ignition systems to provide spark.

Bosch introduced digital motor electronics (DME) in the Motronic system that arrived in the early 1980s, about the same time the rest of the automotive world moved to digital electronics. Motronic systems have used both MAF and MAP-based speed-density engine management. Many Motronic systems provide integrated spark advance using data from a 60-toothed crank (or, in a few cases, flywheel!) triggering system with two missing teeth and a cam-speed 1-tooth trigger providing sync information, though some Motronic EMS packages provide spark using a separate ignition module.

Pre-OBD-II Motronic systems managed the engines of virtually all post-K-Jetronic Porsche, Audi, VW, Ferrari, Mercedes, and BMW vehicles from about 1984 to 1995. Bosch engine management has been installed on various Nissan, Hyundai, Kia, Fiat, and Yugo vehicles. These are all carmakers with a significant enthusiast interest in performance and performance improvements, and Bosch engine management systems have been hacked by firms such as Active Autowerk, Bonneville Motor Werks (DME Editor, Shark Edit, Shark Injector), Autothority, and others. If you have one of these vehicles, you can probably find calibration/PROM software for it, and you can definitely find someone who will make you a custom PROM or flash-calibration for it (for an obscene price, in some cases). These companies have been providing custom tuning and off-the-shelf premium-fuel and high-boost tuning on 1996 and newer vehicles with Bosch engine management systems using a system of ECM swapping or OBD-II re-flashing using a laptop or programmer module that communicates with the ECM using classic OBD-II commands or CAN communications protocols to modify the Bosch ECM calibration.

Ford

Ford electronic engine control (EEC) EMS computers generations 1, 2, and 3 controlled the idle air/fuel ratio and emission control devices on vehicles with electronic carburetors and some of Ford's earliest throttle body injection engines.

Ford released the powerful, relatively modern EEC-IV EMS in 1983 on the 1.6-liter Escort, Lynx, EXP, and LN7 cars, and the EEC-IV stayed in production through 1995 for domestic American vehicles (at which point EEC-V computers arrived for 1996 and newer OBD-II vehicles and engines). The EEC-IV appeared on the 1983–84 Mustang 2.3-liter GT Turbo, and found its way onto the high-performance manual-trans 5.0-liter Mustang GT for 1986 (the 210-horsepower manual-trans 1985 Mustang GT was still carbureted, though the auto-trans model already had throttle body injection).

The EEC-IV was an advanced and flexible system that could be configured to handle virtually any Ford gasoline powerplant. Ford subsequently released EEC-IV applications for all four-, six-, and eight-cylinder engines, with both speed-density and mass flow controls. As was the case with GM TPI and TBI ECMs, the EEC-IV gained in complexity and power as time went on.

All but the earliest EEC-IV controllers had identical 60-pin harness connectors, though the pin assignments sometimes varied with the engine application and how many I/O pins were needed. The EEC-IV controlled spark timing mated to three ignition systems (thin film ignition), EDIS (electronic distributorless ignition system), and motorcraft DIS, all of which had the ability to deliver spark timing autonomously if communication with the ECU failed. In the case of the thin film ignition (TFI), the EEC-IV read a Hall effect sensor and provided a spark-out signal to the ignition when it was time to deliver spark (dwell was sometimes controlled by the EEC-IV, sometimes by the TFI). The EDIS module provides the EEC-IV with crank position information from a 36-1 crank trigger wheel and the EDIS de-multiplexed signals from the EEC-IV to control wasted-spark direct-fire coils. Rather than using the timing of the EDIS-bound pulse to determine spark timing, special code in the EEC-IV encodes timing information into the length of the spark angle word (SAW) returned to the EDIS module. A shorter pulse delivers more spark advance. Though lacking the 36-1 trigger wheel of the EDIS system, Motorcraft DIS ignitions provide distributorless ignition for dual-plug 2.3L powerplants, Thunderbird SuperCoupe, and Taurus SHO.

The J3 test port on the side of the EEC-IV box is for developer use. This is the way aftermarket chipmakers gained access to the EEC-IV. The test connector port contains the micro-controller's multiplexed address/data bus signals, as well as a PROM disable signal. Although more expensive than the simple chip-change technology of similar-vintage GM systems, aftermarket chipmakers and tuners wishing to hack the EEC-IV needed only to design a relatively simple electronic module that plugs into the J3 port, disables the EEC-IV internal PROM, and substitutes its own PROM with modified calibration.

Examples of functions controlled by the EEC processor and subject to modification via recalibration are A/F ratio in closed-loop, acceleration and warm-up transient fueling, EGR, charcoal canister purge, thermactor operation, adaptive control system, control of OBD-I and OBD-II testing (enable/disable, change test values, and so on), main fuel, main spark, MAF calibration, VE table, injector flow, rev limits, speed limits, electronic transmission control, and many more.

The aftermarket EEC-Tuner package provides EEC calibration software, cabling, and hardware to modify EEC-IV and EEC-V processors. Tweecer and Anderson (PMS) provide EEC tuning products and calibrations. EECTuner enables a tuner to effectively modify any hex location in PROM memory on the EEC-IV, and all locations in bank 1 and bank 8 in the EEC-V. The trick is knowing where calibration tables and parameters are located in memory.

In the case of several specific common Mustang V-8 EEC processors and the Mustang 2.3 turbo, the EEC-tuner is preconfigured with the location of calibration parameter data structures in EEC ROM memory. In the case of Mustang speed-density processors and many other EEC systems, you are on your own. Over the years EEC-IV processors have had their memories mapped out and the data structures available for performance

tuning and power-adder conversions, though the ranks have not thinned with age.

EEC-V computers on Ford OBD-II vehicles integrate ignition control into the ECU but retain the 36-1 (40-1 in the case of V-10 powerplants) variable reluctor crank triggering system. The EEC-V is capable of controlling variable valve timing and other complex actuator systems, as well as integrated dash gauge control.

Diablosport, Sniper, Superchips and other vendors provide flash programming tools and performance calibrations for OBD-II Fords.

Japanese

The simplest way to get a handle on what's available to hack Honda, Mazda, Mitsubishi, Nissan, Subaru, Toyota, and other vehicles is to look at the application charts from Hondata, Techtom, and other firms that have focused on recalibrating Japanese engines. In the case of pre-OBD-II engines, changing the PROM calibration of many of these vehicles requires hardware modifications to the motherboard of the electronic control module.

OEM ECU PROM/Flash Recalibrations, Software: OEM ECU PROM/flash calibrations/software

AFE Scorcher: 2003–11 Dodge gasoline V-8 cars and trucks, Chev-Dodge-Ford-GMC diesels)

APR: Audi/VW

Arizona Speed and Marine: LS1, LS2, LS7, and supercharged LSx engine ECU tuning and calibrations for marine and ram-jet powerplants.

Active Autowerke: BMW

Autologic: BMW, Land Rover, Jaguar (diesel only), Mercedes-Benz, Porsche, and VAG Performance Tunes, including turbo-diesel reflash

Autothority: Audi, VW, Ferrari, Rolls/Bentley, Mercedes, Mayback, Lamborghini, Porsche, BMW, Mini chip tuning.

Bonneville Motor Werks: Shark Edit for BMW and other vehicles with Bosch Motronic ECUs, Motronic Editor (older)

Bully Dog: Triple Dog engine management programmer and diagnostic module for Dodge and Ford diesel trucks

Carputing: GM ECU tuning: 2005–12 LS2-edit, '94/95 LT1-Edit, '96/97 LT1/LT4-Edit, '97–06 LS1 cars + trucks, '99–05 Holden LS1

ChipTorque: ECU reflash and interceptors for wide variety of ECUs

Cobb Tuning AccessPORT: Realtime and flash tuning for Subaru, Mitsubishi, Mazda, Nissan, Mini, and BMW

Diablosport: ECU Tuning, diagnostics for a wide variety of vehicles

Edge Products: Gas and diesel ECU recalibration and diagnostics module

EFI Live: GM ECU tuning (www.efilive.com/downloads/index.html)

Eurotek Designs: ECU tuning for Bentley, BMW, Ferrari, Jaguar, Lamborghini, Maserati, Mercedes Benz, and Porsche (www.eurotekdesigns.com)

Fastchip.com: ECU tuning for a variety of GM vehicles and engines

FreeScan: Pre-OBD-II tuning software for Lotus and GM vehicles (www.andywhittaker.com/en-us/ecu/freescan.aspx)

Hondata: Honda ECU/PROM tuning and FlashPRO OBD-II reflash module/software

HPTuners: VCM Suite provides GM, Ford, and Dodge ECU tuning (www.hptuners.com)

HS Tuning: Unitronic ECU tuning software for VW, Audi, Porsche, Ferrari, and Lamborghini vehicles

Hypertech: Gas and diesel power tuning for Cadillac, Chevrolet, Ford, GMC, Infiniti, Jeep Mazda, Nissan, Ram, Suzuki, and Toyota

Jet Performance Products: ECU Tuning for wide variety of GM, Ford, Dodge, and Import ECUs

Jim's Performance: GM performance tuning

JMS: Ford, Lincoln, Mercury programmers, Chips, and Custom Tuning

Kraftwerk Performance: ECU tuning, ECO optimization and performance upgrades for cars, trucks, agricultural vehicles, and boats

Mighty Map: Japanese ECU tuning and recalibration, may require TechTOM/Technosquare ROMboard ECU modification or ECUflash program for OBD-II applications

Power Plus Engineering (PPE): ECU Chip tuning (www.power-plus.be/uk/)

Powertrain Electronics Co.: GM and aftermarket programmable ECU tuning and calibration

RomRaider/ECUflash: Open-source Subaru ECU hacking and recalibration solutions; definition files define ECU data structures for non-Subaru applications

SCT: Ford, Dodge, and GM ECU tuning

Shiftmaster: Ford ECU tuning, EEC-Tuner

Softronic: Ferrari ECU tuning (www.softronictuning.com)

Superchips: Flashpaq hand-held gas and diesel ECU tuner for Ford, GM, Dodge, and Nissan vehicles

Tactrix EcuFlash: OBD-II-based general-purpose ECU re-flashing and editing tool supporting a wide and increasing variety of vehicles

Tech Edge: GM ALDL interface (www.techedge.com.au/vehicle/aldl8192/8192hw.htm)

TTS Power Systems: Ford Powerstroke chips and tuning, GM gas engine tuning via Datamaster software, GM diesel tuning via ECU exchange (www.ttspowersystems.com)

C.A.T.S.: ECU tuning and hacking software: OBDI Tuning via Tuner, RT Tuner, OBDI TDF Editor; OBDII Tuning via OBDII Tuner, OBDII RT Tuner, OBDII Diesel Tuner, OBDII Diesel RT Tuner, WinFlash OBDII, OBDII VDF Editor, OBDII Dealer Kit; software utilities: CalData, WinFlash, Disassembler, Checksum, CompBin, S2bin, and Hex2bin (www.tunercat.com)

Veloce Performance Tuning: OBD-II and pre-OBD ECU tuning for Audi, Bentley, BMW, Ferrari, Lamborghini, Maserati, Mercedes Benz, Mini, Porsche, and VW (www.veloceperformance.com)

Vishnu Tuning: [Procede]

Winhex: Hexadecimal memory editor (winhex.en.softonic.com)

STEVE COLE (TTSPOWERSYSTEMS):

HRM: What do you see in the crystal ball?
SC: The tuning process has recently become more difficult because the OE software guys are laying more traps for criminal types like me. They are actually putting in way too much information, which is bad because I'll have to spend just that much more time deciding what's useful and what's smoke.

HRM: Is it a precursor to OBD-III?
SC: No, that's the Big Brother scenario where the car talks to the authorities about what you've been doing with it. We've got a ways to go before that happens, and by that time, we'll probably be too old to care.

Chapter 8
Tuning with Piggybacks, Interceptors, and Auxiliary Computers

Calibration tables and configuration data control the logic of modern digital factory ECUs in accordance with sensor data to *directly* determine the behavior of the engine, but the advent of sophisticated, affordable, programmable microprocessors provided the possibility of *indirectly* changing stock factory EMS behavior in a number of ways with piggyback computers to change engine tuning without permanent ECU recalibration or replacement.

1. *Brainwash the ECM:* Dynamically change critical calibration data used by the ECU to manage the engine, either by conditionally directing the ECU to read calibration data from an alternate memory source or by dynamically overwriting the contents of calibration data in ECU memory as required on an ongoing basis.

2. *Disobey the ECM:* Conditionally modify output signals from the ECU such as spark trigger or injector ground to change spark advance or injection pulse width with the ECU remaining blissfully unaware of what is going on.

3. *Lie to the ECM:* Modify input signals from engine status sensors such as crank position or coolant temperature to create a false virtual reality for the ECU some or all of the time in a way that causes data-dependent ECU operating algorithms to behave differently.

4. *Disregard the ECM:* Auxiliary ECU installed between the engine wiring harness and the main ECM assumes critical engine management functions from the factory ECM either continuously or only when certain conditions are true.

5. *Assist the ECM:* Auxiliary controller monitors engine status and pitches in at critical times to enhance engine functionality with staged additional fuel injectors, proportional nitrous injection, PWM boost control, or other capabilities.

Almost any auxiliary microprocessor device designed to affect engine operation that remains indefinitely powered up and connected to the engine-control wiring can be—and frequently is!—described as a "piggyback" computer. However, this book makes a distinction between a true *piggyback* device that remains connected permanently to an ECU to modify the behavior of a factory engine management system on an ongoing basis versus

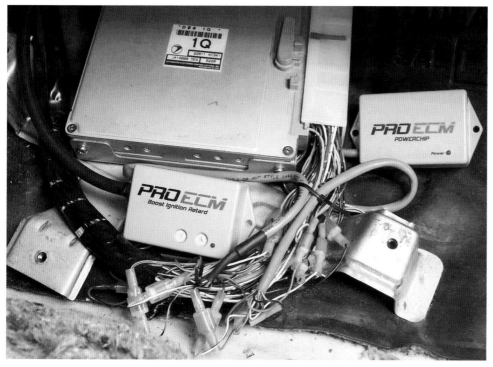

Interceptors can sometimes seem like a Band-Aid approach, but factory calibrations are very hard to beat for streetability. Why mess with the entire calibration if all you need to do is introduce a small delay in the crankshaft position signal to prevent knock with retarded ignition timing or extend the injection pulse to add a little fuel under hard boosted conditions? *ProECM*

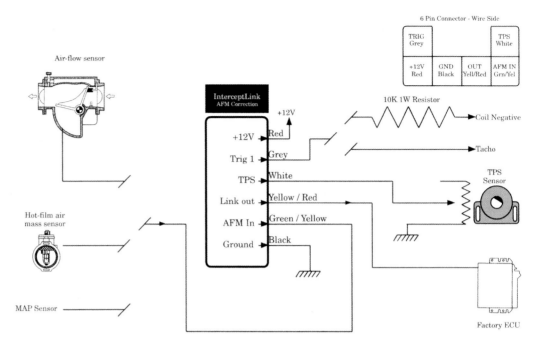

Link Engine Management InterceptLink basically intercepts and conditions engine-loading air (from MAP, VAF, or MAF and throttle position sensors) and combines with engine speed information (from negative coil or tach) in order to lie creatively to the factory EMS to increase performance with VE-improvers or power-adders. *Link Engine Management*

Air-flow sensor

Hot-film air mass sensor

MAP Sensor

6 Pin Connector - Wire Side

| TRIG Grey | | | TPS White |
| +12V Red | GND Black | OUT Yell/Red | AFM IN Grn/Yel |

InterceptLink AFM Correction

+12V — +12V Red
Trig 1 — Grey
TPS — White
Link out — Yellow / Red
AFM In — Green / Yellow
Ground — Black

+12V

10K 1W Resistor

Coil Negative

Tacho

TPS Sensor

Factory ECU

a *programmer* device that may remain in place on the vehicle to log or monitor EMS sensor data but that logically functions *once* to recalibrate the factory computer and has no ongoing role in engine management (unless or until you decide to once again retune the ECM). An *interceptor* is a special class of piggyback installed between the ECM and sensors or actuators that has the ability to block signals and substitute alternative input or output signals. This requires changes to the stock wiring path either by cutting and rewiring the stock harness or installation of an adaptor harness between the main ECM and stock engine harness.

WHY PIGGYBACK?

Why change the behavior of a factory EMS using a piggyback rather than recalibrating the factory EMS or replacing it with a standalone factory EMS?

1. Recalibrating a factory ECU is only possible if someone has succeeded in hacking it, so recalibration may not be an option.
2. Most ECM hacking solutions require at least some hardware, which raises the price.
3. Replacing the factory ECM with a standalone aftermarket EMS can be quite expensive. Piggybacks are usually much less expensive and require less supporting hardware.
4. Direct-injection engine management can be incredibly complex compared to port EMS, with multiple schemes for injection timing, charge stratification, air/fuel ratio, and so on. Recalibrating a DI engine with significant modifications is not something many people have the expertise and equipment to take on. Piggyback interceptors can vastly simplify hot rodding direct-injection powerplants that are turbocharged and can gain significant horsepower from overboosting.
5. It is a challenge to equal the quality of a factory EMS with an aftermarket system. There is a huge investment or time, resources, and expertise in a modern factory EMS. It is, and always has been, extremely difficult to perfectly optimize

electronic engine management for a particular application. Optimizing drivability, efficiency, and emissions under all conditions while achieving maximum torque numbers where it matters most in the operating envelope is not for the faint-of-heart. It typically takes months of work, even years, for automakers to build the "perfect" calibration for a particular engine in a particular application. This type of exhaustive, perfectionist work cannot be profitable on a one-off basis for aftermarket tuners, which is the reason even fully qualified expert professional aftermarket tuners seldom achieve perfectly optimal results when they replace factory EFI with a standalone aftermarket EMS or recalibrate a factory EMS to handle substantive changes to the engine's volumetric efficiency envelope. Tuners don't have the time or, in many cases, the resources (like arctic and tropical test facilities!). People who do have the time (retired hot rodders?) are unlikely to have the resources, lab equipment, and expertise to achieve truly superlative results. Original equipment engine and vehicle manufacturers, though, can and do take the time to tune EFI perfectly. They can afford to, because the time investment will be amortized over thousands of vehicles. They have the equipment and the engineering talent to do it right. What's more, with feds ready to levy hefty fines for noncompliance with emissions standards—and with the market ready to pass judgment on engines whose performance is not competitive—vehicle manufacturers clearly have the incentive to get it right. Perfection is the whole point of factory EFI and electronic engine management. Modern factory engine management with multi-port or direct injection is, in most respects, difficult or impossible to beat.

6. Tweaking the stock factory calibration with an interceptor is much easier than installing and calibrating a standalone aftermarket EMS, and many piggyback systems are easier to install and more intuitive to tune for nonengineers than recalibrating the factory ECU.

In order to upgrade the drivability and fun factor of EFI motorcycles, Dobeck Performance needed the ability to selectively increase fuel delivery at idle, light cruise, wide-open throttle, and during sudden increases in throttle opening. A piggyback device with these capabilities had to work in the real world of real people without their own R&D lab, so it had to be easy to understand, install, set up, tune, troubleshoot, and even uninstall—and it needed to have self-diagnosing and validating characteristics. It also had to be affordable. To meet these requirements, the goal was to keep it simple.

The Dobeck TFI system—progenitor of the current AFR-Plus system—tapped into the injector-driver circuitry of a stock bike's stock EFI to selectively append extra pulse width by continuing to ground injectors to hold them open the exact incremental time required for precise fuel enrichment. A bike's onboard computer and wiring harness remained intact, and no wires needed be cut. The stock air/fuel map remained intact, as did its correlation to the engine's volumetric efficiency (breathing) curve.

Dobeck fuel piggybacks are simple to adjust and conceptually similar to tuning and jetting carburetors. Early models used up to five adjustable dials (pots) and circuitry in the control unit to define the breakpoint between cruise and "main-jet" rpm, the length of time and magnitude for auxiliary transitional enrichment, and the incremental enrichment in tenths of milliseconds for the three operating ranges. More recent Dobeck piggybacks replace the pots with green, yellow, red, and blue LEDs and pressure-sensitive plus, minus, and mode switches. Dobeck piggybacks append an adjustable amount of additional injection pulse to various user-definable ranges of a bike's stock air/fuel map—by simulating changes to the adjustment of idle jetting, cruise jetting, full throttle main-jetting, and accelerator-pump jetting on a carburetor. LEDs provide status information to the tuner.

The transition from midrange to main-jet operating range is user-selectable. The piggyback computer is effectively self-diagnosing via simple tests that may include disabling the unit and observing certain results. Returning to stock engine management is simple: Turn off the unit. If adding fuel improves response, you're on the right track for a given performance range. If a range is set to zero additional fuel and adding any fuel worsens response, the EFI was already too rich as stock (usually implying there is an EFI malfunction).

By adding an adjustable fixed amount of additional pulse width to an injection event in a certain operating range, Dobeck piggybacks automatically produce a declining percentage of addition to pulse width as rpm increases. Even unloaded, engines require a longer injection pulse width as volumetric efficiency increases with rpm until you hit maximum engine pumping efficiency peak torque. Since engines become more sensitive to air/fuel ratio with increased rpm as the air/fuel ratio-spread narrows between rich and lean best torque, a declining percentage of enrichment is exactly what's required when you're looking to fix motorcycle factory compromises in air/fuel ratio. The fixed-declining addition method of pulse width–modification provides a user the ability to fix problems in a jetting range without simultaneously corrupting other parts of the range.

At this time of writing, the latest Dobeck Performance AFR-Plus piggyback was equipped with a Bosch wideband air/fuel ratio sensor and analog air/fuel ratio gauge.

TWEAKING EFI AND ELECTRONIC ENGINE MANAGEMENT WITH AUXILIARY DEVICES

There are various ways of using auxiliary "piggyback" devices to alter the behavior of stock engine management systems. In the real world, each method comes with its own price in terms complexity of use, operating limitations, difficulty of implementation, and cost.

Brainwash the ECU

ECU recalibration devices, also know as programmer devices, change the data parameters and tables in an ECU's flash memory or PROM that, along with the basic ECU logic, determine air/fuel ratio, spark advance, boost pressure, and other components of engine performance at various operating points of rpm and loading.

The chapter of this book about recalibrating a stock ECU deals with laptop-based ECU tuning systems. However, there are special-purpose auxiliary microcomputers designed to remain linked to the J1962 connector (or CAN bus) of an OBD-II ECU or tapped into a dual-ported calibration PROM of a pre-OBD-II ECU. These have the potential to change elements of ECM configuration data *on the fly*, based on input from the driver or on the status of OEM engine sensors, dedicated sensors connected to the reprogramming device, or even an operator-actuated interactive input device such as a nitrous switch.

Modifying the calibration of an OBD-II ECU is straightforward in most cases, as most car companies have used proprietary extensions of OBD-II protocols to allow updating of individual blocks of memory containing data tables and scalars on the fly while running. However, complete calibration updates or code replacement via boot-loader cannot occur while the ECM is running the engine. Many aftermarket programmer devices use proprietary OEM commands encapsulated within OBD-II communications protocols to semi-permanently recalibrate the ECM, after which the device can be removed unless it will be used to monitor or datalog the ECM. It is common in the world of diesel hot rodding to see piggyback programmer devices containing multiple calibrations dynamically available for different types of operating conditions (towing, maximum performance, maximum fuel economy, and so on).

MSD's classic Boost Timing Master was a "programmable" coil driver designed to intercept the spark timing signal and introduce an adjustable delay under boosted conditions as an anti-knock countermeasure on turbo, blower, or nitrous conversions that retained the factory ECM. MSD offered a variety of simple and complex timing interceptor devices, many adjustable with a screwdriver or simple dials. Superseded by Digital-6 Plus. *MSD*

HKS PFC

The HKS PFC (programmed fuel computer) F-CON was an interceptor black box that plugs into OEM injection wiring harnesses to enable modification of stock fuel curves—anything from minor enrichment (or enleanment) to the radical pulse-width changes needed to support really big injectors and high-boost forced induction. The idea is to retain as much as possible of the highly developed factory fueling map, modifying only those areas necessary to provide correct fueling for modifications such as turbo or supercharger conversions, increased turbo boost, larger turbos, or nitrous injection.

HKS offers multiple control maps for the PFC for use with various engines based on extensive testing. The unit is not generally sold for universal applications, although HKS will work with manufacturers of performance equipment outside the range of HKS's own specific product line to supply PFC maps for the new applications.

The PFC is designed to plug into factory EFI wiring harnesses and requires no fabrication or surgical skills to install. Once installed, PFC internal dip switches allow selection of gross richer or leaner percentage of the basic program, plus selection of nine separate condition programs. Beyond that, the graphic control computer (GCC) option gives the user a second black box with pots to adjust individual load points of 500, 2,000, 3,500, 5,000, 6,500, and 8,000 rpm, each of which can be adjusted to deliver up to 16 percent more fuel or 12 percent less fuel than the base map. The GCC averages values between the adjustable points for smooth fueling. HKS offers a further optional black box called the electronic valve controller to raise turbocharger maximum boost levels by electromechanically altering boost pressure levels as seen at the factory wastegate/controller. And to work with this, they offer the Fuel Cut Defenser (FCD) black box to defeat the factory fuel shutdown with overboost or high rpm for use with modified engines where such limits are dysfunctional.

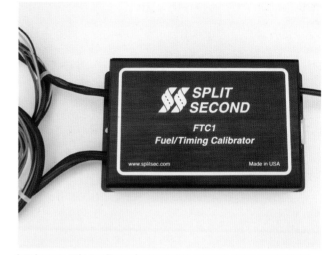

Split Second's FTC1 Fuel/Timing Calibrator offers adjustable timing retard and fuel enrichment for power-adder conversions. The ISF project in Chapter 18 uses an FTC *Split Second*

Most pre-OBD ECUs store configuration data in programmable read-only memory (PROM) that is not electrically erasable and must be removed for modification, but some pre-OBD-II ECUs can be forced to operate in a special diagnostic mode in which calibration data is retrieved from an alternate memory location that *can* be tuned while driving. Alternatively, PROM emulator devices can be used to replace PROM with random access memory or flash memory that makes the calibration data tunable on the fly via special mapping software. An example of older recalibration technology is the Techtom ROMboard solution. A reworked Toyota MR2 ECM reads calibration data from an auxiliary PROM (recalibrated using Techtom's Mighty Map software) installed in a piggyback daughterboard that itself plugs into a PROM socket soldered into place on the motherboard in place of the stock PROM. The stock PROM is itself installed in the daughterboard, but a ROMboard piggyback processor on the daughterboard forces the stock Toyota computer to operate in diagnostic mode on an ongoing basis such that the ECU reads data from the modified PROM.

Disobey the ECU

The simplest *ECU output modification devices* are fuel-trim piggybacks that lengthen fuel-injection pulse width under certain conditions to enrich air/fuel mixtures. Wires from the device tee into the ground circuits of individual port fuel injectors, allowing the piggyback to extend pulse width simply by continuing to ground the circuit after the ECU has dropped ground. The simplest fuel trim devices are calibrated manually by tuning trim pots with a screwdriver or adjusting pressure switches with LED indicators to increase or decrease fuel delivery during acceleration, idle low-end pulse width gain, pulse width gain at peak airflow, and sometimes other adjustment ranges. Idle gain may or may not affect pulse width under all conditions. High-end gain changes peak airflow pulse width, with decreasing effect at lower airflow or rpm (equivalent to changing the slope of the gain in pulse width according to rpm or load). Some fuel trim devices are equipped with their own MAP sensor tot enable tuners to deliver fuel enrichment exclusively during boost conditions for turbo or supercharger conversions. This type of fuel trim piggyback is not technically an interceptor because all output circuits remain in place at all times, allowing output signals only to be extended, not truncated.

The simplest spark-retard devices conditionally introduce a delay into the primary ignition trigger circuit from the ECM, ignition module, or points to the igniter and coil, and are thus able to retard spark timing but unable to *advance* it. Which is fine, because these devices are mainly used to pull timing during boost for turbo or supercharger conversions. In the simplest case, by swapping resistors or adjusting tuning pots or pressure switches with LEDs, a tuner can warp the shape and slope of various regions of the rpm and load timing curves—but always in the direction of less timing advance. Spark-retard devices are indeed interceptors, since the timing control circuit must be cut and diverted through the interceptor, which can then pass a timing pulse directly through without delay, switch the pulse through circuitry that introduces a delay, or block the pulse entirely and fabricate a new timing pulse at a calculated time. Many spark retard devices are bundled with a performance ignition module like the MSD 6 series, a capacitive discharge and multispark coil driver.

Sophisticated general-purpose interceptors sometimes provide output signal manipulation for fuel or ignition trim that is controlled not by trim pots, pressure switches, or resistors, but by sophisticated table-driven software algorithms in a digital microprocessor that rivals the ECU itself in terms of performance and sophistication.

Lie to the ECU

Sensor-manipulation devices are designed to create a false virtual reality around the ECU. These devices are input interceptors that strategically lie to your stock ECM about the status of one or more engine sensors under certain conditions in such a way that the ECU's standard logic provides modified engine management. Sensor manipulation has been successfully used to increase or decrease fuel delivery, spark timing, boost pressure, top speed, redline, or other factors, but one downside is that manipulating sensor data to optimize one tuning parameter can have unintended undesirable consequences for other tuning parameters that must be addressed in some way. This is a bit like taking a drug to fix a medical condition and being forced to take one or more additional drugs that deal with the side-effects of the first.

A common trick that falls within this class involves manipulating temperature sensor data. All factory ECUs use coolant, air, oil, or cylinder head temperature sensor data to deliver fuel enrichment when the engine is cold or warming up as a percentage offset to the base fuel calculation. Reporting a *false* low engine temperature during boosted operations after the engine has reached normal operating temperature can be used to force the ECU to deliver any fuel enrichment percentage available in the warm-up enrichment table(s) between, usually, -60 and 160 degrees Fahrenheit. Temperature-based enrichment schemes are limited to what's available in the warm-up map, but factory ECU must provide the radically rich air/fuel mixtures required to operate at temperatures as low as -60 degrees Fahrenheit, at which point 100 percent enrichment is a common default value in engine temperature compensation maps. Keep in mind that if the stock air/fuel ratio was, say, 12.0:1 at full throttle, adding 100 percent more fuel changes the air/fuel ratio hugely, to 6.0:1! And a 100 percent increase fuel would allow the ECU to maintain a 12.0:1 air/fuel ratio if turbo boost doubled mass airflow into the engine. You might think this implies you could fuel a full atmosphere of boost, that is, a pressure ratio of 2.0, but doubling engine mass flow requires more than an

extra atmosphere of boost pressure, due to density loss from the heat of compression, even with an efficient intercooler removing some of the heat in the compressed air.

What pressure ratio will deliver a *density ratio* of 2.0? Density ratio is pressure ratio corrected for temperature increase:

SPLIT SECOND FUEL TIMING CALIBRATOR

Cell Value	Mode	
	Direct	Signal Modify
0	0.0	-2.5
1	1.25	-2.25
2	0.5	-2.0
3	0.75	-1.75
4	1.0	-1.5
5	1.25	-1.25
6	1.5	-1.0
7	1.75	-0.75
8	2.0	-0.5
9	2.25	-0.25
10	2.5	0.0
11	2.75	0.25
12	3.0	0.5
13	3.25	0.75
14	3.5	1.0
15	3.75	1.25
16	4.0	1.50
17	4.25	1.75
18	4.5	2.0
19	4.75	2.25
20	5.0	2.5

The number entered into the timing map indicates the timing retard in degrees. The value can range from zero to 20.0. The maps for both fuel and timing are overlay maps that are applied on top of the maps in the stock ECU.

TPC Racing used a Split Second FTC1 to control additional injector and retard timing on its Porsche 993 supercharger kit. *Split Second*

$$DR = (T1C / T2C) * PR$$

But what is the temperature increase? Assume compressor inlet air temperature (T_{CI}) is 70 degrees Fahrenheit and you're running 14.7-psi boost and compressor efficiency (**CE**) is .79, an 80 percent effective intercooler. 70 degrees Fahrenheit converts to an absolute temperature (degrees above absolute zero) of 530°R (530 = 460 + 70).

Compressor Outlet temperature T_{CO}) will be:

$$TCO = TCI + (TCI * PR.0283) – TCI) / CE)$$
$$TCO = 530°R + (530°R * 2.0.0283) – 530°R)/.79)$$
$$TCO = 675°R = (675 – 460) = 215°F)$$

Temperature increased 145 degrees Fahrenheit. The 80 percent efficient intercooler removed .8 * 145 = 116 degrees Fahrenheit of the temperature rise. Actual temperature increase after intercooling is 145 – 116 = 29 degrees Fahrenheit. 70 + 29 = 99 degrees Fahrenheit. 99 + 460 = 559°R

Going back to the first equation,

$$DR = (T1C / T2C) * PR$$
$$DR = (530 / 559) * PR$$
$$DR = 1.896$$

A pressure ratio of 2.0 is a density ratio of 1.896, which does not double the mass airflow. But let's work backward assuming a density ratio of 2.0.

$$PR = DR / (T1C / T2C)$$
$$PR = 2.0 / (530 / 559)$$
$$PR = 2.11$$
$$Boost = 2.11 * 14.7 = 15.5 psi$$

The bottom line is that 100 percent additional fuel would maintain a 12.0 air/fuel ratio at 15.5-psi boost using a 79 percent efficient compressor and 80 percent effective intercooler. Meanwhile, since engine temperature compensation fuel enrichment normally declines gradually to 0 as the engine warms to 160 degrees Fahrenheit, an intelligent sensor-manipulation device has plenty of leeway to vary fuel enrichment to compensate for the additional fuel required with boost pressure in the 0-15.5-psi range, depending on the precise false engine temperature it reports to the ECU. Keep in mind that maintaining a certain air/fuel ratio under boost may not be enough because boosted engines may need richer mixtures to fight detonation, which, of course, lowers the maximum boost that's fuel-able with this type of sensor-manipulation scheme.

Temperature-manipulation schemes tend to work well on older vehicles with dumb engine management systems incapable of evaluating the plausibility of sudden changes in sensor data. Sophisticated late-model OBD-II systems are much, much better at recognizing sensor problems with the potential to adversely impact exhaust emissions—like a temperature sensor that apparently never warmed up all the way or one that intermittently reports sudden drastic changes in engine temperature. Which could cause an OBD-II ECU to set check engine trouble codes or to enter some kind of limp-mode operation where it disregards engine temperature and uses a default.

However, even if an EMS is not smart enough to recognize some types of questionable sensor data, there are other potential problems with temperature sensor manipulation. In addition to delivering (desirable) richer air/fuel ratios, reporting falsely cold engine temperature to an ECU may result in advanced spark timing designed to deal with the slower combustion of really cold

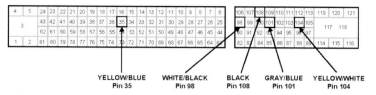

These connections are for the Passat.

All wire connections are made to the wiring harness near the engine computer. The wires are identified by color code and ECU connector location.

| | YELLOW/BLUE Pin 35 | WHITE/BLACK Pin 98 | BLACK Pin 108 | GRAY/BLUE Pin 101 | YELLOW/WHITE Pin 104 |

Connections:

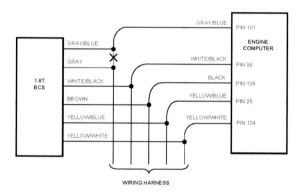

Wiring connections for Split Second's 1.8T VW/Audi Boost Control System illustrate the simplicity of making four taps into the factory ECU connector to the BCS, cutting a fifth wire, and splicing the ends to connections on the BCS. The BCS is an interceptor/display device located between the factory ECU and the VW PWM boost controller that allows a user to increase boost above stock-permissible levels from the cockpit without ECU re-programming from 6 to 14.5 psi with performance gains of 35 rwhp and 43 ft-lbs. *Split Second*

temperatures—the last thing you want during turbo boost. No problem, intercept and manipulate engine position data output from the crank sensor to retard timing, right? Fine, but this could result in retarded valve timing with adverse performance, emissions, or fuel efficiency effects if the engine has electronic valve timing.

Airflow sensors (MAF, VAF, and MAP) represent another class of sensor that is subject to fruitful manipulation strategies. A programmable airflow sensor or interceptor that can be configured to over- or under-report airflow in various segments of the flow range of the engine can be used to "re-jet" an engine in a way that's conceptually similar to adjusting idle mixture, midrange, and peak-power air/fuel ratios in the days of carbureted engines. Yet another trick is underreporting airflow to the ECU by a percentage corresponding to the percentage increase in fuel flow from upgraded fuel injectors, thus forcing the ECU to command shorter injection pulse widths that compensate for oversized fuel injectors. Of course, the point of installing larger injectors is that subsets of the rpm/load map where smaller injectors were unable to deliver sufficient extra fuel can now be handled by adjusting the interceptor or programmable sensor to reduce the amount by which airflow will be underreported in these specific areas. Yet another airflow manipulation trick that can be useful on hot rod engines is

Signal Modify Configuration Using internal MAP Sensor:

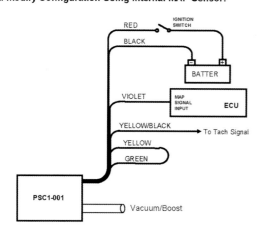

Split Second recommends this configuration for most applications using its programmable signal calibrator, which is used to lie to the ECM about manifold pressure to accommodate injector size changes or to induce fuel enrichment by overstating engine loading to the stock calibration logic. Output to the ECU in this mode is a modified version of the internal MAP sensor signal, which is already close to the desired output. The PSC1-001 uses its internal MAP table to modify the MAP signal as necessary. The range of adjustment in this mode is +/- 2.5 volts. A cell value of 0 will subtract 2.5 volts from the signal. A cell value of 10 will not alter the signal. A cell value of 2.5 volts will add 2.5 volts to the signal. The starting map for this configuration is a map loaded with 10 in every cell. *Split Second*

Typical Connections:

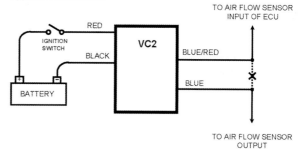

Wire Assignments:

WIRE COLOR	CONNECT TO	LABEL
Red	Switched battery positive (+12V)	BATT +
Black	Battery negative (chassis ground)	BATT -
Blue	Air flow sensor output	FLOW IN
Blue/Red	Air flow sensor input to the ECU	FLOW OUT

Clamp Function (User adjustable):

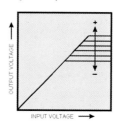

Wiring connections for Split Second's Voltage Clamp 2 (VC2). This interceptor device is designed to condition the output of voltage-based airflow meters, MAP sensors, and mass airflow sensors to avoid a fuel cut in forced-induction conversion applications. Under normal operating conditions, the VC2 outputs a signal that is identical to the signal present at its input. When the voltage of the flow signal reaches a user-adjustable clamp level, the VC2 maintains a constant output voltage at the clamp level as the input voltage rises. The VC2 differs from the VC1 by offering a hard clamp function that is user adjustable. Once in clamp mode, the VC2 maintains the clamp level with high accuracy regardless of overdrive. *Split Second*

programming an interceptor device to clamp the air sensor voltage or frequency just below the value that will trigger an ECU boost fuel cut on many factory ECUs, though, of course, airflow above such a value must then be fueled by some other method.

As with ECM output fuel trim devices, air sensor input manipulation devices are sometimes calibrated with simple trim pots (or pressure switches) that clamp or modify the slope of modifications to standard sensor voltage. In the case of programmable devices, sophisticated air sensor manipulation is possible by defining complex transfer functions under digital microprocessor control capable of falsifying sensor output in complex ways with fine granularity depending on operating conditions.

In some cases, airflow manipulation devices change the method by which airflow is measured or estimated, replacing vane airflow sensors with more sophisticated MAF sensors, or allowing restrictive VAF or MAF sensors to be replaced by a sensor-manipulation device equipped with a MAP sensor, configurable speed-density data tables, and software algorithms that simulate the airflow meter and convert the powerplant to speed-density engine management.

VAF sensors have disappeared from new engines. Modern engines are usually equipped with both MAF and MAP sensors, and modern ECMs have the ability to correlate airflow data from MAF, MAP, and throttle-position sensors if there is any doubt about the veracity of any of the sensors. The market for airflow manipulation devices is no longer what it was, but well-known examples of past airflow-manipulation products include the APEXi Super Airflow Converter (SAFC) and the HKS vane pressure converter (VPC), both of which have been discontinued. The VPC substituted its own user-adjustable (via

trim pot) MAP-based airflow data for data from the stock Vane airflow meter, which was no longer required. The VPC transfer function could also be reprogrammed by changing the internal conversion or transfer tables that drive its overall operation. Some sophisticated interceptors still provide the ability to convert VAF engines to programmable MAF-based airflow metering and are configurable to match the voltage or frequency requirements of the EMS and manipulate an airflow signal to change air/fuel ratio in subsets of the operating envelope or specifically to compensate for larger fuel injectors as described above.

Another important type of input sensor manipulation involves the crank position sensor. Some piggybacks have the ability to monitor crank trigger systems and substitute *fabricated engine position* signals for the stock crank reference signal that provides the ECU with precise engine position data. Lying about engine position by delaying or advancing the crank reference signal is powerful because this type of sensor manipulation can be used to not only retard spark timing but to *advance* it, which is not possible with schemes that simply intercept the ECU-generated timing pulse leaving the ECU.

Problems

Sensor-manipulation schemes sometimes break down if the engine encounters temperature, altitude, or airflow conditions that require some or all of the fuel enrichment you were depending on to deal with boosted manifold pressure to handle normal operating conditions.

For example, if you are depending on a false low-temperature sensor reading to deliver boost fuel enrichment, problems may arise if the engine is boosted while the engine is still warming up and a certain amount of engine temperature compensation is required to deal with poor low-temperature fuel vaporization. A robust sensor-manipulation scheme will take this into account when calculating a false air temperature.

Another type of problem can occur when you are over-reporting engine airflow at high levels of horsepower to instigate increased fuel delivery if calculated false airflow reaches the upper limit of the airflow sensor range. An out-of-range airflow sensor voltage or frequency may be interpreted by the ECU as an indication that the sensor has failed, usually resulting in a fuel cut or limp-mode and check engine light. Sensor range problems of this kind must be dealt with by other means, such as installing larger injectors and recalibrating the airflow transfer table of the sensor-manipulation device, or by clamping the false output

signal to the ECU at an acceptable level and employing an alternative fuel enrichment scheme in the realm—or tweaking injection pulse higher on the output side of things. In some cases, however, a calculated false airflow may be within the range of the sensor but outside the range the ECU will accept as valid. For example, let's suppose the upper portion of airflow sensor range is unused and not reachable by a stock turbo engine, and the stock ECU knows this. Sensor output high enough above the expected peak airflow will usually cause the ECU to deduce that the sensor is bad or that the engine is seriously overboosting, which will trigger a hard fuel cut or limp mode with self-protective countermeasures. This precise situation can occurs with many overboosted factory turbo engines, but also with the stock MAP sensors on certain naturally aspirated Honda engines, which are capable of measuring a half-bar or so of boost pressure. Without countermeasures, an unmodified stock ECU will freak out as described above.

Engine position manipulating can cause problems in the latest OBD-II systems, which may depend on micro-changes in the timing of the crank reference signal to detect unexpected crankshaft acceleration and deceleration that indicate misfires, and the ECU may report malfunctions if an interceptor is manipulating the crank ref signal in the wrong way.

J&S Safeguard individual-cylinder Knock Retard Kit. Includes electronic control unit, knock sensor, AFR gauge, wiring, and connectors.

Assisting the ECM

This type of dedicated EMS enhancement device does not tamper with stock ECM operation, but instead monitors engine operating conditions and works independently to improve performance under certain circumstances in a way that is invisible to the main EMS computer.

One example is the pulse width-modulated nitrous controller, which triggers proportional nitrous and supplemental fuel injection at full throttle when the nitrous system is armed. Most nitrous system suppliers sell PWM nitrous controllers, and most general-purpose piggybacks have the ability to regulate nitrous solenoids, in some cases with PWM capability.

Another type of EMS enhancement device is the *auxiliary injector controller* (AIC), which is configured to kick in when manifold pressure exceeds a certain limit during boost conditions to stage add-on fuel injectors that provide supplemental boost fuel. This may be combined with a voltage clamp on MAP or MAF sensors to prevent the stock ECU from freaking during boost and triggering a fuel cut or limp-mode. Split Second, AEM, AutoSpeed, and others have sold additional injector controllers. In some cases, AIC capability is bundled with other piggyback/interceptor functions.

Still another example of an EMS enhancement device is the electronic *fuel management unit,* which provides functionality similar to an AIC by pinching off fuel return downstream of the stock fuel pressure regulator to raise fuel pressure above normal specifications during boost conditions, usually as a multiple of psi increases in positive manifold pressure. The Superpumper-II is one example of an electronic pressure control device. In some cases high rate-of-gain pressure controllers must be supplemented by activation of an additional fuel pump or increased voltage to the stock fuel pump in order to provide the additional fuel flow required to achieve target super-normal pressure.

Upgrade injector driver devices are equipped with high-power transistors that enhance the stock ECU's ability to control high-flow low-resistance upgrade fuel injectors. Most high-flow aftermarket injectors use low-resistance peak-and-hold coils that will damage stock ECUs designed to handle ordinary high-resistance saturated-circuit stock injectors.

A special case of enhanced engine management involves adding a complete aftermarket engine management system that assumes all major engine management functions, at least some of the time, leaving the stock EMS functional to handle other significant vehicle or powertrain management that is not practical or viable for handling by the aftermarket system. This type of installation sometimes requires a separate piggyback to fabricate inputs to the stock ECU/CAN bus plausible enough to keep the stock ECU functioning normally for the tasks it is still handling. Haltech's Emulator 8 is one example.

ADVANCED INTERCEPTORS

General-purpose interceptors are in a sophisticated and powerful class of programmable piggyback controller designed to "outsmart" or disregard the stock ECU in multiple ways, and as such may rival the power and sophistication of a stock factory ECM. General-purpose interceptors bundle multiple piggyback capabilities described above and are typically programmable in complex ways using a laptop, PDA, or dedicated handheld programming device. Many have some general-purpose I/O channels that are user-definable, and some even provide a facility to incorporate user-written special-purpose programming logic. General-purpose interceptors can be relatively expensive (though

J&S safeguard ECU. Note adjustment pot for sensitivity, boost retard threshold and rate, as well as dip configuration switches that define operation mode. *J&S*

not usually as expensive as a standalone aftermarket EMS) and all require at least some modifications to the ECM-to-engine wiring harness or a harness adaptor that accomplishes the same thing. Advanced interceptors are typically trivial easy to program or tune because they are similar in complexity to standalone aftermarket EMSs and have limitations that standalone systems do not have that can make tuning less straightforward. The interceptor and piggyback tricks required to change the way a stock ECU manages an engine (lying to the ECU, disobeying the ECU, operating aftermarket actuators the ECU does not know about) can have unintended consequences and may have the potential to initiate a fight with your stock computer by triggering ECU countermeasures that attempt to undo what the interceptor is trying to have happen or that attempt to protect the engine by drastically reducing performance.

All interceptors require cutting at least some ECU input or output wires to eliminate a direct connection between ECU and certain sensors or actuators, in such a way that the interceptor can substitute its own signal.

Besides intercepting and directly modifying ECU control signals to ignition or injector circuitry, an interceptor may affect ECU commands indirectly by, airflow, manifold pressure, and so forth.

Advanced interceptors have the ability to:
- Directly increase fuel delivery by extending injection pulse-width signals leaving the ECU
- Directly retard timing by delaying ECU timing pulses to the ignition system
- Indirectly advance and retard spark timing by delaying or advancing the crank reference signal to the ECU
- Indirectly influence fuel delivery by increasing or decreasing the airflow sensor signal used in ECM fuel calculations

Advanced piggybacks have the potential to manage cold-start, knock sensing, temperature compensation, A/C cluthc operation or automatic transmission control, and more.

Dash-mounted Edge piggyback. This type of piggyback usually allows modifications to the operating mode of diesel trucks via turnkey recalibration (that must meet CARB emissions standards for add-on and modified parts!), and/or monitoring of engine functionality via OBD-II connection.

COMPUTER WARS: INTERCEPTORS VERSUS SELF-LEARNING ECMS

Modern ECMs use self-learning strategies to optimize performance, emissions, and durability as pumping efficiency changes when engines age and wear out. Attempts to tune a stock EMS with a piggyback interceptor can run into problems with self-learning factory ECMs that may be working at cross purposes, and this has gotten worse in recent times as factory ECUs have gotten smarter and gained more authority to self-tune at higher power settings based on data from wideband air/fuel ratio sensors.

For example, ECMs with learning strategies trim injection pulse width to target stoichiometric air/fuel ratios using an O_2 sensor. Exhaust gas oxygen content is a good indicator of precombustion air/fuel ratio, assuming there are no misfires or manifold air or exhaust leaks. If trim exceeds a certain threshold, the ECU incorporates it into a matrix of long-term "block-learn" fuel trim values minimize the magnitude of dynamic O_2-based fuel correction necessary by automatically incorporating block-learn correction in the basic fuel calculation. Closed-loop O_2 sensor strategies and long-term corrections are generally clamped to operate within a 14.1-15.5 air/fuel ratio (air/fuel ratio) range, beyond which additional fuel correction is outside the authority of the O_2 sensor and fuel correction logic due to the fact that the apparent need for additional correction is considered evidence of a serious malfunction that calls into question all fuel correction. If this is the case, the ECU will default into open-loop mode in which there is no air/fuel ratio correction. Even a light stab on the throttle can terminate closed-loop mode. Some late-model engines are equipped with wideband air/fuel ratio sensors that are accurate at mixtures much further from stoichiometric, enabling the ECM to read rich AFRs at heavy loading and undo the effects of an interceptor attempting to achieve the authority to trim the richer air/fuel ratios required at heavier engine loading is still limited to the outer limits of the range considered plausible, at which point the ECM will set the Check Engine light. Some advanced interceptors allow a tuner to optimize timing at part-throttle or peak torque, which can help the ECU achieve stoichiometric air/fuel ratios with a state of tune that improves performance.

In a method similar to the handling of long-term fuel trim, many factory ECUs continuously monitor knock sensors in a short-term closed-loop mode of aggressive retard-then-advance timing control strategies designed to stop detonation immediately. Knock-control strategies are critical in avoiding engine damage from detonation on any engine that is knock-limited on regular fuel, particularly turbocharged engines. If unexpected detonation continues to occur, many ECUs will learn the new detonation limits and construct "long-term" timing trim tables similar to the construction of block-learn fuel tables. The difference is that in the case of learned timing, ECU logic is designed to assume that detonation is probably caused by substandard fuel, and the EMS will continue at intervals to test the effect of timing advances in the direction of the default (fully advanced) stock timing on the theory that there is a good chance premium fuel will become available after the next fill-up, at which point the EMS will revert fairly quickly to more efficient stock spark timing. The bottom line is that detonation that occurs while calibrating on a dyno with an interceptor may cause the ECU to work at cross-purposes to the interceptor.

OEM engine management systems use knock sensors specifically designed to react to the detonation frequency of the particular engine. But in some cases, adding performance equipment that changes the amount and kind of normal engine noise can cross the threshold that the ECU suspects to be detonation. Some interceptors have the ability to intercept and modify knock sensor input to the ECU to fix this type of problem, though it may be more fruitful and straightforward to look for a replacement knock sensor more suited to the equipment on the engine, or to move the sensor to a location on the engine less sensitive to spurious engine noise—or to install an adjustable aftermarket knock detection and retard system like the J&S Safeguard for which there is documentation and support available for difficult pseudo-detonation problems.

Some experts flatly recommend never tampering with knock-sensor output with an interceptor (though monitoring the sensor output is always a good idea). If you have a sophisticated engine with factory EMS that is highly modified and are experiencing false-knock indications that cause problems, it is possible you should be working with a standalone programmable engine management system. If you are experiencing genuine knock, you should *never* interfere with the ECU's detonation countermeasures under any circumstances, but should immediately take steps to eradicate knock with higher octane fuel, colder plugs, piston-cooling oil squirters, upgraded combustion chamber cooling, better intercooling, colder air intake, or other tricks that lower the engine's octane number requirement (ONR).

How does a modern ECU know if the engine is producing more power than is good for it? One leading indicator is boost pressure. If the ECU sees over 4.6 volts from the MAP sensor, it may conclude the engine is making more power than is advisable and take countermeasures. In this case, an interceptor can truncate the MAP signal, say, to a maximum of 4.5 to 4.6 volts, preventing the ECU from adjusting boost or implementing other anti-power countermeasures.

Another indication of excessive power is the mass airflow signal. Even if the ECU is only seeing normal manifold absolute pressure, a high MAF signal could alert the ECU to dangerously high power levels. An interceptor can truncate the MAF signal to prevent ECU anti-power countermeasures. Of course, the ECU will probably not inject enough fuel for the true amount of air,

TUNING

Dobeck PowerCard interceptor. Generally used for motorcycles, sleds, or ATV applications, the device has also been packaged by automotive tuners for power-adder kits. *Dobeck Performance*

so the tuner would have to artificially extend injection pulse width (and possibly retard timing).

It used to be true that there was no facility for a standard factory ECU to say that at a particular rpm point and at a certain throttle position, it should see a certain airflow (so the ECU could cope with the effect of altitude and temperature changes, which can have a large influence on engine mass airflow). Older ECUs simply tried to keep mixtures within limits at cruise and to keep ignition timing from impacting the knock sensor circuit. Interceptor tuners did not have to worry much about triggering ECU limp-mode, which was not normally an issue, as the tuner had to do something fairly radical to have this happen. However, the sophistication of the latest ECUs have increased tremendously. ECUs are equipped with precision engine models suitable for torque-based engine management. Some ECUs monitor the slew rate of an accelerating engine—the maximum acceptable rate of change in certain engine parameters under certain conditions, such as vehicle speed or engine rpm at a certain engine loading—and will intervene if things get too out of hand.

How can an interceptor compensate for a factory ECU's closed-loop system tuning out all the adjustments made with an interceptor? Interceptors will not generally need to alter air/fuel ratios if closed-loop is working properly. However, sometimes an aggressive cam requires idle mixtures too rich for stoichiometric closed-loop operation. Only when aggressive camshafts require air/fuel ratios out of the O_2 sensor's narrow operating bandmust the interceptor be used to bring the air/fuel ratios back within range so the closed-loop can again operate correctly to achieve what it thinks are stoichiometric air/fuel ratios at cruise for good economy and throttle response. Such an engine would require an interceptor capable of simulating a near-stoichiometric O_2 sensor signal when mixtures are considerably richer.

If the airflow meter signal is being controlled by an interceptor to bring about changes to injection pulse width, might this affect ignition timing or boost control? The simple answer is, maybe. In fact, one advantage of an interceptor over a simple programmable mass airflow sensor on a super-modified engine is that a sophisticated interceptor can probably control fuel, advance/retard, and boost pressure—not just fuel.

Sophisticated general-purpose interceptors can often control auxiliary injectors and water injection. The basic injection pulse width itself can be controlled with highly sophisticated air/fuel maps that rival the power of a standalone EMS. The internal software will contain extensive table-driven Boolean logic that can be programmed via laptop user interface by setting the tables to make intelligent decisions for control of other actuators.

Powerful interceptors can control boost pressure to a high degree of resolution throughout the rpm range, allowing aggressive boost pressures to be programmed where it is safe to

PERFECT POWER SMT8

The SMT8 is an interceptor and emulator, combined with additional actuator controller capabilities. In addition to basic piggyback fuel and timing modifications, the following are some additional SMT8 capabilities and requirements:

- Designed to tune any engine
- Windows-based user interface for map modification
- Requires laptop
- Average of six wire connections to the OEM wiring loom
- Installation of SMT8 within 30 minutes by experienced installer
- Development kit includes all software, manuals, and 650-car wiring database or available unbundled
- No-tune option to hide setup and maps
- Lambda sensor signal modification via linear mode (tunes according to the voltage of the sensor) and nonlinear mode (tunes according to lambda value)
- Auxiliary output can be enabled according to rpm, airflow, temperature, and analog deflection points
- Frequency modification for airflow sensor input
- High-resolution 384-element rpm-load maps
- Seven steps per degree ignition for fine ignition replica
- Multiple, switchable maps
- Boost control with rate-of-gain
- Wide- and narrow-band air/fuel ratio modification
- Extra injector driver can alternately be used for proportional nitrous injection
- Input for airflow sensors and temp sensors, each having a map to manipulate fuel, extra injector, and ignition

do so (say at midrange), while dialing back boost pressure at higher rpm and coordinating with the correct air/fuel ratio and ignition advance. With sophisticated interceptors, you should not have to run modest boost pressure across the rpm range to keep things safe at higher engine speeds.

Some powerful interceptors can eliminate top-speed mph limitations, fuel cut at high-boost, and rev-limiter maximum rpm limits. Some can data-log engine sensors, injection pulse width, and ignition timing. Some allow multiple configurations to be stored in memory. The tuner is presented with 3-D ignition and fuel maps along with a boost vector. The ignition and fuel maps contain highly granular rpm and load range points, with hundreds of separate adjustments for ignition advance and retard and a large number of boost values spread across the rpm range.

continued on page 128

MSD Digital-6 Plus

SPLIT SECOND APPLICATION NOTE FOR ADVANCED GENERAL-PURPOSE INTERCEPTORS

What Piggyback Tuning Can Do

There are many cases in which piggyback tuning is an excellent solution. Piggyback tuning can be used to change ECM inputs and outputs to achieve the desired results. Mass airflow (MAF) sensor signals can be changed to adjust the fuel mixture and compensate for larger injectors. Crank and cam sensor signals can be delayed to retard timing in boost as needed to avoid detonation. Manifold absolute pressure (MAP) sensor signals can be clamped to avoid fuel cut on supercharged and turbocharged engines. The injector pulse width can be changed to add or take away fuel.

Piggyback tuning can be very effective in tuning aftermarket turbo and supercharger applications. Piggyback methods are widely used to compensate for larger injectors, keep signals within their normal range, retard timing as needed, and adjust for the correct AFR in boost. Manipulating the closed-loop fuel pressure signal on G-DI turbo engines can be very effective in providing fuel enrichment for overboost by forcing the ECM to increase common rail fuel pressure. Applications with boost up to 14 psi and even higher can be served effectively using piggyback techniques.

What Piggyback Tuning Can't Do

The essential limitation is that you are constrained by working within the limitations of the stock engine management system. For example, if the ECM is operating in closed loop AFR mode and you try to change the fuel mixture, the ECM will do everything it can to restore its target mixture. This in turn can be overcome by altering the O_2 sensor feedback to the ECM. Changes to the O_2 sensor readings must be done in a certain way so readings stay within their normal range and continue to respond to fuel mixture changes.

The main limitation when adjusting sensor signals is to keep them within their normal range. For example, it is common for a MAP sensor to have a maximum reading of 4.6V. ECM programming is often set to generate a fault if the reading is greater than 4.7V. That means that when you reach 4.6V on a MAP sensor signal, it's game over. You can't add fuel at that point by simply increasing the reading. In fact, you are more likely to induce fuel cut.

Beyond keeping signals within their normal operating range, you must keep signals within their range of plausibility. ECMs are programmed to expect a range of readings from an MAF sensor given a certain TPS reading. If the MAF sensor deviates outside the expected value range, the ECM will set a fault. This means you can't just do whatever you want

when doing piggyback tuning. You have to operate within the limits that the ECM gives you.

The Engine Management System

The ECM operates as an integral part of the entire EMS. The ECM takes in inputs from sensors that provide critical information about the engine such as coolant temperature, air temperature, barometric pressure, throttle position, air flow, and crank position. These inputs determine the current operating conditions. Based on these conditions and the programmed response, the ECM generates the appropriate outputs to various actuators. The ignition coils, fuel injectors, idle air valve, and other assorted solenoids and switches control the physical processes in the engine.

Piggyback calibration can be used on either the inputs or outputs of the ECM. For example, the MAF sensor signal input can be adjusted to change injector pulse width. Fuel can also be adjusted by intercepting the injector drive signals and changing the pulse width directly. There are pros and cons to each approach. Adjusting the MAF can be accomplished by intercepting a single signal versus multiple signals for each injector. On the other hand, intercepting the injector drive signals provides direct control, while changing the MAF reading is a more indirect method that is limited by ECM programming.

Piggyback Signal Calibration

The reading from the primary load sensor can be modified in order to achieve the desired change in fuel mixture. In most cases, this will be a MAF or MAP sensor. In some cases, some other sensor such as the throttle position sensor (TPS) may be used. As load on the engine increases, the signal from the primary load sensor increases.

It is possible to tune the engine by altering the load signal in a precise way for all the different possibilities of load and rpm. Figure 1 shows a theoretical fuel map for an engine. The axes for the map table are load and rpm. The map contains numbers that represent the on-time in milliseconds. These numbers are not actual numbers that would be used to run an engine. They are calculated based on the total amount of time for one cam revolution.

These numbers are based on the time for a complete engine cycle at different rpms. The actual pulse width will be less than these numbers. Actual injector duty cycle rarely exceeds 80 percent.

		LOAD (%)										
		0	10	20	30	40	50	60	70	80	90	100
	1,000	0	12.0	24.0	36.0	48.0	60.0	72.0	84.0	96.0	108.0	120.0
	2,000	0	6.0	12.0	18.0	24.0	30.0	36.0	42.0	48.0	54.0	60.0
	3,000	0	4.0	8.0	12.0	16.0	20.0	24.0	28.0	32.0	36.0	40.0
RPM	4,000	0	3.0	6.0	9.0	12.0	15.0	18.0	21.0	24.0	27.0	30.0
	5,000	0	2.4	4.8	7.2	9.6	12.0	14.4	16.8	19.2	21.6	24.0
	6,000	0	2.0	4.0	6.0	8.0	10.0	12.0	14.0	16.0	18.0	20.0
	7,000	0	1.7	3.5	5.2	7.0	8.7	10.4	12.2	13.9	15.7	17.4
	8,000	0	1.5	3.0	4.5	6.0	7.5	9.0	10.5	12.0	13.5	15.0
	Theoretical Injection Pulse Width (ms)											

Figure 1. Theoretical Injection Map. The numbers in the 100 percent column are based on 100 percent injector duty cycle at indicated engine rpm. At 8,000 rpm, the cam rotates 360 degrees in 15 ms. Actual injector duty cycle will generally not exceed 80 percent.

In Figure 2, a load trace is shown in red diagonally across the table. This trace roughly describes the path that would be followed if you were to gradually squeeze on the throttle and reach wide-open throttle (WOT) at 8,000 rpm. As you travel along the diagonal trace, the pulse width increases from zero to 15.0 ms. For comparison, the blue trace shows the path you would trace by applying WOT from a low rpm. The green trace shows the path if you lift the throttle abruptly from 8,000 rpm.

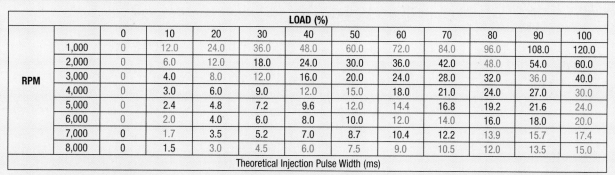

RPM	LOAD (%)										
	0	10	20	30	40	50	60	70	80	90	100
1,000	0	12.0	24.0	36.0	48.0	60.0	72.0	84.0	96.0	108.0	120.0
2,000	0	6.0	12.0	18.0	24.0	30.0	36.0	42.0	48.0	54.0	60.0
3,000	0	4.0	8.0	12.0	16.0	20.0	24.0	28.0	32.0	36.0	40.0
4,000	0	3.0	6.0	9.0	12.0	15.0	18.0	21.0	24.0	27.0	30.0
5,000	0	2.4	4.8	7.2	9.6	12.0	14.4	16.8	19.2	21.6	24.0
6,000	0	2.0	4.0	6.0	8.0	10.0	12.0	14.0	16.0	18.0	20.0
7,000	0	1.7	3.5	5.2	7.0	8.7	10.4	12.2	13.9	15.7	17.4
8,000	0	1.5	3.0	4.5	6.0	7.5	9.0	10.5	12.0	13.5	15.0
	Theoretical Injection Pulse Width (ms)										

Figure 2. MAP Traces for Various Throttle Inputs. The blue trace shows WOT from low rpm. The green trace shows a throttle lift from high rpm. The red trace shows progressive application of throttle with WOT at 8,000 rpm. *Split Second*

Piggyback calibration can be achieved by varying the load reading to the ECM. Figure 3 shows an example range of adjustment. At any given rpm, the fuel can be varied by changing the load reading to the ECM. In this example, the pulse width is 12 ms at 5,000 rpm and can be adjusted from roughly

RPM	LOAD (%)										
	0	10	20	30	40	50	60	70	80	90	100
1,000	0	12.0	24.0	36.0	48.0	60.0	72.0	84.0	96.0	108.0	120.0
2,000	0	6.0	12.0	18.0	24.0	30.0	36.0	42.0	48.0	54.0	60.0
3,000	0	4.0	8.0	12.0	16.0	20.0	24.0	28.0	32.0	36.0	40.0
4,000	0	3.0	6.0	9.0	12.0	15.0	18.0	21.0	24.0	27.0	30.0
5,000	0	2.4	4.8	7.2	9.6	12.0	14.4	16.8	19.2	21.6	24.0
6,000	0	2.0	4.0	6.0	8.0	10.0	12.0	14.0	16.0	18.0	20.0
7,000	0	1.7	3.5	5.2	7.0	8.7	10.4	12.2	13.9	15.7	17.4
8,000	0	1.5	3.0	4.5	6.0	7.5	9.0	10.5	12.0	13.5	15.0
	Theoretical Injection Pulse Width (ms)										

Figure 3. Piggyback Fuel Calibration Range. The fuel mixture can be precisely controlled by varying the load signal input to the ECM for every combination of load and rpm. Fuel is adjusted by moving around on the stock map table. *Split Second*

7.2 ms to 16.8 ms by varying the load signal by ±20 percent. While this example is based on theoretical numbers, it illustrates how varying a load signal can be used to change the amount of fuel delivered to the engine and the resulting AFR. When piggyback tuning by varying a load signal, what you are really doing is moving around on the stock map table. When doing this, you are fundamentally limited by the range of injector pulse width that is programmed into the stock ECM. For example, if the programmed injector pulse width at a given rpm is only capable of reaching a 65-percent duty cycle, that is the maximum duty cycle you can get. This means you have to work within the range that the stock ECM gives you.

Load sensor adjustment is frequently used to compensate for larger injectors. At light load when the new injectors deliver too much fuel per stock programming, the load signal can be shifted to read a lower load which results in a shorter injector pulse width.

There can be unintended consequences when doing piggyback tuning. The most important area of concern is ignition timing. In the process of adjusting the fuel mixture, it is possible to change the load signal in a way that advances timing. In extreme cases, this can lead to engine damage. Figure 4 shows a theoretical timing map. Consider the same variation in load that was used in Figure 3 to adjust AFR, and you see a substantial variance in ignition timing from roughly 25 to 35 degrees of advance. This is why calibrators for use in forced induction applications with larger injectors have the ability to retard timing as well as adjust fuel.

RPM	LOAD (%)										
	0	10	20	30	40	50	60	70	80	90	100
1,000	20.8	20.0	19.2	18.4	17.7	16.9	16.1	15.3	14.6	13.8	13.0
2,000	26.2	25.0	23.8	22.6	21.3	20.1	18.9	17.7	16.4	15.2	14.0
3,000	37.2	35.0	32.8	30.6	28.3	26.1	23.9	21.7	19.4	17.2	15.0
4,000	42.7	40.0	37.3	34.7	32.0	29.3	26.7	24.0	21.3	18.7	16.0
5,000	42.6	40.0	37.4	34.9	32.2	29.8	27.2	24.7	22.1	19.6	17.0
6,000	42.3	40.0	37.7	35.3	33.0	39.7	28.3	26.0	23.7	21.3	19.0
7,000	42.2	40.0	37.8	35.6	33.3	31.1	28.9	26.7	24.4	22.2	20.0
8,000	42.1	40.0	37.9	35.8	33.7	31.6	29.4	27.3	25.2	23.1	21.0
	Theoretical Spark Advance (degrees BTDC)										

Figure 4. Altering the Load Signal Can Change Ignition Timing. As the load signal is varied to tune fuel, it can also change ignition timing. When compensating for larger injectors, a lower load reading can result in dangerous timing advance. *Split Second*

A typical example would be a naturally aspirated engine that has been converted to forced induction with either a turbocharger or supercharger. In order to fuel the motor in boost, it is fitted with larger injectors. The big injectors do a fine job of fueling the engine at the top end but result in a mixture that is too rich in the light-load region. To compensate for the large injectors, the load reading is modified according to an overlay map in the piggyback calibrator. Cell values are chosen in the overlay map that subtract a precise amount from the load signal. As a result, the ECM provides less fuel to the engine by shortening the injector pulse width.

Closed Loop vs. Open Loop Operation

All engines with an O_2 sensor are able to operate in closed-loop mode. In this mode, the ECM fine -tunes the fuel mixture as you drive. The actual fuel mixture is determined by one or more O_2 sensors. These sensors may be narrowband, wideband, or a combination of both. The narrowband O_2 sensor is highly accurate at 14.7:1, which is known as the stoichiometric air fuel ratio (AFR). This AFR is targeted for the best compromise between fuel economy, performance, and emissions. Stoichiometric AFR is essential to the proper operation of catalytic converters.

In closed-loop mode, the ECM uses the readings from the O_2 sensors to adjust the injector pulse width to maintain stoichiometric AFR. This AFR is targeted during idle, cruise, and moderate acceleration. The base fuel or nominal injector pulse width is set according to airflow, rpm, and environmental factors. The base fuel is modified according to O_2 sensor feedback through a process called adaptation. Adaptation occurs both in real time and based on history. Historical adaptation data is stored in volatile memory that can be cleared by disconnecting the battery on the vehicle for 10 minutes.

A large part of the tuning process involves achieving stoichiometric operation over the light-load range. This is the range where we spend most of the time during daily driving. Tuning this region is essential to achieving good drivability. Tuning in the light-load region involves adjusting fuel for minimum adaptation as viewed on an OBD-II scan tool.

ECMs that use narrowband O_2 sensors need to be able to switch off the closed-loop process to achieve enrichment. When the closed-loop mode is switched off, the engine is operating in open loop. In open loop, the ECM no longer uses the O_2 sensor to fine-tune the fuel mixture. Under high load conditions, the engine computer targets a richer mixture than 14.7:1 to safely support the combustion process. An AFR of 12.5:1 is typical for high-load conditions.

Wideband O_2 sensors produce precise readings over a wide range of AFR. ECMs that use wideband sensors are able to stay in closed loop over most of the load range of the engine. Rather than going open loop, the wideband based ECM can get enrichment by targeting a rich fuel mixture and trimming precisely to that mixture.

TUNING

continued from page 125

Piggyback auxiliary engine management computers are, in the end, reliant on the existing ECU to provide fuel and ignition to the engine and are ultimately subject to the limitations of the ECU, its architecture, and its logic.

AUXILIARY COMPUTER AND INTERCEPTOR SOURCES

034 Motorsport: Supplementary injector ECU (additional injector controller)

APEXi: Piggyback AFC neo-digital fuel controller
www.apexi-usa.com

Autothority: VAF-to-MAF conversion, chip tuning, and ECU reflashing
www.autothority.com

Blowerworks: SuperPumper-II electronic fuel pressure management, SuperFueler AIC, and more
www.blowerworks.net

ChipTorque Xede Interceptor, ECU reflash, and turnkey ECU recalibration tools
www.chiptorque.com.au

ECUTek ECU tuning and datalogging for many OBD-II Subaru, Mitsubishi, Mazda, Nissan, Toyota, and Scion vehicles www.ecutek.com

Greddy: eManage ultimate universal piggyback
www.greddy.com

H&S Mini Maxx Race Tuner With Pyrometer for Dodge, Ford, and GM diesel applications
www.hsperformance.com

HKS: F-CONiS piggyback, F-CONiD diesel piggyback, F-Con V Pro standalone EMS, Fuel Cut Defencer, Valve Timing Controller, and so on
www.hks-power.co.jp/en/

Hondata: Piggyback-type Honda ECU add-ons for OE recalibration and expanded capabilities
www.hondata.com

Morego: Piggyback BBR-GTi Interceptor 2000
www.morego.co.uk

Perfect Power SMT8: Standalone engine management, universal piggyback and special-purpose interceptor devices, auxiliary engine electronics modules
www.perfectpower.com

Split Second: Piggyback laptop-programmable signal calibrator, pot-adjustable air/fuel ratio calibrator, additional injector controller, sensor signal conditioners and clamps
www.splitsec.com

Dobeck Performance: Piggyback fuel controller for EFI bikes, watercraft, sleds, and so on
www.dobeckperformance.com

Turbosmart: Electronic and pneumatic fuel cut defenders
www.turbosmart.com.au

Unichip (Dastek): Universal piggyback and plug-and-play calibrations for Infiniti, Jeep, Lexus, Mazda, Mini, Nissan Scion, and Toyota
www.unichip.com

9.1	9.7	10.6	11.7	13.0	14.2	15.2	16.2	17.1	17.9	18.6	19.3	20.0	20.6	21.3	21.6	22.3	22.6	22.6	
10.1	10.8	11.7	13.0	14.4	15.7	16.8	17.9	18.7	19.5	20.2	20.8	21.5	22.1	22.7	23.2	23.6	23.9	24.1	
11.0	11.8	12.9	14.3	15.8	17.2	18.4	19.5	20.4	21.1	21.8	22.4	23.0	23.6	24.2	24.6	25.0	25.3	25.4	
11.9	12.8	14.0	15.6	17.3	18.8	20.0	21.1	22.0	22.7	23.3	23.9	24.5	25.1	25.6	26.1	26.4	26.7	26.8	
12.9	13.8	15.1	16.9	18.7	20.3	21.6	22.7	23.6	24.3	24.9	25.4	26.0	26.5	27.1	27.5	27.8	28.0	28.1	

MAP [kPa]										
100	0.89	0.89	0.89	0.89	0.89	0.89	0.89	0.89	0.89	0.89
80	0.92	0.92	0.92	0.92	0.92	0.92	0.92	0.92	0.92	0.92
60	0.98	0.98	0.99	0.99	1.00	1.00	1.00	1.00	1.00	1.00
40	0.98	0.98	0.99	0.99	1.00	1.00	1.00	1.00	1.00	

Chapter 9
Standalone Programmable Engine Management Systems

Standalone aftermarket engine management systems are designed to provide complete engine management for competition-type vehicles. From the U.S. federal government's point of view, standalone engine management systems are legal—like all other hot rod modifications designed to increase engine performance—*if and only if* the vehicle is old enough that it is exempt from emissions testing or if modifications are installed on race or off-road vehicles that will never be driven on the street. Or if someone has succeeded in getting a prototype modified vehicle though the rigorous and expensive Federal Test Procedure for Add-On and Modified Parts and received an exemption order that proves modifications are relatively tamper-proof and have not increased emissions more than 10 percent above stock. For a variety of reasons, virtually all aftermarket programmable EMSs are illegal for highway use.

Since there are many good (and at least *potentially* legal!) ways to provide excellent engine management for power-adder conversions on late-model fuel-injected road-going vehicles that don't require replacing the stock ECU, standalone aftermarket engine management systems make the most sense as a solution

Holley Dominator Vehicle Management System. Note use of the word "vehicle." Dominator ECMs were designed with a radically powerful processor architecture, and the I/O system allows connections to a very large number of digital and analog input and output devices that monitor engine/vehicle events, or make things happened on the vehicle of engine. Like modern standalone ECMs in general, Holley targeted Plug-and-Play applications aimed at specific vehicles and engines. *Holley*

8.8	9.1	9.7	10.6	11.7	13.0	14.2	15.2	16.2	17.1	17.9	18.6	19.3	20.0	20.6	21.3	21.8	22.3	22.6	22.8
9.7	10.1	10.8	11.7	13.0	14.4	15.7	16.8	17.9	18.7	19.5	20.2	20.8	21.5	22.1	22.7	23.2	23.6	23.9	24.1
10.6	11.0	11.8	12.9	14.3	15.8	17.2	18.4	19.5	20.4	21.1	21.8	22.4	23.0	23.6	24.2	24.6	25.0	25.3	25.4
11.5	11.9	12.8	14.0	15.6	17.3	18.8	20.0	21.1	22.0	22.7	23.3	23.9	24.5	25.1	25.6	26.1	26.4	26.7	26.8
12.4	12.9	13.8	15.1	16.9	18.7	20.3	21.6	22.7	23.6	24.3	24.9	25.4	26.0	26.5	27.1	27.5	27.8	28.0	28.1

MAP											
100	0.89	0.89	0.89	0.89	0.89	0.89	0.89	0.89	0.89	0.89	0.89
80	0.92	0.92	0.92	0.92	0.92	0.92	0.92	0.92	0.92	0.92	0.92
60	0.98	0.98	0.99	0.99	1.00	1.00	1.00	1.00	1.00	1.00	
40	0.98	0.98	0.99	0.99	1.00	1.00	1.00	1.00	1.00	1.00	

The Accel DFI Gen 7 system arrived with a more complex and powerful architecture than the older Gen 6, including an optional volumetric efficiency VE table architecture, which describes how engine breathing varies from a perfectly flat torque curve with changes in rpm and manifold pressure. *Accel*

for (1) race vehicles that never drive on the street, (2) really old (exempt) street vehicles with carb-to-EFI conversions, (3) nonautomotive applications that do not have to pass emissions (experimental aircraft, certain marine engines, and so on), (4) street vehicles converted to burning clean fuels like natural gas or propane that exempt them from emissions testing, and (5) off-highway educational projects designed to teach participants the theory and practice of scratch engine calibration. Such applications are legal, and there's a lot to be said for going legal rather than outlaw.

What is not on the above list are certain classes of vehicles and engines for which programmable EMS makes perfect sense technically but is not legal: (1) All-out race-type vehicles that *do* drive on the street, (2) all-motor street-type hot rods so heavily modified with exotic tricks that stock EFI engine management cannot realistically be made to work well, (3) hot rod performance vehicles whose stock EMS literally cannot be successfully modified with interceptors, (4) scratch-built kit cars, (5) ongoing maximum-effort R&D-project vehicles with heavily modified engines where engine management is a moving target, (6) "streetable" show cars where looks are everything, and (7) anything owned by hot rodders who have no patience dealing with difficult reverse-engineering projects for the stock engine management.

In the real world there are plenty of applications where aftermarket EMS makes all the *technical* sense in the world, one result being that there are plenty of outlaw hot rodders driving on the street with illegal aftermarket engine management systems that are well-tuned, with emissions comparable to stock, many in states lacking effective enforcement programs against illegal hot rodding by sophisticated, smart, motivated hot rodders. That said, it is worth remembering that in states like California, you can pass an ordinary load-based smog test with flying colors and yet fail the smog test if a visual inspection of the vehicle reveals that the engine has been modified in a way that *could* impact emissions. This is true even if the engine tests out with *better* than stock emissions. It is also worth remembering that many standalone aftermarket engine management systems are *not* tuned to within 10 percent of stock exhaust emissions. For that matter, many are simply not optimized.

AEM plug-and-play Infinity EMS for 2JZ-GTE Toyota Supras. An increasing trend in standalone aftermarket engine management systems is the plug-and-play concept, which is designed to allow a replacement ECU to plug into the stock ECU connector with no changes to the wiring, sensors, or actuators. With the need to stand in for increasingly complex and powerful OEM engine control modules, AEM designed a vastly powerful new ECU with great flexibility, which could be used to run a large variety of EFI systems by adapting the ECU pin-outs to the OE requirements of nearly any streetable vehicle. Though AEM supplies generic calibrations for stock engines or common modifications, the company warns that failure to have an expert tune the calibration could damage your engine. Like most aftermarket systems, the AEM ECU is wide open to tuning with a laptop PC. *AEM*

The rest of this chapter discusses standalone programmable engine management systems from a purely technical rather than legal point of view.

CHOOSING A STANDALONE AFTERMARKET EMS

At this time of writing there were a least two dozen companies that developed and marketed programmable standalone engine management systems for the consumer or "prosumer" performance aftermarket. Most aftermarket EMS companies build three or more distinct lines of ECUs targeted to take advantage of the vast price elasticity and differing user requirements in the performance and racing aftermarket. There are more than 50 distinct aftermarket engine management ECUs from which to choose. In addition, there are many standalone programmable aftermarket systems that are no longer sold but are still out faithfully running performance engines on the street or racetrack (or perhaps awaiting your bid on eBay).

How do you compare the scores of features, capabilities, and options of programmable engine management systems, some of which may not be completely analogous, any of which might be truly important or of no consequence whatsoever in managing *your* engine, some of which may not be well documented and not fully understandable without access to proprietary source code? Whether you're a performance enthusiast considering the acquisition of your first programmable engine management system or a veteran of multiple engine calibration efforts on many brands of standalone onboard computers, choosing the best engine management system for a high-performance engine can be daunting.

9.1	5.7	10.6	11.7	13.0	14.2	15.2	16.2	17.1	17.9	18.6	19.3	20.0	20.6	21.3	21.8	22.3	22.6	22.8
7	10.1	10.8	11.7	13.0	14.4	15.7	16.8	17.9	18.7	19.5	20.2	20.8	21.5	22.1	22.7	23.2	23.6	23.9	24.1
.6	11.0	11.8	12.9	14.3	15.8	17.2	18.4	19.5	20.4	21.1	21.8	22.4	23.0	23.6	24.2	24.6	25.0	25.3	25.4
1.5	11.9	12.8	14.0	15.6	17.3	18.8	20.0	21.1	22.0	22.7	23.3	23.9	24.5	25.1	25.6	26.1	26.4	26.7	26.8
2.4	12.9	13.8	15.1	16.9	18.7	20.3	21.6	22.7	23.6	24.3	24.9	25.4	26.0	26.5	27.1	27.5	27.8	28.0	28.1

		0.86 0.86 0.89 0.89 0.89 0.86 0.86 0.86 0.86 0.86 0.86 0.86
MAP	100	0.89 0.89 0.89 0.89 0.89 0.89 0.89 0.89 0.89 0.89 0.89 0.89
	80	0.92 0.92 0.92 0.92 0.92 0.92 0.92 0.92 0.92 0.92 0.92
	60	0.98 0.98 0.99 0.99 1.00 1.00 1.00 1.00 1.00 1.00
	40	0.98 0.98 0.99 0.99 1.00 1.00 1.00 1.00 1.00 1.00

AEM's Infinity system looks a lot like the latest OEM ECMs, which are commonly designed to function and survive in harsh engine compartment environments. *AEM*

This is a good time to point out that if you want to really understand what goes on in the guts of a complex aftermarket EMS, there are ways to go beyond being simply a customer of prefabricated commercial EMS packages with proprietary operating software. The open-source software movement was founded by idealistic computer programmers who believed that human knowledge expands faster and the world is a better place if knowledge is shared freely in a collaborative effort. The open-source movement supports wiki-type software in which operating instructions are viewable, modifiable, or expandable by users who are encouraged to contribute newly developed sofware back into the wiki.

The do-it-yourself and open-source software movements came to aftermarket engine management systems in roughly 1998. There have been a number of open-source EMS efforts, the most important being MegaSquirt, which consists of a selection of modular EMS hardware and software components developed mostly by Al Grippo and Bruce Bowling. Grippo and Bowling were two DIY grassroots hot rodders who happened to be engineers capable of designing an increasingly sophisticated EMS that was unusually affordable due to the reduced manufacturing cost of unassembled or partially assembled electronic components and modules, and the fact that there was less development overhead factored into the price.

The original MegaSquirt design work was essentially donated, and users assembled their ECUs individually by soldering components onto a bare motherboard sold by MegaSquirt and then loaded the operating software themselves. (The original code was firmware, written in assembly language to be more efficient.) Self-assembled versions of the several generations of MegaSquirt ECU hardware are still available at bargain prices compared to most proprietary commercial systems. MegaSquirt's operating software is intellectual property that is legal for use only on MegaSquirt hardware, but the source code has always been openly available for modification or enhancement by any purchaser of MegaSquirt hardware (which is relevant because MegaSquirt has had some problems with third parties selling unauthorized pirate versions of MegaSquirt hardware). There are now multiple generations of MegaSquirt hardware and software available for purchase from multiple vendors/distributors that make MegaSquirt components available in various stages of assembly, from

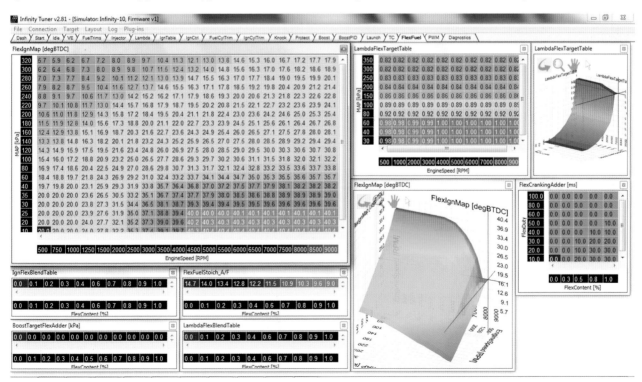

AEM infinity Flex calibration screen, showing spark advance map, lambda table, and cranking adder table. *AEM*

8.8	9.1	9.7	10.6	11.7	13.0	14.2	15.2	16.2	17.1	17.9	18.6	19.3	20.0	20.6	21.3	21.8	22.3	22.6	22.8
9.7	10.1	10.8	11.7	13.0	14.4	15.7	16.8	17.9	18.7	19.5	20.2	20.8	21.5	22.1	22.7	23.2	23.6	23.9	24.1
10.6	11.0	11.8	12.9	14.3	15.8	17.2	18.4	19.5	20.4	21.1	21.8	22.4	23.0	23.6	24.2	24.6	25.0	25.3	25.4
11.5	11.9	12.8	14.0	15.6	17.3	18.8	20.0	21.1	22.0	22.7	23.3	23.9	24.5	25.1	25.6	26.1	26.4	26.7	26.8
12.4	12.9	13.8	15.1	16.9	18.7	20.3	21.6	22.7	23.6	24.3	24.9	25.4	26.0	26.5	27.1	27.5	27.8	28.0	28.1

MAP [kF	150	0.86	0.86	0.86	0.86	0.86	0.86	0.86	0.86	0.86	0.8
	100	0.89	0.89	0.89	0.89	0.89	0.89	0.89	0.89	0.89	0.89
	80	0.92	0.92	0.92	0.92	0.92	0.92	0.92	0.92	0.92	0.92
	60	0.98	0.98	0.99	0.99	1.00	1.00	1.00	1.00	1.00	1.00
	40	0.98	0.98	0.99	0.99	1.00	1.00	1.00	1.00	1.00	1.00

PROGRAMMING STANDALONE SYSTEMS

Electromotive TEC GT EMS. Electromotive is well known for its waste-spark direct-fire ignition coils that deliver spark to pairs of cylinders 360 degrees out of phase. The system is also well known for its 60-tooth trigger wheel, which provides very accurate engine position information.

roll-your-own kits that require wiring harness and ECU assembly (soldering discrete components and integrated circuits onto a bare board), to turnkey, ready-to-go systems comparable to advanced commercial aftermarket systems from outfits like Haltech, Motec, and Edelbrock. MegaSquirt is marketed for off-road competition and educational use—and it is certainly true that the more primitive DIY versions of MegaSquirt require customers to learn a *lot* about the functioning of engine management hardware and software.

The opposite of the DIY EMS solution is the *plug-and-play* EMS solution, which typically provides everything you need to convert a factory EFI vehicle to programmable aftermarket engine management—in some case right down to the calibration files—by plugging the aftermarket into the stock EFI wiring harness with a conversion harness. Always verify whether it's a fully calibrated system ready to rock 'n' roll, or plug-and-play *hardware*, which will definitely require extensive tuning by a human tuner or Auto-Tune algorithms in the ECU in combination with a wideband air/fuel ratio sensor. Obviously any follow-on hot rodding modifications will require additional tuning and in some cases additional hardware. True plug-and-play EMS kits have the appeal that they get you going right away, which is why nearly all of the commercial standalone EMS vendors offer at least some plug-and-play versions of their system for common vehicle and engine applications.

This chapter is designed to provide the gist of what was out there at the time of this writing in the way of standalone programmable engine management systems and to get you thinking about what matters when you purchase one. Like all high-tech electronic markets, the EMS world is a moving target, so after reading this book you'll want to get online and explore what is new. Like camshaft selection, any good decision about the right engine management system involves much more than just reading a chart and looking for the biggest, baddest one on the page. Beyond evaluating what the systems can do, an intelligent choice should include evaluating what your engine really needs

and your own financial and technical capabilities and limitations to find a compatible marriage with the right standalone engine management system.

GENERAL CAPABILITIES

Some of the general capabilities of an engine management system are straightforward. How many cylinders can the ECU manage, and in which configurations (even-fire, odd-fire, rotary, and so on)? Can it handle multi-port or throttle body injection? Sequential injection? What about direct injection? Which kind of ignition configurations can it control? What is the maximum rpm it can handle? Can it handle electronic transmission functions such as torque-converter lockup? Does it have soft, fuel-based rev-limiting capabilities available to keep you from hurting the engine if your supercharger conversion makes it really fun to blast hard through 8,500 rpm? Can it handle drive-by-wire electronic throttles?

On one hand this is not rocket science. If you have a V-6 and plan to run sequential injection, don't buy an ECU that only has four injector drivers. On the other hand, not everything is so obvious. Can a particular ECU with a particular set of high-flow injectors driving a turbo engine with high specific power fire the injectors with *short* enough pulse width to idle well, or will the engine need more than one injector per cylinder and an ECU capable of staged-injector control algorithms to deliver safe maximum power and good idle?

Even the cost of an engine management kit can be difficult to establish if, as is often the case, it turns out you have to buy expensive auxiliary components that are not included in the base price of the kit or fabricate new components. Modern ECUs are flexible about accepting data from a variety of types of engine sensors these days. Most can handle a variety of types of fuel injectors and a variety of igniters, so your stock ones will work in many cases, particularly if you have a common performance vehicle. There is a good chance an aftermarket EMS will support your stock manifold absolute pressure (MAP) sensor. But let's

8	9.1	9.7	10.6	11.7	13.0	14.2	15.2	16.2	17.1	17.9	18.6	19.3	20.0	20.6	21.3	21.8	22.3	22.6	22.8
.7	10.1	10.8	11.7	13.0	14.4	15.7	16.8	17.9	18.7	19.5	20.2	20.8	21.5	22.1	22.7	23.2	23.6	23.9	24.1
.0	11.0	11.8	12.9	14.3	15.8	17.2	18.4	19.5	20.4	21.1	21.8	22.4	23.0	23.6	24.2	24.6	25.0	25.3	25.4
1.5	11.9	12.8	14.0	15.6	17.3	18.8	20.0	21.1	22.0	22.7	23.3	23.9	24.5	25.1	25.6	26.1	26.4	26.7	26 8
2.4	12.9	13.8	15.1	16.9	18.7	20.3	21.6	22.7	23.6	24.3	24.9	25.4	26.0	26.5	27.1	27.5	27.8	28.0	28.1

MAP [kf										
100	0.86	0.86	0.86	0.86	0.86	0.86	0.86	0.86	0.86	0.86
80	0.89	0.89	0.89	0.89	0.89	0.89	0.89	0.89	0.89	0.89
60	0.92	0.92	0.92	0.92	0.92	0.92	0.92	0.92	0.92	0.9
40	0.98	0.98	0.99	0.99	1.00	1.00	1.00	1.00	1.00	1.00
	0.98	0.98	0.99	0.99	1.00	1.00	1.00	1.00	1.00	1.00

say your stock engine used to be naturally aspirated and you are installing an aftermarket programmable EMS because you are doing a turbo conversion. The stock MAP sensor will almost definitely be a 1-bar unit that's unable to measure boost much above atmospheric pressure, so you're going to need a 2-bar or 3-bar MAP sensor, which will add to the cost. That ECU you're lusting for may drive eight fuel injectors right out of the box. But maybe it will drive only four *low-resistance* performance-type peak-and-hold injectors, not the eight you're going to need on your V-8. Is a particular ECU able to manage coil dwell (charging) time for your coil(s) and igniter (some igniters provide fixed dwell, others variable)? In general, be wary of EMS kit pricing. Unless you're buying a turnkey EFI conversion system like Edelbrock's carb-to-EFI conversion Pro-Flow Chevy V-8 system, there will be extras. There may well be extras even on a "turnkey" system.

PRODUCT/TECH SUPPORT

Product support is difficult to quantify, but it is one of the most important features of an engine management system, and this extends to the expert presales consulting that should be available up front to make certain that the unit will work well for you. OK, there may be a toll-free number (or maybe it's not a toll-free number) to call for product support. But how easy is it to get through to a human being? Don't laugh. In some industries there have been documented cases of customer service phone numbers that no one ever answers. How many installed engine management systems is an EMS vendor supporting? How polite, how *helpful* is the person who picks up the phone? What about the fifth time you call late Friday afternoon? Is there anyone there answering the phone in early evening on the East Coast when you call at 2:45 p.m. Pacific time? What about on weekends? Will the person on the phone give good advice that rapidly solves problems?

How good is the manual (some really suck)? Is there a good website with a good online knowledgebase or FAQs, or is the site mainly a selling tool? Is the engineer who actually designed the ECU hardware or software available for consulting as a last line of defense if all else fails or if your application uncovers a hardware or software bug? Is there a dealer in your area, preferably with a chassis dynamometer, who can help get the EMS working on your vehicle if you can't or the performance is disappointing?

Is there another dealer or tuning shop in reasonable proximity if the first dealer turns out to be a disappointment on your application? Is your application standard or are you the first person in the world lucky enough to be trying to get an XYZ Superfreak programmable EMS to work on a 1912 John Deere tractor with 50-jigawatt magnetos that emit so much electrical interference that the rig jams AM radio stations in Calcutta?

Are you about to be an interesting experiment for a supplier or dealer hot for one more sale this month (like that Brand-X muffler guy in the old Midas ad with a really big hammer who announces, "We'll *make* it fit.")? Well-run, stable companies with integrity will walk away from no-win business. They have the technical and financial depth to recover from problematic situations if they made a mistake. And all companies and individuals make mistakes because they're human.

USER INTERFACE

First of all, do you need a laptop PC? This is less important than it used to be because society in general is much more computer-literate than it used to be and there are a lot of laptops around

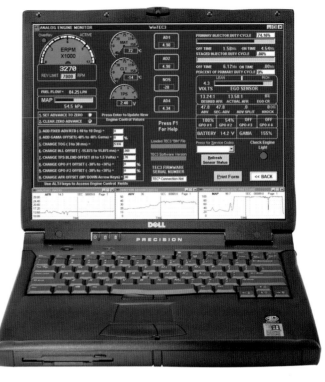

Electromotive TEC3 Analog Engine Monitor.

today. Most—but not all!—EMSs require a laptop with a certain minimal microprocessor speed, operating system, memory size, and interface hardware. You may encounter an EMS that does do not require (or perhaps support) a laptop at all, particularly if it is "pre-owned," and you may or may not find this to be a good thing. If you are buying a laptop to tune your EMS, make sure it will work. As one example, at this time of writing, some EMSs would not work with 64-bit laptops. Some ECUs require an RS232 asynchronous connection, which is no longer standard on most PCs. Some standalone systems are equipped with a proprietary programming module the eliminates the need for a laptop. These usually consist of a module that fits in one hand that is equipped with a small LCD display and four arrow keys to navigate through menus (up, down, right, left), plus a select key and back/deselect key. A newer trend is ECUs that allow a USB- or Bluetooth-connected iPhone or Android smart phone with an EMS app to program or tune the EMS.

Virtually all new aftermarket EMSs now provide a graphical user interface. The friendliness of the graphical or tabular (table-based) user interface is of decreasing importance as your knowledge and experience with a system increase, but really great graphics combined with excellent, powerful datalogging and data *analysis* software can solve problems by making it easier to see anomalies in, for example, the volumetric efficiency or injection pulse width tables. Of course, behind the gorgeous graphics, all tuning maps are matrices or charts of numbers.

If you are not familiar with an engine management system, a trim module, in which turning a dial richens or leans the air/fuel mixture or advances or retards timing or changes maximum turbo boost, can make tuning much easier (though some people loathe the things). The modern equivalent is laptop Global Fuel or Spark trim.

8.8	9.1	9.7	10.6	11.7	13.0	14.2	15.2	16.2	17.1	17.9	18.6	19.3	20.0	20.6	21.3	21.8	22.3	22.6	22.8
9.7	10.1	10.8	11.7	13.0	14.4	15.7	16.8	17.9	18.7	19.5	20.2	20.8	21.5	22.1	22.7	23.2	23.6	23.9	24.1
10.6	11.0	11.8	12.8	14.3	15.8	17.3	18.4	19.5	20.4	21.1	21.8	22.4	23.0	23.6	24.2	24.6	25.0	25.3	25.4
11.5	11.9	12.8	14.0	15.6	17.3	18.8	20.0	21.1	22.0	22.7	23.3	23.9	24.5	25.1	25.6	26.1	26.4	26.7	26.8
12.4	12.9	13.8	15.1	16.9	18.7	20.3	21.6	22.7	23.6	24.3	24.9	25.4	26.0	26.5	27.1	27.5	27.8	28.0	28.1

MAP [kP]											
150	0.86	0.86	0.86	0.86	0.86	0.86	0.86	0.86	0.86	0.86	0.86
100	0.89	0.89	0.89	0.89	0.89	0.89	0.89	0.89	0.89	0.89	0.89
80	0.92	0.92	0.92	0.92	0.92	0.92	0.92	0.92	0.92	0.92	0.92
60	0.98	0.98	0.99	0.99	1.00	1.00	1.00	1.00	1.00	1.00	
40	0.98	0.98	0.99	0.99	1.00	1.00	1.00	1.00	1.00	1.00	

FAST EZ-EFI is a very complete turnkey throttlebody injection system with everything needed for carb-to-EFI conversions.

HARDWARE

Check out the environmental requirements for an engine management system: Some engine management systems are designed to operate reliably only in a temperate environment, which means installation in the cockpit with the driver rather than in the engine compartment or on a heat-soaked firewall near the engine. Electronic circuits generally hate heat, moisture, and vibration, but some engine management systems are hardened and equipped with waterproof connectors, making it possible to install them in the engine compartment. Pay close attention to the environmental and mounting requirements. If you don't, the system may fail.

ECUs with external indicator LEDs, check engine lights or "dash/display" modules are desirable, because they can warn you of incipient or intermittent problems that you would not otherwise see without a laptop connected (which can be dangerous and illegal to use while driving). In case of a serious malfunction, they can immediately steer you in the right direction.

ECU power requirements provide information about the flexibility of the EMS to successfully start the engine with a partially discharged battery and to run it for a longer time if the alternator quits (some ECUs have a wider operating range than others). Power requirements tell you how much current (amperage) the system will consume from the alternator (and it can be significant). Power consumption depends not just on ECU consumption but very much on the number and type of injectors and the number and type of ignition coils and igniters and so forth. Power requirements can increase significantly if you need a special external module to handle direct-injection fuel injectors or to drive an electronic throttle.

ECU physical size and weight are self-evident, but remember that the ECU box is effectively larger when the connector plug(s) and wiring harness are installed.

RESOLUTION AND GRANULARITY

Digital computers approximate fuel and ignition curves with a table of discrete numbers and then compute a moving average for points that fall in between table cells or "breakpoints." A naturally aspirated engine with a flat torque curve does not require many numbers in its fuel and ignition tables to provide an accurate approximation of the curve. But engines with wild or variable cams, turbochargers, variable intake plenums or runners, nitrous and other exotic volumetric-efficiency modifiers may have oddly shaped torque curves that change rapidly in certain areas and thus require complex, sophisticated air/fuel and timing curves for good drivability and power.

The **resolution** of an engine management system refers to the number of cells or breakpoints in the tables being used to approximate the fuel and timing curves over the range of engine speed and loading—that is, the *granularity* of the approximation. A 12,000-rpm engine running 4- or 5-bar boost (a lot of dynamic range) almost definitely needs bigger digital fuel and ignition tables than a naturally aspirated engine with a mild cam and a 5,200-rpm redline. All things being equal, engine management systems with higher resolution are preferable, especially for difficult engines. On the other hand, table resolution is like shoe size: you need enough, but more than that will not help you go any faster.

Engine management systems with the ability to accurately control fuel injectors with good repeatability to very short injection pulse widths will have the ability to make more power on engines with a big dynamic range because they can

FAST XFI fuel injection kit is another turnkey carb-to-EFI conversion system that provides port-EFI conversions usable for forced-induction applications.

produce acceptable idle with the big injectors you need to provide big power at peak torque. The key to providing accurate and repeatable idle at short injection pulse width is sophisticated **injector dead time** tables for specific injectors and compensation tables that accurately model injector fuel flow in the nonlinear range or when they are not yet fully open or closed. Such tables—accurately configured!—are critical for EMS systems that attempt to provide an accurate model of engine performance for torque-based engine management. This means some aftermarket systems and most late-model OEM controllers. Ideally, the aftermarket EMS allows you to specify the model number of the fuel injectors and activate prefabricated dead time and compensation tables.

AIR/FUEL

Some systems equipped with wideband air/fuel ratio sensors provide the ability to define **target air/fuel ratio tables** for various segments of the rpm load range, which is a powerful tool for calibrating the system because the EMS will alert you to modifications in pulse width required to achieve the target air/fuel ratio or even override the current pulse width to achieve a specified air/fuel ratio or function as a critical part of an "auto-tune" self-tuning facility. Target air/fuel ratio tables set to homogenous numbers can be a powerful tool for calibrating the VE table if so equipped because errors in air/fuel ratio correspond directly to required corrections to volumetric efficiency at a particular speed-loading point as described in the chapter of this book that tells how to build a VE table from scratch. Of course, deciding on the *ideal* target air/fuel ratios for various sectors of the speed-loading matrix ultimately requires a load-holding dynamometer.

Fuel pressure detection and pulse width compensation can be very useful, particularly if you're looking to manage an engine with a deadhead (returnless) fuel supply system found in some models of vehicles like the Ford Focus. This is similar to the battery voltage compensation logic used by virtually all modern engine management systems to correct for increasing laziness in injector opening performance as battery voltage decreases with longer injection pulse width. Fortunately, there is a straightforward relationship between rail pressure and fuel delivery per injector squirt, so effective compensation is predictable and accurate. The ECU uses a sensor in the fuel rail to detect pressure and compensates for nonstandard rail pressure with modifications to injection pulse widths.

Volumetric efficiency (VE) tables specify an engine's cylinder-filling efficiency across the range of rpm and loading. That is, how much air mass actually makes its way into the cylinder by the time the intake cycle is completed as a percentage of the amount of air mass found in a cylinder at atmospheric pressure with the engine stopped at bottom dead center. Peak VE can be more than 100 percent with forced induction or resonation-tuned racing engines but will be less than 100 percent on most engines even under ideal conditions at peak torque. Some engine management systems have used VE tables and some have not, though increasingly tuners now have the option on many systems to define a VE table or use simple injection pulse width tables that have no need for VE tables or target air/fuel ratio tables.

Maximum required injection pulse width is always a function of the injector size, fuel pressure, maximum torque at the required max-torque air/fuel ratio. Minimum pulse width is a function of injector size, pressure, and fuel required to idle at the required or desired air/fuel ratio. Everything in between is linear with volumetric efficiency. Electromotive's VE table defaults to all zeros (perfectly flat torque curve across the rpm range), and the base Electromotive straight-line interpolation

8.8	9.1	9.7	10.6	11.7	13.0	14.2	15.2	16.2	17.1	17.9	18.6	19.3	20.0	20.6	21.3	21.8	22.3	22.6	22.8
9.7	10.1	10.8	11.7	13.0	14.4	15.7	16.8	17.9	18.7	19.5	20.2	20.8	21.5	22.1	22.7	23.2	23.6	23.9	24.1
10.6	11.0	11.8	12.9	14.3	15.8	17.2	18.4	19.5	20.4	21.1	21.8	22.4	23.0	23.6	24.2	24.6	25.0	25.3	25.4
11.5	11.9	12.8	14.0	15.6	17.3	18.8	20.0	21.1	22.0	22.7	23.3	23.9	24.5	25.1	25.6	26.1	26.4	26.7	26.8
12.4	12.9	13.8	15.1	16.9	18.7	20.3	21.6	22.7	23.6	24.3	24.9	25.4	26.0	26.5	27.1	27.5	27.8	28.0	28.1

MAP [kPa]										
150	0.86	0.86	0.86	0.86	0.86	0.86	0.86	0.86	0.86	0.8
100	0.89	0.89	0.89	0.89	0.89	0.89	0.89	0.89	0.89	0.89
80	0.92	0.92	0.92	0.92	0.92	0.92	0.92	0.92	0.92	0.92
60	0.98	0.98	0.99	0.99	1.00	1.00	1.00	1.00	1.00	1.00
40	0.98	0.98	0.99	0.99	1.00	1.00	1.00	1.00	1.00	1.00

PROGRAMMING STANDALONE SYSTEMS

Haltech Platinum 1000 Street Kit with wideband AFR sensor. Note the Racepak dash iQ3 unit capable of displaying a wide variety of engine data for a race driver on LCD panel and 14—count 'em, 14!—lights.

fuel calculation between idle and max-torque pulse width will actually start and run most engines with *zero VE correction*. If the target air/fuel ratio table is set at a workable homogeneous number in all cells, the Electromotive VE table can then be tuned with positive or negative numbers in the various cells that reflect the engine's actual breathing efficiency at various points of speed and loading. A target air/fuel ratio table can then be tuned with a wideband air/fuel ratio sensor and/or dyno. Some tuners find it more straightforward to directly tune tables of simple injection pulse width times to achieve the performance and air/fuel ratio they want at particular rpm and load points, but others consider VE table systems more elegant and understandable in their modeling of actual engine behavior with respect to ideal mixture delivery. VE table systems are far more flexible than fuel table systems in accommodating changes like injector size by simply resetting the idle and max-torque numbers and letting the VE and air/fuel ratio tables do their thing without having to take on a massive recalibration project. Keep this in mind when choosing an EMS.

CLOSED-LOOP

Most modern EFI systems have the ability to trim fuel injection pulse width at idle and light-cruise to target the ideal (14.7:1) chemical air/fuel ratio (stoichiometric) for cleanest combustion, based on feedback from an exhaust gas oxygen (EGO) sensor that measures residual oxygen in post-combustion exhaust gases that can be used to deduce what the charge air/fuel ratio was at idle. However, a standard or O_2 sensor is only accurate at air/fuel ratios near the stoichiometric ratio in the 14.0-15.0 range, and stoichiometric ratios do not work for optimizing power at heavier engine loading.

For meaningful air/fuel ratio numbers at the richer mixtures required for best power and torque at heavier loads, an engine management system needs the ability to interface to a more expensive wideband air/fuel ratio sensor that measures not just exhaust gas oxygen but exhaust gas hydrocarbons. To safely trim pulse width at higher, more dangerous levels of power with wideband feedback, or for self-tuning at high power levels, an engine management system needs to have additional smarts, and not all do. Look to see whether or not an EMS has full authority to tune or trim air/fuel ratio at full power, and look to see whether the EMS has the ability to turn on detonation detection and elimination based on feedback from one or more knock sensors, which will make self-tuning or self high-power air/fuel ratio trim much safer.

CALIBRATION, SETUP, PLUG AND PLAY

The availability of a plug-and-play EMS or good pre-existing calibration for your engine and vehicle combination and modifications could in some cases have a material impact on your choice of EMS. Properly calibrating an engine from scratch is laborious and difficult, and there is a risk of damaging a high-output engine from detonation induced by excessive boost, lean mixtures, or too much spark advance, which can destroy an engine in a matter of seconds. Learning to tune an engine for the first time is a bit like a student pilot learning to spin an airplane (which they no longer teach in U.S. flight schools). In the same sense that student pilots start out on easy, low-performance aircraft rather than F-22 fighters, it is better to learn on a simple, naturally aspirated powerplant that is not knock-limited and to use an EMS with intuitive controls and a good prefabricated calibration to get you started.

The best way to calibrate an engine is not to calibrate it but instead to install a known-good calibration that was built by experts on an identical engine in an identical vehicle, which will plug and play on your vehicle. If identical is impossible, then "close" is the next best place to start. A true plug-and-play calibration is gold, particularly if you are not a professional tuner. The availability of one could be a decisive factor in selecting an engine management system. Generic library calibrations invoke the phrase caveat emptor. When it comes to calibrations, close is a matter of opinion, and what you don't know *can* hurt you.

9.1	9.7	10.6	11.7	13.0	14.2	15.2	16.2	17.1	17.9	18.6	19.3	20.0	20.6	21.3	21.8	22.3	22.6	22.8
10.1	10.8	11.7	13.0	14.4	15.7	16.8	17.9	18.7	19.5	20.2	20.8	21.5	22.1	22.7	23.2	23.6	23.9	24.1
11.0	11.8	12.9	14.3	15.8	17.2	18.4	19.5	20.4	21.1	21.8	22.4	23.0	23.6	24.2	24.6	25.0	25.3	25.4
11.9	12.8	14.0	15.6	17.3	18.8	20.0	21.1	22.0	22.7	23.3	23.9	24.5	25.1	25.6	26.1	26.4	26.7	26.8
12.9	13.8	15.1	16.9	18.7	20.3	21.6	22.7	23.6	24.3	24.9	25.4	26.0	26.5	27.1	27.5	27.8	28.0	28.1

MAP												
150	0.86	0.86	0.86	0.86	0.86	0.86	0.86	0.86	0.86	0.86	0.8	
100	0.89	0.89	0.89	0.89	0.89	0.89	0.89	0.89	0.89	0.89	0.89	
80	0.92	0.92	0.92	0.92	0.92	0.92	0.92	0.92	0.92	0.92	0.92	
60	0.98	0.98	0.99	0.99	1.00	1.00	1.00	1.00	1.00	1.00		
40	0.98	0.98	0.99	0.99	1.00	1.00	1.00	1.00	1.00			

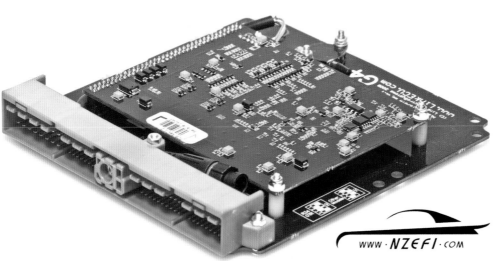

Link Engine Management— formerly Link Electrosystems— G4 plug-and-play ECM for the Nissan Skyline.

Some engine management systems are available with plug-and-play hardware and connectors that enable you to remove a stock ECU, plug in the aftermarket ECU with its adapters, and immediately use the original equipment wiring, sensors, and actuators, possibly with the need to substitute one or more sensors. Wiring and sensors are expensive, and true plug-and-play hardware compatibility could also be a decisive factor in choosing an engine management system. As mentioned earlier, "plug-and-play" does not include the calibration.

When you are learning a new engine management system, the ability to work on the calibration offline is valuable. Calibration wizards that automate the process of building a calibration from a number of configurable parameters that is good enough to get the engine started can be valuable, as can automated mapping features such as the ability to change all or part of the fuel or ignition map by a percentage (very useful if you're changing to bigger or smaller injectors). The sophistication of the models used in map-building algorithms can vary a lot. The more parameters you enter, the better.

DATA LOGGING

The ability to log a series of snapshots of engine sensor and ECU status while the engine is running and driving is extremely valuable, because it means that rather than doing all tuning in real time while the engine is operating (which requires two people to do safely while driving), you can run the engine through its paces, log the data, and then go back and carefully analyze what is right and wrong about the calibration and improve it at your leisure when the engine is safely stopped. Some engine management systems provide tools that automate the analysis of large amounts of logged data, and some bundle in basic data-logging, with "advanced" data-logging an extra-cost option that logs more parameters faster for a longer time and includes sophisticated competition-type analysis software and in some cases the ability to log data from not only the engine but from auxiliary sensors and data sources. Many EMSs log data by sending it to a connected laptop for storage and analysis, but it may turn out to be convenient if your EMS has the capability to log data in the ECU itself without needing to have a laptop connected. Some ECMs are now equipped with removable flash memory cards.

INPUT/OUTPUT

The number of I/O circuits on an EMS can vary greatly and the availability of certain functions can be a zero-sum game. Older ECUs tended to have hardwired I/O designs that wasted unneeded injector output channels if engines had fewer cylinders than the max. Most modern aftermarket EMSs typically provide one or more "wildcard" configurable multipurpose input-output channels that can be customized to do almost any function the EMS supports. However, the availability of a pulse width modulated (PWM) output circuit to manage, say, a boost controller, could depend on whether you already need the output to drive a fuel injector. The same output might also be capable of driving a tachometer, but not if you need it to interface with a boost controller. When reading a spec sheet on an engine management system, beware: It is extremely important to analyze the total number and type of I/O circuits you might need and make sure there will not be conflicts. The good news is that the most sophisticated modern engine management systems are designed so that almost any I/O channel can be configured for almost any function, and the ability to add expander modules to handle even more functions

MegaSquirt MS-208. Many MegaSquirt systems can be hand-assembled by hobbyists, or purchased pre-assembled from a number of distributor/resellers like DIYAutotune.

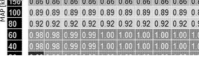

8.8	9.1	9.7	10.6	11.7	13.0	14.2	15.2	16.2	17.1	17.9	18.6	19.3	20.0	20.6	21.3	21.8	22.3	22.6	22.8
9.7	10.1	10.8	11.7	13.0	14.4	15.7	16.8	17.9	18.7	19.5	20.2	20.8	21.5	22.1	22.7	23.2	23.6	23.9	24.1
10.6	11.0	11.8	12.9	14.3	15.8	17.2	18.4	19.5	20.4	21.1	21.8	22.4	23.0	23.6	24.2	24.6	25.0	25.3	25.4
11.5	11.9	12.8	14.0	15.6	17.3	18.8	20.0	21.1	22.0	22.7	23.3	23.9	24.5	25.1	25.6	26.1	26.4	26.7	26.8
12.4	12.9	13.8	15.1	16.9	18.7	20.3	21.6	22.7	23.6	24.3	24.9	25.4	26.0	26.5	27.1	27.5	27.8	28.0	28.1

MAP [kPa]											
150	0.86	0.86	0.86	0.86	0.86	0.86	0.86	0.86	0.86	0.86	0.8(
100	0.89	0.89	0.89	0.89	0.89	0.89	0.89	0.89	0.89	0.89	0.89
80	0.92	0.92	0.92	0.92	0.92	0.92	0.92	0.92	0.92	0.92	0.9(
60	0.98	0.98	0.99	0.99	1.00	1.00	1.00	1.00	1.00	1.00	1.0(
40	0.98	0.98	0.99	0.99	1.00	1.00	1.00	1.00	1.00	1.00	

Megasquirt-based DIY-PNP EMS kit. MegaSquirt was founded by hotrodders who happened to be computer and electrical engineers and designed for people who enjoyed learning about the details of EMS design, and were willing to operate on their own with web-support alone, reprogramming the ECM themselves, if they wanted. More recently an infrastructure has grown up to provide hand-holding and support, if you're willing to pay a little more.

or more cylinders. If it is appropriate, choose an EMS with the headroom to accommodate future plans that require controlling additional functions or reading additional sensors.

SENSORS AND ACTUATORS

The flexibility of an EMS to use the sensors and actuators already on your engine could save you a lot of money. Most modern aftermarket ECUs are flexible about driving fuel injectors of any resistance, but some cannot handle as many low-resistance performance-type peak-and-hold injectors. Most aftermarket ECUs now have software-configurability for multiple types of ignitions, but since the circuitry required to drive multiple coils is expensive, direct-ignition capability is often unbundled as an extra-cost option requiring expansion hardware. A few manufacturers have taken the opposite approach, bundling in direct-fire circuitry, direct coils (in the case of Electromotive, waste-fire coils, each of which fires two plugs at once on cylinders 360 degrees out of phase), and crank trigger wheel and sensors. Bundled direct ignition definitely simplifies ignition compatibility and configuration issues, though you'll need to install the trigger mechanism.

When you are converting an EFI engine to aftermarket programmable engine management, you may find you do not need all the factory sensors. Some sensors are indeed mandatory, in the sense that the EMS cannot run the engine without them, but some sensors are not specifically required if an alternative type of sensor is available. For example, a manifold absolute pressure (MAP) sensor is not required if there is a mass airflow (MAF) sensor and vice versa. Most people installing aftermarket EMS do not want to retain (restrictive) factory MAF sensors, so some aftermarket systems are not designed to use MAF

load sensing. Some sensors are not required in the sense that the engine management system can operate if the sensor fails, but degraded performance must be considered in a cost analysis of a particular engine management solution. For example, an engine management system with a failed or missing coolant temperature sensor will typically run with a default coolant temperature setting of, say, 70 degrees Fahrenheit, but would have trouble starting when cold and run rich at full operating temperature. Most EMSs, though, can function well without the stock Baro pressure sensor by measuring barometric pressure before the engine starts, but will henceforth not have the ability to distinguish between manifold pressure changes due to engine loading versus weather or altitude changes—until the next time the engine is stopped and restarted. Not good if you're driving up Pikes Peak.

NITROUS

Plans to run nitrous oxide injection can have a significant impact on your choice of programmable EMS because there are many options when it comes to nitrous injection. Most EMSs offer some way of controlling nitrous injection, but there is a big difference between an EMS that simply trips a relay to activate a conventional on-off external nitrous system and an EMS that can provide pulse width modulation of a nitrous solenoid to progressively feather in nitrous injection in a way that controls traction while simultaneously modifying fuel-injection pulse width to provide nitrous fuel enrichment through primary fuel injectors. Different aftermarket engine management systems provide a variety of ways of controlling nitrous delivery, corresponding fuel enrichment, numbers of stages of nitrous delivery, or PWM nitrous, and the EMS control algorithms may or may not take into account nitrous-induced changes in intake air density, nitrous-displaced intake air oxygen, changes in nitrous tank pressure, temperature and thermal expansion, liquid nitrous vaporization effects on nitrous and intake air temperature, and so forth.

Pay careful attention to EMS nitrous options if juice is in your game plan for an engine. Although nitrous injection will provide a substantial infusion of cheap power, you are essentially injecting extra oxygen (initially linked to nitrogen atoms), which can easily blowtorch your engine if there are any fuel delivery or mixture distribution problems: Since port-EFI intake manifolds are not designed to handle wet mixtures of air and fuel, providing required enrichment fuel via auxiliary injectors or jets is not a good idea unless they are located in every intake port. Jacking up the fuel pressure to all the injectors when nitrous is flowing to get the required increased fuel delivery is a better idea, though it requires a special fuel pressure regulator and possibly an upgraded fuel pump. The best way to provide enrichment fuel for nitrous to burn is having an ECU capable of delivering the additional fuel via the primary fuel injectors as an offset to ordinary fuel-injection pulse width. This strategy requires injectors large enough to handle the total fuel delivery at maximum torque with nitrous on and, of course, an ECU that can accurately deliver the small pulse width required to idle well.

Some ECUs can *stage* the delivery of nitrous (and fuel) or even gradually increase the nitrous stream to improve traction in drag-type conditions (*progressive* nitrous). If you're planning to use nitrous and convert to a programmable aftermarket EMS, rather than handle nitrous as an add-on, buy an ECU with sophisticated nitrous capabilities built in so the EMS seamlessly integrates nitrous injection with everything else.

PROGRAMMING STANDALONE SYSTEMS

The most recent MegaSquirt system is the MS3 Pro system, consisting of powerful advanced, miniaturized surface-mount circuitry that can do almost anything. This is a bold move into the mainstream of aftermarket standalone engine management.

WIRING

The EMS wiring harness is vital to reliability, and building a truly robust harness is not cheap. Factory wiring harnesses are made to last, because wiring that is insufficiently robust can cause expensive warranty claims and could interfere with emissions functionality, which the U.S. government requires carmakers to warrant for an extended period of time. Faulty aftermarket EMS wiring is the bane of product support because wiring is harder to do than most people think, which is why EMS vendors do not like selling finish-it-yourself wiring harnesses and components unless the customer is demonstrably competent. If it's an option for your application—assuming the vehicle is not too old—you may want to consider reusing the stock wiring with an adapter harness between the connector on the new ECM and the main connector(s) on the stock engine wiring harness. Keep in mind, however, that factory EMS wiring was designed to be reliable under *normal* circumstances in which the engine is never out of the vehicle and EMS components will be connected to the wiring harness *once* (or maybe twice) in the life of the vehicle. "Normal" definitely does not apply to situations where the harness is repeatedly connected and disconnected from components, as is the case with many race cars or R&D-type hot rod projects. Repeated R&R can degrade factory wiring faster than you'd think, especially if it's getting old, which is why sophisticated aftermarket EMSs are often available with mil-spec connectors and wiring harnesses.

The problem of faulty or substandard wiring is so severe with aftermarket standalone engine management systems that some premium race-type engine management systems come bundled with a high-quality custom wiring harness built to user specs that is included in the system price.

Less expensive systems may be priced with a generic engine-wiring loom equipped with connectors designed (typically) for GM sensors and actuators. The problem is, the generic harness connectors may not fit your fuel injectors and engine sensors, and the various segments of the harness may be too short or too long to work really well in your application. This means the harness might have to be extended or shortened at various places or have alternate connectors installed, which requires special tools and expertise to do it right. Bottom line: Pay close attention to wiring when you select an EMS or you will live to regret it.

GENERIC EMS/ECU FEATURES
General
* Microprocessor and co-processors:
* Warranty:
* ECU control software in updatable flash memory?
* Battery transient protection?
* Environmentally sealed electronics?
* Mil-Spec?
* ECU connector type:
* Case size:
* Weight:
* Programmed via [PC, programming module, dash-logger]
* Cylinders:
* Engine cycle: [two-stroke, four-stroke, X-Rotor Wankel]
* Maximum rpm:
* Expandability:
* Expandability with external modules for: [additional injectors, coils]
* Configurable/flexible I/O definitions?
* Open-source ECU firmware or software?
* Ruggedized/potted/mil-spec ECU?
* Plug-and-play vehicle support:
* Data-link protocol: [USB 2.0, nine-pin RS232 Serial, CAN Bus, Bluetooth, 4G-LTE]

Operating Conditions
* High-temp-tolerant ECU?
* Internal temperature range:
* Maximum ambient temperature:
* Operating voltage:
* ECU operating current:
* Reversed-battery protection?
* ECU current protections?
* Sealed automotive/marine-grade connections?

PC computer software
* Software functions: [configuration, tuning, diagnostic and data analysis]
* Laptop computer requirements:
* Built-in help system?
* Data logging analysis: [multiple graph overlays, XY plots, math functions, virtual instrument display, track maps]

Emissions
* OBD-II self-diagnostics?
* Emissions controls: [EGR, purge solenoid]

Anti-Knock
* Dual water/methanol injection (rpm/load dependent)?
* Water/methanol injection as % injector flow (for ideal tuning)?
* Optimized water/meth injectors?
* Duel knock sensing?
* Individual-cylinder knock retard?

Nitrous
* Nitrous oxide fuel-enrichment / ignition-retard?
* Nitrous stages:
* Wet/dry nitrous with closed-loop feedback?
* Lean/rich nitrous safety cutoff?
* Progressive nitrous solenoid control?

8.8	9.1	9.7	10.6	11.7	13.0	14.2	15.2	16.2	17.1	17.9	18.6	19.3	20.0	20.6	21.3	21.8	22.3	22.6	22.8
9.7	10.1	10.7	11.7	13.0	14.4	15.7	16.8	17.9	18.7	19.5	20.2	20.8	21.5	22.1	22.7	23.2	23.6	23.9	24.1
10.6	11.0	11.8	12.9	14.3	15.8	17.2	18.4	19.5	20.4	21.1	21.8	22.4	23.0	23.6	24.2	24.6	25.0	25.3	25.4
11.5	11.9	12.8	14.0	15.6	17.3	18.8	20.0	21.1	22.0	22.7	23.3	23.9	24.5	25.1	25.6	26.1	26.4	26.7	26.8
12.4	12.9	13.8	15.1	16.9	18.7	20.3	21.6	22.7	23.6	24.3	24.9	25.4	26.0	26.5	27.1	27.5	27.8	28.0	28.1

MAP										
150	0.86	0.86	0.86	0.86	0.86	0.86	0.86	0.86	0.86	0.86
100	0.89	0.89	0.89	0.89	0.89	0.89	0.89	0.89	0.89	0.89
80	0.92	0.92	0.92	0.92	0.92	0.92	0.92	0.92	0.92	0.92
60	0.98	0.98	0.99	0.99	1.00	1.00	1.00	1.00	1.00	1.00
40	0.98	0.98	0.99	0.99	1.00	1.00	1.00	1.00	1.00	1.00

Motec M84-based plug-and-play system for the GEN II Hayabusa motorcycle.

- Progressive PWM nitrous control based on: [time, rpm, boost]

Engine Load-Performance Sensing
- Accelerometer input and logging?
- Accelerometer-based control/feedback strategies:
- Combustion pressure input?
- Torque/strain gauge input?
- Torque-based engine management?
- Combustion pressure-based engine management?

Injection
- Types: [batch, sequential, TBI, direct, staged, additional-injector]
- Number injectors:
- User programmable current?
- Individual programmable peak current:
- Individual programmable hold current:
- User-definable battery compensation?
- Twin/triple injector engines?
- Unequal injection angle capability?
- Delayed Sequential Injection?

Fuel Calibration/Control
- Accuracy:
- Load sensor types: [MAP, MAF, TPS, Torque Sensor, Combustion Pressure]
- Rpm and load site definitions user-definable?
- Main table: (# fuel map dimensions, # rpm sites, # load sites)
- End of injection primary and secondary: (# rpm sites, # load sites)
- Individual cylinder trim?
- Individual cylinder trim tables: (# rpm sites, # load sites)
- Secondary injector balance table: (# rpm sites, # load sites)
- Adjustable compensations: [MAP, engine temp, air temp]
- Auxiliary compensations?
- Gear compensation?
- Accel/decel (clamp, decay, sensitivity)
- Tau (wall-wetting) transient compensation algorithm?
- Engine temperature compensation: [parameters]
- Multiple injection pulses per engine cycle?
- Direct-injection modes:
- LB/HR fueling strategy?

- Three-mode direct-injection calibrations [power, stratified charge, stoichiometric]
- Dual fuel (type/octane) control (multiple fuel delivery and injection systems)?
- Return-less fuel pump control?
- Voltage–based fuel pump speed control?
- Closed-loop (fuel) pressure-based pulse width compensation?
- Flex fuel compensation?
- Over-Run fuel cut?
- VE table fueling?
- VE-based Startup?
- Auto-Tune?

Idle/Accel
- Four-wire stepper motor idle speed control?
- PWM idle control?
- Tau (wall-wetting) transient enrichment algorithm?
- A/C, engine fan, power steering idle-up controls:

Ignition Outputs
- Number:
- Integral/native direct-fire ignition?
- Number coils per output:
- OEM ignitions supported:
- Twin/triple plug engines?
- Coil-on-plug?
- Waste-spark?
- Distributor?
- Dual distributor?
- Unequal coil firing capability?
- CDI support?
- Integral multi-spark?

Ignition Calibration
- Accuracy:
- Rpm and load site definitions user-definable?
- Main table: (table dimensions, # rpm sites, # load sites)
- Individual cylinder trim?
- Individual cylinder tables: (# rpm sites, # load sites)
- Adjustable compensations: [MAP, engine temp, air temp]
- Auxiliary compensations:
- Gear compensation?
- Accel advance: (clamp, decay and sensitivity)
- Configurable coil dwell time: (rpm x battery voltage)
- Odd-fire engine capability?
- Rotary ignition split?
- Multi-spark?
- EGT/pyrometer timing compensation/correction?
- Nitrous retard configurable per stage based on rpm/time:

Forced Induction
- Boost main table (dimensions, rpm sites, user-defined sites)
- Boost temperature compensation [engine, air, exhaust]
- Auxiliary boost compensation:
- Boost enhancement (anti-lag)?
- Turbine speed sensor (with boost control)?
- Turbo control functions:
- Open/closed loop turbo pressure?
- Gear-based target boost?
- Speed-based target boost?

9.1	9.7	10.6	11.7	13.0	14.2	15.2	16.2	17.1	17.9	18.6	19.3	20.0	20.6	21.3	21.8	22.3	22.6	22.6
10.1	10.8	11.7	13.0	14.4	15.7	16.8	17.9	18.7	19.5	20.2	20.8	21.5	22.1	22.7	23.2	23.6	23.9	24.1
11.0	11.8	12.9	14.3	15.8	17.2	18.4	19.5	20.4	21.1	21.8	22.4	23.0	23.6	24.2	24.6	25.0	25.3	25.4
11.9	12.8	14.0	15.6	17.3	18.8	20.0	21.1	22.0	22.7	23.3	23.9	24.5	25.1	25.6	26.1	26.4	26.7	26.8
12.9	13.8	15.1	16.9	18.7	20.3	21.6	22.7	23.6	24.3	24.9	25.4	26.0	26.5	27.1	27.5	27.8	28.0	28.1

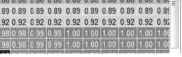

Motec began as a high-end system for sophisticated racers and tuners, but more recently Motec has worked with third-parts tuners to provide cost-effective pre-assembled packages such as this V8 kit from Tuned by Shane T (Shane Tecklenburg, a well-known Motec tuner).

- User-switchable boost control maps?
- Active base PWM map (for easy calibration)?
- Forced-induction pressure valve?
- Intercooler water spray control?

Trigger Sensors
- Trigger types [Hall, magnetic, optical]
- Multi teeth:
- Missing teeth:
- OEM trigger systems: [Ford narrow tooth, Nissan optical, Harley Davidson]
- Digital signal processing/diagnostics:

Sensor Inputs
- Standard sensors: [throttle position, manifold pressure, engine temperature, air temperature]
- Auxiliary sensor inputs (analog):
- Digital inputs: [vehicle speed, driveshaft speed]

Sensor/Setup
- Fuel pressure input?
- Standard/default sensor calibrations:
- Programmable sensor definitions:
- User-adjustable charge temp blend?
- User-configurable rpm and load points
- User-configurable battery voltage compensation tables for injector dead time and coil-on time?
- Map sensor support?
- Multi-inputs configurable for: [0-5V sensor, 0-20V sensor, thermistor temp input, high/low voltage]
- Number analog sensor inputs:
- Sensor inputs configurable: [0-5V/high/low]
- Speed inputs: [number, digital/inductive?]
- Special sensor input: [oil pressure, fuel pressure, oil temp, wheel speed, driveshaft speed, turbine speed and torque sensor, combustion pressure, EGT/pyrometer]

Air/Fuel Ratio Inputs
- Narrow-band air/fuel ratio?
- Wideband air/fuel ratio?

- EGT/pyrometer fuel compensation/correction?
- Integral wideband controller?
- Wideband type: [Bosch LSU, NTK]
- Number wideband sensors:
- Wideband and narrow-band control?
- Lambda range:
- Lambda resolution:
- Usable as auxiliary sensor input?
- Integrated wideband controller?
- Lambda switch?
- EGT/pyrometer?

Data Logging
- Allows logging of all ECU parameters?
- Number log-able parameters:
- Datalogging memory size:
- Individual parameter/rate selection?
- Logging rate (samples per second):
- Available logging time (@ number, rate):
- Interpreter software, type:
- Maximum parameters logged:
- Maximum logging throughput:

Outputs
- Number of auxiliary outputs:
- All outputs PWM and switched capable?
- Four-wire stepper motor capable?
- Number of outputs with high and low side drive:
- Auxiliary outputs configurable for: [turbo wastegate control, idle speed control, fuel used output, tachometer output, shift light, driver warning alarm, rpm and load-dependent device, user definable table, slip warning, fuel pump relay, thermatic fan, A/C fan, A/C clutch]
- Unused injector outputs usable for general auxiliary functions?
- Unused ignition outputs usable for general auxiliary functions?
- Injectors type(s) [low impedance, high impedance, direct]
- Support for external direct-injection controller?
- Number PWM/switched outputs:

141

PROGRAMMING STANDALONE SYSTEMS

- PWM/switched output amperage:
- High/midcurrent output? (for small solenoids or relays)
- Number switched-ground 12V PWM outputs:
- Configurable user-defined, pin-mapped output functionality (no unneeded hard-wired pins wasted)?
- Auxiliary-injector control?
- Number auxiliary injectors?

Diagnostics/Warning/Test

- Injector diagnostics: [open circuit, short circuit, peak current not reached]
- Sensor diagnostics: [open circuit, short circuit]
- Ref/sync noise warning & error diagnostics [noise, runt pulses, amplitude, and so on]
- Operating errors [over-rpm limit, injector over-duty, over-boost, low battery, ref error and so on]
- Color touchscreen LCD: (on-the-fly tuning, datalogging, "dash" data display)?
- Check engine light?
- Engine use histograms?
- Crankshaft oscilloscope calculates tooth pattern and position?
- External data capture [board, storage device]
- Integral device-simulator circuitry?
- Oil pressure input?
- Integrated Engine Protection Strategies:
- Self-dyno datalogging
- Self-dyno feedback engine control strategies?
- Torque-based transmission protection?
- Data-logging: [memory/rate/length-of-time/ number parameters]
- Warning alarms: [sensor high/low]
- Real-time monitoring and data acquisition via telemetry link?
- Telemetry data link type:

Special Functions/Capabilities

- Cam control type:
- Multiple cam phasing and lift?
- Cam control functions: [open/closed loop PWM cam advance control, static offset table, speed- and load-dependent target cam advance table, active base PWM map (for easy calibration), VTEC]
- Drive-by-wire throttle control?
- Drive-by-wire throttle control type: [pedal follower, torque-based]
- Traction control and launch control type:
- Dual wet/dry traction control?
- Narrow-band lambda control?
- Wideband lambda control?
- Gear change ignition cut?
- Gear detection?
- Ground speed limiting?
- Dual rpm limit?
- Air conditioner request?
- Rpm limiter: [hard cut, soft cut, fuel, ignition...]
- GPS logging/controls:
- Map switching? (multiple maps for fuel change, torque limits, and so on)
- Accelerometer input and logging?
- Accelerometer-based control and feedback strategies:
- Emulation outputs to factory ECU (in parallel twin-ECU installation):
- Flexible tachometer output
- Dash switches selection: [fuel/spark/boost map, fans, turbo control map]
- Transmission control: [GM 4L60E/4L80E]
- Drive-by-wire (pedal follower/torque-based)
- Programmer module (on-the-fly tuning, datalogging, data display): [touchscreen LCD, handheld module]
- Temperature-dependent limits: [soft/hard rpm limit, soft/ hard boost limit, vehicle speed limit]

SNAPSHOTS OF PROGRAMMABLE AFTERMARKET EMS CAPABILITIES

What follows is a summary of noteworthy capabilities some common aftermarket programmable engine management systems. This market is a moving target, with companies updating their offering with new capabilities and dropping products that are obsolete or no longer sell well as new vehicles arrive on the scene and older models wear out and disappear. At this time of writing, many EMS vendors were offering three classes of systems: (1) a basic lower-cost turnkey system targeted at the naturally aspirated carb-to-EFI conversion market, sometimes with throttle body injection and a dedicated programmer module; (2) a midgrade street-rodder system that supports power-adders and multi-port EFI engines, basic datalogging, auto-tune capabilities with wideband air/fuel ratio sensor, and so forth; and (3) a flexible high-end system targeting complex V8/V-10/V-12 engines and racers that need more input and output circuits, individual-cylinder fuel and ignition correction, launch and traction controls, progressive/multi-stage nitrous, advanced tuning and datalogging capabilities, and so forth. All three types of systems are in some cases offered in turnkey plug-and-play packages for specific vehicles and engines, in some cases with ready-to-go calibrations. In some instances, less expensive offerings are identical to vendors' higher-end systems, with some capabilities locked out in the ECU firmware or PC software.

AEM (Advanced Engine Management) has focused on providing plug-and-play systems and powerful universal ECUs for the prosumer and weekend-racer aftermarket. **AEM Series 2** systems have supported cam-phasing control, boost control, EGT feedback, and up to 12 injectors and 8 ignition drivers, nitrous control, and multipurpose I/O circuits. Some Series 2 AEM systems have supported drive-by-wire electronic throttles. AEM's flagship **Infinity system** arrived with an advanced 32-bit RISC PowerPC microprocessor and complementary floating-point math co-processor chips packaged in a hardened case designed to withstand harsh racing environments. Infinity capabilities included massive I/O expansion capabilities, dual internal wideband control, flex-fuel compensation, multi-fuel capability, dual-channel adaptive knock control, integrated engine protection strategies, data-logging to USB storage, no-lift shifting, four-wheel speed traction control, three-step launch control, anti-lag turbo strategies, and more. AEM has marketed plug-and-play systems for Dodge Vipers, various Honda models, Ford 5.0 Mustangs, various Mitsubishi, Subaru WRX, various Toyota, and other vehicles.

APEX Integration's PowerFC (full computer unit) represents a complete "total" standalone ECU designed to handle virtually anything up to and including drive-by-wire throttle control that is required to seamlessly replace the factory ECU on Japanese performance vehicles such as the Acura Integra, Honda

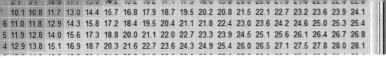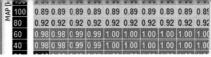

STANDALONE AFTERMARKET ENGINE MANAGEMENT SYSTEMS

Accel/DFI	http://www.prestoliteweb.com/accel/ACCELDFI.aspx
AEM	http://www.aemelectronics.com/
APEX	http://www. apexi-usa.com/
Autronic	http://www.autronic.com.au/
BigStuff3	http://www.bigstuff3.com/
DTA fast	http://www.dtafast.co.uk/
Edelbrock	http://www.edelbrock.com/automotive_new/mc/efi/
EFI Technology	http://www.efitechnology.com
Electromotive	http://www.electromotive-inc.com/
FAST Electronics	http://www.fuelairspark.com/
Haltech	http://www.haltech.com/
HKS	http://www.hks-power.co.jp/en/
Hydra Engine Management Systems	http://www.hydraems.com/
Holley Fuel Systems	http://www.holley.com/Index.asp?division=Holleyefi
Hondata	http://www.hondata.com/
Hydra Engine Management Systems	http://www.hydraems.com/
Link Engine Management	http://www.linkecu.com/
Mass-Flo	http://www.massfloefi.com/
MegaSquirt	http://www.megasquirt.info/
Motec Systems	http://www.motec.com/
Perfect Power	http://www.perfectpower.com/
RetroTek Speed—PowerJection	http://www.retrotekspeed.com/
Simple Digital Systems	http://www.sdsefi.com/
PGMFI.org Grassroots ECU Dev.	http://www.wikitest.pgmfi.org/twiki/bin/view.pl

Civic, Mazda RX-7, Mitsubishi Eclipse and Lancer EVO, Nissan Silvia and Skyline, Subaru Impreza, and Toyota's Altezza, Celica, MR2 Spyder, and Mark-II Chaser. The PowerFC connects to stock EFI wiring via an adapter harness and is designed to keep all critical accessories such as computer-controlled A/C functioning.

BigStuff3 was John Meany's third EMS venture after DFI/Accel and FAST/Fel-Pro. In addition to the more common EMS capabilities, BigStuff3's **PRO SEFI GEN 3** system includes advanced wideband capability with optional methanol support, eight-cylinder coil-on-plug support, individual-cylinder fuel and timing calibration, anti-lag turbo launch control, fuel pump staging, and wide-range ECU environmental capability (-40 to 221 degrees Fahrenheit), as well as optional four-stage nitrous, CO_2 boost controller, engine torque management using spark or cylinder fuel cut-off, dash and display support via CAN bus, EGT monitoring, E10-E85 fueling via GM Flex-Fuel sensor, up to 24 fuel injectors, 4L60E/4L80E transmission control, torque convertor lockup control, 1- to 3-stage boost control, and more. BigStuff3's **GEN 4** was a high-end research system targeting R&D labs, with price and complexity commensurate with what you'd expect. BigStuff3 partnered with damBEST to deliver the damBEST dual-quad "electronic carb" TBI system for V-8s.

DFI (Digital Fuel Injection), later acquired by Accel/Mr. Gasket/Prestolite, was founded by OEM EMS engineer John Meany, who later founded Fel-Pro/FAST and more recently BigStuff3. Accel/DFI is one of the earliest aftermarket EMS companies that is still around. DFI GEN 7 and Thruster systems have supported distributor-type ignitions, Ford EDIS, GM DIS module, and LS1 ignitions. Thruster ECUs have controlled torque converter lockup, A/C compressor control, fan control, single-stage nitrous injection, and two-step rev limiting. In addition to the Thruster/GEN 7 capabilities, DFI GEN 8 systems have supported additional direct-fire ignitions

(including the new Mopar Hemi), PWM boost control, multiple fan control, VTEC-type dual-cam switching, and progressive (PWM) nitrous control. The DFI Pro version is an extra-cost option that unlocks less commonly modified internal ECU tables for advanced tuners. In addition to basic programmable engine management systems, Accel has marketed complete turnkey carb-to-EFI conversion packages, vehicle-specific wiring harnesses, including EFI multi-port intake manifolds for common performance engines, TBI throttle body assemblies, and EFI-related components like fuel injectors, fuel pumps, fuel pressure regulators, and more.

DTA is a British company that designs and builds "cutting edge" engine management systems that are positioned as state-of-the-art and have been installed on a huge variety of performance vehicles and engines. The flagship S100 PRO is an extremely powerful ECU capable of managing 6-, 8-, 10-, and 12-cylinder engines at speeds of up to 20,000 rpm. Interesting capabilities include twin-spark, twin-injector support, genuine two-stroke and four-stroke cycle support, unequal coil-firing and unequal injection angle capabilities, dual main fuel, spark, and boost maps selectable via dash switch, extensive lambda parameters table, auto-tuning function, open- or closed-loop turbo boost control, gear and speed correction for turbo boost, full ALS ignition and fuel maps, ALS valve control with dash-selectable switch, open- or closed-loop PWM cam advance, active load and speed-dependent target cam advance maps, VTEC control, water/methanol injection control, launch control, traction control, full-throttle shift cut, CAN laptop communications via CAN converter, advance datalogging, and flash-upgradable ECU firmware.

Edelbrock, around since the earliest post-World War II days of the hot rodding movement in the dry lakes of southern California, has the clout to be a player in any niche of the

MSD Atomic 2900 throttlebody EFI kit is designed to hide the fuel injectors and some of the electronics in a throttlebody that strongly resembles a Holley 4-barrel carburetor.

performance aftermarket it chooses. Edelbrock has chosen to focus on what it knows best—performance intake manifolds, throttle bodies, throttle body adaptors, fuel systems, and so forth—and to partner with outside EMS specialists for the electronics. The Pro-Flo XT Plus features an ECU designed by EFI Technology, a company that had previously focused exclusively on high-end race systems. The XT includes sequential injection, closed-loop narrow- or wideband fuel trim, on-the-fly user-switchable dual calibrations, boost control, four-stage nitrous, onboard ECU datalogging, and speed-density or Alpha-N load control. Edelbrock has also sold the Pro-Tuner system, mass-flow based EMS featuring an ECU designed by Moto Tron, a builder of OEM engine management systems. The Pro-Tuner supported one or two MAf sensors, distributor ignition, and internal datalogging.

EFI Technology built the Pro-Flo XT system for Edelbrock, but its own market has been high-end EMSs for use in glamour-class pro racing that are cost-prohibitive for most hot rodders. EFI's **X1 Race System** does all the ordinary stuff as well as 12-cylinder injection and coil-on-plug integral-CD ignition, sequential fueling with individual-cylinder ignition and fuel trim, progressive nitrous, air-shifting, launch control, EGT monitoring, cam phasing control, and so forth in a mil-spec hardware package with potted circuitry. EFI markets their own version of the **Pro-Flo** system featuring eight-cylinder sequential injection, four-coil wasted-spark direct ignition, closed-loop wideband fuel control, shift-without-lift function, pit-lane speed limiter, mil-spec main connector, PWM boost control, internal datalogging, and four-stage nitrous control.

Electromotive has long been known for bundling wasted-spark direct-fire ignition into its hardened ECUs designed to live in the engine compartment, which makes sense, given that the company started out developing patented timing control and coil-charging electronics. Electromotive TEC (Total Engine Control) systems use a proprietary 60-2 crank trigger wheel design (sold to fit a variety of engine configurations), but the waste-spark ignition requires cam trigger, which *is* nonetheless required sequential injection phasing. Other TEC capabilities include boost control, nitrous control, data logging, and support for odd-fire engines. Electromotive internal engine-control logic is based on the construction of an accurate volumetric efficiency table.

FAST (Fuel Air Spark Technology), a division of Competition Cams, offered both an entry-level bolt-on carb-to-EFI conversion system called EZ-EFI, and the XFI 2.0. EZ-EFI was designed as a throttle body injection system with LCD interface module that supports up to 1,000 horsepower and features throttle body with four injectors and integral fuel rail and fuel pressure regulator, wideband air/fuel ratio sensor, self-tuning capability, and optional electric fuel pump. FAST's XFI 2.0 was introduced with a powerful microprocessor with four times the speed of previous systems. The XFI standard features included laptop-less tuning, built-in wideband controller, individual-cylinder fuel and spark trim, 5-bar MAP sensor support, boost control, torque convertor lockup control, A/C control, and four calibrations optimized for daily driving, fuel economy, racing, and so forth. Optional features included touch-screen digital dash, coil-on-plug distributorless ignition module for modular Fords, Chrysler Hemi, and GM LSX powerplants, advanced power-adder controls for time-based boost control, progressive nitrous and boost control, intelligent traction control, four-stage nitrous, and internal datalogging, as well as self-learning auto-tuning VE table capability. FAST offers turnkey carb-to-EFI conversion kits, engine swap harness for late-Hemi and LSX powerplants, as well as dual-sync distributors for American V-8s for users not requiring direct-fire ignition.

Haltech has been around for a long time and the Australian company was first to market with an ECU that allowed real-time PC tuning while the engine was running (Haltech's original fuel-only systems would stumble when you updated the calibration) and standard staged-injector fuel control. Haltech EMSs are quite flexible in allowing configurations of I/O channel functionality that permit any particular circuit to be software-defined for fuel or direct-ignition control. The flagship Platinum Sport 2000 offered sequential injection for up to 12 cylinders, and coil-on-plug ignition for six cylinders or waste-spark ignition for up to eight cylinders. Other capabilities included up to 11 user-definable auxiliary inputs, up to 13 user-definable auxiliary outputs, wideband auto-tuning with target air/fuel ratio table, narrow- or wideband closed-loop fuel trim, staged control of multiple injectors per cylinder, EGT-based fuel correction, Alpha-N load control with MAP correction, dual-MAP switching, rally or launch-type anti-lag turbo function,

PROGRAMMING STANDALONE SYSTEMS

144

.1	5.7	10.6	11.7	13.0	14.2	15.2	16.2	17.1	17.9	18.6	19.3	20.0	20.6	21.3	21.6	22.3	22.6	24.1
.0	10.1	10.8	11.7	13.0	14.4	15.7	16.8	17.9	18.7	19.5	20.2	20.8	21.5	22.1	22.7	23.2	23.6	23.9	24.1
6	11.0	11.8	12.9	14.3	15.8	17.2	18.4	19.5	20.4	21.1	21.8	22.4	23.0	23.6	24.2	24.6	25.0	25.3	25.4
5	11.9	12.8	14.0	15.6	17.3	18.8	20.0	21.1	22.0	22.7	23.3	23.9	24.5	25.1	25.6	26.1	26.4	26.7	26.8
.4	12.9	13.8	15.1	16.9	18.7	20.3	21.6	22.7	23.6	24.3	24.9	25.4	26.0	26.5	27.1	27.5	27.8	28.0	28.1

MAP										
150	0.86	0.86	0.86	0.86	0.86	0.86	0.86	0.86	0.86	0.8
100	0.89	0.89	0.89	0.89	0.89	0.89	0.89	0.89	0.89	0.89
80	0.92	0.92	0.92	0.92	0.92	0.92	0.92	0.92	0.92	0.92
60	0.98	0.98	0.99	0.99	1.00	1.00	1.00	1.00	1.00	1.00
40	0.98	0.98	0.99	0.99	1.00	1.00	1.00	1.00	1.00	1.00

VTEC and VANOS cam control, true variable cam phasing control, dual intake runner control, custom sensor calibration, open- or closed-loop boost control, stepper or PWM idle stabilization, alternator control, nitrous switching with fuel/ignition correction, staged shift lights, turbo timer, torque convertor lockup, CAN bus communication to Racepak and Aim Dash systems, flash-able ECU firmware update in the field, and more. Haltech offers an adaptor harness ("plug-in patch looms") to interface the Haltech ECU to fourth-generation Supras, second-gen RX-7, and various other Mitsubishi, Nissan, and Subaru vehicles.

Holley has been building fuel system components since 1903, in particular, the iconic Holley four-barrel carburetor. Holley's **Pro-Jection**, the original Holley EFI system, arrived in the 1980s, a simple TBI system providing carb-to-EFI conversion for American V-8s featuring two or four throats with above-throttle fuel injectors and optional O_2 closed-loop idle control. The Pro-Jection was controlled by an analog (nondigital) ECU that provided Alpha-N throttle position-based load estimation and was tuned with pots that defined idle mixture, full-throttle mixture, midrange, and acceleration enrichment. A Pro-Jection system handled engine management on a 1970 Dodge Challenger big-block featured in an earlier version of this book. The projection throttle body assembly lives on in Holley's **Commander 950** system, which has a modern laptop-programmable digital controller capable of providing speed-density load control as well as Alpha-N like the old Pro-Jection. Holley's flagship EMS at this time of writing was the **Dominator EFI Vehicle Management System**, built around an advanced ECU with a robust potted mil-spec design providing powerful capabilities such as the ability to control a progressive nitrous-injected 12-cylinder turbo engine with two-stage sequential fuel injection, twin drive-by-wire throttles, 12 direct-fire coils, electronic boost control, and methanol-water injection providing detonation suppression, and dual-channel knock control as a last line of defense. The Dominator system is capable of providing 4L60E/4L80E transmission control, and additional capabilities include dedicated fuel and oil pressure sensing, stepper and PWM idle speed control, (13) 0-5V multi-inputs, (30) 0-5V/0-20V sensor inputs, (4) speed inputs, (20) 12V PWM/switched outputs, and (16) ground PWM/switched outputs, the capability to redefine the purpose of I/O circuits to avoid wasting any pins not needed for a particular purpose, and much more.

Hydra Engine Management Systems has specialized in building plug-and-play ECUs for a variety of Japanese vehicles, as well as a smaller selection of European and American vehicles. Nemesis 2.7 ECU capabilities include variable valve timing, boost control, anti-lag turbo management strategies, integral wideband air/fuel ratio controller, sequential control for up to eight injectors, individual-cylinder fuel trim, direct-fire ignitions, quad variable 3D cam control with dual maps, drive-by-wire throttle control, and gear correction for fuel, timing, and boost. Other options include programmable closed-loop knock control, switched ethanol fuel map, flex-fuel capability, full CAN support for dash-display with AC and ABS speed sensors, and programmable traction control based on individual ABS speed sensors. Hydra ECUs are sold with an adaptor harness that connects to the stock vehicle wiring loom to enable replacing the stock ECU, or in some cases operating in parallel.

Link Engine Management is a new Zealand company that provided plug-and-play and universal EMS systems

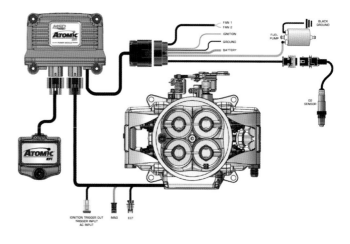

MSD Atomic connection schematic.

built upon the **Link G4** ECU, which was segmented into the lower-priced **Storm**, with fewer I/O channels, and the **Xtreme** system with more. Both G4s are sophisticated ECUs that provide MAP, MAF, or TPS-based load sensing, or blend multiple load sensing sources under user-defined conditions. In addition to the standard fuel and timing controls, the G4 allows individual-cylinder correction. The Storm provides four injector channels and four ignition channels, the Xtreme eight of each. Both systems support boost control, anti-lag turbine speed management, staged injection, stepper and PWM idle control, a variety of variable valve timing controls, fuel pump speed control, multiple fan control, intercooler spray control, check engine light control, purge solenoid emissions control, and many other capabilities. The G4 Xtreme can provide drive-by-wire throttle control.

MegaSquirt originated as a cost-effective do-it-yourself grass-roots ECU kit targeted at self-sufficient hobbyists interested in building their own EMS, right down to soldering and assembling the ECU motherboard and loading the firmware themselves (after modifying the open-source code, if necessary) after which they were responsible for acquiring additional EMS sensors, actuators, and wiring that comprised a workable system. Instructions and support were posted on the Internet, initially by MegaSquirt designers Al Grippo and Bruce Bowling, later as a wiki effort by MegaSquirt users and distributors like DIY-AutoTune that sprung up to distribute packages of MegaSquirt equipment in various stages of completeness, from plastic bags of components, to complete assembled plug-and-play systems indistinguishable from traditional standalone aftermarket programmable engine management systems. From the earliest days, Bowling and Grippo encouraged users and distributors to modify the hardware and source code to expand what MegaSquirt could do. Earliest MegaSquirt designs were relatively simple, fuel-only batch-fire systems, but that soon changed with the additional of ignition control. Most MegaSquirt 1, 2, and 3 equipment is still available, and there is no standard list of features, meaning that there can be a learning curve just to understand which ECU and what features you'll need to order to fit your application. The most powerful systems support eight-cylinder sequential injection, speed-density, Alpha-N, or MAF-based load control, eight-cylinder coil-on plug ignition, PWM boost control, datalogging, and so forth. MicroSquirt is a

PROGRAMMING STANDALONE SYSTEMS

8.8	9.1	9.7	10.6	11.7	13.0	14.2	15.2	16.2	17.1	17.9	18.6	19.3	20.0	20.6	21.3	21.8	22.3	22.6	22.8
9.7	10.1	10.8	11.7	13.0	14.4	15.7	16.8	17.9	18.7	19.5	20.2	20.8	21.5	22.1	22.7	23.2	23.6	23.9	24.1
10.6	11.1	11.8	12.9	14.3	15.8	17.2	18.4	19.5	20.4	21.1	21.8	22.4	23.0	23.6	24.2	24.6	25.0	25.3	25.4
11.5	11.9	12.8	14.0	15.6	17.3	18.8	20.0	21.1	22.0	22.7	23.3	23.9	24.5	25.1	25.6	26.1	26.4	26.7	26.8
12.4	12.9	13.8	15.1	16.9	18.7	20.3	21.6	22.7	23.6	24.3	24.9	25.4	26.0	26.5	27.1	27.5	27.8	28.0	28.1

water-resistant miniature ECU designed for motorcycles and off-road vehicles. Even the latest ready-made MegaSquirt systems with standardized hardware are still open-source, allowing sophisticated users to develop new capabilities.

Mass-Flo systems are turnkey EMS kits with engine load-sensing provided by a factory-style mass airflow (MAF) sensor. Mass-Flo kits are available for AMC, Buick, Cadillac, Chevrolet, Chrysler/Dodge, Ford, Oldsmobile, Pontiac, Studebaker and other V-8 engines. The LSX EFI system includes four-barrel single-plane GM performance parts port-EFI intake manifold and fuel rails, 1,000 cfm Mass-Flo four-barrel aluminum throttle body, Pro-Flo MAF meter (Pro-M Mass-Flo meter optional for draw-through or blow-through forced-induction applications), production sequential-injection ECU, all required sensors (crank sensor not required), eight fuel injectors sized for application with headroom for large power increases, performance billet aluminum distributor with integral ignition (no crank trigger required), and performance coil and mount. The Pro-Flo kit allows installation of aftermarket CDI boxes, boost-retard systems, nitrous controllers, rev-limiters, and shift lights.

Motec targets the high-end hot rodding and full-race EMS marketplace. The current product line includes the M400, M600, M800, and M800 race ECUs for 4-, 6-, and 8- to 12-cylinder engines, as well as rotary powerplants. The relatively new M84 targets the more price-sensitive prosumer market by deleting certain capabilities such as individual-cylinder trim, telemetry, remote logging, knock control, variable cam control, and drive-by-wire throttle control, as well as offering reduced datalogging speed and analysis capability. Late-model Mx00-series Motec ECUs have fast 32-bit microprocessors that allow management of engines running at extremely high speeds up to 20,000 rpm. All late-model Motec ECUs have CAN bus capability and provide standard or optional five-wire lambda control, boost control, nitrous control, dual-stage injection, ground speed limiting, GPS track mapping, overrun boost enhancement (anti-lag), gear-change ignition cut, stepper motor idle control, variable cam control, advance data-logging, and optional I/O and ignition expansion via auxiliary modules. All Mx00 systems provide optional knock control via SKM module, optional mil-spec design, and M8X0 systems provide servo motor control. Motec has a giant catalog of premium-quality competition EMS parts to do almost anything, including esoteric equipment like a mil-spec power distribution module or Motec's ECU-controlled competition digital dash/logger, which can be ordered pre-installed in a competition steering wheel. Motec offers a few plug-and-play ECUs for performance street and race vehicles like the Subaru WRX and the Mitsubishi Lancer Evolution.

Perfect Power is a South African company that builds powerful piggyback engine management computers and two ECU-targeted standalone rally-type applications. The **XMS5B** is an eight-cylinder system with wideband lambda sensing, and the **XMS5A** is a four-cylinder ECU without wideband. XMS5 systems offer sequential fuel injection, drive-by-wire electronic throttle control, launch control, idle control, boost control, and simple straight-line traction control. Other capabilities include automatic and manual map-switching while driving. One interesting XMS5 feature is the built-in dyno, which calculates power and torque on the basis of user-programmable start and end conditions. Dyno start conditions include TPS voltage, rpm, ground speed, and end conditions include ground speed, distance, time, and rpm. XMS ECU include a connection for an optional dash/display, which can optionally be connected in a head-up installation.

The **PowerJection III** from **RetroTek** was designed as a four-barrel throttle body injection system that looks a lot like a classic Holley four-barrel carburetor, with four side-mount fuel injectors housed in what would appear to be float chambers spraying at the four throttle plates. The PowerJection III was optimized for low cost, simple installation, and clean, classic looks, and to that end, the ECU, sensors, and a good deal of wiring are packaged in the throttle body with the injectors, and the basic kit is designed for vehicles that already have a fuel return line, fuel pressure regulator, and an EFI-type electric fuel pump with adequate capacity, and includes braided stainless hose and fitting to plumb into the pre-existing fuel supply and return lines to the fuel tank. Load-sensing is speed-density, with a 2.5-bar MAP sensor integral to the throttle body, allowing up to 20-psi turbo or supercharger boost. The PowerJection III includes a standard wideband air/fuel ratio sensor and "adaptive learning" self-tune algorithms designed to eliminate the need for laptop programming and tuning, except in the case of the most radical engines. The system supports stepper-motor idle air control. Ignition control can be used with a Ford TFI ignition or GM HEI (computer-controlled version). The optional PowerJection return-less kit eliminates the need for the return-type fuel loop required by most EFI systems and includes an auxiliary electronic fuel pump controller and wiring, electric fuel pump with integral heat-sink fins, and inline fuel filter. The returnless components are available in a standalone kit without the PowerJection EMS.

The **Simple Digital Systems (SDS) EM-5** ECU was designed to be simple to use. The company claims it is the "easiest digital standalone EFI system to program on the market today—period." Rather than using 3D maps like most engine management systems, the EM-5 system presents fuel and ignition maps to the user via pairs of 2D maps displayed on a dedicated LCD programmer module that shows the contents of load cells one at a time. In addition to the programmer module, the EM-5 includes a mixture control module with a knob that will temporarily adjust injection pulse width by up to 50 percent while the vehicle is running without changing the internal EMS fueling tables—which is useful for testing the effect of air/fuel ratio changes on actual performance or on sensed wideband air/fuel ratio in advance of actual table modification. Tuners adjust base fueling as a function of rpm and a MAP trim value that applies across the rpm range. EM-5 ECUs are available as fuel-only systems or with ignition control as a flying magnet or 24-tooth crank-triggered fully programmable ignition with optional knock control capable of firing plugs via external CDI box and distributor or optional waste-spark coil modules. The EM5 provides speed-density or throttle-position Alpha-N load sensing and can accept the air/fuel ratio signal from an external wideband controller. The EM-5 injector drivers are designed to fire OEM-type saturated-circuit injectors, but can drive high-flow aftermarket peak-and-hold injectors using a resistor module. SDS systems are limited to and sold with specific engine sensors, and can accept knock and nitrous inputs, and extra output channels can be used to control a fuel pump, radiator fan, check engine-type diagnostic light, and rpm-activated on/off circuit that provide functions such as nitrous triggering. EM-5s have been used on a variety of vehicles, including experimental aircraft, which says something for the reliability.

Chapter 10
EMS/EFI Engine Swapping

Swapping an EFI engine into an alien EFI vehicle is one of the most complex and difficult topics covered in this book. Jaguars That Run, a Livermore, California, firm that specializes in Chevrolet TPI and TBI engine swaps had this to say in their manual on TPI/TBI engine swapping:

"The original intention of this manual was to make it possible for 'average shade tree mechanics' to install Tuned Port Injection or throttle body injection engines into older cars and trucks. However, after testing the manual on several 'average shade tree mechanics' and observing their swaps, we learned that they could sometimes make the engines run, but made numerous mistakes in wiring, fuel systems, hose routing, hose selection, cooling, exhaust, emissions-control equipment, air conditioning—just about everything imaginable. A lot of the mistakes could have been dangerous. In other words, the 'average shade tree mechanic' was not qualified to do the TPI or TBI engine swap, or any engine swap."

Author Mike Knell went on to suggest, "Engine swaps require experience, knowledge, patience, and a willingness to look things up in a book or shop manual. From these experiences, we can only advise most people not to do TPI or TBI engine swaps unless they are experienced mechanics or have experienced mechanics who will carefully inspect the conversion before the vehicle is started, and again before the vehicle is driven. Remember, the purpose of doing an engine swap is to make the vehicle run better, and if you cannot make it better, it is not worth doing."

Vintage TBI/TPI engine swaps—difficult as they can be—are considerably less complicated than swaps involving more modern powerplants installed in vehicles with complex

Some things they should have done at the factory, and the 3.0 V-6 Gen 2 MR2 is one. Swapping a 3.0-liter 1994-plus 1MZ-FE Toyota/Lexus V-6 in place of the 1991-95+ 2.0-liter turbo is at once simpler and more complex than some swaps. Some EMS components (for example, the fuel pump and supply system) work great, but each car has some EMS features that are completely beyond the scope of the other's ECM, an example being a V-6 EMS's desire to see torque converter slip data (the MR2 Turbo is a five-speed-only vehicle).

Lexus V-6 and MR2 Turbo transaxle preparing for a hook-up.

onboard CAN networks consisting of dozens of embedded controllers that interact with each other to handle complex EMS and vehicle-management tasks. At this time of writing, the performance aftermarket was still coming to grips with networked cars in a situation analogous to the mid-1980s, when engine management tasks formerly handled by the physical plumbing of carburetors were suddenly under the control of a black-box onboard computer. It took a little time to reverse-engineer the inner workings and logic of onboard computers and build tools and equipment to deal with PROMs and electronic injectors.

Modern engines and vehicles are more complex and sophisticated than ever, but so are the tools to deal with them. Standards-based and proprietary vehicle networks can have a steep learning curve, but in the same sense that manipulating a few numbers in a computer can be a lot more powerful (and conceptually simpler!) than tinkering with the complex guts of a carb, multi-processor vehicle networks are wonderfully powerful. Interpreting or translating digital data packets that broadcast engine rpm on a network to make a digital tachometer work with a new engine can ultimately be a lot simpler than building a signal processing circuit to change the wave form of a tach driver. We've all seen piggyback interceptors that modify signals going in and out of an EMS ECU to increase performance, and it seems purely a matter of time before we see programmable CAN interceptors that filter, translate, and manipulate CAN messages on a vehicle network to accomplish even more.

The best news of all for performance enthusiasts is that federal and state laws that protect the rights of individuals and service professionals to repair and modify vehicles right down to the data bits offer the promise that there is a bright future for people who know damn well they can do it better than the factory, or at least more the way *they* want it. Which sometimes requires a different engine.

This book contains a number of engine-swap-project-type vehicles. The BMW M3–into 1993 325-ci is an extremely complex EMS-engine-into-foreign-EMS-vehicle swap, which utilized the vehicle's pre-OBD-II EMS and also involved a turbo conversion. The Toyota 1MZ-FE V-6–into 1991 MR2 Turbo was even more complex, using the engine's OBD-II EMS to control and weave together two partially compatible EMS systems (later converted to aftermarket EMS control).

Projects involving previously carbureted recipient vehicles are usually somewhat less complex, but nevertheless very serious projects.

The "Jag-rolet" project in this book involved harnessing a powerful Motec M48 aftermarket EMS to manage a supercharged hot rod TPI Corvette V-8 in its new home in a late-model Jaguar sedan. The project required comprehending an extremely complex set of computer-controlled vehicle-management functions such as automatic load leveling, designing the hardware and wiring to interface such peripherals to the Motec, and then programming the Motec to make everything work.

CRITICAL EMS/EFI ENGINE SWAP ISSUES

Clearly, no EMS/EFI engine swap is for the faint of heart. Even if you are swapping a complete engine and all related engine systems into a vehicle where the swap engine was a factory option, you will almost definitely have to deal with challenges and incompatibilities on a variety of levels, including the following:

- Any engine swap involves ordinary physical swap issues: space, motor mounts, clutch and transmission, shifter/linkage, alternator and belt-driven accessories, intake and exhaust systems, cooling system and fans, fuel supply, and so on. Some will be trivial, others extremely challenging.
- Installing any EFI engine in a carbureted vehicle involves, in addition to the above, the need to provide a high-pressure fuel supply of sufficient volume, and probably a fuel tank return line. And, of course, you'll need to deal with all the issues surrounding installing and mounting the engine management computer and wiring.
- Installing a standalone aftermarket EMS on a swap engine in a foreign vehicle involves, in addition to all the above, issues similar or identical to what you're up against with an aftermarket EMS installation, including the need to deal with calibrating the EMS for the specific engine and vehicle. If the vehicle had OEM electronic engine management, you will almost definitely need to deal with managing certain functions only peripherally related to running the engine (gauges, air-conditioning, fan controls, and possibly much more). In order to do this, will you leave the OEM computer in place and alive and happy enough to function where needed? Or is the aftermarket system powerful and programmable enough to manage special vehicle functions such as ride height adjustment, as was required in the Jag-rolet project.
- In some cases, when installing an EMS engine in a foreign EMS vehicle, you'll have to decide who runs the show: the engine's EMS or the vehicle's EMS (or perhaps a cooperative effort or a standalone aftermarket system). In addition to handling most of the above-mentioned issues, you're going to have to deal specifically with either: adapting the vehicle's EMS to the engine (perhaps changing sensors and actuators, perhaps changing the calibration and so on) or making the engine's EMS work in the vehicle (in some cases opening up a Pandora's box of issues with integrating the foreign EMS with the vehicle's wiring and electrical system and any auxiliary vehicle onboard computers, electronics, and diagnostic wiring) or employing both vehicle and engine EMS, integrating functionality of two different control systems. In the state of California, the legal way to go is to swap in a complete engine and all its EMS and SMOG equipment that is at least as new as the vehicle into which it is swapped to avoid degrading the exhaust emissions of the vehicle (see sidebar about California enigne swapping).

Whether you're working with a stock swap engine, the swap engine's stock EMS, a recalibrated stock EMS, a hot rod swap engine, an aftermarket EMS, the vehicle's stock EMS hacked to work on the swap engine, or some other combination of engine, EMS, and vehicle equipment, you may also have to deal with issues related to the following:

- Transmission control, including converter lockup, shifting, and other transmission issues (particularly if you change from automatic to manual transmission or vice versa; ECU electronics and firmware may vary according to the transmission). Some aftermarket ECMs will handle transmission control for some electronic transmissions and some will not.

- Swap engine sensors and actuators incompatible with alien engine or vehicle systems that require engine sensor data
- Engine/Tach driver signal incompatibility with vehicle tachometer
- Speedometer incompatibility with the EMS or vehicle speed sensor
- Intake issues (including space for MAF meter and possible MAF turbulence issues if it's necessary to modify the air intake)
- Integrated dash and gauges incompatible with alien EMS and engine
- Computer-controlled alternator issues
- Computer-controlled air conditioning issues
- Traction controls that integrate the EMS and electronic braking systems
- Electronic throttle
- Handshake between various computers
- Engine position sensor location and timing problems
- Antitheft, emissions
- In-tank fuel pump and regulator capacity and pressure
- Fan control incompatibilities
- Coolant temperature-control systems
- Direct-fire versus distributor ignition controls
- Combo-meter dash issues where the meter displays data from multiple embedded controllers including CAN-based air bag ECU, cruise control ECU, ECM, and so on
- Multi-mode power steering electronic control problems
- Brake event monitoring
- Knock sensor incompatibilities (if using recipient EMS)
- Altering length of stock harness
- Catalyst and emissions issues, including cat AIR pump control, multiple O_2 sensors, missing cat, and so on
- An engine swap involving a state-of-the-art 2008 and newer EMS vehicle will require dealing with a CAN bus and CAN-based functionality such as dash gauge controls, airbags, door locks, proximity cruise controls, electronic stability control, active suspension controls, braking and ABS, telematics-based remote diagnostics and automatic trouble-reporting and assistance services, and much more (see CAN section).

ACTUAL SWAP PROCESS

1. *Install and mount the engine* (and transmission, if they install together). Obviously, as in any engine swap, you need the right motor mounts that locate the engine with correct geometry so everything fits. You may need to relocate engine components or equipment in the engine compartment, alter engine accessories, or even modify the firewall, radiator bulkhead, radiator, or other components to make the new engine fit in place.

2. *Install exhaust system/catalysts.* Emissions-controlled engines must have legal exhaust manifolds with properly located oxygen sensors, legal catalytic converters, and AIR injection. Vehicles with speed-density EMS may need relatively correct exhausts to keep the engine volumetric efficiency close enough to stock to maintain correct EFI calibration—or a custom calibration. Some tight swaps may require custom headers, which can be a gray area for California street driving unless the header manufacturer has a California exemption order for the modified parts. Clearly, the closer to stock configuration, the better chance a referee will approve the vehicle.

From the *V-8 Conversion Manual* by Jaguars That Run (JTR):

Due to some misinformation, and exaggeration, people across the country think the California-style smog laws are the end of engine swaps. Even in California, many automotive enthusiasts believe it is against the law to perform engine swaps.

The basic intent of the California engine change laws is that when you do an engine swap, the new engine/transmission cannot pollute more than the original engine/transmission. This means the newly installed engine must be the same year (or newer) as the vehicle, and all emissions controls on the newly installed engine must be installed and functional. Also, you can't put a heavy-duty truck engine (over 6,000 lb GVW) into an S-10 Truck because heavy-duty truck engines have less stringent emissions limits than light-duty trucks.

To get your engine swap approved, you must go to a referee station. The referee inspection is less than $40, and it is a benefit for people who do smog-legal engine changes because the engine change can be approved on a visual inspection, current smog laws, and common sense.

The referee station will visually inspect the vehicle and engine/transmission for all the proper smog equipment, and inspect the engine to be sure it is the same year (or newer) as the vehicle. If all is there, they will put an "engine identification" tag in the doorjamb. The "engine identification" tag is not mentioned on any registration papers or ownership papers. It is only on the vehicle.

If your vehicle does not pass the visual inspection, and you feel it should, you can have the Referee Inspector call the engineering office for a ruling. If the engineering office fails your vehicle and you think it should pass, you can always run it through the California Air Resources Board (CARB) for a full Federal Test Procedure (FTD), but that can cost you several thousand dollars, and your vehicle may still fail. Remember, *the Referee Inspection program is a benefit for people who do engine swaps.*

The California smog laws on engine swaps (or engine changes) are consistent with common sense, safety, and emissions reduction.

The EPA recognizes California smog laws as being applicable across the nation. That is, if it is legal in California, then according to the EPA, it is legal in all other states.

Let's assume you've done a California smog-legal engine change to your vehicle. You've installed an engine that is the same year (or newer) as your vehicle, with all of the required smog equipment and controls for both the engine and transmission. The chassis has the correct emissions controls: Catalytic converter, charcoal canister, and fuel filler restrictor (if required). Your next step is to visit a referee station.

The Department of Motor Vehicles (DMV) can get you the phone number required to make an appointment with the referee station. When you call to make the appointment, the person on the phone will ask you why you need to go to the referee station. Your answer will be, "Engine change." (If you say, "engine swap" or "V-8 conversion," the person on the phone may not know what you are talking about, so please, just say, "engine change.")

Next, the person will ask for your name, address, and the vehicle's license number. You will then get an appointment date, which can range anywhere from the very next day to five weeks away. Some areas have appointments on Saturdays if that is more convenient for you. Within a few days, you will receive a postcard in the mail confirming your appointment date, and it will tell you to bring the vehicle's registration papers and any other smog-related paperwork that you may have.

When you arrive at the referee station, be polite, be honest, and be patient. The inspectors rarely see engine swaps. They usually see stock vehicles that have failed the smog inspection. The inspectors are a lot like police officers—they are highly trained, and the public only sees them when there is a problem. Remember, it is their job to make sure your vehicle is smog legal. For all they know, you could be an undercover inspector, so don't expect the inspector to let anything slide, because his job may be at stake.

The inspectors have a general training in smog inspection and will not necessarily be an expert on the type of engine in your car. They see Volkswagens, Fords, Volkswagens, Chryslers, Volkswagens, Datsuns, Volkswagens, Toyotas, Volkswagens, Mercedes, Volkswagens, Chevrolets, and Volkswagens—just about everything ever built, so they cannot be expected to be an expert on every vehicle's smog equipment, unless of course it's a Volkswagen.

The inspection takes anywhere from 30 minutes to over one hour, depending on the inspector and the type of "engine change." Some inspectors will want to be left alone with your vehicle, others may ask for your assistance in locating devices such as the charcoal canister, vehicle speed sensor, or the wiring for the lock-up torque converter. The inspector will check ignition timing and EGR operation.

If your vehicle passes the visual inspection, a sticker will be placed in the doorjamb or engine compartment (see below).

If your vehicle does not pass the visual inspection, you will be given a form explaining what your vehicle will need to pass the inspection. You will need to correct the problem(s) listed on the form and make another appointment with the referee station.

After the visual inspection, the vehicle will be given the tailpipe (or sniffer) test. The tailpipe test is quite lenient. If your vehicle cannot pass the tailpipe test, something is wrong, or your engine has been modified a lot. Generally, a vehicle's tailpipe emissions will be about one-third of the allowable standards if it is running decently.

If your vehicle passes the visual inspection and the tailpipe test, you will get the smog inspection certificate ($7 fee) so that you can register your vehicle. The certificate has no indication of the "engine change" and is the same type of certificate that "normal" vehicles receive for passing the inspection.

We at JTR really do believe in running clean cars. We are located in a high-smog area and we see (and smell) the smog in the air almost every day. Now that we have the technology to make cars perform well and run clean, let's make an effort to keep *our* air clean.

The sticker in the doorjamb (see below) allows the car to be subsequently tested at any smog inspection station. It gives the following information on what smog equipment the vehicle requires.

Explanation of Sticker Contents

VIN No.	Serial number of the vehicle
YR.	Year of the engine (not the vehicle)
Size	Engine size
MFG	Manufacturer of the engine
F/C	Federal/California smog requirements
M/A	Manual/automatic transmission
Site	Where the car was inspected
B/A	Before/after: If the engine was installed before March of 1984, it may not need any smog controls
NOX	NOx emission controls
PCV	Positive crankcase ventilation
TAC	Thermostatic air cleaner
IS	Air injection system
EVP	Evaporative controls (charcoal canister)
FR	Fuel filler restrictor (unleaded gas)
OC	Oxidizing catalytic converter
TWC	Three-way catalytic converter
EGR	Exhaust gas recirculation
PK	Spark (distributor) controls
COM	Computer
C/I	Carburetor/injection
OTH	Other smog controls

EMS/EFI SWAPPING

Lexus V-6 in a 1991 MR2. Now if we only had a passenger side engine mount . . .

3. *Modify the driveshaft* on a rear-drive longitudinal engine/ transmission swap so it bolts to the rear end and transmission, if necessary shortening or lengthening the driveshaft and fabricating a hybrid shaft that joins the transmission end of one shaft and the differential end of another.

4. *Mount the computer and wiring harness.* Except for certain EMS computers hardened to survive the harsh environment of the engine compartment (moisture, heat, vibration, electromagnetic radiation, and so on), the ECU must be mounted in the passenger compartment or trunk in a location where it will stay cool and dry. Beware the hot trunk firewall of a rear- or midengine vehicle. You may need to lengthen parts of the wiring harness to locate the computer in an optimal place and may want to shorten other wiring for a sanitary installation. As long as you use reasonably heavy-gauge wire to extend the wiring harness and make excellent quality crimp joints, signals to and from the ECM will not be affected for most sensors and actuators. If at all possible, get the EMS wiring harness when you acquire an engine, as an OEM wiring harness can be expensive if you have to buy a new one. New aftermarket wiring harnesses are available but make sure that "simplified" harnesses have the capability to connect all components you require on your vehicle (such as torque converter lockup and vehicle speed sensor). Ground wires should ideally be grounded individually to the same lug on the engine block or cylinder head and the block grounded to the negative battery terminal).

5. *Fit/adapt engine accessories.* Emissions accessories such as an air injection pump must be correct for the engine. In the case of the A/C compressor, power steering pump, and alternator, it is usually easier to use the swap engine's original accessories, but in some cases vehicle accessories such as the A/C compressor may work better, since they are definitely compatible with the rest of the A/C system. Engines with MAF sensors may not be compatible with radiator and accessories in tight engine swap situations, requiring you to fabricate air inlet/ MAF ducting out of elbows, pipe, OEM ducting, and so on. This takes time, ingenuity, and resources. It is relatively easy to create air turbulence problems in the air intake that interfere with proper MAF functioning at certain mass-flow rates.

With speed-density EFI engines, you can mount an open-element air cleaner directly on the throttle body, but you will lose torque due to the lack of a cold-air inlet. MAF sensors are delicate and require precise aerodynamics to work right, and they complicate the swap air inlet plumbing task. Some engine swappers have had to relocate or replace radiators and fabricate new engine accessory mounts to relocate accessories to be compatible with the EFI engines. You may have difficulty with the stock knock sensor location. Since the shock wave/sound created by detonation travels well through metal, this sensor can usually be relocated. If necessary, Teflon tape wrapped around the sensor threads may help to reduce the sensitivity of the sensor in the new location.

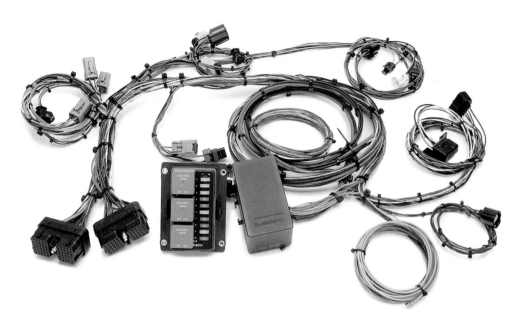

Almost without a doubt, wiring issues will be one of the most challenging aspect of an EFI engine swap. Fortunately, outfits like Painless Performance make complete swap harnesses for some common performance swaps, and they also make some semi-custom harnesses you can adapt in more problematic situations. This harness is designed to help swap a Cummins turbo-diesel into anything. *Painless Performance*

6. *Handle miscellaneous swap hassles:*

- Many late-model vehicles have antitheft systems. In some vehicles the EMS will match data from a coded resistor in the key to stored internal data, while in others, the remote function actuation (RFA) system will interact with a transponder in the key or key fob that must match stored data. Without the right key with the right resistor/transponder, the vehicle will not start. Because all vehicle manufacturers must have a way to deal with lost keys, antitheft systems can usually be defeated with aftermarket electronics or by changing the configuration in the ECM or other embedded controller.

- The vehicle speed sensor (VSS) tells the ECU how fast the vehicle is going. Some engine management algorithms make use of ground speed data to control torque converter lockup, EGR valve, evaporative charcoal canister purge valve, cooling fans, closed-loop air/fuel ratio, and idle speed. There is a lot of ECU logic that depends on the VSS, which will affect the operation of the above devices. You should retain the VSS if you want the engine to run as well as it did stock.

- Depending on your selection of transmission, you may need to make sure the overdrive torque converter lockup is wired and operating correctly.

- EFI wiring is relatively self-contained on many older vehicles and operates independently of most of the rest of the vehicle's electrical system. All 2008 and newer and some older vehicles with CAN buses eliminate a ton of wiring between the module and onboard peripheral devices, but most messaging on the CAN bus is defined by the vehicle manufacturer. On some CAN vehicles, the check engine light, radio volume, electronic speedometer, and other dash gauges and equipment may be wired directly to the ECM rather than communicating through the CAN bus (which only need to carry messaging related to OBD-II). Some vehicles have a combo meter or other dash/gauge control module that receives data from several sources, including the main ECM, but that does not feed data to the ECM and can potentially be eliminated in

engine swaps. Bottom line: Anyone swapping a complex late-model engine into a complex late-model vehicle for the first time is engaged in a complex R&D project that is going to involve a certain amount of reverse-engineering.

- There is often wiring included in the factory EFI wiring harness for connecting devices that have nothing to do with fuel injection or engine management but operate non-EFI appliances that are simply located on the engine close to EFI components (such as oil level or engine temperature gauge senders). These may need to be segregated out of the engine wiring harness for engine/ECM swapping. Minimally, there are several EMS wires that must be connected to the rest of the vehicle electrical system (switched power, ground, and so forth). Depending on how much of the factory harness you use, or whether you are using an aftermarket harness, these include fuel pump wiring, torque converter lockup, and power for emissions-control devices. In general, fuel-injection systems need constant 12-volt+ power, switched 12-volt+ power, starter 12-volt+, tach or crank/cam trigger, and ignition coil, in addition to the EFI sensors and actuators. You may want to consider a simplified aftermarket EFI wiring harness, since it will only include EFI-specific wiring rather than all engine and related wiring. Engine management systems on 2008+ vehicles will need to communicate with other onboard controllers and diagnostic devices on the CAN bus, which may or may not be a significant reverse-engineering project. For much more information on hacking the CAN bus, see Chapter 16.

- You will need to handle throttle linkages and, in some cases, transmission kick-down linkages and clutch linkages or hydraulic hoses. This is standard swap stuff, except that the EFI throttle body may require fabricating different linkages that connect otherwise incompatible accelerator pedals and throttle bodies, and a swap engine with electronic throttle will require an electronic accelerator or conversion to a cable-actuated throttle.

- If you are using special swap headers, you may need to

install a threaded bung to install one or more air/fuel ratio sensors in the exhaust system as close as possible to the first exhaust collector (where it will stay hot) if you are not able to use the stock EFI exhaust system. Weld-in O_2 sensor bosses are available from firms like K&N.

- You will definitely need to assess the total electrical power requirements of the total vehicular package in the swap configuration, including all EMS components (such as fuel injectors and ECM) as well as non-EMS appliances and lights. The alternator must provide sufficient power for worst case, meaning all lights on, wipers on, air conditioning on, all intermittent EMS components (such as staged injectors) in operation. Remember, the EFI system will not function reliably if the battery voltage gets much below 10 volts and may not run below 8 to 9 volts.

7. *Build a fuel supply system* with adequate volume and pressure. Any port-injected engine requires (relatively) high-pressure fuel in the 30- to 70-psi range from an EFI-specific electric fuel pump, while throttle body injection engines require about 20 psi, and gasoline direct-injection engines incorporate special self-contained fuel systems that boost ordinary EFI-type fuel supply line pressure into the 1,500- to 3,000-psi range at the injector rail. Engines with more horsepower obviously require a higher peak volume of fuel than engines with less. You may decide to raise the fuel pressure above stock to tune the engine for special circumstances, and this may require a more powerful pump. If the new engine has a lot more power—and why else would you be swapping in a new engine?—you may need a high-flow in-tank or inline supplementary fuel pump to prevent at all cost lean mixtures or fuel starvation that could result in engine damage.

On most EFI engines, pressurized fuel flows into the injector fuel rail, and excess fuel beyond what's required to supply the injectors is released by a pinch-type pressure regulator downstream of the injector rail and returned to the fuel tank. On a carb-to-EFI conversion, unless you are swapping in one of the relatively few return-less/deadhead EFI powerplants with ECM fuel-pump speed control, fuel rail pressure sensor, and fuel pressure pulse width compensation, you'll have to create a fuel return loop by fabricating a second fuel line to route excess fuel back to the tank. Keep in mind that some EFI vehicles that have only one fuel line going from the tank to the engine are actually equipped with a short fuel loop in or near the tank with a standard pinch-type regulator—and a deadhead spur supply line leading to the injector rail.

A fuel return can often be tapped into the tank at the fuel filler neck or fuel gauge sending-unit panel (though you

Fuel Injection Specialties placed a good number of LTx powerplants in place of carbureted powerplants, GM TBI vehicles, and vehicles like this Pontiac Firebird that was originally equipped with Tuned port Injection. However, if your old TPI Firebird made 200 horsepower, and you've got a hot rod LT4 cranking out 350 or 400 all-motor horses hidden in the closet, we're talking nearly twice the power. You could do this with TPI hot rod parts (or a late-model LSx powerplant), but a PROM-based 1993 LT1 ECM will manage the engine, as will almost any TPI computer with a few calibration or auxiliary fuel-air tweaks, and the swap is straightforward if you've done your homework. This is obviously not a cold-air intake and would make more power if it were.

clearly do not want to have a shower of return fuel spilling continuously onto the gauge sender for obvious reasons). Optimally, return fuel should dump into the bottom of the tank or spray across the tank to prevent aeration near the fuel pump pickup. This may be difficult to arrange and is not absolutely vital. An OEM EFI fuel tank usually has a reserve, a return, a fuel damper, and a submersible high-pressure pump built into the tank. Wrecking yards can supply Walbro-type EFI-type inline external fuel pumps from cars like the old 280Z/ZX. You will need an adequately sized fuel line for sufficient injection pressure and a high-pressure EFI-type inline fuel filter.

In some cases you may want to construct a small external auxiliary fuel tank fed by a low-pressure pump upstream of the primary high-pressure EFI fuel pump to prevent fuel starvation during high G-maneuvers or on steep hills when the fuel tank level is low.

8. *Handle engine cooling.* This has nothing in particular to do with the engine management system, though EFI air cleaner/MAF plumbing on a swap engine with front throttle body can sometimes have clearance problems with the radiator and fittings. Depending on the engine-vehicle configuration, you may need to increase the size of your radiator or have it re-cored for higher cooling capacity. It is critical that the coolant thermostat and EMS warm-up enrichment tables agree on what is normal operating temperature, or the EMS may continue to wet the cylinder walls with cold-running enrichment even after the engine is as warm as it's going to get.

9. *Maintain functionality of all original-equipment emissions controls* on a donor swap engine if you are dealing with an emissions-controlled vehicle that needs to be legal for street use in the United States. The engine can never be older than the vehicle in which it's installed in order that vehicle emissions are not increased by the engine swap, and you cannot install a heavy-duty truck engine in a light truck or car because emissions standards are less rigorous for heavy vehicles. The emissions system cannot be older than the engine, even if the car is. Maintaining emissions functionality explicitly refers to all emissions-control equipment and any engine, engine electronics, or fuel system components that can affect emissions, including intake manifold, throttle body, exhaust manifolds, air pump, charcoal canister, EGR system, computer and relays, fuel delivery system, air cleaner, air cleaner ducting, vehicle speed sensor (VSS), torque converter lockup wiring, and virtually all wiring. You can fabricate your own wiring, or buy an aftermarket wiring harness, but all devices in any way affecting or potentially affecting emissions must be original and working properly to be legal.

If the car is not emissions-controlled (i.e., more than a specified number of years old), you do not need original smog equipment. In this case, anything goes as far as speed equipment, and this goes for larger runners, bigger cams, heads, and so forth. In this case, keep in mind that speed-density systems base fueling on engine speed and manifold pressure and assume a fixed correspondence between rpm/MAP and engine volumetric efficiency—a relationship that goes away when you switch to, say, a cam that doesn't run as much vacuum. EMS recalibration is mandatory.

The digital EMS on modern vehicles is calibrated for a particular weight vehicle, with particular drag, particular thermostat, particular induction and exhaust systems, and particular pollution controls. Changing the engine and EMS to a different vehicle without EMS recalibration could mean engine management is no longer optimal, with degraded engine performance or efficiency. Because MAF engine management systems with mass airflow sensing directly measure rather than estimate airflow, they have some ability to compensate for modifications that influence the factory-assumed relationship between manifold pressure, engine speed, and engine airflow—but only to a point (on some systems as little as 15 percent greater airflow than stock can cause problems). In case you are hoping to adapt EMS components from a vehicle's original engine to a swap engine, keep in mind that fuel flow reaches its limit the moment injectors are continuously open (unless you then increase fuel pressure).

If you are making radical changes to a swap engine for off-highway use or installation in an older vehicle that's exempt from emissions controls, you may want to consider installing a programmable aftermarket computer. Most standalone programmable aftermarket ECUs can be configured to work fine with common OE engine sensors, fueling systems, and speed-density air metering systems. MAF-capable aftermarket ECUs are more rare, but they do exist. Meanwhile, once you install an aftermarket EMS and wiring, converting to speed-density is as simple as replacing the MAF with a section of ducting and installing a MAP sensor with reference line to the intake manifold. Many late-model factory EMSs with MAF and MAP sensors will work very well with the MAF disconnected and can be recalibrated so they will operate in speed-density mode without turning on the check engine light. The newest trend is plug-and-play aftermarket systems that plug directly into factory EFI wiring harnesses and control everything from basic injection pulse width and spark timing to the check engine light to drive-by-wire electronic throttle to torque converter lockup or even shifting electronic transmissions, and there might be one that works well in a swap situation.

If you live in California, registering an emissions-controlled vehicle following an engine swap requires that you have the vehicle approved by a referee at the California Bureau of Automotive Repair (see sidebar), in a process consisting of a robust visual inspection followed by a tailpipe sniffer test. The referee must verify that all stock systems are in place and working properly and that there are no obvious modifications to the swap engine that could degrade exhaust emissions.

SPECIAL ENGINE SWAPPING COMPONENTS

There are a variety of companies that make special parts and equipment to help with EMS engine swapping, including everything from replacement high-volume in-tank fuel pumps to swap wiring harnesses, electronic interceptors, special PROMs or calibrations (in some cases to disable potentially problematic functions like antitheft systems, MAF metering, emissions equipment, and so forth), VSS and speedo conversions, tach conversions, and more. Beware of simplified aftermarket wiring harnesses that eliminate otherwise essential wiring by fooling the engine management system into thinking, for example, that the car is always in neutral or park, which could hurt drivability, fuel economy, emissions, and even power.

Texas concours d'elegance car collector Dee Howard had his technicians stick a Jaguar 4.2-liter in-line six into this 1940s-vintage Studebaker. The guys then installed a triple-Weber DCOE carburetor intake manifold, equipped it with triple TWM throttle bodies incorporating cast-in injector bosses, and installed a Haltech fuel-only engine management system. Sweet. (Though maybe not sweet enough: Howard later decided to convert the car to carbureted Chevy small-block V-8 power!)

GM L98, LTx AND LSx V-8 ENGINE SWAPPING

GM small-block V-8s with multi-port EFI are so important as to merit as special mention in a discussion of EMS engine swapping.

GM built thousands of tuned port injection (TPI) and throttle body injection (TBI) fuel-injected small-block V-8 engines from 1985 through 1996. These 5.0L and 5.7L EFI engines are old now, but there are still some in wrecking yards and available for engine swaps. TPI engines are traditional Chevy small-block 305/350-cid V-8 long blocks with the addition of port-EFI or throttle body fuel-injection components. Factory-stock TPI engines delivered 200 to 245 horsepower. LTx engines are essentially TPI-type engines hot rodded with hotter cams, high-rpm intake runners, reverse-flow cooling, and optical ignition triggering to deliver between 260 and 330 horsepower. However, LT1/4 heads and manifolds are not strictly interchangeable with traditional small-block blocks (in part because of the reverse-flow cooling and all that it entails)—though LTx head conversions can be done by machinists who know what they're doing. As you'd expect, 5.7L Corvette engines are more expensive than 305 or 350 TPI Camaro/Firebird motors because they are the same size and weight but more powerful. The ultimate traditional Chevy small-block has to be the 1993–'95 5.7L 32-valve four-cam small-block that made 405 horsepower in the ZR-1 Corvette. The ZR-1's LT5 powerplant is a super-duty 5.7L short-block hand-assembled at Mercury Marine with special Lotus-designed four-valve twin-cam cylinder heads. They are rare and very expensive—if you can find one.

GM's Gen III LSx engine series arrived in 1997 in the form of the 345-horse LS1 Corvette, and the first Gen IV engines arrived in 2005. GM has delivered factory-stock supercharged

Corvette LSx engines with up to 638 horsepower! LSx engines installed in trucks are equipped with iron-block and aluminum heads, but all LSx engines installed in cars have lightweight aluminum blocks.

LSx engines are a completely different animal from earlier GM V-8s and are in no way interchangeable with L98 or LT1 engines. Iron-block truck 4.8L LS1s had at 270 horsepower, but all LS1 powerplants installed in cars had lightweight aluminum blocks and at least 305 horsepower, with high-output LS6 versions reaching 405 horsepower in 2004. Large-displacement LSx engines have produced over 500 naturally aspirated horsepower in the 427-cid LS7 Z06 Corvette, and 638 horsepower in the 376-cid LS9 ZR-1 Corvette with supercharging. All post-2007 LSx ECMs are designed to work on a GMLAN high-speed CAN bus, and some LSx engines going back to 2004 interact with other embedded controllers on the CAN (see the section of this chapter about hacking the CAN).

If you have a healthy traditional Chevy small-block V-8 that was previously carbureted, you may be considering swapping EFI components onto your engine. This can be done, but there are potential problems: swap-meet EFI components may be missing parts—and you may not know it—and buying additional parts can be expensive. TPI ducting for the MAF sensor and/or remote air cleaner may be incompatible with accessories and/or radiator and hoses on older engines. ECUs are calibrated for a specific engine configuration, and if your EFI-conversion Chevy Small-block engine is different in any respect, the EFI calibration may no longer be optimal. In addition, 1987 and newer TPI lower-intake manifolds have four bolts that are not compatible with older cylinder heads. The newer TPI EFI manifolds must be modified with welding and/or grinding to fit older engines.

The builders of this kit car had the following brainstorm: A Cobra (replica or not) with a huge iron-block 427 Ford V-8 or even a 302 Windsor small-block Ford is packing a lot of front-end weight, and if the goal is handling in a club-race environment, a hot rod Ford 2.3-liter turbo SVO Ford four-banger could make almost as much power and make up the difference through the turns due to better weight distribution and lighter overall weight. A stock 2.3 Turbo maxed out at 205 horsepower, but a chip change and enough fuel could make something like 355 horsepower on an overboosted 2.3. The Texas-based designers of this Cobra replica swapped in an iron-block, alloy-head SVO 2.3 turbo, added a Freon-cooled intercooler, and cranked the boost to 20 psi. As they say in Dallas, Yeeehaaaw!

In addition, the distributor drive gear metallurgy on newer EFI distributors will not be compatible with older cam drive gears, resulting in improper wear unless the gear is changed.

GM EFI engines have used speed-density MAP-based engine management, MAF-sensed engine management, and in newer powerplants, a combination of both. From the point of view of an engine swap, speed-density EFI is often preferable due to the simplified intake plumbing required in the absence of a MAF sensor, though MAF engines tend to be more forgiving of small performance increase. If you modify the airflow of a speed-density engine with MAP load sensing, the EMS will not work right unless you recalibrate the ECU. Surprisingly, MAF-sensed L98 and LT1 GM engines worked fairly well with the MAF removed entirely, due to excellent limp-home strategies that disregard suspect sensors and make do with historical data and data from other sensors (TPS in TPI engines, MAP sensor after 1993) to deduce engine airflow.

GM EFI engine swaps can deliver a powerful and economical street vehicle with the performance of a Corvette. You'll need the stock EFI engine and all accessories and wiring, and you will want to install the engine and components with an absolute minimum of modifications. If you are running off-road or using an older nonemissions-controlled engine, you can modify the EFI engine's airflow and fuel delivery with high-performance parts such as bigger TPI runners and fatter cams and other VE enhancements. You can also recalibrate the GM computer's fueling and spark timing for the new engine configuration with a new PROM chip or install a completely new aftermarket programmable computer to handle the job.

No EFI engine swap is a trivial task, even using the simpler vintage tuned port injection engines from the 1980s and early 1990s. A swap will probably cost more than you think and will require more than average ingenuity. But TPI and the traditional Chevy small-block represent straightforward, fully compatible fuel injection for all 50 million or so Chevy small-blocks and factory V-8-equipped vehicles built between the mid-1950s and 2003, when the last L98 powerplant rolled off the assembly line.

There is vastly more performance equipment available for GM small-block V-8s of all types than anything else around, and it's capable of achieving any level of performance anyone could possibly require from the small-block V-8. Swapping in a TPI engine is a great way to fuel inject your vehicle or improve the performance of your existing non-TPI EFI engine. Chevy small-block V-8s have been swapped into almost any vehicle you can name. If you take your time, start with a complete engine/transmission and do everything right, the task can be fun, and the result will be a rugged and reliable installation.

With an 8.6L stroker Cadillac V-8, twin turbos, and Haltech engine management, a classic GMC motorhome smokes the front tires. Actually, not as big a deal as it sounds; the GMC has six wheels, and Eldorado-type front wheel drive sans limited-slip differential. With what amounts to 1-wheel drive this thing could get stuck on wet pavement! Cadillac's 500 CID V-8 is the largest engine ever installed in a production car, and in 1975, it was also the first American engine to ship with optional electronic fuel injection. Jim Kanomata's GMC ran for a while with the big Caddy motor replacing the stock GM 400, but then Jim wanted more guts for climbing into the high Sierra near Lake Tahoe. The Cadillac EMS was a great jumping-off spot for a super-duty powerplant with programmable aftermarket engine management.

I built a bolt-down hat for the stock Cadillac throttlebody, removed the old fast-idle valve, and installed a Haltech fuel-only EMS. The GMC rig was too big to make it onto any dyno in a FWD direction, so we did a "tailgate party" calibration with a laptop, a Horiba UEGO meter, and a half-dozen friends and hangers-on—first in the parking lot, eventually on Interstate 280 near San Francisco.

For highway cruising and mountain climbing, we built a new Caddy V-8 with a stroker crank, then converted the stock exhaust manifolds to support twin Turbonetics H-trim turbos. For hill-climbing in a heavy vehicle, you've *got* to control thermal loading. I built and installed a turbo system with a giant air-air-intercooler with Spearco cores and put it in the front airstream just below the driver's feet. With the giant left front truck tire removed, the FWD motorhome lends a whole new meaning to easy access.

157

Lotus Europa: Longitudinal, mid-engine, fiberglass body, 1,320 pounds, tiny 1.6-liter wedge-head Renault engine with 82 horsepower. But that was BT (Before Turbocharging) the stock Renault.

With a few modifications (for the cam-driven alternator, for example), this hemi-head Renault Turbo Fuego EFI engine bolts right in a Europa to make 132 stock horsepower at 5,750 rpms at 9.5-psi boost from the intercooled Airesearch T3 turbocharger. T3 uses integral pneumatic wastegate potentially controllable with electronic boost controller to increase the boost pressure.

With more boost, free-flow intake plumbing, computer-controlled 40-horse port nitrous injection, and a DFI Gen 6 EMS, you've got a 200-horsepower engine hauling around 1,320 pounds of backbone frame and fiberglass and everything else. After removing the funky fiberglass luggage compartment from the rear of the engine compartment, the Fuego intercooler installs above the longitudinal transaxle. Note port nitrous lines and "dry" nitrous solenoid, set up for for an ECM capable of delivering nitrous fueling through the electronic injectors. Gen 6 DFI ECM had multi-stage nitrous management capabilities and the ability to calculate nitrous fueling as an offset to the base fuel calculation, a task made more complex by the fact the fuel is injected on a non-continuous per-revolution basis, but nitrous is injected continuously as a function of time (well, neglecting changes in nitrous delivery due to thermal contraction and pressure changes as the self-pressurizing nitrous tank cools during use).

EMS/EFI SWAPPING

158

Chapter 11
Roll-Your-Own EFI

This chapter examines the following options for fuel-injecting your performance engine.

CARBURETED ENGINES

1. **Swap in a complete fuel-injected engine** and supporting equipment such as the high-pressure fuel pump. Many transmissions currently mated to old carbureted engines will mate to a newer version of the engine that is virtually identical except for the addition of EFI/electronic engine management.

Examples of this include:
- Ford 5.0L and 5.8L port-EFI V-8s that Ford began installing after 1985 are modernized versions of the low-block 260-289-302 and raised-block 351W engines used in many '60s, '70s, and '80s Mustangs and other Ford-Lincoln-Mercury vehicles.
- Ford 8.0L port-EFI V-8s installed in Ford trucks after the mid-1980s are modernized versions of carbureted 429 and 460 V-8s used in '60s- and '70s-vintage muscle cars.

- Chevy/GM 5.0 and 5.7L tuned port injection V-8s fitted to GM cars of the 1980s and 1990s are modernized versions of 265-400 Chevy small-blocks installed in millions of GM vehicles since the mid-1950s.
- Chevy/GM 7.4-liter TBI or MPI big-block V-8s fitted to various GM trucks in years after 1986 (including the performance 454SS) are modernized versions of 396-402-427-454 Chevy Mark IV big-block V-8s installed in countless muscle cars, cars, and trucks since its initial appearance in the 1965 Corvette.
- Porsche flat-six 3.6 engines were equipped with electronic port fuel injection starting in the mid-1980s, though some continued with mechanical K-Jetronic injection for a number of years. Vintage Porsche carbureted engines from the 1960s and 1970s can be replaced with later Porsche powerplants and even turbocharged.
- Jaguar upgraded its 4.2-liter inline-six powerplant from multiple carbs to EFI in the mid-1970s, and the engine

Roll-your-own Carb-to-EFI Ford 460 powerplant designed for a 1985 Bronco, originally equipped with a 5.0L Ford V-8 with speed-density EFI. Note the 90-degree adaptor designed to mount a horizontal port-injection throttlebody on a 4-barrel manifold milled to accept port-injectors on D-section fuel rail, and an Accel throttlebody. Engine used Haltech EFI.

Bell Engineering had in mind the best Cobra in the world, and they built the CB1 Cobra replica car from the ground up with many advanced features that Carroll Shelby never dreamed of in the 1960s. The CB1 was a built twin-turbo 351 Ford with custom intake and turbo system and an Electromotive TEC3 EMS.

continued in production until 1992. The engine is a modernized version of carbureted 3.4L-3.8L-4.2L powerplants installed in various Jaguar cars from the late 1940s to the 1980s.

- Many Ford and GM EFI V-8s will mate to older transmissions as far back as the 1950s, in the case of GM, or 1960s, in the case of Ford. Ford's original thin-wall Windsor V-8 arrived in 1962 displacing 221 cubic inches. GM's 265 small-block V-8 came out in the mid-1950s. These blocks are similar or identical externally to the EFI V-8s of the same family manufactured until 2003. You may be able to find a junkyard EFI small-block GM V-8 in good shape for a few hundred dollars.

The job then will be to adapt the EFI engine to your car. A number of aftermarket suppliers sell simplified wiring harnesses designed for engine/injection swapping. It is legal to swap in a later model engine (complete with all emissions-control devices) into an earlier vehicle, though you will have to have the vehicle and engine inspected at a referee station if you live in California. It is typically not legal to install an older engine and engine management system in a newer vehicle, given that piston crown geometry, compression ratio, displacement changes, and other factors could impact exhaust emissions.

Typically, late-model EFI engines are available from commercial wrecking yards for $1,500 to $1,750 or less, with older EFI engines in running condition less. Obviously, engines can be obtained from private parties on the Internet for substantially less, though caveat emptor is the rule. Make sure you get all required parts, including wiring and ECU, which may or may not be included in the asking price. It will be much more expensive to buy additional EFI parts one by one after.

2. **Adapt port-EFI equipment** (manifolds, fuel rails, throttle bodies, and even ECU and wiring) from an equivalent EFI engine to an existing previously carbureted engine using the principles discussed above. Swapping the ECU as well will work if your existing engine is in strong condition, yet very similar in cam specs, cylinder head CFM, and displacement to the donor factory EFI engine.

The danger is that engine variations that affect volumetric efficiency—particularly cam specs—would prevent OEM EFI engine management from providing correct air/fuel ratios or spark advance on your engine. Swapping EFI components onto a carbureted engine could still be a good choice, even with a heavily modified engine, as long as you recalibrate or otherwise modify operation of the factory engine management system to provide correct air/fuel ratios and timing. PROM changes, fuel pressure changes, add-on black boxes and interceptors that change injector pulse width, larger injectors, extra injectors, and other hot rodding techniques are available to rework the stock engine management parameters. In the case of a common engine with common modifications, there may well be plug-and-play options, though none of this comes for free.

Older OEM EFI parts may still available dirt-cheap in a salvage yard, though increasing numbers of older EFI vehicles have been crushed, which will eventually drive up the price again. Intake manifolds and parts can be polished for an excellent look on a custom car. This book illustrates swapping Jaguar XJ-6 Bosch L-Jetronic EFI system onto a 1969 Jaguar XKE 4.2 engine in a later chapter and explains what's involved in swapping GM TPI EFI components onto a carbureted Chevy small-block V-8.

There's almost nothing you can't find out there to convert nearly anything to EFI and electronic engine management. Hilborn developed this EFI conversion for 426 Hemi engines, and although it's computer-controlled, the look is definitely radically stacked mechanical fuel injection.

FIS supercharged big block. Roll-your-own EMS includes giant tunnel-ram intake with port fuel injectors and Vortech supercharger.

Look Ma, no carb! Here's the classic "old school" supercharger, based on the Roots blower architecture originally used to "blow" air at near-atmospheric pressure into a 2-stroke Detroit Diesel truck/bus engine. These superchargers originally had 2-lobe rotors with extremely poor thermal efficiency, and many still require "wet" mixture in which fuel introduced upstream by carburetion or fuel injection cools the rotors enough to maintain safe internal rotor clearances. Note that although you can see an auxiliary injector at the rear of the blower hat that provides fuel cooling for the rotor assembly, what you can't see is the custom Norwood Autocraft port fuel injection system located *inside the intake manifold below the supercharger.*

3. **Bolt on an aftermarket throttle body injection system**. These two- or four-butterfly throttle body injection systems are relatively inexpensive, easy to install (since the throttle body with integral injectors and fuel pressure regulator bolts onto a four-barrel manifold exactly like a carb) and are true electronic fuel-injection systems with many of EFI's advantages—but not all! These are single-point injection systems in which all fuel is injected near the throttle plate. So, like a carbureted engine, the intake manifold must handle a wet mixture, which imposes constraints that do not exist on a dry port-EFI manifold.

Older TBI conversions systems such as the analog Pro-Jection were tuned with pots on the ECU, but newer carb-to-EFI systems use a modern digital control unit, which may or may not require a laptop for calibration. You'll probably need to install some additional relatively inexpensive parts not supplied with the kit, such as materials to construct a second fuel line to return unused fuel from the throttle body back to the tank. The

The author's three-turbo Jaguar 4.2L I6 arranged here for light run-in of a newly rebuilt version of the engine prior to dyno-testing. The engine was an upgraded Jaguar 4.2L XKE powerplant originally converted to EFI using a Bosch L-Jetronic system from a '79 XJ-6, and later with this TWM manifold designed to put triple Weber DCOE carbs on a 4.2. This is the twin-injector per bore version, which allowed construction of a 12-injector staged system with triple turbos.

Dodge Challenger project in this book shows how to roll your own TBI.

4. Install an aftermarket programmable ECU and OEM EFI components (or a complete engine). That is, use factory air-supply equipment (EFI manifold, throttle body, and so on), factory fuel-metering equipment (injectors, fuel rail, and so on), with an aftermarket computer, wiring, and (perhaps) engine sensors.

This book covers the installation of aftermarket EFI controls onto a V-6 Gen II MR2, Honda CRX, and big-block 1970 Challenger.

5. Bolt on a plug-and-play multi-port EFI conversion package, that has virtually everything you'll need to convert the engine to fuel injection. Some may even have a legal emissions exemption order, making the kit legal on certain emissions-controller vehicles of certain years, with the rest legal for off-highway usage

or on older vehicles that are not emissions-controlled. There are several such packages for small-block Chevy V-8s, small-block Fords, and Chrysler A- and B-block V-8s. We installed an AEM plug-and-play system on the del Sol project.

6. Fabricate a complete roll-your-own add-on fuel-injection system, in which you:

- Modify a carburetor intake manifold to install port injector bosses (or buy an aftermarket EFI manifold).
- Construct a fuel rail and mountings to supply port fuel injectors.
- Select and install a fuel pressure regulator, filter, supply and return lines, and injectors.
- Build (if you're a machinist) or acquire a throttle body with correct CFM capacity and adapt the throttle cable.
- Purchase an aftermarket electronic control unit, engine sensors, and wiring loom as in 5 above.

Just a red '56 Chevy "Shoebox," still popular among older hot rodders, equipped with the original small block Chevy V-8, of which the General would eventually manufacture and install about 60 million in trucks and cars into the 21st century with power ratings from about 100 SAE horsepower to 405 in the high-water' mark early-'90s ZR1 'Vette. Its age made this car perfect, street-legal hot rodding material that would forever be exempt from modern emissions requirements—and yet cleaner than it had ever run when carbureted.

The "Last, Best Speed Secret"—high compression V-8 power, programmable EFI, and turbocharging—turned this old dog into a raging power freak that could idle smoothly.

Left: A 5.7L custom cross-ram EFI system with programmable aftermarket injection and twin turbos seemed like a much better idea than the stock V-8.

Bob Norwood made a pretty good living building hot rod beasts like this modified Ferrari 308 with 16 giant fuel injectors pissing 1,800-horses worth of gasoline into the motor. Using Motec engine management, the bow-tie big-block GM powerplant managed to push the 288-GTO-paneled 308 to a one-way record of 267 miles per hour at Bonneville.

Hot rod twin-turbo Norwood big-block powerplant uses turbochargers the size of a spare tire to achieve the prodigious levels of power required to approach 300 miles per hour in the thin, 6,300-foot elevation of the Bonneville Salt Flats. The Motec engine management system's altitude compensation greatly reduces the tuning effort required when carbureted or mechanical-injection vehicles arrive at the high desert dry lake in the summer.

Dee Howard's '32 Pierce Arrow land-speed-record car ran a heavily modified P-A flathead V-12 with twin turbos and methanol fuel. The original fuel system was constant mechanical injection. For improved performance at the Bonneville Salt Flats, Bob Norwood converted the car to Motec electronic control and port EFI.

Speed-record '32 Pierce-Arrow V-12 is equipped with a custom plenum and twin throttlebodies. Gigantic 1,600-cc/min electronic injectors spray methanol into the modernized V-12 powerplant at a stoichiometric air/fuel ratio of 6.5:1, roughly twice that of gasoline. Methanol makes about 10 percent more specific power per air mass than gasoline, mainly due to the significant cooling effect of vaporizing alcohol, which greatly increases air density and can negate the need for an intercooler on efficient turbo systems running modest boost pressure. Gasoline-type injectors will work with methanol, but must be large to handle the volume. *Bosch*

Such a system will typically include a speed-density ECU and sensors, fuel pump, fuel injectors, fuel-pressure regulator, single-plane manifold plus modifications, and throttle body.

This option is explored in this book in a nitrous-injected, triple turbo Jag XKE, a Chevy 350 twin turbo, and a big-block Mopar 383.

FUEL-INJECTED ENGINES

TBI-to-MPI conversions. In case your engine is already equipped with throttle body injection (for example, certain 1987–95 GM trucks and cars), you can buy or fabricate a kit of parts to convert to the improved fuel distribution of port fuel injection. Edelbrock's kit provides replacement port-EFI intake manifold with injectors and fuel rail, upgraded fuel pump, injector harness, and other conversion parts, retaining the stock computer, throttle body, and much of the stock engine wiring harness.

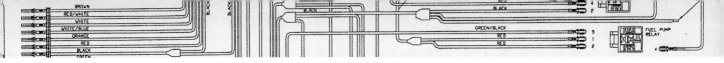

Chapter 12
Installation and Start-up Issues

For a successful, trouble-free EMS installation, you'll need to deal with some or all of the following issues: electrical and wiring; power draw; electrical interference; mounting and connecting the ECU; ignition system compatibility, installing sensors, vacuum/boost source; laptop computer interface; installing fuel maps; and fuel injectors.

ELECTRICAL WIRING INSTALLATION

Engine management system problems are almost always caused by wiring or problems with sensors or actuators, but virtually never by the ECU itself. I have seen experienced professional EMS experts make false assumptions about wiring integrity that wasted countless hours of troubleshooting time.

Good electrical wiring is essential to reliable engine management, and you'll need the right tools to do custom wiring. The nightmarish EMS wiring that regularly arrives on customer vehicles entering a performance shop for troubleshooting—wires twisted together to make connections and sloppily wrapped in electrical tape, poor-quality plastic-shrouded crimp-type connectors "crimped" with a hammer or some other inappropriate tool, multi-wire OEM connectors that have been separated by force rather than the correct special tool and held together with cable ties, and so forth.

It is always false economy to settle for substandard wiring. Poor wiring always fails in the end, usually when it is most inconvenient. And if your luck runs out, bad wiring will fry something expensive in the process.

You'll definitely want to have a schematic and a pin-out diagram of the EFI electrical system, which is usually obtainable from the ECU manufacturer. This will be extremely useful when things don't immediately work right on initial startup and you're not sure what's wrong. A schematic and a continuity tester are a godsend when this happens.

When routing the EFI harness, be sensible about running it away from noisy electrical sources—as well as heat or sharp or abrasive components like braided steel hoses that can, over time, damage wiring by rubbing against it.

Engine sensors that report such things as throttle position, intake air temperature, coolant temperature, velocity airflow, and other engine conditions work by changing resistance based on some physical condition of the engine. Beware of modifying an EFI wiring harness in any manner that would change the resistance of a sensor by adding additional resistance on the way to the ECU. For example, suppose you bought a standard wiring harness that cannot reach a coolant temperature sensor without extension. Use the proper gauge wire if you must extend it, and use a resistance meter to verify that the wiring modifications have not changed the signal as seen at the ECU. In the case of some aftermarket engine electronics, you may discover that any wiring changes void the warranty. However, in most cases, if you

Wiring is one of the most critical areas of any EMS installation, and poor wiring will eat your lunch in troubles immediately or down the line. You need the right tools and the right tricks, but there are entire books about wiring. Norwood Autocraft built a custom wiring harness for this four-cam stroker big-block Chevy with Motec EMS. Note the monster custom throttle bodies and intake plumbing under construction. Basically your typical aluminum Chevy big-block with Batten B-4 DOHC cylinder heads. Definitely a roll-your-own situation. Norwood Autocraft built a system from the ground up using Motec engine management.

plan ahead it may be possible to have the manufacturer build a special wiring harness to your specification, which can actually save you money in the long run.

A really good crimping tool can crimp a connector to a wire so securely that the wire will tear before the connector releases the wire. But you must have the right crimping tool for a connector and the right connector for a given wire size, and I am talking about a heavy-duty ratchet-type crimping tool. I find that having the right tools can actually make good wiring fun, whereas the wrong tools can make it hell.

Most professional EMS installers never solder anything because if a wire works or moves in the vicinity of a solder-on connector, the strands that make up the wire can gradually break—one by one—where the wire was heated and where it entered the solder, and the connection can eventually fail. My view is that soldering is definitely preferable to poor-quality plastic-shrouded consumer-grade crimp-on connectors of the type you find at the corner auto parts store. Such things may work OK for a trailer hitch (at least for a while), but not for a computer EMS wiring harness. The problem is, it is hard to have the right wiring tool for every situation if you are not an EMS pro because pro ratchet crimpers can easily cost over $100. You will not want to be running out to buy obscure crimping tools on a case-by-case basis in the middle of wiring something, and the right tool can be expensive or difficult or impossible to find

Honda del Sol project turbo conversion under construction. What do you do when Hondata's programmability conversion for the Honda computer is missing a calibration and the car needs to drive 300 miles to Dallas? You cut jumpers on the ECM to activate the stock calibration and drive very carefully. The moral of the story is: Plan ahead.

Fuel Line Size Chart

Horsepower	Rigid Line Size	-AN Hose Size	Pump GPH at System Pressure	Pump GPH Free Flowing
200	5/16"	-04	17	46
350	3/8"	-06	29	81
550	1/2"	-08	46	127
800	5/8"	-10	67	184
1200	3/4"	-12	100	276

at the last minute. If you are doing an ambitious EMS wiring job, buy the right tools in advance and pay what it costs to get good quality tools. In an emergency, unless you have access to the right high-quality ratchet-type crimp-on connectors and the right crimping tool(s), soldering could be a better choice.

Give some thought to layout of the system wiring harness before installing ECU or sensors. Connect the sensors and ECU to the harness and drape the wiring in place and spend the time to get a feel for what will work the best.

POWER DRAW

All ECUs have the ability to correct injection pulse width for the state of charge of a battery, which affects how long it takes the injectors to open. However, most ECUs have a threshold below which they will not start the engine. This is usually around 8 volts. Fuel pump maximum pumping volume declines with voltage (just as it increases with voltage when aftermarket Boost-a-Pump devices jack up the voltage to super-normal levels to run the pump faster and harder when required during boosted engine conditions).

An engine management system will consume a certain amount of power that would not be required on a carbureted engine, depending on engine speed and injector resistance. Electronic ignition systems require power as well, as do electric fuel pumps—all of which is in addition to the power requirements of accessories such as air conditioning, headlights, wipers, and so on. Add up all the electrical requirements of the vehicle under worst conditions and compare them to the output of the vehicle's charging system, and to verify the current capacity and resistance of critical wires delivering electrical power to high-draw appliances. With everything on, your battery may be slowly draining. Eventually, the engine will stop. In some cases you may have to install a larger alternator as part of an EFI conversion or engine swap.

You can probably increase the capacity of a performance fuel pump by running a heavy-gauge wire directly to the battery and using the ECU's pump output to trigger a heavy-duty relay in the wire. Do not depend on the ECU to directly energize a fuel pump—use it to trigger a relay.

If you don't know the pumping capacity of your fuel pump, use a pressure source to pump up the reference port on the fuel pressure regulator to maximum manifold pressure (at maximum boost, if applicable) and test the fuel pump by diverting the fuel return line into a closed container of known size, activate the fuel pump by jumpering it to a +12V source (without creating sparks near gasoline fumes), and measure how long it takes to fill the container. Using the formulas described in the section of this book on actuators (of which the fuel pump is one) you can determine the fuel pump capacity at rail pressure. Keep in mind that the fuel pump will have a lower capacity at 12 volts than it would at 13.9 volts (with the engine running). Make sure fuel pump capacity is higher than what's required for the most optimistic horsepower case at the most pessimistic brake-specific fuel consumption for the engine (explained elsewhere in this book). If applicable, factor in the fuel required during nitrous boost.

ELECTRICAL INTERFERENCE

High-output ignition systems with extremely high voltages (particularly with wire-core plug wires) produce electromagnetic radiation (radio waves) that can interfere with the proper operation of an engine management system. Most engine control modules should be used exclusively with resistor-core (rather than wire-core) plug wires and the ECM mounted inside the vehicle or in the trunk, away from the heat, moisture, and electrical interference of the engine compartment. Even if an ECM is approved for installation in the harsh environment of the engine compartment, it is *better* to mount it inside the vehicle if at all possible. Electronic components do not like heat, and heat can diminish life expectancy, even if it does not kill components.

ENGINE CONTROL MODULE

It is essential to provide high-quality constant and switched power to the ECM, and best to route constant power directly from the battery. Switched power must be connected to a source that is not turned off during cranking (or drained to less than 8 or 9 volts). Some ECMs provide cranking enrichment based on a reference wire to the starter circuit; if this is the case, make sure it is triggered by a power source that is only active during cranking, or the system will run rich.

When mounting the ECM, be aware that the case often functions as a heat sink. Mount the ECU in a cool place away from the exhaust system and heater where dry cool air will help to cool it, and where heat can transfer directly from the case into the bulkhead to which it is bolted. Never mount the ECU on the floor of the vehicle, which could become flooded and permanently ruin the electronics. Finally, make sure the user-interface port will be accessible once the is in place for connecting the communications cable to configure and calibrate the system.

Like everything electrical, GM Weatherpak connectors require the right tools to assemble. You slide on the rubber sleeve, strip the wire, crimp on the metal connector, crimp the connector around the rubber sleeve, and insert the prong into the main plastic connector until you feel it click. Removal requires a special tang to release the connector, though there are circular tools with many tangs for various types of connectors. If you don't have the right tools, you'll be tearing out your hair before the connector comes apart.

The weld-in or epoxy-in injector boss can be critical for building a custom port-EFI engine management system, for example, if you need to convert a wet intake manifold to port injection or if you're adding additional injectors somewhere in the intake system. *MSD Fuel*

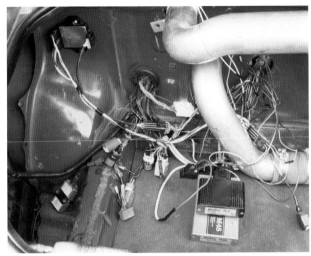

The greatest challenge will not be to build from-scratch wiring, but partially disassembling stock wiring and combining it with new wiring for aftermarket electronics. This in-progress wiring from the MR6 project in this book involved several varieties of Toyota MR6 wiring connectors, Motec connectors, GM Weatherpak connectors, Bosch connectors, and more. You NEED the right tools (especially to disassemble factory connectors without destroying them) and patience.

IGNITION SYSTEM COMPATIBILITY

ECMs require an electrical signal to determine how fast the engine is turning and—for sequential injection or spark control—to determine crankshaft position. Many fuel-only or batch injection systems with distributor or wasted-spark ignition can utilize a low-voltage signal from the negative side of the coil as a trigger to determine engine speed. ECMs delivering sequential injection or coil-on-plug ignition require a crank ref trigger and cam sync trigger—or a cam position sensor.

If you are using a multi-spark capacitive-discharge module on a distributor-ignition, most aftermarket ECMs require that the CDI provide a special tach output signal to the ECM, since the multiple-spark capability of a capacitive system can damage the ECM. Most aftermarket ECMs will work with OEM ignitions found on common performance vehicles, common aftermarket ignitions, standard points ignitions, and a variety of special ignitions. In some cases, an ECM may require dip-switch settings or factory hard-wiring to properly determine trigger threshold, but trigger threshold is software-configurable to most modern aftermarket engine management systems. Check with the manufacturers of the EMS and the ignition for compatibility. The Motec M48 EMS used on one of the projects in the book allowed you to configure the ignition as one of: rise trigger; fall trigger; Mazda three-rotor; Mazda Series 5 or Series 4; Ford SAW 4, 6, or, 8 cylinder; Ford SAW 10 cylinder; and Ford SAW special.

You'll also have to configure the EMS for the precise triggering system used to fire ignition and injectors and so on, meaning you'll need to know the number of reference teeth or flying magnets on crank angle and cam angle sensors and the number of missing or additional teeth used to sync top dead center on the trigger wheel.

Bear in mind that the purpose of programmable ignition is a good hot spark at the plug electrode. Make sure to select plugs that are the correct heat range for your application. If the application involves a turbo conversion or a lot of overboost,

you almost definitely need colder plugs than stock and should probably set the gap smaller than stock, even with a high-powered ignition. Check with the coil/coil-driver vendor, but many pros assume the gap on a hot rod turbo application should be no larger than 0.029.

Whatever you do for ignition, you're going to need a way to drive a tachometer. If you are using the stock ignition module or coil-driver, there is probably a tach driver signal you can continue to use. If not (say, if the stock ECM provided a conditioned tach signal but you've changed to aftermarket), the aftermarket ECM probably has a tach signal that will work, or one that can be inverted with a little wiring and a resistor. If you're swapping in a powerplant with a different number of cylinders than stock (see the MR6 project in this book), you may find your ECU can provide a pulse width modulated signal of programmable duration and frequency that will work with the stock tachometer.

INSTALLING SENSORS

You will almost definitely need an air temperature sensor, coolant temperature sensor, a throttle-position sensor (TPS), a MAP sensor, one or more oxygen or wideband air/fuel ratio sensors, and probably crank and cam sensors.

Heat soak from surrounding metal can be a problem with some air-temperature sensors. Try to locate the sensor in such a way that engine heat does not soak the body of the sensor, giving a falsely high reading (which may lean out the mixture or richen it, depending on circumstances). Make sure the air temperature sensor is fast enough to react to the rapid changes in temperature that occur with turbo-supercharged and intercooled induction systems so that the air temperature sensor can be installed downstream of an intercooler where it belongs to react intelligently to temperature changes.

Oxygen sensors do not work well until they heat up to about 600 degrees Fahrenheit, so it's important to locate a standard O_2 sensor as close as possible to the exhaust ports, subject to measuring exhaust from all available cylinders. Oxygen sensors with onboard heating circuits can be located farther from the exhaust ports, for example in a header collector or downstream of a cat or turbine housing. A heated O_2 sensor has the advantage that it will become effective sooner after startup and stay warm enough to work properly during prolonged idling.

If you are building a custom or heavily modified exhaust, it is likely you'll need one of these weld-in O_2 sensor bosses. *Painless Performance*

If the EMS does not support multiple O_2 sensors, you might still want to install two oxygen sensors on a V-configuration engine, with an A-B toggle switch regulating which sensor gets used in order to reduce the chance that variations in exhaust gas oxygen content from bank to bank would impact engine management. Keep in mind that if an engine develops degraded fuel distribution due to dirty injectors or begins to misfire due to poor spark-plug condition, one or two cylinders emitting way too much or too little oxygen into the exhaust can result in air/fuel ratio readings that are wrong for all cylinders.

Throttle position sensors come in many varieties. Even though most modern aftermarket engine management systems are capable of learning TPS electrical characteristics at idle and wide-open throttle and interpolating throttle position in between, be careful if you're using an existing original equipment TPS with an aftermarket ECM, as not all variable resistors have the same increase in rate of gain. Fortunately, most programmable ECMs have the ability to display the percentage of throttle opening they think the sensor is reporting. Check the TPS at closed and open throttle to make sure it's working properly as seen at the ECU, and make sure physical throttle positions in between translate into plausible readings on the EMS virtual-dash engine data page.

Many ECMs do not pay much attention to the TPS voltage as such, but are rather more concerned with the rate of change in voltage on speed-density systems that indicate transitions from one engine speed to another that demand transition enrichment or enleanment. However, *absolute* throttle position is a factor that ECMs will use to trigger closed-loop fuel trim and idle speed stabilization logic. But even if the ECM is not programmable for absolute throttle position, do not automatically assume there is a problem if the sensor's full range is not available to the EMS.

Make sure the TPS turns in the same direction as the throttle shaft, and never use the TPS as a throttle stop. If the ECM can program itself for TPS voltage or frequency, make sure that the throttle stop is backed off all the way when you install and clock the TPS so the TPS can never prevent the throttle from closing all the way. Once the TPS is clocked, adjust up the throttle stop to the proper position, probably opening the throttle a tiny bit, and then go through the EMS-TPS learning procedure. If the ECM requires a specified voltage for idle, with the engine off and the key on and the throttle stop adjusted where the throttle will be when it is considered closed, with the EMS virtual dash displaying throttle position, clock the TPS until it the virtual dash shows a throttle opening of 0.

EMSs that provide spark control require engine position data from a sensor. Syncing engine position relative to the power stroke for a particular cylinder can only be provided by the camshaft, since a crank sensor has no way of knowing whether a given position represents compression or exhaust stroke on a four-cycle engine. Cam-speed devices reveal the exact position

in the engine cycle, and it may be tempting to derive engine position from the distributor or camshaft, but if you are using a flying-magnet-type system with only one or two position events per cylinder (versus, say, a 36- or 60-tooth gear read optically or magnetically at crank speed), the ECU cannot react as quickly to micro-changes in engine speed. And cam-based position information could be affected by slop in the cam belt. Most ECUs that need to know engine position get it from a crank sensor, with the cam/distributor sensor used purely to sync the crank position to compression on the number one cylinder.

VACUUM/BOOST SOURCE

Speed-density engine management systems require accurate manifold pressure to provide proper fueling. This is particularly critical at idle. Some wild-cammed engines are not suitable for speed-density EFI because the manifold pressure at idle is unstable. Engines like this should use throttle-angle (Alpha-N) load sensing, or a derive engine loading from a *blend* of MAP and TPS where the EMS switches over to TPS load-sensing or a combination of TPS and manifold absolute pressure (MAP) sensor data at idle to prevent a wandering MAP signal from causing the engine to hunt.

A problem can occur if you're running multiple throttle bodies, since the manifold pressure reference signal from a single port only indicates the vacuum of this one port and might fluctuate rapidly at idle, confusing the EMS. In this case, it is essential to construct a vacuum accumulator of 2-cid volume with vacuum lines as short as possible running to reference ports on all intake runners, and reference the MAP sensor to the accumulator. This type of accumulator will dampen fluctuations yet is small enough in volume to react quickly to changes in manifold pressure.

You should always endeavor to have the shortest possible manifold pressure reference line to a MAP sensor, or even mount it directly on the manifold with an O-ring as is the case in some OEM applications. The larger the volume of the reference line, the lazier the MAP sensor data will be in relation to actual manifold pressure, which could cause problems with acceleration and deceleration enrichment. Metal or hard plastic reference lines can help because they will come up to full pressure slightly faster than softer rubber vacuum hoses that will expand a little before they reach full pressure—a bit like a balloon.

BOOSTED APPLICATIONS

Some aftermarket engine management systems are not suitable for turbos or superchargers, a good example being an EMS that only uses throttle position to estimate engine loading (since the same throttle position can yield vastly different engine VE, depending on turbo compressor speed). Speed-density engine management systems designed for nonboosted engines are not suitable for forced induction without installing a multi-bar MAP sensor and recalibrating the ECM. The point this raises is that it helps to know where you are ultimately going with a project before you decide what your EMS strategy will be.

Some engine management systems are not suited for managing integrated nitrous oxide injection, while others have highly sophisticated nitrous capabilities. If you are planning to boost the engine with nitrous (some day?), acquire an EMS with nitrous capabilities that provide fuel enrichment using the electronic injectors, and plumb the intake manifold with port nitrous jets. The closer to the intake valves that you inject fuel and nitrous, the smaller the likelihood of distribution problems,

Injector Static Flow Rate, In C.C. of Fuel/Minute, Toyota 3S-GTE, MR2 Turbo

1	723.0
2	718.3
3	720.4
4	721.0
AVG:	720.7

TOTAL SYS. LBS./HR.-STATIC:	274.54
CC FUEL/MIN/H.P.-STATIC:	6.78
B.S.F.C./@ 80%/@ EST. H.P.:	0.52
DUTY CYCLE AT EST. B.H.P.:	0.85

Horsepower At 80% Duty Cycle at listed Brake Specific
Fuel Consumption
@ .65: 337.9
@ .55: 399.3
@ .50: 439.3

COMMENTS: SYSTEM BALANCE IS AT 0.7%

If what you have is used fuel injectors, avoid troubles during start up and tuning by having the injectors cleaned and flow-tested. RC Engineering did the job on these. An engine with funky injectors will never run really right.

and the less chance of turning the intake plenum into a pipe bomb in case of a backfire. You should *never* inject fuel upstream of an intercooler for the same reason.

Do not make the mistake of trying to inject nitrous oxide and fuel (a fogger nozzle, for example) at a single point unless there is no other way to do it. Port EFI manifolds are not designed to handle wet mixtures, and you could burn down the engine if there are distribution problems (see the Honda CRX project in this book). It may also be tempting to inject nitrous at one place near the throttle body, but resist the temptation: You could have uneven nitrous distributions depending on exactly where you inject the nitrous upstream of the throttle body, and if too much nitrous goes to one or two cylinders, you could still have a lean burn-down situation even if the nitrous enrichment fuel is perfectly distributed through the port electronic injectors.

PERSONAL COMPUTERS/INTERFACE

The vast majority of programmable engine management systems are designed to use a personal computer as a user interface for tuning and monitoring the EFI system. You will need to have a rudimentary knowledge of the Windows operating system, although most EMS user interfaces provide a fairly complete set of self-contained commands that will do the job to create and modify fuel maps, and to manage them on CD or hard disk.

It is important to have a laptop computer so you can calibrate or troubleshoot the vehicle while it's operating, but never attempt to tune and drive at the same time; get a friend to drive the vehicle while you tune. Many expert tuners claim that some road tuning is required even if the raw fuel map was created on a dyno with an air/fuel-ratio meter or gas analyzer. It is definitely not safe to drive and tune at the same time, so either drive the car while logging data and use the datalogs to tune while the car is stopped, or be smart and get someone else to drive while you tune.

Edelbrock Pro-Flow systems, SDS's EMS, FAST EZ-EFI, MSDAtomic and certain interceptor/piggyback systems that modify the actions of the factory computer are available with

their own user interface—usually with a keypad and an LCD display—which means you do not need a PC (though some of these can use a laptop if you have one or don't want to buy the proprietary interface device). However, given the nontrivial cost of a programmable engine management system, the superior friendliness and usability of a big-screen laptop user interface, and the ease of borrowing or renting a laptop, laptop concerns should not be an issue to most people.

Most programmable EFI systems support an optional mixture-timing-boost trim module or software equivalent that enables a tuner to vary the air/fuel mixture by an adjustable percentage rich or lean by turning a knob on the interface. This allows you to easily change the mixture and instantly "feel" or analyze the effects. Some provide an across-the-board trim that simply modifies the "final" injection pulse width, timing, or maximum boost calculation by the selected percentage. Others have provided a separate adjustment for, say, idle versus wide-open-throttle. Once you know what percentage change is required at a certain speed and loading to improve the calibration, you can program the change permanently into the EMS. Unless you are quite experienced, you may find this method more reliable and easier than immediately altering the raw fuel map—even with the help of a wideband air/fuel-ratio meter!

If you have a good wideband air/fuel ratio meter, it's a simple matter to set the engine speed and loading at a particular breakpoint and trim the module until the air/fuel ratio is where you want it (or where torque is optimized on a dyno). You can then stop, look at the percentage trim it took to optimize the mixture (or timing, or maximum boost), then modify the injection pulse width or VE-fueling at the speed-loading point (and smooth the points surrounding the chosen test breakpoint, since virtually all engine management systems average pulse width or timing with surrounding data to arrive at the final fuel or timing calculation unless the engine is at the precise rpm and airflow of the breakpoint). Many EMSs now automate this kind of air/fuel ratio-based update.

To repeat, if you do not smooth the data in surrounding speed-density cells, you will not get the pulse width or timing you expected due to averaging. Most engine management systems will display the speed-density cell from which an engine is being managed as well as the current injection pulse width. If the value in the current cell is not the same as the actual injection pulse width, there is either averaging going on with other cells, or some kind of warm-up enrichment or closed-loop O_2-based trim going on.

Practice navigating through the menus (screens) of the laptop EMS user interface before attempting to tune the car, and read the software manual several times, memorizing the features and commands. Things can happen very fast while tuning, and some can damage an engine. You do not want to be fumbling around reading the manual while you tune. Tuning a high-performance vehicle involves a certain amount of risk. Lean mixture or detonation under high power can damage your engine.

Always save all your fuel maps so you can recover to an earlier fuel curve if you reach a point where things are not working well on the current map, or if you accidentally erase something (force yourself to do this).

Keep a *detailed* log of everything you did and change only one thing at a time. One good way to do this might be with a hand-held recorder, as long as background noise is not unacceptably loud.

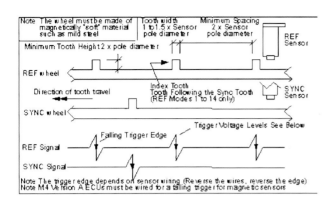

Many aftermarket EMSs are configurable regarding how the system reads engine position sensors. Setting Rising versus Falling edge can make a significant difference in the timing, and the engine may not start or stay running if the EMS is listening for the wrong type of signal. VR sensors *must* be installed with correct polarity.

FUEL AND TIMING MAPS

When installing an EMS you will need a map close enough to optimal to start the engine. Professional engine builders and tuners have collectively spent a huge amount of time building precise fuel (and spark) maps for various engines. It is always a complex and painstaking process to build a map from scratch, and it's impossible to optimize maximum power and efficiency if you don't have access to an exhaust-gas analyzer, exhaust-gas-temperature sensors, and a chassis or engine dyno.

The good news is that many fuel maps already exist for common engines and modifications, not to mention plenty of uncommon engines with uncommon modifications. Keep in mind, any changes from the original engine configuration or even the vehicle configuration could potentially cause a prebuilt map to be less than optimal on your vehicle. What's more, an otherwise identical vehicle and engine configuration will require some rescaling of the prebuilt map if the injectors or fuel pressure are different from the engine on which the calibration was built. But it is always better to start with an optimized, preprogrammed map from a similar or identical engine if you can find one.

If this is not possible, many engine management systems have software that will automatically build a startup calibration based on a set of parameters you enter about your engine, vehicle, fuel, and ignition systems.

As a last resort, use the from-scratch method in the tuning chapter of this book, or use the closest map you can find and then rework it for your engine. Even if the calibration is not that close, if it was a good calibration for a real engine, it will be better than nothing.

FUEL INJECTORS

Fuel injectors are usually not included in a standard aftermarket EMS kit because they are not cheap and because they must match the horsepower and dynamic range of a particular engine

application. As discussed in detail in the chapter on actuators, it is essential to select and install injectors that provide a small enough amount of fuel to idle properly without pulse width much below 1.5 to 2.0 milliseconds (below which the injection events may not be precisely repeatable) and still provide adequate high-end fueling without going static.

Injectors are rated in terms of resistance to current flow. Low-resistance coils in high-flow injectors draw more power and require heavier-duty drivers. Such injectors are usually a peak-and-hold design. Make sure your ECU has the capability to reliably power the injectors you plan to use.

Many ECUs have the ability to fire multiple injectors per injector driver without overloading the circuitry (it all depends on the resistance of the injectors, the current draw, and the capacity of the drivers). This means that you can potentially use two or more injectors per cylinder. It also means you might be able to add more injectors to handle more cylinders than the system was originally designed to handle if you're using batch-fire injection—just by wiring in more injectors to existing drivers. Some ECUs have the ability to stage injectors, providing idle and low-end fueling by pulsing one primary injector per cylinder, while providing wide-open-throttle fueling by pulsing one or more secondary injectors per cylinder once fuel requirements reach a certain threshold.

There are a number of aftermarket devices that provide fuel enrichment for factory EFI systems by staging one or more additional injectors (sometimes as many as four, six, or eight), typically located usually at a single point upstream of the throttle body. This solution can work reasonably well if executed carefully on the right engine with the right intake manifold. But theoretical problems are several: You may be forcing a dry manifold to handle a wet mixture, which can cause distribution problems. And since you are probably providing enrichment for a power-adder conversion, lean cylinders can quickly lead to disaster. The extra injector(s) must pulse at a rate that provides correct fueling and at the same time provides consistent enrichment to all cylinders.

Some tuners have installed a standalone aftermarket programmable EMS to help an OEM injection engine with fuel delivery by providing fuel enrichment under turbo boost. Supertune Bob Norwood applied a fuel-only Haltech ECU to control two gigantic alcohol injectors when building an Acura NSX turbo—successfully fueling 10 pounds of boost on an engine with a 10.5:1 compression ratio. Bell Engineering Group of San Antonio installed a fuel-only Haltech ECU and four additional injectors when building a super-high-output turbo system for a Mazda Miata. In both cases, the Haltech unit was not activated until the engine entered turbo boost, and the Haltech did not use temperature or TPS sensors since the factory injection system provides cold enrichment, acceleration enrichment, and so forth.

A related option is the parallel ECM setup (described elsewhere in this book), where one EMS (typically the stock system) handles some engine or vehicle-management tasks at least some of the time while a second takes delivers fuel and spark some or all of the time, in some cases with a separate fuel system and/or ignition.

Chapter 13
Designing, Modifying, and Building Intake Manifolds

Intake manifold design really matters. A great intake manifold design can provide really substantial performance advantages over a less optimal one. Clever naturally aspirated designs have taken advantage of high airflow characteristics, inertial effects, and pressure-wave tuning to achieve air density in cylinders that substantially exceeds atmospheric pressure with as much as 10-psi positive pressure at the intake valve.

Sooner or later, you may want to fabricate a custom intake manifold for a fuel-injected engine. Important intake manifold design goals typically include the following:

- Low resistance to airflow
- High air velocity for a given flow rate
- Excellent fuel and air distribution among the various cylinders
- Runner, plenum, and air intake sizes that take advantages of RAM and tuning effects
- Overall intake volumes that combine good response with smoothing

A wet intake manifold—designed for handling both air and fuel flow for carburetion or throttle body injection systems—has substantially less freedom of design for optimizing airflow, because the overriding priority is always to keep the air and fuel well mixed and to distribute fuel originating at a central point as evenly as possible to all the cylinders. Single-carb or TBI manifolds use many tricks and kludges to correct air- and fuel-flow problems, and it is seldom feasible to build such a manifold with any method other than mold building and casting. Computational fluid dynamics is one of the more complex types of computer modeling and simulation, and there is still a lot of trial and error in manifold design. If you need a wet intake manifold, buy one.

On the other hand, building a tunnel-ram manifold for a port EFI powerplant is quite feasible, and construction may be rather simple on inline engines once you know the correct runner size and length for your application, as well as the ideal plenum volume. Of course, V-type engine manifolds are more difficult to fabricate, but, again, are simple compared to single-point wet manifold designs. This is because there is usually a way to design the runners so every one is perfectly symmetrical with the others in such a way that all runners have even lengths and take-off points, and all merge into the plenum in precisely the same way.

TYPES OF DESIGNS

Intake manifolds consist of hollow runners that mate to the intake ports on a cylinder head. Runners may or may not merge into one or more larger chambers called *plenums*, into which air enters through a throttle body or carburetor that is connected to the air cleaner and atmosphere (or perhaps to a supercharger or turbo compressor) via an intake ram tube.

Whether wet or dry, there are several classes of intake manifolds.

Dual-plane manifolds divide the cylinders into two groups, which are separated into a divided plenum, i.e., two smaller plenums. This type of manifold produces better low-end torque and better throttle response than most other manifolds.

Single-plane manifolds route all intake runners into a single common plenum, which smooths out induction pulses better

A millennium-vintage problem: the un-modifiable plastic intake manifold. It's cheap to build, and it helps insulate charged air from engine compartment heat. This GM Ecotec manifold also has long, narrow runners optimized for low-end torque. *GM*

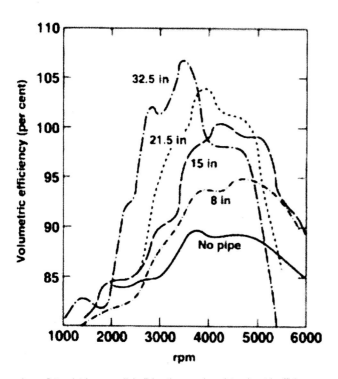

Jaguar D-type intake runner ("pipe") length comparison plots volumetric efficiency for various engine speeds with 32.5, 21.5, 15, 8, and zero inch pipes, indicating the effects of inertia and resonation effects on cylinder filling. Clearly, the two longest pipes achieved a supercharging effect below 4,000 rpm, while the 15-inch pipe was better above 4,000. The 8-inch and zero pipe were suboptimal to at least one of the longer pipes under all conditions.

than the dual-plane design and typically provides better peak power at the expense of low-end torque. Higher-revving engines should use a single-plane intake design.

Tunnel-ram manifolds are a special case of the single-plane design, except that all intake runners are straight and meet symmetrically at a common plenum. This design is, of course, still good for top-end power, with the added benefit of intrinsically excellent fuel distribution. The tunnel-ram typically has a fairly large plenum, which tends to reduce the signal strength of induction at a carburetor venturi and hurt throttle response. Designers typically work hard with tuning effects to improve the responsiveness for adequate streetability.

Individual-runner manifolds eliminate the tunnel-ram plenum and equip each runner with its own throttle. There is a tremendous amount of pulsing through each throttle, which can actually improve low- and midrange performance due to increased peak runner velocities. However, with no plenum to dampen the induction pulses, high-rpm tuning is more problematic. There tends to be a lot of fuel standoff above each throttle on carbureted individual-runner manifolds.

Dual-resonance (VarioRam) manifolds are basically a cross between a dual-plane and a tunnel-ram manifold. The system uses a large plenum divided into two smaller halves by a wall fitted with a large throttle plate. The throttle plate can close to route intake air for half the runners through a smaller dual-plane plenum that functions as a collector for matched sets of cylinders that Y together into a ram tube effectively extending beyond the throttle. When the plenum throttle opens at higher rpm, the dual plenums become a large single tunnel-ram plenum collecting all runners into a single-plane plenum. Both the dual-

plane and tunnel-ram configurations use advanced tuning effects to optimize airflow, inertia, and resonation effects for improved performance in either mode of operation (see sidebar).

No matter which type of manifold is in use, swirl resulting from air moving past the throttle plate should be dampened out by a restrictor to avoid biasing airflow to certain cylinders. Similarly, there must be no sharp corners or edges in any of these manifold types in order to avoid turbulence or eddies that might bias volumetric efficiency to particular cylinders.

INTAKE (AND EXHAUST) MANIFOLD TUNING

The intake and exhaust systems of a running engine constitute a highly complex system of high- and low-pressure waves resonating and bouncing around inside the plumbing. Such waves are caused by the inertia of the air and the opening and closing of the valves at a certain frequency. If an engine designer can arrange to have high-pressure waves approach an intake valve just as it opens or closes (or to have low-pressure waves approach an exhaust valve from the exhaust system as exhaust valves open), volumetric efficiency will increase and the negative effects of valve overlap will decline.

Pressure waves can actually move from the exhaust system through the exhaust valve and combustion chamber out through the intake valve into the intake manifold. Intake and exhaust tuning must harness these effects to force more charge into the engine as the intake valve closes or fight reversion when the intake starts to open. It is unfortunate but true that tuning that is optimal for one engine speed usually degrades performance at some other part of the power band.

Engineers use two main models to predict the effects of manifold tuning on engine volumetric efficiency. The first approximates a plenum-runner manifold with a quarter-wave organ pipe combined with a Helmholtz resonator, assuming that either component can operate either independently or in combination as a system, assuming that there are no more than four runners per plenum and that the cylinders sharing a plenum must be even-firing, with pulses entering the plenum at even intervals. The second models manifold behavior as a function of wave motion within the manifold, varying according to rpm.

In either case, the intake manifold (and the intersections and terminations of its runners, plenum(s), intake ram tubes, and so on), valves, cylinders, and pistons constitute a complex system containing resonant cavities formed by cylinders with open ports and manifold branches leading to closed ports. Elements of the system change impedance (resistance to the net movement of alternating gas flow) where a pipe alters a cross-sectional area.

WHAT HAPPENS IN TUNED INTAKE AND EXHAUST SYSTEMS?

The intake system on a four-stroke automotive engine is designed to get as much charge air/fuel mixture into the cylinders as possible. One way to help with this is by tuning the lengths of the pipes.

When a piston is moving down and the intake valve is open, atmospheric pressure forces air into the cylinder at a very high speed. When the intake valve suddenly closes, the column of intake air still has velocity and inertia, producing a shock wave as the air smashes into the valve, sending a pressure pulse backward into the intake manifold at the speed of sound. At certain frequencies of valve opening and closing events, the air column in the runner will start to resound or echo in a coordinated way otherwise known as resonance, which can cause energy from reflected pressure waves to combine with the force of static air pressure to push more air into the cylinder than would happen from air pressure alone. Designing intake pipes, plenum sizes, and runner size and length to take advance of positive and negative inertial and resonation effects to supercharge the volumetric efficiency of an engine is known as intake tuning.

RESONATION EFFECTS

- The exhaust valve opens and an acoustic pulse (+) goes down the pipe at the speed of sound (which varies according to exhaust temperature).
- The wave arrives at the end of the pipe and enters the atmosphere, triggering a negative pressure wave that travels back up the pipe. If the pipe length, rpm, cam overlap, and duration are tuned correctly, the low-pressure wave reaches the combustion chamber just before the exhaust valve closes.
- This helps suck out the last of the exhaust gas.
- The negative pressure waves continue on through the combustion chamber (valve overlap happening) and out the intake valve, where it helps to get the sluggish intake charge started into the combustion chamber.
- The negative wave travels up the intake port and into the tuned intake manifold runner where it again meets the atmosphere.
- At this point the powerful wave is once again reflected back as a positive pressure wave traveling back down the intake runner. If the length is correct, the remaining energy is expended, propelling extra charge into the combustion chamber just as the intake valve closes.
- Power increases are commensurate with multi-psi positive boost pressure.
- At all other rpm but the target "sweet" engine speed, the effect is negative—subtracting volumetric efficiency—and making for a peaky motor.
- Engineers use box structures in the intake system to dampen strong pressure waves and flatten the torque curve.

The air space in the intake-system box acts as a spring, and the air in the intake tube acts as a weight. At a target frequency the air in the tube vibrates back and forth without actually departing the tube. The volume of the box and the length and diameter of the tube determine the frequency of the system. Strong pressure waves excite the box into resonance at a matching impedance, dampening the pressure waves and flattening the torque curve.

This is a complex situation. Another manifestation of intake tuning is as follows:

When an intake valve is open on an engine, air is being pushed by atmospheric (or boost) pressure into the combustion chamber at high velocity (sometimes at supersonic speed). The piston creates a negative pressure wave as it recedes down the bore that travels through the intake valve until it hits the plenum, where it is inverted and returns to the intake valve as a positive pressure wave that can help supercharge air into the cylinder if it arrives at the right time while the valve is still even partly open.

When the intake valve suddenly closes, incoming air slams to a stop against the valve and inertia causes it to stack up on itself, forming a region of high pressure that makes its way up the intake runner away from the cylinder in a high-pressure wave. When the pressure wave reaches the end of the intake runner, a negative pressure wave will be produced that bounces back down the intake runner, crashes into the now-closed valve,

and is reflected back a second time as a negative pressure wave that again moves up the runner toward the plenum at the speed of sound (1,250–1,300 feet per second in hot intake air). At the plenum the wave is again inverted—this time to a positive pressure wave—which returns again to the intake valve where it can help boost air into the cylinder, given the right engine speed.

A well-tuned intake will have a high-pressure wave at the intake valve as it's opening and again at the same time the engine is in its overlap period with both intake and exhaust valves open. If the exhaust is tuned to the same rpm range, there will be low pressure in the exhaust at the same time due to scavenging and negative pressure waves returning from the exhaust system to the vicinity of the exhaust valve.

With the intake above atmospheric pressure and the cylinder much lower than atmospheric, air blasts into the cylinder, causing a rapid drop in pressure that moves away from the cylinder through the intake. On the heels of this, as the piston accelerates down the bore, a second negative wave moves through the intake valve into the manifold, one right after the other. The various pressure waves can create as much as 10 psi of positive boost pressure at the intake valve, which can raise volumetric efficiency above 100 percent in high-rpm racing engines.

How long would an intake runner have to be to take advantage of pressure-wave tuning? Assume the engine is turning over at 5,000 rpm. On a four-stroke engine, each intake valve opens once every 720 degrees of crankshaft revolution. Assume it stays open for 250 degrees. This means that there are 470 degrees between the intake valve closing event and the next opening event. It will take the engine 0.012 seconds per revolution at 5,000 rpm, and since 470 degrees is about 1.31 revolutions, each intake valve will remain closed for 0.0156 seconds. At the speed of sound—1,300 feet per second—the pressure wave would travel about 20 feet in this time, which is 10 feet up and 10 feet back.

Unfortunately, the tuning effect is only true within a narrow range—around 5,000 rpm—meaning the pressure wave will be out of sync at, say, 3,250 or 4,250 rpm. Variable intake systems like Porsche's VarioRam can create more than one sweet spot, but peaky power is just the name of the game in pressure-wave tuning. The other problem is that 10-foot runners are way too long to fit in a car.

But any even divisor of 10 feet—say 2.5 feet, or 30 inches—allows the pressure wave to resonate up and down the pipe four times before the intake valve opens again, arriving at the valve at the right time.

Intake aerodynamics are complex and tricky and offer tradeoffs. High-velocity intake air is a good thing, because intake air moving into the cylinders at high speed has more momentum and increases turbulence that helps the air and fuel mix and increases the speed of combustion and helps fight detonation. But if you increase the air velocity by forcing intake air to enter the engine through a smaller-diameter intake runner, at higher engine speeds with high-CFM airflow, small runners will produce a pressure drop that degrades volumetric efficiency. So it is better to have large-diameter runners at peak-power engine speed.

Some four-valve engines are designed with primary-secondary runner systems that use one (sometimes smaller diameter) primary runner at lower engine speeds when super-high charge velocities will improve cylinder filling. A butterfly valve blocks the secondary (sometimes larger diameter) runner at

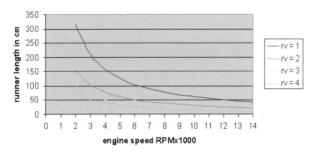

Runner length tunning speeds

lower speeds, then opens up at higher engine speeds to reduce the pressure drop at peak power, increasing maximum horsepower.

RUNNER LENGTH

Longer, narrower intake runners are better for optimizing low-rpm performance because they have a lower resonant frequency, and the smaller diameter helps increase the air velocity and enhances inertial cylinder-filling effects at lower engine speeds. Shorter, wider runners are better for high rpm because they have a higher resonant frequency, and the larger diameter is less restrictive to all-out airflow.

Grape Ape Racing has a workable method of computing intake runner length using wave motion theory, which is designed to provide reasonable results compared to known-good tuned manifolds.

Begin by computing an effective cam duration (ECD), which typically involves subtracting 20 to 30 degrees from the advertised cam duration. Use 30 degrees for solid-cam drag motors, 20 degrees for less radical powerplants.

ECD = 720 - Adv. duration - 30

> **For a 305-degree duration race cam:**
> **ECD = 720 - 305 - 30**
> **The ECD of that cam would be 385.**

The formula for optimum intake runner length (L) is:

L = [(ECD x 0.25 x V x 2) ÷ (rpm x RV)] - (D ÷ 2)

Where:

> **ECD = Effective cam duration**
> **V = Pressure wave speed (400–1,250 ft/s)**
> **RV = Reflective value – the utilized pressure wave set**
> **D = Runner diameter (inches)**

If an engine with a 305-degree race cam needed to be tuned to 7,000 rpm using the second set of pressure waves (RV=2) and had a 1.5-inch diameter intake runner, the optimum runner length formula would look like this:

> **L = [(445 x 0.25 x 1300 x 2) ÷ (7,000 x 2)] - 0.75**
> **19.91 inches would be the optimal runner length.**

The equation produced the above graph, verifying the requirement for longer runners at lower engine speeds to produce tuning effects as well as indicating the effect of using various reflective values.

Note: Runner length includes the length of the intake passage from the manifold plenum all the way through the head intake port to the intake valve, which includes the set-length passage from the manifold gasket to the valve in the cylinder head. The researchers in this example were working with a Suzuki motorcycle engine with head ports estimated at 13 centimeters in length. This length had to be subtracted from the

total runner length to derive the intake manifold portion of the runner length. At 10,500 rpm, using the second set of pressure waves to reduce volume, improve response, and save space, the total runner length is 28.5 centimeters. So the intake manifold runners would be 28.5 – 13 = 15.5 centimeters.

Manifold designers should terminate manifold runners in the plenum with trumpeted stacks to reduce the loss of air entering the runners.

RUNNER AREA

In contrast to tuning runner length (which affects power in a narrow rpm range), tuning the diameter or area of the runners affects power at all engine speeds. If the port is too small, it will restrict top-end flow. If too large, cylinder-filling velocity will suffer, and this will hurt low-end power. As a rule, the larger the runner, the less strength pressure waves will have.

Since the intake valve is the most restrictive part of an intake system, intake runners should be sized to optimize airflow through the valve area. Equipped with a camshaft that is a good match, most decent cylinder heads will flow air through the valve area equivalent to that of an unrestricted port with about 80 percent the area of the valve(s), while some excellent racing heads can be ported to flow 85 percent of the valve area. For example, a 2.02-inch valve with 3.20 square inches of area will flow the same as an open tube with about 2.56 square inches of area (this is 80 percent of 3.20). Therefore, the port area should be about 2.56 square inches in the area of the port leading directly up to the valve.

INTAKE PORT TAPER

For best cylinder filling, it helps to have a high flow velocity at the back of the valve, because faster air exerts less pressure (this is the Bernoulli effect). To increase velocity, the intake port can be tapered. To be effective, there should be a 1.7–2.5 percent decrease in intake runner area per inch of runner approaching the valve, which represents a 1–1.5 degree taper.

For example, let's say you want a 2 percent increase in taper per inch of runner for the 2.02-inch valve discussed above, which has a port area of 2.56 square inches near the valve. A 10-inch runner with a 2 percent taper and final area of 2.56 inches near the valve should start out with 3.12 square inches of area 10 inches away from where the port joins the plenum. As taper approaches 2.5 percent, you are at the limit of what taper can do to help airflow.

PLENUM VOLUME

The purpose of a plenum is to permit charge gases to slow down and gain density and to help isolate the resonant pulses of the individual runners from a desirable overall smooth flow of air through the throttle. An intake manifold plenum can be effective over a fairly wide range of volume, and general design rules work pretty well in calculating optimal volume. This lack of sensitivity is fortunate, since there is no simple answer to the plenum volume requirement for a given application or rpm range. But general rules work fairly well. The tradeoffs involve supplying sufficient plenum volume to deliver plenty of airflow versus keeping the volume low enough to keep throttle response from becoming sluggish.

The rule for plenums without tuned runners and with airflow restrictors is to design an intake plenum with one to two times the engine displacement in order to provide a large amount of available reserve air. In this case, air volume acts as a

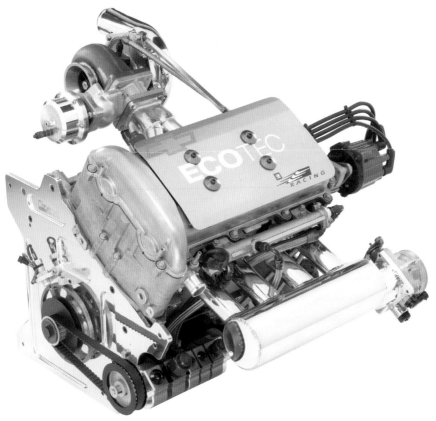

Ecotec turbo dragger powerplant with GM Racing custom manifold. When GM Racing decided to build this super-duty Ecotec powerplant, the plastic intake had to go, and the name of the game for super-high boosted power in the 600–900 horse range is shorter, larger runners. The shorter runners and space-frame chassis permit flexibility of manifold design, and the shorter-than-stock runners simplify geometry compared to the long plastic runners of the stock 2.0-liter Ecotec. The manifold is a rather simple construction, with throttle body and head flanges, four straight pipes, and a round plenum. Runner length and diameter and plenum volume are critical to optimal power, as is radius-ing the various piping that enters and exits the plenum. *GM*

The Helmholtz resonator is a small auxiliary plenum/chamber that attaches to the main plenum/induction system with a narrow neck and uses sound waves to improve air flow.

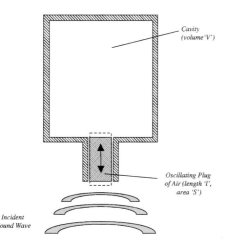

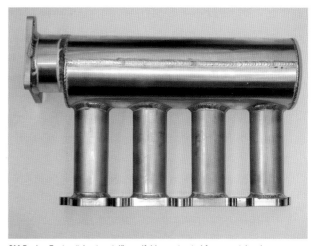

GM Racing Ecotec "sheet metal" manifold, constructed from scratch using aluminum pipe and aluminum plate.

low-pass filter (capacitor) between the engine and the restrictor, smoothing the flow through the restrictor. Without a plenum, the engine would choke the air through the restrictor with each intake stroke of a piston. Using this method with the above example predicts a plenum of 1.2 liters.

The rules change when a Helmholtz resonator is being used. A Helmholtz resonator is a small auxiliary plenum or chamber that attaches to the main plenum or chamber through a narrow neck. The Helmholtz plenum makes a dense charge by use of pressure waves, using the same physics as a tuned-port intake runner.

For engines operating at a maximum rpm in the 5,000 to 6,000 range, Grape Ape Racing recommends the following guidelines for plenum volume: V-8s sharing one large plenum do not work well as far as resonation-effects tuning, but the optimal tuning size would be 40 to 50 percent of total cylinder displacement. For a four-cylinder, 50 to 60 percent of displacement works well. For three cylinders or a six with twin plenums, each plenum should be 65 to 80 percent of the displacement of the three cylinders being fed. For engines operating closer to 7,000 to 7,500 rpm, reduce plenum volume by 10 to 15 percent. For a power boost at 2,500 to 3,500, the plenum should be 30 percent larger.

Using a tuned plenum and tuned intake pipes requires a plenum volume of approximately 300 cc in the previous Suzuki example, which applies specifically to engines that use tuned intake pipes.

Cavity (volume 'V')

Oscillating Plug of Air (length 'l', area 'S')

Incident Sound Wave

INTAKE MANIFOLDS

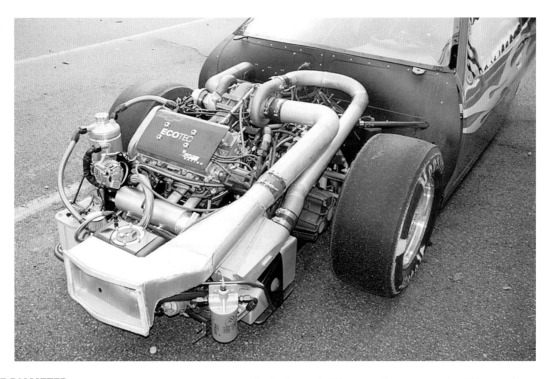

Super-duty Ecotec engine in GM Racing Cavalier drag car. The powerplant was capable of 1,200 horsepower on methanol.

INTAKE RAM PIPE DIAMETER

The velocity in the plenum intake ram pipe should always remain at less than 180 feet per second at maximum rpm and horsepower.

Grape Ape Racing's formula to compute the diameter of a plenum intake pipe is:

D = SQR (CID x VE x rpm) ÷ (V x 1130)

Where:

D =	**Pipe diameter**
SQR =	**Square root of**
CID =	**Cubic inch displacement**
VE =	**Volumetric efficiency**
V =	**Velocity in ft/sec**

(for liters, change cubic inch displacement to liters and the constant to 18.5)

Example:

153-ci four-cylinder engine with 85 percent VE, revving to 6,000 rpm and 185 ft/sec:

D= SQR (153 x 0.85 x 6000) ÷ (180 x 1130) = 1.96 inches

If you are using more than one throttle bore to feed the cylinders, the ram pipes associated with each bore should be half of the total required. To get the diameter, use the formula for the area of a circle—area = π r^2—in reverse as, diameter = 2 x SQR (area ÷ π), where SQR = square root.

A dual-bore ram pipe for the above example would replace a single 3.02-square-inch 1.96-inch diameter pipe with twin bores each of 1.39-inch diameter.

INTAKE RAM PIPE LENGTH

Grape Ape Racing suggests adjusting the length of the intake ram pipe last, using a pipe that can be easily adjusted in length for dyno or airflow testing

Start with a 13-inch-long ram pipe to provide airflow enhancement at about 6,000 rpm. For each 1,000-rpm change in speed from 6,000, add or remove 1.7 inches, shortening the

pipe for higher rpm. The inlet of a ram pipe should have at least a 1/2-inch radius on the intake for smooth flow.

On the dyno, experiment with a 1/2-inch adjustment in either direction to see what this does for both peak and average power and torque. Grape Ape suggests tuning the intake ram pipe about 1,000 rpm lower than the intake runner length tuning speed for increasing average power. Obviously, a target speed of 8,000 rpm does not require a very long ram pipe.

HOW TO FABRICATE AN INTAKE MANIFOLD

(This information was provided by Simple Digital Systems.)

This section details the complete fabrication process on a custom intake manifold for a developmental Mazda RX7, but the basic design can be easily adapted for almost any engine design. Required tools include a drill press, lathe, band saw, hole saws, files, and a TIG welder. SDS constructed this manifold from mild steel for ease of assembly, but in most ways aluminum is easier to fabricate and is the material of choice for intake manifolds.

The plenum type design uses a single throttle body attached to a plenum with separate intake runners for each port. Port injectors are mounted in each runner.

The main flange is constructed from 1/4-inch plate to reduce warpage during welding. An intake manifold gasket can be used as a guide to trace the flange outline and mark the port and bolt holes, and the flange plate can be cut out using a band saw or plasma-arc cutter. Bolt holes can be drilled on a drill press. Intake runner tube holes can be made with a hole saw, or a plasma arc if they are not round.

Try to design the port holes so the ID of the tubing used for the runners is the same as that for the finished port size in your head. If this is not possible, you can probably open up smaller runners with porting or using the extrude-hone process. The runners should be spigotted inside the flange hole for ease of jigging.

Runners are made from 0.050 to 0.065 tubing. Runner lengths can be adjusted within the space constraints to help boost torque within the desired range. Short runners are good for high-rpm torque as used in racing. Long runners are more applicable for street use at lower rpm. For most street engines, try to keep the length from the end of the runner to the valve at least 9 inches long and preferably longer. Available space usually limits this dimension when using straight runners, so curved runners using 90-degree mandrel bent tubing can sometimes be used to increase the runner length.

As applied to engines with oval or square ports, you will have to form the tubing into the port shape, which is considerably more complicated. Tubing should be cut off at precise lengths with a tubing cutter and carefully deburred. For maximum airflow, tapered runners with velocity stacks inside the plenum can be made if you can do this type of work. While time consuming, this design shows a 20 to 25 percent increase in flow over straight tubing runners.

Depending on engine displacement and the throttle body used, the intake plenum is typically constructed from 3-inch diameter 0.065 wall tubing for engines under 1,600 cc or 4-inch diameter for most other engines. Holes must be cut in the plenum tubing with a hole saw for the intake runner tubes and throttle-body tube. The throttle body may also be placed directly on one end of the plenum in place of an end plate, depending on component layout. 4-inch tubing is a common size. The plenum should be made at least 2 inches longer than the dimension of the outside intake ports to allow better airflow to the outer ports. This is a good time to plan and drill any manifold vacuum ports for brake boosters, MAP sensors, and so on.

Build end plates from 0.050- to 0.066-inch plate stock to cap the plenum ends. Cut them out with a band saw or plasma arc. Make them about the same size as the plenum tubing OD. If you plan to mount the throttle body on one end of the plenum, this end cap should be made from 3/16–1/4-inch plate to allow for tapping threads to hold the throttle body. If the throttle body will be mounted on a ram tube, use 1/4-inch plate for the TB flange. Tap directly into the plate with fine threads for maximum strength.

Throttle body options are numerous. Select a throttle body that can flow the desired amount of air and fits within the space limitations. Think about the suitability of the throttle body for plumbing in an air cleaner, intercooler, or turbocharger. Too large a throttle body for street use will often mean a very sensitive tip-in throttle response, which can hurt drivability. There is also no need for a giant 3.5-inch throttle body if your turbo plumbing is only 2.25 inches. Acquiring a throttle body with a potentiometer-type TPS already installed will save time and trouble. For many applications, Ford 5.0-liter and 4.6-liter V-8 throttle bodies work well. They are cheap, available, and relatively compact. Ford Motorsport and Edelbrock make larger sizes in 5-millimeter increments. The 4.6-liter throttle bodies are compact and have a minimal amount of extra clutter. All Ford throttle bodies have a potentiometer-type TPS sensor. Ford 65-millimeter 4.0-liter Explorer throttle bodies are easily available used or from a Ford dealer. These are relatively inexpensive and include minimal garbage on the outside. Put some thought into a throttle linkage at this point also.

SDS recommends fabricating injector bosses out of 1-inch bar stock and sealing the vacuum side of the injector with a 5/8-ID, 3/4-OD O-ring slid over the nose of the injector body. You can pull off the stock O-ring and pintle cap. Bore the bar stock to 0.640–0.650, straight through. This allows a slight air gap between the boss and the injector to reduce heat transfer and fuel boiling. Machine a 0.740 counterbore, 0.040 deep at the end for O-ring retention and sealing. Cut off the bosses at 45 degrees so that they are about 1.35–1.5 inches long. This is a good entry angle for many injectors into the runner and is an easy angle for sawing.

The fuel rail is typically made from 3/4-inch square tubing with a 0.050 to 0.065 wall. This shape allows much easier drilling and jigging. One-quarter-inch holes can be drilled at the port spacing interval. The upper O-ring bosses machined from 3/4-inch bar stock will be welded over the top of these holes. These will usually be about 1/2-inch long and have a 0.540- to 0.545-inch hole drilled for the O-ring to seal on. Carefully chamfer the entry side for easier O-ring fit. End caps for the rail are made from 1/4-inch plate and tapped for 1/8-inch NPT fittings.

Once all of the pieces are cut out and deburred, if possible clamp the head flange to a scrap cylinder head to reduce warpage during welding. Carefully jig the plenum and runners to the flange and measure for straightness. Tack weld the pieces lightly and recheck for straightness. You should still be able to move things around a bit at this stage. Tack the opposite side of each joint and re-check again. Once you are satisfied, TIG weld all of the joints. Weld on your end caps and TB flange. Let everything air cool.

Now cut holes in the runners for the injectors. Scribe a line across the runners where you want the center of the injectors to be. Now intersect each mark on the runner with another line down the center of each tube. Punch mark and drill a 1/4-inch hole. Now drill straight through with a 1/2-inch drill. Once you pierce the tubing, slowly lean the drill over at 45 degrees to oval the hole. The injector bosses must be positioned over these oval holes; make sure before starting that you have enough room around the boss and flange so you will be able to get the welder in close proximity for welding.

Assemble the injectors into the rail and slide the bosses over the injectors. Carefully align the assembly so the injectors are dead center through each injector hole in the runners. Clamp in position and recheck. Lightly and quickly tack each boss in position. As soon as this is completed, either pull the injectors out or water quench each tack to avoid heat damage to the injectors (very easy to do). Once you are satisfied that everything is straight, remove the injectors if they're still there and finish welding the bosses. Be aware that the bosses must be very straight and at identical depth for proper sealing.

You can weld bolt-down tabs onto the fuel rail and weld attachment points for the bolts onto the manifold. A couple of long, 1/4-inch bolts usually suffice. The manifold can now be thoroughly cleaned with soap and hot water, then lacquer thinner. A quality engine enamel or powder coating will provide a nice-looking finish.

Chapter 14
The Science and Practice of EMS Tuning

THE LANDSCAPE OF DIGITAL PERFORMANCE TUNING

Programmable engine management systems permit (and require) a tuner to define the basic raw fuel and ignition curves for an engine with digital ignition and electronic fuel injection by developing tables of numbers that enumerate representative breakpoints of spark timing advance and fuel delivery as a function of engine speed and airflow. Such tables are typically represented to the tuner (calibrator) in graphical or tabular format via software on a laptop computer running Windows or some version of Unix.

This PC-resident software has the ability to interact, typically via a serial data cable, controller area network (CAN) bus, or Bluetooth, with the electronic control module (ECM) that actually manages the spark and fuel requirements for an engine. The PC software allows the user to transfer data back and forth on the fly between the laptop and ECM memory for tuning purposes.

Typically, programmable engine management systems provide both the ability to interactively modify particular operating parameters and table cells in the ECM that affect

Supercharged Cadillac Northstar 4-cam V-8 on the engine dyno. Calibration engineers spend many months or even years developing perfect engine calibrations that optimize power and efficiency under all operating conditions. It is impossible to do better, though you can make a little more power on most engines if you're willing to eliminate factory safety margins that protect owners from damaging their engines with poor-octane fuel or extremely severe race-type driving. It's almost impossible to optimize spark timing for maximum torque without a load-holding dynamometer.

49	49	51	60	67	70	70	71	71	73	77	96	102	102	102	98
49	49	51	60	67	70	70	71	71	73	77	90	96	96	96	98
49	49	51	60	67	70	70	71	71	73	77	85	89	89	89	87

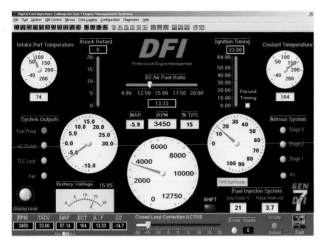

Laptops are great for displaying EMS sensor status in a highly readable format like this "virtual dash" screen from Accel's Gen 7 version of CalMap EMS software. There is a lot of great data on this page, and it's very readable. In some cases, you can set alarms to warn of dangerous conditions.

tuning while the engine is running with a PC, as well as the ability to upload the entire set of all engine management tables and parameters into a Windows PC for subsequent offline recalibration and eventual download back to the ECU.

A programmable engine management system thus consists of the onboard ECM with its firmware logic and calibration data, and a laptop computer with tuning software and data-link hardware connecting it to the ECU. In a few cases, an alternate dedicated interface/programming hardware module replaces the laptop. Once the ECM is configured and calibrated, it is self-sufficient, but without the laptop present and connected, the ECM on most EMSs is in no sense programmable.

The user interface and graphical method of representing ECU internal data tables will vary with the brand of EMS. The underlying resolution or granularity of the tables often varies as well. But behind the scenes the basic engine management operating concepts are the same: When it is approaching time for the ECM to schedule the next fuel injection or spark event, it checks data from engine sensors to get a snapshot of how fast the engine is turning and how much air it is ingesting. The ECM then looks up tuning data for the current speed and airflow in fuel and spark-advance tables to determine when to open and close the fuel injectors and how many degrees before top dead center to trigger an external igniter or coil to fire the next spark plug. If engine speed or airflow fall in between the defined breakpoints in an engine management table, the ECM determines base injection pulse width and spark advance by applying a weighed average of the closest breakpoints surrounding the actual rpm and airflow.

Regardless of the exact means used, the process of calibrating or tuning an engine management system has the ultimate goal of optimizing the engine's torque *or* fuel economy *or* emissions at every breakpoint of engine speed and loading defined in the fuel and ignition tables (there are usually between 24 and 800 such points).

In theory, building an EMS engine calibration is a laborious process. It is a sobering fact that OEM carmakers frequently spend months or even years perfecting the engine management calibration for a particular engine in a particular vehicle. In the real world of performance tuning, the calibration process can often be expedited or eliminated by deploying pre-existing calibrations from similar or identical engines. Where that's not possible, many EMS brands now offer sophisticated computer modeling algorithms that are quite good at building calibration maps based on basic information about engine displacement, horsepower, injector size, rpm range, and so forth.

Even if you are forced to build a calibration from scratch, the scope of the task is mitigated by the reality that there are always many combinations of engine speed and airflow in a typical calibration table that the engine can never reach (i.e., very high airflow at very low engine speed). Tuners normally define unreachable breakpoints by extrapolating from the closest breakpoints the engine *can* reach to prevent implausible data in unreachable breakpoints just beyond the edge of the engine's operating range from being averaged into the fuel or spark calculation for nearby rpm and airflow points (and because the graph looks prettier). Even within the range of speed and airflow the engine you are tuning *can* reach, the calibration task is expedited by the fact that there are large areas of any tuning map in which the slope of changes to timing or fuel with changes in rpm and airflow is *linear*. This means that by optimizing fuel or timing for a subset of rpm and airflow breakpoints, you can rapidly fill in others using manual interpolation or extrapolation or automated routines. Some engine management systems now provide a sophisticated option to automate some or all of the air/fuel calibration process using self-learning routines that use feedback data from wideband O_2 sensors, torque sensors, EGT sensors, knock sensor, or even cylinder-pressure transducers to monitor and set the air/fuel ratio (and sometimes timing) while a human operator puts the engine through a series of routines that enable the ECU to optimize tuning.

BEFORE TUNING: SKILLS AND TOOLS REQUIRED TO GENERATE A SCRATCH CALIBRATION

"While we believe that our system is the simplest on the market to install and program, it is still beyond some people's capabilities. This is not a magic bullet that will solve all of your problems without any work. Have realistic expectations and goals for your project. We get many people contacting us saying that they intend to have a streetable 10-second car that gets great fuel economy and idles like a watch. This probably will not happen in reality. Evaluate your skills and knowledge....

"After installation, you must program the system properly. Even though we supply very complete instruction manuals, if you have no idea about the concepts of rich and lean, basic EFI theory, or ignition timing requirements then you will probably not be able to program the system properly. We suggest that you explore our Tech Page and Manuals online thoroughly to gain as much understanding of basic theory and the system as possible before you decide to buy.

"If things seem way over your head after this, our system may not be for you. You will need patience and understanding to be successful with our system. There is a learning curve with all systems, including SDS. Be prepared to spend some time understanding the various parameters and what effect they have."

Sincerely,

Simple Digital Systems (whose design goal was to be the simplest EMS around)

An alternative to the laptop is a dedicated programmer module like this user interface from SDS or a similar unit from Edelbrock, FAST, and one or two other firms. You can accomplish most of the functionality of a laptop, but you are peering through a tiny window into the EMS environment. Of course, once the system is calibrated, the user interface is of no consequence when driving. You're not trying to calibrate it by yourself while you're driving, are you?

The difficulty of the calibration process for aftermarket tuners is partially ameliorated by the *sensitivity* of gasoline in combustion, that is, the *range* of air/fuel ratios over which the engine produces maximum brake torque. Best torque occurs not at a single point but rather over a range of air/fuel ratios. In a naturally aspirated gasoline-fueled powerplant that does not require surplus fuel for combustion cooling and knock control, the spread between rich best torque (RBT) and lean best torque (LBT) at wide-open throttle is typically 11.5 to 13.3 [lambda .78–.90] with mean best torque in the 12.0 to 12.5 range [lambda .82–.85]. This spread narrows at high engine speeds where the highest possible flame speed becomes increasingly critical to achieving complete combustion in the available time.

All late-model engine management systems give a tuner the ability to dynamically modify a wide range of fuel, timing, and enrichment maps, on the fly, while the engine is running. A tuner does this by editing a graphical or tabular representation of a given map on the laptop screen. The tuner then launches an immediate ECU update, at which point the modified data is uploaded to the ECU at high speed to replace the appropriate parameter or table item for directing engine management operations for the next combustion event.

In addition to giving users the facility to create and edit engine management tables from scratch, programmable engine management systems provide users with the ability to load complete pre-constructed library calibrations (maps) stored on a Windows PC into the ECU. Similarly, users can work in the opposite direction, uploading entire ECU-resident calibrations into a PC for viewing, analysis, modification, or propagation to other ECUs. Beginning in 1996 (and as early as 1994 in a few cases), factory ECUs with Level II onboard diagnostics (OBD-II) provide this same type of capability (password protected by a security seed). Pre-OBD-II factory ECUs typically required a PROM change to install a new calibration.

Most programmable engine management systems allow a tuner to manipulate a mixture trim device or software global mixture trim in order to dynamically enlean or enrich fueling by a percentage determined by the position of the dials. Mixture trim devices have typically consisted of one or more linear potentiometer dials that change the air/fuel ratio across the

entire range of speed and loading or in some cases only at idle or wide-open throttle. This is analogous to turning the mixture-adjustment screw on a carburetor with a screwdriver. Air-fuel trim can be a valuable tool in making an instant determination (via air/fuel-ratio meter, exhaust gas temperature gauge, dyno display, or other means) of the empirical effect of changes to air/fuel ratio. Mixture trim devices provide a quick way to determine the percentage change in fuel delivery required to fix a problem area in the ECU's internal calibration.

In addition to calibrating base fuel and ignition tables, programmable engine management systems offer the ability to define special enrichment or enleanment during acceleration or deceleration, when the engine suddenly changes speed, resulting in fast changes to intake airflow that can upset the equilibrium of vaporized intake fuel versus injected fuel sticking to the walls of the intake system that has not yet vaporized (sometimes referred to by the Greek letter *Tau*).

Programmable systems also provide the ability to calibrate enrichment (and sometime timing) changes during startup and cold-running operations when the engine temperature has not yet reached normal operating ranges and the heavier fractions of gasoline do not vaporize well, and most systems also allow configuration of fuel or ignition corrections for changes in air temperature, which affects the need for cold-running enrichment. Most engine management systems separate cold-running enrichment into cranking enrichment, after-start enrichment, and warm-up enrichment. Most systems provide programmable idle speed correction and faster idle after cold startup via an IAC throttle air bypass.

In addition to basic fuel and spark control, many aftermarket engine management systems provide configurable nitrous injection control, boost control, knock sensor ignition retard, and other functionality. More sophisticated systems provide individual-cylinder calibration of fuel and spark to account for variations in volumetric efficiency, temperature, and injector flow. Some systems provide programmable compensation for variations in fuel pressure, and some can control fuel pressure by controlling fuel pump speed or managing electronic fuel pressure regulators.

VE VS. INJECTION PULSE WIDTH

Some engine management architectures require a tuner to directly calibrate fuel delivery at the available breakpoints of engine speed and airflow by adjusting numbers in a table that represent injector open time or the percentage of maximum injection pulse width. Some engine management systems allow tuners to calibrate fuel delivery by defining tables of target air/fuel ratios. In some cases, target air/fuel ratio algorithms in the ECU use feedback from a wideband O_2 sensor to dynamically modify fuel calculations based on injection pulse width tables to chase the target air/fuel ratio. More sophisticated engine management systems provide the facility to model engine behavior across the range of engine speed, loading, and temperature using a concept called the VE Table. A VE table is quite simply a table of numbers that represents the amount of air an engine will ingest compared to its displacement across the operating range VE-table.

In a VE-table EMS, the tuner begins by specifying a maximum injection time at full engine loading for a specific injector size and may then define and tweak the minimum injection time for the engine at idle if it varies from the linear interpolation between peak pulse at full load and a zero pulse at zero load. These two points define pulse width at all loading

EMS TUNING

49	49	51	60	67	70	70	71	71	73	77	96	102	102	102	98
49	49	51	60	67	70	70	71	71	73	77	90	96	96	96	98
49	49	51	60	67	70	70	71	71	73	77	85	89	89	89	87

points in between, with engine speed assumed not to be a factor due to a perfectly flat torque curve at all engine speeds.

However, since the torque curve will *not* be perfectly flat across the range of operation on most engines, the VE-table tuner must provide offsets to the raw computed linear pulse width values for speed-load sites with sub- or super-normal volumetric efficiency.

DO YOUR HOMEWORK

To tune a running engine that has an unfamiliar engine management system without making things worse or risking damage to the engine while you learn, you're going to need to gain a working familiarity with the engine management software that enables you to quickly grasp what is happening and then react quickly. You definitely do not want to be trying to read the manual to find out what to do when detonation or thermal loading is threatening a melt down on your new performance powerplant. And for that, you're going to need patience, judgment, and experience with the software and ECU data structures, as well as familiarity with the datalogging software you will definitely need in order to calibrate power-adder engines in boosted-power ranges.

The ability to work fast without making stupid mistakes is important, because running engines do not necessarily remain in a steady state: They heat-soak in all sorts of interesting ways that can affect the tuning and power. The oil gets thinner. Resistance to detonation degrades. Engines in a dyno cell pollute the air with hydrocarbons, carbon monoxide, and heat, which affect intake air temperature, volumetric efficiency, intercooler efficiency, combustion quality, and other running parameters. The ability to react quickly is important for reasonable tuning efficiency. Once an engine warms up out of a certain range on the warm-up enrichment map, for example, it will probably be hours before it cools off enough to give you another crack at calibrating the colder start-up temperature ranges.

If you're buying dynamometer time for tuning, slow tuning abilities can be costly. Slow reaction time can even be dangerous. A poor state of tune can damage the engine if it takes the tuner too long to recognize and figure out how to correct the problem, or if the correction is in the wrong direction. As Ray Kurzweil points out in *The Age of Spiritual Machines*, human beings are lightning-fast at recognizing a pattern and taking specific preplanned action (like realizing a kid has run in front of your car and hitting the brakes), but we think quite slowly when faced with new situations that call for reasoning through a problem.

To calibrate most programmable engine management systems, you will first need to have at least minimal familiarity with the operating environment of a Windows laptop PC. In the first place, you're going to have to install the EMS software that you'll be using to interface to the onboard engine management system in order to calibrate engine-control tables and parameters. Later, you will need to use the laptop keyboard to enter configuration data and to use the arrow keys or pointing device (mouse, trackpoint, and so on) to change the shape or height of fuel and ignition graphs, and so on.

Once the tuning software is up and running, you'll need sufficient familiarity with the engine management software environment to be able to dynamically track (while the engine is running) which portions of the main fuel, main ignition, cold-running, and transient enrichment maps are being used by the engine management system to manage the engine. Virtually all engine management systems provide some kind of engine data

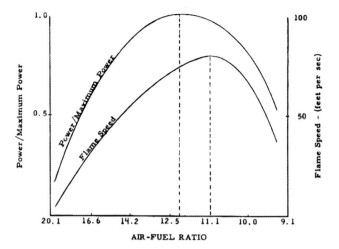

Here's the heart of the matter in fuel calibration: Power and flame speed vary greatly with the air/fuel ratio. In this graph we see typical power and flame speed versus AFR curves for constant-speed operation. Peak power with gasoline fuel occurs at an air/fuel ratio of about 12.0:1. The cooling heat of vaporization of such rich mixtures along with the high flame speed helps fight detonation.

page that can be used to monitor engine sensor values and actuator commands (current injection pulse width, ignition timing, etc.), and determine the map table cells and corrections currently being used in the engine management calculations.

The main fuel, main ignition, engine temperature compensation and other tables typically provide some sort of highlighting, bolding, pointer, or other indication of which cell or graph is currently being used to manage the engine. Many systems have some sort of hot key that a tuner can press to instantly jump to the currently active map or map cell for immediate editing.

So you're going to have to practice working with the user interface of the EMS software and calibrating the parameters and tables.

Assuming you understand the software environment, you still have to have tuning skills and diagnostic tools to do the job well. Professional tuners persistently complain of computer-savvy customers with editing access to programmable engine management systems and little or no tuning experience. Some of these customers insist on tampering with a good calibration in an effort to make more power and succeed only in degrading the state of tune. They then must bring their vehicles back to the pro tuner to be fixed. This sort of unintentional de-tuning is so common it's virtually epidemic.

TUNING TOOLS

A tuner with a great deal of experience with a particular type and brand of engine with specific types of modifications and a specific brand of engine management system may be able to do a reasonable calibration based on past knowledge. Otherwise, you must have the right diagnostic tools. Here's the thing: It is not possible for most people to tune an engine well by seat-of-the-pants, "butt-dyno," trial-and-error methods.

A fact of life is that the less experienced you are, the more you need sophisticated tuning tools like fast, wideband air/fuel ratio meters, multi-gas analyzers, exhaust gas temperature sensors, and chassis dynamometers to do an adequate calibration. This is even

76	49	49	51	60	67	70	70	71	71	73	77	96	102	102	102	
50	49	49	51	60	67	70	70	71	71	73	77	90	96	96	96	
25	49	49	51	60	67	70	70	71	71	73	77	85	89	89	89	

V E tables are useful for engines that must be able to run well without mass airflow sensors and which therefore rely all or some of the time on manifold absolute pressure and engine speed to estimate engine airflow. VE tables correct for the fact that only engines with a perfectly flat torque curve have a perfectly linear relationship between manifold pressure and engine airflow across the rpm range.

VE tables add a kind of elegance to engine management system design that does not exist on EMSs that simply look up fuel injection pulse width or timing advance in a table of rpm and manifold pressure cells. Although any speed-density table of timing or pulse width data is going to correlate to some extent with engine VE, a pure VE table describing the engine's breathing efficiency across the range of operation is uncomplicated by competing purposes such as the desire to optimize some portions of the operating range for efficiency or low emissions and others for maximum power or the need to warp fuel delivery or timing to cool combustion or fight detonation in certain areas of the map. All of these will cause a speed-density-pulse width table to depart from perfectly describing VE. An engine management system in possession of reliable engine VE information in effect knows actual mass airflow into the engine and can use this information in a variety of ways to optimize engine management in various types of self-learning and targeted optimization strategies.

The engine management system's volumetric efficiency table is a critical chart of numbers that represents the engine's breathing efficiency across the range of engine speeds and loading. The VE table essentially tells the engine management system what percentage of the engine's displacement will make it into the cylinders at every possible combination of rpm and manifold pressure. Manifold pressure is itself a function of engine breathing capabilities, throttle angle, and power-adder boost. VE is a function of the basic engine design, including head design, camshaft profile, power-adders, engine speed, and other factors.

Engine VE intake design, intake air heating, and turbine back pressure can vary from 100 percent in both directions (usually negative), depending on what the engine is doing and how it is designed. Once the system knows how much air there is in the cylinders, computing how much fuel the engine needs is simple.

There are an infinite number of possible engine speed and loading numbers, so various engine management systems settle for VE tables that define a fixed number of cells (such as 16x16 or 20x40), with points falling in between the resolution of the table calculated as a weighted average of the closest defined cells (sometimes referred to as breakpoints). If an engine is breathing an amount of air equal to 100 percent of its displacement, the VE is 100 percent. Depending on the table, this number may be represented as a percentage (1.00), or a plus-or-minus offset (0.00), or offset from linear increase.

If extra fuel is being used to cool combustion under boosted conditions as an anti-detonation countermeasure, or if spark retard is similarly being used to fight detonation, the numbers in such a table will depart from engine VE in these areas. Which is why some EMSs have a pure VE table one step removed from the actual base injection pulse width or timing. As mentioned above, the numbers in a main fuel table will also not correlate perfectly with engine VE if injection pulse width is optimized for varying air/fuel ratios to achieve varying purposes at various engine loadings (for example, maximum power at full throttle, maximum efficiency at light cruise).

The table of optimal spark timing advance values will also correlate highly to the VE of the engine and take into account time per degree of engine rotation at various speeds, since denser charge mixtures at points of higher volumetric efficiency burn faster and require less spark timing.

Logically, a VE table looks something like a big spreadsheet with the numbers in each cell representing VE for a particular breakpoint of engine speed and loading. The good news is that, once defined, the VE table of an engine remains constant unless the powerplant begins to wear out (or if you modify engine breathing with new hot rodding equipment).

From one point of view, a VE table projects or normalizes the convoluted surface of a 3-D graph describing engine airflow (therefore, torque) onto a flat surface, such that other calibration tasks can assume the torque curve to be flat. If torque is flat (or there is a VE table), a straight line drawn between maximum injection at peak torque rpm and minimum injection at idle rpm accurately intersects all other points, so all you have to do to tune the engine is to define these two points.

truer for engines with nitrous or forced-induction power-adders, but it's also true of the simple stuff, such as tuning well for a good idle: How do you tell the difference between a rich mixture that's producing a rough-running engine and a lean mixture that is causing the engine to misfire? Many people would not know the difference unless they could see rich black smoke. Ironically, the more you need diagnostic tools, the less likely you probably are to have them.

SCIENTIFIC METHODS

Experienced or not, you'll need to be very organized, patient, and logical, as well as familiar with scientific methods of experimentation (for example, changing one—and only one—variable at a time so you establish true cause-and-effects in an unambiguous way). Like a scientist doing an experiment, you'll need to keep good notes for later analysis and tracking.

On occasion, you'll need the patient ability to shut down the motor, sit quietly, and think logically. What are the possible reasons an event may have happened? What are the implications of the event? What are the possible actions? Are there any risks? What are the possible outcomes of various actions? Which is the highest priority action to try first?

To effectively calibrate an engine with power-adders without damaging it, you'll need a strategic tuning plan firmly rooted in good modeling theory. Particularly on a power-adder engine, you must start with a timing map known to be conservative (on the retarded side of the scale, but not ridiculously so), and a fuel map known to be safely on the rich side at higher loads. This will require either a calibration from an identical or nearly identical engine, or calculated maps built with modeling software or hand calculations.

Even then, you'll need to sneak up on boosted conditions, datalogging quick forays deeper and deeper into boosted territory, analyzing the data, and correcting encountered speed-loading points and points beyond them at higher boost you have not yet actually encountered if timing and air/fuel ratios seem headed in the wrong direction. One thing you can count on is that higher levels of boost will not want less fuel and more timing.

Even with plausibly conservative maps, when you complete the easier idle and light cruise tuning and are ready to tune for high specific power on a boosted engine, it is essential to arrange for fast, accurate data, a dyno or strap-on inertial accelerometer like the G-Tech, and ideally EGT data.

If at all possible, there should be a good way to correlate the wideband air/fuel ratio data to logged sensor data from the EMS (the Motec M48 EMS used in several projects in this book will log wideband O_2 data). Things are happening too fast at

49	49	51	60	67	70	70	71	71	73	77	96	102	102	102	98
49	49	51	60	67	70	70	71	71	73	77	90	96	96	96	98
49	49	51	60	67	70	70	71	71	73	77	85	89	89	89	87

From another point of view, if you know the mass of air entering an engine, fuel-injection pulse width is one simple calculation for best power, another simple calculation for best economy. If you've got a good VE table, tinkering with a few values at the extremes defines everything else. If you have a pulse width table, the surface will look a lot like the surface of the engine VE table except that the pulse width table will be warped higher in the richer high-power areas in relation to other light-cruise sectors of the map where you're probably tuning for leaner lambda 1.0 mixtures. In any case, if your EMS has a VE-table architecture, getting the VE table right turns your MAP sensor into an accurate meter of actual engine breathing.

One possible way to build a VE table is to fill the fuel tank with race gas, install a known-conservative timing table, and use a wideband O_2 sensor to target identical air/fuel ratios in all speed-loading points, which is made easier by the fact that many EMSs now have a target air/fuel ratio table. If you have a wideband O_2 sensor, you could set all cells in the target lambda (air/fuel ratio) table to, say, 12.8:1, which should be safely rich enough to set VE in cells referencing high power and torque settings on all but high-boost powerplants (but not so rich as to harm idle quality or produce surging at light cruise).

Turn off the parameter that deactivates closed-loop auto correction in conjunction with the target air/fuel ratio table, but make sure the O_2 sensor readout stays active.

It is a good idea to get some idea of which cells are being used by the EMS to fuel the engine by using a cell highlight if there is one to mark the speed-density cells as you operate the engine. This will enable you to concentrate on correcting the most important cells first.

Working cell by cell on the road with a tuner riding shotgun with the laptop and a driver with one foot on the gas and one foot on the brake (hopefully on a deserted country road or test track) working to achieve target rpm and engine loadings (or, even better, using a load-holding engine- or chassis-dyno), adjust as many cells as you can reach in the VE table to bring the actual values in the target air/fuel table back to the identical target 12.8:1 (or 13.2) air/fuel ratio. The trick is to work methodically, staying away from sudden acceleration, stabilizing the vehicle at the various breakpoints before moving to the next.

Keep in mind that the trick is changing not just one cell, but smoothing in the surrounding cells to form a smooth slope or graph. If you do not change surrounding cells along with the target cell, you will probably not see the full magnitude of changes reflected in actual injection pulse width, since the EMS will average out sharp peaks and valleys. So change one breakpoint a modest amount, then switch over to graph mode and pull the surrounding cells up or down as required to make a smooth slope. If this is not enough, do another iteration. What will not work well is to yank one cell to ridiculous heights before getting around to other nearby cells.

On some systems you can datalog the actual air/fuel ratios as you drive the vehicle through the range of speeds and loading and have the system tell you the pulse width required to achieve entries in the target ratio table—or even do the actual pulse width compensation. Using datalogging this way can be efficient because a relatively quick test run can be made to encounter many cells in the air/fuel or VE table, which can then be fixed following the run, offline if you like. If is also safer, because a brief foray into each cell is enough, with no requirement to linger in high-power cells while you make sense of what is going on and modify the VE or injection pulse width. However you do it, work your way through the table, adjusting VE to bring the actual air/fuel ratio values in the fuel table back to 12.8:1 (or 13.2:1 if narrowband).

Note: Some highly sophisticated EMSs do not use a special VE table. Instead, they use VE-type tables of pulse width and timing advance data to manage the engine. You will have to optimize each entry for best power, efficiency, or lowest emissions. Even if you do have a VE table, once the VE table is built you'll need to optimize the target air/fuel ratio table, since on a modified engine, it is difficult or impossible to predict in advance what the optimal air/fuel ratios will be. For that, the trick is to use a load-holding dynamometer, which will then enable you to optimize spark advance when fuel delivery is optimal.

high boost to make corrections, and when an acceleration run is over, it is very difficult to figure out what was happening when without a datalog.

Normally aspirated street powerplants seldom generate enough thermal and mechanical loading to hurt themselves with poor tuning unless the compression ratio is very high and you are running the vehicle at top speed and wide-open throttle for a long time. Not so with boosted powerplants at higher loading, when small mistakes can damage the engine catastrophically.

Incorrect spark timing and lean fuel mixtures can induce immediate severe knock that can, in turn, overheat the combustion chamber and result in uncontrolled pre-ignition. Boosted and nitrous-injected engines can break ring lands within seconds if the engine knocks due to incorrect calibration parameters (and will break the apex seals on a rotary engine like the RX-7 *immediately*. As they say, a rotary engine will knock once, and then be broken).

But there is more to think about than the fuel and ignition maps. It will not help to get the timing and pulse width perfect if required fuel exceeds the capacity of the fuel supply system such that fuel rail pressure drops, or if the pulse width required to get a certain weight of fuel in the cylinders exceeds available time for injection at higher rpm and the injectors go static (constantly open).

NITROUS INJECTION

Nitrous is a special case, and nitrous tuning is both easier and more difficult than other types of calibration. Of course, no one should ever begin nitrous tuning until normally aspirated tuning is perfect. On one hand, nitrous is eminently capable of causing catastrophic engine damage when air/fuel mixtures or timing are wrong. Nitrous injection can torch valves in seconds or less, crack pistons, and break rods or even crankshafts.

On the other hand, nitrous is so dangerous that nitrous system manufacturers these days virtually always sell fail-safe cookbook nitrous solutions that require zero tuning and are virtually incapable of damaging the engine if installed correctly (though they require a stock-quality nonboosted calibration and adequate fuel supply). Bottom line: If you do not have experience calibrating engine management systems, do not attempt to learn on a boosted or nitrous motor. Boosted and nitrous motors absolutely cannot be safely tuned with trial-and-error methods; it's simply too dangerous.

THINGS FALL APART

If you are exploring strange new worlds with your tuning project, pushing mechanical and thermal limits that are unknown and difficult to predict, things can and will break. Ask yourself if you have the financial resources to deal with engine damage. If your resources are severely limited, get help from an expert to compute what is a highly safe state of tune for various critical parts, and do not go beyond it for any reason.

If you cannot afford engine damage, it is worth considering that more expensive engine management systems usually offer improved logic, capabilities, and alarms that make it safer to push the limits. An example of this would be the ability of an engine management system to receive, process, and take action based on data from exhaust gas temperature (EGT) probes—one of the most reliable early warning signs of impending engine damage from lean mixture thermal loading. A computer can push back the throttle or institute other countermeasures faster than a human can react to prevent damage.

If you do not have much tuning experience, you may be able to benefit from self-tuning ECUs.

VIRTUAL CARBURETORS

Some old-timers and bike tuners have a lot of experience tuning carbureted engines, and they know a lot about how people tuned engines before there were fast exhaust gas analyzers, wideband air/fuel-ratio meters, or affordable chassis dynos. This can be dangerous. It is certainly true that a good basic knowledge of how and why engines take fuel and spark timing at various speed and loading ranges is important. It is also true a lot of carbureted engines weren't operating at a very accurate and high state of tune. The mixture distribution between cylinders was often terrible, with some single carb cylinders running much leaner than others and tuning efforts directed toward making sure the leanest cylinders were running safely rich. Many hot rodders did not ever attempt to change the spark advance curve of mechanical timing systems, only adjusting basic static timing.

What's more, the specific power (horsepower per cubic inch) of muscle car-era performance engines was vastly less than recent sport-compact turbo engines, and even the gross horsepower was often less. There are plenty of 1.8-liter turbocharged Hondas making more horsepower than a 1970 426 street Hemi.

Not only were older engines stressed less than today's super-high-output powerplants, but—fortunately or unfortunately— points, ignitions, and carburetors manufactured for specific engines were, practically speaking, limited in their adjustments. Most people would adjust idle-air-screws to set air/fuel mixture at idle, and they might swap main jets around a little to tune for best acceleration near wide-open throttle, but they were less likely to make radical changes to basic components like venturis that greatly affect midrange air/fuel ratios. Where they made changes, these were likely to be incremental, in ways that affected one particular area of the timing or fuel curve and that left alone the basic shape or slope of a fuel or timing curve.

There were never many carbureted turbo motors (for really good reasons), and without the requirement to deal with boosted engines, hot rodders tended to follow a cookbook approach to performance tuning for specific normally aspirated performance engines. For, example, "a stock compression 350 Chevy motor with a Com Cams x_1 grind, x_2-inch tube headers, and a Holley x_3 carb needs Holley x_4 main jets, x_5 power valve, with the accelerator pump rod in the x_6 position, and you need x_7 centrifugal advance springs in your distributor and x_8-degrees total timing."

Jet-swapping is smelly, time-consuming, and costs actual cash-money for the precisely machined jets (unlike key strokes on a computer, which are free), so tuners were less likely to make the kinds of radical changes that would completely screw up

fuel delivery. Bottom line, in the old days it took real work and money to royally screw up physical engine management systems, so it didn't happen as much as it does today when computers have greatly increased the efficiency with which people can deliver a poor calibration with electronic management systems.

One trend in engine management modifications is what I like to call the "virtual carburetor," that is, modifying a stock engine management system for a power-adder conversions to fix bad OEM behavior with a potentiometer-equipped electronic interceptor box that gives a tuner the semi-automated option of tuning selected subsets of the fuel and timing curves by turning a knob—and without the challenge of building a scratch calibration equal to the factory's. Companies like Dobeck Performance do a great job of providing the ability to make incremental changes targeted at specific areas of injection and timing, keeping it simple, and protecting people from themselves—just like in the old days.

HOW TO HIRE SOMEONE ELSE TO DO THE CALIBRATION/TUNING

Many performance shops pride themselves on their engine management problem-solving abilities. They love it when they get a chance to be heroes, fixing a problem created by a customer or (even better) a competing performance shop, especially if it involves selling expensive new parts or equipment. "We'll have to change out the Framajigger for a Whatsahoosits; a Framajigger isn't worth a damn and could never work on your 1912 John Deere Super-60-powered trike. Squirrel Performance should never have installed it, but since they're under 60 counts of fraud and a death sentence for incompetence, you get what you pay for."

Some performance tuners are very good at looking you in the eye and conveying absolute certainty about their ability to achieve low-earth-orbit with a 1912 John-Deere-powered trike, even if they aren't actually sure what one is. Many performance shops have a very hard time turning down targets of opportunity that are outside their ordinary specialization and expertise.

The deadly combination of pride and greed can lead to shops taking on tuning projects that, by definition, require on-the-job training or dusting off old expertise on systems they haven't seen in a long time. Some shops welcome the chance to get paid to learn a new engine management system—which could result in unnecessary parts and equipment changes. The worst outcome would be if a shop damaged your engine or vehicle working on a system with a steep learning curve.

The following are some rules of thumb that can help you to avoid this sort of heartache:

- I would not use a tuning shop that lacked extensive experience with your specific engine management system. Preferably, they should be a dealer.
- Unless the tuner is a wizard who I know to be a wizard, I would probably want references from customers. Previous customers can verify satisfaction with a tuner's technical expertise, and customers will also have opinions about support capabilities, financial policies, and fairness.
- I would not normally use a tuning shop for engine management calibration that did not have its own in-house chassis dynamometer. Under exceptional circumstance, this rule might be modified if a tuner had a close working arrangement with a dyno shop that did have a dynamometer. Yes, it is possible to do a good tuning job with a strap-on (no, not that kind of strap-on!) accelerometer-type wideband air/fuel-ratio data. However, I am more comfortable with a shop that has made the

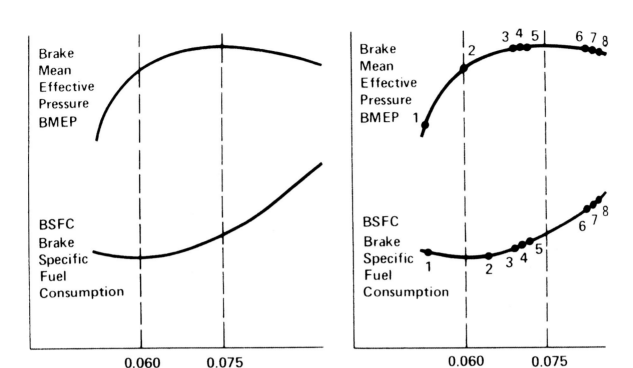

Another way to look at the calibration task is through the lens of peak break mean effective cylinder pressure (BMEP) and brake specific fuel consumption (BSFC), which do not occur at the same air/fuel ratio. In an engine operating with perfect distribution, for best power, a fuel-air ratio of 0.075–0.080 produces the lowest fuel consumption. For best fuel economy, a fuel-air ratio of 0.060 is optimal, though produces less power. The right graph charts the fact that single-point (carb or TBI) wet manifolds produce suboptimal fuel distribution. Cylinders 6, 7, and 8 are too rich, producing less power and wasting fuel. Cylinders 1 and 2 are too lean. To prevent detonation in 1 and 2, all would have to be enriched to bring 1 and 2 to the flat part of the curve, meaning only 1 and 2 would produce peak power with minimal fuel consumption for that output. *Holley*

investment in a $20,000-plus dynamometer than one that has not. What's more, a shop that owns the dyno does not have to buy dyno time, so you're likely to get more extensive dyno tuning and probably a better calibration than a situation where your tuner himself is on the clock.

- Possession of an engine dyno (for example, a Superflow) torque cell is a leading indicator of great seriousness. You can drive a car onto a chassis dyno and rip off a pull or two in a few minutes; an engine dyno is more complicated. Hooking up to one was easier in the days of carbureted distributor-ignition engines but attaching a fuel-injected powerplant to an engine dyno and connecting or fabricating everything it takes to make it work outside the engine bay of a car typically takes hours. However, when they calibrate engines in Detroit or Munich or Japan or wherever, they start with water-brake or eddy-current engine dynos that enable engineers to hold the engine as long as necessary at any precise combination of speed and loading (including combinations not achievable at sea level on the road with street tires) to set best torque at precisely the perfect air/fuel ratio.

- A tuner with a lot of experience is, of course, extremely desirable: How many scratch calibrations has he done? Assuming he has a dyno, how many dynoruns or pulls does he have in his archives? And how many of these involved calibrating an EMS on the dyno (there should be many dyno pulls in such a case). Ask to see the run notes associated with dynoruns. Does he keep good, scientific documentation of the tuning progress? Does he keep records as equipment and settings change

(possession of such can be very useful in the future on a similar vehicle)? Lots of calibration dyno runs on either an engine or chassis dyno, and lots of good anal-retentive documentation are very good signs. I do want to add that I know some excellent supertuners who do not keep very good documentation; in part, because they are so confident and experienced that they don't need it as much anymore. However, many shops with Dynojet chassis dynos are beginning to do a better job of documenting tuning sessions than they did at first.

- Desirable additional diagnostic equipment for a tuner should include fast, wideband air/fuel-ratio meters (for example, a Horiba), exhaust gas analyzers, OBD-II diagnostic analyzers, oscilloscopes, and so forth. I absolutely would not consider using a tuner who lacked a Horiba, Motec meter, or similar.

- How long has he been in business? The longer, the better. Not only is this an indication of experience, it is an indication of someone who knows how to run a successful business, and tuners that go out of business can't offer good product support.

- Is the owner still doing the heavy lifting on calibrations? What other responsibilities does he have? Engine calibrations can be risky, so most tuner-owners let their grease monkeys handle the installations and take care of the tricky stuff on the dyno themselves. I personally think an owner-tuner is preferable to an employee working on your calibration.

- A history of racing indicates a tuner has—or used to have—some money. Winning experience indicates he knows what he's doing, is careful and scientific, and has (or

EMS TUNING

185

76	49	49	51	60	67	70	70	71	71	73	77	96	102	102	102
50	49	49	51	60	67	70	70	71	71	73	77	90	96	96	96
25	49	49	51	60	67	70	70	71	71	73	77	85	89	89	89

used to have) some money. Someone who calibrates race cars that win can tune my engine any time.

- Have there been many articles about the shop or the owner in various performance car magazines? This can be a good thing, but there are plenty of articles these days that magazine people refer to internally as "advertorial," an unhappy compounding of the words advertising and editorial. Sometimes such articles are also called blow-job stories, particularly when they are puff-pieces about advertisers. Most good tuners and performance-equipment suppliers who want magazine PR know how to get it, and it's out there. Many technical articles about tuners and shops are honest and fairly complete. But some articles may not tell the whole story, especially about advertisers. And there are articles out there about people who have more expertise with how to get PR than they do with calibrating engines. Magazine PR is not proof that the tuner is someone you want working on your car!

WHAT IF A PRO TUNER BREAKS YOUR ENGINE?

I interviewed several tuners on this question.

Calibrating somewhat super-high-output engines is inherently risky, and when you are doing an R&D engine project, pushing the limits of strange new worlds, experimenting to find out how much power is possible or how much torque engine components can stand, something may break and this is really not the fault of the tuner. You wanted more power, and neither you nor he knew for sure the mechanical or thermal limits of critical parts. You are basically hiring the tuner to do the job to the best of his ability, and you should understand that you may have to replace some parts in an R&D effort. That's why it's called R&D.

A tuner is not responsible if mechanical parts on your vehicle break, unless he breaks parts through negligence by over-boosting or over-revving the engine. Broken rods or pistons, blown head gaskets, or other damage unrelated to tuning are not the fault of the tuner.

On the other hand, a professional tuner is expected to have a high degree of expertise, and not to destroy parts and equipment through negligence or carelessness. According to Dallas supertuner Bob Norwood, a professional performance tuner should never hurt your engine with lean mixtures or wrong ignition timing. A pro tuner should not detonate your engine.

But.

In the real world, a tuner is unlikely to have insurance that would cover engine damage from R&D or any other reason. The personal resources of the tuner are usually limited. If a tuner destroys your high-dollar engine through negligence, he might be unable to fix it for free even if he is so inclined. Discuss this issue ahead of time and come to an agreement. If it would be catastrophic if your engine breaks, make sure the tuner understands this. A tuner might work differently—more carefully, farther from the ragged edge—if it is essential to avoid damage versus if the highest priority were to search for the absolute limits of deliverable maximum power.

The bottom line is that the reason factory vehicles often have the capability to be hot rodded to higher power levels is that automakers must warrant them and therefore always design them to run at power levels a conservatively safe distance from mechanical and thermal damage. Actually, in the distant past, back in the 1960s, there were a few vehicles sold by automakers for street or track use without warranty for racing use with radical hairy engines like Chrysler's 426-ci Race Hemi, Ford's SOHC Cammer 427, and a few others. Today, all streetable vehicles have to pass emissions and have warranties, and no one sells them without a warranty.

Basically, if something breaks on the dyno while tuning and it is clearly the tuner's fault through egregious negligence, the tuner may want to fix it to protect his reputation. If this happened essentially through dishonesty or fraud (he sold you junk that was bound to break or to break the engine in your application), you could sue him, and maybe you'd win. And if you won, maybe there'd be something to take. But those are big ifs.

The best insurance is to find a good, experienced tuner with a good reputation, tools, and financial resources. Pay his high prices and expect him to do his best for you.

And if something goes wrong that is beyond his and your control, tell yourself, "That's racing."

ENGINE TUNING THEORY

To tune an engine effectively, you will need to understand the theory of volumetric efficiency, burn rate, spark advance, air/fuel ratios, temperature, air-pressure, detonation, and fuels.

Volumetric Efficiency and Engine Fuel Requirements

A piston engine is, in a sense, a self-propelled air pump that breathes in a quantity of air through the throttle related to the displacement of the engine, and exhales nitrogen and combustion products through the exhaust. But even at wide-open throttle (WOT), the amount of air that enters a spark-ignition piston engine can vary considerably. There are many factors that affect how much air actually enters the engine's cylinders under various operating conditions, but inducted air is almost always less than the static displacement of the engine except in the case of highly optimized performance engines utilizing resonation-effects tuned intake and exhaust systems, or on turbo or supercharged engines, which may easily operate at 100 percent or more of static displacement. The efficiency with which an engine fills its cylinders is known as the volumetric efficiency or VE.

Torque is the instantaneous twisting force an internal-combustion engine is able to impart to the crankshaft, averaged over the combustion cycle by the mass of a flywheel. Over time, torque can be used to do work such as accelerating a car or pushing through the air at high speed. On a well-tuned engine, peak torque occurs at the engine speed and loading at which an engine (with power-adders, if present) is most efficient at ingesting air into the cylinders. Therefore, peak torque is also peak VE. Peak torque requires the largest amount of fuel per combustion cycle, hence, the longest injection pulse width. Even though engine breathing is less efficient at speeds above peak torque such that each "putt" is less powerful, more combustion events are occurring per time, so most engines will make peak horsepower at a faster speed than peak torque. Due to the definition of power as a function of Torque/5,250, power and torque are always the same at 5,250 rpm. A properly tuned engine will always use the most fuel per time at peak power.

Engineers strive to design modern naturally aspirated street engines to have as high a VE as possible across the range of engine operating speeds. One hundred percent VE is the amount of air that would be in the cylinder of an engine at bottom dead center at rest, minus the combustion chamber clearance volume (the displacement of the engine). It is extremely difficult to achieve 100 percent VE when the engine is running, because it takes a

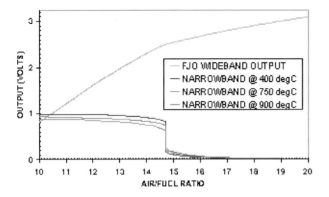

A wideband or UEGO is not the same as any old O₂ sensor, heated or not. Standard O₂ sensors—heated or not—have little ability to distinguish changes to air/fuel ratio except as a rich-lean indicator very near 14.68:1, the stoichiometric air/fuel ratio. What's more, the temperature of the standard-type sensor away from stoich has an effect on the voltage output that is greater than the effect of large air/fuel ratio changes. Standard sensors are useless for power tuning and should be left to do their work to produce low emissions at idle and light cruise.

certain amount of time for air to rush into the cylinders, and there is a limited amount of time (eight or nine thousandths of a second at 7,000 rpm). And there are restrictions in the way.

A number of factors conspire to limit the pumping efficiency of a piston engine. There is normally at least a slight pressure drop through a throttle even when wide open, particularly if the engine is carbureted due to the need for a restrictive venturi that sucks fuel into the air. All throttles restrict airflow, producing a pressure drop when the throttle blade is partially closed (which is the whole idea). Intake ports and valves offer at least some restriction at some engine speeds. The exhaust stroke cannot expel all burned gases and some exhaust remains in the clearance volume to dilute incoming fresh charge. The exhaust valves and exhaust pipes offer some restriction as well. The camshaft profile of an engine has a huge effect on the VE of an engine at various speeds and loading, generally with inevitable tradeoffs between high- and low-speed torque. The bottom line is that most street piston engines cannot achieve anything like 100 percent VE, settling instead for 70 to 90 percent.

If a normally aspirated engine had a perfectly flat torque curve across the rpm range, injection pulse width would not vary at all with engine speed, but would be a function only of engine loading. If VE is entirely independent of engine speed, then the amount of air entering a cylinder on the intake stroke will depend entirely on the amount of air pressure in the intake manifold, hence, injection pulse width is a linear function varying precisely with the voltage from a manifold absolute pressure sensor, with peak VE and torque occurring at the highest achievable manifold pressure. Since many modern street engines do have a relatively flat torque curve, a calibration in which pulse width varies in a linear fashion from 0 milliseconds at 0 kPa manifold pressure to a maximum-power pulse at full achievable manifold pressure is a good approximation of an ideal steady-state air/fuel table optimized for peak power.

Given the varying VE of an engine, the amount of air in a cylinder at any given speed-density breakpoint is not perfectly predictable. Again, you can assume that the maximum VE occurs at the point of peak torque. This will be the point of maximum injection pulse width, with pulse width falling off both below and above this unless significant fuel is being used for combustion cooling at peak horsepower. Maximum power will usually occur at a higher rpm than peak torque, at which point the engine is making more power strokes per time increment that are less efficient than they are at peak torque and will therefore normally require less fuel to be injected per power stroke.

In some cases, engine torque and VE vary considerably with rpm. Naturally aspirated engines optimized to run efficiently at very high speed with resonation-effects intake runner and exhaust tuning at the expense of very weak low-rpm torque capabilities are a good example. Some engines with tuned intake and exhaust systems have achieved as much as 10-psi positive pressure at the intake valve from inertial and resonation effects. Another example of varying VE is turbocharged engines optimized for high-speed operation that cannot boost at low rpm.

Even if the torque curve is not flat, given the relatively broad range of air/fuel mixtures at which an engine will still produce peak torque or near-peak torque, a straight-line approximation of injection pulse width from minimum to maximum may still produce relatively good performance even with no VE corrections. Most production engines, including high-output DOHC engines, can be made to run acceptably well with no volumetric efficiency table offsets to the raw fuel curve, even when fitted with individual throttles on each cylinder.

As an engine wears out, its VE decreases, but this may not occur evenly across all rpm and load ranges or even between the various cylinders. The newest OE factory engines vary less than 1.5 percent in power from spec, but historically, factory-built engines have varied greatly in VE due to significant variations in cam lobe profiles and other machining, with perhaps 5 percent very fast (high VE), 15 percent very slow, and the rest somewhere in the middle.

If the load-measuring device for an engine management system is a mass airflow (MAF) sensor with output highly dependent on engine speed, then the basic fuel calculation is MAF voltage divided by engine rpm. Note that MAF-based fuel calculations require no temperature correction for air density, since the MAF reading already reflects the effect of air density on mass flow into the engine.

Flame Speed

Normal combustion in a spark-ignition engine occurs after the spark plug ignites the compressed air/fuel mixture, starting a flame front that spreads out in a wave from the plug in all directions, something like dry grass burning in a field, only in three dimensions. It takes time for the flame to spread in the air/fuel mixture, exactly as it takes time for a fire in a field of dry grass to burn away from where it began. During normal combustion, the flame front in a combustion chamber moves across the chamber until it reaches the other side, burning smoothly and evenly.

Special cameras recording the combustion event through a porthole in a cylinder reveal that flame-front speeds for gasoline-air mixtures vary from 20 feet per second to more than 150 feet per second, depending on air/fuel ratio, density, compression ratio, turbulence among the charge gases, and combustion chamber design. Flame speed is fastest at rich mixtures near 0.75 lambda (11.1:1 air/fuel ratio on gasoline), falling off dramatically in both the rich and lean directions from this point (especially in the rich direction). The slower the flame front speed, the greater the chance of abnormal combustion.

187

176	49	49	51	60	67	70	70	71	71	73	77	96	102	102	102
150	49	49	51	60	67	70	70	71	71	73	77	90	96	96	96
125	49	49	51	60	67	70	70	71	71	73	77	85	89	89	89

Lambda Table

Load\RPM	0	500	1000	1500	2000	2500	3000	3500	4000	4500	5000	5500	6000	6500	7000	7500	8000	8500	9000
333	0.85	0.85	0.85	0.85	0.85	0.85	0.85	0.85	0.85	0.85	0.85	0.85	0.85	0.85	0.85	0.85	0.85	0.85	0.85
300	0.85	0.85	0.85	0.85	0.85	0.85	0.85	0.85	0.85	0.85	0.85	0.85	0.85	0.85	0.85	0.85	0.85	0.85	0.85
267	0.86	0.86	0.86	0.86	0.86	0.86	0.86	0.86	0.86	0.86	0.86	0.86	0.86	0.86	0.86	0.86	0.86	0.86	0.86
233	0.87	0.87	0.87	0.87	0.87	0.87	0.87	0.87	0.87	0.87	0.87	0.87	0.87	0.87	0.87	0.87	0.87	0.87	0.87
200	0.88	0.88	0.88	0.88	0.88	0.88	0.88	0.88	0.88	0.88	0.88	0.88	0.88	0.88	0.88	0.88	0.88	0.88	0.88
167	0.88	0.88	0.88	0.88	0.88	0.88	0.88	0.88	0.88	0.88	0.88	0.88	0.88	0.88	0.88	0.88	0.88	0.88	0.88
133	0.9	0.9	0.9	0.9	0.9	0.9	0.9	0.9	0.9	0.9	0.9	0.9	0.9	0.9	0.9	0.9	0.9	0.9	0.9
100	0.9	0.9	0.9	0.9	0.9	0.9	0.9	0.9	0.9	0.9	0.9	0.9	0.9	0.9	0.9	0.9	0.9	0.9	0.9
67	0.9	0.9	0.9	0.9	0.9	0.9	0.9	0.9	0.9	0.9	0.9	0.9	0.9	0.9	0.9	0.9	0.9	0.9	0.9
33	0.9	0.9	0.9	0.9	0.9	0.9	0.9	0.9	0.9	0.9	0.9	0.9	0.9	0.9	0.9	0.9	0.9	0.9	0.9
0	0.9	0.9	0.9	0.9	0.9	0.9	0.9	0.9	0.9	0.9	0.9	0.9	0.9	0.9	0.9	0.9	0.9	0.9	0.9

High-compression engines make more power because they are more efficient at getting energy from the air/fuel charge mixture. Normally, combustion pressure rise is 3.5 to 4 times the initial compression pressure. The difference in pressure gain in an 8.5:1 compression engine versus a 10:1 compression engine can easily be 50 percent, as much as 250 psi. A typical 160-psi compression pressure rises quickly to over 600 psi following combustion. Pressure rise rates can exceed 20 psi per degree of crankshaft rotation. Cylinder pressures are highest at wide-open throttle and are lowest at idle and light cruise, when intake manifold vacuum is very high and engine VE very low. Combustion proceeds faster under higher compression.

Engineers carefully design turbulence into combustion chambers. Some swirl will produce greater flame speed, more efficient combustion, and even help resist knock by spreading the flame front more quickly. Too much swirl will produce undesirable disturbance of the quench layer around the combustion chamber, increasing heat loss into the cylinder walls.

The actual performance of fuel in an engine is closely related to the release of energy in the combustion process. This is affected by dissociation of the reactants and products of combustion (splitting of molecules into smaller molecules or single atoms or ions), and heat transfer through the combustion chamber. Increased heat in the combustion chamber makes power, but heat can also cause detonation. At wide-open throttle at high speed, heat transfer amounts for about 15 percent of the fuel's thermal energy. This heat loss decreases with increased brake mean effective pressure in the cylinder. The heat transfer is maximized at stoichiometric air/fuel ratios, decreasing with the higher fuel flow rates of rich mixtures. Heat transfer into the block and water jacket also depends on gas turbulence near the combustion chamber surfaces, and it increases with knock and other violent combustion conditions.

Given that engines induct a fairly constant mass of air for a given speed, manifold pressure, camshaft timing, and intake temperature, the need to improve the horsepower of spark-ignition engines for racing has led to two main strategies in an effort to increase the amount of fuel that can be burned in the combustion chamber. The first involves increasing the mass of oxygen intake by supercharging or supplementary oxygen injection, mostly in the form of nitrous oxide. The second involves burning fuels with higher energy yield per air mass, i.e., fuels that burn with less oxygen.

In addition to engine's octane number requirement (ONR) to avoid detonation, high-performance engines have other performance requirements for fuels, including volatility, flame speed, weight, and volume.

Spark Advance

Spark advance, which is optimally timed to achieve best torque by producing peak cylinder pressure at around 15 degrees ATDC, increases octane requirements by a half to three-quarters of an octane number per degree of advance. Spark advance increases cylinder pressure and allows more time for detonation to occur.

Engine speed range and fuel burn characteristics affect ignition timing requirements. As an engine turns faster, the spark plug must fire at an earlier crank position to allow time for a given air/fuel mixture to ignite and achieve a high burn rate and maximum cylinder pressure by the time the piston is positioned to produce best torque. This is dependent not only on engine speed but on mixture flame speed, which, in turn, is dependent not only on the type of fuel but on operating conditions that change dynamically, such as air/fuel mixture.

Therefore, an independent variable affecting the need for spark advance as rpm increases is the need to modify ignition timing corresponding to engine loading and consequent volumetric efficiency variations, which demand varying mixtures. Throttle position, for example, affects cylinder filling, resulting in corresponding variations in optimal air/fuel mixture requirements.

An important factor that affects VE—and potentially flame speed—is valve timing. Remember, a denser mixture burns more quickly, and a leaner mixture requires more time to burn. Valve timing has a great effect on the speeds at which an engine develops its best power and torque. Adding more lift and intake/exhaust valve overlap allows the engine to breathe more efficiently at high speeds. However, the engine may be hard to start, idle badly, bog on off-idle acceleration, and produce bad low speed torque. This occurs for several reasons. Increased valve overlap allows some exhaust gases still in the cylinder at higher than atmospheric pressure to rush into the intake manifold exactly like EGR, diluting the inlet charge—which continues to occur until rpm increases to the point where the overlap interval is so short that reverse pulsing is insignificant. But big cams result in gross exhaust gas dilution of the air/fuel mixture at idle, which consequently burns slowly and requires a lot of spark advance and a mixture as rich as 11.5 to 1 to counteract the lumpy uneven idle resulting from partial burning and misfires on some cycles. Valve overlap also hurts idle and low-speed performance by lowering manifold vacuum. Since the lower atmospheric pressure of high vacuum tends to keep fuel vaporized better, racing cams with low vacuum may have distribution problems and a wandering air/fuel mixture at idle, which may require an overall richer mixture in order to keep the motor from stalling, particularly with wet manifolds. Carbureted vehicles with hot cams may not have enough signal available to pull sufficient mixture through

49	49	51	60	67	70	70	71	71	73	77	96	102	102	102	98
49	49	51	60	67	70	70	71	71	73	77	90	96	96	96	98
49	49	51	60	67	70	70	71	71	73	77	85	89	89	89	87

the idle system, leaning out the mixture, requiring a tuner to increase the idle throttle setting (which may put the off-idle slot/port in the wrong position, causing an off-idle bog). Obviously, this is not a problem with fuel injection.

Short-cam engines may run at stoichiometric mixtures at idle for cleanest exhaust emissions. Beginning with the Acura NSX, some high-performance engines began to make use of a dual-mode cam profile, in which one set of cam lobes is used for low speed conditions and another for high rpm.

Coming off idle, a big-cam engine may require mixtures nearly as rich as at idle to eliminate surging, starting at 12.5–13.0 gasoline air/fuel mixtures and leaning out with speed or loading. Mild cams will permit 14.0–15.0 gasoline mixtures in off-idle and slow cruise.

With medium speeds and loading, the bad effects of big cams diminish, resulting in less charge dilution, allowing the engine to happily burn gasoline mixtures of 14 to 15:1 and higher. At the leaner end, additional spark advance is required to counteract the slower flame speed of lean mixtures. Hot cams may produce problems for carbureted vehicles when changed engine vacuum causes the power valve to open at the wrong time. Changed vacuum will affect speed-density fuel-injection systems but have no effect on MAF-sensed EFI. Where air/fuel mixtures are inconsistent or poorly atomized, flammability suffers, affecting many other variables.

With a big cam, the spark advance at full throttle can be aggressive and quick; low VE at low rpm results in slow combustion and exhaust dilution, lowering combustion temperatures and reducing the tendency to knock. Part-throttle advance on big-cam engines can also be aggressive due to these same flame speed reductions resulting from exhaust dilution of the inlet charge due to valve overlap.

Turbulence and swirl are extremely important factors in flame speed—more important, within limits, than mixture strength or exact fuel composition. Automotive engineers have long made use of induction systems and combustion chamber geometry to induce swirl or turbulence to enhance flame speed and, consequently, anti-knock characteristics of an engine. Wedge head engines, with a large squish area, have long been known to induce turbulence or swirl as intake gases are forced out of the squish area when the piston approaches top dead center.

In the 1970s, automotive engineers began to de-tune engines to meet emissions standards that were increasingly tough. They began to retard the ignition timing at idle, for example, sometimes locking out vacuum advance in lower gears or during normal operating temperature, allowing more advance if the engine was cold or overheating. Since oxides of nitrogen are formed when free nitrogen combines with oxygen at high temperature and pressure, retarded spark reduces NOx emissions by lowering peak combustion temperature and pressure. This strategy also reduces hydrocarbon emissions. However, retarded spark combustion is less efficient, causing poorer fuel economy, reduced power, and higher heating of the engine block as heat energy escapes through the cylinder walls into the coolant. The cooling system is stressed as it struggles to remove the greater waste heat during retarded spark conditions, and fuel economy is hurt since some of the fuel is still burning as it blows out the exhaust valve, necessitating richer idle and main jetting to get decent off-idle performance. If the mixture becomes too lean, higher combustion temperatures will defeat the purpose of ignition retard, producing more NOx. Inefficiency of combustion under these conditions also requires the throttle to be held open farther for a reasonable idle speed, which, combined with the higher operating temperatures, can lead to dieseling (not a problem in fuel-injected engines, which immediately cut off fuel flow when the key is switched off). By removing pollutants from exhaust gas, three-way catalysts tend to allow more ignition advance at idle and part throttle. Undesirable products of combustion include formaldehyde, NOx, CO_2, and fragments of hydrocarbons.

In any case, various high-performance fuels vary in burn characteristics, particularly flammability, flame speed, emissions, and so on, which all affect spark timing requirements. Gasoline engines converted to run on propane, natural gas, or alcohol require a different timing curve due to variations in combustion flame speed of the air/fuel mixture.

Air/Fuel Ratios

Air/fuel ratio has a major impact on engine octane number requirement (ONR), increasing octane requirements by +2 per one increase in ratio (say from 9:1 to 10:1). Ideally, air/fuel ratio should vary not only according to loading but also according to the amount of air present in a particular cylinder at a particular time (cylinder VE). Richer air/fuel ratios combat knock by the intercooling effect of the heat of vaporization of liquid fuels and a set of related factors. The volatility of fuels affects not only octane number requirement but drivability in general.

The chemically ideal air/fuel mixture (by weight), at which all air and gasoline are consumed in combustion occurs with 14.68 parts air and 1 part fuel, which is usually rounded to 14.7. This ratio is referred to as stoichiometric. Stoichiometric mixtures vary according to fuel, from nitromethane's 1.7:1, to methanol's 6.45:1, ethanol's 9:1, up to gasoline at 14.7:1 and beyond to natural gas and propane, which are in the range of 15.5–16.5:1. Mixtures with a greater percentage of air than the stoichiometric ratio are called lean mixtures and occur as higher numbers. Richer mixtures, in which there is an excess of fuel, are represented by smaller numbers. Air/fuel ratios are often expressed as a percentage of stoichiometric, usually referred to as lambda. Therefore, the stoichiometric air/fuel ratio is 1.0 lambda; the mean best torque AFR for gasoline (12.2:1) is 0.83 lambda.

At high loading and wide-open throttle, richer mixtures give better power by making sure that all air molecules in the combustion chamber have fuel to burn. At wide-open throttle, where the objective is maximum power, all four-cycle gasoline engines require mixtures that fall between lean and rich best torque, in the 11.5 to 13.3 gasoline range. Since the best torque mixture spread narrows at higher speeds due to the increased importance of high flame speed, a good goal for naturally aspirated engines is 12.0 to 12.5, and richer if fuel is being used for combustion cooling in a turbo/supercharged engine.

Typical mixtures giving best drivability are in the range of 13.0 to 14.5 gasoline-air mixtures, depending on speed and loading. At higher engine speeds, reverse pulsing through a carb in engines with racing cams tends to enrich the mixture as reversion gases pass through the venturi twice. Obviously, this is not a problem with fuel injection.

EFI engines are not susceptible to hot weather percolation, in which fuel boils in the carb in hot weather when a hot engine is shut down, flooding into the manifold. This is somewhat dependent on the distillation curve of the fuel, which varies according to the weather for which it is intended. Hot weather percolation can be aggravated by high vapor pressures produced by fuel boiling in the fuel pump or fuel lines, forcing additional fuel past the float needle. Similarly, vapor lock—produced by

Injection Solutions' datalogging provides a highly sophisticated record of critical engine parameters. The data shown here as a function of time are injection pulse width, air/fuel ratio, spark timing, manifold pressure, and rpm.

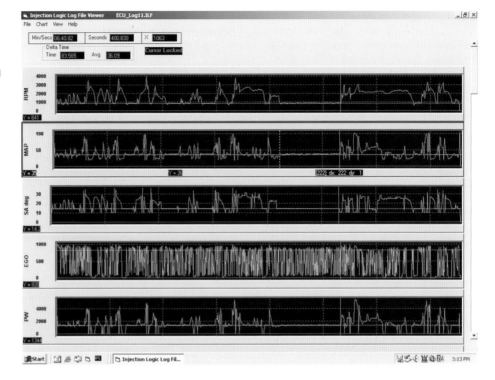

mechanical fuel pumps supplying a mixture of gas and vapor to a carb and eventually uncovering the main jets as fuel level drops—is not usually a problem with EFI, due to increased system pressure increasing the boiling point of fuel.

Computer-controlled engines eliminate compromises in fueling and spark control. Multi-port injection eliminates distribution and inconsistency problems of handling wet mixtures in the intake manifold associated with less than one carb per cylinder, often resulting in improved cold running, improved throttle response under all conditions, and improved fuel economy without drivability problems.

Computer engine management with individual cylinder-adjustable electronic port fuel injection really shines on extremely high-output engines with high effective compression ratios. For peak horsepower, any engine must be treated as a gang of single cylinder engines, each of which should be optimized to deliver peak torque.

On NASCAR engines—until recently restricted to single-point carburetion—this was done by custom modification of the compression ratio, rocker arms, and cam lobes for individual cylinders. But using sequential programmable EFI with fuel and ignition calibration on an individual cylinder basis, whatever the volumetric efficiency of each "single-cylinder engine," optimal timing and mixture can be provided by computer to every cylinder.

Historically, individual cylinder calibration was good for 50 horsepower on a typical high-output small-block Chevy V-8. Not only does individual cylinder calibration improve power, but it saves engines from knock damage while allowing a higher state of tune. By contrast, common practice on street carbureted engines or batch fuel injection is to tune to the leanest cylinder (read best-flowing). A traditional Chevy V-8 with dog-leg ports typically varied 10 percent in airflow between best and worst cylinder, and it was typical that V-type motors responded better than inline motors to individual cylinder calibration. On a dyno, best and worst cylinders that are within 100 degrees EGT of each other is considered excellent. Leaning out an engine on a dyno or track will frequently make more power until one or two cylinders suddenly die from lean mixtures. In the meantime, cylinders with suboptimal VE are running rich. Some advanced engine management systems have implemented EGT-feedback closed-loop systems that equalize EGT from all cylinders at a target level with individual-cylinder calibration, simultaneously providing best power across the board. With this system, every cylinder can reach maximum power at very high compression ratios with the best high-octane gasoline.

Testing by Smoky Yunick for *Circle Track* magazine some years ago showed that the traditional small-block Chevy test engine was prone to detonation on three of the eight cylinders. This was thought to be due to unequal distribution or coolant circulation that caused those cylinders to run hotter. "Now we could have cut these three cylinders to 14:1 compression," wrote Smoky, "and maybe run the other five cylinders at 15:1 and gained some power. Don't know, but I do know this, you are going to get a safer, more powerful engine if you adjust the compression, timing, and distribution to each cylinder."

Temperature

Inlet air temperature increases octane requirement by 0.5 octane number per 10 degree increase. Temperature affects fuel performance in several ways. Colder air is denser than hotter air, raising cylinder pressure. Colder air inhibits fuel vaporization. But hotter air directly raises combustion temperatures, which increases the possibility of knock.

EFI systems normally have sensors to read the temperature of inlet air and adjust the injection pulse width and spark timing to compensate for density changes and fuel volatility limitations. Engines will make noticeably more power on a cold day because the cold, dense air increases engine volumetric efficiency, filling the cylinders with more molecules of air. This is bad news for a carb, which has no way of compensating (other than manual jet

EMS TUNING

190

49	49	51	60	67	70	70	71	71	73	77	96	102	102	102	98
49	49	51	60	67	70	70	71	71	73	77	90	96	96	96	98
49	49	51	60	67	70	70	71	71	73	77	85	89	89	89	87

Characteristic curves.

DFR (dynamic flow range): Variation ratio between minimum and maximum injected fuel quantity at maximum 5% deviation from the linearized flow function. Periodic time $T = 10$ ms.

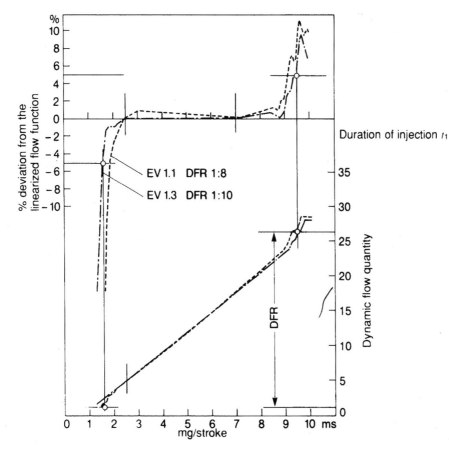

EV 1.1 DFR 1:8
EV 1.3 DFR 1:10

This chart effectively illustrates the performance of Bosch fuel injectors at various pulsewidths. For a workable calibration, it is critical to stay within the range of excellent repeatability for the injectors in use, since the variation ratio between minimum and maximum injected goes beyond the critical 5-percent limit at very short and very long pulse widths. *Bosch*

changes—one size per 40 degrees temperature change). Piston-engine airplane pilots must know the ambient air temperature in order to estimate take-off distance (much longer on hot days), and aircraft fuel systems (including carbureted systems) allow dynamic manual adjustment of air/fuel mixture. As you'd expect, racing automotive engine designs always endeavor to keep inlet air as cold as possible. Even stock street cars often make use of cold-air inlets, since each 11 degrees Fahrenheit increase reduces air density 1 percent.

Cold engines require enrichment to counteract the fact that only the lightest fractions of liquid fuel may vaporize at colder temperatures while the rest exists as globules or drops of fuel that are not mixed well with air. The actual vaporization/distillation curve of various gasolines and fuels differs, depending on the purpose for which the fuel is designed, and gaseous fuels like propane and methane do not require cold running enrichment and have no intercooling effect once in gaseous form. But in a cold engine, most of a liquid fuel like gasoline will be wasted.

Liquid fuels do not vaporize well in cold air, though the oil companies do change their gasoline formulation in an effort to counteract this by increasing the vapor pressure in cold weather (which could lead to a rash of vapor lock in sudden warm spells in winter in the days of carburetors). Choking systems in carbureted vehicles and cold-start fuel enrichment systems on EFI vehicles are designed to produce a rich-enough mixture to run the vehicle even when much of the fuel exists not as burnable vapor, mixed with air, but as droplets of non-burnable liquid fuel suspended in the air or on the manifold walls and combustion chambers. Most air pollution is produced by cold vehicles burning mixtures as rich as 3 or 4:1 (or even 1:1 during cranking). Engine management systems sense coolant temperature in order to provide cold-start enrichments (cold prime, cranking, after start, and warm-up). Electronic injection systems usually spray fuel straight at the intake valve into the swirling turbulent high velocity air that exists there, which greatly improves atomization and vaporization. In general, the higher the pressure of injection, the better, which is why so many OE systems now use gasoline-direct-injection, with pressure in the 2,500-psi range producing excellent shear of fuel droplets for the best quality atomization. EFI does not normally need the exhaust-gas heating that carbs require to provide acceptable warm-up operations, though EFI manifolds may use coolant heating of the manifold to increase vaporization at idle in very cold weather.

Unlike carbs, which are susceptible to fuel starvation if ice forms in the carb as vaporizing fuel removes heat from the air and from metal parts of the carb in cold weather, EFI systems will deliver fuel even if ice forms in the throttle body. In any case, EFI is not as susceptible to icing since fuel vaporizes (stealing

76	49	49	51	60	67	70	70	71	71	73	77	96	102	102	102
50	49	49	51	60	67	70	70	71	71	73	77	90	96	96	96
25	49	49	51	60	67	70	70	71	71	73	77	85	89	89	89

heat) at the hot intake valve, rather than the throttle body. EFI systems require no choke stove to heat inlet air for cold-start driving like carbureted vehicles.

Increases in coolant temperature generally increase octane requirements by roughly one octane number per 10 degree increase from 160 to 180 degrees Fahrenheit.

Air Pressure

Increasing altitude reduces octane number requirements by about 1.5 octane numbers per 1,000 feet above sea level. Supercharging, which provides a denser breathing atmosphere, has the opposite effect—increasing ONR due to the increased density and higher effective compression ratio, as well as the fact that compressors heat intake air, increasing combustion temperature. Air density varies with temperature, altitude, and weather conditions. For a given pressure, hot air, with greater molecular motion, is less dense. Air at higher elevations is less dense, as is air with a higher relative humidity. Air is less dense in warm weather, and air that is heated for any reason on the way into the engine tends to become less dense and thus will affect the weight of fuel required to achieve a correct air/fuel ratio. Intake system layout can have a large effect on the volumetric efficiency of the engine by affecting the density of the air the engine is breathing. Air cleaners that suck in hot engine compartment air will reduce the engine's output and should be modified to breathe fresh, cold air from outside for maximum performance. Intake manifolds that heat the air will produce less dense air, although a properly designed, heated intake manifold will very quickly be cooled by intake air at high speed and will probably improve distribution at part throttle and idle.

Turbos and blowers, which output heated, turbulent air, are known to enhance air/fuel mixing and atomization, particularly if fuel travels through the compressor.

Octane Requirements

A fuel's octane rating represents its ability to resist detonation and preignition. Factors influencing an engine's octane requirements are listed below:

- Effective compression ratio
- Atmospheric pressure
- Absolute humidity
- Air temperature
- Fuel characteristics
- Air/fuel ratio
- Variations in mixture distribution among an engine's cylinders
- Oil characteristics
- Spark timing
- Spark timing advance curve
- Variations in optimal timing between individual cylinders
- Intake manifold temperature
- Head and cylinder coolant temperature
- Condition of coolant and additives
- Type of transmission
- Combustion chamber hot spots.

When an engine knocks or detonates, combustion begins normally with the flame front burning smoothly through the air/fuel mixture. But under some circumstances, as pressure and temperatures rise as combustion proceeds, flame fronts and pressure waves may collide, and remaining end gases explode violently all at once rather than burning evenly. This is detonation, also referred to by mechanics as knock or spark knock. Detonation produces high-pressure shock waves in the combustion chamber that can accelerate wear of an engine or actually cause catastrophic failure. Preignition, also known as surface ignition, is another form of abnormal combustion in which the air/fuel mixture is ignited by something other than the spark plug, including glowing combustion chamber deposits, sharp edges or burrs on the head or block, or an overheated spark-plug electrode. Heavy, prolonged knock can generate hot spots that cause surface ignition, which is the most damaging side-effect of knock. Surface ignition that occurs prior to the plug firing is called preignition, and surface ignition occurring after the plug fires is called post ignition. Preignition causes ignition timing to be lost, and the upward movement of the piston on compression stroke is opposed by the too-early high combustion pressures, resulting in power loss, engine roughness, and severe heating of the piston crown. It can lead to knock or vice versa. Dieseling or run-on on carbureted engine is usually caused by compression ignition of the air/fuel mixture by high temperatures, but can be caused by surface ignition.

Historically, apparently identical vehicles coming off the same assembly line could have octane requirements that vary by as much as 10 octane numbers, though modern engines are built to much more exact standards. The octane number requirement (ONR) for an engine in a particular vehicle is usually established by making a series of wide-open-throttle accelerations at standard spark timing using primary reference fuels with successively lower octane ratings until a fuel is found that produces trace knock.

The single most important internal engine characteristic that requires specific fuel characteristics is compression ratio, which generally increases the ONR +3 to +5 per one ratio increase (in the 8–11:1 compression ratio range). High compression ratios squash the inlet air/fuel mixture into a more compact, dense mass, resulting in a faster burn rate, more heating, less heat loss into the combustion chamber surfaces, and consequent higher cylinder pressure. Turbochargers and superchargers produce effective compression ratios far above the nominal compression ratio by pumping additional mixture into the cylinder under pressure. Either way, the result is increased density of air and fuel molecules that burn faster and produce more pressure against the piston. Another result is an increased tendency for the remaining gases to spontaneously explode as heat and pressure rise.

High peak cylinder pressures and temperatures resulting from high compression can also produce more NOx pollutants. Lower compression ratios raise the fuel requirements at idle because there is more clearance volume in the combustion chamber that dilutes the intake charge. And because fuel continues burning longer as the piston descends, lower compression ratios raise the exhaust temperature and increase stress on the cooling system.

Until 1970, high-performance cars often had compression ratios of up to 11 or 12 to one, easily handled with vintage high octane gasolines readily available in the 98–99 ((R+M)/2) range. By 1972, engines were running compression ratios of 8–8.5:1, with some turbocharged engines running compression in the 6's. In the 1980s and 1990s, compression ratios in computer-controlled fuel injected vehicles were again showing up in the 9.0–11:1 area based on fuel injection's ability to support higher compression ratios without detonation, coupled with the precise air/fuel control and catalysts required to keep emissions low. Race car engines typically run even higher compression ratios. In air-unlimited engines, maximum compression ratios with gasoline run in the 14–17:1 range.

49	49	51	60	67	70	70	71	71	73	77	96	102	102	102	98
49	49	51	60	67	70	70	71	71	73	77	90	96	96	96	98
49	49	51	60	67	70	70	71	71	73	77	85	89	89	89	87

Ratios above 14:1 demand not only extremely high-octane fuel (which might or might not be gasoline), but experienced racers employ countermeasures like uniform coolant temperature around all cylinders, low coolant temperature, and reverse-flow cooling. Extremely high compression ratios require excellent fuel distribution to all cylinders, retarded timing under maximum power, very rich mixtures, and individual cylinder optimization of spark timing, air/fuel ratio, and volumetric efficiency.

BEFORE TUNING

There is simply no way to fully optimize an engine management system without a dynamometer and wideband air/fuel-ratio meter. The combination of target air/fuel ratio tables and closed-loop operations using wideband O_2 and knock sensors can produce good drivability and compensate for funky base maps. But to find 100 percent of the "free" power where you need it and best economy where you want it, you'll need a load-holding dynamometer with wideband air/fuel ratio capabilities. You will no longer be searching for a particular air/fuel ratio, but instead looking for mean or even lean best torque. You may decide to use exhaust gas temperature probes as a safety measure to detect dangerously rising EGT before it is too late. If you do not have a dyno, you will definitely need a good air/fuel ratio readout for tuning. If you are extremely patient and methodical, air/fuel ratio information and an inertial chassis dyno can yield good results. If there is no dyno at all, I'd spend the $140–250 for an accelerometer device like the G-Tech that essentially turns your vehicle into an inertial dyno. If not, it is virtually guaranteed that your map will be suboptimal. To get it really right you need scientific backup. Seat of the pants will not cut it, and do not believe anyone who says otherwise.

However, an engine calibrated exclusively on a dynamometer of almost any kind will almost definitely run sub-optimally rich on the street and track. To produce smooth performance under all conditions, when you are done with a dyno calibration, you'll need to road test and recalibrate to eliminate hesitation, stumbling, and surging in ordinary driving, as well as hunting at idle. An accelerometer device is invaluable for street tuning, as is a wideband readout. But be on the lookout for black exhaust smoke and lazy response, which indicates rich mixtures, or intake backfiring, coughing, and misfiring, which indicates lean mixtures. And always listen for engine-damaging detonation, meaning never tune with the stereo blaring and the air conditioning at full roar.

MAKE SURE YOUR ENGINE IS HEALTHY AND TUNABLE

A performance engine must not burn oil, which will tend to act as a pro-knock agent due to motor oil's octane rating of about 49. The powerplant must have low oil consumption past the piston rings, turbo shaft seals, valve stems, and so on. Obviously, an engine must not be leaking water internally (which will turn oil white), nor should there be excessive scale in the engine cooling jacket.

The motor itself must be mechanically sound, with adequate oil pressure under all circumstances. Most sophisticated engine management systems can monitor oil pressure and sound an alarm and take countermeasures to stop the engine if oil pressure drops dangerously low. There are labs with the ability to analyze used engine oil to check for abnormal metal content and to analyze the source of abnormal metals, which can be very useful in evaluating internal engine health.

If the powerplant is a super-duty engine with power-adders, the pistons should be thermal-coated or cooled with gallery oil-squirters or rods equipped with an oil-spraying orifice angled toward the piston wrist pin that provides a pressurized spray of oil against the undersides of the piston. Or both.

The engine management system and sensors must be working correctly.

The external coolant system must have integrity, with the radiator working efficiently. The fans and shroud must be working efficiently, and if the car is on a stationary chassis dyno, there must be good, powerful fans to route cool air toward the vehicle's own cooling system. Particularly if the engine exhaust is not scavenged to the outdoors, cooling fans in a dyno cell or shop must also be adequate to keep exhaust gases from feeding back into the engine intake, which will reduce the oxygen content of air and increase hydrocarbons and carbon monoxide. Besides killing human brain cells, inadequate ventilation will hurt uncorrected performance by heat-soaking the air (perhaps unevenly in such a way that the dyno's weather station might not compensate correctly for temperature changes, which would produce inaccurate horsepower and torque readings).

ANALYZE COMBUSTION CHAMBERS

A tuner should have a good concept of combustion chamber geometry. The purpose of spark advance is to account for the lag time following spark ignition for combustion pressure to peak at 15-20 degrees after top dead center. Combustion chambers with a large volume, and combustion chambers with a relatively long distance or an obstructed or non-direct pathway from the plug to the farthest "end gases" in the chamber require more time to burn, so more ignition timing advance. The longer the burn, the greater the possibility of remaining unburned gases exploding before normal conclusion of the burn (detonation). Engines with bigger bores and lower effective compression ratios (sum of cranking compression and boost) almost always require more timing advance. Four-valve pentroof combustion chambers tend to be very effective in supporting fast, efficient combustion and resisting detonation. Traditional wedge-head combustion chambers almost always have excellent squish, where charge gases are squished away from certain areas as the rising piston comes into very close proximity with the head in the final stages of the compression stroke, producing combustion chamber turbulence that enhances air/fuel mixing and spreads the flame front faster throughout the chambers.

Engines with combustion-chamber and piston-crown thermal coatings enhance horsepower and speed up combustion by keeping heat in the combustion chamber and out of the engine cooling jacket. Heat makes power by producing higher gas pressure against the pistons. Thermal coatings also resist detonation and pre-ignition by keeping metal hot spots from forming on piston crowns or head chambers.

Not being designed for racing, many street cars—particularly turbocharged cars—are not actually capable of withstanding abnormally lengthy episodes of thermal loading, but thermal coatings can help here. The idea is that even though a really fast sports cars making full boost does not have the ability to sustain continuous full throttle at maximum speed without thermal loading overheating and eventually killing the motor, such a vehicle will reach illegal and dangerous highway speeds long before the engine is damaged.

A car on a load-holding chassis dyno will often reach cooling system and other thermal limits faster than you'd think. A tuner

176	49	49	51	60	67	70	70	71	71	73	77	96	102	102	102
150	49	49	51	60	67	70	70	71	71	73	77	90	96	96	96
125	49	49	51	60	67	70	70	71	71	73	77	85	89	89	89

is wise to know whether or not an engine's combustion chambers have been coated. OEM turbo engines typically use piston-cooling oil squirters to protect the piston crowns from thermal damage, but this strategy does not keep heat from stressing the cooling system and the engine oil, nor does it keep the heat in the combustion chambers to make power (and energetically spool turbochargers).

LIBRARY STARTUP MAPS

Startup maps are basically generic fuel or VE maps designed to approximate actual requirements of a similar engine well enough so the engine can be started and run to be calibrated precisely. When it comes to startup maps, engine displacement is less important than the cam specs, because volumetric efficiency is independent of displacement. In other words, a mild-cammed 350-ci Chevrolet small-block will be closer in fuel requirements to a mild-cammed Chevy 400-ci small-block than two 350s are to each other—if one is mild cammed and the other is wild.

TARGET AIR/FUEL RATIOS, PULSE WIDTH, AND TIMING

Can we provide a handy formula for programming an ECU off-line that will give excellent results for all load-speed combinations immediately upon startup? It is relatively easy to calculate or estimate the volume of a cylinder and therefore the weight of air that enters the cylinder under ideal operating conditions. It is also fairly easy to make a good guess at how long an injector should stay open to spray in an amount of fuel that is a particular fraction of the weight of the air (such as the 14.7:1 stoichiometric or chemically correct air/fuel ratio).

Of course, a complicating factor in designing a fuel curve is that even if you know how much air is entering the cylinders at a given time, it is not necessarily clear what air/fuel mixture is optimal. Most hot rodders want the maximum power possible at wide-open throttle, using the least possible fuel to accomplish this (lean best torque). But under some circumstances, it may be desirable to run at rich best torque (or even richer) in order to design in a safety factor to help prevent detonation with bad gas.

And what about throttle response versus efficiency at part throttle? Are you willing to sacrifice some idle quality for fuel economy or reduced emissions? Does the overlap of your cam dilute the idle mixture so you need a particularly rich mixture for an acceptable idle? These kinds of questions complicate tuning even further.

Additionally, there's the real-world performance of the circuitry that activates the injectors and the physical response of the injectors themselves, which can vary from injector to injector.

Given the complexity of designing a theoretically correct fuel map, most tuners don't even try. If possible, they use a pre-existing map from a similar vehicle or engine. Otherwise, they build a startup map designed purely to be rich enough to get the vehicle running and warmed up. This is made easier by the fact that warmed-up fuel-injected engines will run with mixtures as rich as 6.0:1 or as lean as 22.0:1, and even cold engines are fairly flexible about air/fuel mixtures that will run the motor after a fashion.

With the engine running, ideally on a dyno, tuners adjust the engine at each breakpoint combination of speed and load, and, using test equipment and a mixture trim module, set ignition timing and injection pulse width to achieve low emissions, best torque (lean or rich), or a specific air/fuel mixture—or some combination of all three. Then they road test the vehicle and fine tune it under actual driving conditions, also fine tuning the enrichment maps.

If your ECM has closed-loop capability and is running in a speed-throttle position range in which closed-loop operation is activated, it may be able to tell you what the mixture would have been running open-loop based on what amount of mixture correction was required to achieve a stoichiometric air/fuel mixture. You can then make corrections to the raw fuel map based on this information.

TARGET AIR/FUEL RATIOS

Gasoline, being a stew of hydrocarbons of varying structure, is not a single homogenous molecule that burns with oxygen in a precisely predictable fashion. Nonetheless, given unlimited time for combustion and a perfectly mixed batch of fuel and air, it takes between 14.6 and 14.7 pounds of air to burn a pound of gasoline in a reaction that produces 100 percent water and carbon dioxide (in this ideal reaction, the nitrogen in air is purely along for the ride). So an air/fuel ratio of 14.7:1 is the chemically correct or stoichiometric ratio, sometimes abbreviated by the Greek letter lambda, as in lambda of 1.0. For example, lambda of 0.9 translates as 0.9 x 14.7, or 13.23 air/fuel ratio.

In reality, in a high-speed piston engine, there is limited time for combustion, the air and fuel are not perfectly mixed, and tiny amounts of nitrogen will be burned by hot combustion temperatures and pressures. And inevitably some gasoline molecules will not be burned and some oxygen will not find any fuel to burn. Best power always occurs when there is at least a small fuel surplus above stoichiometric because air (oxygen) is the scarce commodity in spark-ignition piston engines. The best power strategy is therefore always to make sure there is enough fuel available so that virtually every molecule of oxygen finding its way into the engine will be able to burn fuel. The best economy strategy is to make sure there is a small oxygen surplus so that every bit of fuel will get burned. The best emissions strategy is complicated by the fact that lowest hydrocarbon (HC) emissions occur, as you'd expect, with an air surplus, but such lean mixtures produce hotter combustion, which burns more nitrogen and increases oxides of nitrogen, known as NOx. The best overall emissions strategy, therefore, turns out to be to target 1.0 lambda, the stoichiometric ratio, which does not minimize either HC or NOx, but minimizes the sum of both.

Let's first consider target air/fuel ratios for steady-state operation, when an engine is operating continuously at a particular speed and power output and the various engine fuel, air, and cooling systems have reached equilibrium.

Assuming the engine is not knock-limited and therefore does not require additional surplus fuel to cool combustion via heat-of-vaporization effects, for best torque with optimal fuel economy at wide-open throttle, aim for a 12.5:1 air/fuel ratio midway between lean and mean best torque (12.8–12.2 air/fuel ratio). If you're willing to sacrifice a little torque, mixtures as lean as 0.92 lambda (13.5:1) on mild street engines that are not turbocharged will produce excellent peak-power fuel economy at the cost of about 4 percent power. Bob Norwood typically "safes" up a calibration by removing 2–3 percent timing and adding the same percentage of fuel.

On turbocharged or other boosted powerplants that are knock limited, at a very minimum you are aiming for mean best torque of 0.82 lambda (12.2 air/fuel ratio), if not rich best torque of 0.8 lambda (11.76 air/fuel ratio. This has the side benefit at very high speed of increasing flame speed (which increases all the way to 0.75 lambda, at which point a healthy flame front will move

49	49	51	60	67	70	70	71	71	73	77	96	102	102	102	98
49	49	51	60	67	70	70	71	71	73	77	90	96	96	96	98
49	49	51	60	67	70	70	71	71	73	77	85	89	89	89	87

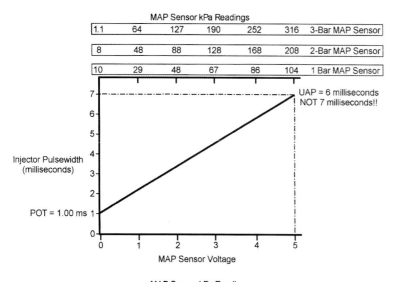

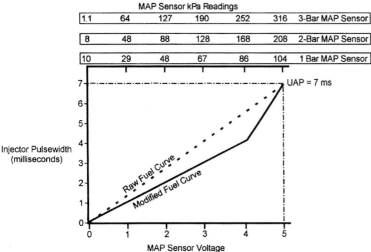

The scope of fuel calibration is reflected in these Electromotive graphs. The company's TEC3 logic defines raw injection pulse width in terms of a line defined on the left by the minimum "Pulse width Offset Time" as MAP voltage approaches 0, and on the right by the maximum "User Adjustable Pulse width," the maximum possible injector open time at maximum MAP voltage. The bottom graph shows how this raw fuel curve can be modified by adjusting a separate VE table to reflect changes in maximum torque with engine speed on engines where engine VE varies significantly from a flat torque curve. *Electromotive*

The lambda table used by the Motec M48 on the MR6 project in this book as tuned by Bob Norwood set target lambda at 0.82 at one atmosphere of boost, increasing to 0.9 lambda at atmospheric pressure, and increasing to 1.0 lamda as manifold pressure decreases to higher ranges of vacuum.

During transient operation—when an engine is starting, warming up, accelerating, or decelerating rapidly—ordinary target air/fuel mixtures are no longer applicable; instead, the engine management system will apply corrections to the base air/fuel ratios to supply additional fuel.

COMPUTING TARGET PULSE WIDTHS

But let's not give up, let's actually compute some target injection pulse widths. Keep in mind that injectors are not accurate much below about 1.7 milliseconds (a millisecond is 0.001 of a second). In addition, some injection systems will not open the injectors more than 16 milliseconds under any conditions. Also keep in mind that the amount of time available for injection is determined by the speed of the engine. At some point, the available time for injection and the required pulse width crisscross, and the injectors become static, that is, open all the time. When in this realm, you have lost control of fuel flow in relation to engine fuel requirement changes, and additional engine speed will decrease the total fuel injected and available per power stroke per cylinder. Since this would most likely occur under conditions of high loading at high speed, additional loading could lead to disastrously lean mixtures. Check to make sure that the injection pulse width is less than 56,000 divided by rpm. For example, at 6,000 rpm, the available time for injection is 56,000/6,000, which is 9.3 milliseconds, so a specified pulse width greater than 9.3 milliseconds would drive the injectors static. Most OEM fuel-injection systems are designed to never require an injector duty cycle greater than about 80 percent, and research by fuel-injection expert Russ Collins indicates there is good reason for this. According to Collins, injectors can begin to fibrillate at such duty cycles, becoming nonlinear in fuel delivery, potentially causing lean-out problems. In practice, I've seen engines run great to pulse widths of 100 percent or above, but it is not a good idea.

If you don't have a VE chart, but know the peak torque speed for the engine, assume 80 percent VE for a street engine at peak torque, 90 to 100 percent for racing engines, and 100 percent or more for supercharged engines. This figure can be used to compute peak fuel-injection requirements, and is identical to what Electromotive calls user-adjustable pulse width,

through this air/fuel mixture at 80 feet per second). Under very high vacuum (deceleration conditions), run 15.5:1 or 16.0:1 air/fuel ratios (1.05–1.09 lambda) or even fuel cut on deceleration to prevent lean exhaust system backfiring.

Mild-cammed engines with tuned runners and little valve overlap operating at full operating temperatures will idle at 14.7:1, but such a 1.0 lambda mixture is fairly close to producing misfires, and most engines produce a better, smoother idle and less stalling with richer air/fuel ratios. It is common practice to set idle lambda at 0.9 (within the correction range of the oxygen sensor) and allow the closed loop system to pull mixtures leaner to stoichiometric at idle and light cruise under O_2 sensor control. If, for any reason, the O_2 sensor fails, the engine will only idle better. Big-cammed engines will not idle well at stoichiometric mixtures, needing at least 13.0–13.5:1 mixtures (0.88–0.92 lambda) to idle as smoothly as possible, even at full operating temperatures.

Subject to engine VE distortions, for best drivability, air/fuel mixtures should smoothly increase fuel in a linear fashion from light cruise at low rpm toward heavier loadings and peak-torque speeds. Build in smooth increases in mixture as the engine increases in speed toward best torque and as loading increases.

176	49	49	51	60	67	70	70	71	71	73	77	96	102	102	102
150	49	49	51	60	67	70	70	71	71	73	77	90	96	96	96
125	49	49	51	60	67	70	70	71	71	73	77	85	89	89	89

the required pulse width when the MAP sensor is reading full scale (though some forced-induction engines cannot achieve or safely operate at full scale on a multi-bar MAP sensor).

To compute fuel-injection requirements, first compute the weight of air in the cylinders. Convert static displacement to displacement at volumetric efficiency (80–100 percent). Divide displacement in cubic inches by cubic inches per cubic foot (1,728), which gives you engine displacement in cubic feet. Multiply this by pounds of air per cubic foot (0.07651) at standard temperature and pressure, which gives you pounds of air that enter the engine per two revolutions. Divide this by the number of cylinders to get air weight per power stroke at each cylinder (injector). Divide this figure by the target air/fuel ratio to get pounds of fuel per power stroke. Divide this number by the number of injections per power stroke (usually one for sequential injection, two for batch-fire port injection), which gives you the weight of fuel per injection. Compute the pounds of fuel injected per millisecond of injector pulse by dividing the pounds per hour of fuel flow by 3,600,00.

And, finally, divide the weight of fuel per injection by the weight of fuel per millisecond of injector pulse to get the number of milliseconds of pulse width to set calibration. Here's an example:

> 454-ci engine x 0.9 VE = 408.6-ci air drawn into engine at peak torque
>
> 408.6 ÷ 1728 = 0.236458333 cubic feet of air drawn into engine
>
> 0.236458333 x 0.07651 (pounds per cubic foot air) = 0.018091427 pounds of air entering engine per two revolutions
>
> 0.018091427 78 = 0.002261428 (pounds per power stroke at each cylinder)
>
> 0.002261428 ÷ 12.5 (target air/fuel ratio, peak torque) = 0.000180914
>
> 0.000180914 ÷ 2 = 0.000090457 (pounds fuel per injection, batch fire)
>
> 30 lb/hr injectors ÷ 3,600,000 = 0.000008333 = pounds fuel per millisecond
>
> 0.000090457 ÷ 0.000008333 = 10.85millisecondspulse width at peak torque with 30 pounds per hour injectors on 454-ci engine at 90 percent VE

Remember, most EFI regulators vary fuel pressure to keep it constant in relation to manifold pressure. If necessary, convert fuel volume to weight (using formulas in the injector selection section). Convert fuel flow in weight per hour to flow per second by dividing by 3,600. For example, 24 pounds per hour divided by 3,600 equals 0.0066667 pounds per second.

Now, divide the fuel flow in weight per time by the fuel weight calculated to achieve the desired mixture. This will tell you the fraction of a second you need to open an injector in order to inject the right amount of fuel. Injectors do not open instantly, but assume this is figured into the pulsed flow rate. Convert this time to thousandths of a second, if necessary, always rounding upward. Don't forget to divide this in two if your injection system uses two batch fires per power stroke. Perform the necessary math if you are using fewer throttle body injectors. Make sure the pulse width is less than the lesser of 16 milliseconds or 56,000 divided by rpm, but greater than 1.7 milliseconds.

Most EFI system software gives you the ability to set multiple speed-load points at once and to modify multiple points by a given percentage or to a given slope. You should not have to manually set all 256 or 512 breakpoints in the startup map.

Maybe you don't want to mess with theoretical mixtures. Given the flexibility of engines to run with widely varying air/fuel mixtures, in the old days Haltech simply recommended building a startup map by setting light-load bars for all rpm ranges to 2.5 milliseconds, sloping pulse width smoothly upward to 7.5 milliseconds in the higher manifold pressure or wider throttle angle bars.

These days, of course, in many cases, a wizard will do most of the math for you.

ACTUAL EMS CALIBRATION
Preliminary Pre-start Checklist

- Make sure there is a working fire extinguisher within easy reach.
- Verify good ground connections to the engine, heads, and intake.
- Verify switched and constant power to critical sensors and actuators.
- Connect a laptop with the appropriate (latest revision) EMS software to the electronic control unit (ECU), and—with the key on, engine stopped—verify that the ECU, sensors, and actuators are communicating with each other, with plausible data from all sensors via the engine data page screen:

  a) Engine temperature gauge (coolant or head temperature) on a cold engine should read ambient temperature, though it may lag if ambient temperature is increasing rapidly.

  b) Intake air temperature (IAT) should read ambient temperature.

  c) MAP (manifold absolute pressure) sensor should read atmospheric pressure 1 bar (about 100 kilopascals).

  d) The O_2 sensor should heat up (you should always use an electrically heated sensor), meaning the sensor body should feel warm after a little while. If the O_2 sensor is out of the exhaust system, you should see the tip get red hot shortly after you energize it by turning the key to on.

  The throttle position sensor (TPS) should move from 0 to 100 percent when you open the throttle; if not, virtually all EMSs now have a calibration facility that allows you to mark the closed and fully open TPS voltages as 0 and 100 percent throttle.

- If the ECU has injector test functions, you may want to test each injector, listening for a rapid clicking noise from every injector.
- Make sure the spark plugs are new, of the right heat range, and gapped correctly for the engine in its current configuration. Turbo conversion engines usually run a much narrower gap than stock (that is, 0.029 or less, versus, say, 0.044)
- Cranking an engine when the injectors are washing the cylinder walls with raw fuel while there is no functioning spark to light off the engine is not something you want to happen. If the ECU has spark test functions, pull the high-tension coil plug wire and set the end near a grounded metal surface of the engine, run the test, and watch for rapid sparking. If the engine has direct-fire capability, you may need to unscrew the spark plugs, re-insert each in the coil-on-plug connector, and ground the plugs. In some cases—like the Motec M4-8 with direct-fire expander module—you may need to redefine the ignition as

49	49	51	60	67	70	70	71	71	73	77	96	102	102	102	98
49	49	51	60	67	70	70	71	71	73	77	90	96	96	96	98
49	49	51	60	67	70	70	71	71	73	77	85	89	89	89	87

single-coil and then jumper spark to each individual low-voltage coil wire at the ECU connector to watch for a spark at each plug. If there are no spark test ECU routines, disable the injectors—or make sure there is no fuel pressure—and crank the engine to test the ignition as above.

- Check the firing order one more time—for plugs or direct-fire plugs, and injectors if it's SEFI. Make sure you have the official engine firing order and know how the engine manufacturer numbers the cylinders. With a distributor ignition engine stopped at top dead center at number-one cylinder on the crankshaft timing mark on the compression stroke (both valves closed), make sure the rotor is pointing at the number-one distributor lead and that the successive distributor wires in the direction of distributor rotation are routed to the correct cylinders in the firing order. A direct-fire ignition module is normally hardwired with certain pins on the connectors designated first to fire, second to fire, and so forth. Make sure the wiring is right.

- Attach a pressure gauge to the fuel rail. Jumper the fuel pump to prime the system and check for pressure of 39–45 psi with no leaks. De-energize the fuel pump and watch the rail pressure closely. The fuel pressure regulator should hold steady pressure for a long time, meaning minutes rather than seconds (the shop manual for the car may have a design pressure drop per time specification). If pressure drops rapidly (seconds rather than minutes), the regulator is defective or stuck partly open with dirt or debris, or one or more injectors are stuck open. Injectors that have sat for a long time in a wrecking yard are particularly susceptible to sticking. When you're done testing, duct tape the pressure gauge in place on the windshield or other location where it can be seen after the engine starts and eventually in early test driving or on the chassis dyno.

- If there is any possibility one or more injectors are leaking, it is critical to remove the spark plugs and injector wiring and crank the engine to purge any gasoline from the combustion chambers—and then fix the problem by replacing or cleaning the injector(s). When a piston is stopped very near before top dead center and a leaking injector is filling up the combustion chamber, the crankshaft will have extreme leverage against a combustion chamber full of gasoline because the crankshaft moves many degrees of rotation to produce the tiniest piston movement. This type of Hydro-lock may not just stop the engine dead in its tracks; it can break rods and pistons and smash broken rods though the block.

- Attempting to start an engine without an rpm or crank trigger signal can be a really bad idea. Disconnect the injector wiring so the engine will not start (unplug the injector harness or unplug all the individual injector connectors), and crank the engine. Verify that the rpm display on the engine data page of the laptop shows a plausible non-zero cranking rpm.

- Once you definitely have a correct rpm, connect a timing light to the number one cylinder and verify that the spark timing as shown by the timing light matches the laptop's reported timing on the engine data page. If it does not, if the engine uses an adjustable distributor ignition, the distributor might be indexed wrong, or the ECU might be incorrectly configured for crank trigger offset. Rotate the distributor until the actual timing matches the ECU's target timing. If the distributor indexing cannot be adjusted or if the engine uses direct-fire ignition, reconfigure the crank trigger angle in the EMS software until actual timing matches the ECU's current timing.

- It is critical to verify that the fuel injectors are sized correctly for the engine so they are small enough to idle well and large enough to fuel the engine at maximum torque and power, preferably at less than 80 percent duty cycle. Injectors that are too big will never idle well, and injectors that are too small could kill a super-high-output, boosted, or nitrous engine with lean mixtures and detonation. Verify that the fuel pump is big enough to deliver enough fuel at maximum power at the required pressure.

- Is your application beyond the envelope of the EMS in a way that is at all questionable?

- Analyze potential risks and remember Murphy's Law (if something can go wrong, it will).
  - Do you have high enough octane in the fuel to protect the engine from detonation while you are calibrating it (unleaded racing gasoline is available up to about 114 octane, leaded to about 118)? Too much octane never hurt anyone, but too little has killed many an engine.
  - Are the plugs cold enough and gapped narrow enough (a turbo conversion should use 1–2 ranges colder than stock and a maximum of 0.030 plug gap)?
  - What is a realistic redline (even with super-duty parts)? Too much rpm will try to stretch rod bolts when the rod tries to pull the piston away from TDC on the intake stroke when there is no pressure helping move the piston, and rod stretch is typically much harder on the rod that boosted combustion pressure.
  - How will you know if the engine is knocking? It can be difficult or impossible to hear.
  - What could make the engine knock? Nothing—if you're running sane levels of boost, enough octane, enough fuel, safe coolant temperatures, cold enough plugs, and enough ignition retard. Is there a strategy in place to prevent boost overrun and overboost?
  - Do you have warnings in place (gauges, audible, warning lights, ECU warnings, helper[s] watching gauges, and so on) in case of dangerous lean mixtures, knock, fuel pressure drop, injectors at 100 percent, low oil pressure, overheating, overboost, leaks, and so on?
  - Are you checking the plugs between test runs for signs of thermal overloading or other problems?
  - Should you be running EGT probes in the headers to watch for serious combustion over-temperatures?
  - Have you taken the easy way out on anything that might matter? For example, is your aftermarket knock sensor in the best place or just the easiest?
  - And last, but not least, how close to the hairy edge can you afford to push it? Can you afford to have the engine fail?

INITIAL STARTUP

You will need a calibration sufficiently accurate to get the engine started—at which point the engine can be accurately tuned using feedback methods—but many aftermarket engine management systems have now automated the process of building a safe and workable startup map. Many systems are equipped with modeling software that will construct a custom startup map for your engine good enough to get it running the first time—based

76	49	49	51	60	67	70	70	71	71	73	77	96	102	102	102
50	49	49	51	60	67	70	70	71	71	73	77	90	96	96	96
25	49	49	51	60	67	70	70	71	71	73	77	85	89	89	89

on a set of configuration parameters you enter via the laptop user interface (number of cylinders, estimated horsepower, injector size, and so on). Some are very good at building a workable map that will actually run and drive the vehicle quite well.

If there is no auto-map software for your system, select the closest library calibration that's available for your EMS on CD or at the vendor's website, and download it into the ECU. A map from an identical engine would be ideal, but there are so many factors affecting what makes the optimal calibration that even minor modifications could render an otherwise perfect map suboptimal. What's more, even a really great map developed by experts in white coats on a million-dollar research dyno from an otherwise identical engine will be wrong if the injectors used in the calibration were a different size (and there is virtually always a range of injector sizes that will work for a given engine). Even if the injector sizes were the same, the perfect calibration might not work perfectly if, for example, the fuel rail pressure was different at the dyno. You simply cannot assume any calibration is perfect without experimental evidence proving this is the case. It is disheartening how many engines are driving around that could have free power and better fuel economy from a more optimal calibration. In any case, a good candidate startup map must be from an engine with the same number of cylinders, with relatively similar VE characteristics (including power-adders or the lack thereof, cam timing, and head-flow characteristics), displacement, and similar-sized injectors. If the injector size is wrong, there is probably a way of rescaling the map's injection pulse width to match the variation in injector flow.

You will almost definitely have to enter some configuration data that defines certain global operating characteristics required to match the EMS with the engine (number of cylinders, ignition type, firing order, and so on).

At this point, the library or auto-map calibration will probably start the engine. If not, the EMS may have a trim module with one or more dials or a global fuel trim parameter you can tweak to provide across-the-board enrichment or enleanment, usually in the plus or minus 10 to 30 percent range. Swinging the trim pot(s) while cranking may help get the engine running, particularly if the problem was a lean mixture. Global trim can be very useful during the initial start and warm-up.

Once the engine is running, try to keep it running at 2,000 rpm until fully warm. If the engine is a brand-new, 0-miles powerplant, make sure to look for leaks and perform all the other maiden-voyage checks required to make sure a new engine doesn't get damaged from low oil pressure, lack of coolant, or incorrect assembly.

When the engine starts, the manifold pressure (MAP) sensor readout should instantly switch from atmospheric pressure to a high-vacuum low-flow airflow rate much closer to 0 kilopascals if the system uses a MAP sensor to estimate engine airflow. As the engine warms up, the engine temperature sensor readout should begin to climb from ambient temperature toward normal operating temperature in the 180 to 200 range. Make sure the EMS is set up for Fahrenheit or Celsius, depending on which you're more comfortable using. The heated O_2 sensor readout should begin to display a plausible air/fuel ratio, which may be displayed as lambda, the ratio of the air/fuel ratio divided by the 14.68:1 chemically ideal stoichiometric air/fuel ratio. Thus, an air/fuel ratio of 13.5:1 is about 0.92 lambda. Once the O_2 sensor is hot and alive, when the engine is warming up and in open-loop mode (no automatic mixture trim), adjusting

global mixture-trim should cause the O_2 sensor readout to vary with changes in mixture trim in the expected direction. Beware being misled by a narrow-band O_2 sensor; such sensors are only accurate at air/fuel mixtures very close to the stoichiometric ratio. Keep in mind that if mixtures are far enough away from optimal to cause misfiring, wideband O_2 sensors can be fooled into reporting falsely lean mixture due to the presence of large gusts of unburned oxygen).

By the time the engine reaches about 140 degrees Fahrenheit, if configured to allow closed-loop mixture trim, the EMS will start feedback mixture trim based on data from the O_2 sensor. At this point, the EMS will have some means of indicating that it is in closed-loop mode. For example, a readout may start displaying the amount of fuel the engine is adding or subtracting to achieve stoichiometric ratios. Some EMSs have air/fuel ratio tables that allow a tuner to specify non-stoichiometric target mixtures for various speed and loading segments of the engine operating range.

The trick with closed-loop operations is to tune the engine so it runs great under all circumstances even if closed loop is turned off, perhaps a little rich of stoich at idle, which will go away in closed-loop. Under no circumstances should uncorrected mixtures ever be leaner than the stoichiometric ratio. If the O_2 sensor fails, the system will default into open-loop mode, which you always want to be perfect or a little on the rich side. The base fuel maps should be constructed so the closed-loop system is always either idle or pulling fuel, never working to add fuel to the base map. Keep in mind that the O_2 sensor is not in the combustion chamber but rather is located downstream somewhere in the header(s) or exhaust system, and there is a varying degree of lag in the O_2 sensor reading, depending on engine speed and exhaust velocity. This may be configurable. A properly calibrated EMS should fail safe, which, in this case, means fail rich. Typically, OEM EMS closed-loop systems are clamped to limit the maximum fuel trim to a rather small percentage; if the system is adding or subtracting huge amounts of fuel, something is wrong. Later on, we will discuss using exhaust gas temperature readings to tune safely at high power levels, but even EGTs have lag time, and combustion temperatures are typically much hotter in the chambers than even a short distance downstream in the exhaust. Bottom line, the base fuel map should err on the rich side, but never by more than about 5 percent.

Whether or not you plan to run closed loop once the EMS is optimized, you will need wideband capability to dial it in. Keep in mind, narrowband O_2 sensors are not capable of providing accurate readings very far from 14.68:1, that is, below 14 or much above 15. The automatic start-up mapping facility may produce a map that will start and operate the vehicle with decent drivability, but air/fuel ratios and timing will almost definitely not be optimal. Therefore, you're going to need wideband O_2 capability to find the "free" power and efficiency in your engine. It is a fact of life that virtually all pro tuners work with wideband O_2 sensor data in all tuning operations, and many Dynojet chassis dynos are now equipped with wideband capabilities that log air/fuel ratio information and graph it along with power and torque. Many EMSs have a wideband option, which allows the EMS to read and log data from a five-wire O_2 sensor, though not necessarily to use for closed-loop feedback operations. Narrowband O_2 sensors deliver a voltage between nearly 0 and nearly 1 volt (a few are frequency-based), and wideband sensors typically deliver a 0–5 volt signal that is not compatible unless you install a resistor-divider. More rarely, some EMS systems can

49	49	51	60	67	70	70	71	71	73	77	96	102	102	102	98
49	49	51	60	67	70	70	71	71	73	77	90	96	96	96	98
49	49	51	60	67	70	70	71	71	73	77	85	89	89	89	87

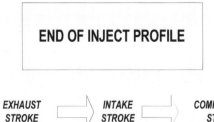

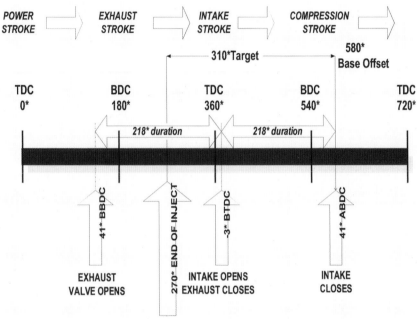

With sequential port fuel injection you will probably have the option to define injection phasing, in particular, the engine position in the 720-degree four-stroke cycle by which injection must conclude (or start). Injection timing can typically be adjusted at various rpm points and optionally at various efficiency points. Adjusting the injection timing allows the fuel to be injected at the optimum point in the engine cycle so the fuel is used most efficiently. Engine power, emissions, economy, and idle stability may be optimized by adjusting the injection timing.

now work with a conditioning processor that converts wideband O2 data to the 0–1 volt signal needed for actual closed-loop trim operations (an example is Link's UEGOlink).

Another option is employing a standalone wideband air/fuel-ratio meter that is not part of the EMS but instead indicates the air/fuel ratio in real time on a digital display or analog gauge needle. Wideband sensing of any variety greatly increases the accuracy of tuning under all conditions, and is accurate in detecting air/fuel ratios from about 10:1 all the way to above 16:1. The trouble is, standalone air/fuel ratio meters cannot be correlated with datalogging information from the EMS, but they are very good, nonetheless.

Most ambitiously, some EMSs now have an auto-mapping capability that enables the ECU to work with a wideband sensor to build correction tables that trim injection pulse width to achieve the values in a target air/fuel ratio table (assuming you know the ideal air/fuel ratios, which frequently vary according to the engine or engine type). Such systems are good for driving around town and allowing the system to tune itself at light and midrange power settings, but I would not trust such a system to find optimal air/fuel ratios for high-boost, high-power operations. You're going to want to sneak up on dangerous high-power air/fuel ratios manually.

VE TABLES

When you've configured an ECU's sensor inputs and set up fuel injector constants, ignition firing order, and other actuator parameters on VE-based systems, it's time to define and calibrate the all-important volumetric efficiency table, which provides a reference for engine pumping efficiency across the operating range on VE-based engine management architectures with a target air/fuel ratio (air/fuel ratio) table.

In a VE table, each cell is related to the ratio of the quantity of air charge inducted into a cylinder under current conditions to the quantity of air charge that would occupy the sweet area of the cylinder under static conditions. VE-based engine management systems use the values in a VE table entry along with cylinder displacement on a continuing basis to calculate a *relative cylinder volume*, which is one of the critical variables required to calculate cylinder air mass in the fundamental operating equation used in speed-density engine management systems:

$$\text{Air Mass} = \frac{(\text{Displacement} * \text{VE}) * \text{MAP}}{(0.28705 * \text{Temperature}_{abs} * \text{# Cyl})}$$

where . . .

Air mass = Cylinder air mass (grams/cylinder)
Displacement = Engine displacement (liters)
VE = Volumetric efficiency (percent)
MAP = Manifold absolute pressure (kPa)
0.28705 = Molar density of air (kg/mol)
Temperature_{abs} = Absolute intake air temperature (degrees K)
Cyl = Number of engine cylinders

It is very important to build an accurate model of engine volumetric efficiency, since adjustments to the VE table impact virtually all other aspects of EMS and engine operation. An accurate VE table allows the engine management system to correctly model engine airflow under all conditions, allowing the EMS to customize fuel delivery at various subsets of the operating envelope according to a tuner-defined table of target air/fuel ratios chosen to maximize torque, minimize exhaust

76	49	49	51	60	67	70	70	71	71	73	77	96	102	102	102
50	49	49	51	60	67	70	70	71	71	73	77	90	96	96	96
25	49	49	51	60	67	70	70	71	71	73	77	85	89	89	89

GM Racing at Bonneville, final adjustments before racing in the thin air of 6,000 feet. If is very common for sea level tuning to run poorly at Bonneville. Electronic engine management with barometric pressure compensation helps, but many racers wait in line and run multiple times before they finally get it right.

emissions, or maximize fuel economy. An accurate VE table with high resolution at engine speeds in the vicinity of idle allows a tuner to increase the dynamic stability of idle on problematic engines by calibrating breakpoints just below design idle speed and manifold pressure with air/fuel ratio and spark advance tuning that instantly delivers increased torque to maintain design idle speed in case of increased loading. An accurate VE table allows a tuner to straightforwardly adapt the EMS to equipment changes such as upgraded injector size or increased fuel rail pressure, simply by redefining injector flow rate and opening constants with no need to modify a large number of fuel table entries.

When calibrating an EMS, it is almost always better to work with prefabricated tables developed for a similar or identical engine developed by a competent tuner or computer model. But if there is no pre-existing calibration and nothing generic available from the EMS manufacturer for an engine of your size and type, you'll need to create the VE table from scratch.

This chapter describes a method of populating the VE table of a speed-density EMS starting from nothing. Using this method, you'll manually calibrate volumetric efficiency at all or most reachable breakpoints of speed and loading until the EMS delivers a single homogeneous air/fuel ratio across the non-boosted operating envelope of the engine. This is easiest if lambda = 1.0, which is a good final air/fuel ratio at idle and light cruise on most engines without big cams. Basically, you're be

using an engine's fuel injectors as a precision metering device, whereby any error in measured versus target air/fuel ratio at any particular speed-density breakpoint in the operating envelope of the powerplant is assumed to result exclusively from an incorrect VE table entry that led to incorrect air mass estimation, which resulted in a precisely calculated and delivered fuel mass that delivered incorrect air/fuel ratio.

VE table calibration using this method requires dealing with a number of issues that must be handled rigorously for the method to be accurate.

PREREQUISITES FOR SCRATCH-CALIBRATING A GOOD VE TABLE

1. The table-builder algorithm described here presupposes that injector *fuel delivery is accurate and repeatable under all conditions* such that 100 percent of any measured error in air/fuel ratio is exclusively a result of incorrect air mass estimation originating in the VE table. Thus, *any* departure in fuel delivery from the ECU's expectation will result in incorrect assumptions about engine airflow being preserved in the VE table. It is therefore critical to make sure that injected fuel mass is precisely what the ECU expects under all conditions.

One potential source of error in fuel mass delivery arises when an ECU does not correctly adjust final commanded injection pulse width to account for injector opening and closing delays and nonlinear fuel flow peculiar to the operating

49	49	51	60	67	70	70	71	71	73	77	96	102	102	102	98
49	49	51	60	67	70	70	71	71	73	77	90	96	96	96	98
49	49	51	60	67	70	70	71	71	73	77	85	89	89	89	87

characteristics of the installed fuel injectors. Fuel mass flow from an electronic injector is never a perfect linear function of injection pulse width for a number of reasons. For one thing, there is always a tendency for injector inlet pressure to drop slightly after the initial burst of fuel spray, which introduces a small amount of non-linearity. Secondly, injectors cannot open or close instantly. Injector *closing* delay depends on fuel pressure, spring force, and the mass of the injector pintle valve. Injector *opening* delay is influenced by the same factors plus the available driver voltage and the design of the electromagnetic coil in the injector. Meaning it takes electronic injectors longer to open than close. The difference between the greater opening delay and the lesser closing delay is referred to as injector *offset*. Offset reduces the effective fuel flow of any length injection pulse. Obviously, injected fuel mass is non-linear during the finite transition period when injectors are *partly* open or closed. The above factors combine to produce an injected fuel mass that is not an absolute function of injector open time, meaning the basic fuel mass calculation must be corrected to avoid error.

It is worth pointing out that any error in fuel mass delivery becomes increasingly significant in percentage terms as commanded pulse width *decreases*. Boosted engines with fewer cylinders and very high specific power and large dynamic range will require very large injectors to meet fuel requirements at max torque within the time available in the four-stroke cycle, but in order to idle at all, such injectors require very short injection pulse widths, which may require operating in the nonlinear range of injector flow. In a worst case, the commanded pulse is so short there is no longer time for injectors to open all the way before it is time to close, at which point the injectors are at least partially closed 100 percent of the time—which will greatly warp the linearity of fuel delivery and may interfere with repeatability.

Combined injector opening and closing time is typically 0.2-0.4 millisecond in the case of low impedance injectors with peak-and-hold driver circuitry, and 0.4-0.8 millisecond in the case of high impedance saturated-circuit injectors. In the case of a calculated pulse width of 14 milliseconds under heavy load, if the injector offset is 0.8 millisecond, only about 5 percent of the driver circuit's energizing pulse would be consumed getting the pintle valve open. But if the calculated pulse width at idle is 1.5 milliseconds, *over 53 percent* of the pulse would be spent opening the pintle. In some cases the injection pulse width may be too short for perfectly repeatable fuel mass delivery and steady air/fuel ratio. Where injectors large enough to provide sufficient fuel for maximum power simply cannot open for a short enough period, the engine will require multiple injectors per cylinder and an EMS capable of staging them.

The good news is that many engine management systems provide for specification of installed characteristics affecting injector flow across the plausible range of fuel pressure and injector-driver voltage so that the ECU can correctly and precisely model injector fuel delivery to correct the initial injection pulse width calculation to deliver the intended fuel mass from the installed fuel injectors. To build a VE table that is not warped incorrectly at low engine speeds when you are using air/fuel ratio to correct estimated VE, it is very important to configure injector constants correctly.

Beyond accurate injector modeling, it is critical that the fuel pump, supply line, injector rail, and pressure regulator deliver consistent expected *fuel pressure* to all injectors under all circumstances without deviation so that fuel mass delivery remains an exclusive function of injection pulse width. In particular, the fuel pump must have the capacity to deliver the worst-case fuel flow without a pressure drop. It is worth noting that poor injector rail design can result in pressure fluctuations or a pressure drop at some injectors that impacts fuel mass delivery, particularly as the fuel delivery system approaches its limits.

When you're using the fuel injectors as precision metering devices for VE table calibration, it is critically important that the fuel pressure regulator maintains a *constant pressure drop* through the injector nozzles so that injected fuel mass is unaffected by manifold pressure. Mechanical regulators accomplish this by supplying intake manifold reference pressure to a port on the side of the regulator housing that surrounds the diaphragm spring. As manifold pressure increases from high vacuum to atmospheric pressure or even positive boost, pressure in the regulator housing increases, which adds to the effective spring pressure against the regulator diaphragm. The result is a linear increase in fuel pressure corresponding exactly to the increase in manifold pressure, the effect of which is to maintain a constant pressure drop through injection nozzles spraying into the intake manifold as manifold pressure changes.

It is essential that the installed *fuel injectors are in good condition* and ideally tested on a flow machine to verify that fuel flow meets specs so that the injectors are well-matched with each other and deliver the expected fuel mass to all cylinders.

There is one additional factor worth considering. It's not usually talked about very much, but consistent *fuel temperature* can be important to prevent thermal expansion from materially impacting the fuel mass injected per millisecond per psi fuel pressure. Fuel mass declines about a half a percent per 9 degree Fahrenheit increase in temperature. Therefore, if gasoline temperature increases from 40F to 120F, fuel mass per volume declines by nearly 5 percent, which will, for example, change a 13.0 air/fuel ratio to nearly 13.7. Ambient temperature in the fuel tank changes with the weather, of course, but fuel may also be heated above ambient temperature on the way into the engine if fuel supply lines pass in close proximity to hot exhaust or engine components or through a hot engine compartment. The fuel tank itself may begin to heat soak if a lot of fuel returns again (and again!) to the hot engine compartment, in the process of which a portion of fuel is heated before returning to the fuel tank due to the effect of time spent in a hot environment as well as from churning by the fuel pump and the trip through the fuel supply plumbing—all of which will be worse in the case of an oversized fuel pump that forces the fuel pressure regulator to bypass a lot of fuel back to the tank when the engine is lightly loaded. Over time, the fuel tank can heat soak. In some cases it may be worthwhile to monitor fuel supply temperature and insulate fuel supply components. In the case of boosted engines with high specific power and great dynamic range, it could be worthwhile replacing a giant fuel pump with a primary and a staged booster pump, or installing a fuel pump voltage-regulation device to slow down the pump at light engine loading to prevent excessive fuel churning and recirculation through the hot engine compartment.

2. Accurate VE table calibration depends on achieving a consistent *cylinder intake temperature* for charge throughout the tuning process (which is different from inlet air temperature). Cylinder intake temperature is a function of the temperature of air entering the intake tract plus the effect of any heating and cooling that occurs on the way into the cylinders (such as the

76	49	49	51	60	67	70	70	71	71	73	77	96	102	102	102
50	49	49	51	60	67	70	70	71	71	73	77	90	96	96	96
25	49	49	51	60	67	70	70	71	71	73	77	85	89	89	89

heat of compression of a non-intercooled supercharger), plus the temperature and heat of vaporization of injected fuel or nitrous oxide. The most sophisticated ECUs have multiple tables that enable the system to model charge heating as a function of airflow rate, boost pressure (if applicable), and the temperature of engine coolant or specific intake system components, including, if applicable, manifold intercooler temperature.

In practical terms, outside of advanced engine research labs, controlling air and fuel temperature normally means 1) having the engine at normal operating temperature prior to making adjustments to the VE table, 2) doing the best you can to control the temperature of the environment the engine or vehicle is in throughout the data collection process, and 3) providing time for engine components and environment to return to equilibrium temperature following heavy loading.

3. Tuning VE to achieve a precise air/fuel ratio is intrinsic to this method of VE table calibration, so you'll need an *accurate wideband O₂ sensor* with a sophisticated controller. Most air/fuel ratio meters have the same Bosch or NGK universal exhaust gas oxygen (UEGO) sensor, but economy wideband air/fuel ratio meters are likely to have less sophisticated controllers, which may have little or no ability to correct raw sensor data for the effects of varying exhaust pressure or temperature that may occur during the tuning process, or for the longer term effects of sensor aging. More expensive wideband systems have powerful controllers that condition raw data to deliver more accurate air/fuel ratio measurements. Some engine management systems allow direct connection of wideband sensors to the ECU, and have excellent built-in sensor control algorithms and offer the advantage over standalone wideband air/fuel ratio meters of the ability to generate datalogs in which air/fuel ratio is sequenced with the data from all other engine sensors. Some ECUs provide a "self-calibrating" capability based upon direct-connect wideband data.

What standalone air/fuel ratio meters or ECU-based wideband metering may or may not have is a method of correcting for *transport time delay* between combustion and exhaust gas arrival at the wideband sensor, which is virtually never located in the immediate vicinity of the exhaust valve, and may be located several feet away at the turbine discharge of a turbocharger or the header collector flange of long-tube headers or as far away as the tail pipe discharge at the rear of the car, many feet from the exhaust valve. Where engine speed or load are changing rapidly, incorrectly correlated UEGO sensor data may represent *historical* data unrelated to what is going on in the current snapshot of logged engine data. The importance of rigorously eliminating transport delay from wideband UEGO data is an excellent argument for holding an engine in *steady state* while calibrating individual breakpoints in a VE table.

4. Calibrating a VE table to the highest standards of accuracy is much simpler if you have the use of a load-holding engine or chassis dynamometer. With an engine loaded at steady state, there is no question about whether the measured air/fuel ratio is current. You can also be certain that no transient enrichment algorithm is altering the final fuel mass calculation such that measured air/fuel ratio is no longer derived exclusively from VE. A load-holding dyno not only allows a calibrator to fine-tune VE table entries to achieve the target air/fuel ratio in real time while the engine is working, but once VE is set, a load-holding dyno provides the facility to optimize spark advance (and target air/fuel ratios) at all points to maximize torque.

The bad news is that running a performance engine continuously at high power levels will frequently generate thermal loading that exceeds the capacity of a stock automotive cooling system to shed heat—particularly in the environment of a chassis dyno where airflow through the radiator is dependent on auxiliary electrical fans rather than the movement of the vehicle through the air, and where the dyno room itself may heat soak. When operating under very heavy engine loading at moderate-to-high rpm, it is safer to abandon tuning at steady-state in favor of automated *ramp runs*. In ramp runs, also known as dyno *sweeps*, the dyno computer automatically manages engine loading to stabilize the powerplant briefly at a series of discrete rpm steps across the speed range of the engine while datalogging rpm, horsepower, torque, EGT, and Air/fuel Ratio. Following which the engine can be idled or shut down while the tuner uses logged air/fuel ratio data to correct the VE table at any and all speed-loading breakpoints encountered during the ramp run at which measured air/fuel ratio was off-target.

An alternative to steady-state calibration on the load-holding dyno is calibrating VE on a test track while holding engine speed and loading steady by simultaneously applying both brake pedal and accelerator in one of the higher gears. Realistically, calibrating on the street literally from scratch without some sort of basic set of prefabricated EMS maps will be difficult, since initial drivability is likely to be very poor. Doing it safely requires two people with a lot of patience (a skilled driver and a skilled calibrator), plus an empty track or deserted road.

An alternative is to calibrate the VE table using an inertial chassis dyno while loading the engine with *acceleration*, during which you log MAP, rpm, and air/fuel ratio data for recalibrating VE after the fact. After the load sequence is finished, the calibrator adjusts VE upward or downward at all speed-density breakpoints encountered in the datalog according to the percentage error in air/fuel ratio. On an inertial dyno, it is *critical* to disable acceleration enrichment or operate in a high gear that will slow the rate of acceleration enough to make certain that calculated fuel mass at a given breakpoint of speed and manifold pressure remains an exclusive a function of VE table entries rather than transient enrichment that comes into play during sudden acceleration.

5. Before beginning the actual VE table calibration, make sure that the VE table has enough resolution in areas of the table where VE changes relatively rapidly as a function of either rpm or manifold pressure. There was a time when rpm ranges were set at fixed intervals along the X axis of EMS tables and loading ranges were set at fixed intervals on the Y axis, but most modern engine management systems allow nonlinear customization of speed and density ranges that concentrate resolution where it's needed. There is no point in wasting rpm ranges on speeds beyond the redline of the engine, and there's no point in wasting load ranges on very low-manifold pressure that is unreachable on some engines, particularly big-cam engines that idle with very low vacuum. Similarly, there's no point in defining load ranges above atmospheric pressure if the engine is not equipped with a turbo or blower. On the other hand, you're going to want a lot of table resolution at speed ranges below 2,000 rpm where VE may change quite rapidly in a non-linear fashion.

6. To prevent tuner and EMS from working at cross purposes, before attempting to start an engine and begin calibrating the

49	49	51	60	67	70	70	71	71	73	77	96	102	102	102	98
49	49	51	60	67	70	70	71	71	73	77	90	96	96	96	98
49	49	51	60	67	70	70	71	71	73	77	85	89	89	89	87

VE table, it is critical to make sure that the EMS parameter that deactivates closed-loop feedback in conjunction with the target air/fuel ratio table is set to force the EMS to operate in Open-Loop mode. However, make sure the UEGO sensor readout stays active and that the EMS is set up to highlight the active cell of any table that's being used to manage the engine.

VOLUMETRIC EFFICIENCY AND MAP VS. MAF

It may have occurred to you to wonder why fool around with *estimating* volumetric efficiency based on measured air/fuel ratio at speed-density breakpoints when you could populate a VE table by installing a MAF sensor during the calibration process to *measure* engine airflow across the operating range of engine speed and manifold pressure?

For any particular engine rpm and intake air temperature, mass airflow is a good linear function of manifold absolute pressure. That is, increasing manifold pressure translates directly to increased cylinder air mass. One implication of this is that at a particular engine rpm, as long as intake air temperature remains constant—which can be a challenge on forced-induction engines under boosted conditions!—calibrating VE at a single high and a single low point of engine loading does a rather good job of accurately defining the slope of change in VE versus manifold pressure for the entire operating range of engine loading. To take advantage of this, most modern engine management systems include an automated function that will interpolate and/or extrapolate the entire range of VE table entries for a particular rpm based on two defined points.

Obviously, MAFs are used all the time to accurately measure airflow on factory engines with great success, but there are a number of potential problems with using a MAF as a VE measuring device. One is that the act of measurement itself may alter what is being measured: Any airflow restriction from the MAF sensor itself that's sufficient to warp the pumping efficiency of the engine at any airflow will defeat the purpose of the exercise.

Another problem is that there is always R&D involved in installing a MAF sensor in the intake tract of a particular engine in such a way that the MAF's hotwire air-measurement system is not significantly misled by turbulence or uneven airflow. And when you've done the best you can with this, you'll still need to calibrate/correct the transfer function by which the EMS maps raw frequency or voltage data from the MAF into precision mass airflow numbers suitable for use in the air mass calculation of a particular engine configuration.

Bottom line, using a MAF to populate a VE table is no panacea because it's very unlikely to be a plug-and-play exercise.

WHY TARGET LAMBDA = 1.0 FOR VE TABLE CALIBRATION?

Depending on the fuel formulation, stoichiometric combustion on gasoline takes place in the range of 14.64-14.7 air/fuel ratio, depending on the precise composition of the hydrocarbons and the percentage of any oxygenated additives such as ether or ethanol. For reasons discussed elsewhere in this book, stoichiometric combustion will not usually deliver maximum torque at any combination of engine speed and loading, though any engine with a compression ratio designed to work on the street running conservative spark timing and premium gasoline should be able to run with an air/fuel ratio of lambda = 1.0 up to about 105 kPa manifold pressure, which encompasses the range of naturally occurring atmospheric pressure.

So why target lambda = 1.0 while calibrating a VE table? In the first place, lambda = 1.0 works great as the final air/fuel ratio on many engines at idle and light-moderate cruise, providing decent torque, good fuel efficiency, and excellent emissions, particularly when the vehicle is equipped with a catalytic converter. When you've calibrated the VE table at lambda = 1.0, a good portion of the speed-density operating envelope is finished, nothing more required. Conveniently, a target air/fuel ratio of 1.0 lambda means that measured lambda is exactly proportional to the required correction to the appropriate VE table cell.

Here's how it works: Let's say that actual measured air/fuel ratio delivered by the active VE table cell is 1.06 lambda and that current VE is set at 50 (percent). Lambda 1.06 represents a gasoline air/fuel ratio of roughly 15.6, which is 106 percent of target lambda, i.e., approximately 6 percent lean of the stoichiometric ratio. Therefore, the VE estimate in the current VE table call must be 6 percent low. Correcting it is simple: Multiply the current entry of 50 by lambda—1.06—which gives 53. Increasing the VE table entry from 50 to 53 should yield a measured lambda of 1.0. Technically there should actually be a divide by target lambda involved in the calculation, but in this case the divide is not required since target lambda is 1.0, and a divide by 1 changes nothing.

It is worth noting that virtually all piston engines will make more torque at air/fuel ratio mixtures rich of the stoichiometric ratio, and some may require richer mixtures to run smoothly. This is true not only at heavy loading, but at idle, where big cams with a lot of lobe overlap may dilute fresh intake charge at low engine speeds with a substantial amount of exhaust gas. If this is the case, there is nothing to prevent you from calibrating a VE table using a global target lambda of 0.95 (or even 0.90 or less if you're not worried about loading the plug) lambda instead of 1.0, though the math of calculating VE table cell corrections requires an additional division.

For example, let's say target lambda is set across the board to 0.95 lambda instead of 1.0 lambda, and that actual measured lambda at a particular VE table cell is 0.98. How incorrect is 0.98 lambda? The answer is found by dividing measured lambda by target lambda, i.e., 0.98 / 0.95 ≈ 1.03. Measured lambda is 103 percent of target, which is lean. Therefore estimated VE in the active VE table cell must be low and needs to be increased to 103 percent of the current value, which will increase the air mass calculation, which will, in turn, increase the fuel mass calculation and cause more fuel to be injected, richening the mixture. If current VE in the appropriate VE table cell is, say, 60 (percent), corrected VE will be 60 * 1.03 ≈ 62. We adjust this 60 VE entry up to 62, which increases the calculated air mass and therefore the injected fuel mass, resulting in a new measured lambda of .95, which is right on target.

Target air/fuel ratio can usually be set as low as 0.87 lambda (12.8:1 air/fuel ratio on gasoline) without encountering rich surging at light cruise, but, as always, over-rich mixtures are undesirable because they increase engine wear by washing lubricant off cylinder walls and could eventually load the spark plugs enough to cause misfires.

You should not target lambda = 1.0 under any circumstance when the intake manifold pressure is boosted above atmospheric pressure by a turbo or supercharger, due to the chronic need to fight knock by reducing combustion temperatures with fuel-cooling, but, again, with premium gasoline, lambda 1.0 should be fine all the way up to wide-open throttle. However, I would

176	49	49	51	60	67	70	70	71	71	73	77	96	102	102	102
150	49	49	51	60	67	70	70	71	71	73	77	90	96	96	96
125	49	49	51	60	67	70	70	71	71	73	77	85	89	89	89

Volumetric Efficiency Table

MAP (kPa)

	700	800	900	1100	1200	1500	1800	2000	2400	2800	3200	3600	4000	5000	6000	7000
203	49	49	51	60	67	70	70	71	71	73	77	102	109	109	109	104
176	49	49	51	60	67	70	70	71	71	73	77	96	102	102	102	98
150	49	49	51	60	67	70	70	71	71	73	77	90	96	96	96	98
125	49	49	51	60	67	70	70	71	71	73	77	85	89	89	89	87
111	49	49	51	60	67	70	70	71	71	73	77	82	86	86	86	83
100	49	49	51	60	67	70	70	71	71	73	77	79	83	83	83	81
90	48	48	50	59	66	68	69	70	70	71	76	79	81	81	81	80
81	45	45	47	55	62	64	65	66	66	69	72	76	79	79	79	77
70	44	44	45	53	59	61	62	63	64	66	69	73	76	76	76	74
64	44	44	45	52	57	59	60	61	63	64	67	70	73	73	73	72
60	40	40	41	49	55	57	58	59	61	62	66	70	73	73	73	72
56	39	39	40	47	52	54	55	57	59	60	64	67	70	70	70	69
50	33	33	34	40	44	53	54	55	58	59	59	62	65	65	65	63
45	29	29	30	35	39	46	47	48	50	51	54	57	59	59	59	58
41	24	24	25	29	32	38	39	40	42	43	46	48	50	50	50	49
28	20	20	20	23	26	31	32	33	34	34	36	38	40	40	40	39

RPM

VE Table example. Building a VE table from scratch involves mapping as much of the table as possible with target AFR set to the same value (such as 14.7), such that any errors in target AFR can be assumed to result exclusively from airflow errors in the VE table and can be corrected according to the magnitude of the required AFR correction as a percentage. Working with the same VE in all table cells that's capable of starting the engine, we work from 2,000 rpm at zero load, initially correcting the entire table to the correction required at 2,000 rpm at zero load to get the AFR correct. At this point, we work upward to higher rpm-load breakpoints from the initial table cell, correcting entire areas of the table to reflect the trends of required correction, gradually sculpting the surface of the table to reflect the pumping efficiency of the engine at all achievable speed-density points.

not attempt to calibrate a VE table on a load-holding dyno at wide-open throttle using street gasoline. High-octane unleaded racing gasoline is cheap insurance, with the only downside being the high cost and a slower burn rate that may require additional spark advance to optimize torque. As always, make sure that you are tuning for an air/fuel ratio or percentage of lambda appropriate for the specific formulation of fuel, given that some unleaded racing gasolines have oxygenated content that can significantly alter the stoichiometric air/fuel ratio.

ACTUAL VE TABLE CALIBRATION PROCESS

1. Begin by populating the naturally aspirated range of the target-air/fuel ratio table up to 105 kPa with target lambda set to 1.0, an air/fuel ratio where measured lambda corresponds exactly to any required corrections to VE.

If the engine is boosted with a supercharger or turbo, set target lambda to 1.0 below MAP of 105 kPa, but set target air/fuel ratio table to lambda = 0.78 at all loading cells in the supercharged realm above 105 kPa. Richer mixtures here provide some insurance against detonation in the case of unintended excursions in boosted territory.

2. Assuming you are starting from scratch, begin the calibration process by populating the entire VE table with the same number in every cell. The goal is to select a plausible VE number that will get the engine started with target air/fuel ratio set to lambda = 1.0 and enable it to run at 2,000 rpm. Two thousand rpm is a very forgiving engine speed, since most normal gasoline-fueled engines turning at 2,000 rpm can operate with air/fuel ratio as rich as 0.61 lambda or as lean as 1.36 lambda (gasoline air/fuel

ratio of 9.0-20.1). Two thousand rpm will keep most automotive engines from stalling long enough to warm up even with fairly dreadful tuning.

The trick is to pick a somewhat optimistic VE number that will produce an air/fuel ratio that's fairly rich to help the engine start easily and warm up. Perhaps a VE of 40 percent will work? Set the entire table to all 40s and crank the engine. If the engine catches but stalls, try setting the VE table at all 50s or 60s. Do not hesitate to make fairly aggressive global changes to estimated VE in the range of 15-30 percent when searching for a mixture that will start the engine.

3. When the engine starts, throttle it up to 2,000 rpm. Do not waste time trying to make the engine idle, which is a lot more challenging to achieve during warm-up due to ongoing dynamic changes to several moving targets that must be balanced to achieve a steady idle without flaring or stalling. These include 1) changes in engine friction due to thermal expansion and heat-induced changes in oil viscosity, 2) increases in effective mixture strength as heavier fractions of gasoline begin to vaporize, 3) decreases in commanded injection pulse width in accordance with the declining fuel enrichment values specified in default warm-up enrichment tables as the powerplant heats, and 4) changing spark timing requirements as a function of all of the above.

If the engine runs roughly at 2,000 rpm with zero loading when it reaches normal operating temperature, note measured lambda and use global calibration functions to adjust *all* VE table cells at once until the engine runs better. Otherwise, let it be and move on to calibrating VE under load. Let's say

49	49	51	60	67	70	70	71	71	73	77	96	102	102	102	98
49	49	51	60	67	70	70	71	71	73	77	90	96	96	96	98
49	49	51	60	67	70	70	71	71	73	77	85	89	89	89	87

all VE table cells were initially set to 65 percent pumping efficiency, and that measured air/fuel ratio at 2,000 rpm and 30 kPa is 0.88 lambda. This is a rather rich air/fuel mixture (12.9 on gasoline), but the engine is running smoothly and we know VE is likely to increase at higher manifold pressure, so instead of leaning out the entire table, we'll leave it where it is for now and recalibrate the table globally when we begin to load the engine. Keep in mind that wideband lambda sensors (including heated ones) will not function properly until they reach minimal operating temperature, and that economy wideband air/fuel ratio meters are unlikely to be very accurate at colder temperatures. Most engine management systems will have default values in the warm-up fuel enrichment table(s) that cause ECUs to begin pulling fuel as coolant temperature rises during a cold start.

4. Prior to loading the engine with a dyno, the engine should be at normal operating temperature, running a plausible but *known-conservative* base timing map. Even with a conservative spark advance map, an add-on individual-cylinder knock sensor system with timing retard is good insurance against engine damage, as it can detect detonation and initiate timing retard only on the knocking cylinder(s) much faster than a human being can hear knock and get out of the throttle to stop it. That said, detonation vibration frequency varies according to the engine design and knock sensor location, so installing a knock sensor system does not relieve a driver or dyno operator of the need for a prudent testing regime or the need to be vigilant for the sound of detonation so you can get out of the throttle the instant you hear the telltale sound of "bee-bees in a tin can."

Assuming you are working with an engine or chassis dynamometer with load-holding capability, configure the dyno for constant-speed testing. In this mode the tuner brings engine speed up to a particular rpm range that's available in the VE table and engages the dyno. With the dyno active, increases in engine torque from increased throttle angle or boost pressure will not change engine rpm as the dyno automatically increases (or decreases) resistance under computer control to maintain rpm or wheel speed using a water brake or eddy current load-absorber. In constant-speed dyno testing, changes in throttle angle increase or decrease engine loading (MAP) within the same speed range, allowing a tuner to move the engine vertically up or down through the loading ranges of a particular rpm range of the VE table.

On a manual transmission vehicle, many tuners using chassis dynos prefer to work in fourth gear. This way the engine is not lugging in overdrive, and the dyno is not forced to deal with the substantial torque multiplication of lower gears, thus achieving a more direct connection between dyno and crankshaft speeds.

Automatic transmission vehicles are more difficult. Unless there is a way to lock the torque converter, on a chassis dyno precise steady-state calibration is not possible with high loading below the stall speed of the torque converter due to the variable converter slip rate preventing the dyno from controlling speed. If possible, lock the torque converter once the wheels are turning and focus initially on calibrating VE table cells that *can* be held in steady state, after which you can deal with calibrating VE cells at lower MAP values. The good news is that at within a particular rpm range, VE will be a smooth linear function of MAP across large swaths of manifold pressure, meaning that VE correction percentages established at moderately high engine loading can often be applied accurately all the way up to WOT and down

to minimum kPa MAP. Obviously, a better (but more expensive and time-consuming) alternative for automatic transmission engines is to calibrate the VE table with the engine out of the vehicle on a torque cell *engine dyno*.

5. The process from this point on is to work on defining the landscape of the VE table under circumstances where any error in target air/fuel ratio is exclusively a function of incorrect VE, entering accurate values in as many VE cells as possible using steady-state or ramp-run methods. Later on, with the VE table calibrated, you will proceed to optimize *target air/fuel ratio* across various subsets of the operating envelope and finally adjust spark timing across the board to optimize torque.

Keep in mind that the slope of changes in VE as a function of MAP and rpm are predictable enough that it is often unnecessary to manually adjust every single cell in the VE table, which can be an extremely time-consuming process on engine management systems with very high resolution VE tables that may have over a thousand breakpoints. This process is alleviated by the fact that some cells in a VE table are literally not reachable (such as high levels of supercharged manifold pressure at, say, 500 rpm). That said, you should enter plausible values everywhere, as most engine management systems will average VE values from unreachable cells into the air mass calculations for nearby bordering breakpoint cells that *are* reachable.

6. With air, fuel, and coolant temperatures stabilized, begin the load-based calibration process by measuring lambda and correcting the VE table at a single moderate engine speed under light loading.

Most engine management systems have a dozen or more loading breakpoints spread across the kPa range of the MAP sensor, with breakpoints typically arranged in a *nonlinear fashion* on both axes to deliver more resolution in the areas where VE changes most quickly as a function of speed and/or manifold pressure. Most street engines with mild cams idle with manifold pressure somewhere in the range of 17 to 21 in-Hg vacuum (50-27 kPa MAP). Engines with more radical cams will see 10-15 inches of vacuum at idle but will probably pull additional vacuum at zero load as rpm increases a bit. Therefore, you'll probably want to begin calibrating VE at an engine speed around 2,000 rpm at a load range somewhere around 60 kPa.

Increase throttle until rpm is stable at 2,000 rpm (or whatever the closest speed range is on the high side), and engage the load-holding dyno. Now add throttle until MAP increases to the 60 kPa manifold pressure range (or 64, or whatever it is) while the dyno absorbs load to maintain rpm. Keep the throttle steady and make a note of measured lambda. If target air/fuel ratio is set to lambda = 1.0, any measured air/fuel ratio besides a reading of 1.0 indicates that the volumetric efficiency estimation in the active cell of the VE table needs to be corrected according to the percentage error of measured lambda. Let's say the measured lambda at 60 kPa and 2,000 rpm is 1.02. Percentage error in air/fuel ratio is:

Percent Error = Measured lambda / Target lambda

Therefore, if target lambda is 1.0:

1.02 / 1.0 = 1.02

Air/fuel ratio is lean, so we should increase the VE estimate by multiplying the current VE of 65 by percent air/fuel ratio error, as in:

65 * 1.02 ≈ 66

Motec's 3D Main Fuel Map plots injection pulse as a percentage of the maximum defined injection pulse (IJPU) as a function of engine rpm and loading in kilopascals (in this case 200 is the maximum due to the 2-bar MAP sensor). Most EMSs allow you to view and modify the fuel curves as either tables or graphs, most of which are very similar to this chart. The surface of the chart should roughly correspond to engine volumetric efficiency—keeping in mind that tuners almost always optimize pulse width at wide-open throttle for power, at light throttle for fuel economy.

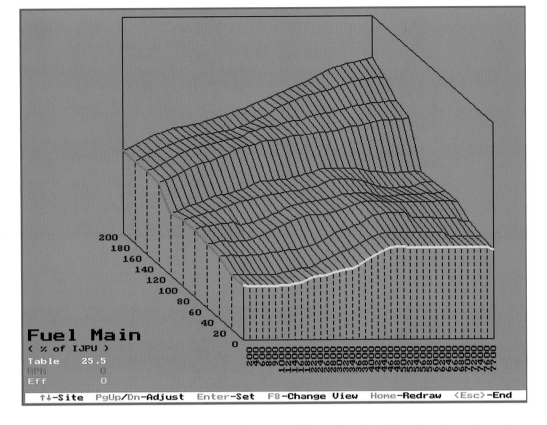

EMS TUNING

Estimated VE goes from 65 to 66, which will lead to a slightly higher airflow estimate. With a slightly higher airflow estimate, the fuel calculation will deliver a slightly greater injected fuel mass, resulting in an air/fuel ratio of lambda = 1.0.

7. However, rather than simply correcting VE at a single speed-density breakpoint of 2,000 rpm and 60 kPa, to speed up the calibration process and begin shaping the larger VE table, we'll apply the percentage VE correction to the VE table entries of *all* rpm ranges at all load ranges greater than or equal to the current manifold pressure, working on the assumption that whatever increase (or decrease!) in pumping efficiency there may be at the current engine loading will tend to persist as load increases toward WOT and as engine speed increases toward maximum torque. Therefore, we'll go ahead and correct *all* VE table cells at or above the current 60 kPa loading by multiplying current VE by the percentage error in lambda at the current speed-density loading point, which is 102 percent. Select all table cells at all rpm ranges at loading of 60 kPa and above and multiply by 1.02, converting the upper part of the table to all 66s.

Note: Most modern engine management systems have a set of powerful table-manipulation functions available that allow you to select multiple table cells and perform operations on them, such as the fill cells with a particular value, or perform arithmetic functions like multiply that are needed to correct VE according to the percentage of deviation in measured lambda. Many ECUs also have an *Interpolate* function that allows you to perform operations such as filling in the cells between two selected points in a row or column according to the linear slope defined by the selected points. Some Interpolate functions allow you to select a *region* of numbers in a table and fill in the value of cells according to the slope of the lines defined by the cells at the upper and lower bounds of the selected area. Interpolate functions are a powerful tool for rapidly building an EMS table, due to the fact that many VE trends are linear within subsets of the operating envelope.

8. Now increase throttle angle to load the engine to the next highest MAP breakpoint, which will be something like 64 or 70 kPa. Let's say it's 70. Once again, the trick is to stabilize the engine with steady throttle at precisely 70 kPa MAP while the dyno computer holds engine speed at 2,000 rpm with increased resistance. Check lambda and implement any required VE correction based on the percentage error in air/fuel ratio. At 70 kPa, if we measure lambda at, say, 1.08 (a gasoline air/fuel ratio of roughly 15.9), we'll need to multiply VE at the current breakpoint (already corrected from 65 to 66) by 1.08. Therefore, 66 * 1.08 ≈ 71.

Again, we'll apply the correction to all table cells at or above 70 kPa: Select all VE table cells in all speed ranges with loading at or above 70 kPa, and select the multiply function and enter 1.08 to increase VE at *all* speed ranges in the VE table to from 66 to 71 percent.

9. If you are running into lean mixtures as engine loading increases, you may want to consider manually *extrapolating VE* at heavier loading in advance of high or WOT load testing. Cylinder air mass tends to increase in a linear fashion with increases in manifold pressure, so examining the slope of increase in VE as a function of changes in MAP can be highly predictive of VE at higher loading at full throttle or positive manifold pressure, if the engine is boosted with a blower or turbo. It is possible to use the linear slope of changes in VE as a function of MAF both to *extrapolate* data points at heavy engine loading beyond anything

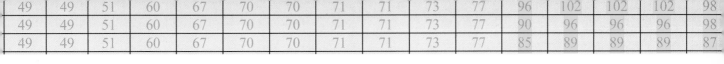

49	49	51	60	67	70	70	71	71	73	77	96	102	102	102	98
49	49	51	60	67	70	70	71	71	73	77	90	96	96	96	98
49	49	51	60	67	70	70	71	71	73	77	85	89	89	89	87

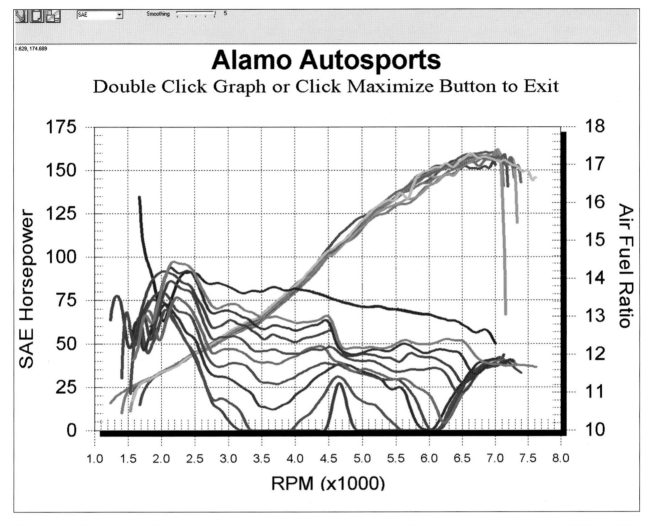

Alamo Autosports
Double Click Graph or Click Maximize Button to Exit

This chain of Dynojet dynoruns graphs Honda horsepower and air/fuel ratio (from dyno's wideband sensor) as Alamo Autosports worked to optimize the del Sol's Hondata high- and low-speed VTEC cam fuel tables, working, of course, from rich to lean.

EMS TUNING

actually tested. It is also possible to *interpolate* values of VE cells between MAP breakpoints already tested to speed up the work of populating a VE table.

There are many sophisticated methods for fitting various types of curves to data points using nonlinear regression in order to extrapolate or interpolate additional data points, but fitting a straight line to two data points to extrapolate or interpolate additional data points can be effective when the slope of the data points is linear or linear over a narrow enough range such that a series of straight lines can be made to approximate a curve and thereby provide a tool with which you are interpolating data points in between the end points of a line segment.

The formula for linear slope is:

Slope = Rise / Run

In the case of a VE table:

Slope = Change in VE / Change in MAP
= (ΔVE) / (ΔkPa)
= (VE2 − VE1) / (kPa2 − kPa1)

Let's say you have used steady-state testing to establish two points in the VE table within a particular speed range defined by

(VE = 0.66, MAP = 60) and (VE = 0.71, Map = 70),
Slope = (0.71 − 0.66) / (70 − 60)

= 0.05 / 10
= 0.005 VE / kPa

Therefore, VE increases 0.005 per increase of 1 kPa, i.e., $Ve_{increase}$ = (.005 VE) * kPa

Let's say you want to extrapolate the next loading breakpoint at 80 kPa, i.e., 10 kPa above 70.

Therefore:

ΔVE = Slope * ΔkPa
= 0.005 * 10
≈ 0.05

Adding 0.5 VE to the 0.71 VE value at 70 kPa gives the projected VE table entry at 80 kPa:

VE = 0.05 + 0.71
= 0.76

We could extrapolate VE at 100 kPa (30 kPa above 70):

ΔVE = (0.005 VE / kPa) * (30 kPa)
≈ 0.15 VE

Adding 0.15 VE to the 0.71 VE value at 70 kPa gives the projected VE table entry at 100 kPa:

VE = 0.15 + 0.71
= 0.86

76	49	49	51	60	67	70	70	71	71	73	77	96	102	102	102
50	49	49	51	60	67	70	70	71	71	73	77	90	96	96	96
25	49	49	51	60	67	70	70	71	71	73	77	85	89	89	89

We might also manually use linear slope to *interpolate* VE at breakpoints between dyno-tested kPa—say, 64 kPa—based on dyno testing we've already done at 60 and 70 kPa:

Assume 64 kPa is the next loading breakpoint above 60 kPa, an increase of 4 kPa.

Therefore:

$$\Delta \text{VE} = (0.005\ \text{VE} / \text{kPa}) * (4\ \text{kPa})$$
$$\approx 0.02\ \text{VE}$$

Adding 0.2 VE to the 0.66 VE value at 60 kPa gives the projected VE table entry at 64 kPa:

$$\text{VE} = 0.02 + 0.66$$
$$= 0.68$$

Note: If you are extrapolating VE ahead of corrections to VE based on measured lambda according to the slope of VE changes determined by testing at lower engine load points, you may decide to apply percentage air/fuel ratio-based VE corrections only to the current load range rather than all higher ranges.

10. Increase throttle angle to load the engine to the next highest MAP breakpoint, such as 80 kPa. Suppose at 80 kPa we measure lambda = 1.01 (air/fuel ratio ≈ 14.9 on gasoline)? To correct the VE table we multiply current VE at 80 kPa (already corrected several times from 65 to 66 to 71) by 1.014.

$$71 * 1.014 \approx 72$$

We correct VE at 80 kPa once again, this time to a value of 72. But as before (unless we have extrapolated VE to higher load points and have decided to apply corrections only to the current load range), we'll correct not just this one entry, but apply the correction factor of 1.014 to VE table entries for *all* speed ranges at or above 80 kPa loading.

11. If the engine is not boosted with forced induction or running extremely high static compression that requires race fuel, you may decide to continue steady-state load calibration all the way up to the WOT zero-vacuum 100 kPa manifold pressure breakpoint. If the engine is boosted but there is a way to disable the blower or turbo(s) by removing the supercharger belt or blocking the turbo wastegate open (or perhaps removing the turbocharger), WOT testing at zero boost should be feasible. Make sure to avoid boost creep on turbocharged engines in case there is insufficient wastegate exhaust gas flow capacity when the wastegate is wide open to foil all boost. Alternately, it may be possible to stay out of boost with careful feathering of the throttle (or an adjustable throttle stop) such that you achieve 100-105 kPa MAP without having the throttle wide open.

A non-boosted powerplant in good health with streetable compression ratio at normal operating temperature running plenty of octane should operate without detonation at wide-open throttle and lambda = 1.0, but if you hear knock, back off the throttle IMMEDIATELY and verify that the engine is not overheating and that the spark advance table is reliably conservative for the engine. Since spark knock increases thermal loading in the combustion chamber, allow the engine to cool following detonation and verify that the fuel octane is definitely suitable for current operating conditions. If you are not already running high-octane racing gasoline, this would be a good time to drain the fuel supply tank and substitute race gas (only enough to tune the VE table, however, unless you will be routinely running race gas, as you will definitely want to optimize air/fuel ratio and spark timing for maximum torque using real-world fuel on any engine that might be knock-limited due to a high effective compression ratio).

If the engine knocks and nothing else is wrong and the global spark advance map is in general plausibly conservative for the powerplant, go into the main spark advance table and remove timing from speed-density breakpoints in the vicinity of the active VE cell(s) running the engine when it knocked. Retard timing in increments of at least 2 or 3 degrees until detonation disappears. It is fine to be aggressive in pulling timing, and do not worry at this time about excessive spark retard. Right now you're just calibrating the VE table, and when you're finished populating the table you will definitely be richening up target air/fuel ratio in the heavier, more knock-prone loading ranges to make power, also a highly effective anti-knock countermeasure. Even if you are forced to retard timing now at stoichiometric combustion, fuel enrichment may cool combustion enough later on to allow you to dial in full spark advance on the dyno when you're working to optimize performance by progressively increasing steady-state spark advance from known-conservative values until torque begins to fall off or you encounter detonation. What's important right now is to kill knock with spark retard so you can finish calibrating the naturally aspirated portion of the VE table with a homogenous air/fuel ratio. Retarding spark timing will eliminate any knock unless it is being caused by preignition (which is an indication of combustion chamber overheating that *must* be dealt with at all cost before continuing). Once again, keep an eye on engine, air, and fuel temperatures and, if necessary, allow things to cool and stabilize before continuing with testing. Remember, a VE table can be calibrated, if necessary, at a target global lambda richer than 1.0.

If you're concerned about detonation or excessive mechanical or thermal loading while dyno-calibrating under heavy loading, you may decide you want to stay away from full-throttle, steady-state VE calibration and flesh out the rest of the VE table. By the time you are through, full-throttle VE will have been corrected to a certain degree based on measured lambda at lower loading ranges, and the slope of VE trends approaching WOT will be well defined and available for linear extrapolation at WOT. At that point you may decide it is safe to finish the VE calibration in steady-state, or you may decide to run dyno sweeps to quickly get a reading on air/fuel ratio at full throttle across the rpm range (more in a moment).

12. Once you've corrected VE entries for the load ranges at 60 kPa and above at 2,000 rpm, back off the throttle and calibrate VE for the various loading ranges *below* 60 kPa. Measure lambda at, say, 50 kPa, and correct VE at all load ranges at or *below* 50 kPa at *all* rpm ranges, according to the percentage error in lambda at 50 kPa and 2,000 rpm. Continue downward until you've arrived at the lowest manifold pressure reachable at the current engine speed in steady-state conditions. The lowest kPa MAP the engine can ever see is reachable only during the high-manifold vacuum of heavy deceleration or using a special motoring torque-cell dyno equipped with an electric motor to simulate the effect of steady-state deceleration by applying power to turn the crankshaft to a specified fixed speed with the throttle closed or nearly closed. It is important to keep in mind that if the lowest achievable manifold pressure during hard deceleration at a given engine speed is between load ranges in the VE table, the VE estimation at the closest VE table breakpoints above and below the actual manifold pressure will be *averaged* into the air mass calculation, and the lower will not actually be reachable. If this is the case you might have to reconfigure the VE table such that there is a load range at rather below the lowest achievable manifold pressure.

MegaSquirt Generated VE Table (10psi)

kPa								
215								
195								
170	140	142	145	146	145	143	139	132
150	130	132	135	136	135	133	129	123
125	118	120	122	123	123	121	117	112
105	109	110	112	113	113	111	108	103
85	99	101	103	103	103	101	98	94
65	90	91	93	93	93	91	89	85
40	78	79	80	81	81	79	77	73
20	68	69	70	71	71	69	67	64
RPM	500	1000	2000	3100	4100	5200	6200	7300

MegaSquirt generated initial VE table (10psi). Based on Toyota 35-GTE engine with 600 rpm idle, 24 Hg idle vacuum, 7,200 redline, 245 hp at 6,000 rpm, 225 lb.-ft. at 3,200 rpm torque, 2.0L displacement, running 10 psi boost.

MegaSquirt Generated VE Table (10psi)

kPa								
260								
235								
205	137	139	141	143	142	139	136	129
180	126	128	131	132	131	129	125	120
150	114	115	118	119	118	116	113	108
125	103	105	107	108	107	105	102	98
100	93	94	96	97	96	95	92	88
75	82	84	85	86	86	84	82	78
45	70	71	72	73	73	71	69	66
20	59	60	61	62	62	61	59	56
RPM	500	1000	2000	3100	4100	5200	6200	7300

MegaSquirt–generated initial VE table (15psi). Based on Toyota 35-GTE engine with 600 rpm idle, 24 Hg idle vacuum, 7,200 redline, 245 hp at 6,000 rpm, 225 lb.-ft. at 3,200 rpm torque, 2.0L displacement, running 15 psi boost.

13. When you're finished calibrating the VE table at 2,000 rpm up to whatever maximum load range you're comfortable dealing with in steady state on a dyno, it's time to begin testing at a higher rpm range. Modern naturally aspirated automotive street engines are designed to have very flat torque curves, but pumping efficiency normally increases with the increasing frequency of valve opening events and increasing air charge inertia until rpm reaches peak torque, above which VE will begin to fade. Depending on the camshaft and intake runner design, you can expect to see at least some degree of improvement in VE at, say, 2,400 versus 2,000 rpm.

At this point in the scratch calibration process, the VE table cells in the 2,400 rpm column will be identical to those in the 2,000 column, having been previously corrected for load according to lambda error at 2,000 rpm. At this point, all VE table estimates in the 2,400 rpm column are likely to be low, which will show initially as lambda *lean* of the stoichiometric ratio at 2,400 and 60 kPa.

Throttle up the engine to 2,400 rpm and engage the dyno. Now increase throttle to bring load up to precisely 60 kPa once again, and measure lambda to make the first 2,400 rpm correction. This time, use measured lambda as a multiplier to scale the *entire* 2,400 rpm column at all loading ranges *plus* the rectangular region that includes all rpm ranges at or above 2400 at loading equal to or greater than 60 kPa. This is usually displayed as the upper right corner of the VE table.

14. With VE corrected at 60 kPa in the 2,400 rpm range, increase throttle to raise MAP to the next loading range—64, or 70 kPa, or whatever it is—and take a lambda reading. This time use measured lambda to scale the rectangular region of the VE table representing speeds greater than or equal to 2,400 rpm and loading at and above the current range, once again working on the assumption that trends in pumping efficiency tend to persist with changes in speed and loading.

15. Continue on up the 2,400 rpm column correcting VE to the lesser of 100 kPa or the highest manifold pressure you are

176	49	49	51	60	67	70	70	71	71	73	77	96	102	102	102	
150	49	49	51	60	67	70	70	71	71	73	77	90	96	96	96	
125	49	49	51	60	67	70	70	71	71	73	77	85	89	89	89	

comfortable dealing with on a load-holding dyno in steady-state. At each step measure lambda and use it to correct all entries in the upper right corner of the VE table in the region bounded by the current rpm and load. *Do not* at this time allow manifold pressure to go positive if the engine is equipped with a blower or turbo.

Note: If the EMS has five load ranges spanning 60 to 100 kPa MAP, by the time you reach WOT at the top of the second rpm range, you may have batch-corrected the 100 kPa entry in the second speed range as many as 10 times, with each correction sculpting the 100 kPa portion of the table closer and closer to correct VE, thus minimizing the required final correction when you measure air/fuel ratio on the dyno at 2,400 rpm and 100 kPa MAP.

16. When you are finished correcting the high-speed, high-load corner of the VE table as high as you are willing to go, throttle back and work *downward* through the load ranges less than 60 kPa, progressively applying each correction at a particular loading cell downward to *all* cells in all load ranges at or below the current MAP range for all rpm ranges *at or above* the current 2,400 rpm range (the lower right corner of the VE table on most engine management systems).

When you're finished, throttle back and allow the engine and dyno environment to cool and stabilize.

17. Now move to the next higher speed range above 2,400 rpm. Well, perhaps not the *next*. Some engine management systems have VE or injection pulse width tables with 40 or more rpm ranges spread across the rpm range of the engine and 20 or more ranges spread across the pressure range of the MAP sensor. If a table has 41 speed and 21 loading ranges, we're talking 861 speed-density breakpoints. In practical terms, if it took even one minute to measure and calibrate each breakpoint, calibrating all 861 breakpoints would take over 14 hours. Depending on how carefully you've configured the VE table to locate speed and load ranges where they are most useful, some proportion of table cells will not be reachable on most engines, but if you calibrated only 75 percent of the breakpoints, it would still take nearly 11 hours at one minute each. Depending on the resolution of the VE table, you may want to skip testing certain rpm ranges where VE is unlikely to vary much between adjacent ranges. For example, if the VE table has rpm ranges at 200 rpm intervals, you might want to focus on measuring correcting every other one between 2,000 rpm and redline. Skipping ranges can be a tremendous time-saver, but below 2,000 rpm, where VE changes with engine speed are less likely to be linear, you'll probably want to test and calibrate *all* speed ranges.

Throttle the engine up to the next rpm range, engage the dyno to hold speed, and add throttle to increase MAP to the same initial load you used when testing at 2,400. If you're at 2,800, as before, measure lambda and make corrections to the high-speed, high-load, upper right corner of the VE table bounded this time by 2,800 rpm and 60 kPa, using measured lambda at the current speed-density breakpoint. Scale the entire region as a percentage using measured lambda as the multiplier. Proceed iteratively upward toward WOT, making VE corrections to the diminishing region of the table at and above the current engine loading and speed ranges as you did at 2,400. After that work downward as before below 60 kPa toward idle.

Unless the engine is out of the vehicle for testing on a torque-cell engine dyno with a very robust cooling system (containing perhaps thousands of gallons of water!), you will probably begin to encounter thermal loading issues as you test at higher levels of horsepower. Pay careful attention to managing engine and air temperature in order to 1) avoid detonation and prevent engine damage from excessive thermal loading in the combustion chambers, and 2) make sure that estimated cylinder air mass is not adversely affected by engine or dyno room heat soak in such a way that calculated fuel mass and VE are based on false assumptions about air density entering the cylinders. If you cannot maintain an even cylinder air intake temperature, lambda error that is actually a result of heat-induced air density changes may be misinterpreted as reduced pumping efficiency. A flawed VE table calibrated on this assumption will not be internally consistent and will not reflect true pumping efficiency across the operating range of the engine.

It may or may not be possible or practical to calibrate the VE table all the way to redline in steady state due to thermal loading issues, but from a safety point of view the good news is that horsepower is almost always on the way down as you approach redline, and pumping efficiency will have been headed downward ever since peak-torque rpm. By the time you get anywhere near redline, multiple corrections to the VE table based on testing at lower rpm will previously have sculpted the region of heaviest loading near redline multiple times. Under these circumstances, halting VE table calibration short of redline above peak horsepower simply results in overly optimistic VE estimates at very high engine speed, and, therefore, overly rich fuel calculations and cooler combustion unlikely to cause overheating or knock. However, the right way to "safe-up" the high-speed, high-load operating range of an engine is with rich target air/fuel ratios and retarded timing, not an inaccurate VE table. A far better idea than simply quitting while you're ahead is to *extrapolate* WOT VE near redline based on VE trends at the highest rpm ranges actually tested, making sure that you err on the high side to keep combustion cool by avoiding lean mixtures. And then, with the VE table plausibly populated all the way up to redline and maximum MAP using dyno test air/fuel ratio results or extrapolation of test results into the boosted load ranges if the engine is supercharged, you're ready to correct the upper reaches of the table in actual testing using WOT dyno *sweeps*.

18. But first we'll want to set VE at speed ranges below 2,000 rpm where VE falls off with speed in a nonlinear way. Keep in mind that at this point, VE table values at all speed ranges below 2,000 rpm will be identical to the values at 2,000 at all load ranges, and that engine pumping efficiency can be expected to decline as engine speed drops below 2,000.

Reduce engine speed to the next lower rpm range, say 1,600 rpm, engage the dyno in speed-holding mode, and increase throttle as before to 60 kPa, and observe measured lambda, which will probably be rich due to a VE estimate that is correct for a higher rpm. Use measured lambda to correct the entire VE table at and below 1,600 rpm for all load ranges by scaling down the VE cells according to measured lambda. This initial correction should account for the bulk of the required correction to all load ranges at this engine speed, since load-based pumping efficiency changes at 1,600 rpm should be very similar to 2,000 rpm.

Work upward to higher load ranges, correcting the upper left corner of the VE table at the higher load ranges, applying corrections to all load ranges at or above the current breakpoint at all speeds equal to or less than the current rpm. Pay close

49	49	51	60	67	70	70	71	71	73	77	96	102	102	102	98
49	49	51	60	67	70	70	71	71	73	77	90	96	96	96	98
49	49	51	60	67	70	70	71	71	73	77	85	89	89	89	87

attention for the possibility of spark knock, which readily occurs as the engine lugs to heavy loads at lower engine speeds.

With the upper left corner of the VE table handled, work downward from 60 kPa to minimum MAP, this time applying corrections to all speeds less than or equal to the current range at all load ranges less than or equal to the current load range.

Downward-based VE corrections will begin to sculpt VE at idle as soon as test speed drops below 2,000 to the extent that by the time you reach a fast idle of 1,000 rpm or so, air/fuel ratio at idle should be very close.

Continue VE mapping to as low a stable engine speed as possible, if at all possible to a speed minimally at least 100 to 200 rpm below the final target idle speed, which will allow the EMS to accurately calculate air mass if the engine bogs due to clutch release or sudden loading due to power steering, A/C, or other accessories at idle.

19. If you have not already mapped VE at full throttle due to concerns about continuous heavy loading or continuous high speeds, particularly in the supercharged range of manifold pressure on a boosted engine, you may want to map VE under these conditions using datalogging and quick dyno sweeps. One significant advantage of the WOT dynorun on an inertial chassis dyno like the popular Dynojet 248 has always been that the relatively quick duration of the pull increases the likelihood that an engine with questionable tuning or longevity at high speed and/or high power levels will finish the run before there's time for mechanical or thermal loading to cause engine damage. Load-holding dynamometers provide a conceptually similar capability in the form of the automated "ramp run" or "sweep," wherein rather than holding engine speed constant, the computer-controlled dyno load absorber holds the powerplant at a rapid-fire succession of rpm steps within a specified range according to a configurable rate of acceleration and step size. A ramp run on a load-holding dyno does not literally provide continuous acceleration like a an inertial dyno, but instead a discontinuous series of accelerations separated by brief pauses at which the engine is held momentarily at a fixed speed before being allowed to accelerate to the next higher step. A fast ramp run *sounds* kind of like a single full-throttle inertial pull that sweeps across the rpm range of the powerplant, and it's over at light speed compared to the steady-state testing we've been discussing up to this point. The output of a dyno sweep is a chart of logged rpm, horsepower, and torque, and, optionally, airflow, MAP, EGT, lambda, and other engine parameters. *The logged data can be used to correct VE table cells based on measured lambda error at cells encountered in the ramp run.*

Note: If you can eliminate transient enrichment by turning it off and/or running in a high gear at a fixed throttle angle (such as WOT), there is no reason that sweep-type runs cannot be accomplished on an inertial chassis dyno like the Dynojet.

Healthy naturally aspirated engines with conservative timing and fuel appropriate to the compression ratio should be able to tolerate full throttle and lambda = 1.0 without knock, and if that's the case, you may already have calibrated the upper reaches of the VE table at 100 kPa in steady-state. If you're running automated dyno sweeps to populate a VE table at high load and rpm as a result of concerns about overheating or engine damage in steady state dyno testing or because the engine is boosted with a blower or turbo, some preparation is required before running the first WOT dyno sweep.

In all cases before commencing automated sweeps to optimize VE, air/fuel ratio, or torque under heavy loading, richen up target air/fuel ratio at the higher naturally aspirated and boosted load ranges. You should not be sweep-testing the powerplant under boost just yet, but setting rich target air/fuel ratios in boosted load ranges where VE was initialized with extrapolated data provides some protection against knock in case of unintended boost. Go into the air/fuel ratio table and set the table cells at all speed ranges for load ranges starting around 90 kPa to a target lambda of 0.85. Then set target air/fuel ratio at all speed ranges for boosted load ranges above 105 kPa to lambda = 0.78. Remember that the mathematics of correcting VE are slightly more complex at target air/fuel ratios other than lambda = 1.0. Keep in mind that if manifold pressure exceeds a load range such as 105 kPa, most if not all engine management systems will begin averaging in target lambda and VE from the next higher load range above 105 kPa into air, fuel, and timing calculations, which could have a material affect on measured lambda in dyno testing and, therefore, the accuracy of the VE table calibration in this region.

If the engine is boosted with a turbocharger—which by definition has a variable-speed drive system—achievable manifold pressure at heavier engine loading will be heavily dependent on turbine energy available to drive the compressor. Which, for a given turbine configuration, will be dependent on the rate of acceleration of the engine, engine rpm, engine loading, exhaust gas temperature, turbine heat soak, the inertial mass of the turbo rotating assembly, and other factors. And the thermal efficiency of the centrifugal compressor at the applicable pressure ratio and compressor speed and the basic pumping efficiency of the engine.

Less efficient engines force the compressor to build more boost pressure to push a given mass airflow through the powerplant. Bottom line, the achievable manifold pressure of a turbocharged engine at any particular combination of engine rpm and throttle position could range anywhere from a bit less than ambient atmospheric pressure (100-105 kPa or zero boost) all the way up to the maximum pressure ratio of the compressor. You'll need to map the VE table of a turbo engine at all achievable manifold pressures and engine speeds, and the place to begin if at all possible is when the naturally aspirated portion of the table has been mapped to WOT and zero boost with the turbocharger ineffective and the pumping capacity of the engine essentially that of the equivalent powerplant without power-adders.

To calibrate the VE table of a boosted engine at the top of the naturally aspirated load range in dyno sweeps, you'll need to foil boost so that manifold pressure and intake air temperature remain at ambient levels. The options are 1) temporarily de-install the turbo or blower, 2) temporarily remove the blower belt on a supercharger, 3) jam open the wastegate on a turbo system if it's capable of bleeding off enough exhaust energy to prevent boost. 4) If that's not possible, try to regulate the throttle carefully or install a temporary adjustable throttle stop to throttle angle in such a way as to limit airflow through the throttle body to less than 105 kPa.

In preparation for WOT dyno sweeps, the timing map should be *very conservative*. The fuel should be racing gas, or at a minimum, premium street gasoline. An individual-cylinder knock-retard system is good insurance against damaging knock, though a generic aftermarket system will not automatically be optimized to detect knock frequencies on your particular engine, meaning the knock-retard system could miss detonation, meaning you are not relieved of the burden of listening for

49	49	51	60	67	70	70	71	71	73	77	96	102	102	102
49	49	51	60	67	70	70	71	71	73	77	90	96	96	96
49	49	51	60	67	70	70	71	71	73	77	85	89	89	89

knock and aborting the run immediately if you hear any. At this point you are not trying to optimize power and torque, simply calibrating VE based on target versus measured lambda. The fact that target air/fuel ratio at heavy loading is no longer lambda = 1.0 means that rather than simply multiplying current VE by measured lambda, you'll need to *calculate* a correction factor before you can use it to adjust estimated VE.

Plan to begin the first dyno sweep at the lowest rpm that will deliver smooth, acceleration at wide-open throttle, somewhere around 1,500 rpm. Datalog rpm, MAP, and lambda on both the dyno and the EMS if possible. If the engine is installed in a vehicle on a chassis dyno, standard practice is make ramp runs in third or fourth gear at a sweep rate of 300 rpm/sec all the way up to redline. Be ready to abort the run immediately if the engine begins to knock or air/fuel ratio goes lean of lambda = 1.0.

20. Launch the first sweep, and when it's finished, stop the datalog(s) and idle or shutdown the powerplant and search the logs for speed-density breakpoints encountered in the run at which measured lambda deviates from target air/fuel ratio. Depending on the dyno and the EMS configuration, rpm and loading points encountered in the sweep may or may not precisely match speed-density breakpoints in the VE table, meaning do the best you can with the measured air/fuel ratio you have from nearby breakpoints. Most engine management systems have "interpreter" programs for searching and analyzing and graphing logged data. Hopefully manifold pressure will have remained at 100 kPa throughout the run, at which measured air/fuel ratio should now be compared to target lambda of 0.85. If something went wrong and manifold pressure rose into the boosted range above MAP =105 kPa, measured air/fuel ratio will be influenced by target lambda of 0.78 at intermediate load points between 105 kPa and the next higher load range, which will be something like 120 (above which measured air/fuel ratio will be 100 percent a function of lambda = 0.78). Before making another ramp run take steps to prevent a reoccurrence of boost.

Go ahead and correct the VE table at any breakpoints where lambda failed to meet the target. At points of lambda error, divide measured lambda by target lambda, which will yield the percentage air/fuel ratio error and the required correction factor to VE that should put lambda where it belongs. Let's say that at 3,000 rpm and 100 kPa MAP, measured lambda is 0.82 instead of the target 0.85, meaning the air/fuel ratio is overly rich. Lambda error is $(0.85 - 0.82) / 0.85 = 0.03 / 0.85 \approx 0.0353$, an error of 3.53 percent.

The VE correction factor is:

Correction = Measured lambda / Target lambda
= 0.82 / 0.85
≈ 0.9647

Multiplying current VE by 0.9647 adjusts estimated VE in the breakpoint at 3,000 rpm and 100 kPa MAP downward. This will automatically result in a lower air mass estimation the next time the engine operates at the 3,000 rpm/100 kPa breakpoint, and consequently a lower delivered fuel mass. This will deliver a leaner measured lambda, and, assuming the fuel injectors were correctly modeled in the EMS setup, lambda should end up precisely where it belongs at 0.85.

21. Exhaustively correct every VE table cell at breakpoints reached in the dyno sweep where lambda was wrong (or at breakpoints *very close* to speed-density points encountered in the run). The trick to mapping is changing not just one cell, but blending in the surrounding cells to form a smooth slope or graph. Some tuners will change one breakpoint a modest amount, then pull the surrounding cells up or down as required to make a smooth slope. If you do not adjust cells surrounding the target cell, you will probably not get the full magnitude of changes, as the EMS will average out sharp peaks and valleys. A good way to handle blending in ramp-run corrections is to call up a graphical representation of the VE table and adjust VE table cells near the erroneous VE cells to smooth the transition to nearby cells and previously mapped regions of the table so that there are no abrupt changes in VE between adjacent cells. This is critically important because VE table cells adjacent to a corrected cell will begin to be weighted into the air mass calculation as soon as rpm or MAP deviates at all from the exact coordinates of the corrected breakpoint. Pay special attention to regions of the VE table where target air/fuel ratio changed to make sure you are using the correct target air/fuel ratio in the correction calculations if target lambda is not 1.0. Run another WOT sweep to verify that the calculated VE corrections worked to correct lambda. It is possible you may want to run a sweep that targets MAP one loading range down from full atmospheric manifold pressure by running less than 100 percent throttle if the range was not previously calibrated at steady state. Alternatively, you'll want to manually map, say, the 90 kPa range in steady state once VE is known to be correct at WOT.

22. With 100 kPa out of the way, if the engine is naturally aspirated, you're done calibrating the VE table and can move on to the target AFR table.

If the engine is boosted with a turbo or supercharger there's still testing to do under more extreme conditions. If you are not already running race gas, switch over now. When the boosted regions of the VE table are calibrated, you'll need to downgrade to whatever fuel will be used under normal circumstances before adjusting target air/fuel ratio and spark timing to optimize torque and fight knock.

Before running boosted ramp runs, *extrapolate VE* into the boosted range of the VE table based on recent VE corrections in the high-load ranges of the naturally aspirated ranges of the table from previous ramp runs. As before, compute the linear slope of VE increases at the highest tested loading breakpoints and then extrapolate VE rise for the various speed ranges in the boosted region of the VE table.

If you are working on an engine dyno with a high-capacity cooling system, you may decide to continue steady-state calibration right on up into the boosted ranges of the table. Otherwise, the cooling capacity of most cars and light trucks is rarely up to continuous loading under boosted conditions, in which case the only choice is to run a series of sweeps of increasing amplitude into boosted manifold pressure and allow the engine to cool while you're correcting VE in between runs. Using some means of limiting maximum boost pressure (such as a wastegate controller on a turbo engine or a electronic bleed valve on a supercharged engine), incrementally work your way upward through higher and higher ranges of manifold pressure using WOT dyno sweeps. As before, correct VE according to datalogged lambda error and smooth adjacent cells to eliminate abrupt changes in VE. Extrapolate any changes in VE upward to all higher loading ranges before increasing boost for the next ramp run at the next highest load range. As always, be vigilant to manage thermal loading. If you hear detonation, abort the run immediately, and, if necessary,

49	49	51	60	67	70	70	71	71	73	77	96	102	102	102	98
49	49	51	60	67	70	70	71	71	73	77	90	96	96	96	98
49	49	51	60	67	70	70	71	71	73	77	85	89	89	89	87

pull timing from breakpoints in the spark advance table at datalogged speed-density points where the powerplant knocked. Continue all the way to maximum boost.

When you are through, graph the VE table and examine the landscape of the surface showing VE as a vertical function of engine rpm and load. An engine is a positive displacement air pump, and pumping efficiency will only change gradually, with no sharp peaks or ridges or sudden deep trenches or holes. In general, volumetric efficiency rises with both rpm and loading, with some falloff in VE in upper rpm ranges. In fact, the amplitude of VE at WOT at or near 100 kPa MAP should match the torque curve of the engine, with VE and torque peaking somewhere in the middle. If intake, exhaust, and camshaft are selected to optimize resonation effects to pressurize the intake valve at a particular engine speed, this will bulge VE upward in this area. It may be difficult or impossible to reach the highest loading cells in the lowest rpm ranges, or lowest loading cells at very high rpm. Most tuners populate unreachable areas of the table by extrapolating VE downward from higher rpm or upward from low rpm.

23. Afterthoughts

An alternative to mapping high-load regions of the VE table with sweeps on a load-holding dyno is to calibrate VE on the track with a tuner riding shotgun with a laptop and a driver executing acceleration runs at maximum throttle. Following each acceleration run, adjust the VE table cells encountered in the run to bring measured air/fuel ratio to target air/fuel ratio (lambda = 1.0, lambda = 0.85, or lambda = 0.78). The trick is to work methodically in a higher gear, staying away from sudden throttle increases to avoid contaminating lambda readings with acceleration enrichment.

Some tuners routinely apply ramp run-type methods to calibrating VE at lower loading. On the street (or perhaps an inertial chassis dyno), datalog the actual air/fuel ratios as you drive the vehicle through the range of speeds and loading, and have the system tell you the air/fuel ratio correction factor required to achieve targets in the air/fuel ratio table. This can be an efficient method of tuning because a relatively quick test run can encounter many cells in the air/fuel or VE table, which can be fixed following the run. You may decide to make acceleration runs with an adjustable throttle stop limiting maximum throttle below 100 percent to derate maximum manifold pressure for calibrating at a repeatable maximum engine loading. The goal should be to accelerate by increasing throttle angle and holding the throttle at a fixed angle in a high gear to eliminate transient enrichment from impacting measured air/fuel ratio. Work your way through the table, adjusting VE at speed-density breakpoints to bring measured air/fuel ratio back to target, adjusting surrounding cells to smooth the transition to the surrounding table. Beware the most dangerous high-boost cells on a 2- or 3-bar boosted engine.

Some highly sophisticated engine management systems do not use a special VE table. Instead, they manage the engine using Fuel Tables populated with data corresponding to injection pulse width at the speed-density breakpoints. In this system you adjust pulse width (or percent user-defined maximum pulse width) to optimize individual fuel cells for best torque, or efficiency, or lowest emissions. If there is a VE table, you will still want to experiment on a dyno to optimize the target air/fuel ratios, since it can be difficult or impossible to predict in advance what the optimal air/fuel ratios will be, particularly on a modified engine.

The ideal way to optimize fuel and spark for maximum torque is to work in steady state on a load-holding dynamometer so you can watch the effect on torque of dynamic changes to air/fuel ratio (and spark advance in what is sometimes referred to as a spark hook test). An alternative is to employ an inertial chassis dyno like the Dynojet 248 or an accelerometer device like the G-Tech to generate and overlay multiple acceleration runs to compare the effect of timing and air/fuel ratio changes on torque.

OPTIMIZING AFR

With the VE table defined, you'll need a dynamometer and a way to measure air/fuel ratio to find 100 percent of the free power where you need it and best economy where you want it. There is simply no way to fully optimize an engine management system without a dyno and wideband air/fuel ratio meter or fast exhaust gas analyzer. At this stage in the tuning process you will be looking for mean or even lean best torque at high load range via target air/fuel ratio and then timing changes. Ideally you'll have installed exhaust gas temperature probes as a safety measure to detect dangerously rising EGT before it is too late to prevent engine damage.

An engine calibrated exclusively on a dynamometer of almost any kind will almost definitely run sub-optimally rich on the street and track. To produce smooth performance under all conditions, when you are done with a dyno calibration, you'll need to road test and recalibrate to eliminate any hesitation, stumbling, and surging in ordinary driving, as well as hunting at idle. An accelerometer device is invaluable for street tuning, as is a wideband readout. But be on the lookout for black exhaust smoke and lazy response, which indicates rich mixtures, or intake backfiring, coughing, and misfiring, which indicates lean mixtures. Always listen carefully for engine-damaging detonation—meaning never tune with the stereo blaring and the air conditioning at full roar.

To avoid detonation and lean-mixture meltdowns at high loading (torque) when calibrating to optimize power, always work from rich to lean. Start by tuning the engine at idle in open-loop mode but with the O_2 *readout* turned on. The precise target idle air/fuel ratio for engines with mild, streetable cams is 14.68:1, also known as stoichiometric, but if the production vehicle will run in closed-loop mode at light cruise and idle, you may want to tune slightly richer than lambda = 1.0 and let the closed-loop system pull fuel under actual operations. Lambda = 1.0 will produce a good idle on street-type engines without racing cams (though probably not the absolute fastest idle, which occurs rich of stoichiometric) and is most compatible with catalytic converters and narrowband closed-loop O_2 feedback operations.

Engines with big cams may need richer air/fuel mixtures in the range of lambda = 0.89-0.95 (gasoline air/fuel ratio in the 13s) to idle well due to overlap-induced reversion that can blow the mixture back into the intake runners and EGR-type charge contamination with exhaust gases. If you are not using timed sequential fuel injection, converting to sequential injection can really help, and if you are, you may find that changing the phasing of the end-of-injection can help to minimize the impact of idle-spoiling reversion effects.

Engines with truly radical cams (with a lot of duration and overlap) may hunt at idle even with rich air/fuel ratios due to an inherently unstable and wandering manifold pressure causing the EMS to chase its own tail, so to speak. If such an engine has an MAF sensor, MAF accuracy and operation could be compromised by reversion and turbulence in the inlet tube near the MAF sensor, and variations in airflow could, again, feed back into the fuel calculation and make it even harder for the engine to idle well. Throttle position, however, will not change when an engine is idling, so an EMS is likely to achieve a better idle with difficult engines by disregarding the MAP signal and using throttle position sensor (TPS) data as an indicator of engine loading instead of manifold absolute pressure (MAP). Alpha-N systems manage nonboosted engines quite well using throttle position for the load estimate across the speed range. Alpha-N can work well on some engines, particularly on light vehicles like performance motorcycles, but it does not work well on engines that require significant changes to fueling based on minor loading changes when there might be zero change in throttle position. Some engine management systems like the Electromotive TEC3 and the Motec M4-8 provide the option to *blend* TPS and MAP data such that the EMS fuels the powerplant at idle and light loads using on throttle position, but transitions to MAP-based fueling at higher levels of engine load (particularly during boosted operation when manifold pressure can rise above atmospheric pressure with zero change in throttle position or rpm). ECUs configured to estimate engine load based on throttle position may need a fairly steep increase in pulse width at light loads, particularly on systems with large throttle areas in which there is a large change in airflow for a small throttle angle change.

When you have a good idle, turn on the air conditioning, which will noticeably load the engine harder. Some engines have an EMS-actuated dashpot that immediately kicks in when the engine is really cold or when the air conditioning is energized to initiate a fast idle. You might want to consider using it with an aftermarket programmable EMS or just wiring it to the air conditioning clutch circuit to come on when the air conditioning compressor comes on. Although most EMSs now have idle speed stabilization logic that can regulate an IAC stepper-motor to bypass air around the throttle plate to the degree required to maintain a target idle speed under all conditions, the IAC system may not be fast enough to deal with air conditioning–induced load changes at idle without a bothersome momentary drop in rpm when the air conditioning kicks on.

Ideally, the sudden load of an air conditioning compressor will cause the EMS to switch to another speed-loading cell, which can be optimized for the best idle with the air conditioning on (perhaps with a little more timing or fuel to stabilize the idle almost instantly). It is for this sort of reason that sophisticated EMS systems provide for user-defined nonlinear granularity of rpm and loading ranges. You can create loading or speed breakpoints that are closer together where required to allow the EMS to change fueling and/or spark advance in response to subtle changes in engine speed or loading.

Most modern EMSs now have sophisticated IAC logic that enables you to command the interval at which the EMS reexamines idle speed for possible corrective action, as well as the magnitude of the initial step in a corrective direction based on the magnitude of deviation from target idle speed. Careful configuration and calibration of the IAC control system can help a lot. Some EMSs have special functions to handle air conditioning problems.

Move to higher rpm ranges, still with zero load, stabilize the engine at a target speed and hold it there while you trim fuel until the air/fuel ratio readout shows slightly rich but no more than 5 percent rich of stoichiometric (lambda = .95). For now, do not get involved at this time in optimizing acceleration enrichment.

The target air/fuel ratio for light cruising is 14.5–14.9 or 0.99–1.01 lambda, though you may be able to successfully tune an engine with very mild cam specs for good fuel economy at light loading with air/fuel mixtures approaching 16:1.

Again, a mixture trim module or global fuel trim can be very useful for instantly testing percentages of enrichment or enleanment.

At medium engine loading, you'll need to target richer mixtures in the neighborhood of 13:1.

As the midrange starts to get fleshed out, bring up the graphing function and work ahead on the graph to keep higher throttle settings in line with how the midrange is shaping out and consistently richer than what is proving to work in the midrange. Again, the trick is to make brief forays into high-loading conditions, the rate of acceleration, torque, and drivability, fleshing out the active target AFR or pulse width cells and adjacent cells. Some people find it much easier to tune tables in graphical format, using mouse and/or arrow keys. Others find it easier to edit numbers in the table, perhaps flipping back and forth between tabular and graphical format (there will usually be a hot key for this purpose). However you do it, getting an occasional look at a 3-D graph of the fuel or VE table is very valuable, because you'll begin to get a sense of the overall surface of the map, and you'll also be able to see any anomalies in the surface that probably don't belong there. You'll find that only a relatively small portion of the fuel map is used much and that you have to work to get the engine running very far off the beaten path, so to speak. If you started with a plausible startup map and have already mapped out a main VE table, what we're doing here is just fine tuning, but always stay on the rich side.

For normally aspirated street vehicles or boosted engines that are not severely knock-limited, mean best torque (MBT) should fall in the 12.2:1 range at the highest engine load points, though boosted engines often require additional fuel (or water injection) for combustion cooling to fight knock and prevent meltdown. If, as recommended, you are running really high-octane unleaded racing gasoline to minimize the effect of lean mixture mistakes, runaway boost, or poor tuning technique, knock should not be a problem, particularly with a conservative timing map, and, preferably, a good EMS knock-sensing and retard EMS strategy or possibly an add-on knock control device like the J&S Safeguard. At some point, you will have to turn off the knock-retard program in order to optimize basic safe timing and safe-up timing, fuel, and boost to work with the gasoline octane you'll be running, but not quite yet.

Dallas tuner Bob Norwood points out that super-duty engines always make the most power as you lean them out just before they burn down. Really experienced, brave tuners like Norwood searching carefully for every last horsepower on a race car will sometimes run high-power air/fuel ratios leaner than 12.4:1, but such a mixture is definitely more dangerous in really high-output engines, and—as Norwood, who has set a variety of land-speed records at the mile-high Bonneville Salt Flats, can testify. The increased rpm at peak-horsepower will definitely produce greater mechanical stress on mechanical parts like connecting rods, and peak horsepower will result in more thermal loading to the cooling system and so forth (which can increase the tendency for detonation). But it is peak torque that makes the most cylinder pressure, and peak torque thus requires slightly richer mixtures than peak power. Many tuners

EMS TUNING

214

49	49	51	60	67	70	70	71	71	73	77	96	102	102	102	98
49	49	51	60	67	70	70	71	71	73	77	90	96	96	96	98
49	49	51	60	67	70	70	71	71	73	77	85	89	89	89	87

recommend optimizing a high-power calibration by tuning from a known over-rich setting and then carefully leaning the mixture until torque falls off slightly, then quicklymoving in the rich direction until you achieve peak torque.

If you develop the fuel map on a chassis or engine dyno, you will almost definitely need to lean out the map for best performance in the real world of competition or street performance. For one thing, dynos cannot accurately create real-world conditions like underhood airflow at speed or ram-air effects. What's more, load-holding dynos capable of keeping the engine indefinitely at a certain speed and loading provide extremely high thermal loading that demands safe-rich mixtures that may be suboptimal for achieving maximum performance on the street under less severe conditions.

Exhaust gas temperature (EGT) data can be invaluable to warn you of danger before it is too late in high-power tuning. You can take it to the bank that a gasoline piston engine that is not knock-limited will make peak power at an air/fuel ratio between lambda 0.80 and 0.88 (11.8-13.0 on gasoline). However, the EGT at peak power AFR is less predictable and depends on many factors, including ignition timing, cams, pistons, headers, and so on. EGT at peak power might be anything between, say, 1,250 and 1,800 degrees, or even a bit hotter. Typical peak EGT on a performance automotive street engine would be more likely in the range of 1,350 to 1,550 degrees. Peak EGT typically occurs at about 75 degrees Fahrenheit lean of best power, and temperature falls off from there in both the lean and rich directions.

Virtually all piston-engine aircraft have a mixture control used to richen the mixture for maximum safe climb performance, to optimize the air/fuel ratio at cruise, and to kill the engine at shutdown. Pilots operating in cruise conditions (steady state) use exhaust gas temperature (turbine inlet temperature on turbocharged aircraft) measured by a pyrometer to lean the air/fuel ratio for peak power or best economy. The exact procedure is specific to a particular engine type in a particular aircraft, but you typically begin leaning from a specific rich mixture that's used to provide a high-power safe climb out based on a particular flow in gallons per hour on the fuel flow meter. In level cruise flight the standard procedure is to set the throttle for a specified engine rpm (or manifold pressure, in the case of a constant-speed prop) and gradually lean the mixture for best economy manually until the EGT reaches a peak temperature (typically measured at the turbine inlet), and then continue leaning until EGT is 50 degrees cooler than peak.

Continuous EGT above 1,550 degrees would be a cause for concern on many engines. If you log EGT on an engine working at a known optimal peak-power air/fuel ratio, then a rapidly rising EGT moving out of the expected range will warn you that something is dangerously wrong in time to manually take countermeasures (or the EMS might be configured to sound an alarm and take automatic countermeasures such as adding large amounts of fuel, retarding timing, and backing off an electronic throttle). Detonation will rapidly increase combustion temperature and EGT, but would not affect the exhaust gas oxygen content as seen on a wideband air/fuel ratio sensor. An EGT pyrometer has the additional advantage that it is not damaged by leaded fuel, which neither wideband nor narrowband O_2 sensors can tolerate for an extended time.

Spark plug condition can tell you a lot about steady-state combustion at peak torque or peak power. Check the spark plugs after hard acceleration to get a snapshot of air/fuel mixture. The way to do this is to abruptly shut off the engine at full load (making sure you don't lock the steering if you're actually driving rather than on a dyno) and immediately check the plugs. Overly light or white plugs indicate a lean mixture, while dark, sooty plugs imply too rich a mixture. When the tuning is correct, normal plugs should be light brown immediately after a hard run. Metal sparks are evidence of detonation.

A wideband closed-loop system can be very useful to speed up tuning and smooth out variations in air/fuel ratio at midrange and high-power settings once you're in the neighborhood of optimal. When you've built up a number of islands of correct fueling (not just single cells) and have some idea of the optimal air/fuel ratio, you can probably use an interpolation function to build a smooth linear surface connecting the known-good islands. Now calibrate the target air/fuel ratio table cells in the vicinity with plausible air/fuel ratio values, and turn on wideband closed-loop fuel correction and run the engine. Note the amount of correction the EMS is applying to reach the target air/fuel ratio at various cells, then correct the fuel table to minimize the amount of auto-correction (the main fuel table should always be constructed so auto-correction is in the direction of *pulling out* fuel).

Some interceptor devices present a user interface which, in effect, is that of a programmable standalone ECU—in which case calibration is the identical process (only easier, since you are starting with a known-excellent factory calibration and working to hot rod critical (boosted) areas of the calibration, in most cases to add fuel and remove timing for a power-adder conversion).

If you are working with an entirely independent add-on auxiliary fuel or timing device such as an additional injector controller (AIC) or timing boost-retard processor, the first thing is to verify that it is installed correctly and functioning properly. AIC operation will be triggered by a configurable combination of loading and rpm, so test the AIC system by disconnecting the AIC load reference line from the intake manifold and connecting it to a hand air pump and operating the engine at a speed that's within the A/C trigger rpm range but below the trigger loading point (above which the engine *needs* fuel enrichment). Then pump up the manifold pressure reference line with the hand pump until pressure at the AIC reference is above the configured threshold triggering pressure, and use an injector tester to verify that all auxiliary injectors begin operating when they're supposed to as pressure reaches to the trigger point. Alternately, bleed off fuel pressure to the addition injector(s), and using a mechanic's stethoscope, listen to hear an additional injector clicking rapidly. Alternatively, watch a wideband air/fuel ratio meter to verify that the air/fuel ratio richens up. As a last resort, test the AIC with at least one of the additional injectors spraying into a safe container so you can actually see it operating (this could be dangerous if you are not extremely careful). Before actual loaded testing on the road or dyno, make sure to verify that the fuel-supply system had adequate reserve capacity to fuel all primary and additional injectors without a pressure drop.

When you actually begin testing the AIC under a load, the trick, as always, is to work from rich to lean using high-octane fuel and a known-conservative timing map. In the case of a boost-retard device, work from a conservative timing setting in the direction of more timing advance, ideally with a load-holding dyno measuring torque at a fixed engine speed as you increase throttle. Since a turbocharger adds approximately 10 percent torque per pound of boost (this will tend to fall off at higher boost), you can figure needing at least 10 percent more fuel per psi boost, plus any additional fuel required to cool combustion as an anti-knock countermeasure. If possible, check out the main fuel map pulse width in the target speed-loading cells that will be boosted, and set the AIC to deliver at least 10 percent extra fuel per-psi boost, compensating for any differences in injector fuel-flow capacity. If you do not know the stock pulse width, there are pulse width meters that can be used to measure injection pulse width. Otherwise, estimate the additional horsepower or torque you expect to generate per-psi boost and apply the correct formula to the amount of fuel required per horsepower per cylinder at a 12.0–12.5 air/fuel ratio. Follow the instructions on the AIC, and test with careful forays into boosted territory, using a wideband O_2 sensor and preferably a knock sensor to help protect the engine from knock or lean-mixture damage.

OPTIMIZING SPARK ADVANCE

As EMS supplier Electromotive writes in the TEC3 user manual, "Perhaps the most important step in tuning an engine is establishing the required ignition advance. An engine with too much timing will detonate, regardless of how much fuel is thrown at it. An engine with too little timing will perform poorly and overheat the exhaust in short order."

Late ignition timing can make an engine run roughly, and it will definitely increase the exhaust gas temperature (since the mixture continues burning later in the combustion cycle). If the exhaust headers are glowing, you know there is too little spark advance; if the engine is knocking, timing may be too advanced.

Optimal spark timing varies, with the overall goal being to light off the charge mixture in time so that peak combustion pressure occurs when the piston is at 15 degrees after top dead center on the power stroke. A critical overarching requirement, however, is also to avoid engine damage by delaying light-off to the degree required to avoid having unburned portions of the charge explode as combustion pressure and heat build during the burn (as the piston may still be compressing the mixture). The optimal amount of timing advance varies inversely with volumetric efficiency because denser mixtures burn faster and require less lead time to achieve the 15-degree peak.

Therefore, engines need more advance at low-load, small throttle settings when VE is poor. At the same time, when the engine is running at high speed, a combustion event of fixed length in time consumes more degrees of crankshaft rotation, requiring more timing advance. Combustion speed and crank degrees per millisecond are thus independent variables. VE is poor at idle, but engine speed is slow, so 8–20 degrees of timing typically works well. As the crank quickly accelerates off-idle, a huge infusion of spark advance produces the best torque and responsiveness, with some wild-cammed engines with very poor low-end VE requiring as much as 28 degrees total advance. Engines cranking to start turning at 200–300 rpm require moderate spark advance with nearly as much timing as idle.

As the throttle opens and the engine speeds up toward peak torque-peak VE, combustion speeds up along with VE and thus requires less spark advance. Peak timing usually occurs by 3,000 rpm on most engines. On the other hand, high engine speeds at very light loading require huge amounts of advance—in some cases as much as 40 degrees or so. If the engine is turbocharged, the onset of boost increases the effective compression ratio, and combustion speeds up dramatically, requiring less timing, and simultaneously increases the risk of detonation. Maximum timing at 1.0-bar boost is typically in the range of 23 degrees at any engine speed, and 2.0-bar boost might only need 22 or even 21 degrees of timing advance. All things being equal, bigger engines need more timing advance because it takes the flame longer to burn its way across a large bore than a smaller one. Engines with small combustion chambers need less timing (opposite reason), and engines with pop-up pistons or other irregularities that slow down flame travel in the combustion chamber need more timing.

Spark advance maps plot spark timing as a function of engine rpm and engine loading (normally manifold pressure or mass airflow). Unlike conventional distributors with mechanical springs and advance weights and vacuum-advance diaphragms, mechanical devices incapable of providing timing advance that varies except as a smooth curve or straight line, computer-controlled timing can dance all over the place if that's what's optimal. It can deliver a complex 3-D surface with various peaks and valleys if that's what produces the best performance on a complex engine with multiple power-adders and numerous accessories and so on.

Conventional distributors with auto-advance smoothly increase timing with engine speed. Though two springs of varying strength may be used to bring in some timing advance quickly with initial speed increases, then bring in more as rotating weights overcome the force of the second spring bending the linear increase to a new slope. In some cases, high vacuum at light loading was used to add timing. It would be a simple matter for EMS designers to provide two separate timing tables—one for rpm advance, a second for load retard—but one additive timing table makes it simpler to calibrate, and, besides, the real trick is an exhaustive search for power on a dyno while the engine is running.

A modern EMS with knock-sensor/spark-retard logic should be calibrated with enough timing to provide peak torque across the board using a fuel of specific octane, but may rely on knock-sensor-feedback logic to pull timing to protect the engine from occasional light knock in case of a poor tank of fuel or if the engine is unusually hot (or if anything else unusual is happening that makes the engine especially knock prone). However, tuners should work rigorously to calibrate timing conservatively enough that the knock sensor normally never becomes active—by eliminating excessive timing advance in any area of the timing map where the knock sensor sounds off in order to clamp maximum timing within a normally safe range. Setting maximum timing by advancing timing as far as possible to the ragged edge of knock-sensor activation will probably yield best fuel economy though not necessarily best torque. (It was once common to set timing on older carbureted engines with distributor-points ignition by advancing the distributor in actual road testing to the ragged edge of incipient spark knock.) Over-advanced timing may also cause the engine to surge at cruise, and will diminish torque.

Aftermarket mechanical-lifter hot rod valvetrain parts may generate enough background noise to falsely trigger the knock sensor. If this is the case, keep in mind that any knock sensor should ideally be selected to match the frequency of the detonation characteristics of a particular engine, which might not be true of a particular generic aftermarket sensor. There are a lot of knock sensors, and another one tailored for a different frequency might work better. For example, an original-equipment sensor selected specifically for your engine—or, if your engine has been modified and you are getting false positives, a non-OEM sensor. Normally, a small four-cylinder engine should have a knock sensor designed for a small four-banger and so on.

A possible alternative to changing sensors would be to experiment with changing the location of the sensor in the

49	49	51	60	67	70	70	71	71	73	77	96	102	102	102	98
49	49	51	60	67	70	70	71	71	73	77	90	96	96	96	98
49	49	51	60	67	70	70	71	71	73	77	85	89	89	89	87

block or head(s) or even mounting it with Teflon tape or other insulating material around the threads to decrease sensitivity. Some aftermarket knock-sensor control systems have the ability to tune or condition the EMS or knock-controller response to various types of knock-sensor signals to narrow the response to what is actually detonation as opposed to engine noise. However, if the engine is simply too noisy for a knock sensor and you have the bucks and like experimenting, you could install in-cylinder pressure transducers, some of which are bundled with special spark plugs to detect knock pressure spikes and provide a readout of torque or brake mean effective pressure (BMEP). Measuring cylinder pressure is actually much more accurate than listening for knock-like vibrations using a knock sensor.

Anything that affects engine VE or efficiency (displacement, heads, cams, power-adders, compression) will change the shape of the optimal spark advance map. And it is worth the effort to optimize timing, because there is free power in optimized timing—sometimes a lot. To optimize spark timing throughout full-throttle acceleration runs, you need a dynamometer (or a drag strip-type highway and a datalogging accelerometer like the G-Tech). As with fueling, it is much better to start with an optimized map from a similar or identical engine, but, remember, engine wear effects VE, and carbon buildup in combustion chambers raises the compression ratio, which increases combustion flame speed.

VE increase on brand new engines for as much as 20,000 miles as the rings wear in, but eventually VE heads slowly south, so no engine is truly identical to another. As with fuel calibration, it is much better to start conservatively and feel your way toward maximum safe power. The default EMS timing map should be a good, conservative place to start on the retarded side, and timing will be too advanced when the engine exhibits trace spark knock. Keep in mind that it's sometimes hard to hear knock, and by the time you do, it could be too late. A knock-sensing and retard interceptor like the J&S Safeguard will protect the engine but show you graphically when the device is fighting knock with retard, enabling you to search for optimal advanced timing. In the case of fuel, conservative means rich. In the case of timing, it means less spark advance.

KEEP IN MIND:
* Emissions considerations will affect optimal timing and may conflict with maximum performance or responsiveness.
* Maximum safe timing can be influenced by the gear, and some EMSs have special maps to trim spark for certain gears.
* You might want to safe-up your engine by pulling timing and adding more fuel at peak power or above if you occasionally like to rage along at full throttle in top gear and want to save the engine at the cost of a little power. This is a typical OEM strategy, which is why tuners sometimes remove fuel and add timing to make a little more power on a stock engine.
* At light cruise, as much as 44 degrees timing advance could enhance fuel economy.
* A small-block wedge-head V-8 like the traditional small-block Chevy with traditional heads wants about 38 degrees maximum total timing, though fast-burn aluminum heads can lower this to, say, 34 degrees.
* OEM engineers sometime use timing (or even cam phasing) to smooth over transitions from gear to gear on an automatic-transmission vehicle. Honda has done some

of this to smooth out the transition from the low- to high-speed cam on VTEC engines. Some tuners have dialed in more than 40 degrees of timing in the midrange to match the torque converter flash point, again pulling timing in speed-loading cells where the converter lugs down.

When you are done optimizing the timing map, it can pay dividends to return to the fuel map, particularly if you find the spark map was way wrong. Because air/fuel ratio affects the tendency to detonation and the flame speed of combustion, experienced supertuners like Bob Norwood move back and forth between the fuel and timing maps as they home in on an optimal calibration. Timing and fuel interrelate because they both have an effect on the tendency of an engine to knock, and because air/fuel mixture affects flame speed (which affects ideal timing), air/fuel mixtures burn faster with increasing richness all the way to an 11.1:1 air-gasoline mixture (which is richer than rich best torque).

For example, let's say you started tuning a turbocharged engine at 11:1 air/fuel ratio, then began to take out fuel in the direction of 12.2:1 to make power. Flame speed would be slowing down as you leaned the mixture. You'd now have more power at 12.2:1, but if you optimized timing correctly for 11:1, assuming the fuel octane was high enough, you'd now discover that you could make more power by advancing the timing to make up for the slower flame speed of 12.2 combustion. On the other hand, if the engine required fuel to fight detonation at 11:1, you might need to retard timing at 12:2 before pulling fuel because there'd be higher cylinder pressures at the higher power 12:2:2 air/fuel ratio levels and less surplus vaporizing fuel available to fight knock. Which is one great reason to tune with really high octane fuel: you can experiment with more combinations of spark and fuel than you could otherwise safely reach.

COLD-START AND WARM-UP
Gasoline is a stew of various hydrocarbons of various weight and chemical composition. The heavier components, in particular, do not vaporize well when the air or internal engine surfaces are cold. Engine management systems, therefore, must deliver extra fuel to start the engine when it is cold and while it is warming up to keep it from stalling. Cold-start tables will be populated by the EMS vendor with default data, but—unlike, say, battery-voltage compensation tables—cold-start tables will almost definitely need to be customized to perform really well on your engine with good drivability and no stalling. This is especially true if you are running really large injectors, really large displacement, unusual intake manifold designs, injectors with unusual geometry, injectors that are farther than usual from the intake valve, or radical, unusual combination of hot rod parts.

Most engine management systems can now provide the following:
* Cold-running enrichment as a percentage of the ordinary fuel pulse width calculation, with the percentage declining with increases in coolant or cylinder-head temperature until the engine reaches maybe 140 degrees Fahrenheit.
* Cold-air enrichment based on intake air temperature (which may disappear if the intake system heat-soaks). Note: it is critical to locate the intake air temperature (IAT) sensor in a place where it is measuring the intake air temperature, not the temperature of the intake manifold or air-intake tube.
* Special priming enrichment while the engine is cold and cranking to deliver the super-rich mixtures needed to fire up fast when the engine is stone-cold. On early OE

EFI engines, this almost always involved energizing an additional cold-start injector (a spray valve, typically aimed at the throttle body), though increasingly, the priming enrichment is delivered through the main port injectors.

- After-start enrichment, which typically continues for a fixed number of engine revolutions (say 250) to prevent stalling.
- Idle-air control enrichment, which typically might increase idle speed when the engine is very cold.
- Hot temperature enrichment to help protect a hot engine via the cooling effect of fuel evaporating. Also called the heat of vaporization, meaning the heat required to vaporize something.
- Air-temp enrichment.
  Some EMSs can provide the following:
- Temperature-based increases in acceleration enrichment, as a percentage.
- Temperature-based increases in spark timing to compensate for the decreased flame speed when a lot of raw fuel is floating around the combustion chambers in tiny droplets rather than fully vaporized.
- Temperature-based limitations to maximum boost to prevent engine damage while the oil is still thick.
- One-second temperature-based start enrichment.
- One-second constant enrichment. In some cases, the EMS will inject a burst of fuel to all cylinders if TPS exceeds, say, 70 percent with the ignition key on before cranking.
- Fixed one-second starting pulse width.

Many cold-running tables are designed as a final percentage modification to the ordinary fuel and timing calculations, which is why it is essential to get the EMS working really well at normal temperature before you mess with the cold tables. However, once the engine is running great under ordinary conditions, it is really simple to wait until the engine is fully cold, bring up the warm-up map as a graph, start the engine, and adjust the map up or down at the current temperature (an arrow or something similar will highlight the current coolant temperature) until the engine runs smoothest, then repeat the process as the engine warms up and the temperature increases.

A cranking engine will typically be affected by both warm-up and cranking enrichment, and initially it can be hard to tell if you need more cranking fuel and less warm-up or the reverse. Immediately after starting, it can be hard to tell if you need more or less after-start enrichment or if you should be modifying the main warm-up map. One clue would be to watch what happens when the cranking and after-start enrichments disappear. Does optimal warm-up enrichment suddenly decrease or increase? A heated narrow-band sensor will reveal if exhaust gas oxygen is where you want it, i.e., if enough excess fuel is available to consume the oxygen in the air.

A typical engine might need 10 to 15 percent enrichment immediately after a cold start in order to achieve a 12–12.5:1 air/fuel ratio on a mild street engine (perhaps as low as 11:1 on more radical engines), and this requirement will decline to nothing somewhere at or above an engine temperature of 140 to 180 degrees Fahrenheit, with more enrichment required in really cold climates. When cranking in really cold winter weather, the engine may need grossly rich priming air/fuel ratios in the neighborhood of 4:1 to start the engine fast. Beware a sudden cold snap or, say, a trip to a mountain ski area from palm-lined Los Angeles if you have never had a chance tune below 50 or 60 degrees. You might be unable to start the engine without a laptop. Though in a pinch you could probably start the engine by spraying starting ether, carb cleaner, or WD-40 into the manifold plenum through an unplugged vacuum reference line.

The engine must be stone cold to set cold cranking and warm-up enrichment accurately, which means you will want to attack the problem first thing in the morning after the engine has cold-soaked over night. You really want the coolant temperature at 70 degrees or lower to begin the process.

It may work best to adjust the throttle plate to a reasonable setting for cold-running idle and later work to program the IAC for an ideal cold idle speed after the mixture is right. As always, a wideband O_2 readout may be useful, though the goal of cold-running enrichment is purely to eliminate stalling and improve drivability, so you never want more or less fuel than what is obviously needed for this purpose. A mixture-trim module or global fuel trim could be very useful when you are working to optimize the air/fuel ratio for fastest cold idle.

Start the engine and experiment with greater or lesser cold enrichment percentages until the engine runs best. As always, modest trim changes are best, since a few percent can make a large difference in how the engine runs. The EMS will not have an infinite number of temperature cells. Stay on top of it as the engine warms up and moves to a higher temperature range. You may notice the engine change speed or sound when the engine moves to a new discrete segment of the warm-up map.

If an engine with reasonable timing will not start, it is either because there is too little enrichment or because the engine is flooded. A flooded engine will typically smell strongly of gasoline. To confirm flooding, you can remove the plugs to check if they are wet. If the engine will not start when cold and the plugs are not flooded, there is probably not enough fuel.

ACCELERATION ENRICHMENT

Some people compare acceleration enrichment on a port-EFI system to the accelerator pump typically used to squirt raw fuel down the throat of a traditional Holley four-barrel carb when the throttle rotated. Though EFI typically needs less acceleration enrichment than a carb because bogs in air velocity that affect a carb's mechanical ability to get fuel in the air have no effect on EFI and there is less likelihood of cylinder wall-wetting. The accelerator pump was something of a Band-Aid heavily related to air velocity and problems with the fuel equilibrium in a wet air/fuel manifold.

Acceleration or transient enrichment (or enleanment) is critical to responsive drivability, and all EMSs will arrive with plausible default data designed in. However, there is almost always room for improvement, and sophisticated EMSs offer a large and powerful set of acceleration enrichment functions to make sure there is never a problem with transitional enrichment that cannot be handled in some way.

Transitional enrichment is the final major fuel system to optimize and should be attacked when everything else is in good shape. If you mess with it before the main fuel tables are right, it could confuse the process of calibrating normal operation. Transient enrichment is normally used to keep the engine from stumbling when you suddenly open the throttle (not normally a problem on port-EFI systems), and to make sure that the engine is as responsive as possible when you suddenly stab the throttle.

Most EFI systems can now provide acceleration enrichment based on increases in throttle angle and/or sudden changes in manifold pressure. Providing enrichment based on falling MAP is

49	49	51	60	67	70	70	71	71	73	77	96	102	102	102	98
49	49	51	60	67	70	70	71	71	73	77	90	96	96	96	98
49	49	51	60	67	70	70	71	71	73	77	85	89	89	89	87

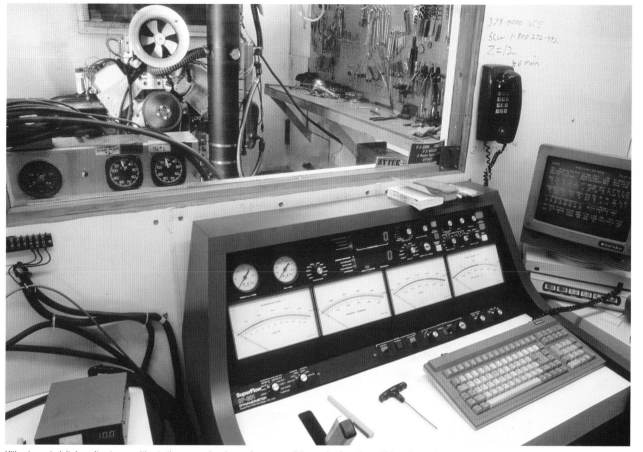

Ultimate control. It doesn't get more ultimate than an engine dyno, where you pull the engine from the vehicle and mate it to a computer-controlled load-holding water brake or eddy-current dynamometer with extensive instrumentation.

somewhat analogous to the way a Holley carb used a power valve to fix a lean hesitation and surge when there was a large drop in vacuum prior to a corresponding increase in throttle angle.

The main components to acceleration enrichment are basically attack (sensitivity) and sustain, and there the EMS may provide separate rules for enrichment at low rpm (when the vehicle can probably accelerate very hard) and at higher rpm. Attack is the percentage of enrichment that should be commanded while the throttle angle is increasing at or above a threshold rate. Sustain specifies how fast to phase out the enrichment. Electromotive points out that the typical duration of required transient enrichment on acceleration is around one second.

There is no diagnostic tool that will tell you when the accel is right. Inertial chassis dynos like the Dynojet will measure increases in torque and power as you roll on the throttle. But the Dynojet is not very good at dealing with partial throttle situations because it is difficult to distinguish the human factor in banging down the gas a certain amount, versus how the engine responds (one imagines robots increasing the throttle an exact amount at an exact rate of increase).

However, if you have the time and the dyno, Dynojet could possibly help you optimize accel enrichment. In any case, sooner or later, you'll need to hit the road, and the trick here is basically a lot of patience and intuition, and plenty of trial and error. If you are working on the dyno, it may be easier to see rich, black smoke from too much accel. When you are road testing the calibration, it could be very useful to have a helper in a chase vehicle watching for black smoke on enrichment (and possibly exhaust flames, particularly on deceleration).

Adjust the acceleration increase, sensitivity, or whatever it is called upward if there is an instant bog, and add to the sustain if there is a slightly delayed bog. You may also be able to clamp acceleration enrichment to a percent of total pulse width for various loading or rpm ranges if some conditions result in over-enrichment.

Most engines will not require any acceleration enrichment over 4,000 rpm and will require more enrichment accelerating from lower engine speeds. Ideally, your EMS will provide multiple cells to define acceleration enrichment at various ranges of loading or rpm, enabling you to define decreasing transient enrichment with increased engine speed.

If you reach 100 percent increase (or maximum acceleration enrichment) and the engine still lean-coughs, the base fuel map is too lean somewhere, or the engine data configuration is wrong, or the ECU hardware is wrong for your application. Engines with very large throttle area (such as one throttle blade per cylinder) will greatly increase manifold pressure with a slight turn in throttle angle, and might require MAP-based acceleration enrichment, less throttle area, or possibly some method of multiplying the change in throttle angle at lower rpm (for example, a gear-driven, variable-rate-of-gain TPS). Engines with positive-displacement superchargers with bypass valves can require very large enrichment off-idle with sudden throttle application.

76	49	49	51	60	67	70	70	71	71	73	77	96	102	102	102
50	49	49	51	60	67	70	70	71	71	73	77	90	96	96	96
25	49	49	51	60	67	70	70	71	71	73	77	85	89	89	89

IDLE SPEED CONTROL

IAC units are stepper motors or PWM valves under computer control that work to stabilize engine rpm at idle. If the IAC is configured wrong, it may do nothing (for example, if the throttle plate is already opened enough to force rpm above the target IAC idle speed), or it may hunt. Hunting occurs when the computer is slow to react to a change in idle speed, but then overreacts, and idle speed can surge up and down forever, failing to stabilize. Some EMSs now have the ability to configure high and low thresholds for corrective action. You should also be able to program the magnitude of the corrective action, possibly depending on how wrong idle speed is and how fast it got so wrong. Work with the IAC parameters until idle stays where you want it.

ADVANCED STUFF: INDIVIDUAL CYLINDER INJECTION AND SPARK TRIM

Some engine management systems provide a set of advanced features that can be useful if you want to optimize engine performance under all circumstances. Examples of such features include the following:

- Individual-cylinder fuel trim
- Individual-cylinder timing advance trim
- End-of-injection phasing (crank angle)
- VE correction to target air/fuel ratios
- Engine coolant temperature VE correction
- VE correction coefficient versus estimated intake port temperature (density decreases with temperature, but hotter air pumps more easily)
- Knock-sensor functions (threshold definition, rate of knock-induced advance retard, rate of advance increase on recovery, maximum retard allowed)

Many of these advanced features are useful only within the lab-type environment of an engine dynamometer equipped with substantial diagnostic equipment, or on an exhaustively instrumented race-type vehicle with a large datalogging capability. As an example, individual-cylinder trims can be useful to correct for minor variations between cylinders in volumetric efficiency, thermal loading, and so forth. Even on a well-designed and built engine, some cylinders may run a little hotter or colder, some cylinders may have slightly more tendency to knock, some cylinders may have slightly different intake or exhaust runners that can affect VE under certain circumstances. Remember, a V-8 is acutally a gang of single-cylinder engines working together.

In the days of high-output single-carbureted V-8 engines with points ignitions, fuel distribution could be terrible and certain cylinders almost always had better cooling than others. Unfortunately, there was no choice but to tune the carb rich enough to avoid dangerous mixtures and detonation in the leanest cylinders and to set timing to avoid detonation in the hottest cylinders. Modern port-EFI engines obviously avoid most problems with mixture distribution, though testing and matching injectors for perfect flow definitely makes sense if you are gearing up to optimize individual-cylinder performance. There can also be minor differences in cooling and VE that are not practical to eliminate, but which can at least be optimized: an eight-cylinder engine is actually a gang of eight single-cylinder engines.

To make any sense, individual-cylinder tuning requires individual-cylinder instrumentation. Accurate, fresh EGT probes on each cylinder are critical, as are wideband AFR sensors, which have come down in price to about $50 on Amazon, though you may need a standalone controller (or controllers). In-cylinder pressure transducers are extremely effective in measuring the effect of individual-cylinder tuning strategies, and there are spark plugs with built-in probes. You clearly need the ability to measure small changes in torque, which is, after all, the bottom line. You clearly want a dynamometer with load-holding capability; a race-type engine full-instrumented with torque-measuring strain gauges on the transmission input shaft, or an EMS with the ability to estimate micro-changes in individual-cylinder torque by looking at tiny differences in acceleration and deceleration of the crankshaft. Such an EMS can effectively turn an engine and EMS into its own dyno, but this is almost science-fiction-type stuff that's within the repertoire of only the most sophisticated automotive engineers. Practically speaking, aftermarket tuners and racers—if they do this at all—are going to take on individual-cylinder tuning using EGT probes on a load-holding engine dyno.

The trick is to search the rpm and loading range, allowing the EGT probes to stabilize (good, fresh probes are important), and checking for cold or hot cylinders. Since most EMSs only permit individual-cylinder trim as a percentage (not a complete, separate fuel map for each cylinder), you're looking for the worst differentials, at speed-density points that matter. Now, work to trim any individual slackers that are running too cold or too hot with individual fuel trim, watching the dyno for increases or decreases in torque. When you think you've fixed the problem as well as it can be fixed, log a full-throttle pull to redline, and compare with before results to make sure that you didn't make things worse somewhere else. Now, optimize individual-cylinder timing to optimize torque in each cylinder.

INEQUALITY FOR ALL: INDIVIDUAL-CYLINDER ENGINE MANAGEMENT

What is a V-8 engine, really? Eight single-cylinder engines hooked up in a line, doing their best to work together. These cylinders are not identical engines, however. This is why the most sophisticated aftermarket engine management systems offer not only sequential injection, but individual cylinder calibration of injector open time (pulse width), injection start time (phasing), and spark timing. Such systems produce higher output and cleaner power on otherwise identical engines.

Variations in the intake system, cylinder head, and exhaust system, even with equal-length runners, cause airflow to resonate slightly differently for different cylinders, resulting in slightly varying volumetric efficiency. "Even with identical header length," says EFI expert Graham Western, "some exhaust tubes are more forgiving than others. On true racing engines, fuel pulse width trim of 1 to 2 percent correction is required to eliminate mixture variations due to this slight breathing differential."

While batch injection is reasonably efficient on ordinary multicylinder engines with little pulsing in the intake, on high-rpm, wildly pulsing competition motors, sequential phasing is more effective, particularly at peak torque where tuned intake and exhaust systems are most efficient. On race engines, where charge density can sometimes be improved by taking advantage of the intercooling high heat of vaporization by injecting farther upstream, spraying at the wrong time can result in fuel being blown back out the stacks or directly through into the exhaust system on valve overlap, producing distribution problems or wasted fuel and high emissions.

In order to eliminate standoff distribution problems, it is critical to inject fuel when the intake valve is open so that fuel

49	49	51	60	67	70	70	71	71	73	77	96	102	102	102	98
49	49	51	60	67	70	70	71	71	73	77	90	96	96	96	98
49	49	51	60	67	70	70	71	71	73	77	85	89	89	89	87

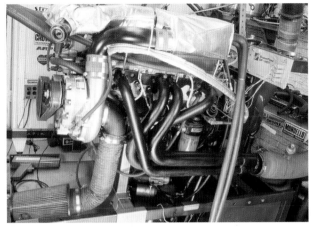

This supercharged and intercooled Pontiac LT1 powerplant did its thing on Kim Barr Racing's Superflow dyno. Note the EGT probes in each exhaust port. Exhaustive calibration is a matter of manually holding a load at a wide selection of rpm and loading cells within the EMSs main fuel and main timing tables. Unlike an inertial chassis dyno's 5- to 15-second dyno pulls, an engine calibrated this way on an engine dyno will have proven itself in the hell of continuous loading at high power.

does not hit the closed valve and bounce back along with the decelerating, bouncing air column. On a plenum-stack turbo engine with compressed air entry at one end, depending on the resonant frequency, standoff fuel can be blown to the stacks farthest away. Individual cylinder pulse width or injection-phasing adjustment can correct for distribution problems related to resonant differences in the airflow to each cylinder (particularly when the injectors are open a lot)—realizing as much as 8 percent more power. According to Western, a 60 to 70 percent injector duty cycle usually makes best power. Larger injectors get all fuel in the cylinder while the valve is open, but the tradeoff with short injection time is degraded vaporization and intercooling.

Western says you always see power increases over batch fire injection at mid- to high-range torque; a six-cylinder truck that tested at 280 horsepower with batch-fire injection will pick up 20 lb-ft of torque at peak torque and 12 to 16 horsepower at peak power with sequential injection. A 700-horsepower racing engine might make up to 5 percent more horsepower due to general phasing correctness.

Individual spark trim is usually associated with detonation-limited engines. Retarding timing on just the offending cylinders (typically 2 to 3 degrees) lowers peak combustion temperature and cylinder pressure, helping fight detonation. Where exhaust gas temperatures are too high on turbo motors, tuners may run a little extra fuel or spark timing in the cylinder causing problems—or increase overall compression ratios. Raising compression is preferable to advanced timing. The increased expansion ratio of gases from a smaller combustion chamber results in greater loss of temperature than retarding timing, and the increased compression ratios improve peak and average cylinder pressures instead of simply peak cylinder pressures.

AIR/FUEL OPTIMIZATION PROCEDURES ON A PISTON-ENGINE AIRCRAFT

Modern turbocharged aviation piston engines, which typically run at 75 percent power settings more or less constantly, and which must run at high takeoff power settings for long minutes or tens of minutes at a time on takeoff and climb-out, typically leave airports running full-rich, which would typically be 100 to 150 degrees rich of peak EGT (75 degrees rich of peak typically makes maximum power). The EGT gauge is critical to the leaning procedure used to arrive at an optimal power and air/fuel ratio setting for cruise flight and illustrates something about the meaning of safe. Obviously, if you burn down an aviation engine, you cannot simply coast over to the side of the road.

Engines with poor mixture distribution are sensitive to leaner mixtures and will run roughly on the lean side of peak EGT. Many aviation engines, which typically still use carburetion or constant mechanical fuel injection, vary in air/fuel ratio by 8 to 12 percent among the various cylinders But on well-balanced aviation engines, an excellent procedure for arriving at mixtures producing high levels of safe power is to begin the leaning procedure with the engine running more than 100 degrees rich of peak EGT, with manifold pressure slightly down from full throttle. The pilot or flight engineer then carefully leans the turbocharged engine until EGT peaks (which would often be in the neighborhood of 1,500 degrees Fahrenheit). At this point, the procedure is to continue leaning until EGT cools to 40 to 60 degrees below peak EGT (this would typically be only 15 to 30 degrees lean of peak on a normally aspirated engine).

Consulting an aviation EGT chart for a common piston engine, we see that EGT falls off fairly evenly on both the rich and lean side of peak EGT, whereas cylinder head temperatures on an air-cooled engine were 35 to 40 degrees cooler on the lean side of peak EGT, and fuel flow was markedly lower.

However, power is down on the lean side, right? Well, yes, assuming you continue to run the same manifold pressure. If a plane requires more power in cruise flight, in this procedure, the pilot increases the throttle to raise manifold pressure to the required power setting with a few more inches of manifold pressure. High-performance aircraft engines typically have constant-speed propellers that use hydraulics to vary the angle of attack of the prop to maintain a particular manually adjusted prop speed. Within a particular operating envelope, such engines will not increase in speed with more throttle.

This procedure requires good mixture distribution, or the engine will run a little rough due to uneven mixture distribution. But the implication of this procedure is interesting for EFI automotive engines with excellent mixture distribution, running high octane gasoline. Leaner mixtures stress the cooling system less, and the EGT is not higher. Power might be down a mite, but more boost handles that, at less fuel flow. Something to think about, because a piston aviation engine pulling against a constant-speed prop is a lot like a piston automotive engine pulling against a steady-load engine dynamometer.

Chapter 15
EMS Troubleshooting

All EFI systems are ultimately controlled by an onboard computer that, as we've already discussed, has been referred to by various automakers as an electronic control unit (ECU), engine-control module (ECM), or powertrain control module (PCM).

Automotive ECUs seldom fail. They are extremely rugged and are built to withstand the harsh automotive environment of vibration, freezing winters, baking-hot summers in the sun (or, sometimes, under-hood temperatures), high humidity, electrical interference, and other factors, and perform with the precision required to calculate engine fueling, spark, and other management tasks in millisecond time frames. The ECU must perform perfectly on a -10 degrees Fahrenheit morning in Buffalo, as well as a baking-hot south Texas summer afternoon just after a thunderstorm, in 100-percent humidity. It must perform perfectly in a four-wheel-drive vehicle, jouncing and vibrating through extremely rough off-road conditions.

Automotive engineers sometimes put the ECU in the engine compartment, but prefer to locate it inside the vehicle or trunk where the cooler, drier environment is kinder to electronic components. Why tempt fate any more than you have to? However, it is possible to design an ECU that will withstand the incredibly harsh engine-compartment environment in which underhood temperatures can reach hundreds of degrees, where the electromagnetic and radio interference close to high-voltage ignition components can induce killing voltage in normal nearby wiring, and where vibration can shake apart sensitive

electronic components—not to mention mechanical parts. Some Corvettes, for example, are equipped with computers that live in the engine compartment. The transmission controllers on some late-model GM vehicles are installed *in* the transmission!

Mil-spec (military specification) equipment—designed in some cases to withstand the electromagnetic pulse of a nuclear blast—is shielded from radio interference by the enclosure, and protected from humidity and vibration by a bath of hardened plastic resin that is poured into the enclosure, completely surrounding, strengthening, reinforcing, protecting all components. Mil-spec cabling and harnesses use fail-safe connectors and attachment systems. However, such systems are difficult to justify if the simple alternative consists of locating sensitive components out of harm's way inside the vehicle's passenger compartment or trunk. But on race cars and nuclear reentry vehicles, you go mil-spec. There are a few hardened automotive ECUs available in the aftermarket, including race units from companies like Motec, EFI Technology, Zytek, and others, which can sell for many thousands of dollars. All electronic control units are very rugged, but it is only common sense when designing an EFI system to mount your ECU and wiring so the ECU stays happy.

Assuming the engine itself is healthy, in most cases, if there's a problem with an engine management system, the problem is not with the computer but with the data it is receiving from its sensors—or some related electrical or physical air/fuel system

A chassis dynamometer like this bolt-on Dynapack tells you if tuning or equipment changes made things better or worse. There is just no substitute—well, except for an engine dyno. An engine that has not been tuned on a dyno with air/fuel-sensing ratio data will virtually always have "free power" waiting to be unleashed.

problem. Low fuel pressure, clogged injectors, defective sensors, leaky vacuum hoses or fittings, and electrical system shorts or incorrect wiring can drive you crazy when trying to troubleshoot an EFI system.

It is important to go about troubleshooting in a methodical, scientific way, with the right tools, checking one thing at a time, substituting one part at a time, checking the results, then moving on to the next step. You may not want to do this, but if you accurately follow a good troubleshooting algorithm, it is inevitable that you will isolate the problem.

It is important to realize that troubleshooting a modern computerized EMS is a little like playing chess with a hidden opponent. The computer itself—with its own bag of tricks—will be doing its best to analyze or work around or compensate for problems. Of course, the ECU's view of the world is completely through the sensors. A problem like a small vacuum leak can fool some ECUs into assuming a lean condition exists, causing it to erroneously enrich the mixture. One bad injector—stuck either closed or open—can throw off the average air/fuel mixture as perceived by the computer based on a single sensor measuring exhaust gas oxygen coming from a group of cylinders. If there's only a single exhaust sensor, located on one bank of a V-configuration engine, the effect of one malfunctioning cylinder will be magnified.

Incorrect fuel pressure will result in unexpected fuel mass delivered per injection pulse width, giving the wrong air/fuel ratio. This will show up immediately in systems operating in open-loop mode with predetermined injection pulse width, but an ECU operating in closed-loop mode at idle and light cruise will attempt to compensate for incorrect air/fuel ratio. The fuel pressure problem may thus be masked at idle, only to show up disastrously at full throttle when closed loop is still rarely an option.

A bad EGR valve can cause the ECU to believe the mixture is lean. A plugged fuel filter may only show up during very heavy loading or high rpm, or intermittently at other times, causing a closed-loop computer to constantly chase correct mixtures. Many OEM computers maintain internal lists of long-term (Block Learn) correction factors designed to compensate for changes in engine VE due to aging or other such factors.

Modern ECUs make use of algorithms that allow them to disregard suspect sensors under certain circumstances and operate in a safe mode with default sensor values selected to prevent engine damage while allowing the vehicle to continue operating with reduced performance (typically referred to as "limp mode"). An ECM may outsmart itself in attempting to correct for unusual circumstances, in some cases making things worse. When the computer attempts to compensate for an inaccurately perceived lean condition by enriching the mixture at idle, the engine may run roughly and produce a rotten-egg smell at the exhaust.

Throttle position sensors that are broken or out of adjustment can cause the engine to stumble at certain throttle positions or on sudden acceleration.

If the EMS incorporates knock sensing, ECM strategies to prevent engine damage from detonation may mask other problems. Bad gas, plugged injectors, new platinum spark plugs, or oil introduced into the mixture by turbochargers or positive crankcase ventilation (PCV) systems can all cause detonation. Since the ECU may retard timing to prevent detonation, the problem may be masked. What the user sees is reduced power.

In virtually all cases, EMS problems can be traced to the computer somehow receiving inaccurate data or some

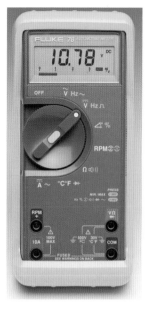

Fluke 78 Automotive Multimeter provides a read-out of volts, amps, continuity and resistance, frequency for "pulsed-DC" and AC frequency tests, PWM Duty Cycle, direct reading dwell for 3, 4, 5, 6 and 8-cylinder engines, Temperature in degrees Fahrenheit or Celsius up to 1839° Fahrenheit or 999° Celsius (thermocouple bead probe and adapter plug accessories included), min/max recording work with all meter functions, precision analog bar graph, RPM80 inductive pickup (optional accessory) for both conventional and distributorless (DIS) ignitions, and 10 megohm input impedance.

other physical problem outside the ECM. And for efficient troubleshooting, to start with, you need the right tools.

EMS TOOLS
Accelerometer Performance Meters

To optimize the performance of an engine management system on a particular vehicle, you need a way to accurately measure power and torque before and after tuning changes or VE modifications.

Once you know a vehicle's exact weight (including driver and payload, fuel and fluids, and so on), accelerometer performance meters can do an excellent job converting acceleration data into precise torque and horsepower and complete data acquisition. For as little as $200 or so, an enthusiast can record acceleration runs and analyze shift points, delivered horsepower, and reaction times. You won't necessarily know what percentage of crankshaft power is lost to drivetrain and rolling losses (you wouldn't on a chassis dyno either), though some performance meters like the Vericom will report various types of friction. Either way, like an inertial chassis dyno, an accelerometer performance meter is great for recording before and after maximum-performance acceleration runs to determine the effect of performance modifications.

The ubiquitous G-TECH/Pro Performance Meter Competition is a sophisticated automotive tuning tool designed to be used in place of an inertial chassis dynamometer. The G-Tech Pro measures reaction time; 0 to 60 feet time; 0 to 330 feet time; 0 to 60 miles per hour time; 1/8 mile E.T. and speed; 1,000 feet time; quarter-mile E.T. and speed; horsepower; torque; rpm; braking distance; handling Gs; accelerating and braking Gs; rpm versus time graph; horsepower and torque versus rpm graph; speed versus time graph; speed versus distance; and Gs versus time graph.

Similarly, Vericom's performance meter provides braking performance; speed; longitudinal G-force; drag factor; time; lateral G-force; braking force; distance; vertical G-force; coefficient of friction; horsepower (corrected standard); gradient; dynamic friction; torque; static friction; rpm; delta velocity; slip friction; and gear ratio (revolutions per foot), in English or metric units.

It doesn't take buying too many dynoruns before you could've had your own onboard "dyno."

their communications cables and recharging power cords get ripped from them. People have crashed cars because a laptop started to leap off the passenger seat during a high-G maneuver and the driver saved the laptop at the cost of the car.

There are ruggedized mil-spec laptops and computers where you wear the keyboard on your belt and the system unit in a fanny pack. There are laptops designed to survive a nuclear electromagnetic pulse. There are also foam pads, Velcro, and big, industrial-strength cable-ties and there are turnkey laptop protector solutions. It is really worth thinking about how to protect your automotive laptop from an early demise.

Diagnostic Systems for Laptops/PDAs

With the right cabling and hardware interface, a Windows laptop or PDA can become a diagnostic scan tool for enthusiasts and professional repairers who need to retrieve and clear malfunction codes, scan and log high-speed data while driving, and diagnose faults using dynamic vehicle testing, sometimes referred to as bi-directional controls that enable you to manually control functions in real time, such as controlling cooling fans, fuel pressure, and other functions. In some cases, wideband air/fuel ratio, 5V analog voltage and thermocouple inputs allow you to integrate data from external sensors directly with the logged data stream. Some systems can provide specialty DVT controls such as crank angle sensor error relearn (CASE), cylinder power balance test and manual idle control.

When the flash/scan tool connects to a vehicle, it performs a series of automated requests to determine the status of the vehicle's PCM. The program can typically retrieve and display interface cable type and com port properties, the OBD-II protocol detected, VIN, PCM number, generic and enhanced parameters supported by the PCM, number and type of modules connected to the Class-II data bus, system readiness tests, EPA test results, non-continuously monitored systems' test results (manufacturer specific), oxygen sensor test results, MIL status, diagnostic trouble codes (if present), history data if present, and customer-specific data associated with the detected VIN.

A typical virtual dashboard allows the user to configure tabular data, gauges, and scrolling charts in the same window. The gauges may be customized to different shapes, sizes, and colors, including large, crisp digital displays that can be read up to 10 meters away. Each gauge has its own audible and visible alarms. Gauges can be customized with your own bitmap images to give them a genuine look and feel. EFILive will interact with transparent portions of a custom bitmap to display visual alarms. When things go wrong, most upscale diagnostic software is designed to provide comprehensive help that may be retrieved online, allowing the software to display the error message, what went wrong, and the steps you can take to rectify the problem. If the problem cannot be resolved easily by the user, the diagnostic vendor provides backup support.

Unlike some rugged professional scan tools designed for a shop environment, if you drop a laptop or PDA, it will probably break. For this reason, some people will tell you the laptop/PDA solution is better for the sophisticated enthusiast than the dedicated professional.

Diagnostic Charts and Algorithms

A diagnostic algorithm can be a computer-resident or a hardcopy flow chart. It can be vehicle/engine specific or generic. A good diagnostic chart or algorithm is guaranteed to solve the problem

Fluke's 190C Color ScopeMeter provides continuous capture of waveform sample points, with 27,500 points in deep memory in up to a 48-hour time span. A metering oscilloscope can be invaluable for diagnosing difficult problems with almost any engine management or automotive electrical system, and many people find they are much less complicated to use than they expected. *Fluke*

Code Access Keys

Typically these devices look like a cross between an ignition key and a paperclip. Their job is to plug into the driver-compartment diagnostic connector of specific vehicles in order to induce the engine management system to flash out malfunction codes using the check engine light. A code access key is convenient and inexpensive; on the other hand they don't do anything you can't do with slightly more effort using a jumper wire or a paper clip. Unlike a paperclip, code keys are specific to a particular vehicle or class of vehicle.

Personal Computers

You're almost definitely going to need a laptop Windows PC to tune and modify engine management systems. Yes, there are a few systems with their own proprietary calibration modules, but they are the exception, and on such systems a laptop will usually provide a more powerful user interface than the calibration module.

If you're on a budget, there are a lot of used laptops out there, and you don't necessarily need a very powerful one, especially if you only use it to calibrate engines. That said, if you can afford it, a good laptop that runs a modern version of Windows will be far more robust and less subject to crashing than earlier versions of Windows, and keep in mind that a laptop that crashes in the middle of updating some factory engine management systems can permanently damage the ECM.

One important factor in a calibration laptop is the ability to survive abuse. Every pro tuner I know has trashed multiple laptop computers in the harsh environment of road testing and dyno tuning. It happens: Laptops slide off fenders and roofs and smash on the concrete. Laptops get slammed in doors, they get overheated and cooked, they get sprayed with brake cleaner, if you follow the algorithm and do the testing correctly. The algorithm also functions as a kind of checklist of possible problems and considerations. Airplane pilots know the value of a checklist, and the FAA requires that pilots use them before start, before takeoff, before landing, and at other times when forgetting something could be catastrophic. If you follow the checklist, you will not forget to put the landing gear down, and if you follow a problem-solving checklist, you will not decide to rip the engine out of the car for a rebuild because you forgot that something like low fuel pressure could cause the same symptoms you're experiencing. No matter how experienced you are, checklists are a great way to avoid embarrassing and expensive diagnostic mistakes. Many shop manuals, aftermarket EMS installation and user guides have diagnostic charts.

Dial-back Timing Lights

New factory engine management systems typically do not permit adjustment of engine position sensors or distributor clocking, but if you install an aftermarket EMS you're going to need a way to verify that spark timing is what the computer thinks it is (and to correct it if not). You may need to verify that one or more plugs are firing. A good timing light will trigger not just from a high-voltage source like a plug wire, but from the low-voltage circuits that fire direct coils. A good timing light's dial-back capability allows you to set cam timing, to precisely set adjustable cam sprockets on both banks of a four-cam powerplant, and to strobe other cam-speed events that occur far from TDC. Dial-back capability simply allows a tuner to dial-in *delay* to the strobe flash with a calibrated dial that provides a readout of the correction required to dial-in a particular event to Top Dead Center.

For example: To determine the advance you want at 2,500 rpm, use a dial-back timing light. Set the amount of advance you want—say 35 degrees—on the dial-back timing light. Connect the dial-back timing light to the number one cylinder. Some EMSs allow you to disconnect a wiring jumper that forces timing to a certain advance at a specific rpm, like 2500. Pull the jumper, run the engine at 2,500 rpm, and rotate the engine position sensor until the TDC timing mark is centered at TDC (you may have to find TDC and mark the crankshaft on some modern engines). You will now have the amount of advance you dialed into the timing light. Tighten any standoffs and verify that timing has not shifted.

Digital Multimeters

A digital multimeter can be an essential tool for troubleshooting automotive engine management and electrical systems. The Fluke 88 Deluxe Automotive Meter with rpm has been around a long time and is typical of an excellent automotive-oriented multimeter. The Fluke 88 provides volts, ohms, amps, continuity and diode testing, milliseconds injection pulse width measurements, rpm measurements with inductive pickup, min/max/avg recording, frequency and duty-cycle measurements (for MAF meters, IACs, and so forth), low ohms function, 10 megohm input impedance, parameter change alert, smoothing, and a sleep mode. The Fluke 88 provides leads with interchangeable test probes and wide-jaw alligator clips.

Dynamometers

A dynamometer enables you to optimize performance in a scientific manner. If you're looking to measure peak power and torque, a few baseline dyno pulls on an inertial chassis

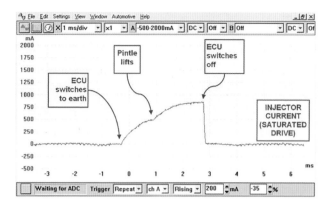

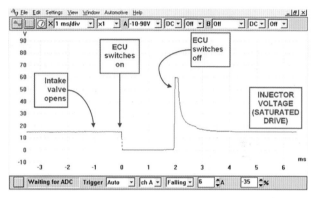

Oscilloscope trace can be extremely valuable in troubleshooting injection pulsewidth and crank sensor issues.

dynamometer will probably cost around $50-100 and take a few minutes. For R&D, you may want to buy dyno time by the hour or the day.

Professional automotive engineers at places like General Motors use super-expensive load-holding dynamometers that cost in the six- or seven-figure range to calibrate and test engines, to measure the power and torque output under varying conditions, and to record emissions data while the vehicle is operating under tightly controlled conditions. Compared to data acquisition from road testing or competition telemetry, dynamometers provide a controlled environment that makes it vastly easier to evaluate what is going on in an engine and optimize tuning for particular types of operation.

There are many different types of dynos, but automotive engine dynos are designed to connect to the flywheel or flex-plate of an engine that has been removed from a vehicle, while chassis dynos are designed to interface with the driving wheels of a vehicle as either a rolling road or as devices that bolt to the lug nuts of a vehicle in place of the driving wheels. Typically, a vehicle drives onto a set of rotating drums (one large roller under each driving wheel or two smaller rollers) and is fastened in place with tie-down devices, which allow the vehicle to operate its powertrain against the rollers while remaining stationary.

The rollers are attached to various sensors that measure speed, loading, time, and other essential information that can be crunched in a computer to analyze performance. Inertial dynos measure horsepower and torque by measuring the rate of acceleration of an engine at wide-open throttle working to accelerate a heavy mass of known weight and rolling resistance, usually a set of heavy drums (Dynojet 248 chassis dynamometers usually have two 1,600-pound drums). Although chassis dynos have been around since the 1930s, Dynojet Research revolutionized the performance aftermarket in the early 1990s for bikes, cars, and light trucks with an affordable, easy-to-use inertial chassis dyno costing less than $30,000. Before the Dynojet, most claimed performance increases for aftermarket parts were optimistic guesses, and street-car enthusiasts typically had no idea whether a performance modification had made things better, done nothing, or was even performance-negative.

Most inertial dynos are chassis dynamometers, but there are inertial engine dynos that attach to the flywheel of a powerplant (Dyno-mite, for example). Whether engine or chassis types, inertial dynamometers are most effective working at full throttle, and have no way to hold a precise, steady engine load at a given engine rpm. For that, you probably need a water brake, oil brake, eddy-current brake, generator, or other active power-absorbing dynamometer technology that can hold a precise braking force on the flywheel of an engine. Some inertial dynamometers also have optional water brakes or eddy current power converters.

The big disadvantage of an engine dyno is that you have to remove the engine from a vehicle before you can work with it on the engine dyno. Compared to the old days of self-contained carbureted engines, there may be a discouraging amount of interfacing work on EFI engines to make all cooling, fuel, and exhaust systems work in the dyno environment. On the other hand, once a powerplant is on an engine dyno, it is much easier to work on than it is in the engine compartment of the vehicle. For example, if a head gasket blows, replacing it is trivial on an engine dyno compared to the hours of R&R work required in a tight engine compartment.

Inertial chassis dynamometers are very repeatable and accurate, very simple to use, and easier on the vehicle and engine than brake-type dynos. The passive inertial mass of the inertial dynamometer will often be less than the weight of the vehicle itself, and the dynorun is typically over in 5 to 15 seconds, with little time for mechanical or thermal forces to become critical.

Load-holding dynamometers load an engine and force it to do work. You set the throttle to a particular rpm, engage the dyno, and the dyno computer will increase or decrease the load to hold rpm as the throttle increases or decreases. Many pro EMS calibrators insist that a load holding-dyno is the only way to properly calibrate an engine in a process whereby you set air/fuel ratio and timing at all breakpoints of rpm and loading in the EMS tables. They have a good point, because a load-holding dyno allows you to adjust spark advance to maximize torque, fuel efficiency, or exhaust emissions under all engine operating conditions. There is a detailed explanation of how to build VE and timing tables from scratch on a load-holding dyno in the chapter of this book about tuning.

Whatever unknown translation factor is required to convert from wheel horsepower on a particular vehicle to SAE crankshaft horsepower (rolling resistance and the weight of all components in the powertrain as well as tire and rolling resistance will affect measured horsepower on an inertial dyno), inertial dynos are extremely good for providing before and after comparison testing of aftermarket performance parts. On the other hand, installing heavier tires and wheels can change the inertia of the drivetrain enough to show a horsepower gain (although, indeed, a *lighter* drivetrain allows the vehicle to accelerate faster). The equation used to convert acceleration to horsepower is Horsepower = [(Mass x Acceleration x Drum Circumference) ÷ (Time x 550)]. Torque can be derived from horsepower with the formula Torque

= [(Horsepower ÷ 5250) ÷ Engine Speed]. Chassis dynos capture engine speed from an inductive pickup attached to a plug wire or direct-fire coil.

Exhaust Gas Temperature Gauges and Sensors (Pyrometers)

Virtually all piston-engine aircraft are equipped with EGT gauges, which pilots use as feedback for manually adjusting the air/fuel ratio control on the basis of target EGTs for best safe power and best cruise economy on the basis of specifications in the aircraft operating manual. EGT gauges are very common on diesel hot rodding packages, due to the fact that burning up more of the air surplus in a diesel engine can raise the EGT to dangerous levels. Many serious spark-ignition race engines are equipped with individual-port EGT probes that can be used for calibrating individual-cylinder fuel and spark trim and for datalogging EGT under race conditions. Some aftermarket EMSs can be equipped with at least one or two EGT probes that can be datalogged with user engine sensor data, and in some cases configured to use EGT feedback for closed-loop air/fuel ratio control. EGT data is extremely useful if you are working on a max-effort turbo engine project and want to optimize timing and run the leanest safe mixtures possible for maximum turbine energy or when calibrating an anti-lag system that intentionally burns some of the fuel in the exhaust system upstream of the turbocharger. Individual-port EGT probes are optimal, but a single EGT-probe providing turbine inlet temperature for each turbocharger provides very useful information.

Electronic and Electrical Components

Where do you go for PROMs, computer cables, wiring, relays, switches, and so forth? Radio Shack, Digikey, Fry's Electronics, Newark Electronics, and so forth.

Electronic Stethoscopes

For $100–200 you can purchase an electronic stethoscope designed to pinpoint noise and locate bad bearings, bushings, dirty fuel injectors, wind and air leaks, and noisy valves and filters. Typically, a flexible shaft reaches tight areas and an ultrasensitive microphone and amplifier provide the full range of sounds needed for diagnosis, with seven sound level control settings from 60 dB to 120 dB.

Fuel Pressure Gauges

Fuel pressure is critical to proper operation of electronic fuel injection. Without an accurate, high-pressure gauge, you are guessing about fuel rail pressure. You need a good gauge with a selection of fittings for common NPT, flair fittings, and air conditioning–type Schrader valves. Yes, the water-pressure gauges from hardware stores are less expensive, but they are not reliable, and who wants fuel spraying into a hot engine compartment at 40–60 psi? An alternative on some aftermarket engine management systems would be to install a pressure sensor on the fuel rail and record and datalog the data to a virtual dash via EMS software, with a warning alarm set if pressure drops below a critical level.

Ignition and Spark Tools

You think the plugs are firing fine. You think the spark is hot and true. But removing a plug to verify this is a major operation on some cars. While nothing substitutes for actually watching

PLX's Kiwi provides a car-to-smartphone datalink using WIFI or Bluetooth that allows Android and iOS smartphones and tablets running diagnostic software (such as Palmer Performance DashCommand) to interface to the vehicle's OBD-II system wirelessly. A scan tool that taps into the diagnostic port of a factory EMS is extremely valuable for viewing and logging factory engine data from sensors while the engine is running. This PDA-based system provides a lot of data in a small full-color user interface, but it is very lightweight and convenient for use while driving. Note barometric pressure, engine rpm, and moving graphs of mass airflow rate and intake air temperature. *Palmer Performance*

the ignition fire the actual plug that will light the fire, spark-gap testers are quick, simple, and cheap. If you've ever experienced a full-bore high-voltage shock trying to hold a plug against a ground with your hand, you probably already understand the value of this tool.

Injector Tester

Yes, you can sometimes hear injectors clicking when they are working. But if the injector is not clicking is it because the injector is stuck or because the wiring is bad? An injector tester will provide the answer. A good one should have adapters for all possible injector connectors. If it can read out the injection pulse width, so much the better. Some powerful automotive multi-meters can display injection pulse width.

OBD-II/CAN Bus Diagnostic Scanner

If a post-2007 factory EMS is acting up, the onboard diagnostics system can be helpful for troubleshooting the problem, and there are a huge variety of scan tools that interface to the OBD-II port and access all embedded controllers on a controller area network (CAN) vehicle network. One cost-effective option is to install an OBD-II-to-USB interface/cable and diagnostic software on your Windows laptop, Android smartphone or tablet, iPhone, or iPod. You'll be able to display current sensor data, including engine rpm, calculated load value, coolant temperature, vehicle speed, short term fuel trim, long term fuel trim, intake manifold pressure, timing advance, intake air temperature, airflow rate, absolute throttle position, oxygen sensor voltages and associated short term fuel trim, fuel system status, fuel pressure, and many other important parameters.

Oscilloscope

Diagnostic scan tools are only as good as the ECM, which may confuse injector problems with sensor faults. Multi-meters are cheap, but too slow to see injectors opening and closing. An oscilloscope is far more versatile: It displays the changing voltage on the switched side of a fuel injector and, with a current clamp, can even show the current through the injector coil. You can scope all the other electrical components in the vehicle, including the ignition.

An oscilloscope is a type of electronic test instrument that allows observation of constantly varying signal voltages, usually displayed as a two-dimensional graph of one or more electrical potential differences on the vertical or y-axis, plotted as a function

of time on the horizontal or x-axis. Many repeating signals can be converted to voltages and displayed this way. Because signals are often periodic and repeat constantly, multiple samples of a signal which is actually varying with time can be displayed as a steady picture. Many scopes can also capture nonrepeating waveforms for a specified time, and show a steady display of the captured segment. Yes, you can pay $20,000 for a special-purpose lab-quality oscilloscope (a.k.a., "scope"), but you can also buy a useful hand-held digital automotive scope for $100.

PROM Tools

If you are recalibrating an old EPROM-based OEM engine management system, you will need a PROM burner, which allows you to download and burn a calibration from a laptop PC. There are a number of USB EPROM burners that will do the job.

PROM Emulators can be used to convert a PROM-based factory EMS to dynamic programmability (while running and driving). The emulator replaces the ECU's program memory with its own internal dual-ported RAM, which can be used in conjunction with a laptop computer and the tuning software to monitor and change the PROM-based calibration. In the days before flash memory when the calibration tables of most factory engine management systems were stored in Programmable Read-Only Memory (changeable only with a PROM-burning device that uses ultra-violet light to write the PROM), knowledgeable tuner could use a general-purpose binary editor like WINHEX to modify anything in the PROM image in the emulator's RAM with the engine running on a dyno, and later burn a new PROM when finished tuning. The right EMS-calibration software package can provide user-friendly graphical access to specific tables and parameters in the EPROM for specific engine management systems and vehicles. Age has decimated the fleet of PROM-based EMSs that are alive and well, which has, in turn, decimated the ranks of PROM-tuner software packages that are still available and supported. If you are wrestling with an old PROM-based car, you can probably find what you need to calibrate it by searching the web for professional tuners who cater to the mark and by checking out the websites and message boards of owner's clubs.

Scan Tools

A scan tool is designed to provide a window into the factory EMS computer, and there are now some good packages that convert

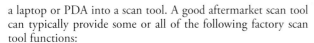

a laptop or PDA into a scan tool. A good aftermarket scan tool can typically provide some or all of the following factory scan tool functions:

1. Display and clear check engine error codes
2. Sensor display: airflow sensor, throttle position sensor, rpm, injector pulse width, battery/system voltage, coolant temperature, barometer, O_2 sensor, spark advance, ISC stepper position, EGR temperature
3. Switch position: idle, park/neutral, air conditioning request, air conditioning control, power steering
4. Turn on/off each of the actuators: injectors, fuel pump relay, purge solenoid, fuel pressure solenoid, wastegate solenoid
5. Datalogging: fuel trims, knock sensor, air volume, acceleration enrichment

Scan tools and digital multi-meters have some overlap in functionality. Scan tools:

1. Provide easy access to trouble codes
2. Provide easy checking of temperature sensors
3. Are good at finding intermittent wiring problems (wiggle test)
4. Monitor events while driving
5. Record readings while driving for later playback
6. Can sometimes measure pulse width
7. Show commands issued by ECU, but can't show if executed (pre-OBD-II)

Service Manuals
Modern engines and vehicles are very complex, and the factory shop manuals are virtually always better than aftermarket manuals. Of course, they are more expensive. Some genuine factory manuals cannot be ordered from a dealer but only from an outside supplier.

Soldering, Crimping, Circuitry, and Wiring Tools
Bad wiring is the cause of a huge number of EMS problems. Let me repeat: Bad wiring is the cause of a huge number of EMS problems! If you are planning to do any automotive wiring, you need a pro-quality crimping tool. This means ratcheting crimping tools with the correct jaw for all common size metal connectors. Such tools usually cost $50–150 but they are infinitely superior to the crap-quality crimping tools you find at places like Pep Boys that are supposed to crimp plastic-cased wire connectors (you should not be using plastic-cased connectors but rather good metal connectors that will be insulated with heat-shrink tubing). Some good crimping tools are available with removable jaws that can be changed out for a large number of applications, which can definitely save money, but my experience is that they don't cover all automotive connectors. You can find good wiring tools through EMS vendors like DIY AutoTune, and Motec, plus Amazon, Howard Electronics, Pace (eBay), Metcal Gear (eBay), Radio Shack, Paladin Tools, Altex, Fry's Electronics, and so on. As always, the right tool is *critical*.

Thermometers and Temperature Instruments
A cooling system thermometer can be useful if you are struggling with flaky sensors or if you're attempting to locate a heat-soaked air- or coolant-temperature sensor that measures temperature more representative of the actual air or coolant temperature. Gun-type non-contact infra-red thermometers are really fast and convenient.

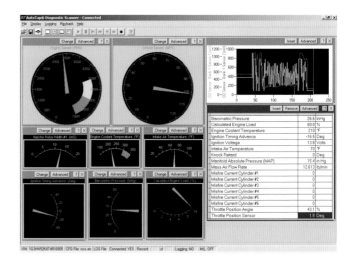

A PDA-based scan package is nice, but there is nothing like the large color screen of a laptop for providing the complete picture of what the EMS thinks is happening in the engine and vehicle. Note the "Calculated Engine Load" virtual meter and the individual-cylinder misfire displays. OBD-II monitors can be really useful for onboard diagnostics. *Auto Tap*

Vacuum/Pressure Pump
Devices like MAP sensors, wastegate actuators, oil pressure sensors, and fuel pressure regulators all require a pressure source to function properly. A hand pump with a gauge readout and a selection of plumbing to interface the tool to various types of sensors and vacuum/boost-operated devices can be really valuable to operate these types of devices without the engine running to verify they are functioning properly or to properly simulate operating conditions if you are, say, testing fuel pump output at a certain pressure. How many hours of wasted time does it take to justify this tool? Not many, especially if measuring the response of a wastegate actuator or a MAP sensor keeps you from destroying your engine.

VOM meters (Volt-Ohm-Millimeter) and Digital Multimeters
These devices are commonly used for sensor testing of O_2, MAP, MAT, TPS, Knock, CTS, and IAC. You might decide to acquire a digital multimeter in place of a scan tool. Compared to a scan tool, the digital multimeter:

- Tests same sensors as scan tool (with more effort)
- Performs tests without influence by wiring or ECM problems
- Tests sensors that scan tools cannot test (IAC, cam position, and crank position)
- Tests injector pulse width and resistance
- Tests traditional electrical components (alternator, regulator, starter, coil, plug wires)
- Finds bad connections and high-resistance circuits
- Finds average or maximum readings using recording/averaging feature without having to watch the meter

Wideband Air/fuel-ratio Gauges, Meters, and Sensors, and Exhaust Gas Analyzers
Most aftermarket air/fuel ratio meters are based on Nernst pump cell wideband air/fuel ratio sensors commonly available from Bosch and NTK/NGK, and they have five or six wires. Five-

wire sensors always require sophisticated closed-loop controllers to measure the air/fuel ratio. Five-wire wideband sensors allow the switch-point zone to be moved around to different air/fuel ratios, meaning they are in effect equipped with an electronically controllable target air/fuel ratio in their reaction cavity.

Wideband air/fuel ratio gauges are widely available in the $150 to $300 price range, with datalogging available in the higher-end models that are more properly referred to as meters.

If your EMS supports wideband air/fuel ratio sensors (most now do), you should absolutely get one. Keep in mind that the EMS may have integrated wideband controller capability, which would allow you to install a simple wideband sensor available in the $50 to $100 range. If not, you will need a wideband sensor kit, complete with controller, which will be more expensive.

Virtually all exhaust gas analyzers measure exhaust gas carbon monoxide using infrared light, and some can measure exhaust hydrocarbons and NOx. Good ones can be calibrated with test gases or known content. Exhaust analyzers are useful if you are having difficulty passing a smog check, but they are also valuable if you are evaluating combustion efficiency at a particular state of tune.

TROUBLESHOOTING SENSORS

Car companies have worked hard over the years to increase the self-diagnostic capabilities of original-equipment engine management systems from the bad old days when 80 percent of drivability problems didn't result in a trouble code in the computer. OBD-II vehicles are greatly improved in their ability to detect and comprehend engine system troubles, but intermittent problems, such as loss of ECU ground or a bad sensor, still may not show up in the diagnostics trouble codes.

How can we look at sensor data to decide if there is a sensor problem?

In the first place, you are going to need either a scan tool or a Digital Multimeter (DMM) for more comprehensive troubleshooting. (If you have an oscilloscope, that's even better for some situations). Some engine management systems require an analog multimeter or a digital multimeter (DMM) with analog simulation so you can see trouble codes spelled out as pulses. The scan tool's ability to function while you drive is nice, but it reflects what the ECU *thinks* is happening, not necessarily what is actually occurring. A meter that measures physical pulse width at the injector—rather than assuming actual pulse width by analyzing the situation at the ECU—can point out a bad injector driver.

Exhaust Gas Oxygen Sensor

The exhaust gas oxygen sensor is very important because many factory ECUs evaluate data from the O_2 sensor with the highest priority. A functioning O_2 sensor offers a good snapshot of how the engine is running (though it too can be fooled). It can be a good idea to routinely replace the sensor with a new one before proceeding. O_2 sensors are relatively inexpensive and a known-good, new sensor is a valuable aid in diagnosing other problems, such as other bad sensors. The O_2 sensor is used in feedback mode by the ECU to trim the air/fuel mixture and thus directly affects injector on-time.

The voltage output of a normal narrowband sensor to the ECM is 0.1 to 0.9 volts, with 0.5 representing the stoichiometric or theoretically ideal mixture and the sensor sensitive to air/fuel ratio changes in the 14.1-15 range, making the sensor useful for determining if the engine is operating

above or below the stoichiometric ratio, indicating whether the EMS should lengthen or shorten injection pulse width by a tiny amount to keep the mixture where it belongs for lowest exhaust emissions. Wideband air/fuel ratio sensors are a different story. The ubiquitous Bosch LSU wideband is designed for a 5-volt reference signal and analog output is within the 0- to 5-volt range, though 2.5 volts does not necessarily represent a stoichiometric air/fuel ratio, depending on how the sensor is set up. Some Toyota wideband sensors receive a 3-volt reference and output 0-3 volts.

Exhaust gas sensors must be heated to roughly 600 degrees Fahrenheit to function accurately, so modern sensors have a supplemental heating circuit to bring the sensor up to temperature within 10 or 20 seconds of start, and modern EMSs typically use after-start tuning strategies designed to aid in the process by heating the exhaust very quickly (with retarded timing a critical component).

Narrowband oxygen sensors swing from rich to lean by design, but it is possible to check these oscillations with a scan tool or digital multimeter (DMM). The sensor voltage should jump from rich to lean every few seconds as the EMS chases the stoichiometric air/fuel ratio. If this doesn't happen, or if the sensor voltage stays in the 0.3- to 0.6-volt range, or stays lean, the sensor is bad.

Some DMMs have an averaging feature that allows you to read the idle mixture and provides maximum high and low values, giving you some idea of the sensor's condition. A scan tool lets you look at the block learn counts that will tell you if the ECM is drastically altering the air/fuel mixture. As an example, some GM ECMs show 128 as the normal block learn count. Above 138, the ECM is interpreting sensor data as implying lean air/fuel ratio, and will add fuel. Below 118, the reverse is true.

The oxygen sensor must remain connected to the ECU in normal closed-loop operation during measurement, but you can measure sensor output by removing insulation from the wire or make use of a breakout box connected between the sensor and wiring to connect the meter. Remember, we are talking about using a *digital* multimeter. An *analog* multimeter can damage the sensor by drawing too much current. Check a shop manual for the wire function in multiple-wire sensors.

Since low voltage corresponds to a lean mixture, failing sensors seldom erroneously indicate a rich condition. Sometimes an O_2 sensor will intermittently quit, which shows up as rich running, with the check light occasionally coming on. This could show up in an ECU trouble code, indicating that the O_2 sensor seemed to be staying lean too long (voltage went below 0.5 and stayed there for a long time).

The following procedure tests for possible wiring problems between the O_2 sensor and the ECU:
1. Disconnect the O_2 sensor connector.
2. Tap into the sensor wire with a probe.
3. Leave a meter hooked up to the sensor.
4. Hold the probe in one hand while touching the positive battery terminal with the other (safe with battery voltages).
5. The ECU will see a high voltage, interpret this as a rich condition, and lean out the mixture, causing the motor to stumble and possibly die.
6. The meter connected to the O_2 sensor will indicate voltage dropping to 0.1 volts or below.
7. Switching your hand to the minus or negative battery terminal should cause the ECU to enrich things considerably, indicating 0.8 volts or above on the meter.

If you drive the system lean, a new sensor will indicate below 0.1 volts, while an old tired sensor may not go below 0.2 volts. The reverse is true at the rich end of the scale.

To verify whether you have a bad oxygen sensor circuit or whether there is something wrong in the ECU that's causing a problem with closed-loop mode, connect a scan tool to the ALDL and with the ignition on, engine off, disconnect the sensor lead, and ground the lead. The scan tool should indicate 0.2 volts or below.

If you have a DMM, with engine off and ignition on, check the voltage at the ECU lead, which should be 0.3 volt or below. Verify that the ECU is very well grounded!

Temperature Sensors

When an EFI engine is cold, until the oxygen sensor reaches full operating temperature and becomes effective, basic fuel-injection pulse width is computed based on the mass airflow calculation (engine speed and mass airflow or manifold pressure corrected for engine and air temperature. Temperature sensor data is also used to determine warm-up enrichment, and whether or not the engine is allowed to operate in closed-loop air/fuel ratio mode.

You can test a thermistor-type coolant-temperature sensor by checking the resistance across the two leads (one usually being a ground routed to the ECU, which supplies a high-quality conditioned ground to most sensors) with the connector removed using a DMM. The coolant temperature sensor is usually located on the intake manifold, sometimes on the water pump or cylinder head. Check for corrosion on the leads; anything affecting resistance through the sensor

GM/CHRYSLER TEMPERATURE SENSOR RESISTANCE

Temperature (deg F.)	Resistance (ohms)
210	185
160	450
100	800
70	3,400
40	7,500
20	13,500
0	25,000
-40	100,700

FORD TEMPERATURE SENSOR RESISTANCE

Temperature (deg F.)	Resistance (ohms)
248	1,180
230	1,550
212	2,070
194	2,800
176	3,840
158	5,370
140	7,700
122	10,970
104	16,150
86	24,270
68	37,300
50	58,750

wiring would change the sensor reading. Compare resistance to the sensor specification, then verify the figures with a known-good thermometer.

The MAT (manifold air temperature) and IAT (inlet air temperature) sensors, if fitted, can be tested the same way. Look for these sensors in the manifold or air cleaner ducting. If the engine has cold-soaked overnight, all temperature sensors should read the same in the morning. When reconnecting the sensors, make sure the connectors are seated correctly and that none of the connector pins push out of the connectors (some can!). Electronics supply houses sell chemicals that help to prevent corrosion on connectors.

Mass Airflow Sensors

There are two kinds of MAF sensors, those that output variable DC voltage like most sensors, and those that output a variable frequency. For frequency-type MAF, you'll need a scan tool or oscilloscope. MAF failures typically begin with intermittent symptoms that are followed by total failure. For example, you're driving down the highway and feel a momentary loss of power, usually accompanied by the service engine light flashing on and off. If the MAF does fail completely, the light will stay on, though the car should still be drivable in limp mode.

Tapping on the MAF with the engine running may indicate a failing MAF if the engine stumbles. If the engine is running rich or lean, and disconnecting the MAF helps, this indicates a failure. Jumper wires can enable you to connect a DMM to the MAF to read voltage. MAFs usually have three wires: ground, ECM reference voltage in (usually 0-5 volts, occasionally 0-12 volts), and sensor output. You can connect the DMM to the ground and sensor output, which typically yields about 2.5 volts on GM systems. Switching to DC volt frequency allows you to look for big frequency changes in response to small changes in engine speed. You can blow through the MAF with something like a

MASS AIRFLOW SENSOR TESTING VALUES

MAF output	DC voltage	Frequency (Hz)
Idle	2.599	45
5-psi boost (second gear)	2.613	118
10-psi boost (second gear)	2.620	125
17-psi boost (second gear)	2.635	142

hair dryer, tapping the MAF to see if it's affected. Road testing is possible with the scan tool or a DMM with extended test leads. A scan tool will read grams per second of air, which, for example, might be 4–7 at idle on a V-6 engine, varying from 3–150 grams per second across the operating range of the engine. A failed MAF will show up on the scan tool as the default output by the ECU. DMMs show frequency variance from 32–150 hertz. The idea is to look for null output or suspicious output. Remember, the scan tool displays what the ECU thinks is happening at the sensor rather than what is actually happening.

The following results came from testing on a 3.8-liter turbo V-6 Buick:

MAP and BP Sensors

The MAP (manifold absolute pressure) sensor outputs a signal based purely on absolute pressure, not relative to the altitude the vehicle happens to be at right now. Before diagnosing the

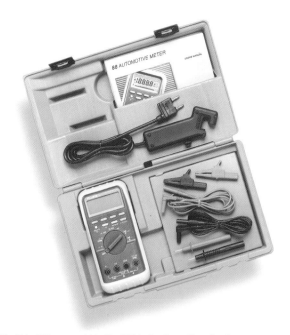

The Fluke 88 is a powerful tool for EMS testing. It provides volts, ohms, amps, continuity, diode testing, milliseconds pulse width, rpm (with inductive pickup), frequency and duty-cycle measurements, min-max-average recording, and more. *Fluke*

MAP sensor, check the hose feeding the sensor for any leaks. Like the MAF, MAP sensors come in two breeds, those that output varying voltage (GM) and those that output a square-wave 5 volts DC that varies in frequency (Ford), requiring a DMM that can measure frequency in hertz. It can be hard to get documentation on what the output of a MAF should be; consider measuring a known-good vehicle first and compare it to the one in question.

Troubleshooting Hall Effect Sensors

Wiring shorts, loose or corroded connectors, or arcing damage to internal sensor circuitry can cause problems with the Hall effect sensor. Most aftermarket engine management systems will immediately detect Hall effect faults such as missing crank REF or cam SYNC and report the problem to a connected laptop, while OEM systems will set the malfunction indicator light (MIL). To troubleshoot OE Hall effect sensors, Wells Vehicle Electronics (which builds a variety of automotive sensors, actuators, and engine management components) recommends using a self-powered indicator-light type of Hall effect tester that flashes when the sensor's output signal changes.

"If the sensor is being tested on the vehicle," says Wells, "simply plug the tester into the sensor, then crank the engine and observe the indicator light. It should wink on and off while the engine is cranking. If the sensor is being tested off the vehicle, plug the tester into the sensor connector and observe the indicator light. It should remain on steadily. Then insert a metal blade into the sensor's magnetic window (air gap). The indicator should go off while the blade is in the window, then wink back on when the blade is removed. No change would indicate a faulty sensor."

Wells points out that on-car sensor problems can be caused by several things:

The sensor must have the proper reference voltage (VRef) power supply from the computer. If the sensor is not receiving the required voltage, it won't work. Measure the supply voltage between the sensor's power supply wire and ground (use the engine block for a ground, not the sensor's ground circuit wire). If you don't see the specified voltage, check the sensor's wiring harness for loose or corroded connectors.

The sensor's ground circuit must be in good condition. A poor ground connection will have the same effect on the sensor's operation as a bad VRef supply. Measure the voltage between the sensor's ground wire and the engine block. If you see more than 0.1 volts, the sensor has a bad ground connection.

If the sensor has power and ground, the next thing to check would be sensor output. The voltage output signal should switch back and forth from maximum to near zero as the engine is cranked. No change would indicate a faulty sensor. Watching the sensor's voltage output on an oscilloscope is a good way to spot problems that might escape normal diagnosis. You should see a nice, sharp square-wave pattern that goes from maximum to near zero (or vice versa) every time the sensor switches on and off. The sync pulse signal from a crank/cam position sensor should also stand out and be readily apparent in the waveform. If you see rounded corners, spikes, excessive noise or variations in amplitude from one pulse to the next, the erratic operation of the sensor may be causing the computer to miss signals or pick up false signals.

Wells recommends testing an electronic ignition system with Hall effect pickup in the distributor by inserting a steel feeler gauge, pocket knife blade, or similar object, into the sensor window with the ignition turned on to see if this fires the ignition coil, making sure the spark has a proper path to ground via a spark-gap tester. For you old-timers, blocking the magnetic window in a Hall effect sensor should have the same effect as opening the points in a breaker point ignition system.

A Hall effect sensor must be aligned correctly with the interrupter ring or shutter blade to generate a clean signal, and any contact between moving parts and the sensor might cause idle problems or fatal damage. A worn, stretched, or jumped timing chain or belt can affect the timing of the sensor's output (which is one reason why using any cam-speed component to provide precision timing information is riskier than using the crank). Failure of the crank position sensor usually causes the engine to die immediately since the EMS no longer has a reference for ignition and fuel injection.

On older Chrysler Hall effect ignition systems, the shutter blades under the distributor rotor must be properly grounded to produce a clean signal. Wells recommends using an ohmmeter to check continuity between the shutter blades and distributor shaft. "If the blades are not grounded, the sensor will check out OK but won't produce a good signal when the engine is cranked with the rotor in place," says Wells. "On Ford applications with Thick Film Integrated (TFI) ignition distributors, the Hall effect signal is called the 'Profile Ignition Pick-up' (PIP) signal. Corroded connectors between the Hall effect PIP unit in the distributor and the TFI module on the distributor housing are common." Replacing the sensor on these applications requires R&R of the distributor shaft.

Troubleshooting Throttle Position Sensors

With the engine stopped and the ignition turned off, unplug the electrical connector and attach an ohmmeter between the center terminal and one of the outer two terminals on the TPS. Manually open the throttle slowly to operate the TPS. The ohmmeter reading should increase or decrease smoothly as you operate the TPS through its complete range of travel.

Connect the ohmmeter between the center terminal and the other outer terminal as above. Again, the ohmmeter reading should increase or decrease smoothly as you work the sensor. Momentary Infinity (open), full continuity (0 ohms), or erratic readings indicate a defective or shorted sensor.

Check the reference voltage from the computer with a digital voltmeter or oscilloscope. If the sensor is not receiving a full 5 volts from the ECM, it will be unable to generate the correct range of return signals. Less that 5 volts on the VRef indicates a possible wiring or computer problem (assuming the battery is not excessively low). Verify good continuity between the TPS ground wire terminal and ground with the key on. Verify that the voltage reading indicates less than 0.1 volts. Voltage output between the signal wire and ground with the key on should vary from less than 1 volt at idle up to nearly 5 volts at wide-open throttle.

A scan tool or laptop computer can also be used on most OEM and aftermarket engine management systems to observe the TPS output voltage as seen by the onboard computer system. Note that since the scan tool displays the TPS output voltage as a digital reading, the display may not update quickly enough for you to detect a momentary skip spot in TPS output as you open and close the throttle.

Troubleshooting O_2 Sensors

Oxygen sensor performance tends to diminish with age as contaminants accumulate on the sensor tip and gradually reduce its ability to produce voltage. According to Wells Vehicle Electronics, which builds replacement OE-type O_2 sensors, "The sensor becomes sluggish and takes longer to react to oxygen changes in the exhaust causing emissions and fuel consumption to go up. The effect is most noticeable on engines with multi-port fuel injection (MFI) because the fuel ratio changes more rapidly than on the throttle body or feedback carburetor applications. If the O_2 sensor fails, the computer may go into open loop operation." Contaminants include lead, silicone (from internal coolant leaks or inappropriate types of RTV sealant), phosphorus (from oil burning), and sulfur.

The operation of the O_2 sensor, according to Wells, should be checked any time there's an emissions or engine-performance problem. Wells recommends that the O_2 sensor be checked when the spark plugs are replaced, or if the vehicle has a maintenance reminder light calling for a check of the O_2 sensor. Reading O_2 sensor output voltage with a scan tool or digital voltmeter while the engine is running and warmed up can tell you if the sensor is producing a signal, but the digital numbers will jump around too much to enable an accurate determination if the sensor is good. A high-impedance analog voltmeter is somewhat better for viewing O_2 sensor voltage transitions, but may respond too slowly to be conclusive on systems with higher voltage transition rates. However, a digital storage oscilloscope (DSO) will display the sensor's voltage output as a wavy line that shows both amplitude (minimum and maximum voltage) as well as the frequency of transition rate from rich to lean. A good O_2 sensor will produce an oscillating waveform at idle that transitions from minimum voltage (0.3 volts or less) to maximum (0.8 volts or higher).

Try making the fuel mixture artificially rich by feeding propane into the intake manifold, which should cause the sensor to respond almost immediately (within 100 milliseconds) and go to maximum (above 0.8 volts) output. Creating a lean mixture by opening a vacuum line should cause the sensor's output to drop to its minimum (0.3 volts or less) value. If the O_2 sensor

voltage does not change back and forth quickly enough, it needs to be replaced. A sluggish O_2 sensor may not set an MIL code, so don't assume the O_2 sensor is OK just because there is no code.

Alternately, the O_2 sensor can be checked by removing it from the vehicle, connecting a digital voltmeter to the sensor, and using a propane torch to heat the sensor element. With a unheated zirconia O_2 sensor, connect the positive test lead to the sensor's wire lead and the negative test lead to the sensor housing or shell (ground). Hold the sensor with pliers, then use the propane torch to heat the sensing element. The flame consumes most of the oxygen, so the sensor should generate a rich voltage signal of about 0.9 volts within 60 seconds or less. Now remove the flame while observing the voltmeter. If the sensor is good, the sensor reading should drop to less than 0.1 volt within three seconds.

To test a sensor's heating circuit, connect an ohmmeter across the sensor's two heater wires. Set the meter on the low scale. If the heater circuit is OK, the ohmmeter will register a resistance reading. The precise reading is unimportant as long as the meter registers other than an open circuit.

Titania O_2 sensors change resistance rather than generating a voltage like zirconia sensors. However, a Titania O_2 sensor can also be tested with an ohmmeter and propane torch. Connect an ohmmeter across the black and gray sensor leads, setting the meter on the 200K scale. Heat the tip of the sensor with the torch as above, and note the ohmmeter reading. A good sensor should show resistance that varies with flame temperature, and good sensor should return to infinity after removing the flame.

Troubleshooting Engine Temperature Sensors

A coolant temperature sensor (CTS) is critical in triggering many engine functions, which means a faulty sensor or wiring can cause a variety of warm-up performance problems and emissions failures.

Symptoms that might be caused by a bad coolant sensor include the following:

* EMS fails to launch closed-loop feedback mode once the engine is fully warm
* Poor cold idle due to excessively rich fuel mixture, no early fuel evaporation (EFE), or lack of heated air
* Stalling due to excessively rich mixture, retarded timing, or slow idle speed
* Cold hesitation or stumble due to lack of EFE or excessively early EGR
* Poor fuel mileage due to rich mixture, open loop, spark retarded

Keep in mind that such problems may not indicate sensor failure but might result from wiring faults or loose or corroded connections. An engine thermostat that is too cold for the application can also upset cold-running EMS strategies, as can low coolant due to incomplete filling or cooling system leaks. The sensor element must be in direct contact with liquid coolant to generate accurate data.

The easiest way to test a coolant temperature sensor is with a sweep test with an ohmmeter. To conduct a sweep test:

1. The engine must be cold.
2. With the key off, disconnect the wiring connector from the thermistor.
3. Attach an ohmmeter across the sensor leads and note the resistance.
4. Reattach the CTS connector. Run the engine for 2 minutes and then shut it down.
5. Repeat steps 2 and 3.

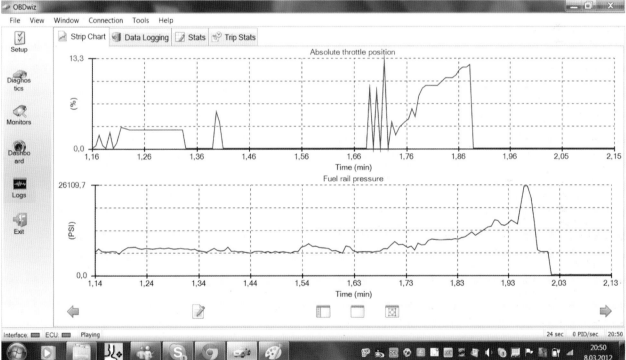

ECMScan OBDwiz provides a powerful set of tools that help analyze and log sensor problems in OBD-i engines.

6. There should be a difference of at least 200 ohms between the two readings.
7. If not, the sensor is defective or possibly coated with cooling system sludge that insulates it from changes in engine temperature.
8. Try cleaning the sensor element and then retest.
9. Good shop manuals will contain a chart specifying coolant sensor resistance for various engine temperatures. Verify that the reading meet specs.
10. Alternately, check the sensor's operation signal as the engine warms up with a voltmeter: Measure the CTS reference voltage (normally 5 volts) and returned voltage (3–4 volts when cold, dropping to less than 2 volts at normal operating temperature).
11. No change in returned signal voltage (or lack of a return signal) indicates a faulty sensor.
12. Incorrect VRef indicates a wiring problem.
13. Alternately, observe the sensor's waveform with a digital storage oscilloscope (DSO).
14. If an EMS provides live sensor data through its diagnostic connector, you can also read the coolant

continued on page 249

STARTING PROBLEMS

A healthy engine with fuel, air, and spark MUST run. If it's not running properly, there MUST be a problem with one of more of these parameters.

TROUBLE: ENGINE WILL NOT START

Possibilities:

Injectors are not operating because:
ECU is not receiving 12 volt switched power.
ECU is not receiving 12 volt constant power.
Insufficient ground.
Ignition system is not compatible with ECU.
Bad ECU.
Check connections, fuses, relays, plug wires.
ECU not receiving an rpm signal from the ignition system.
Check wiring for proper connection, ignition compatibility, ignition system operation.
Voltage drops below 9 volts during cranking.
Check battery voltage, connections.

Injectors are operating but:
Fuel mixture is too lean.
Fuel mixture is too rich (spark plugs will be wet with fuel).
Check plug condition and adjust fuel delivery bars as required.

Injectors do not have proper fuel pressure.
Check pump operation, fuel rail pressure.

Engine is not receiving ignition spark or engine ignition timing is incorrect.
Check ignition system function, and timing.

Engine must have a small amount of air to start.
Engine is not receiving enough air to start.
Check throttle-stop setting, IAC system configuration parameters.

NO-START ALGORITHM

1. Check for spark; if spark exists, go to 2.
1.1 On fuel-only EFI system with standalone ignition: Disconnect EFI tachometer wire from ignition system; if still no spark, repair ignition; otherwise go to 1.2.
1.15 On fuel-spark EMS, check for rpm reading as viewed from a laptop or scan tool. Verify crank sensor alignment and air gap with the trigger wheel. Verify crank sensor resistance (typically 600-700 ohms***).
1.2 (Electrical problem in EFI system) Disconnect ECU; if spark, substitute spare ECU known to be good and recheck; otherwise go to 1.3.
1.3 (Bad EMS wiring harness) Check EMS wiring harness.

2. Check fuel pump—with ignition on, pump should audibly run a few seconds, then stop. If pump runs, go to 3; otherwise go to 2.1
2.1 (Bad fuel pump or electrical problem in ECU) Check switched and continuous power to ECU, check all grounds. If bad, fix; otherwise go to 2.15.
2.15 Check pump fuse and all other fuses. If blown, go to 2.3; otherwise go to 2.2.
2.2 (Fuse OK) Check pump power and ground for several seconds after activating ignition. If power OK, replace fuel pump; otherwise check wiring harness and if good, substitute replacement ECU.
2.3 (Fuse blown) Replace the fuse (make sure it's the correct rated fuse!). If fuse again blows, go to 2.4
2.4 (Fuse blows again) Check wiring harness, repair if necessary; otherwise go to 2.5.

2.5 Disconnect fuel pump, injectors, and other sensor connectors from the ECU and try new fuse. If the fuse blows again, substitute new ECU; otherwise go to 2.6.
2.6 Reconnect EFI components one by one until the fuse blows, and then replace the faulty component.

3. (Fuel pump runs, engine will not start)
Check fuel flow direction at pressure regulator and pump. If correct, check fuel rail pressure with a high-pressure gauge (upstream of regulator, if there is one or more!) for 10 seconds after energizing the EMS. The fuel pressure should increase to the rating of the fuel pressure regulator (typically 39-43 psi with no manifold pressure). If pressure is OK, go to 4; if pressure is low or there is no pressure, go to 3.2; otherwise go to 3.1.
3.1 (High pressure) Check return line for blockage. If OK, replace regulator.
3.2 (Low pressure) There is either air in the line or the regulator has malfunctioned. Trying running the pump for a minute or two by jumpering +12V to the hot side of the fuel pump. If pressure increases with air bleeding, continue. Otherwise, clamp off return line, then retry. If pressure builds to a high pressure, replace regulator; otherwise go to 3.3.
3.3 Check supply line from pump to injectors and regulator and fix if blocked (blocked fuel filter, pinched hose, blocked fuel feed screen at tank, low fuel, and so on). If OK, replace fuel pump.

4. (Pressure in fuel rail OK)
With ignition on, crank engine with coil wire disconnected. Fuel should pulse in 0.01 second squirts from one or more injectors (listen for a loud clicking from the injectors; this will be easier with a mechanic's stethoscope or with a screwdriver tip against the injector and the other end placed against the ear). If fuel pulsing is OK, EMS is OK (replace coil wire, check ignition timing, firing order of the plugs, check at least +9V battery voltage to the ECU during cranking, and so forth); if no fuel is pulsing, go to 4.1; if continuous fuel flow from one or more injectors, go to 5.
4.1 (No fuel pulsing). Verify valid Crank Ref or Tach signal to ECU. If signal is OK, check +12V power to injectors with a test light with the ignition turned on to one terminal on one injector. If +12V is present on one terminal, check for continuity between the other terminal and the injector driver/channel of the ECU, which pull to ground to fire the injector. If you have an oscilloscope, look for a +12V square wave at the injector connector. If not, the ECU could be defective, and this would be a great time to substitute a known-good ECU (with the correct MAP installed). Verify in the EMS software that the injection pulsewidth table is not zero-ed out completely, resulting in NO INJECTION. If the electrical tests show no problem but the injectors are not clicking, consider that one or more injectors might be stuck fully closed or even fully open. An injector stuck closed will not click or flow any fuel; an injector stuck open will rapidly flood the cylinder, and can hydro-lock the cylinder and destroy pistons or even put a rod through the block JUST CRANKING THE ENGINE!! Try substituting one or more known-good injectors into the fuel rail. Otherwise go to 4.2.
4.2 (No tach signal or crank reference). Check wiring harness and connectors/pins to all components, then check ECU. Check ignition components that generate the tach signal or the crank trigger mechanism that generates the Crank Ref signal.

5.(Continuous fuel from one or more injectors)
Disconnect electrical connections on injectors, recheck for spray. If no injector sprays, check wiring harness, connections, and ECU; otherwise go to replace damaged injector(s). **Note:** Stuck-open injectors can hydro-lock the engine and cause catastrophic damage! If you suspect excessive flooding might be a problem, immediately remove the spark plugs before cranking for further troubleshooting efforts.

6. (Insufficient air)
Crank engine with the throttle manually opened a small amount. If the engine starts, adjust IAC motor settings for proper start-up.

TROUBLE: ENGINE STARTS, THEN DIES (FULLY WARM)

Possibilities:

> **Tach/Crank Ref source problem**
> **Sensor problems**
> **Intake air leaks**
>> Check sensors, tach signal source, integrity of intake system.

Start-Stall Algorithm:

6. Check critical engine connections (Crank Position, tach lead to tach source for fuel-only batch-fire injection (coil, tach driver), lead to coolant temperature sensor, ground connection, MAP/MAF sensors, and so on). Correct problem if required; otherwise go to 6.1.

    6.1 Check resistance of tach-to-ECU or Crank Ref circuit. If required, replace any wiring/connectors; otherwise go to 6.2.

    6.2 Check other sensors for legitimate electrical values based on known physical conditions (temperature vs. legitimate coolant sensor resistance, air pressure in manifold vs. MAP signal, and so forth). Replace sensors if bad; otherwise go to 6.3.

    6.3 Check for major air leaks in intake system (throttle body, runners, vacuum hoses and ports, and so on).

    6.4 Check for other ignition problems.

TROUBLE: DIFFICULT COLD START, POOR OPERATION WHEN COLD

Possibilities:

> **Bad coolant temperature sensor**
> **Warmup map needs more enrichment at lower temperatures**
> **Zero-rpm map needs more duration on cranking bars**
> **Cranking primer needs more duration**
>> Check coolant sensor, maps for proper adjustments.

Difficult Cold-Start Algorithm:

7. Disconnect coolant temperature sensor, check resistance of the sensor to ground (need chart of resistance per degrees temperature) with ohmmeter (in the case of thermistor-type sensor). Verify that Zener diode-type sensor is good or substitute known good sensor. If bad, replace sensor and retry running; otherwise go to 7.1.

    7.1 (Good coolant sensor) If the engine is not hard to start, adjust the prime fuel injection pulse width under warm conditions; otherwise go to 7.2.

    7.2 Verify operation of startup enrichment devices (extra injector or injectors, thermo-time switch, fast idle equipment, and so on). If bad, replace; otherwise go to 7.3.

    7.3 (Incorrect startup enrichment on programmable system) Reprogram the warmup enrichment percentage(s), verifying that the values are correct when the system is again cold (which may take some time).

    7.4 Engine flooded (use "clear flood" mode if it exists).

    7.5 Low battery voltage (below 8.5volts) when cranking. Try starting with additional voltage or by powering the ECU with a separate battery.

    7.6 Unusual fuel pump condition (vapor-locked, overheated motor, and so forth).

TROUBLE: DIFFICULT HOT START

Possibilities:

> **Engine flooded.**
> **Air temperature sensor (if installed) is heat soaking.**
> **Fuel lines are heat soaking.**
> **Fuel pump problem.**
>> Check air temperature sensor mounting location, fuel line routing (shield from engine/exhaust heat).

TROUBLE: FUEL PUMP DOES NOT OPERATE

Possibilities:

> **ECU is not receiving power or ground.**
> **Fuel pump relay is not operating. Pump is not receiving power or ground.**
>> Check connections, relays.

TROUBLE: TACH READING IS INCORRECT ON FUEL-ONLY BATCH-FIRE EMS

Possibilities:

> **Number of cylinders or other data entered incorrectly to ECU.**
> **Incompatible ignition type.**
>> Check ID page, ignition compatibility chart.

RUNNING PROBLEMS

DRIVABILITY IMPROVEMENT TO ENGINE THAT RUNS

8. Verify correct prime engine sensors (MAP, MAF, tach signal, and others). Replace if bad; otherwise go to 8.1.

    8.1 Check fuel pressure setting during running conditions with gauge connected to fuel rail.

    8.2 Check for air and vacuum leaks.

    8.3 Check injectors for correct operation. Injectors should match flow at all duty cycles as closely as possible (for racing, injectors must be individually cleaned and matched by experts).

FUEL ECONOMY IMPROVEMENT FOR ENGINE THAT RUNS

Possibilities:

> **TPS poorly calibrated**
> **Wrong air-fuel mixture**
> **Acceleration enrichment problem**
> **Leaky injectors**
> **Other engine problem**
>> Check TPS, mixture, acceleration enrichment maps, injector balance test.

FUEL ECONOMY IMPROVEMENT ALGORITHM

9. Check TPS for calibration (incorrect setting could cause undue acceleration enrichment).

    9.1 Check air-fuel mixture at idle and cruise (14.7:1 is correct stoichiometric; smooth, lean idle is best). Check content of exhaust gases for carbon monoxide (CO), hydrocarbons (HC), and so forth.

    9.2 Check acceleration enrichment percentage and sustain. Back off the enrichment until the vehicle begins to bog slightly, then enrich slightly. Adjust sustain according to manufacturer's recommendations, then try backing off until vehicle bogs, and enrich slightly again. Poor economy is probably not due to faulty acceleration enrichment if drivability is good. Black fuel smoke under heavy acceleration is a good indicator that acceleration enrichment is excessive.

    9.25 Check for leaky injector(s).

    9.3 (EFI system good) Check distributor curve, engine timing, vacuum advance, and other functions.

TROUBLE: ENGINE RUNS RICH

Possibilities:

> **ECU adjustments set too high**
> **TPS calibrated incorrectly**
> **Leaky injector(s)**
> **Excessive fuel pressure**
> **Nonfunctional temperature sensor**
> **Bad ECU**

EMS TROUBLESHOOTING

TROUBLE: ENGINE RUNS LEAN

Possibilities:

ECU pulsewidth adjustments set too low
TPS bad or incorrectly adjusted
Low fuel pressure
Low switched or continuous power to ECU
Bad ECU

TROUBLE: ENGINE REVS TO AN RPM AND DEVELOPS A MISFIRE

Possibilities:

Incompatible ignition
Check rpm signal on engine data page.
Fuel mixture changes drastically from one rpm range to the next
Fuel mixture is too rich
Fuel mixture is too lean
Check fuel delivery maps for proper adjustments.
Engine is running out of fuel
Check fuel pressure.

TROUBLE: SLOW THROTTLE RESPONSE

Possibilities:

Fuel delivery maps too rich.
Ignition timing retarded.
Check fuel maps, ignition timing.

TROUBLE: ENGINE COUGHS BETWEEN SHIFTS

Possibilities:

High-rpm light throttle areas of maps too rich
High-rpm light throttle areas of maps too lean
Accelerator pump values too rich
Accelerator pump values too lean
Check accelerator pump maps, fuel delivery maps.

TROUBLE: ENGINE COUGHS UNDER RAPID THROTTLE MOVEMENT

Possibilities:

Accelerator pump enrichment too lean
Accelerator pump enrichment extremely rich
Fuel maps too lean at part throttle
Ignition timing retarded
Check accelerator pump maps, fuel maps, ignition timing.

TROUBLE: ENGINE MISFIRES UNDER CORNERING

Possibilities:

Improper fuel pressure
Fuel pickup problems
Check fuel pressure.

TROUBLE: ENGINE PERFORMANCE WILL NOT REPEAT FROM ONE TEST TO THE NEXT

Possibilities:

Fuel pickup /pressure problems
Crank Ref or ignition tach signal problem (on fuel-only EMS)
Fuel maps adjusted erratically
Engine warmup map adjusted erratically
Poor or erratic manifold vacuum signal (speed-density units)
Battery voltage fluctuating
Check fuel pressure, tach signal on engine data page, fuel maps for proper adjustment, vacuum signal, battery voltage.

TROUBLE: ENGINE SURGES UNDER LIGHT CRUISE CONDITIONS

Possibilities:

Fuel mixtures too rich
Fuel cut on deceleration feature is on
Check fuel maps, fuel cut problem.

TROUBLE: POOR OR ERRATIC IDLE

Possibilities:

Throttle plates are not synchronized (multiple butterfly systems)
Fuel maps adjusted erratically in idle area
Poor manifold vacuum signal
Check throttle synchronization, fuel maps, manifold vacuum.

TROUBLE: ENGINE MISFIRES UNDER HARD ACCELERATION

Possibilities:

Fuel maps too lean
Fuel maps too rich
Improper fuel pressure
Ignition system failing
Battery voltage falling
Check fuel maps, fuel pressure ignition system, battery voltage.

TROUBLE: ENGINE LACKS PERFORMANCE/POWER

Possibilities:

Full-throttle settings are too rich (black smoke from exhaust)
Full-throttle settings are too lean (high exhaust gas temperatures)
Check fuel maps.

TROUBLE: PROBLEMS AT LOW-, MEDIUM-, AND HIGH-LOAD

Possibilities:

Air-Related Load Problems
Check air-related load problems arising from improperly sized throttles. Make sure that a throttle can flow enough air for an engine. Stock throttles on heavily modified engines will typically cause upper-rpm performance problems.

FUEL-RELATED LOAD PROBLEMS

Fuel pressure dropping with load because:
Fuel pump cannot keep up with the engine's fuel needs
Fuel pressure regulator is not functioning properly
Check fuel pressure under load (should increase by 1psi with every 1psi of boost on turbo or supercharged engines (unless a rising rate regulator is installed, in which case it should increase 4-8 psi per psi boost).
Injectors Undersized
Check injector flow rate.
Tuning issues
EGO Sensor Correction Problems
Check tuning recommendations, O_2 sensor tuning recommendations.

SPARK-RELATED LOAD PROBLEMS

Calibration.
Secondary Ignition Failure
Improper Wiring.
Check coil or direct-fire coil units are wired correctly before proceeding.
Check tuning (software timing problems can seem like spark-related problems). An engine that is detonating has too much timing in the Timing Advance Table, or is not receiving enough fuel. An engine that is not performing well may have too little timing, or too much timing. Try adding timing until light detonation is detected, then back off a bit (but do not attempt to run a rotary into detonation!).
Check for secondary ignition failure (often blamed for load-based ignition problems), including the spark plugs and spark plug wires.
Check the coil screws tightness.
Check direct-fire coil units for proper ground operation (If misfiring occurs under load, loose coil screws or ungrounded Direct-fire coil units are often the culprit).

Of course you're going to need a standard set of mechanics' tools for tuning and modifying engine management systems, but since wiring is so important, it is worth having a really good ratchet-type crimp tool with the correct slots for a handling a variety of crimping jobs. This MSD tool has multiple, interchangeable jaws with a variety of connector gripping slots. Such a tool can (and should) cost a few bucks, but remember that a broken or shorted wire could destroy your vehicle.

sensor's output directly with a scan tool (usually in degrees Celsius or Fahrenheit).

15. Aftermarket programmable engine management systems will display engine temperature sensor readings along with other sensor values on an engine data page via laptop computer.

Troubleshooting MAP Sensors

A faulty MAP sensor, shorts or opens in the wiring circuit, or vacuum leaks in the sensor hose or intake manifold can cause drivability symptoms that include rough or erratic idle, black exhaust smoke (rich fuel condition resulting in high hydrocarbon emissions), stalling, hard starting, hesitation, engine misfires, pinging, poor fuel economy, and bad general engine performance.

There are various ways to check out a MAP sensor that you suspect has problems. It is trivial to use a laptop attached to most programmable engine management systems to display the MAP sensor data and watch how it changes as you load and unload the engine. A scan tool can check for MAP sensor trouble codes on OEM systems. A digital storage oscilloscope can observe the sensor's output as a waveform. A multimeter can compare the sensor's output voltage or frequency to specifications in a manual. And the following two relatively simple procedures will quickly tell you whether or not a MAP sensor is responding to changes in intake vacuum.

General Motors and Chrysler MAP sensors can be tested on a vehicle using a digital voltmeter (DVOM) and two jumper wires. The following test verifies that the MAP sensor is responding to changes in engine vacuum. If the reading does not change, it means the sensor is faulty or the vacuum hose is plugged or leaking.

- Disconnect the MAP sensor's electrical connector.
- Connect one jumper wire between the connector and the MAP sensor's terminal A.
- Connect another jumper wire from the connector to terminal C.
- Connect the positive lead on the DVOM to terminal B (the sensor's output terminal) and the negative DVOM test lead to a good engine ground.
- Turn the ignition key on and observe the voltage. If the reading falls in the voltage range of 4 to 5 volts (2 to 3 volts for turbocharged engines) at sea level, the sensor is functioning properly at this point.

- Verify the vacuum hose between the MAP sensor and engine is in good condition and does not leak. Then start the engine and let it idle. An idling engine will produce a large amount of intake vacuum, which should pull the MAP sensor's voltage down to a low reading of 1 to 2 volts (note: readings will vary with altitude).
- You can also do this test with the key on, engine off by applying vacuum to the MAP sensor's hose with a hand-held vacuum-pressure pump.
- On Ford applications, you'll need a multimeter that can display frequency required to check the sensor's output, or you can use an ordinary diagnostic tachometer (tachs display a frequency signal) as follows:
- Set the tachometer to the four-cylinder scale (regardless of how many cylinders the engine has).
- Connect one tachometer lead to the middle terminal on the MAP sensor and the other tachometer test lead to ground.
- Connect the two jumper cables the same as before, attaching each end terminal on the sensor to its respective wire in the wiring connector.
- If you want to measure engine vacuum so you can correlate it to a specific frequency reading, connect a vacuum gauge to a source of manifold vacuum on the engine, or tee the gauge into the MAP sensor hose.
- Turn the ignition on and note the initial reading. The reading on the tachometer should be about 454 to 464 at sea level, which corresponds to a frequency output of 152 to 155 hertz.
- Start the engine and check the reading again. If the MAP sensor is functioning properly, the reading should drop to about 290 to 330 on the tachometer, which corresponds to a frequency output of about 93 to 98 hertz. No change would indicate a defective sensor or leaky or plugged vacuum hose.

Troubleshooting VAF Meters

Vane airflow sensors are no longer used on new vehicles, but you may encounter one on a classic vehicle. There are special testers for troubleshooting VAF sensors, but you don't always need one to check sensor operation. By watching the VAF sensor's output with an analog voltmeter or ohmmeter (or better yet an oscilloscope), you can look for a change in the sensor's output as airflow changes. One simple check is to look for a voltage change as you slowly push the airflow flap all the way open. A good sensor should produce a smooth and gradual transition in resistance (ignition off) or voltage readings (ignition on) all the way from full-closed to full-open. If you see any sudden jerks in the movement of the needle (analog ohmmeter or voltmeter) or dips or blips in the scope trace (similar to sweeping a TPS), the VAF sensor needs to be replaced.

Changes in the sensor's voltage output should also produce a corresponding change in fuel injector duration when the engine is running. Injector duration should increase as the VAF flap is pushed open.

On Ford EFI systems, you can use a breakout box and voltmeter to check VAF sensor voltage readings. Pushing the flap open should cause a steady and even increase in the sensor's output from 0.25 volts when the flap is closed to about 4.5 volts with the flap fully open. The reference voltage to the airflow sensor from the computer should be 5 volts.

Ford's trouble codes that apply to the VAF include: code 26 indicates a VAF reading out of range, code 56 indicates sensor input too high, code 66 is sensor input too low, and code 76 indicates no sensor change during the goose test.

Most manufacturers also give specific resistance specs for the various VAF terminals in a shop manual. Bosch, for example, lists the following for some of its applications:

Terminals 6 and 9	200–400 ohms
Terminals 6 and 8	130–260 ohms
Terminals 8 and 9	70–140 ohms
Terminals 6 and 7	40–300 ohms
Terminals 7 and 8	100–500 ohms
Terminals 6 and 27	2,800 ohms max at 68F

Troubleshooting MAF Sensors

MAF problems will normally cause the ECU to set a trouble code on OEM engine management systems. An engine with a bad MAF sensor may be hard to start or stall after starting. It may hesitate under load, surge, idle rough, or run excessively rich or lean. The engine may also hiccup when the throttle suddenly changes position. However, keep in mind that low engine compression, low vacuum, low fuel pressure, leaky or dirty injectors, ignition misfire, and excessive exhaust backpressure (plugged converter) can produce similar drivability symptoms.

MAF sensors can be tested either on or off the vehicle in a variety of ways. You can use a MAF sensor tester and tachometer to check the sensor's response. If testing on the vehicle, unplug the wiring harness connector from the sensor and connect the tester and tachometer. Start the engine and watch the readings. They should change as the throttle is opened and closed. No change would indicate a bad sensor. The same hookup can be used to test the MAF sensor off the vehicle. When you blow through the sensor, the readings should change if the sensor is detecting the change in airflow.

Another check is to read the sensor's voltage or frequency output on the vehicle. With Bosch hot-wire MAF sensors, the output voltage can be read directly with a digital voltmeter by back-probing the brown-and-white output wire to terminal B6 on the PCM. The voltage reading should be around 2.5 volts. If out of range, or if the sensor's voltage output fails to increase when the throttle is opened with the engine running, the sensor may be defective. Check the orange and black feed wire for 12 volts, and the black wire for a good ground.

Power to the MAF sensor is provided through a pair of relays (one for power, one for the burn-off cleaning cycle), so check the relays too if the MAF sensor appears to be dead or sluggish. If the sensor works but is slow to respond to changes in airflow, the problem may be a contaminated sensing element caused by a failure in the self-cleaning circuit or relay. With GM Delco MAF sensors, attach a digital voltmeter to the appropriate MAF sensor output terminal. With the engine idling, the sensor should output a steady 2.5 volts. Tap lightly on the sensor and note the meter reading. A good sensor should show no change. If the meter reading jumps or the engine momentarily misfires, the sensor is bad and needs to be replaced. You can also check for heat-related problems by heating the sensor with a hair dryer and repeating the test.

This same test can also be done using a meter that reads frequency. The older AC Delco MAF sensors (like a 2.8-liter V-6) should show a steady reading of 32 hertz at idle to about 75 hertz at 3,500 rpm. The later model units (like those on a 3800 V-6 with the Hitachi MAF sensor) should read about 2.9 kilohertz at idle and 5.0 kilohertz at 3,500 rpm. If tapping on the MAF sensor produces a sudden change in the frequency signal, it's time for a new sensor.

On GM hot-film MAFs, you can also use a scan tool to read the sensor's output in grams per second (gps), which corresponds to frequency. The reading should go from 4–8 grams per second at idle to as much as 100–240 grams per second at wide-open throttle.

Like throttle position sensors, there should be smooth linear transition in sensor output as engine speed and load change. If the readings jump all over the place, the computer won't be able to deliver the right air/fuel mixture, and drivability and emissions will suffer. So you should also check the sensor's output at various speeds to see that its output changes appropriately.

Another way to observe the sensor's output is to look at its waveform on an oscilloscope. The waveform should be square and show a gradual increase in frequency as engine speed and load increase. Any skips or sudden jumps or excessive noise in the pattern would tell you the sensor needs to be replaced.

Yet another way to check the MAF sensor is to see what effect it has on injector timing. Using an oscilloscope or multimeter that reads milliseconds, connect the test probe to any injector ground terminal (one injector terminal is the supply voltage and the other is the ground circuit to the computer that controls injector timing). Then look at the duration of the injector pulses at idle (or while cranking the engine if the engine won't start). Injector timing varies depending on the application, but if the mass airflow sensor is not producing a signal, injector timing will be about four times longer than normal (possibly making the fuel mixture too rich to start). You can also use millisecond readings to confirm fuel enrichment when the throttle is opened during acceleration, fuel leaning during light load cruising and injector shut-down during deceleration. Under light load cruise, for example, you should see about 2.5 to 2.8 milliseconds duration.

Troubleshooting Knock Sensors

For this test you need a strobe gun so you can physically see the timing change via the cam belt or the timing mark on the crank pulley wheel.

- Inspect the KS connector and its pins for good condition and ensure that there is no damage to the cable form like cuts, splits, burns, and so on.
- Check that the connector plug fits home on the KS and is not loose and that the pins make good contact. Spray the contacts with WD-40.
- Using the strobe gun, attach the probe of the inductive pick to the HT lead of cylinder number one (follow manufacturer's instructions if you don't know how to do this).
- Turn on the engine and allow to idle.
- Gently tap the engine block close to the number-one cylinder with the handle of a screwdriver.
- The timing should be seen to retard.

Testing a Vehicle Speed Sensor

The VSS can be tested using a scan tool or an oscilloscope scope, but vehicle manufacturers' test procedures vary widely. A road test with the scan tool or lab scope hooked up is often the most effective way to test a VSS. Compare your scan tool readings with the manufacturer's specifications. When using the lab scope, you

EMS TROUBLESHOOTING

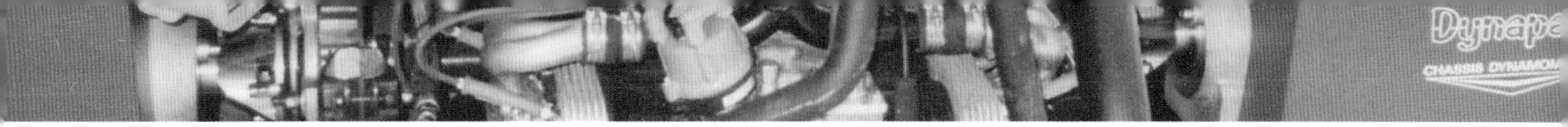

may see either a square-wave pattern if the VSS has an integrated buffer circuit or an AC sine wave if the buffering and conversion are done within the computer. In some cases, you can even count VSS cycles with a DVOM. Use the analog bar because the digital display usually won't be fast enough or accurate enough to give reliable readings.

If the readings on your scan tool or lab scope match the manufacturer's specifications, then the VSS is working properly and the problem is most likely in the computer. If the readings don't match the specs, check the sensor wiring harness and connectors for damage, corrosion, and high resistance. If the wiring and connections are good, the sensor is bad and must be replaced.

One final note on VSS, changing to a tire size that differs from original equipment may cause problems, especially if the change is excessive and the buffer has not been recalibrated. The speedometer readings will be wrong and there is a chance other vehicle systems may be affected because the VSS signals will no longer show actual vehicle speed.

Troubleshooting IACs

A common condition is an idle-air-control bypass valve that's fully extended (closed). This is often a symptom of an air leak downstream of the throttle, such as a leaky throttle body base gasket, intake manifold gasket, vacuum circuits, injector O-rings, and so on. The computer has closed the bypass circuit in a vain attempt to compensate for the unmetered air leak that is affecting idle speed.

Incorrect idle speed (too high) also can be caused by a shorted air conditioning compressor clutch wire or defective power steering pressure-sensor circuit. To troubleshoot a GM idle-air control circuit, disconnect the IAC stepper motor, then start the engine to see if the idle speed increases considerably. Turn the engine off, reconnect the IAC and start the engine again. This time the idle speed should return to approximately the previous rpm. If it does, the problem is not the IAC circuit or motor. Check for vacuum leaks or other problems that would affect idle speed. If the idle speed does *not* change when the IAC is unplugged or does not decrease after reconnecting the unit, use a test light to check the IAC wiring circuits while the key is on.

Ford uses a PWM idle-air bypass that is also commonly used on aftermarket EMSs to control idle speed. The diagnostic procedure is to turn the engine off, unplug the bypass air-solenoid connector, then restart the engine to see if the idle rpm drops. No change would indicate a problem in the solenoid, wiring, or ECM.

A Ford ISC solenoid can be checked by measuring its resistance. A reading of between 7.0 to 13.0 ohms would be normal. Also check for shorts between both ISC solenoid terminals and the case. If the ISC checks out OK, check for battery voltage between the ISC connector terminals while the key is on. Voltage should also vary when the engine is running. No voltage indicates a wiring or EEC processor problem.

On late-model vehicles with OBD-II, the following codes may indicate a problem with the idle-air-control system:

P0506—idle too low
P0507—idle too high
P1508—idle-air-control stuck closed
P1509—idle-air-control stuck open
P1599—engine stall detected

When installing a new GM IAC or Chrysler AIS motor, the pintle must not extend more than a certain distance from the motor housing. The specs vary, so check the manual. Chrysler says 1 inch (24.50 millimeters) is the limit, while some GM specs allow up to 28 millimeters on some units and 32 millimeters on others. If the pintle is overextended, it can be retracted by either pushing it in (GM) or by connecting it to its wiring harness and using actuator test #03 to move it in (Chrysler). You can also use a digital storage oscilloscope (DSOs) to view IAC wave forms.

Chapter 16
Emissions, OBD-II, and CAN Bus

EMISSIONS-CONTROL DEVICES

Air pollution has been a major problem in heavily populated areas of the United States since the late 1950s and early 1960s when the first major smog formed from the photochemical action of sunlight on air pollution in southern California. The state of California has required air pollution control devices of one form or another on cars since 1961, when the state began requiring car companies to scavenge crankcase vapors rather than vent them into the atmosphere.

California laws dealing with automotive emissions became stricter after 1965 and 1972, with the other 49 states eventually following California's lead. California currently has laws requiring all owners of light trucks, cars, and RVs newer than 30 years old to put their vehicles through load-based emissions testing to certify that HC, NOx, and CO emissions are within specs for the particular vehicle and engine.

The law also requires a visual anti-tampering check designed to make sure no one has removed emissions-control devices or made other modifications that might affect emissions (such as changing to a different carburetor, modifying the ignition, changing heads, or modifying the exhaust system, the camshaft, and so on), which includes almost any hot rodding mods that affect engine volumetric efficiency. Aftermarket manufacturers that build products that are not simple OE-type replacement parts—and might affect emissions—must get an Exemption Order from the state of California in order for the vehicle to be street legal. Getting an exemption order requires that aftermarket manufacturers follow a structured procedure at a certified lab designed to prove that vehicles' emissions are within 10 percent tolerances of original vehicle emissions. Both manufacturers and end users have been subject to fines of $2,500 for each violation (in contrast to the old days when the government more or less penalized only the installer/manufacturer).

New federal laws took effect in 1991 that put the rest of the country in sync with California on emissions requirements (other than the fact that performance parts for 49-state vehicles do not require an explicit EO; manufacturers must self-test the parts). In fact, 49-state manufacturers are supposed to emissions-test their products on a kind of honor system in which they are expected to obtain and maintain evidence that their products are legal, if the government should request such evidence.

As a practical matter, there are still states and cities that don't yet have an emissions testing procedure in place (depending on the administration in Washington, they have sometimes come under a degree of federal pressure to implement one). Many manufacturers are now seeking California EOs for performance parts, since California is a huge market for car parts, and since a California EO automatically provides compliance with federal laws.

By 2000, air pollution had become a worldwide problem. The most polluted city in the world was no longer Los Angeles,

The standard OBDII connector

Pin 1 - Proprietary
Pin 2 - J1850 Bus+
Pin 3 - Proprietary
Pin 4 - Chassis Ground
Pin 5 - Signal Ground
Pin 6 - CAN High (J-2284)
Pin 7 - ISO 9141-2 (K Line)
Pin 8 - Proprietary

Pin 9 - Proprietary
Pin 10 - J1850 Bus-
Pin 11 - Proprietary
Pin 12 - Proprietary
Pin 13 - Proprietary
Pin 14 - CAN Low (J-2284)
Pin 15 - ISO 9141-2 (L Line)
Pin 16 - Battery Power

The standard J1962 OBD-II connector is the pathway into all 1996-plus and some 1994-plus engine management systems. This 16-pin connector provides really valuable diagnostic data, and it also provides a marvelously simple access to reflash the EMS calibration—if you've got the proprietary security seed to gain access. Fortunately, there are brilliant hackers who are also car guys, hence, products like LS1edit exist to recalibrate performance engines like the LS1/6 'Vette. *OBDII Diagnostic Secrets Revealed*, Peter David

which has benefited from air pollution control measures, but Mexico City, which is terribly overpopulated and has virtually no air pollution measures—mostly because air pollution controls cost money and may have an adverse economic impact. Add-on pollution-control devices for an engine cost money. The situation had become so critical in Mexico City that on bad days, only half the cars in the city could drive (which in itself has an economic impact). Newspapers regularly showed people wearing surgical masks or gas masks just to go outside. Los Angeles and California had experimented with laws requiring a certain percentage of cars sold there to be zero emissions (electric), though the government had backed away from requiring a specific percentage by 2003.

Smog is a result of the photochemical action of sunlight on unburned hydrocarbons (HC) and oxides of nitrogen (NOx). These pollutants combine under the action of sunlight to make a brown haze that irritates human eyes, noses, and throats. Smog is harmful to plant and animal life, and can damage plastics, paint, and rubber parts used in cars and other human-built structures. Los Angeles, with lots of vehicles, lots of sun, and a bowl-like layer of mountains surrounding the city that tends to hold pollutants in place, is a perfect place for smog.

Required by laws to deal with the problem, car companies were forced to contend with three kinds of vehicle emissions: Crankcase blow-by and oil fumes that would otherwise enter the air through crankcase breathers, exhaust gases that enter the atmosphere from a vehicle's tailpipe, and evaporative emissions from the vehicle's fuel system.

Crankcase emissions were one of the easier problems to fix. Before 1963, crankcase emissions spewed directly into the atmosphere through a vent tube designed in such a way that an air draft produced by the vehicle's forward motion tended to suck or scavenge fumes from the tube into the atmosphere. These combustible fumes could easily be sucked into intake manifold along with the charge mixture and burned.

It was an easy thing to design a positive crankcase ventilation (PCV) system that used engine vacuum to suck fumes from the valve cover into the intake manifold near the throttle plate. Open PCV systems use a PCV valve located inline in the hose connecting the valve cover and intake manifold that contains a small orifice and a spring-loaded check valve that is sucked closed at idle or other times of high vacuum, only allowing suction through the small orifice. During heavier engine loading, spring action overcomes lower engine vacuum to allow more flow. The oil filler cap contains a mesh filter that allows air to enter the valve cover from the atmosphere. At very low or zero vacuum, heavy blow-by could still escape into the air through the filler cap.

In 1968, this system was modified to be closed so the oil filler cap was not vented to the air, but to a location inside the air cleaner, taking advantage of the fact that fumes could be sucked into the air cleaner at times of very low-manifold vacuum when there is a lot of air being sucked into the engine through the air filter. At idle, or other high vacuum conditions, crankcase emissions would enter the engine downstream of the throttle plate via high-manifold vacuum. This strategy of handling crankcase emissions was successful and took care of one-third of all engine emissions.

Handling exhaust emissions was a different story. The struggle to clean up exhaust emissions continues today. The problem is that when you improve one component of exhaust emissions, you tend to make other emissions components worse. Although perfect combustion produces heat energy plus harmless water and carbon dioxide, in reality, combustion is not perfect. Rich mixtures (lack of oxygen) produce CO_2, water, and carbon monoxide (CO), a deadly gas capable of asphyxiation by replacing oxygen in the blood of humans, plus unburned hydrocarbons, i.e., gasoline that made it through the combustion process without burning.

Carbon monoxide disappears from exhaust gas as mixtures lean, but as mixtures lean further hydrocarbons rise again due to lean misfires when there isn't enough fuel. The surplus of oxygen and the abnormal heat of lean burn mixtures around 16:1 also tends to produce peak oxides of nitrogen, a problem which begins to occur at stoichiometric air/fuel ratios. A perfectly tuned engine with no emissions-control devices produces excellent (although not peak) power at stoichiometric mixtures, which implies high heat and high pressure in the cylinder. High cylinder pressure with heat will break down small amounts of normally inert diatomic nitrogen gas and oxidize it to form NOx, a component of smog. HC and CO both fall off nicely at 14.7 parts air to fuel. But with mixtures leaner than 13:1 or so, excess oxygen becomes available to oxidize free atomic nitrogen. NOx emissions reach a peak at about 16:1 and then fall off with even leaner mixtures as combustion pressure falls off. Unfortunately, lean mixtures are exactly what you want for best economy, particularly at less than full throttle.

In 1966, the state of California applied standards to tailpipe exhaust emissions and toughened these again in 1973. Vehicles had to be certified by undergoing a test that simulated a 20-minute drive through downtown Los Angeles. Test equipment

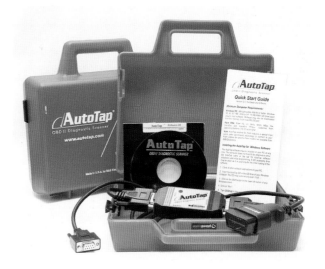

Auto Tap's OBD-II diagnostic scanner plugs directly into the 16-pin diagnostic port to tell you what the factory EMS thinks is going on in the engine and related sensor systems, as well as a vast array of specific malfunction codes. The purpose of OBD-II is to keep engine system components from breaking in ways that pollute the air without anyone knowing, but its usefulness goes way beyond emissions.

collected the exhaust gases, producing weighted average emissions figures for the three pollutants. In 1973, the U.S. government came up with the Federal Test Procedure (FTP) in which vehicles are tested on a chassis dyno that simulates a 23-minute, 7.5-mile drive after a 10-hour cold soak period to make sure the vehicle is undergoing a true cold start (the time when it produces the worst emissions). The chassis dyno is loaded in proportion to the actual vehicle's induced drag and weight. Exhaust gases are mixed with atmospheric gases in a specified proportion (while monitoring the composition of the atmospheric gases to correct for pollutants in the ambient air). Gases are collected in plastic bags.

For 1975 cars, the FTP was extended to include a rerun of the first 8.5 minutes after a shutdown to simulate a hot start. and averaged in with the 8.5 minutes after the initial cold start. More recently, California began to require emissions inspections of certain heavier vehicles, such as motorhomes and some trucks, even if these were not required to pass emissions testing when new. California requires CARB Exemption Orders for these vehicles. Since there may be no emissions data from the vehicle model when new, manufacturers of add-on or modified parts for these vehicles may discover they have to run comparison testing of the vehicle without the modified parts, and then again with the parts, and possibly a third test with the parts removed.

The emissions problems automotive engineers must deal include formation of CO in rich mixtures with too little oxygen to support full combustion. CO can never practically be eliminated completely, because even with a combustion chamber filled with an overall perfect air/fuel mixture, the gases are not perfectly distributed and local pockets of richness exist. Gasoline, consisting of numerous molecules containing hydrogen and carbon, releases heat energy when these are oxidized by burning in air. Hydrocarbon emissions in the exhaust gases are the products of gasoline that made it through the engine without burning completely. Eliminating CO and HC emissions is inconsistent with making maximum power, because to get best power you want to make sure sufficient fuel is present to make use of every bit of oxygen that you have been able to coax into the engine.

ONBOARD DIAGNOSTICS

The 1990 Clean Air Act specified emissions-related requirements for new cars in the 1990s and beyond as well as organizing requirements for aftermarket automotive equipment. The act extended the prohibition against removal or rendering inoperative the emissions-control devices to the consumer. It would now be a violation to manufacture, sell, or offer to sell parts where the principal effect is to defeat the emissions-control devices.

EPA memorandum 1A states that those who might be subject to claims of tampering as a result of installation of certain parts can be certain there will be no such claims if the manufacturer of the part(s) is able to certify that the vehicle with the parts in question installed could pass the Federal Test Procedure—or if they have received an Exemption Order (EO) from the California Air Resources Board. Any entrepreneur who wants to manufacture parts that might interfere with emissions-related systems on a vehicle (almost anything related to the combustion cycle of the engine) can obtain the "Procedures for Exemption of Add-on and Modified Parts" from the California Air Resource Board.

ENGINE SWAPS

According to the California Bureau of Automotive Repair (BAR), an "engine change" is the installation of an engine in an exhaust-controlled vehicle that is different from the one that was installed originally in the vehicle and does not qualify as a replacement engine. A replacement engine is defined as a new, rebuilt, remanufactured, or used engine of the same make, size, and number of cylinders as the original engine with all original emissions controls reinstalled, or an engine that matches a configuration offered by the manufacturer for that year, make, and model of the vehicle with the appropriate emissions controls for the installed engine and chassis components present and connected. Licensed California smog check stations must refer vehicles with engine changes to the BAR for referee inspection. Once a vehicle has been inspected by the referee and a BAR label attached to the doorpost (listing the required emissions-control equipment), any licensed smog check station may thereafter perform an inspection. The vehicle must have all the emissions-control equipment listed on the BAR label.

In California, cars more than 30 years old are considered non-exhaust-control vehicles, and may have any year engine installed and only require PCV (and appropriate retrofit devices, if required). These vehicles may be inspected at licensed smog check stations and do not need referee intervention. For newer vehicles, note the following explicit regulation: "An automotive repair dealer shall not make any motor vehicle engine change that degrades the effectiveness of a vehicle's emissions controls."

ONBOARD DIAGNOSTICS, LEVEL II

Onboard Diagnostics, Level II (OBD-II) is a series of regulations intended to reduce in-use vehicle emissions by requiring the OEM engine management system to continuously monitor the powertrain and its emissions-control systems for failures or deterioration. OBD-II includes provisions for standardization of diagnostic, repair, and other service-related information. The system was designed to reduce high in-use emissions caused by emissions-related malfunctions, to reduce time between occurrence of a malfunction and its detection and repair, and to assist in the diagnosis and repair of emission-related problems.

To be OBD-II compliant, an EMS must monitor virtually all emissions-control systems and components that can affect emissions. OBD-II requires a malfunction indicator light (MIL) visible to the vehicle operator that must be illuminated and a fault code set when either there is a failure of a monitored component/system or when any of the sensed parameters deteriorates to the extent that the vehicle's emissions would exceed the relevant standard by approximately 50 percent. In most cases OBD-II must detect malfunctions within two driving cycles.

OBD-II provides for strict enforcement to be implemented through increased penalties for noncompliance for both vehicle manufacturers and consumers. Prior to renewal of the vehicle's registration, a motor vehicle owner must provide proof that any required repairs have been made and that no fault codes are present.

OBD-II immediately required vehicle manufacturers to provide more robust warranty coverage for emissions-related engine and EMS systems. It required that the increased durability requirements of the new, more stringent emissions standards would be accompanied by stricter reporting of component defects and failures along with lower triggering limits for recalls. The reading of fault codes during state emissions tests would now identify virtually all failures.

THE CLEAN AIR ACT AND WARRANTIES

The Federal Clean Air Act requires vehicle makers to provide a production emissions warranty as well as a performance emissions warranty. The production emissions warranty requires a vehicle maker to warrant that the vehicle has been engineered and manufactured so that it conforms with emissions requirements at the time of sale. The performance emissions warranty requires a vehicle maker to warrant that the vehicle will continue to comply with emissions requirements as tested in state vehicle emissions inspection programs for the warranty periods specified in the law. For model year 1995 and later vehicles, the warranty is two years/24,000 miles for all emissions-related parts and eight years/80,000 miles for the catalytic converter, electronic emissions-control unit, and onboard diagnostic device. The performance warranty is conditioned on the vehicle being properly maintained and operated.

Like the Magnuson-Moss Act, vehicle manufacturers may not refuse warranty repairs under the Clean Air Act's performance and defect warranties merely because aftermarket parts have been installed on the vehicle. The only circumstance under which the vehicle manufacturer can void the emissions warranties is if an aftermarket part is responsible for (or causes) the warranty claim.

OBD-II grew out of the more primitive OBD-I standard, which was adopted in 1985 for 1988 and later vehicles, and was designed to monitor ECU input devices and the EGR system. OBD-II was adopted in 1989 for all 1996 and later vehicles and OBD-II was implemented on some 1994 and 1995 vehicles. It was designed to address certain shortcomings in OBD-I. OBD-II expanded the scope of monitored data to determine if a component or system had malfunctioned. And OBD-II provided substantial diagnostic information to help service technicians identify and repair problems.

Key OBD-II monitoring requirements include the following systems:
- Primary emissions control systems/components
- Catalyst
- Misfires
- Evaporative system
- Fuel system

- Oxygen sensor
- Exhaust gas recirculation system
- Secondary air injection system
- Heated catalyst system
- Comprehensive components

OBD-II requires that the connectors through which the emissions-control diagnostic system would be accessed for inspection, diagnostic service, or repair are standard and uniform on all motor vehicles and motor vehicle engines, and that access to the emissions-control diagnostics system through such connectors is unrestricted and does not require any access code or any device that is only available from a vehicle manufacturer. OBD-II requires that the output of the data from the emissions-control diagnostics system through such connectors should be usable without the need for any unique decoding information or device.

OBD-I/OBD-II COMPARISON

OBD-I	OBD-II
Oxygen Sensor	Oxygen Sensor (enhanced)
EGR System	EGR System (enhanced)
Fuel System	Fuel System (enhanced)
Electronic Input Components	Electronic Input Components
Diagnostic Information	Electronic Output
Fault Codes	Components
	Catalyst Efficiency
	Catalyst Heating
	Engine Misfire
	Evaporative System (leak check/function)
	Secondary Air System
	Diagnostic Information
	Fault Codes
	Engine Parameter Data
	Freeze-Frame Engine Parameters
	Standardization

BENEFITS OF OBD

OBD-II was designed to provide certain clear benefits. In addition to reducing air pollution, one of the most important benefits was standardization. Standardized interfacing, diagnostics, and datalogging were of great concern to independent repair shops that might otherwise find it prohibitively expensive to acquire proprietary diagnostic tools for every make and model of vehicle serviced. OBD-II standardization reduced the cost and complexity of diagnosis by providing a known communications protocol for handshaking between the ECM and diagnostic devices.

OBD–II provided a physical diagnostic connector that would be the same on all 1996 and later vehicles (and a few 1994 and later vehicles) and—bottom line—allowed one diagnostic device to connect to any vehicle sold in the United States. Standardization basically enabled one scan tool to work on any vehicle. OBD-II provided a set of fault codes designed to help identify faulty components. OBD-II provided for real-time diagnostic information and, thus, continuously updated engine parameter data. It provided a facility to supply freeze-frame information, in which the system would store engine operating conditions upon detection of a malfunction.

OBD-II was later expanded by 2008 to include Controller Area Network (CAN) protocols by which multiple onboard controllers could communicate with each other and diagnostic equipment to synchronize operations in a prioritized scheme that allowed critical communications to propagate at very high speed.

OBD-II'S EFFECT ON VEHICLE DESIGN

OBD-II had a significant impact on the engineering of new OEM engine management systems. Compared to earlier factory engine management systems, powertrain control modules became much faster, with much more memory and more features, and cost and complexity increased significantly. OBD-II required additional components and systems for many of the monitors, including additional oxygen sensors, fuel tank, and EGR pressure sensors. Existing components/systems required substantial upgrades. Achieving higher standards required higher accuracy, durability, and reliability in addition to design changes that compensate for differences in the duty cycle or function of parts.

In addition to effectively revising existing functions, the global effect of OBD-II was to require that the base operating strategy, or algorithm, of the EMS be completely retooled to incorporate new features specific to OBD-II. Since the system required a substantial amount of monitoring to be performed while driving, a considerable effort was required to make sure monitoring was completely transparent to the driver. Older OBD-I diagnostic routines had to be significantly revised to support repairing malfunctions identified by the gamut of new monitors. Standardization of terms and equipment helped to some degree, but although the increased complexity of the overall system vastly improved diagnostics, it could actually result in more difficult repairs.

SMOG CHECKS AND OBD-II

OBD-II was designed for full integration into the smog check procedures required in many states and cities. At the time of the smog check, technicians would verify that the MIL was not illuminated (light and computer indication), that the I/M readiness code was fully set, that no fault codes were stored, and that proper calibration was installed.

The Specialty Equipment Marketing Association (SEMA)—the organization of aftermarket automotive equipment suppliers—has noted that various government agencies have been highly interested in implementing countermeasures to stop people from tampering with OBD-II engine management systems. Such agencies, says SEMA, "want to prevent passing of vehicles that have had their fault codes erased (or readiness code set) illegally by 'hackers.' The potential for such activity is purely speculative; there has been no proof it is occurring."

SEMA notes that the same agencies have had a strong interest in preventing consumers or non-OEM technicians from any tinkering whatsoever (recalibration/tuning) that would make adjustments to the vehicle's computer—effectively locking the hood.

SEMA points out that the OBD-II standard made no provisions for non-OEM calibrations and limited the performance aftermarket's ability to develop and sell many current emissions-compliant products since such calibrations would automatically fail I/M. Limiting parts and service to dealerships, says SEMA, reduces consumer choice and could raise costs.

In the meantime, says SEMA, aftermarket calibrations/computer chips have proven they do not increase emissions and many have California Air Resources Board (CARB) exemption orders. In fact, SEMA notes, CARB has agreed that aftermarket recalibration should remain possible under VC 27156/38391,

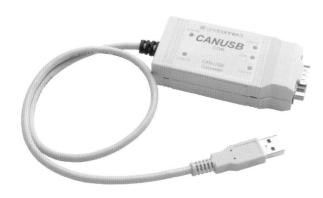

CAN-USB-COM converter provides bi-directional communication between a USB COM Port Serial interface and a CAN 2.0A/B (ISO 11898) Network. Features include:

- Fast Cortex-M3 32-bit microcontroller
- Easy setup using "Configuration Push Button"
- Virtual Serial Baud Rates up to 1 Mbps
- CAN Messages formatted in ASCII or binary
- Integral Help menu for set-up/configuration commands.
- Automatic set-up of "bit-time" and "slew rate," adjustable via configuration commands
- Usable with any COM Port based software, including HyperTerminal and TeraTerm.
- Standard Drivers for Windows XP-plus, MAC and Linux.
- Usable in command or virtual circuit mode

though the OBD-II standard does not explicitly allow this. "Bottom line," says SEMA, "electronic tampering has never been verified as a real problem. It is unlikely it ever will be since the required sales volume, equipment investment and knowledge are prohibitive for all but the aftermarket [industry itself, not individual consumers]. The latter are too responsible/visible to consider such risks." The above statement is fairly true.

TAMPERING

In fact OBD-II initially required that computer-coded engine operating parameters should not be changeable without the use of specialized tools and procedures, for example, soldered or potted computer components or sealed (or soldered) computer enclosures. However, subject to executive officer approval, manufacturers could exempt from this requirement those product lines unlikely to require protection. Criteria to be evaluated in making such an exemption included—but were not limited to—current availability of performance chips, high-performance capability of the vehicle, and sales volume.

Manufacturers using reprogrammable computer code systems (for example, flash memory) were required to employ proven methods to deter unauthorized reprogramming, which could include copyrightable executable routines or other methods. Beginning with the 1999 model year, manufacturers were called upon to implement enhanced tamper-protection strategies including data encryption with countermeasures to secure the encryption algorithm, as well as write-protect features requiring electronic access to off-site computers maintained by the manufacturer.

By 1997 it was clear that specialty products could still be used on pollution-controlled motor vehicles. SEMA was making a strong point of the distinction that SEMA members' products made provisions for emissions-control devices or were considered replacement parts; they were not defeat devices. It was clear by this time that the use of add-on or modified parts would not be considered a form of tampering if the product has been granted a CARB EO number (California and 49 states) or meets the requirements of the EPA's antitampering policy document, Memorandum No. IA (49-state only).

Hundreds of products of all types had been granted EO numbers for thousands of applications, with many specialty products sold by OEMs with EO numbers and many manufacturers representing their products as meeting Memorandum 1A. It was clear that such products did meet emissions and applicable criteria for an EO or Memo 1A, and that enforcement provisions/penalties designed to prevent fraud would be considered adequate to prevent fraud. In fact, elimination of components present in the originally certified configuration would be allowable under certain circumstances (for example, GM's Camaro package).

BARRIERS TO ENTRY: THE PERFORMANCE AFTERMARKET AND OBD-II

OBD-II presented a challenge to aftermarket firms in the business of providing performance recalibrations on PROM-based OEM engine management systems. Using the new flash memory technology, OEMs in some cases implemented write-protect features that removed the ability to perform aftermarket recalibrations required for compatibility/compliance for performance equipment packages.

OBD's sensitivity to changes and modifications increased the risk of incompatibility. The need to uniquely calibrate each engine family further added to the complexity. Extended warranties and increasingly higher vehicle useful life requirements have expanded emissions liability for both OEMs and the aftermarket, providing more chances for unexpected use, wear, adaptations, failures, and so on. To make street-legal products, aftermarket performance firms need a full understanding of the powertrain control/OBD system operation to minimize potential incompatibilities and false MILs over the vehicle's useful life. Given that OEMs continue developing OBD systems while they are being produced, OEMs have a nearly insurmountable advantage in having the information needed to maximize compatibility of aftermarket parts.

With the world going OBD-II in 1996, SEMA launched a lawsuit against the federal EPA, California's EPA, and the California Air Resources Board, basically to prevent these governmental organizations from enforcing OBD-II and the Clean Air Act of 1990 in ways that were economically ruinous and anti-competitive toward legitimate aftermarket equipment and performance suppliers capable of building parts and equipment that genuinely did not degrade vehicle emissions or even improved emissions performance. SEMA was looking to force OEMs to meet the following conditions with respect to the $200B specialty equipment aftermarket:

1. Provide initial calibration development training on applicable power trains.
2. Designate a liaison from each participating OEM.
3. SEMA acts as specialty aftermarket liaison.
4. Provide information to aftermarket for product development/recalibration.
5. Provide access to equipment/tools needed for development.
6. Provide ongoing training/communication as vehicles are updated.

ANATOMY OF AN OBDII MESSAGE

The diagnostic scanner and the vehicle communicate with each other by exchanging small pieces of information, called diagnostic messages. The message transmitted from the scanner to the PCM is called a command. The message transmitted back from the PCM to the scanner is called a response.

Once the OBD11 scanner tool is connected, it will transmit a command message to the vehicle. The PCM microprocessor will receive the message and verify it. If the message is valid, the PCM will respond.

A typical scanner command looks as follows:

C4 10 FI 23 FF 06 8D

C4	Required Header Byte
10	Destination (PCM)
F1	Originator (Scanner)
23	Command ("Request data")
FF 06	Data ("Address FF06")
8D	Message checksum

In the above message, the scanner is requesting data from the PCM memory at address FF06.

7. Provide specifications, documentation, and other items needed to get an exemption order (information could be provided to J2008/central databases).

Aftermarket manufacturers would be liable for proper use of information and equipment provided, as well as security.

In spite of the above challenges, after some initial pessimism, aftermarket companies and individuals have succeeded in reverse-engineering the EMS of many of the most important OEM performance vehicles to the point of making aftermarket recalibration feasible, so OBD-II has not been the lock on the hood that some people feared. New software like LS1edit was developed that readily hacked into the flash memory of the millennium C5 Corvette and other LS1/6 vehicles, and the software has been expanded and upgraded in the years since to interface with a large number of GM vehicles and engines. With highly sophisticated piggyback and interceptor computers able to manipulate OBD-II systems so effectively, government and OEMs seem to have understood that it was somewhat pointless to worry too much about providing insurmountable barriers to entry around the sacred OBD-II OEM calibration.

HACKING THE CAN BUS

Understanding the CAN-standard vehicle network is vital to a successful engine swap involving any U.S.-market vehicle or engine built after 2007 and some vehicles or engines built much earlier, starting with the 1986 BMW 850 coupe. Engine data broadcast on the CAN by the engine control module may be required by other embedded controllers to work properly. Obvious examples include rpm data that's required by a dash controller to operate the tachometer, vehicle speed data required by a body control module to lock or unlock the doors above a certain speed, or engine rpm, manifold pressure, and vehicle speed required by a transmission control module to shift the gears of an electronic automatic transmission.

Bosch pioneered the controller area network (CAN) serial data-link protocol in the early 1980s and licensed a number of semiconductor vendors to develop and produce controller chips. Twenty-five years later, starting in 2008, the U.S. government required all cars sold in the U.S. to support CAN protocol for OBD-II diagnostics. CAN specified what's called the *data-link layer* of a networking protocol stack, and left the physical layer and all higher layers open to be implemented by automakers as they saw fit. CAN does, however, specify that the *physical layer* must support an active (i.e., dominant) state for a zero bit and a passive (i.e., recessive) state for a one bit, which is critical to resolving collisions between messages of differing priority

Many organizations have developed differing physical layers that support CAN. GM, for example, developed GMLAN, a representative onboard network which defines two physical layers along with the higher level layers that provide standards by which all of a vehicle's various processors or nodes cooperate to accomplish diagnostic, bulk data transfers, ECU reflash or recalibration, and so forth. CAN uses a Non-Return-to-Zero protocol, NRZ-5, with bit stuffing, and the network implements Carrier Sense Multiple Access with Collision Resolution (CSMA/CR). GMLAN consists of two linked CAN buses: a high-speed dual-wire CAN for high-speed (EMS and brake) nodes and a lower-speed single-wire CAN for other nodes (in some cases there may be a medium-speed bus). The primary purpose of GMLAN was to improve reliability and lower costs by reducing the numbers of wires, connections, and special-purpose circuits in a vehicle. GMLAN promotes synergism between vehicle nodes to provide features that would not be feasible without a network.

CAN does not include addresses in the traditional sense, but is a publish-and-subscribe communications module. Each packet is physically broadcast to all nodes, which decide for themselves whether to process the message packets. Packets include no authenticator fields, meaning any embedded controller can indistinguishably send a packet to any other. There is a defined challenge-response sequence designed to protect the system against certain actions without authorization. Thus, a given ECU may participate in zero, one, or two challenge-response pairs for: (1) reflashing and memory protection (for upgrading the firmware), and (2) tester capabilities (on GM, DeviceControl diagnostic service used during manufacturing and servicing operations).

Normal messages are the messages broadcast between controllers. Data varies depending on the electronics systems, and being undefined by CAN/OBD-II, is defined by vehicle manufacturers, most of which have taken a similar approach. Normal message data does not need to be requested but is typically sent at a periodic rate by a controller as fast as it needs to be sent so that listening controllers get a timely value.

Diagnostic messages are command/response messages. If you want to get data from an embedded controller, you have to send it a request. The controller will then respond to that request using a common diagnostic protocol. There are only a handful of protocols that are used and these are typically specific to the OEM; however, there is not much difference between OEMs on how they have implemented their flavor of diagnostic messages.

DeviceControl protocol takes an argument (parameter) called a control packet identifier, which specifies a group of controls to override. DeviceControl is used for situations that require exporting control commands from one ECU to other embedded controllers on the CAN bus.

Connector typically has access to all of the ⟨net⟩works so that engineers and techs working on ⟨...⟩ the data easily. When the vehicle is released ⟨from man⟩ufacturing, the networks usually remain accessible from the OBD-II connector, though there have been cases where a gateway device was installed to block hackers from accessing all CAN data from the OBDII connector—which was the situation with some FiatChrysler vehicles. In such cases, access to the powertrain or body CAN buses, requiring finding the appropriate bus somewhere on the vehicle and tapping into the one- or two-wire (or fiber-optic) network. Happily, FiatChrysler has phased out the gateway, at least in some cases. The body network of the 2011 Town and Country is accessible on pins 3 and 11 of the OBD-II connector and could be found as well on the OBD-II connector of the new Fiat 500 destined for the U.S. marketplace.

SERVICES

In standard OBD-II, functions performable by an embedded controller are usually referred to as **services** or **modes**. In diagnostic messaging protocols, there is always a command and virtually always a response from the controller under command. When sniffing raw CAN bus messages, you will discover the service is specified in the second or third, or occasionally the fourth data byte. Almost all vehicle manufacturers have implemented ISO 15765-2, where the service is Byte 1 following the transport protocol header.

A CAN Bus OBD-II sequence to retrieve engine rpm (service $01) would thus be:

Request:	**$7DF 02 01 0D 00 00 00 00 00**
Response:	**$7E8 04 41 0D 01 FE 00 00 00**

COMMON OBD-II SERVICES /MODES

$01 -	Request current powertrain diagnostic data
$02 -	Request powertrain freeze frame data
$03 -	Request emission-related diagnostic trouble codes
$04 -	Clear/reset emission-related diagnostic information
$05 -	Request oxygen sensor monitoring test results
$06 -	Request onboard monitoring test results for specific monitored systems
$07 -	Request emission diagnostic trouble codes detected current or last-completed driving cycle
$08 -	Request control of onboard system, test or component
$09 -	Request vehicle information
$0a -	Request emission-related diagnostic trouble codes with permanent status

Services $10 and more are non-OBD-II services known as enhanced diagnostics that are not government-mandated and are based upon proprietary specifications. In the case of GM, vehicles use GMLAN. Ford uses UDS (ISO-14229), after previously using ISO-14230.

GMLAN ENHANCED SERVICES

$10 -	Initiate diagnostics
$12 -	Read failure record
$1A -	Read diagnostic ID (DID)
$20 -	Return to normal
$22 -	Read data by parameter ID (PID)
$23 -	Read memory address
$27 -	Security access
$28 -	Disable normal communications
$2C -	Define dynamic data packet ID (DPID)
$2D -	Define PID by memory address
$34 -	Request download
$36 -	Transfer data
$3B -	Write DID
$3E -	Tester present
$A2 -	Report programming state
$A5 -	Enter programming mode
$A9 -	Check codes
$AA -	Read DPID
$AE -	Device control

A GM enhanced diagnostics CAN bus sequence to retrieve engine rpm (Service $22) would be:

Request:	**$7E0 03 22 0D 00 00 00 00**
Response:	**$7E8 04 62 00 0D 01 7E 00 00**

FORD (ISO-14229) ENHANCED DIAGNOSTICS

$10 -	Diagnostic session control
$11 -	ECU reset
$14 -	Clear diagnostic information
$19 -	Read diagnostic trouble codes (DTC)
$22 -	Read data by ID
$23 -	Read memory by address
$24 -	Read scaling data by ID
$27 -	Security access
$28 -	Communications control
$2A -	Read data by periodic ID
$2C -	Dynamically define data ID
$2E -	Write data by ID
$2F -	Input / output control
$31 -	Routine control
$34 -	Request download
$35 -	Request upload
$36 -	Transfer data
$37 -	Request transfer exit
$3D -	Write memory by address
$3E -	Tester present
$83 -	Access timing parameter
$84 -	Secured data transmission
$85 -	Control DTC setting
$86 -	Response on event
$87 -	Link control

Generic diagnostic services that you'll find in common across virtually all diagnostics systems include the following:

- **Tester present** (typically 0x3E) is used to inform embedded controllers that there is a tester present and a command to enter a diagnostic or augmented state where certain capabilities or services are available that otherwise would not be. A recurring tester present signal from the scan tool keeps embedded controllers in the altered state. When this happens there needs to be some way of maintaining that state while the tool that initiated the state is still connected to the diagnostic connector. If the scan tool is disconnected or turned off for more than three seconds, the absence of the tester present message allows embedded controllers to return to the normal state, so scan tools will typically broadcast the message every 1 to 2.5 seconds.

- **Read data by PID** can be used to read data from embedded controllers on virtually any new vehicle. **Service 0x01** is the OBD-II standard read data by Parameter ID, in which PID is a 1-byte number representing the data you wish to read. **Service 0x22** is the enhanced diagnostic method for reading data, typically a 2-byte sequence representing the parameter you wish to read. Sometimes the 2-byte parameter can be used in conjunction with a different enhanced diagnostic service to *write* the data as well, but this is definitely not standard.

- **Security access (0x27)** is used to prevent (or *provide*) privileged access to an embedded controller in order to read or write sensitive proprietary calibration data that manufacturers are required to restrict. Security access "unlocks" data on the controller. The controller "unlock" procedure is a multi-step procedure in which a scan tool must (1) broadcast a request for a security seed, (2) receive the seed, (3) run a proprietary algorithm against the seed to generate a security key, (4) broadcast the key to the embedded controller, and (5) receive a positive response indicating the controller is unlocked. There can be multiple levels or subfunctions of security access that provide increasingly unrestricted access to sensitive data on a "need-to-know" basis in order to provide limited privileged access for one type of access (e.g., locksmith activating a new ignition key) without having to unlock all levels. Security access seed-key transaction occurs in odd-even pairs in which subfunction **0x01**, for example, would be the seed request, **0x02** the key response. **0x03** is paired with **0x04**, **0x05** with **0x06**, and so on.
- **Other important diagnostic services** that are not standardized include the following:
- **Stop normal communications** (GMLAN and others) is designed to stop the controller area network, or at least drastically limit communications between all embedded controllers. The purpose is normally to clear the bus prior to transfer of large amounts of data (such as an ECU flash) over the CAN bus. On GMLAN this service is **0x28**, making the complete message looks like this: **0x7E0 01 28 00 00 00 00 00 00.**
- Stop normal communications should cause engine controller normal messages to virtually disappear, making the command a useful hacking tool if you want to prevent interference when you are trying to simulate messages a controller would send and wish to avoid disabling the controller entirely or having to gateway the CAN as discussed elsewhere in this section. Embedded CAN controllers are supposed to be designed with fail-safe code that does not allow muting of critical messages if someone with a diagnostic tool attempts to stop the network completely while driving and prevents reflashing the operating software while the engine is running, but this is not always the case, so it is not wise to attempt doing so while the engine is running.
- The stop normal communications service requires tester present (0x3E) packets on a continuing basis every two seconds or so to keep communications stopped. To restart normal network communications, send a return to normal (0x20) message: **0x7E0 01 20 00 00 00 00 00 00**. Or simply stop sending the tester present message, which will automatically restore communications after three seconds.

Input/output control (UDS/ISO 14229) provides a way to command controller outputs that make things happen. I/O control service (**0x2F**) requires (1) DID (data ID), (2) control record, and (3) control mask. DID is a 2-byte ID describing

Auterra's Dyno-Scan turns your Windows laptop or Android device into a powerful automotive scan tool and road dynamometer. *Auterra*

the output (or input!) you are modifying. Control record describes what should happen (up, down, on, off, and so on). Control mask is a bitwise mask that indicates which of one or more parameters will be modified. For example, if **0x1122** is the DID, **0x07** is the control record, and **0x0100** is the mask, a random sample I/O control message would be: **0x7E0 06 2F 11 22 07 01 00 00 00**, but hacking the command from scratch to investigate what is going to require exhaustively stepping through the various possible control masks, many of which will elicit a negative response from the controller: **0x7E8 03 7F 2F 13 00 00 00 00**, where **0x13** is the negative response code (NRC). Other NRCs include:

0x13 –	Incorrect message length or invalid format
0x22 –	Condition not correct
0x31 –	Request out of range
0x33 –	Security access denied
0x80-FF –	OEM specific

EXTENDED ID

CAN Extended ID is a concept that expands frame identification for special situations. All CAN messages have an ArbID header that (1) identifies the data contents of the frame and (2) arbitrates which packet gets priority when two CAN messages are sent at the same time in order to prevent a low-priority ArbID frame halfway through being sent from being preempted by a higher priority ArbID. **Extended IDs** comprise the ArbID *plus* one or more additional data bytes from the frame. Extended ID is useful in the case that non-OBD-II specifications require use of a particular ArbID for certain *classes* of data (e.g., engine sensor data). In many cases you will see multiple data parameters bundled into the same message under the same ID, with each type of data allocated to a specific location in the message, but if you had more data to send than one frame could hold or you wanted to restrict all parameters to byte 5 of every frame, you could allocate byte 1 as the extended ID, with each parameter assigned a new ID. Each engine parameter could be assigned an ID with engine rpm identified by 0x0C, coolant temp by 0x05, and additional engine parameters in the form 0x0Y.

Thus, with an overall ArbID of 0x444, **engine rpm** frames would be:

0x444 0C 03 00 FF 22 00 00 00 00, and **coolant temp** frames would be:

0x444 05 04 00 FF 10 00 00 00 00

Extended IDs have been used for diagnostics messages. As one example, Toyota has used extended IDs for diagnostic requests and responses, with a Toyota enhanced diagnostic request beginning with 0x750, to be followed by destination controller address as byte 1. Vehicle manufacturers such as GM, Ford, and Chrysler that assign an ArbID for each ECU destination address must live with a situation where the more embedded controllers you have allocated as diagnostic identifiers, the fewer ArbIDs are available for other purposes.

NETWORK MANAGEMENT

Most vehicles have high-speed and low-speed CAN buses, and the high-speed powertrain network comes alive when the key turns to the start position. Automakers employ network management for the low-speed body network, which requires a system to wake up nodes to deal with an unlock command from the key fob, or in some cases with remote commands from a long-distance (cellular) network, as well as a system that allows controller nodes to go to sleep when the vehicle is parked. There are many different proprietary systems that operate above the physical link-layer CAN, one of which is GMLAN.

GM uses network management on their single-wire low-speed network to wake up nodes sleeping in low-current mode. To communicate with a sleeping node, two events must take place:

1. Send a high-voltage wake-up command. The physical layer of a low-speed single wire CAN is typically an active high, 0-5V line in which 0V represents a low value, and 5V represents a high. The wake-up command occurs as a special battery voltage (9-16V) signal that is typically arbitration ID **0x100** and NO data, though the voltage *is* the command and any data format (or none) will do the job. Most nodes require another "wake-up" signal that tells them to begin listening for data.

2. Send the virtual network management frame (VNMF), the purpose of which is to wake up particular virtual networks or groups of nodes associated with common systems such as "lighting control" or "entry systems" such as doors. Before communicating with a door ECU to unlock the doors, you would want to wake up the virtual network for doors. Lacking a proprietary list of all the nodes involved in a particular virtual network or system, you may wish to wake up *all* with a sign command: **0x621 01 FF FF FF FF 00 00 00**.

The mechanism stems from the fact that all VNMFs have 11-bit IDs (even on a 29-bit network!) in the range of 0x620-0x63F, such that any ID within that range is interpreted as a VNMF by all nodes. The ID—in this case $621 (body control module)—is the source node, and the first byte of the VNMF is either *0x01* (meaning initiate the following virtual networks) or *0x00* (meaning continue the following VNs), wherein the next three or four data bytes contains a bit-encoded list of all VNs, where 1 commands wake-up and 0 does not. Thus, sending 0xFF wakes up all eight VNs encoded in that byte. Each node will hear it and wake-up. To wake a particular VN without proprietary documentation you'll need to search bit-by-bit (which should be relatively quick as there are so far seldom more than 20 VNs on

any particular vehicle). VNs remain awake for up to 3 seconds after the initiate command; to keep the network awake, you must send continue frames **$621 00 FF FF FF FF 00 00 00** within that period.

VNMF format: ArbID, B1, B2, B3, B4, B5, B6, B7, B8
Example: $620-$63F, 01 or 00, XX, XX, XX, XX, 00, 00, 00

Where XX = some bit-encoded value where each bit represents a single VN. Must be exactly eight bytes.

NETWORK SECURITY

Embedded ECUs are supposed to use a fixed-challenge (security seed), which is stored in the ECU along with the corresponding security key, thus avoiding storage of the challenge-response algorithm that converts a seed into a key in the ECU firmware, where it could be read out easily in the case that an external flash chip were used. In fact, the CAN reference standard states that, "under no circumstances shall the encryption algorithm ever reside in the node." The encryption algorithm instead resides in the testing device so it can compute the key. The standard requires that ECUs permit a key attempt every 10 seconds, which means that a 16-bit key can be cracked in no more than about 7.5 days (or in no more than roughly 3.5 days if the hacker removed the embedded controller from the vehicle in order to power-cycle the ECU every two attempts). There is no concept in CAN of access-control rights on a per-user basis.

Exactly how do you unlock a controller? Assuming you don't have the security access algorithm that acts upon a controller-supplied security seed to calculate the key to unlock the controller, you'll need to use a brute force technique to get the key, in which you sequentially guess what it might be and test. GM was kind enough to make this easier by using a static seed (which doesn't change each time it is requested). The logic of brute-forcing a controller follows below, but you will almost definitely want to automate the process by writing a laptop computer program or procedure that can run unattended. Security countermeasures against brute-forcing the security key include a retry timer and a maximum retry counter designed to massively slow down the hacking process, but there is nothing you can do about it. On the other hand, that's what computers are for.

1. **Initialize: Set key-ID to the initial state of 1** (00 01).
2. **Send seed request** to the controller: [7E0 02 27 01 00 00 00 00].
3. If the controller response to the seed request was **negative, *go to negative seed.***
4. **If the controller sends the security seed, send key-ID** [7E0 04 27 02 00 01]
5. If the **key-ID was correct**, the controller response will be positive [7E0 01 67], meaning **you have found the security key. *Go to success.***
6. The odds are high that any particular key ID guess will be wrong, which will illicit a negative (wrong key) response from the controller: [7E8 03 7F 27 35].
7. Compute new key and try again: **Add 1 to the previous key ID** (such as, 00 01 + 1 = 00 02). *Go to send seed request.*
8. ***Negative seed:*** *If the controller negative response to seed request was [7E8 03 7F 27 37],* it was too soon to request **another seed**. Wait 1-2 seconds. *Go to send seed request.*
9. If the controller response to the seed request is negative [7E8 03 7F 27 36], you have **exceeded the controller's maximum number of retry attempts,** another countermeasure against brute-forcing. Manually or automatically **reset the power on the controller. *Go to send seed request.***

10. **Success.** Once you have the key it will work for the controller type every time (*though not for* all *controllers*).

REVERSE-ENGINEERING THE CAN
Getting Information

Suppose you need information about the workings of an embedded controller. You can buy the data or reverse it from an existing scan tool. If you want to buy the data, you have to be a member of the Equipment and Tools Institute (ETI), which gets you access to most OEM data, though in the case of GM and Chrysler you may require an extra-cost license specific to the OEM. An ETI tool membership requires a multi-thousand dollar investment up front, at which point getting the OEM controller data may require a significant additional investment. The OEM data may be in Excel files, Access Databases, or sometimes PDF files, so you'll have to massage the data to fit your application. In all cases you are required to use ETI data in a commercially available tool within one year of joining.

To reverse-engineer data from a scan tool that already has the data, connect the scan tool to a device such as a neoVI or ValueCAN and a laptop with Vehicle Spy software, which will allow you to simulate the vehicle's network. By connecting the scan tool this way you can respond with properly formatted diagnostic responses to scan tool requests, which will allow you to vary the data portion of the message to derive parameter identifier, data position, and scaling. For example, if you want to find the enhanced ID for engine speed you would setup the scan tool to request engine speed, instigating a message with engine speed parameter ID (0x000D). By changing the data in the response message from 0x00000000 to 0x**ff**000000 to 0x00**ff**0000 to 0x0000**ff**00 to 0x000000**ff** you will discover that the engine rpm is located in the first and second bytes of the response message. At this point you can set the response data to 0x0001 and you will discover the scaling for the message equals the signal value (0.25). You can do this for each of the parameters for which you are searching. It will take about 30 seconds per parameter once everything is set up.

Suppose you are reverse-engineering a CAN BUS, but *don't know the baud rate*. You have two different choices:

1. Go one-by-one through a possible list, trying different rates. CAN BUS baud rates tend to be 33,333 bps, 50 Kbps, 83,333 bps, 100 Kbps, 125 Kbps, 250 Kbps, 500 Kbps (most common), 800 Kpbs, and 1,000 Kbps. The last two are the least common as they suffer from reduced network length issues. Anything higher violates the CAN BUS specification. It is possible to effectively decapitate the network by having the wrong baud rate set in your tool. So make sure you are not switching baud rates while the vehicle is in motion.

2. Use an oscilloscope or logic analyzer. The foolproof way of measuring any serial data network such as CAN BUS is to use a tool that can measure the one-bit time. Baud rate is simply the inverse of one-bit time. Simply take 1/(one bit time) in seconds and you have your baud rate.

Behavior Modification

How might you *change the behavior of a device on the CAN*? Let's say you're tired of hearing a car chime or beep at you when the key is in the ignition with the door open or if you're not wearing a seat belt on a dyno and wish to stop it. You will need to connect to the lower speed GM single wire (SW) CAN bus, which is on PIN 1 of the OBD-II DLC connector and runs at 33,333 bps, the standard rate. The GMLAN 29 bit ID is broken into three pieces: priority, parameter ID, and source address. Priority is the first 3 bits of the ID and is designed to allow more important messages greater access to the network in the case of congestion (0 is the highest priority, 4 the lowest). The remaining 26 bits are divided evenly amongst the parameter ID and the source address (i.e., 13 bits each). Parameter ID identifies what will be sent in the data portion of the frame, and source address uniquely identifies the node that sent the message.

Chime has a parameter ID of 0x0F, meaning commands relating to chime require 0x0F starting at the 26th most significant bit. 0x0F in binary is typically 600–700 ohms. Thus, "0x1001E060" represents a Priority 4 chime command (0xF) sent from node 0x60. In binary, 0x0F is #b0:0000 0000:1111. Putting the whole ID together, as priority followed by parameter ID and source address gives #b1:00**00 0000:0001 111**0:0000 0110:0000 (parameter ID is in bold).

The 5-byte data portion of the command defines the characteristics of the chime, which can be a long chime, short chime, a click sound, or a ding sound, which is executed once or multiple times.

- The first four bits of the first byte (the most significant nibble) specifies which speaker will emit the sound. Front driver-side speaker is controlled by bit 7 (the most significant bit) of the byte, Front passenger speaker by bit 6, rear driver side bit 5, then rear passenger speaker by bit 4. Making a sound in only the driver speaker then you would send 0x8X in the first byte (where X is irrelevant).
- The second nibble of the first byte describes the type of sound, typically a beep or a click.
- The second byte describes the intonation of the chime.
- The third byte commands the number of repetitions.
- The fourth byte describes the duty of the chime.

Thus, if you wanted to cancel a chime, you could arrange to have software on a CAN-resident scan tool or PC monitor the CAN bus for a chime command and effectively cancel it by overriding it with a fast chime with 0-percent duty cycle.

RFA

Most modern vehicles have distributed electronic systems where the **remote function actuation** (RFA) module that receives commands from the key or key fob is separate from the controller that actuates the door locks themselves, such that door lock/unlock is accomplished via a CAN BUS message. The trick is to connect to the vehicle's *body* CAN bus, which is usually separate from the powertrain bus or OBD-II CAN bus. Once you've found the correct network, you'll have to monitor it for the unlock or lock commands by using the factory key fob and watching for a new message that shows up or data that changes at the same instant that you press the key fob lock and unlock buttons. Do this a few times and you'll find the message that controls the unlock and lock commands and then test the data by broadcasting a message with the same arbitration ID and data. If the doors lock and unlock, you've found it, but if not you may have discovered a message *related* to a door unlock/lock procedure (such as dome light status). Note that the lock/unlock *is not always done via the CAN bus.*

Off the CAN

Quite a bit of time can be wasted trying to reverse-engineer **CAN commands that are not applicable** to a vehicle because the functionality is not implemented using the CAN bus. A

UC-SD/UW'S INVESTIGATION OF CAN BUS VEHICLE SECURITY

When University of California San Diego and University of Washington computer science researchers set out to investigate vehicle security, they decided to launch a representative series of sophisticated attacks against two identical 2009 Chevy Impalas equipped with a low-speed and a high-speed CAN bus.

Hacking tools included the following:

(1) A Windows laptop equipped with a CANCapture ECOM cable, an off-the-shelf CAN-to-USB interface used to interact with the high-speed bus, (2) an Olimex AVR-CAN Atmel AT90CAN128 development board used to interact with the low-speed CAN, (3) custom "CARShark" Windows software installed on the laptop, and (4) a custom-built CAN bus analyzer and packet injection tool used to process and manipulate OEM proprietary extensions to CAN. Off-the-shelf CAN sniffer and OEM diagnostic tools could have accomplished limited testing, but the researchers needed to read out ECU memory, load custom code into embedded ECUs, and generate *fuzz-testing packets* over the CAN interface.

The investigation determined that any attacker who is able to infiltrate *any* CAN device could (1) bypass rudimentary network security, (2) maliciously bridge between the low- and high-speed CAN networks, and (3) leverage this ability to completely circumvent a broad range of safety-critical systems to implement heinous tricks such as disable brakes at speed, selectively lock the brakes on individual wheels on demand, and stop the engine, in all cases regardless of driver input.

UCSD/UW attack points included (1) the OBD-II diagnostic port, (2) the CD/DVD player, (3) short-range wireless networks (vehicle Bluetooth and vehicle Wi-Fi hotspot), (4) dealer diagnostic tools connected wirelessly via Wi-Fi diagnostic device connected to the OBD-II port, (5) telematics systems (GM OnStar, Ford Sync, and so on), (6) digital over cellular voice channel, (7) 3G cellular (used for automatic crash response, remote diagnostics, and stolen vehicle recovery).

Hacking methodologies include the following:

- *Packet sniffing and targeted probing* to observe the CAN bus while turning on various components such as headlights. Replay and informed probed revealed how to control the radio, instrument panel, and a number of body control functions but was less useful in mapping the interface to safety-critical powertrain components.
- *Fuzzing* (interactive testing of random or partially random packets) revealed that significant attacks did not require a complete understanding or reverse-engineering of even a single component on the vehicle. DeviceControl functions discovered largely by fuzzing included controlling the engine (ECM), body components (BCM), brakes (EBCM), and heating and air conditioning systems (HVAC).
- *Reverse-engineering* was used to explicitly understand how certain hardware features were controlled. This involved dumping the embedded controller code via the CAN ReadMemory service and running it with a debugger (IDA Pro).
- *Stationary testing* with vehicle immobilized on jack stands allowed safe testing in simulated driving to observe the effect of sending packets on the corresponding module, the resulting actions, and determine the following: (1) Could the result of the packet be overridden manually (for example, by pulling the manual door unlock lever)? (2) Did the result of the packet change when the vehicle was traveling more than 40 mph? (3) Did the module in question need to be unlocked with the DeviceControl key before the packet could achieve a result?

The study found that although the CAN standard stated that some access-controlled operations—such as reading sensitive memory areas like the ECU operating program or security keys—could be denied outright if considered too risky and some memory addresses defined as locations that the ECU will not permit to be read under any circumstances, experiments verified that this was (surprisingly) not implemented in some cases, even for the DeviceControl Security Key required for reflash operations.

Although the CAN standard stated that the CAN communications and reflashing service should be disabled while the vehicle is moving, this was not always implemented. In one case, when an OBD-II test device commanded a reflash, instead of rejecting the programming event, the engine stopped while driving and the reflash proceeded.

The **radio** could be controlled completely: user-control disabled, messages displayed, volume changed and locked, clicks and chimes produced for various durations at various intervals.

The **instrument panel cluster** could be controlled completely, including displaying arbitrary messages, falsifying fuel level and speedometer reading, changing illumination, and so on. Disabling communications to and from the engine control module (ECM) when the wheels were spinning reduced the speedo reading to 0. Disabling communications to and from the body control module (BCM) froze the instrument cluster in its current state. The engine could be turned off in this state but then would not restart without re-enabling communications to the BCM.

The **engine** could be controlled to (1) change idle speed, (2) change engine timing by recalibrating the crankshaft angle sensor error, (3) disable all cylinders simultaneously, (4) disable the engine so it knocked excessively when restarted or would not restart at all, (5) disable the engine by forging a packet with the "airbag deployed" bit set, and more.

The **brakes** (revealed via fuzzing) could be controlled without needing the security key to unlock the EBCM via DeviceControl to (1) lock individual brakes, (2) lock all brakes, (3) lock a brake semi-permanently (resistant to attempts to unlock via manual override, shutdown, and battery removal), and (4) release the brakes and prevent them from being enabled at speed. Track-testing revealed essentially identical behavior except that EBCM has to be unlocked over 5 mph to affect the CAN controls.

parameter like vehicle speed tends to be universally available on the CAN bus, and knowing it's there, should be simple enough to capture and scale, but more obscure parameters can be more difficult. Before fruitlessly searching for a CAN command that may not exist on a vehicle, review the wiring to see if it appears to be hardwired some other way. But assuming some function is thought to be accomplished via a command sent over the CAN bus (such as an unlock command originating from a key fob receiver module thought to be on the CAN), you can capture all CAN messages while you press the unlock button and then play those messages back to the network a few times to see if the doors unlock. Why does this work? If the message was sent over the CAN bus then playing all of the messages back on the bus should produce the same result as pushing the key fob (including parking lights flashing, horn honking, and so on). In this case, you can assume the message is broadcast over the CAN bus.

Diagnostic Services

Diagnostic data is built on top of ISO 15765-2_transport protocol, which can be used to determine which diagnostic service a particular vehicle supports and which parameters or

The **HVAC** could be controlled to (1) turn fans on and off, (2) turn the A/C on and off, (3) turn the heat on and off, and (4) disable manual override of these components.

Successful composite hacks included:

Falsifying speed by intercepting speed update packets on the low-speed BCM and transmitting maliciously crafted packets with falsified speed.

Disabling interior and exterior lights (while the lighting system set to "automatic"), including headlights, brake lights, auxiliary lights, interior dome light, and instrument panel cluster illumination.

A "self-destruct" demo featuring a 60-second countdown displayed on the driver information center accompanied by clicks at an accelerating rate and horn honks in the last few seconds. (Required less than 200 lines of code in CARShark, mostly for timing the sounds and countdown display.)

Bridging the two internal CAN networks allowed OE and aftermarket devices on the low-speed CAN to impact devices such as the electronically controlled brake module on the high-speed CAN bus by reprogramming the telematics controller that, along with the BCM, operate on both local area networks to enable the telematics ECU to act as a bridge.

Hijacking the Telematics unit by (1) initiating a programming request to the telematics controller (running the UNIX-like QNX Neutrino Real-Time operating system) via the low-speed CAN, (2) uploading a few hundred firmware instructions (less than 1,200 bytes) to the telematics controller's RAM via the low-speed CAN. Special telematics code ran *instead* of the ordinary code (meaning telematics services were not available while it was running). More sophisticated attacks could insert a new code into the OE Telematics environment by storing new code in RAM or reflashing the Telematics ECU.

Gaining access to the rich UNIX-like Telematics operating system to control GPS, Audio Capture, Cellular Link, via software libraries such at OpenSSL and standard OS interfaces to additional hardware. Instructions inserted into RAM by bridging from the low-speed CAN disappear the next time the controller reboots, with the only evidence remaining the lack of telematics records. Special hacked code inserted via reflash could potentially erase any evidence of its existence following whatever event it was designed to facilitate via sophisticated but straightforward measures that reflashed controller code to original-equipment status.

The study concluded that because some CAN/ECU hacks were possible due to weak or unenforced protections of the diagnostic and reflashing services, vehicle manufacturers could address vulnerabilities by locking down these capabilities after the car leaves manufacturing, but this ignored the needs of legitimate stakeholders:

- Enthusiasts should be able to tune or customize some aspects of their vehicle and engine management systems, a right that is codified in the proposed federal Motor Vehicle Owners Right to Repair Act, which was passed in 2012 in a statewide ballot measure in Massachusetts with the motivation of fostering competition in the automotive industry. The Right to Repair Act requires manufacturers to provide diagnostic information and tools to vehicle owners (and service providers), and to provide information to aftermarket tool manufacturers that enables them to make functionally equivalent tools.

- Mechanics have had access to OE internal servicing information on a voluntary basis via the National Automotive Service Task Force (NASTF), a cooperative involving 63 organizations (including carmakers plus auto service and equipment and tool companies) that established a website providing reference for all technicians on obtaining service information and tools from manufacturers. Independent service and replacement of components could be difficult or impossible in a fully locked-down environment. Even relatively simple CAN security mechanisms could be at odds with the Right to Repair act.

The UCSD/UW automotive security study suggested the core security problem is a lack of access control for the use of highly valid services and proposed that a solution must (1) prevent arbitrary ECUs from being able to issue diagnostic and reflashing commands, (2) require validation before the issuing of any diagnostic or reflashing command, and (3) require physical access to the vehicle in order to issue any "dangerous" command.

However, even if diagnostic and reflashing services were secured, modern vehicles leave the factory with multiple third-party ECUs, and owners add aftermarket components such as stereo and radio components on the CAN. All such devices contain controllers that could potentially "spoof" packets that appear on the CAN during normal operation, presenting vehicle manufacturers with the choice of ultimately either trusting all third-party components or locking down the CAN such that no third-party component can affect the state of the vehicle. The researchers proposed that owners could be permitted to install an external filtering or interceptor device between an untrusted component such as a radio to restrict all traffic to and from the device and the CAN bus to an approved set of packets. Yet another possibility would be installation of a device to monitor, detect, and *correct* rather than *prevent* security problems, recognizing the stringent reality that (1) automotive design and manufacture requires swift and efficient integration of parts from different manufacturers and multiple sources that may change over time, (2) competitive pressures drive vendors to reuse designs, which tends to increase heterogeneity, (3) it is not uncommon for every embedded controller to use a different microprocessor and software architecture, (4) some vehicles use multiple communications architectures between ECUs that are grafted onto each other to integrate a vendor assembly and get the vehicle to market in a timely manner. The reality that many automotive functions are safety-critical means that introducing any delay into the processing of, say, braking system commands is unsafe.

subfunctions the service may support. To determine supported services and subfunctions, proceed as follows:

1. Sniff the network to discover the diagnostic IDs of the various nodes (including the physical ID and response IDs)

Exhaustively sending a tester present request (Service 0x3E) to each CAN bus ID works well with 11-bit systems (Unfortunately, 29-bit systems require a shortcut because 29 bits encompasses too many IDs for it to be practical to sequentially request the ID from every possible ID, necessitating some sort of shortcut.) Keep in mind that any generated ID that is also a functional ID will result in more than one node responding to the request.

Start by sending tester present to ARB ID 0x001 of the form: 0x001 01 3E 00 00 00 00 00 00. Alternatively, 0x001 02 3E 01 00 00 00 00 00 may work (test to see).

You will know that a node has a diagnostics service available if you receive a response such as 0x7E8 01 7E 00 00 00 00 00 00 (0x7E is the positive response to the 0x3E request).

Log or write down the request ID as well as the response ID.

Increment the arbitration ID by one: 0x001, 0x002, 0x003, . . . 0x7FF and reiterate, until you encounter the next positive response. Note that CAN bus errors may occur in this iterative process, in which case resend.

If the diagnostic ID is also a functional ID, you may notice unintended effects (such as a windshield wiper move or a turn signal flashing) if you happen to send a packet that is interpreted by another controller as a function command.

2. Find Supported Services

Some services may require a certain message length, and once in a while you may have to have 0x04 in the first data byte to get a positive response from the embedded controller. Keep in mind that the service ID for a diagnostic command is found in the second byte: ARBID, B1, **B2**, B3 . . .

A first request might be: 0x7E0 01 01 00 00 00 00 00 00, where there's no protocol data and byte 2 contains the service. Diagnostic services are broken into ranges, as the request IDs and positive response IDs do not overlap. Since we're not interested in sending the responses, it's OK to remove the positive response IDs from the requested services. Service request IDs are: 0x01-0x3E, 0x80-0xBE. Keep in mind that 0x3F is reserved, 0x7F is used for negative responses and 0x40-0x7E and 0xC0-0xFE are reserved for positive responses from the embedded ECUs.

Knowing what the range is, the trick now is to send a request and deduce from the response if the service is supported. Suppose we send 0x7E0 01 01 00 00 00 00 00 00 and get back 0x7E8 03 7F 01 12 00 00 00 00? Since there is a 0x7F in the second *data* byte, the response is a negative. This tells us there was a problem with our request but does not prove that the service is not supported. Byte 4 indicates the reasons that the request failed. In this case byte 4 was a 0x12 negative response code (NRC), which means **subfunction not supported**. The service *is* supported but the subfunction (not sent in this case) is not. Other NRCs are:

NRC	Long Name
$11	Service not supported
$12	Subfunction not supported—invalid format
$22	Conditions not correct or request sequence error
$31	Request out of range
$35	Invalid key
$36	Exceed number of attempts
$37	Required time delay not expired
$78	Request correctly received—response pending

The relevant NRCs are 0x11 and 0x78. NRC 0x11—service is not supported—is a definite indication that the service in question cannot is not available on the electronic control unit. NRC 0x78—response pending—is not actually a negative response but an indication that an additional NRC or a positive response will follow. Other than NRC 0x11, a lack of response within 100 milliseconds (ms) is proof that the particular service is not supported on the controller.

3. Find Parameters

This step is trickier because it requires some understanding of the service, which could have a subfunction or a service that has an argument of variable length. Thus, a lot of testing will required to cover all the bases. Prepare for a lot of negative responses.

To find parameters, iteratively send the request, incrementing the bytes as follows:

0x7E0 02 01 00 00 00 00 00 00, 0x7E0 02 01 01 00 00 00 00, 0x7E0 02 01 02 00 00 00 00 00, and so on.

If you are getting positive responses back from the controller, great. In the case of a negative response, you'll be forced to adapt. Suppose you receive a response NRC 0x22, which means conditions not correct, sequence error? This vague response might indicate that the key must be in the ignition, or that you must send a start diagnostic command first, or something of that order, which will require that you do some detective work to determine what is wrong or missing. On the other hand, an NRC 0x12 tells you immediately that the subfunction or this parameter ID is not supported by this controller, allowing you to move on to the next one. Ideally, you'll be able to automate the process: Writing each message and handling each response can be a challenge.

CHANGING THE VIN

How can you change the VIN stored in an embedded CAN controller?

The first question is, does the controller actually store the VIN? You can discover this on OBD-II controllers by sending a CAN message formatted like this:

Arb ID = 7E0, DATA = 02 09 02 00 00 00 00 00, so Message = [7E0 02 09 02 00 00 00 00 00]

If the VIN is on the controller, this will get the first part of it. A typical response might appear thus:

Arb ID = 7E8, DATA = 10 13 49 02 31 39 48 31, so Message = [7E8 10 13 49 02 31 39 48 31]

You could send a flow control message [7E0 30 00 00 00 00 00 00 00] to get the remainder of the data bytes, but the goal here is simply to discover if this controller stores the VIN. If we get a negative response [7E8 03 7F 02 12] then we know it does not and thus we cannot change something that isn't there.

Assuming you know the controller stores the VIN, the procedure to *write* the VIN will be OEM-specific and may not always be possible without extraordinary means (like desoldering and dumping a flash chip or dumping the controller code and running it through a debugger to understand the firmware code and then modifying the code and reflashing it onto the controller). In the case of setting VIN on a GM CAN BUS vehicle employing the GMLAN diagnostic protocol for enhanced diagnostics (GMW 3110 spec is downloadable from the Internet), the VIN is stored in the controller as a data identifier (DID). Service 3B is used to write DIDs. The VIN, however, is considered a protected DID, requiring that you unlock the controller using security access first.

With the security key found and the controller unlocked, you can now use Service 3B to write the VIN as follows in a series of three messages in which the [31] represents digits of the 17-digit VIN:

1. [7E0 10 13 3B 90 31 31 31 31]
2. (Wait for flow control frame): [7E8 30 00 00]
3. [7E0 21 31 31 31 31 31 31 31]
4. [7E0 22 31 31 31 31 31 31 31]

90 is the VIN DID and on GM controllers the 3B is the service, the 013 is the length of the data in hexadecimal. The 1, 21, and 22 are ISO 15765 diagnostic layers.

If the VIN write is successful you should get a positive response: [7E8 02 7B 90]

SIMULATION OR SPOOFING

Simulation can be a powerful tool for modifying the behavior of system on a CAN. Discovering the meaning and function of the data packets flowing through the CAN buses on a vehicle is useful on many levels, not the least of which is the potential to *simulate* normal packet flow in order to replace or delete fundamental equipment on the vehicle such as the engine, engine-control module, seats, and so forth without controllers on the CAN that are designed to cooperate with each other from generating error messages or modifying behavior in ways that interfere with normal vehicle or engine functioning in ways that are dysfunctional. Even if you are not looking to replace or delete CAN-based systems, the ability to simulate or *spoof* controller packets can be very useful if the goal is to enhance normal vehicle or engine functioning. Perhaps you have modified the powertrain in ways that change the noise levels under some circumstances and wish to adjust the amplitude of automatic changes in stereo system volume, or perhaps you want to change the circumstances under which the automatic door lock-unlock procedure kicks in. Perhaps you want to mute the door-open chime so you can calibrate the EMS on a chassis dyno with the door open without annoying sounds from the vehicle-management systems.

The process of simulating CAN packets begins with research:

- What is the arbitration ID of the message you want to simulate?
- What is the length of the data?
- Is the data static or does it change?
- Are message packets event-driven or periodic?
- What happens if a controller is getting contradictory command packets from an OE controller that remains on the CAN and an add-on controller that is simulating the original controller with new commands packets designed to deliver different results (say, in the face of headlights-on and headlights-off commands) what happens?

Having established the above information, we can begin. Assume we've observed that a message generated by an embedded controller has an arbitration ID of **0x555** and a data field of 8 bytes of static data such that a command sent every 100 milliseconds looks like: **0x555 00 00 00 00 00 00 00 00**. We observe that if we disable the embedded controller and send a simulated message on the CAN with the first byte changed from **0x00** to **0x01**, the sideview mirror steps upward a tiny bit. What's more, we observe that as long as we transmit the **0x555 01 00 00 00 00 00 00 00** every 100 millisecond, the mirror moves smoothly upward and continues to move until we stop transmitting or transmit messages with the data byte changed back to **0x00**.

Next we activate the embedded controller and now observe that the movement of the mirror is not as smooth. What is happening is that we are spoofing a message already present on the CAN at 100-milliseconds intervals, causing the embedded controller that actuates the mirror stepper-motor to interpret our simulated message as an up command and the original controller's message as a stop command. If we press the down arrow on the mirror control switch which spoofing up commands, the results are unpredictable and depend on the robustness of the code running on the controller and how fault-tolerant it is at handling error-type conditions that should not normally be possible. Conflicting messages can definitely cause adverse results with a simulation-based system we want to build and can result in a plethora of CAN bus error frames. To keep the mirror movement smooth, we'll need to prevent the embedded controller from sending **0x555** messages. There are several possibilities.

1. The problem could potentially be handled by the quick and dirty solution of disconnecting or powering down the controller (which could have intolerable unintended consequences but is otherwise the easiest solution).
2. Alternatively, it may be possible to ask the embedded controller to stop sending by using diagnostic services

Bureau of Automotive Repair

ENGINE IDENTIFICATION

VIN NO. RJ01120	I 0056875				
YR	SIZE	MFG	F/C M/A	SITE	B/A NOx
89	5.7U	CHEV	C A	206	A

PCV	AIS	FR	TWC	SPK	C/I
X	X	X	X	X	X
TAC	EVP	OC	EGR	COM	OTH
X	X	X	X	X	X

| E.O.NO. | | ECS | | OTH | 2CATS |

to send a command with a name like "disable normal communications." Unfortunately, the format of such a message and the rules pertaining to it can vary considerably between vehicle manufacturers, which could require extensive reverse-engineering to discover or purchasing the documentation from the manufacturer, which could be expensive. And the results could, as with disconnection or powering down, cause unintended problems with other controllers that are expecting packets from the disabled controller.

3. A final trick is to build a gateway/interceptor between modules where you disconnect sending or receiving modules in order to intercept all messages to a receiving module except the (simulated) messages you want to get through, allowing you to maintain the flow of messages and data to other CAN modules while maintaining complete control of what gets in and out of the embedded controller you are hijacking. The CAN interceptor device needs the processing power to support at least two identical CAN bus channels and handle easily configurable transaction processing of packets on both.

OBD-III

OBD-III is a proposal designed to minimize the delay between detection of an emissions malfunction by the OBD-II system and repair of the vehicle. In the service of this, the two basic elements are the ability to read stored OBD-II information from in-use vehicles and the authority to direct owners of vehicles with fault codes to make immediate repairs. There are three proposed ways to send/receive data: roadside reader, local station network, and satellite.

Proposed enforcement mechanisms include the following:

Incorporate into biennial I/M program (read fault code to screen for vehicles that need complete testing, pass or short test for vehicles with no fault code)

Out-of-cycle inspection (compile and screen data, mail notice to vehicle owner requiring out-of-cycle inspection within 10 days, require certificate of compliance on next registration/resale or within 30 to 60 days, issue citation for noncompliance, enforce citation via court or DMV penalty at next registration, and so on)

Roadside pullover (CHP flags down vehicles with fault codes, technician verifies problem by inspecting or testing vehicle, issuance of notice requiring out-of-cycle inspection, and so on)

The concept of OBD-III is rife with legal issues. OBD-III imposes sanctions based on "suspicionless mass surveillance" of private property. The concept includes random, possibly frequent, testing. There would be no advanced knowledge the vehicle will be tested. The results of testing would not be immediately available (unless roadside pullover follows). There might be no opportunity to confront or rebut, and there is the possibility of the system's use for other purposes (police pursuit/immobilization, tracking, cite speeders).

OBD-III raises Fourth Amendment search and seizure privacy issues: "The right of the people to be secure in their persons, houses, papers and effects, against unreasonable searches and seizures shall not be violated." From a legal perspective, the scope of the OBD-III concept is unprecedented; previous cases have looked at surveillance of individuals.

CARB has requested proposals for incorporation of radio transponders into vehicle onboard diagnostic systems, with the objective "to demonstrate the feasibility and cost effectiveness of replacing the current emissions-based periodic Inspection and Maintenance (I/M) program with automated inspections based on the OBD-II system and an on-vehicle radio transponder. The study will test, evaluate, and demonstrate the viability and cost of equipping new vehicles with various transponder technologies and assess how these technologies can be effectively used to improve the convenience, effectiveness, and cost-effectiveness of the I/M program."

The idea was to save money. Currently the entire vehicle fleet must be tested in order to identify the relatively small number of vehicles that are likely to fail, and 10 million vehicles per year are required to undergo an I/M inspection that results in passing scores for 70 percent of the vehicles.

The idea was that transponder signal receivers would be capable of performing these functions storing a query and received data in a database format that would include the following:

* Date and time of current query
* Date and time of last query
* VIN
* Status (OK, Trouble, or No response)
* Stored codes
* Receiver station number

Besides emissions-related functions, authorities were very interested in cooperative techniques for police pursuit/mobilization. The California Air Resources Board noted that, "The cooperative techniques comprise devices that are installed on automobiles, which would receive a coded radio frequency signal that would produce a progressive speed reduction or shut down the automobile. The speed reduction and shut down could be incorporated in the Onboard Diagnostic (OBD) III system, which is planned to have a radio transponder for reading out automobile status including vehicle number and smog equipment fault codes."

The major obstacle to overcome, notes CARB, "is to get public acceptance of a device that they have to pay for and that can disable their automobile. One way to obtain public acceptance may be to offer incentives by including this device as part of a package that provides other benefits. These benefits could be an antitheft device and/or a smog readout device. The smog readout device could eliminate the need for costly and time-consuming periodic inspections at smog stations. With the idea that the only time you would need to go to an inspection station is when the automobile exceeds smog-generating limits. In addition to public acceptance, this approach will require federal government, state government, and car manufacturer cooperation. The use of a cooperative device has strong appeal because of effectiveness, safety, and ease of use. Incorporating the overall system as part of a larger subsystem would reduce cost and make it more attractive."

THE PHYSICS OF PASSING EMISSIONS

A three-way **catalytic converter** will decrease tail pipe emissions substantially by supporting the following chemical reactions in the exhaust gas:

Concerts nitrogen oxides (NO_x) to nitrogen (N_2) and oxygen (O_2):

$$2 \text{ NO} > N_2 + O_2$$
$$2 \text{ NO2} > N_2 + 2 O_2$$
$$2 \text{ NOX} > N_2 + X O_2$$

Converts carbon monoxide (CO) to carbon dioxide (CO_2):

$$2 \text{ CO} + O_2 > 2 CO_2$$

Oxidizes unburned hydrocarbons (HC) to carbon dioxide (CO_2) and water (H_2O):

$$2 \text{ CXHY} + (2X+Y/2) O_2 > 2X CO_2 + Y H_2O$$

Due to a cat's limited ability to store oxygen, to work most efficiently, catalytic converters require a stoichiometric engine air/fuel mixture. If the air/fuel ratio is too rich, there will be insufficient oxygen to burn hydrocarbons and carbon monoxide. If the air/fuel ratio is too lean, oxides of nitrogen can't be completely reduced by the removal of oxygen (which is why outlaw tuners sometimes pipe pure oxygen into the cat when emissions-testing a dirty hot rod that might otherwise fail). Fortunately, a narrow-band O_2 sensor is extremely effective at targeting a 14.7 stoichiometric air/fuel ratio. To catalyze exhaust components ,a catalytic converter must reach its 400-600 degrees Fahrenheit "light off" temperature, which is why it is critical that a cat heat up very quickly on start-up. Which is why calibration engineers use retarded timing and rich mixtures to maximize exhaust gas heat during warm-up.

If you anticipate trouble passing an emission test, there are a number of things to consider.

* Make sure a good three-way cat is installed and in good working order.
* Ideally the engine should idle with a stoichiometric air/fuel ratio for best cat operation, but engines with long-overlap cams will see relatively larger than normal charge contamination by exhaust gases, which could result in misfires that degrade idle and idle emissions (which is why engines with "big" cams can have a lumpy idle). Engines with big cams that idle poorly may need a richer than stoich idle mixture to eliminate misfires, which can degrade emissions more than a richer idle air/fuel ratio. Turn off Closed Loop mode at idle to prevent the EMS from attempting to undo the richer air/fuel ratio by trimming idle mixtures back toward a dysfunctional stoichiometric mixture. Tune idle air/fuel ratio to achieve the highest possible manifold vacuum.
* Make sure than a long overlap cam is not causing trouble on a speed-density EMS with a pulsating signal to the MAP sensor. Depending on the intake manifold configuration, you may need to build a plenum with references to all intake runners. Some people have had success smoothing out a pulsating MAP signal by installing a 1mm restrictor orifice and a small plastic inline fuel filter in the MAP sensor reference line.
* If an engine seems is hunting at idle, slightly fluctuating rpm and MAP signals may accentuate the problem by causing the EMS to operate from a different speed-density cell. Consider redefining speed-density breakpoint in the EMS timing and VE or fuel tables to bracket conditions at idle so that the operative cell remains the same with small changes in rpm and MAP.

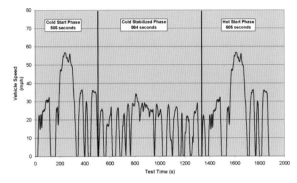

EPA Federal Test Procedure (FTP)
Duration = 1874 seconds, Distance = 11.04 miles, Average Speed = 21.19 mph

- If you are running large, low-impedance fuel injectors and having difficulty with idling, verify that EMS current and timing thresholds are set to optimize the ability to tune tiny changes to injection pulse width in a realm where pulse width is very small compared to the available time for injection.
- To lower emissions by running leaner mixtures during deceleration (which can greatly improve overall fuel economy and allow you to tune more spark advance under such conditions), you may want to define separate ranges for starting verse idle at very low (vacuum) manifold pressure. If the engine has problems with stalling on deceleration, calibrate an anti-stall "wall" of rich air/fuel ratio and advanced timing at rpm just below idle speed and loading just above idle manifold pressure. Idle spark timing itself should be significantly retarded to provide a reserve of torque that will come into play as above to keep the engine from stalling if rpm drops too low, which should give the leeway to maintain a fuel cut on decelerating to a higher rpm.
- To prevent misfires that will greatly amp up HC emissions (and poison the exhaust gas with unburned oxygen that can mislead closed loop EMS operation), make certain the ignition system is in excellent condition by replacing any maintainable components such as spark plugs, plug wires,

rotor, distributor cap, and any other replaceable emissions components such as PCV valve and EGR.
- Make sure the narrowband O_2 sensor or wideband air/fuel ratio sensor is calibrated correctly if the sensor or EMS permit or require this. The narrowband switch point should be 0.450 volts. Wideband should be whatever it needs to be for stoichiometric, usually 2.500 on a 5-volt range sensor.
- Consider retarding ignition timing by a bit (few degrees) to heat up the exhaust gas to prolong the burn and keep the cat(s) good and hot, even though it may amp up the NO_x a bit.
- Consider increasing idle speed a bit, at least 100 rpm above the minimum point at which the engine idles well without stumbling, which will increase intake velocity—which should help to improve fuel vaporization and charge consistency.
- Make sure the thermostat has not been swapped for a low-temperature unit, and consider configuring the electric fan to kick ON in the 200-215 degrees Fahrenheit range, which will tend to reduce engine friction and improve fuel vaporization for more complete combustion and improved consistency between all cylinders.
- Consider changing over from an oiled lifetime aftermarket air cleaner to a standard air cleaner to avoid the possibility that oil in the filter could be sucked into the engine, raising HC emissions.
- Always make certain that the engine is running at full operating temperature before emissions testing to avoid the possibility that 1) the EMS is delivering any warm-up enrichment, 2) unusually cold intake surfaces are adversely impacting combustion efficiency, or 3) the three-way cat is not being warmed enough by hot exhaust gases to operate at full efficiency.
- Consider oxygenating the fuel a bit by filling the tank with a fresh oxygenated blend of gasoline. Depending on where you live, the gasoline may be treated with 5-10 percent alcohol in winter months or year around. Unleaded race gasolines in particular usually achieve their ultra-high octane rating in part with especially high ethanol content or by treating the gasoline with an external source of oxygenation such as ethanol or ether.

	Baseline	Timing Retarded 10°	Timing Advanced 10°	Mixture richened	Mixture leaned
HC	1.00	0.78	1.14	1.39	0.88
CO	14.5	11.6	13.0	81.0	9.8
NO_x	2.91	1.89	5.18	0.71	3.03
O_2 Not usually tested	22.3	19.8	23.8	17.4	25.4
CO_2 Not usually tested	305	307	298	246	310

Testing of spark timing and air/fuel ratio changes on one engine with a MegaSquirt aftermarket standalone EMS and no Cat showed that retarding timing and leaning air/fuel ratio a bit produced the best CO-HC-NOX compromise, increasing NOX slightly. With a cat installed, emissions would be best with a stoichiometric air/fuel ratio and retarded timing. *MegaSquirt*

Chapter 17
Project: Supercharging the 2010 Camaro SS

There are plenty of aftermarket supercharger conversion kits out there. For some common performance vehicles like the 426-horse 2010 Chevy Camaro, you'll find multiple supercharging options, both in terms of competing vendors offering kits for the same vehicle or engine, as well as multiple packages from the same vendor that offer various "stages" of increasing levels of supercharged performance. When it comes to engine management, this chapter is a case study of the simplest type of supercharger conversion, a low-boost Magnusen TVS supercharger on a 2010 Camaro, where a recalibrated stock GM ECM provided the required revised engine management during boost. The "MagnaCharger" kit was designed to deliver power gains of approximately 120 horsepower and 120 lb-ft of torque at the rear wheels at 6-psi boost on 2010–12 Camaro V-8s, turning the vehicle into a 546-horse supercar. Fueling this much horsepower requires upgrading to high-flow electronic fuel injectors.

Most supercharger kit suppliers will tell you their kit has the best numbers, at least in some area, but in fact it is great engine management—not the highest horsepower numbers at some subset of the dyno graph—that is critical to achieving the

kind of drivability that makes a car really perform and genuinely fun to drive.

SUPERCHARGING EMS CONSIDERATIONS

There are a number of critical EMS considerations to keep in mind when considering supercharging a late-model vehicle like the 2010 Camaro.

- Even on a "low-boost" conversion, you need significant engine management changes to provide fuel enrichment and spark retard during boosted operations. But how is this accomplished? Are boost fuel enrichment and spark engine management correct at all breakpoints of engine speed and loading? Some supercharger kits throw a bunch of fuel at the engine under boost conditions that is only really correct under worst-case conditions, like a stopped clock that is right twice a day. The Magnuson kit was designed to get the job done the ideal way, by recalibrating the stock EMS in the boosted portions of the engine-operating envelope.
- Will the kit require super-premium fuel to avoid detonation on your vehicle? Is the kit design conservative enough that you will not be fighting endemic detonation

The 2010 Chevrolet Camaro LS-3V-8 is typical of what you're up against with relatively hot rod–friendly late-model performance vehicles. The Camaro is popular raw material for performance modifications because it appeals to people who like to go fast—and then they want to go even faster. The performance aftermarket tends to focus on vehicles like the Mustang and Camaro because there are plenty of them out there, and in the case of a GM vehicle, the reflashable ECMs have been extensively hacked by multiple ECU-tuning vendors, and installing a power-adder calibration is no problem. For people who like a solid edge, the only modifications worth considering are supercharging, turbocharging, and nitrous injection.

The SCTflash device connects to the J1962 OBD-II port, located within easy reach of the driver's seat under the dash.

When supercharging specialists Magnuson products decided to build a turnkey supercharger kit for the 2010+ Camaro V-8, they developed a calibration on in-house engine and chassis dynamometers and went to SCTuners to create a pre-loaded flash device for the Camaro.

problems if you install the kit correctly and operate the vehicle the way people operate vehicles when they install supercharger conversion kits? In the case of the 2010 Camaro kit, the Magnuson calibration required a minimum of 91-octane premium, which is what there was at California gas stations when the kit was designed. Magnuson recommended using the best street premium available in your state.

- Are the instructions complete and well written, with good supporting drawings, photography, and videos? In the case of the Magnuson kit, all were excellent.
- Does the kit vendor offer high-quality telephone tech support and hand-holding from people who are polite and articulate and know what they're doing? In advance of a sale, will the vendor supply references of customers who made use of tech support? In this case, yes.
- Is the kit emission-legal in all 50 states? Supercharger kits are *never* legal for street use in the United States unless the vehicle is quite old or the supplier has obtained an Environmental Protection Agency (EPA) or California Air Resources Board (CARB) exemption order granted to aftermarket specialty equipment that are able to prove to the EPA or CARB in a rigorous test procedure that proves installation of the product does not degrade emissions

more than 10 percent when operated in a specific driving cycle on a chassis dynamometer. The Magnuson 2010 Camaro kit did indeed have a CARB exemption order, making it legal in all states.

- How much power and torque does a supercharger conversion kit really make as installed? In this case, the Magnuson kit dynoed at 492 horsepower.

INSTALLING THE 2010–12 MAGNUSON KIT

Before installation:
- Run the vehicle nearly out of (regular) fuel and fill up with premium gasoline of at least 91 octane.
- Relieve the fuel system pressure before servicing fuel system components in order to reduce the risk of fire and personal injury. After relieving the system pressure, a small amount of fuel may be released when servicing the fuel lines or connections. In order to reduce the risk of personal injury, cover the regulator and fuel line fittings with a shop towel before disconnecting. This will catch any fuel that may leak out. Place the towel in an approved container when the job is complete.
- Magnuson recommends installing a new GM fuel filter at the time of supercharger installation. Use stock spark plugs with stock plug gap.

Keep in mind:
- Magna Charger Camaro systems are manufactured to produce 20 rwhp per pound of boost at sea level. High altitudes will produce different numbers.

1) Open the SCT Device Updater Software Click the **Load Custom File** button.

2) Click the **Locate Custom Tunes** button.

3) Select Tune to load. If none listed, go back and use the browse button.

4) Select the file position, and type a name for the tune file. Press the **Program** button.

The reflash procedure is quite simple, with a few simple precautions. The engine must NOT be running. The battery must be fully charged, and many people recommend connecting a high-quality battery charger to the battery so than system voltage remains constant throughout the reflash procedure, which requires minutes rather than seconds. A reflash is a serious procedure that can potentially leave the ECM in an inconsistent state and unable to function if interrupted, so NEVER disconnect the flash device until the reflash is complete. Once in a while something goes wrong and you'll never need to run a second reflash. Do not panic.

A special J1962 connector cover that warns against reflashing is a great idea, because some dealers and repair shops routinely update the ECM code to the latest version if the vehicle is ever in for servicing. A dealer reflash will obviously wipe out a special supercharger calibration.

- The kit is designed for engines in good mechanical condition only. Installation on high-mileage or damaged engines is not recommended and could result in engine failure.
- Magna Charger is not responsible for the engine or consequential damages.
- Aftermarket engine recalibration devices that modify fuel and spark curve (including, but not limited to programmers) are not recommended and may cause engine damage or failure.
- Use of non-Magna Charger approved programming will void all warranties.

KIT INSTALLATION PROCEDURE

Basically, you are going to disconnect some stuff around the front and top of the engine, remove the intake manifold and valley cover, remove the fan shroud and disconnect the top radiator support brackets, and remove the serpentine belt. After that, you'll begin modifications: Drill and pin the harmonic balancer and install a replacement valley cover with added clearance, the supercharger-intercooler-intake assembly, the intercooler water-cooler heat exchanger in front of the radiator, and the intercooler pump and reservoir. Move some OE parts like the throttle body from components that will not be needed like the stock intake manifold to the supercharger. Finally you're going to reinstall some stock parts such as the airbox/MAF assembly, and then rock 'n' roll.

The installation manual is detailed and exhaustive, but the specific procedures for supercharger kit installation begin with preparation: Drive the car until it is virtually out of fuel and fill it up with premium fuel. It is critical that the tank is virtually empty before fueling up with premium, as regular fuel can detonate and damage your engine within seconds, especially if the fuel is old (for example if it's a project vehicle that has been sitting for a long time, particularly in hot weather, which can boil off the high-octane components of gasoline first).

With premium fuel in the tank, you're ready to begin the installation. The first thing to do is to reflash the stock onboard computer.

REFLASHING THE CAMARO E38 PCM

When you convert an engine to supercharging, you need to retard spark timing during boost to account for the higher flame speed for supercharged combustion and maintain or even increase the richness of the air/fuel ratio when the airflow increases during boost. Lean mixtures and overly advanced spark timing under boost can damage the engine within seconds the first time you accelerate hard. The designers of Magnuson Products' 2010–12 Camaro supercharger kit handled fuel and timing changes

ADDITIONAL REFLASH CAPABILITIES

SCT SF3 Power Flash modules for the 2010–13 Camaro SS V-8s were designed to interface with Windows PC software that allowed data and program files to be downloaded over the Internet to a PC and transferred to the SF3 unit via USB cable. At this time of writing, generic SF3 functionality included

Diagnostic codes—Reads and clears OBD-II DTC trouble codes.

Dual analog inputs—Monitors EGT temps, air-fuel ratio and other popular sensor data.

Adjustable parameters—These are user adjustable parameters for tuning your own vehicle.

Rear O_2s disabled—Disables the rear O_2s and eliminates CEL caused by rear O_2 removal.

Fuel injectors—Allows you to adjust for different sized fuel injectors.

CMCV delete plates—Allows you to disable the Charge Motion Control Valve (CMCV) in your vehicles PCM to prevent a check engine light and other issues associated with removing the CMCV plates in your vehicle.

Speed limiter—Allows you to remove, increase, or decrease the vehicles speed limiter.

Idle speed—Allows you to increase or decrease the vehicles idle speed.

Traction control—Allows you to disable the vehicle's traction control without using the button in the vehicle.

Spark modification by rpm—Allows you to add or remove timing by rpm range. (0–2,000)(2,000–4,000) (4,000–8,000)

WOT fuel—Allows you to add or remove fuel at wide open throttle.

Shift firmness control—Allows you to change automatic transmission shift pressure. Controls how firm the shifts will feel.

Axle ratio—Allow you to set the axle ratio (gear ratio) to correct shift patterns and the speedometer on your vehicle.

Tire size—Allows you to set the tire size to correct shift patterns and the speedometer on your vehicle.

Store stock tune—Stores a true copy of your vehicle's stock file before programming. Typically used for warranty repairs and unlocking the programmer.

Supports custom tune—Supports and holds up to three custom tunes.

Fan control—Lowers the temperature at which the fan turns on.

Rev/rpm limiter in drive—Allows you to remove, increase, or decrease the vehicle's rev/rpm limiter in drive.

Rev/rpm limiter neutral—Allows you to remove, increase, or decrease the vehicles rev/rpm limiter in neutral.

Speed limiter—Allows you to remove, increase, or decrease the vehicles speed limiter.

Fan control—Lowers the temperature at which the fan turns on.

Axle ratio—Allow you to set the axle ratio (gear ratio) to correct shift patterns and the speedometer on your vehicle.

WOT shift points by gear—Allows you to increase or decrease the wide open throttle shift points of each gear individually.

by building a custom blower calibration for the stock ECM on a chassis dyno, which was propagated into Magnuson kit installations with an SF3 Power Flash programmer module from SCTuners. Reflashing the stock ECM should be the first step before installing the rest of the supercharger kit, which will make sure that no one tries to drive the supercharged car without proper tuning after the kit is installed.

Magnuson MP2300 supercharger/manifold/ intercooler assembly for GM LS3 V8.

Magnuson 2010-2011 Camaro SS supercharger kit.

The SCT SF3 Power Flash programmer, which becomes VIN-locked to the vehicle once it is used, is equipped with an OBD-II cable designed to interface between the SCT SF3 Power Flash and the Camaro PCM. The 2010 Camaro OBD-II cable/port can be used to (1) re-program the stock ECM, (2) datalog from the PCM, and (3) view parameters in real-time. The Camaro is located, as on all OBD-II vehicles, within easy reach of the driver, in this case under the dash on the left side of the car. Some OBD-II connectors are equipped with a cap covering the pin connector that are labeled as a diagnostic port, and if the vehicle had previously been reflashed with, say, a premium fuel performance calibration before it was supercharged, it may have a special "*do not reflash*" cap on the OBD-II connector installed to prevent dealers or other tuners from accidentally erasing the performance reflash.

The SCT SF3 programming module comes equipped with interface software and a USB connection for communicating between the SF3 and a Windows PC, which allows you to update the SF3 module with new data files downloaded to the PC over the Internet from SCT. There are six main keys on the SF3 Power Flash keypad. The arrow-up and arrow-down keys are the primary keys used to scroll through the main menu and submenu options. The arrow left and right keys can be used within the submenu screens to view multiple options or other features. The select key chooses individual menus or submenus and selects options. The cancel key de-selects or cancels operations in the submenus and allows you to go back to the last screen viewed.

BEFORE YOU BEGIN

- Remove the fuel pump fuse and fan fuse. Be sure heater fans, windshield wipers, or any other current draw is minimized during flashing.

- Do *not* interrupt the flashing process once it has begun, by disconnecting the cable of battery or pulling the diagnostic cable.
- Never attempt to reflash on the fly or with the engine running. This will damage the SF3 Power Flash and processor.

ACTUAL REFLASH PROCEDURE

1. With the engine stopped and key off, plug the programming module into the vehicle's OBD-II port, which will power up the module.
2. Leave the ignition key in the OFF position and select the SF3 **program vehicle** main menu option to begin.
3. When the **program vehicle** submenu appears, use the arrow up and down keys to navigate to the menu option you want. The **install tune** option is the default. To program a tune file, press the select key to enter the install tune submenu. The **pre-loaded tune option** is the default.
4. Press the select key. You will be prompted to turn the key on without starting the motor, which will begin the tuning process.

5. During the reflash process you will be prompted to turn the ignition key on and off multiple times *without starting the vehicle*. *Do not* unplug the OBD-II cable at any point during this process.

6. Completely loading the Magnuson supercharger calibration may take around 5 to 7 minutes, after which it is safe to remove the device from the OBD-II port and start your engine.

7. In the event the SF3 Power Flash does not successfully flash the vehicle it will display an error message. If this happens, you must recover the ECU. Turn the key off and program the vehicle with the *return to stock* option, at which point you can make a second attempt.

With the Camaro reflashed and the GM E38 engine control module ready to provide supercharging engine management via upgrade fuel injectors, you can now proceed to install the rest of the supercharger kit. The main procedures include:

- Remove a bunch of small external stuff: battery, fuel cap, engine cover, air box and air inlet tube, vent tube, heater hoses, fuel line, radiator overflow, steam vent hose, fan shroud assembly, harmonic balancer bolt, serpentine belt, belt-tensioner pulley, wire loom covers, and two direct-fire coil brackets with four coils. Drain the radiator. Disconnect certain vacuum, PCV, and emissions hoses. Remove the EMS sensor and actuators: MAP sensor, eight stock fuel injectors, throttle body.

- Drill the harmonic balancer and install two pins that positively prevent additional load on the crank pulley from twisting the balancer; install a new harmonic balancer bolt.

- Remove the OEM intake manifold, and replace the OE valley cover with new unit.

- Install intercooler water-cooler and heat-exchanger in front of the radiator.

- Install the supercharger assembly on the block after installing the MAP sensor, electronic throttle, throttle O-ring, and brake boost valve from the stock intake manifold.

- Install replacement high-flow fuel injectors, replacement (smaller) belt tensioner pulley, electronic throttle (ETC) extension harness, MAP sensor extension harness, new heater hoses, replacement fuel line, replacement intake air temp (IAT) connector, various EVAP, PCV, brake booster hoses, add-on check valves, and PCV hoses. Install the replacement (extended) serpentine belt. Reinstall the air box/MAF unit and plug in the harness connector.

- Clamp the intercooler pump and reservoir bottle to the vehicle frame rail. Cut the I/C cooler hoses to length and route to the various hose barbs. Install wiring for intercooler water-cooling system. Fill the intercooler system with 50-50 antifreeze. Refill the cooling system with (saved) water-antifreeze solution.

- Affix the replacement vacuum hose diagram and belt-routing diagram in a conspicuous place and attach the "Use Premium Fuel Only" decal to the gas tank fill cap or door.

- Test the supercharged engine: Start and run the engine without driving and check for leaks. Shut off the engine and check engine and intercooler fluids and top off if necessary. Some people believe in jacking up the vehicle to help bleed out air. Test drive the vehicle for a few miles under ordinary driving conditions, listening for any abnormal noises, vibrations, misfires, or anything else

that does not seem normal. You will hear the supercharger make a slight whining noise under boost conditions. After the initial test drive, stop and retension the serpentine belt after the initial test drive. As you gain confidence that all is well, work gradually up to full-throttle runs. It is *critical* to *listen carefully for detonation*, which sounds something like bees rattling against metal. If you hear any knock, something is definitely wrong when it's a turnkey supercharger kit like the Magnuson 2010 Camaro system, which should work perfectly out of the box. *Throttle back instantly to prevent very rapid engine damage!* The most likely cause of knock is regular fuel left in the tank, but do not run the engine under boost again until you investigate thoroughly and figure out what is wrong. Assuming you didn't try anything unusual—like installing custom overdrive blower pulleys in the initial installation—by far the most likely scenario is that the Camaro will work perfectly and kick ass from the get-go.

- Last but not least, get ready to rock 'n' roll!

1. Camaro engine cover before removal.

2. Removing the stock Camaro intake manifold.

3. Installing the air-water intercooler heat exchanger in front of the stock radiator.

4. Installing gaskets on the blower intake manifold before installation.

5. Lowering the supercharger assembly into place on the Camaro engine. Get help.

6. Bolting down the supercharger manifold.

7. Ribbed supercharger pulley drive (top), idler pulley (left), and tensioner.

8. Camaro SS with installed Magnuson supercharger kit, ready to rock 'n' roll.

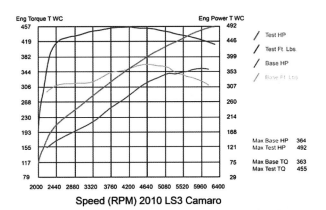

9. Before and After dyno results. The blower kit adds over a hundred lb-ft torque, pretty much everywhere, which translates to a peak power increase from 364 to 492 at 6,400 rpm, a gain of 128 horsepower.

Chapter 18
Project: Twin-Turbo Lexus IS-F

Q: How do you turbocharge a Lexus IS-F with a 416-horsepower, direct-injection V-8 with 11.8:1 compression?

A: Very *carefully.*

The IS-F arrived in the United States in 2007 with a 416-horsepower four-cam 5.0L V-8 pushing around 3,780 pounds of tuner car via the world's first eight-speed automatic transmission—aimed like a rocket straight at the M in BMW M3. My brother bought a '08 model, which I drove often enough to know that when you've got 416 horsepower and a really elegant modern eight-speed transmission with sophisticated torque-based engine/transmission controls, there is *always* more than enough torque under your right foot to go wild at a moment's notice under any and all conditions. And I do mean *always.*

When Dallas supertuner and exotic car builder Bob Norwood decided to hot rod a '08 IS-F with forced induction, he had as much or more experience with ultra-high-performance street and race engines as anyone in the world.

He was going to need it.

In order to avoid the U.S. gas-guzzler tax while meeting the highest standards of exhaust emissions and maximum power, the IS-F was equipped with gasoline-direct injection (G-DI). G-DI engines are able to run in three distinct fuel delivery modes with very high efficiency, including full power, stoichiometric, and ultra lean burn. G-DI engines achieve very high fuel efficiency at idle and light cruise with stratified air/fuel mixtures relatively rich near the spark plug but too lean overall for ordinary port EFI. In some cases, G-DI engines further improve fuel efficiency by operating with the throttle wide open at very low power settings to avoid throttle-induced pumping losses, which requires very precise engine-management algorithms executed by powerful ECMs with enhanced memory and processing capabilities.

The G-DI IS-F was equipped with extremely sophisticated electronic engine management that made use of MAF-based, high-authority AFR-sensing, torque-based electronic throttle control, quad spark-knock sensors, variable cam phasing, variable runner area, variable plenum volume, air-grabber hood, 11.8:1 compression, traction control, and something like 17—count 'em, 17!—onboard electronic control units that collaborated with each other to kick ass and take names by communicating on at least two onboard controller area (CAN) networks. On this type of system, accelerator pedal position is interpreted as a request for torque rather than a particular throttle position, leaving it up to the ECM how to fulfill the driver's torque request. With traction control disabled, an IS-F will smoke

2008 Lexus IS-F with twin-turbo conversion. The stock 416-horse IS-F was an extremely sophisticated factory tuner car designed to take on the BMW M3 with Gasoline-Direct Injection and every performance trick in the book except forced induction. Many people were looking for a way to amp up the performance to supercar levels, but Toyota Motor Company is one of the least hot rod–friendly carmakers in the world, and ECU tuning is virtually impossible, making hot rodding the IS-F a radically difficult project. Dallas supertuner Bob Norwood employed twin turbochargers, a Split Second piggyback interceptor, and Motec ECM controlling auxiliary fuel injectors to add over 100 horsepower.

Strapping the stock IS-F to a Dynojet chassis dynamometer to get baseline power and torque results. The 4-cam engine delivered about 365 horsepower at the wheels, indicating drivetrain and tire rolling loses below 14 percent, which is excellent.

IS-F 2UR-GSE powerplant with the engine cover removed. There is an engine under the plastic.

the tires unmercifully. If the wheels start to slip when traction control is active, the ECM immediately scrams throttle, sucking the oxygen out of the car's performance in a heartbeat.

Anyone looking to hot rod a G-DI IS-F using forced induction (and *lots* of people were aching to do exactly that for a number of reasons, not the least of which was the desire to cut their teeth on hot rodding G-DI, the performance engine of the future) would need to modify fuel delivery and spark timing to provide boosted combustion within the context of a stock ECM designed to deliver torque-based engine management. Torque-based engine management means the IS-F is equipped with a sophisticated multi-dimensional model of the implications for torque of myriad interactions involving G-DI combustion mode, variable intake configuration, variable valve timing, spark timing, fuel mass delivery, fuel timing, throttle position, gear selection, shift firmness, torque convertor slip, and so forth. Not your father's engine management system.

Setting aside the fact that an IS-F has one of the most complex and sophisticated production engine management systems on planet earth, improving the performance of *any* premium-fuel stock 5.0L powerplant already making 400 horsepower and change at nearly 7,000 rpm is not for the faint of heart. A stock 3,780-pound IS-F is capable of a 0–60 time of 4.2 seconds and 12.6 in the quarter, governed to 170 mph at the top end. Other than establishing the luxury IS-F's redline at 6,800 rpm—far below the 8,000 redline of an M3—Lexus engineers had used every other trick in the book to make a lot of all-motor power on premium pump gasoline. Including 11.8:1 compression. What is the *effective* compression ratio of an 11.8 engine boosted to, say, 5 psi positive manifold pressure? A lot! Try 16:1. The risk of detonation is really all about brake mean effective pressure, which depends on a lot of things, including camshaft specs. Yes, you can flood an engine with fuel or water injection and pull timing like crazy to fight detonation. Texas tuners working with 93-octane street premium have a little more slack than California tuners forced to deal with 91-octane California gasoline, but wherever you are, if you're hot rodding an 11.8:1 engine, you're definitely going to want stellar engine management and the best fuel you can get to keep such an engine running on the happy side of engine-killing spark knock.

REFLASH ME?

Hot rodding the calibration of a G-DI engine management system is obviously not for the faint of heart, but in the case of the

DI-G COMBUSTION MODES

G-DI engine management systems are far more complex than port injection due to the fact that G-DI systems dynamically choose between three combustion modes on an ongoing basis: full power output, stoichiometric, and ultra lean burn, the difference being widely varying target air/fuel ratios and the tactics required to achieve them. The stoichiometric (chemically ideal) air-fuel mass ratio for gasoline is 14.7:1, but G-DI ultra-lean mode can deliver ratios up to 65:1 (or even leaner in some engines for very limited periods).

Full power mode is used for high-loading situations such as hard acceleration, steep hills, or trailer towing, when maximum power is required. Fuel is injected into the combustion chamber at up to 3,000 psi during the intake stroke. The air-fuel mixture is homogeneous and richer than stoichiometric, typically 12.0–13.0 in the case of non-boosted powerplants, or even richer in the case of knock-limited high-output forced-induction engines that use excess fuel as an anti-detonation countermeasure. After the first fuel charge has been ignited, with direct injection it is uniquely possible to inject additional fuel as the piston descends. The benefit of injecting fuel more than once is increased power and fuel efficiency, but exhaust valve erosion has been observed with certain octane fuels.

Stoichiometric mode is used for moderate engine loading. Fuel is still injected during the intake stroke, creating a homogeneous air/fuel mixture throughout the combustion chambers. For reasons related to the scarcity of oxygen in most spark-ignition piston engines, stoichiometric combustion delivers less torque than richer AFRs but results in relatively clean exhaust with balanced NOx, hydrocarbon, and CO emissions suitable for further cleaning by catalytic converter.

Ultra lean burn or stratified charge mode, is used for light loading at constant or reducing engine speeds, and it can only be accomplished with direct injection. Fuel is injected and ignited *late in the compression stroke* in a toroidal- or ovoidal-shaped concavity in the surface of the piston as it approaches the roof of the combustion chamber. Depending on the location of the direct injector, the combustion cavity may be centrally located in the piston crown or displaced to side. The cavity is architected to induce charge swirl that places a small cloud of air/fuel mixture locally rich enough to be combustible optimally close to the spark plug electrode. The combustible charge is surrounded by air and residual gases that keep the fuel and the flame away from the cylinder walls. Decreased combustion temperatures lower NOx formation, and reduced heat losses and gas dilation deliver additional torque.

Operating modes of a Gasoline-Direct Injection powerplant. In addition to operating in stoichiometric and full-power modes, in which fuel injection occurs during the intake stroke, G-DI engines like the IS-F can operate with extremely high fuel efficiency in stratified charge mode under very light cruise loading or deceleration by injecting fuel into a combustion pocket formed by the head and a cavity in the piston crowns late in the compression stroke. The charge air/fuel mixture is normal in the vicinity of the spark plug, but surrounded by almost pure air, for an overall air/fuel ratio of up to 65:1.

Stratified mode

Homogeneous mode

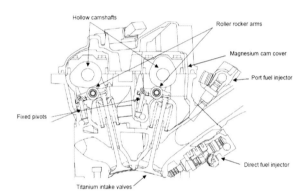

Rather than using hydraulic lifters, the IS F twin-cam aluminum DOHC cylinder heads was designed with low-friction rocker arms that pivot on fixed points, which helps ensure accurate valve operation. Due to their minimal weight, titanium intake valves can be very large in diameter. The lightweight hollow camshafts were mirror-polished to minimize friction. The result? Low friction and light weight permit a high-lift, high speed valvetrain designed that provides maximum all-motor performance and efficiency at 6,600 rpm, far less than the 8K rpm redline of a BMW M3. The heads are equipped with lightweight magnesium cam covers.

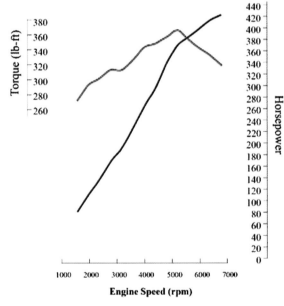

Stock IS-F dyno graph published by Lexus. Power increases above 420 at 7,000 RPM, but the engine has a 6,600 rpm redline, at which the engine is good for 416 horses.

IS-F, it was a moot point because the engine was built by Toyota Motor Company, which has to be the least hot rod friendly of any major car company in the world. If there was a way to design an electronic control unit with an architecture that requires hardware modifications to alter calibration data, Toyota found a way. If there was a way to select a microprocessor architecture in which non-volatile memory was embedded into the processor chip, Toyota made it happen. If there was a way to design a non-standard OBD-II interface, Toyota got the job done. And when Toyota was forced by the U.S. government to design an engine management system serviceable and reflash-able by independent repair shops using OBD-II/CAN diagnostic tools, they designed nearly bulletproof anti-tampering security requiring a secure download targeted at one specific vehicle and designed the ECU so that it could be reflashed once—and only once—at which point you needed a new ECU. Well, unless you had the expertise (and the cajones) to 1) de-solder and extract the flash memory device from the ECM motherboard, 2) dump the contents of memory, 3) separate the code from the data, 4) reverse-engineer the meaning of the data and what it means in terms of engine

management, 5) modify the calibration to hot rod the engine, 6) write the revised calibration on a new flash memory device, and 7) solder the memory device back onto the motherboard. Any or all of which could be illegal due to the Digital Millennium Copyright Act of 1997 (DMCA).

There have been a number of aftermarket outfits claiming to provide custom Toyota ECU reflashing, but when it comes down to it, the only outfit known to have a valid hot rod reflash that was definitely more than vaporware in the immediate years following IS-F introduction was Toyota Racing Development (TRD), which operated semi-independently of Toyota Motor Company to provide specialty performance parts for selected late-model Toyota vehicles that allowed the owner to retain the factory warranty. Over the years, TRD had marketed a number of low-boost supercharger kits designed to function with the stock ECM recalibration, but when TRD decided the Scion tC supercharger

0-60 magazine based their IS-F hot rodding project around a positive-displacement supercharger. This type of blower produces highly predictable boost pressure.

Fox Marketing's IS-F was turbocharged, but used rear-mounted turbos. The turbos and plumbing look great from the back, and there's plenty of room, but the location far from the exhaust manifolds can lose heat energy. *Fox Marketing*

kit *really* needed an ECM reflash, they were rumored to have made an end run around Toyota's conservative attitude regarding aftermarket performance and gained ECM access for certain Toyota trucks and SUVs by hiring a Denso engineer experienced with the Denso electronic control units that provided Toyota engine and vehicle management. Then someone in the larger Toyota organization assigned a calibration engineer to build a special ECM reflash calibration for TRD supercharger kits and made it available through the service departments of Toyota dealers as part of the Toyota Technical Information System (TIS) download/reflash system. Unfortunately, TRD's supercharging calibration was designed for Toyota trucks with port EFI, not for a three-mode G-DI powerplant with electronic throttle and torque-based engine management and the rest of it. And in any case, TRD wanted nothing to do with a hot-rod Lexus ISF.

"TRD wouldn't even talk," said Norwood. "There was NO way to reflash the Lexus ECM."

Again, assuming you even wanted to, given the likelihood that reworking the stock calibration to handle forced induction while retaining Lexus-type drivability could be an R&D project of near-biblical proportions.

FORCING INDUCTION

In any case, engine management aside, an IS-F forced-induction conversion by itself is not for the faint of heart.

Simply installing a V-8 into an IS at the factory was a significant challenge. The F project that shoehorned a 5.0L V-8 engine into a space designed to accommodate inline-four and V-6 IS 250/350 engines required a variety of vehicle and engine modifications, including a carbon hood with a V-8–sized hood bulge. Aftermarket tuners contemplating where to put turbochargers in an ISF were staring at a sea of mechanical equipment filling up the engine compartment. Some blinked and retreated to the idea of an Eaton-type positive-displacement blower, which required an even higher custom hood and significant engine and induction modifications. Almost without exception, turbo conversions for the ISF, when they arrived, took the easy way out, installing rear-mount twin turbos under the chassis at the rear corners of the vehicle just ahead of the exhaust tips, routing boost-air 15 feet forward to intercoolers at the far front of the 183.5-inch vehicle—and from there several feet backward to the top of the engine. You can lose a fair amount of turbine energy in 12 feet of exhaust, which is definitely not

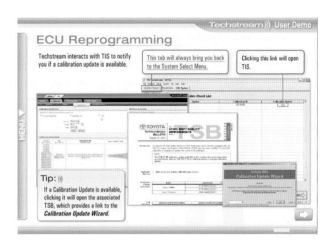

Modern Toyota ECMs can be reflashed using the Techstream ECU reprogramming system, but you need to be a dealer or an independent repair shop willing to fork over thousands to subscribe to the online-calibration download service. The only reflash calibrations available were stock Toyota or TRD supercharger calibrations, and each download was targeted at a specific vehicle, and the ECM could only be reflashed ONCE, after which it must be replaced. At this time of writing it was not clear that a single aftermarket ECU tuning vendor had managed to crack Toyota's ECM reflash security, meaning that the only way to modify the flash memory device was to de-solder the Toyota memory/processor chip and dump the contents for analysis. Digital Copyright legislation in the U.S. makes it a federal crime in some cases to hack or reverse-engineer computer software.

helpful if you're looking for low-rpm boost. You're never going to see rear-mounted turbos on a factory vehicle, but if you're an aftermarket tuner, you do what's gotta be done.

You compromise.

Not Bob Norwood. With a five-axis CNC mill available to carve custom parts out of stainless steel and aluminum, Norwood set about building what would be the most space-critical turbo system he'd ever had to design among several scores of custom turbo systems in a lifetime of exotic hot rodding. The trick was working with extremely compact turbochargers, in this case Garret GT28-series turbos with Tial stainless turbine housings that made use of V-band turbine inlet plumbing and a remote wastegate. With enormous

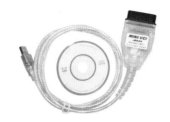

Mini VCI USB-OBD-II interface cable allows a flash device to interface to the Toyota/Lexus ECM for diagnostics or reflash, but you need the security seed for reflashing.

Tial GT2871R turbocharger consists of a Garret compressor and center section mated to a custom Tial stainless steel turbine housing with extremely compact design requiring an external wastegate. Space for turbochargers below the IS-F exhaust headers is tight, to say the least. Note V-band turbine inlet and outlet connection.

The IS-F twin-turbo project made use of twin Tial external wastegates, with boost pressure seen at the wastegate actuators tightly managed by Motec PWM boost-control logic driving a boost-control solenoid that raises maximum boost by limiting the amount of manifold pressure reference available at the wastegate actuator.

Norwood IS-F twin turbo system. In some cases clearance is measured in fractions of an inch.

Tial turbos mount on exhaust heads using a V-band connection that avoids wrenching bolts in very tight spaces. Turbos mount ahead of the cats, which are relocated slightly downstream.

IS-F dual intercooler system under construction. Limiting combustion temperatures was critical to avoiding detonation on an engine with 11.65:1 compression.

Split Second Fuel/Timing Calibrator FTC1 interceptor allowed Norwood Autocraft to: one, prevent the Lexus ECM from instigating countermeasure against air flow signals above 4.6 volts; two, retard spark advance by delaying the Crank Ref signal to the stock ECM; and three, manage the wideband AFR signal to prevent the stock ECM from fighting the Motec under boost when eight auxiliary port fuel injectors kicked in to provide boost-appropriate rich air/fuel mixtures designed to increase power and fight spark knock.

Lexus IS-F turbo boost fuel enrichment system consisted of adding eight additional fuel injectors under Motec control. Note the twin D-section auxillary fuel rails (with blue Earl's fittings). Duel to limitations of the stock fuel delivery system, Norwood installed a complete parallel port-injector fuel delivery system with in-tank submersible pump and regulator, with a single fuel line leading to the injector rails on the engine.

difficulty, GT2871R/Tial turbochargers could be made to fit immediately below the IS-F's stainless headers if you relocated the catalysts a short distance downstream.

IS-F ENGINE MANAGEMENT GOALS

When the turbo IS-F project kicked off, there were a number of more or less non-negotiable goals:

- Significantly quicker than stock
- Excellent stock drivability not degraded
- No internal engine modifications required (i.e., retains stock compression ratio)
- Luxury car sound levels not impacted by hot-rodding modifications
- Retain stock knock-control system
- Connects to J1962 OBD-II scan device and works correctly without problems
- Does not obviously fail emissions testing

Project Chronology

With agreed-upon goals, the project proceeded as follows:

1. Set modification strategy:
   a) Twin turbocharger in the engine compartment
   b) Dual air-air intercoolers in front of stock A/C condenser and radiator
   c) Stock ECM running the engine all the time
   d) Interceptor piggyback modifying/censoring input data to the ECM in a way that keeps the ECM happy enough to prevent it from setting malfunction codes or, worse, going into limp-mode
   e) Fuel-only port-injection system managed independently by Motec M4-8, operating in parallel to the stock ECM
2. The first thing was to connect a CAN-capable OBD-II scan tool with datalogging to the car and observe the air/fuel ratio during all modes of driving. The scan tool revealed that the ECM delivered AFR as rich as 12.1 AFR (0.82

lambda) at maximum torque rpm (5,200) as a safety margin on a premium-fuel engine with a high static compression ratio. This was good news, because a well-designed turbo engine running moderate boost should be able to function at 0.82 lambda at maximum loading. It meant that the Lexus EMS would probably tolerate moderately richer full-throttle mixtures in open loop mode and that the ECM would definitely not be trying to lean out AFR above 0.82 lambda under any circumstances at heavy loading in closed loop mode. It should be possible to control spark knock with achievable AFRs and retarded timing.

3. After extensive street time flogging the piss out of the IS-F with datalogging enabled, Norwood conducted official "before" dynoruns on a Dynojet 248C inertial chassis dynamometer with all instrumentation in place. The 416 crankshaft horsepower at 6,600 rpm translated to 360 wheel horsepower, indicating 13.5 percent drivetrain/rolling losses.

Twin-turbo Lexus IS-F engine. FTC1 interceptor is located near the front on the passenger side of the engine.

					LOAD (%)						
		0	10	20	30	40	50	60	70	80	90	100
	1000	0	12.0	24.0	36.0	48.0	60.0	72.0	84.0	96.0	108.0	120.0
	2000	0	6.0	12.0	18.0	24.0	30.0	36.0	42.0	48.0	54.0	60.0
	3000	0	4.0	8.0	12.0	16.0	20.0	24.0	28.0	32.0	36.0	40.0
	4000	0	3.0	6.0	9.0	12.0	15.0	18.0	21.0	24.0	27.0	30.0
RPM	5000	0	2.4	4.8	7.2	9.6	12.0	14.4	16.8	19.2	21.6	24.0
	6000	0	2.0	4.0	6.0	8.0	10.0	12.0	14.0	16.0	18.0	20.0
	7000	0	1.7	3.5	5.2	7.0	8.7	10.4	12.2	13.9	15.7	17.4
	8000	0	1.5	3.0	4.5	6.0	7.5	9.0	10.5	12.0	13.5	15.0

Theoretical Injection Pulsewidth (ms)

Figure 1. Theoretical Injection Map. The numbers in the 100% column are based on 100% injector duty cycle at indicated engine rpm. At 8,000 rpm the cam rotates 360° in 15ms. Actual injector duty cycle will generally not exceed 80%.

					LOAD (%)						
		0	10	20	30	40	50	60	70	80	90	100
	1000	0	12.0	24.0	36.0	48.0	60.0	72.0	84.0	96.0	108.0	120.0
	2000	0	6.0	12.0	18.0	24.0	30.0	36.0	42.0	48.0	54.0	60.0
	3000	0	4.0	8.0	12.0	16.0	20.0	24.0	28.0	32.0	36.0	40.0
RPM	4000	0	3.0	6.0	9.0	12.0	15.0	18.0	21.0	24.0	27.0	30.0
	5000	0	2.4	4.8	7.2	9.6	12.0	14.4	16.8	19.2	21.6	24.0
	6000	0	2.0	4.0	6.0	8.0	10.0	12.0	14.0	16.0	18.0	20.0
	7000	0	1.7	3.5	5.2	7.0	8.7	10.4	12.2	13.9	15.7	17.4
	8000	0	1.5	3.0	4.5	6.0	7.5	9.0	10.5	12.0	13.5	15.0

Theoretical Injection Pulsewidth (ms)

Figure 2. Traces for Various Throttle Inputs. The blue trace shows WOT from low rpm. The green trace shows a throttle lift from the high rpm. The red trace shows progressive application of throttle with WOT at 8,000 rpm. *Split Second*

					LOAD (%)						
		0	10	20	30	40	50	60	70	80	90	100
	1000	0	12.0	24.0	36.0	48.0	60.0	72.0	84.0	96.0	108.0	120.0
	2000	0	6.0	12.0	18.0	24.0	30.0	36.0	42.0	48.0	54.0	60.0
	3000	0	4.0	8.0	12.0	16.0	20.0	24.0	28.0	32.0	36.0	40.0
	4000	0	3.0	6.0	9.0	12.0	15.0	18.0	21.0	24.0	27.0	30.0
RPM	5000	0	2.4	4.8	7.2	9.6	12.0	14.4	16.8	19.2	21.6	24.0
	6000	0	2.0	4.0	6.0	8.0	10.0	12.0	14.0	16.0	18.0	20.0
	7000	0	1.7	3.5	5.2	7.0	8.7	10.4	12.2	13.9	15.7	17.4
	8000	0	1.5	3.0	4.5	6.0	7.5	9.0	10.5	12.0	13.5	15.0

Theoretical Injection Pulsewidth (ms)

Figure 3. Piggyback Fuel Calibration Range. The fuel mixture can be precisely controlled by varying the load signal input to the ECM for every combination of load and rpm. Fuel is adjusted by moving around on the stock map table. *Split Second*

4. With "before" performance established, Norwood Autocraft designed and built a twin turbo system on the IS-F with two huge front-mounted air-air intercoolers.

5. After investigating a number of interceptor piggyback options, the project team installed a Split Second FTC1-017B Toyota interceptor, a sophisticated laptop-configurable piggyback interceptor with 3D load/rpm-based timing retard and airflow increase/decrease tables capable of increasing or decreasing fuel delivery by 20 percent in either direction.

6. At this point, they removed the stock intake manifold and plenum and machined it to accept eight weld-in port injector bosses in the intake runners, and installed eight cc/min Bosch peak-and-hold fuel injectors and twin D-section fuel rails with adjustable fuel pressure regulator and plumbed supply and return lines into the low-pressure section of the Lexus G-DI fuel system.

7. Now the Norwood team installed a Motec M4-8 ECM with a two-bar manifold absolute pressure (MAP) sensor and a calibration designed to provide null supplemental fuel delivery below engine loading of 100 kPa airflow, with fuel delivery increasing progressively as engine loading increased into positive boost *above* one-bar MAP.

8. The M4-8 also managed a PWM boost controller that regulated the amount of manifold pressure reference seen at the Tial wastegates set up with 3-psi nominal wastegate spring pressure, such that the Motec could deliver boost pressure anywhere from 3 psi to blowup.

9. Meanwhile, the FTC1 was configured to
a) Progressively retard spark advance during boost as far as 6 degrees later than normal Lexus ignition timing by delaying the crank trigger signal to the ECM.
b) Clamp MAF voltage to less than 4.6V to prevent fuel cut.
c) Optionally manage reported AFR from wideband sensors to prevent malfunction codes.
d) Optionally manage reported closed-loop G-DI common fuel rail pressure in a way that caused the Lexus ECM to increase stock injection pressure.

e) Optionally increase fuel in non-boosted areas of the operating envelope by misreporting the MAF signal to compensate for unintended artifacts of Interceptor operation (see sidebar).

10. Initial FTC1 modifications resulted in a number of problems:
    a) Timing error at startup
    b) Crank sensor voltage error
    c) Lean mixture on bank one or two

11. After concluding that FTC1-017B was failing to react quickly enough to prevent the Lexus ECM from repeatedly setting malfunction codes, Split Second upgraded the IS-F's FTC1 to a more powerful Split Second E-model processor custom-tailored as a Lexus-specific interceptor with integral Split Second EGO Signal Conditioner functionality.

12. The FTC1-102 solved most check engine problems, though the Norwood team still encountered lean mixture on bank one or two about once a week.

13. Meanwhile, the IS-F turbo system began delivering measurable boost at 2,100 rpms.

14. After extensive dyno testing, Bob Norwood calibrated the FTC1 to pull 6 degrees of timing at 6-psi boost. During the tuning process, the slightest spark knock detected by any of the IS-F's four knock sensors caused immediate aggressive throttle closure and massive ignition retard by the Lexus ECM.

15. With the IS-F working reasonably well at 6-psi boost, with power up by nearly 100 crankshaft horsepower at 5,500 rpms, Bob Norwood experimented by cranking up the boost to as much as 12-psi positive pressure. With the FTC1 retarding timing and the Motec M4-8 pouring fuel into the 5.0L IS-F powerplant, it was possible to avoid detonation under all conditions.

16. However, at boost above 6 psi, the IS-F engine was too powerful and accelerated too fast. The IS-F's internal tables must permit the maximum acceleration under heavy load achievable at maximum throttle going down a steep hill, but beyond that, there are limits. Depending on the gear, too much boost increased torque beyond the allowable slew rate in the ECM's internal tables for various combinations of torque and rpm—that is, the maximum allowable rate of increase in engine speed achievable by a stock engine under best-case conditions plus a margin—which would cause the ECM to instigate retard timing to kill performance. The fuel cut could be partially or completely overcome by programming the Motec to pour in fuel, but the engine sounded very pissed off, and when slew rate and torque got too high, the ECM instigated a rotating fuel cut that killed performance.

17. The trick was to prevent the engine from over-torqueing itself. Bob Norwood discovered that the ECM would tolerate higher levels of peak torque at full throttle if you used the paddle-shifters to manually upshift at 5,500 rpm instead of allowing the transmission to auto-upshift at even higher rpm, which would trigger ECM throttle push-back.

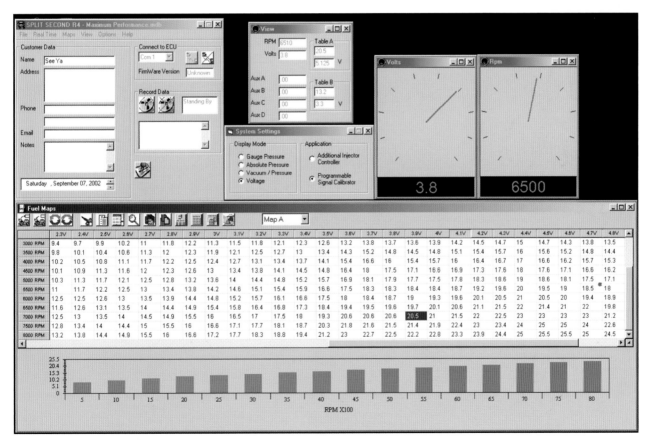

Split Second R4 laptop PC window showing interceptor fuel map.

Chapter 19
Project: Supercharged Jag-Rolet

Here was a company with the vision and cojones to build a multi-carb DOHC cross-flow six in the '40s with more deep-breathing going on than an obscene phone call—at a time when most automobiles were still powered by wheezing flathead powerplants with all the high-technology and specific power of a prewar farm tractor. The Jaguar XK engine powered a legacy of performance sports cars and sport sedans in the glory days that included the XK-120, the D-type, the Mark II sedan, and the legendary E-type—a car so gorgeous there are plenty of car people whose first sight of a new E in full flight will surely pass before their eyes in their final moments.

With such a legacy, one truly has to marvel that Jaguar managed to find the executive "talent" that replaced the E-type with the XJS, introduced some of the more gutless cars to ever carry the "Jaguar" marque in the 1970s and 1980s, and formulated the brilliant strategy of milking a good name rather than wasting time and money producing cars with genuine thoroughbred performance like Porsche or Ferrari or BMW.

Jaguar management did all of the above, but it was downright decent of the company to faithfully make sure there was always sufficient space in the big cat's engine compartment to install an American V-8 without too much fuss. Jaguar also faithfully made sure there'd be a weight reduction as well as a performance advantage to be gained by junking your DOHC Jaguar six or V-12 and installing a dirt-cheap high-performance

pushrod American V-8. For a time, the supply of dirt-cheap gutless Jag sedans in the United States and the even larger supply of Chevrolet small-block V-8 engines made the mating of the two a marriage made in heaven.

It is only now that Ford-owned Jaguar has lashed back viciously against its modern detractors by introducing a scratch-built four-cam V-8 in 1996 that made it a legitimate question whether tuners armed with a humble hot rod pushrod American V-8 as a weapon were still up to the Jaguar factory's challenge. Jaguar's AJ-V-8—supercharged, no less!—delivered up to 420 crankshaft horsepower from 3.2-5.0, which might make you wonder how even the best Chevy-Jag V-8 conversion could possible measure up to the new supercharged V-8 sedan (when it finally arrives in the United States). The follow-on 2009 Jaguar V-8 was a 5.0L powerplant with direction injection, continuously variable cam-phasing, VTEC-like cam profile switching, variable-length intake runners, and optional supercharger with 385-510 horsepower. Of course, there are Corvette LSx engines around with up to 638 horsepower, and there are hot rod GM V-8s with a lot more than that.

Dallas superturner Bob Norwood was the perfect candidate to respond to the latest figurative shots Jaguar had fired across the bow of American V-8 swappers with the newly introduced Jaguar V-8s. Norwood's response was a custom V-8 conversion of a 1990 EFI Jaguar sedan.

Bob Norwood had a fuel-injected late-model Jag sedan with the 4.0-liter inline six—and a love for supercharged Chevy V-8 power. Converting to a hot rod L98 Chevy small block while maintaining all the original engine and chassis electronic functionality would be a massive challenge.

1991 350 Corvette Challenge small block Chevrolet crate motor coming together with Vortech Race supercharger. Note toothed belt for high-boost dyno testing without belt slip, definitely not recommended for street use if you want the blower drive to last.

Norwood chose a 1989 Jaguar XJ6 3.6, which weighs in at more than 4,000 pounds stock, and when he pulled out the 3.6-liter naturally aspirated Jaguar six, he had to cut a claw and a half from each of the front springs to lower the ride height due to the nearly 200-pound weight advantage of a 1991 5.7L Chevy small-block V-8, with Motec programmable engine management and a Vortech high-efficiency S-Trim centrifugal supercharger—along with a GM 4L80E programmable four-speed overdrive electronic transmission. The brand-new Chevy engine that arrived in Dallas straight from GM in a crate was something special: The Corvette Challenge Chevy crate motor is a special version of the L98 TPI V-8 with 11:1 compression, rated by General Motors at 375 horsepower, and designed especially for Corvette Challenge Series factory racers. Although a later-model Corvette LT1 engine with low-lash hydraulic cam would have been an attractive option for the swap, Norwood needed a motor with a distributor drive to power a load-leveling Jaguar hydraulic pump, hence the L98.

Mind you, 375 horsepower was before Norwood went through the engine to maximize it with improved large-runner Accel intake manifold with huge plenum and tuned runners, camshaft, and improved Motec engine management, not to mention the GM 4L80E electronic automatic transmission—the only unit Norwood found to be capable of handling the super-duty torque he planned to direct through the unit's torque converter. And this was way before Norwood went so far as to custom-fit an S-Trim Vortech centrifugal supercharger to the Chevy V-8. Curb weight for the Norwood-Jaguar was 3,824 pounds, roughly a 200-pound advantage compared to the stock supercharged XJR sedan.

The swap looked good on paper, but when you're looking for fast-car bragging rights, these days you head straight to the dyno to measure the actual horsepower and torque delivered to the wheels. And when it comes to measuring real-world acceleration and speed, in Dallas you head for the Ennis Motor Speedway—a quarter-mile drag strip—to check out acceleration. Reliable data from the dyno and the drag strip made it possible to compare the supercharged Norwood Jag-rolet to the new factory blown V-8.

In fact, the 303.4 rear-wheel horsepower found by the Dynojet on a factory XJR represents a rather typical drivetrain and tire power loss of 18 percent under Jaguar's advertised SAE horsepower. Magazine tests show the factory car can be flogged to 0 to 60 in 5.6 seconds, with the standing quarter-mile requiring 14.2 seconds and achieving a trap speed of 101 miles per hour, which is clearly about what you'd expect.

NORWOOD FIREPOWER

Testing on a Dynojet inertial chassis dyno confirmed that the Norwood car produced 432.1 rear wheel horsepower at 5,000, and 484.7 lb-ft torque at 4,000 at the rear wheels, which is a calculated 540 horsepower at the crankshaft. At the strip, the car managed 0–60 in as little as 3.8–3.9 and drove through the quarter-mile in the high 12s or low 13s depending on the driver and track conditions.

These are the bare-bones statistics. But what is the character of this Norwood-built tuner car, and how and why did it come to be born?

There have always been tuners who produced enhanced Jaguars built for racing or performance street use—including hybrid cars like the famous postwar Lister-Jaguar—that mostly

Jag-rolet Main Tables

Fuel (% IJPU)

Eff\RPM	0	150	300	450	600	750	900	1050	1200	1350	1500	1650	1800	1950	2100	2250	2500	2750	3000	3250
200	27.00	27.50	27.50	27.50	27.50	27.50	27.50	27.50	27.50	27.50	28.00	28.00	28.00	28.50	29.00	29.50	30.50	31.00	33.00	35.00
180	28.50	28.50	28.50	29.00	29.00	29.50	29.50	29.50	29.50	29.50	30.00	30.50	31.00	31.50	32.00	32.50	34.00	35.50	37.00	39.00
160	30.50	30.50	30.50	30.00	30.00	30.50	31.00	31.50	31.50	31.50	31.50	31.50	32.50	33.00	34.50	36.50	37.50	39.50	41.50	43.50
140	31.50	31.50	31.50	31.50	32.00	32.50	33.00	33.00	32.50	32.50	32.50	33.00	34.00	35.50	36.50	39.00	41.00	44.00	45.50	46.50
120	19.00	21.00	21.50	22.50	24.00	25.00	25.50	26.00	27.50	30.00	32.00	33.00	34.50	36.50	38.00	40.50	42.50	44.50	46.00	47.00
100	16.50	20.00	21.00	23.00	24.00	25.00	26.50	27.00	28.50	30.00	31.00	32.00	33.00	34.00	36.50	38.50	40.00	41.00	41.50	42.50
80	15.00	17.00	18.50	20.50	22.00	23.50	25.50	27.00	28.50	30.00	30.50	31.00	31.50	32.00	33.00	33.50	34.00	35.00	35.50	35.50
60	14.00	15.50	17.00	18.00	19.50	21.50	23.00	25.00	25.50	27.00	28.00	29.50	30.00	30.50	31.00	31.50	32.00	32.50	32.50	32.50
40	15.50	17.50	19.00	20.00	21.00	21.50	22.50	22.00	24.00	24.50	25.00	26.00	26.50	26.50	26.50	27.00	27.00	27.00	27.50	28.00
20	15.50	16.50	17.00	18.00	18.00	18.00	18.50	18.50	18.00	17.50	16.50	17.00	17.00	17.00	17.50	18.00	18.50	19.50	20.00	21.00
0	13.50	13.50	13.50	13.50	14.00	14.50	15.00	15.00	15.00	15.00	15.50	15.50	15.00	15.50	16.00	16.50	17.00	19.00	19.50	19.50

Ignition (Degrees BTDC)

Eff\RPM	0	150	300	450	600	750	900	1050	1200	1350	1500	1650	1800	1950	2100	2250	2500	2750	3000	3250
200.00	22.00	22.00	22.00	22.00	22.00	22.00	23.00	23.50	23.50	23.50	23.50	23.50	23.50	23.50	23.50	23.50	23.50	23.50	23.50	23.50
180.00	22.00	21.50	22.00	22.00	22.00	22.00	22.00	22.00	22.00	23.00	23.00	23.00	23.00	23.00	23.00	23.00	23.00	23.00	23.00	23.00
160.00	21.00	22.00	22.50	22.50	22.50	22.50	22.50	22.50	22.50	22.50	22.50	22.50	23.00	24.00	24.00	24.00	24.00	24.00	24.00	24.00
140.00	10.00	21.50	22.50	23.00	23.00	23.00	23.00	23.00	23.00	23.00	23.00	23.00	23.00	23.00	23.00	24.00	25.00	25.00	25.00	25.00
120.00	7.00	16.00	20.50	22.50	24.50	25.50	27.00	27.50	28.00	28.00	28.00	28.00	28.00	28.00	28.00	28.00	28.00	28.00	28.00	28.00
100.00	5.00	10.50	16.00	19.50	22.50	24.50	25.50	26.50	28.00	29.00	30.50	31.50	33.50	34.50	35.00	35.00	35.00	35.00	35.00	35.00
80.00	5.00	8.00	13.00	18.00	21.00	23.00	24.00	26.00	27.00	28.50	30.00	32.00	34.00	35.50	37.00	38.00	38.50	38.50	38.50	38.50
60.00	5.00	8.00	11.00	18.00	20.00	21.00	23.00	24.50	26.00	28.50	30.00	32.00	34.00	36.00	39.50	43.00	43.50	43.50	43.50	43.50
40.00	5.00	6.00	9.50	14.50	17.00	19.00	20.00	21.50	23.50	25.00	27.00	30.50	34.00	40.50	44.00	44.50	45.00	45.00	45.00	45.00
20.00	5.00	6.00	8.50	10.50	13.00	15.00	17.50	20.50	22.50	25.50	29.00	32.00	36.50	41.00	45.00	45.00	45.00	45.00	45.00	45.00
0.00	5.00	6.00	7.50	9.50	11.50	13.00	16.50	19.00	22.00	26.00	29.00	31.50	35.00	40.00	43.00	45.00	46.00	47.00	47.00	47.00

used Jaguar powerplants, but also a few Chevy V-8s. Anyone who remembered glory-days Jaguar performance of the past would not be disappointed by the Norwood-Jaguar package, which was designed with a goal of nothing less than producing the fastest, most powerful, streetable Jaguar sedan ever built, while maintaining all of Jaguar's refinement and luxury.

1. The Raw Material:

1990 Jaguar XJ6. The Challenge: Seamlessly Mating British and U.S. Electronics.

"The Jag sedan was just a sweetheart of a car—a nice-running bone-stock '89 four-valve 3.6-liter sedan with a perfect body I bought from a customer," said Bob Norwood. He and his crew of technicians pulled the Jaguar 3.6 engine and set to work building a viciously powerful supercharged Chevy V-8 conversion for the '89 Jaguar, envisioning a genuine supercar (and also, with its purely stock Jaguar exterior, something of a stealth supercar).

From the beginning, Norwood designed the conversion around a Motec engine management system. This aftermarket programmable onboard computer system had the power and flexibility to allow all stock '89 Jaguar systems to function seamlessly with a new engine, transmission, and engine management system—a far more complex task than the typical V-8 conversion done so frequently on earlier Jaguar cars due to complex new Jaguar electronics introduced in the 1990s to handle electronic fuel injection, computer-controlled ignition, OBD-II emissions controls, electronic transmission controls, self-leveling hydraulics, computer-controlled anti-lock brakes, and more. Even with a powerful Motec EMS system doing the thinking, this was not going to be easy.

In fact, the commitment of time, technical resources, and financial resources involved in the complex R&D required to analyze, research, or reverse engineer all Jaguar electronic and hydraulic systems—and then design the special custom mechanical and electronic equipment required for an EFI V-8 engine conversion that maintained 100 percent functionality of all systems on both the Jag chassis and the Chevrolet 350 V-8 engine—had already bested some well-known Jaguar conversion experts. In fact, the difficulty of a late 1980s-plus conversion was perhaps best illustrated by the brand-new but unused 1989 Jaguar sedan at a certain well-known Jaguar V-8 conversion facility and conversion kit supplier in Texas, which had been moldering silently, frozen in place, partially disassembled, for almost a decade, the V-8 conversion effort in suspended animation.

2. The Chevrolet Engine

Norwood acquired a Corvette Challenge 350 V-8 as raw material for the supercharged powerplant. The Corvette Challenge engine was a special engine that was used at General Motors R&D for development work. The L98 engine was the last of the traditional-design small-block Chevy pushrod V-8s. It was available in 1985 to 1991 Corvettes, Z-28 Camaros, Trans-Am Firebirds, Chevrolet Impalas, and some Cadillac vehicles, and had roots and backward-compatibility going all the way to the first overhead-valve (OHV) Chevrolet 283-ci V-8 engines built in 1955.

Beginning with the Challenge motor, Norwood Autocraft installed a performance-oriented Cam Motion low-lash mechanical roller blower camshaft, and a special Accel port fuel injection intake manifold, designed with large plenum and much-bigger-than-stock volume intake runners that connected the lower manifold to the floor of the plenum and could be equipped with bolt-on port-matched extension tubes of tunable-length that protrude into the plenum a variable distance according to the application and rpm range of the engine.

The cam profile was designed to move a greater quantity of air through the supercharged engine, with special emphasis on additional lift and duration on the exhaust side. Along the

Jag-rolet Main Tables

Fuel (% IJPU)

3500	3750	4000	4250	4500	4750	5000	5250	5500	5750	6000	6250	6500	6750	7000	7250	7500	7750	8000	8250	Eff\RPM
36.50	38.00	38.50	39.50	40.00	40.50	41.00	41.00	41.50	41.50	41.50	41.50	41.50	41.50	41.50	41.50	41.50	41.50	41.50	41.50	200
40.50	41.50	41.50	42.00	42.50	42.50	43.50	43.50	43.50	43.50	43.50	43.50	43.50	43.50	43.50	43.50	43.50	43.50	43.50	43.50	180
44.50	44.50	45.00	45.00	45.50	45.50	45.50	46.00	46.50	46.50	46.50	46.50	46.50	46.50	46.50	46.50	46.50	46.50	46.50	46.50	160
46.50	46.50	47.00	47.00	47.50	48.00	48.00	48.50	49.00	49.50	49.50	49.50	49.50	49.50	49.50	49.50	49.50	50.00	50.00	50.00	140
48.00	48.50	49.50	50.00	50.00	50.50	51.00	51.50	51.50	51.50	51.50	51.50	51.50	51.50	51.50	51.50	51.50	51.50	51.50	51.50	120
43.50	44.00	44.50	44.50	44.50	44.50	44.50	44.00	43.50	42.50	42.50	42.00	41.00	40.50	39.50	38.50	37.50	36.00	35.00	33.50	100
36.00	36.00	36.00	36.50	37.00	37.00	37.00	36.50	36.50	35.50	35.00	35.00	34.00	33.00	33.00	32.50	32.00	32.00	30.50	28.50	80
32.50	33.00	33.50	34.00	34.00	33.50	34.50	34.50	35.00	34.50	33.50	33.00	32.00	31.50	30.50	30.00	29.00	28.50	28.00	27.00	60
28.50	28.50	29.00	29.00	29.00	29.50	30.00	30.00	30.00	30.00	29.50	29.50	29.00	28.50	27.50	27.00	26.00	25.00	24.50	24.00	40
22.00	24.50	25.50	26.00	27.00	27.50	28.00	28.00	27.50	27.00	27.00	26.00	25.50	25.00	24.50	23.50	22.50	21.50	21.00	19.50	20
19.50	20.00	20.00	20.00	20.00	19.50	19.50	19.50	19.00	18.00	18.00	17.50	17.00	16.00	16.00	15.00	15.00	14.50	14.50	14.50	0

Ignition (Degrees BTDC)

3500	3750	4000	4250	4500	4750	5000	5250	5500	5750	6000	6250	6500	6750	7000	7250	7500	7750	8000	8250	Eff\RPM
23.50	23.50	23.50	23.50	23.50	23.50	23.50	23.50	23.50	23.50	23.50	23.50	23.50	23.50	23.50	23.50	23.50	23.50	23.50	23.50	200.00
23.00	23.00	23.00	23.00	23.00	23.00	23.00	23.00	23.00	23.00	23.00	23.00	23.00	23.00	23.00	23.00	23.00	23.00	23.00	23.00	180.00
24.00	24.00	24.00	24.00	24.00	24.00	24.00	24.00	24.00	24.00	24.00	24.00	24.00	24.00	24.00	24.00	24.00	24.00	24.00	24.00	160.00
25.00	25.00	25.00	25.00	25.00	25.00	25.00	25.00	25.00	25.00	25.00	25.00	25.00	25.00	25.00	25.00	25.00	25.00	25.00	25.00	140.00
28.00	28.00	28.00	28.00	28.00	28.00	28.00	28.00	28.00	28.00	28.00	28.00	28.00	28.00	28.00	28.00	28.00	28.00	28.00	28.50	120.00
35.00	35.00	35.00	35.00	35.00	35.00	35.00	35.00	35.00	35.00	35.00	35.00	35.00	35.00	35.00	35.00	35.00	35.00	35.00	35.00	100.00
38.50	38.50	38.50	38.50	38.50	38.50	38.50	38.50	38.50	38.50	38.50	38.50	38.50	38.50	38.50	38.50	38.50	38.50	38.50	38.50	80.00
43.50	43.50	43.50	43.50	43.50	43.50	43.50	43.50	43.50	43.50	43.50	43.50	43.50	43.50	43.50	43.50	43.50	43.50	43.50	43.50	60.00
45.00	45.00	45.00	45.00	45.00	45.00	45.00	44.50	44.50	45.00	45.00	45.00	45.00	45.00	45.00	45.00	45.00	45.00	45.00	45.00	40.00
45.00	45.00	45.00	45.00	45.00	45.00	45.00	45.00	45.00	45.00	45.00	45.00	45.00	45.00	45.00	45.00	45.00	45.00	45.00	45.00	20.00
47.00	47.00	47.00	47.00	47.00	47.00	47.00	47.00	47.00	47.00	47.00	47.00	47.00	47.00	47.00	47.00	47.00	47.00	47.00	47.50	0.00

Norwood Autocraft, which specializes in building and tuning complex and powerful EMS systems on exotic cars, made the TPI engine fit in the Jag with the sanitation of a factory installation.

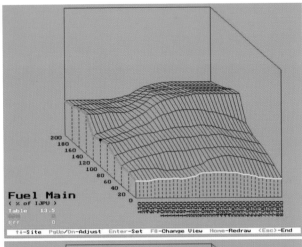

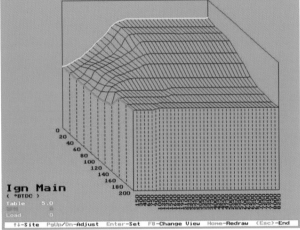

Norwood Autocraft Chevy V-8 "Jag-rolet" Fuel and Ignition maps for supercharged application.

SPECIFICATION

Engine: 1991 350 Corvette Challenge crate motor, Norwood Autocraft custom supercharging and other VE improvers

Crankshaft horsepower: 375 (nonsupercharged Corvette Challenge engine)

Wheel horsepower: 500 (as tested on Dynojet's 248C chassis dynamometer)

Intake manifold: Accel

Compression ratio: 11:1 (static)

Supercharger: Vortech S-Trim, 800 cfm capacity (uses adapted Chevy truck mounting kit for serpentine belt system and custom Norwood bottom pulley)

Engine management system: Motec M48 (Jaguar computer removed)

Camshaft: Cam Motion mechanical roller cam with solid roller tappets, 113 lobe separation

Intake lift: 0.483 (net of 1.5 ratio roller rockers)

Exhaust lift: 0.496 (net of 1.5 ratio roller rockers)

Intake duration at 0.050: 221.3 crankshaft degrees

Exhaust duration at 0.050: 231.1 crankshaft degrees

Headers: Norwood custom stainless-steel tube headers with ceramic thermal coating, copper-seal exhaust header gaskets, Bosch four-wire wideband O_2 sensor mounted in each, EGT sensor probes in each runner for Motec engine management

Cooling system: Mr. Gasket high-performance electric fan, custom alloy radiator (16 x 27, three rows)

Air conditioning: Stock 1990 Jaguar, excepting Chevy Vortec pickup truck compressor, brackets, and tensioner. Custom hoses.

Exhaust system: Twin 2.5-inch pipes to twin Flowmaster mufflers with vacuum-operated dump valves

Fuel system: 1990 Jaguar, with Walbro staged high-volume, high-pressure fuel pump, adjustable fuel pressure regulator

Transmission: GM 4L80E with Accel/DFI Tranmap programmable electronic transmission controller. Adjustable shift points, line pressure. Huge 4L80E converter adapted by Norwood to fit a small-block flywheel. Starter gear notched for small bolt, small starter gear ('Vette lightweight) to clear headers.

same lines, the engine was equipped with custom stainless steel headers of 1.75-inch diameter tubing welded to 3/8-inch-thick flanges sealed with copper-seal exhaust header gaskets, both collectors equipped with Bosch wideband O_2 sensors for precise air/fuel closed-loop mixture control and safe tunability under full supercharger boost conditions.

The header collectors fed into twin 2.5-inch exhaust and twin Flowmaster mufflers, each with two outlets—one that feeds into the stock mufflers and tailpipes, the other connected to an exhaust-pressure-activated dump-valve that was normally closed to provide quiet running during ordinary driving but opened for maximum performance at higher levels of supercharger boost under control of a modified turbocharger wastegate actuator diaphragm.

3. The Supercharger System

The Jag-rolet used a Vortech S-trim centrifugal supercharger selected to produce 10 pounds of boost at 6,000 rpm. The system used a custom Norwood Autocraft billet-aluminum crank pulley and 10-ribbed serpentine belt system. Centrifugal superchargers provide the highest thermal efficiency of any supercharger design, meaning they heat the air the least amount over the minimum theoretical adiabatic heating of compression predicted by thermal dynamics equations. The S-Trim blower provided 72 percent maximum efficiency and as much as 800

cfm maximum airflow without overspeeding the compressor wheel and gears. Like any compressor, pumping efficiencies are increased by intercooling. Jaguar used air-water intercoolers on the Eaton blower, but by limiting boost to 10 psi, Norwood got by without intercooling by using a high-efficiency blower, fuel-enrichment combustion cooling, and boost-retard. An intercooler would make more power, but Norwood achieved his horsepower target the old-fashioned way, with 10-psi boost.

THE NORWOOD JAGUAR V-8 CONVERSION
Auxiliary Engine Equipment

A 16 x 27-inch three-row custom radiator and Mr. Gasket high-performance electric fan provided cooling for the most extreme levels of power on hot Texas summer days with the air-conditioning system on full-blast, simultaneously providing sufficient clearance for the supercharger system.

The air conditioning system on the Norwood-Jaguar conversion was stock with the exception of a 1997 Chevy truck A/C compressor, brackets, and tensioner.

Transmission

The super-duty 350 V-8 mated to a 4L80E GM super-duty four-speed electronic automatic transmission, used by GM on 454 truck motors or 502-ci performance engines. Normally controlled by a GM Powertrain Control Module (PCM) that managed both engine and transmission, the 4L80E transmission electronics on the Norwood-Jaguar were controlled by an Accel/DFI programmable transmission computer that operated independently of the Motec engine management system and allowed the Norwood team to program customize shift points and line pressures to control the speed and harshness of gear changes.

Needless to say, a robust transmission was required to survive under the power and torque of the boosted hot rod small-block engine, and the 4L80E had a large torque converter. According to Norwood, the biggest problem in mating the engine and transmission was getting the huge torque converter to work with the 350 engine's relatively small flywheel. A specially machined flex-plate and reduced-diameter starter gear provided sufficient header clearance.

Norwood adapted a GM performance aluminum driveshaft to the Jag's 3.58 rear end, designed for a six-cylinder engine.

Hydraulics and Accessories

The stock XJ-6 Jaguar hydraulic system delivered 1,100-psi pressurized mineral oil (Rolls-Royce "Green") to operate the self-leveling suspension and the ABS brakes, and the three-cylinder hydraulic pump provided energy for anti-lock braking as well as ordinary braking power boost, with fail-safe hydraulic pressure provided by hydraulic fluid kept under pressure by a 1,200-psi nitrogen gas cylinder/accumulator.

Where to drive the pump on a Chevy V-8? With ignition provided by Mitsubishi direct-fire ignition coils, Norwood was free to eliminate the stock Chevy distributor. Instead, Norwood's swap team mated the Jaguar hydraulic pump to a custom-fabricated billet distributor-type drive assembly powered by the distributor/oil pump cam gear. In addition to the hydraulic pump, the assembly housed a Hall effect sensor that allowed Motec computer to sync with top dead center compression stroke number one cylinder to provide sequential fuel injection and direct-fire ignition.

Norwood discarded the Jaguar alternator in favor of an 1989 GM high-capacity unit and swapped the power-steering pump for a 1989 GM unit, and installed an Edelbrock water pump on the L98.

INSTRUMENTATION, ELECTRICS, AND COMPUTER CONTROL

With the Jaguar onboard computer a thing of the past, Norwood calibrated the Motec M-48 on a chassis dyno and set about to recreate some of the more esoteric Jag computer tricks. The original AJ-6 engine and computer used low-current earth-line switching in which a switch only carries signals, the stock Jaguar electronic control module providing all diagnostics and warnings. "We decided to run the Jag microprocessor just for diagnostics, but now the Jag gets diagnostic information from the Motec," says Norwood. The Motec M-48 computer had logic that could be used to drive the dashboard interface and warning system, to check for correct fluid levels and provide dash error messages.

Fan control strategies were based on programmable voltage readings that can be customized to the particular sensors available and the appropriate temperatures/sensor voltages on which to activate or deactivate electric fans.

Mating the Lucas tachometer to a foreign electronic control unit was not trivial and involved reverse-engineering the Jaguar tach signal. "Making the dash work exactly as stock was a substantial amount of work," says Norwood. In the end, the signal needed to drive a tachometer (designed to register the pulses from a six-cylinder engine was a matter of dedicating one of the Motec M-48 auxiliary outputs as a tach driver, and programming it to synthesize a customized pulse width modulated (PWM) signal with six-cylinder frequency.

HOT RODDING

The Jag-rolet's Vortech S-Trim compressor was driven by a 10-rib serpentine belt, with a stock six-ribbed belt running all other accessories. The Vortech delivered 8–11-psi boost, depending on the drive ratio of the pulleys. Norwood performed minor head porting, and opened the combustion chambers a bit and smoothed the surfaces. With the stock pop-up pistons and small-cc chambers providing a compact combustion chamber, and the Wedge head configuration providing significant squish and quench, the Motec M-48 was able to deliver fuel and spark timing that ran the engine at 10-psi boost on 93 octane pump gas without detonation.

Why not turbocharging? "I actually built a turbo Jag a long time ago," says Norwood, "and if I'd kept the four-valve AJ-6, I'd probably have built a bomber four-valve inline turbo six. But with the Chevy V-8 in a jag engine compartment, clearances were more of a problem. You've got a V-shaped engine compartment with no room at the rear for turbo manifolds. Instead, we've got a blower mounted out front, on the left side, with rubber mounts attaching it to the frame, and anti-torque struts to make sure the engine doesn't lift. We adapted the Vortech plumbing for a remote (cold air) air cleaner."

The stock oil cooler was located in front of the radiator, but Norwood moved it downward to the left side of the radiator, such that trans-cooler was on one side of the radiator, the power steering cooler on the other, with the advantage that the radiator cools the fluids when they're hot, but warms them when they're ice cold.

DRIVING IMPRESSIONS

"I drive it every day to work," said Norwood, who clearly appreciated the Jag's comfortable yet precise ride over the mean streets of Dallas and enjoyed the performance capabilities of the car as equipped with a supercharged hot rod Chevy V-8. The 1990 Jaguar was designed with a relatively low 0.37 coefficient of drag, which made high-speed cruising all that much easier. With 540 horsepower on tap, the engine was rpm-limited rather than power-limited at top speed.

The Jag-rolet was a unique creation that combined stock Jaguar luxury and handling with the brutal hot rod characteristics of a competition NASCAR-type blown-V-8 powerplant tamed to the relative docility required for a reasonable auto-transmission idle. The hybrid V-8/Jaguar held its own in acceleration with not only the stock supercharged Jag XJR (both inline six and newer V-8), but just about any European tuner sedan as well.

Chapter 20
Project: 1970 Dodge Challenger B-Block

What did it take to change a 1970 Dodge Challenger B-block from a dinosaur into a creature of the new millennium? Good modern tires and wheels, some suspension tricks, hardened valve seats in the heads, and an upgrade to electronic fuel injection (and timing).

Although Mopar V-8s of the 1960s and early 1970s were famous for high-performance, high-output Mopar V-8 engines departed the scene in the mid-1970s, and big-block Mopar V-8s disappeared from everything but trucks—and high performance Mopar V-8s did not start to come back until 1992, when Chrysler introduced Magnum upgrades to their 5.2 and 5.9L V-8s. However, it is very possible to retrofit electronic fuel injection and computer-controlled spark advance, and even emissions controls to older carbureted Mopars. I had a 1970 Dodge Challenger with the big-block 383 V-8, and electronic fuel injection seemed like a right-on idea.

PHASE 1. THROTTLE BODY INJECTION

Holley's original TBI Pro-Jection system was designed as an affordable self-contained injection system simple to understand, install, and tune. It was designed to replace the four-barrel carb on older V-8s, and two- and four-barrel versions are still available that are controlled by a digital microprocessor instead of the analog circuitry and logic used in the original versions. The original TBI Pro-Jection was tuned by adjusting five pots on the side of the control unit with a screwdriver. Holley began with a single-point-injection throttle body with two injectors that essentially had been developed as an OEM replacement part for certain 80's- and 90's-vintage engines with single-point injection, and made it part of a kit that also included an MSD-designed and manufactured control unit, wiring, a sensor or two, and some miscellaneous mounting adapters. The Pro-Jection was simple and cheap.

Naturally, there were tradeoffs.

An installer who did a carb-to-EFI conversion on an older vehicle with a Pro-Jection 2 kit could expect the following:

- Hard acceleration and cornering or harsh terrain could not degrade the operation of the fuel system as it could with a carb due to absence of a float bowl.
- Precise Fuel delivery infinitely variable infinitely variable to a granularity of less than a thousandth of a second.
- Adjustable enrichment for cold starting, and fast-idle solenoid.
- Tunable with a set of screwdriver-adjustable dashpots while driving or on a chassis dyno (an obvious advantage compared to the repeated disassembly that may be required when making jet changes on a carb).
- Wild-cammed engines not subject to mixture problems resulting from reversion pulses flowing backward through

1970 Dodge Challenger B-block 383 four-barrel with side pipes: the early-'70s retro look.

a carb with a single plane manifold that can result in a carb over-richening the mixture by adding fuel to the air twice as it reverses direction.
- Dieseling impossible due to instant fuel cut when you turn off the key.
- Vapor lock is much less likely under the 12–20-psi Pro-Jection fuel pressure, compared to the reduced pressure of a stock mechanical vacuum pump sucking fuel forward to the engine.
- Hot air percolation, in which gasoline boils and overflows the float bowl(s) in a carb in hot weather—additionally pressurized by the action of vapor pressure in fuel lines—is not possible with the Pro-Jection.

On the other hand:
- One of the tradeoffs of throttle body injection is that fuel is injected from only two injectors at one place. TBI ability to deliver equal fuel and air to every cylinder is subject to the limitations and design flaws of any intake manifold that must handle a wet mixture. Gasoline tends to fall out of suspension in the air of the intake manifold during cold starting or sudden throttle openings that rapidly change manifold pressure—and then tear off the surface of the manifold unpredictably in sheets of liquid in a way that can produce unequal distribution to individual cylinders. Higher air velocity is required to keep fuel suspended in the air at low rpm, which eliminates the possibly of more radical dry manifolds found on port fuel-injection systems that provide great high-end breathing while relying on port injection to put fuel directly into the swirling dry air at the intake valve at low speed for good idle and equal distribution.
- The Pro-Jection 2 did not control ignition spark advance or other emissions-control devices.
- The Pro-Jection 2 ECM was an Alpha-N system estimated air mass entering the engine based solely on throttle

This car started out life as a 290-horse 383-ci two-barrel big block. With four-barrel Carter AFB carburetion and some other mild hot rod parts (Edelbrock "Streetmaster 383" single-plane manifold, better cam, headers, and so on), we guessed the "Commando" V-8 was mostly up to the standard of the factory 335-horse "Magnum" four-barrel. Everything worked, including the air conditioning.

position, rpm, and temperature, with no provision for measuring actual mass airflow (MAF) or manifold absolute pressure (MAP), which meant the system could not be used with forced induction.

• Obviously, the Pro-Jection could not time fuel injection for individual cylinders like a sequential multi-port or direct-injection system to improve emissions and fuel economy.

The L code on the VIN revealed that the '70 Challenger had originally been built as a 290-horsepower two-barrel 383. The engine was now equipped with a new Carter AFB four-barrel carburetor. When this project began, the car was running a single-plane Edelbrock Streetmaster 383 aluminum intake manifold and an ancient Carter AFB carb on. The engine was still running the stock compression ratio (9:1) but had been upgraded to a fairly hot auto-transmission Competition Cams bumpstick.

With fresh paint and interior on the Challenger plus a freshly rebuilt engine, a new air conditioning compressor and a host of other details like a new wiper switch and door handles, it was time to install the Pro-Jection. Although the Pro-Jection 2 used a two-barrel throttle body system, it would not fit on a stock two-barrel manifold. The throttle body was designed to bolt to an adapter plate designed to fit on most small- and medium-displacement four-barrel American V-8s, and could flow up to 650 cfm.

The Pro-Jection was easy to install. You began by designing a way to return fuel to the gas tank. Like virtually all injection systems, the Holley system required constant pressure to the injectors, regardless of the engine fuel requirements. As usual,

this was done by providing a fuel loop that supplied gasoline from an electric fuel pump near the fuel tank to a pressure regulator in the engine compartment near the fuel-injection unit and returned excess fuel back to the tank. The regulator, referenced to manifold pressure, was integral to the throttle body in Pro-Jection systems, and worked by pinching off fuel flow to the degree required to maintain a preset pressure in the fuel supply line *with respect to manifold pressure*. The amount of excess fuel returning to the tank thus varied depending on engine fuel consumption. On this type of system, a lot of fuel is returning at idle, and little or none of the engine fuel consumption approaches or exceeds the capacity of the fuel pump under high-rpm heavy loading.

For obvious reasons (right?) *you can't simply drill a hole in the tank* to install a fuel-return line. However, one neat trick that can work rather quickly is to return fuel to the filler neck. With this in mind I removed the pipe, cleaned it carefully, and welded on a fitting to attach a hose barb for the fuel return line. An alternative that would have worked in this case would have been to remove the plate that held the fuel gauge sending unit and drill it and attach a return fitting. If it is necessary to remove the tank for drilling or welding, you should have the work done by a fuel tank specialist. An empty fuel tank—inevitably loaded with fuel vapor—is incredibly explosive!

When mounting an inline electric fuel pump, what you're looking for is a safe location near the fuel tank in a low spot where it will be primed by gravity rather than the reverse. Holley suggested mounting the Projection fuel pump no higher than

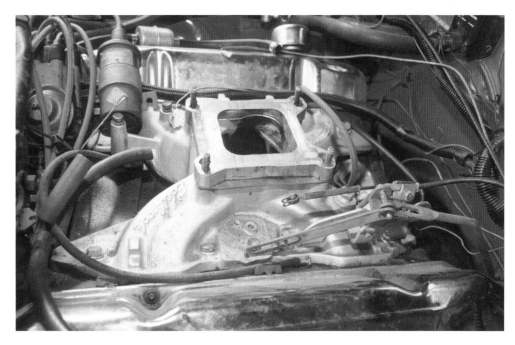

The old 383 2-bbl had been modified with an Edelbrock Streetmaster 383 4 bbl manifold and carb spacer plate.

the top of the tank and locating the pump at the bottom of a loop of fuel line so the pump would always have liquid fuel to pump when it first starts. The problem is that when you turn on the key, the EMS activates the electric fuel pump for only a second or two to pressurize the injector supply line. If fuel is not immediately available to the pump before the injectors begin squirting, the engine may be very hard to start. On an old dog like a '70 Challenger, you'll want to remove the mechanical fuel pump from the engine, and blank off the hole in the block with a plate (still available at most speed shops or online).

The next step was removing the old carb, mounting the Holley adapter plate and throttle body, and connecting the fuel supply and return lines to the throttle body. Old Mopar vehicles with automatic transmissions used a mechanical kick-down linkage and thus required an adapter to attach the linkage to the Pro-Jection. Holley built a Mopar adapter, but did not include it in the standard universal Pro-Jection kit, but I found one in stock at a local speed shop and they are still available online from places like Summit Racing. The linkage on the Challenger had been doctored in the conversion to the Carter AFB four-barrel and thus required refurbishing to work perfectly.

Aftermarket ECMs almost always work better in a temperate environment, away from engine or exhaust heat and electrical interference—meaning inside the car or in the trunk. The Pro-Jection ECM mounted nicely on the console ahead of the shifter where it could tuned easily, and the wiring harness routed to the Pro-Jection throttle body, Holley EFI fuel pump, and EFI water temperature sending unit (which I'd mounted in a 1/8-inch fitting in the water pump) through an existing hole in the firewall. Several wires on the harness connected to constant positive 12-volt, switched +12 voltage, and negative 12-volt coil or tach-drive voltage.

START UP TIME

Since an EFI fuel pump usually only runs a second or two when it's energized before cranking, it's a good idea the first time to jumper the fuel pump to +12 battery voltage to fill the fuel system with gasoline. Some ignition switch connections specifically do

not provide voltage while cranking (for non-essential accessories that drain power you might need to start the engine), so make sure that the ECM and fuel pump (and relays, where applicable) are connected to the right source.

With the fuel pump working, I verified that the dashpots on the computer were at the positions specified by Holley for initial start up, at which point (with the air cleaner removed from the throttle body) I cranked the ignition and watched the injectors. It is easy to see big throttle body injectors spraying fuel downward at the throttle plate, and the next moment the engine came to life. I immediately went to work on the idle mixture dashpot, hunting for the position that would give the smoothest idle. Disconcertingly, smoothest idle required the idle pot to be pegged at the leanest possible setting.

Consulting the manual, I decided that perhaps the throttle position switch (TPS)—a linear potentiometer mounted on the throttle shaft on the side of the throttle body—must be clocked wrong. Since the computer determines engine loading directly from throttle position and rpm, it is essential that the switch read the right voltage. Using a digital resistance meter and some jumpers, I watch the resistance of the switch change as I opened the throttle. Bingo! The switch was reading too high with the throttle closed. Loosening the Pro-Jection TPS, I was able to rotate the sensor until the meter showed the correct voltage for a closed throttle. Starting the engine, the idle mixture dashpot now yielded the best mixture farther up the scale, as it should.

Holley's installation manual listed procedures for tuning the midrange and high-end power, which basically involved tuning for best mixture at 3,000 rpm (unloaded in neutral), then using a stopwatch to tune-and-time acceleration runs at wide-open throttle (WOT) until the Pro-Jection delivered best power as indicated by the stopwatch. Pro-Jection 4 units have an extra pot for tuning high-end power. Of course, the best procedure is to attach a wideband air/fuel-ratio meter and tune for 12.5–13.5:1 mixture, or tune on a chassis dynamometer for best torque.

Out on the highway, I noticed an interesting thing: Although the car felt—seat of the pants—as if it had better torque, what was missing was the sudden burst of power under

Holley no longer makes the Pro-Jection-2 system for street use, but this Pro-Jection 2 Marine system is very similar down to the calibration ports.

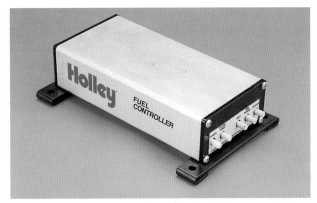

Holley Pro-Jection 2 fuel controller is actually a hardwired analog computer tunable exclusively with adjustment pots for Choke, Accel Pump, Idle, Mid-Range, and Power.

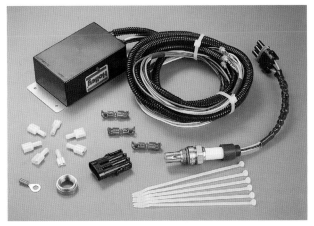

Optional add-on O_2 sensor controller provides closed-loop mixture control at idle.

hard acceleration you get with a four-barrel as the secondaries open up at wide-open throttle.

The Pro-Jection 2 system on the big-block Challenger was undoubtedly a vast improvement over the carburetor. It started quickly in all weather, provided fast idle when cold, and was free of the hot weather starting problems encountered by the AFB in the heat of a south Texas summer. Throttle response was good under all conditions. The system had no way of compensating for the air conditioning compressor coming on line, but the big-block only dropped a small amount of rpm, and had it really mattered, I might have rigged a relay to trigger the cold-start solenoid.

PHASE 2: PORT FUEL INJECTION

At this point I obtained a Haltech F3 ECM (fuel only) capable of controlling multiple port injectors on a V-8, and converted the Challenger to multi-port EFI under digital control. Given the modifications for Holley TBI, the multi-port conversion turned out to be extremely easy. There was a fuel return line. There was a mounting point for a coolant-temperature sensor. The throttle position switch on the Holley throttle body was compatible with the Haltech ECM, and the injector/regulator/ fuel supply assembly was a one-piece unit that bolted to the main section of the Holley throttle body with three Allen screws that could be easily removed. I fabricated an aluminum blank-off plate that allowed the Holley throttle body to be used as a multi-port throttle body.

Happily, the single-plane Edelbrock manifold on the Challenger used runners that were perfectly in line with each other. I milled holes for injector bosses into the ceiling of the intake runners working through the intake ports from the underside of the manifold where the flat planes that joined the manifold to the cylinder heads could be used to align the mill so the injectors were aimed with perfect geometry, and then I welded the injector bosses in place from the bottom, grinding the excess boss material away so as not to interfere with airflow. I installed O-ringed Lucas disc fuel injectors in the bosses that were fitted for hoses on the fuel input side, and constructed a two-piece D-section fuel rail with eight hose barbs connecting the injector hoses to the fuel supply. The two-piece fuel rail linked together at one end with a section of high-pressure, high-flow EFI fuel line.

The biggest problem had to do with the fact that 1970 Chryslers used a mechanical kick-down linkage that had originally connected to the carb linkage. Later, with adaptations, I had attached it to the Holley throttle body. Unfortunately, the left fuel rail and injector assembly was now located exactly where a linkage support had bolted to the intake manifold. Fortunately, it was possible to move the kick-down linkage outboard of the left bank of injectors by cutting the linkage support in two pieces and welding it back together with the addition of some mild steel bracketing. I cut the linkage and inserted a 3/4-inch inward offset so it could connect properly to the Holley throttle body.

It was an easy matter to connect the fuel supply and return lines to the fuel rail (using 900-psi hose). I installed a 39-psi MAP-referenced fuel pressure regulator from an L-Jetronic injection system, and robbed the Bosch fuel pump I'd used in the original XKE turbo-EFI system featured in another chapter of this book and installed it in the fuel loop on the return side of the fabricated Challenger fuel rail. The fuel L-Jet pump was necessary since the Pro-Jection 2 electric pump is designed for a lower pressure TBI system that does not need to provide stable fuel pressure to eight batch-fire port injectors.

Wiring the Haltech ECM was simple, and programming is discussed in detail in other sections of this book. Suffice it to say that the Haltech ECM was not equipped with auto-tune

Beginning the installation, the first thing is to remove the carb and install an adapter plate for the two-barrel throttlebody.

You're going to need a fuel return line. We did it the easy way, adding a hose barb to the fuel filler neck so unneeded fuel that bleeds from the fuel rail can return into the fuel tank. We also installed a coolant temp sensor, fuel return line, and a few other tricks.

Holley 15-psi electric fuel pump replaces the stock mechanical fuel pump, which is replaced with a blank-off plate. Obviously the Pro-Jection system is not intended for forced-induction applications. Throttlebody injection puts all the fuel through two giant fuel injectors, and 15 psi fuel rail pressure gets the job done.

capabilities. Haltech provided a startup map designed for a "modified V-8" that provides a set of base fuel maps designed to produce safe rich mixtures as a good starting point for a car like the Challenger. The big-block Mopar 383 engine is not tremendously radical, but given the hotter-than-stock cam, the headers, and the large-port intake manifold, the modified V-8 map seemed like a good place to start, as it is always preferable to begin rich and work lean when calibrating an engine.

I installed a Haltech-compatible air temperature sensor in the air cleaner inlet, which was preferable to milling a port hole in an intake manifold runner, as it was less likely to heat-soak the sensor and lean out mixtures.

I removed the Holley wiring harness and equipment and set it aside and mounted the Haltech ECM inside the car on the side of the transmission hump near where the Pro-Jection system had been. It would be easy enough in the future to replace the Holley throttle body with something else and use the whole Holley system on some other project. The final detail was building a connector to adapt the Holley TPS connector to the foreign Haltech wiring harness and plugging in the new harness to all sensors and actuators and connecting the harness to constant and switched power and ground.

Multi-port injectors spray fuel at high pressure directly into turbulent air at the hot intake valves only an inch or two away from the injectors on a setup like the Challenger, and there is a wonderful crispness when everything is right. The Haltech ECU offered excellent resolution, basically providing a 512 element matrix of speed-load breakpoints that define the engine fuel map. Obviously, this provides greater flexibility than the Pro-Jection system that defines the base fuel map with three control knobs.

CONCLUSIONS

Is multi-port injection worth the additional expense over a throttle body system like the Pro-Jection?

The fairest thing to say about whether it's worth it depends on what you are asking the simpler Pro-Jection system to do. How good is the manifold you're using for wet mixtures? How smooth and consistent is the volumetric efficiency of the engine as power and airflow increase? How peaky is the engine in its torque curve; how much does torque vary from a truly flat curve? How high is the compression? How important is fuel consumption? Is the engine boosted with turbos or blower? Do

Fuel-injected B-block Dodge, something that never happened at the factory on any big-block Mopar.

you have the equipment and patience required to really take advantage of the programmable port EFI system's flexibility? It you have a radical manifold on a peaky engine with a lot of compression, it is very important to have the flexibility to build an oddly shaped fuel curve to match torque, and then you'd clearly want a programmable multi-port engine management system. But on many engines, considering only peak power at wide-open throttle, a throttle body system like the Pro-Jection is right up there with the best of them. It does not have the wonderful low- to mid-range broad torque range of a tuned multi-port injection system with long runners. But that's a different story.

Starting with the Pro-Jection TBI system made the subsequent port-injection conversion a little easier. I removed the two big injectors from the throttle body, drilled and welded-in injector bosses, constructed a fuel supply rail, and installed a high-pressure inline fuel pump. The Haltech EMS generic harness plugged into the injectors and sensors straightforwardly. We plugged in a laptop, fired up the car with a library calibration, and tuned the car for drivability with the Haltech mixture trim module as best we could on some Texas back roads. Later on we found some free power with a Horiba wideband AFR meter.

Chapter 21
Project: Real-World Turbo CRX Si

The defining characteristics of a Honda CRX Si are front-wheel-drive, ultra-light 2,100-pound curb weight, and a 1.6-liter SOHC aluminum powerplant with 9:1 compression. Honda is known for building a jewel of an engine that was lightweight and powerful for its size. The CRX 1.6-liter engine is a 16-valve design, with a single overhead cam (SOHC) aluminum head bolted to an aluminum block. The cylinders were aluminum, with nonsleeved silica-aluminum (hardened) bores. Pentroof four-valve heads breathed extremely well for the valve lift, and this combustion chamber was an excellent shape for resisting spark knock. Pentroof chambers provide a short path from the centrally located spark plug to the farthest end gases in the combustion chamber—improving the chances normal combustion will progressively and smoothly burn the air/fuel mixture before any of it has a chance to explode in the increasing heat and pressure of combustion. All good for turbocharging.

What would it take to hot rod the power of a 2,100-pound CRX by 55 percent, from the stock 97 wheel horsepower at 6,200 to, say, 150? To calculate potential turbocharged power, a ballpark assumption is 8 percent more torque per psi of additional boost. With 6-psi boost, torque would be up approximately 48 percent at 6,500 to 121.36. Converting this to horsepower, gives 150.25. A 10-psi boost makes 148 lb-ft of torque at 6,500, or a calculated 183 rear-wheel horsepower. At 7-psi boost, the Honda's effective compression ratio increased from the static C/R of 9.0:1 to roughly 11:1, perhaps 12:1 at 10-psi. With intercooling, fuel enrichment, and timing-retard anti-knock countermeasures, a four-valve pentroof engine like the Honda could be made to handle 9- or 10-psi boost on 93 octane fuel without detonation. Without intercooling, probably 6 or 7.

When it comes to hot rodding, the 1.6 engine's biggest problems were the cast pistons and lightweight rods, designed for a lightweight, high-revving engine making less than 100 driving-wheel horsepower. According to Alamo Performance of Arlington, Texas, if you could prevent the 1.6 Honda from detonating, you'd bend the rods first with too much power. Otherwise knock would kill the pistons first. Meanwhile, head gaskets could blow, the piston ring lands could break, and as a worst case, cast pistons could melt from too much boost.

We decided to see how much power we could make without opening the engine. Effective engine management would be critical. It is worth noting at the outset that the stock CRX had almost none of the factory countermeasures found on factory turbo cars, such as overboost warnings, overboost fuel-cut, boost ignition retard, alternate fuel and spark maps, or knock sensor.

The Honda PFI engine management system calculates injection pulse width using the speed-density model, with airflow calculated based on engine rpm and manifold absolute pressure (MAP) corrected for temperature. With MAP limited to slightly above 1 bar, boost fuel enrichment can be supplied by

1989 Honda CRX on the Alamo Autosports Dynojet. The 17-inch wheels looked good, but they actually made the car slower due to higher final gear ratios, and added weight. Higher inertia will actually lower the power measured by an inertial chassis dyno.

(1) altering the Honda computer's calibration, (2) dynamic fuel pressure increases, (3) an additional injector system, or (4) an aftermarket programmable computer system.

The Honda CRX fuel delivery system—centrifugal high-pressure fuel pump, regulator, fuel lines, and so on—was designed to supply 100 wheel horsepower worth of fuel plus a small margin, and will run out of capacity quickly on a hot rod turbo conversion. The stock fuel injectors are out of capacity by 6-psi turbo boost, which is about as much boost as much it's worth bothering with on a turbo or supercharger conversion. The stock CRX fuel pump has a 60-psi bypass valve, meaning that the fuel pressure cannot be raised enough to support a full 6-psi boost without a replacement or additional high-pressure fuel pump. The stock pump's volume has little capacity beyond stock horsepower, and essentially all turbo conversions—whatever the fueling strategy—require a fuel pump upgrade. Fuel lines do not require upgrading for high-output street turbo cars.

But first, nitrous.

SATURDAY NIGHT DISASTER

I had a nitrous fogger kit and knew people who'd used just such a wet kit on the 1.6 Honda with great results, and the whole thing bolted on in a few hours. This is a binary sort of kit in which a fixed amount of nitrous and enrichment fuel are injected at a single point from a single fogger nozzle just upstream of the throttle body. On a CRX, a 50-shot nitrous kit adds 50 percent more power and blasts torque to the stratosphere at low rpm.

I made a single awesome nitrous run with the fogger kit—pulled the CRX onto the Dynojet, and made a benchmark run at stock power, brought the engine back up to 2,500, put

With stock Honda EMS, the first thing we tried was a wet nitrous kit, which operates independently of the Honda EMS. It can be tricky getting enrichment gasoline introduced just ahead of the throttle body to distribute well in a dry EFI manifold. On about the third dynorun, we crisped three exhaust valves.

the hammer down hard to 100 percent, and as the engine revved through 3,000, flicked a dash-mounted arming switch to bring the nitrous on-line. The CRX's engine let out a low-pitched growl like Frankenstein's monster clearing his throat, gained super powers, and spun up those two giant 1,200-pound Dynojet rollers in a nitrous-enhanced dash to the redline, then reverted instantly back to its mild-mannered secret identity as a Honda CRX economy car when I dumped the throttle. We graciously accepted the applause of the onlookers and drove (fast) to the local saloon for beers, where pretty young barmaids draped flowers around our necks and kissed us on the lips.

Unfortunately, that last sentence never happened. As the CRX's roar fell back to an idle on the dyno, it was instantly clear something was very wrong. The car was stumbling and missing, hitting on maybe half the cylinders. Following exactly one nitrous run (which actually made pretty good power before nitrous fried the engine), the CRX was left with approximately enough guts to labor off the dyno under its own power and limp across the lot into an empty parking spot where it immediately stalled into a deep coma. The crowd of on-lookers stood around

in the sudden stillness, letting out half-hearted rebel yells and making farting noises with their underarms.

As expected, testing revealed the 1.6 engine's two center holes had zero compression. I hoped the problem was something easy—for example, a blown head gasket. But forensic analysis by yours truly on a marathon Saturday night cylinder-head R&R session revealed that three of the Honda's eight exhaust valves appeared to have been attacked with an oxyacetylene cutting torch. In the space of a few Saturday night hours at Alamo Autosports, I removed, disassembled, and resurfaced the head, replaced and lapped the bad valves, made sure everything else (pistons, and so on) appeared to be in good shape, then cleaned and block-sanded the deck surface of the block, reinstalled the head, and buttoned up the engine.

Following emergency surgery to the head and valves after the nitrous fiasco, we fired up the newly repaired engine at about 2 a.m. Sunday morning. None of us looked too good by this time, but I must have been living right. The engine fired up immediately and ran like a top. The Dynojet proved the 1.6 had almost exactly as much power as before I flame-torched the three

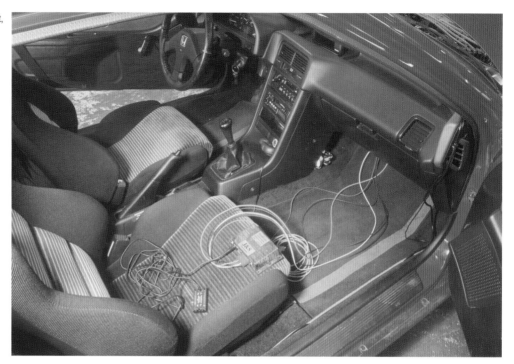

Following the burned-valve incident, we installed a J&S Safeguard individual-cylinder knock-retard system, which also functions as an igniter.

valves. Things could've been much worse—for example, melted or cracked pistons, broken ring lands, squeezed or broken rings, or flame-torched valves.

Analysis: Clearly, there was a lack of gasoline in the center cylinders. Possibly this had to do with an interaction between freezing-cold boiling nitrous and chilled gasoline vapors that subsequently condensed into drops of liquid while dodging past the throttle blade or turning a corner in a dry intake manifold that was never intended to carry liquid fuel, and departed the air stream, resulting in a dearth of enrichment gasoline in cylinders two and three. Clearly, the Honda's two center holes had received a surplus of nitrous that oxidized the hell out of all the available gasoline and then, with nothing better to do, burned up three exhaust valves where they'd been preheated from previous combustion cycles.

They no longer sell fogger systems for naturally aspirated EFI cars like our Honda. Wet EFI systems often worked well, but they could nuke an engine under the right conditions. When Honda fogger systems *didn't* work right, the problem is virtually always enrichment fuel starvation at one or more cylinders. The fluid dynamics of freezing-cold vaporizing nitrous and raw gasoline entering through a fogger nozzle in the air intake and then blasting around the throttle plate and finding a way into the howling winds of a long-runner EFI manifold can sometimes be a little unpredictable.

Keep in mind that old-style fogger systems mix nitrous and fuel in one nozzle near the throttle and spew this "fog" mixture into the intake charge. You have to hope the air, fuel, and nitrous stay nicely mixed all the way past the throttle and through the dry intake manifold plenum and runners, so that each cylinder gets the proper dose of nitrous, gasoline, and air in one well-mixed homogenous cloud of vapor. The trouble is, liquid gasoline and gaseous nitrous have different fluid dynamics, and don't always corner the same in the byzantine twists of an intake manifold.

Dry-port EFI manifolds like CRX's are designed to use inertial and resonance tuning effects to cram the maximum amount of air in the cylinder—with no consideration given to keeping gasoline suspended in air like wet carb or throttle body-injection manifolds. EFI manifolds are designed to get the maximum equal air charge to all cylinders, but they're not required to deal with distributing gasoline evenly to the cylinders (the port fuel injectors do that).

A fogger system would've probably worked fine on a turbocharged CRX engine. Dumping gasoline and nitrous near a turbocharger blasting out hot air at maybe 100,000 rpm is a little like dumping a load of manure through the prop of an old B-29 bomber on a maximum-performance engine run-up. Nothing bigger than a quark is going to survive, and you know the stuff's gonna get spread around. Actually, according to NOS and Alamo Autosports, a lot of people ran fogger systems on EFI Hondas with good results, sometimes with 80-shot or bigger nitrous jets. Our engine coulda-shoulda-mighta lived with the fogger nozzle in the perfect place.

EFI NITROUS: THE SEQUEL

At this point we installed a state-of-the-art NOS 5122 50-horse EFI kit on the CRX. This was very much a fail-safe type of kit. You have to be really clever to hurt your car with one of these.

The NOS EFI kit injects nitrous liquid near the throttle like a fogger system, in a steady stream, independent of engine speed. But the EFI nitrous kit supplies enrichment fuel not by dumping enrichment fuel in with the nitrous but by jacking up fuel pressure in the injector rail by artificially raising the pressure to the fuel pressure regulator MAP reference port. When you arm this type of EFI nitrous system and put the pedal to the metal, a throttle-activated microswitch opens a nitrous solenoid that allows nitrous gas to escape from the main nitrous supply line through a mini pressure regulator to the reference port on the fuel pressure regulator via a T-fitting inserted in the manifold reference line (a one-way valve between the T and the intake manifold prevents nitrous from entering the manifold through the reference line). The heightened reference pressure quickly raises fuel pressure from the normal 36-psi max to 65 psi, at which point each fuel injector squirt delivers significantly more gasoline to be burned when the nitrous arrives. When fuel rail pressure pushes through 50 psi, a fail-safe NOS pressure switch in the fuel rail/supply line allows the main nitrous regulator to open. Located downstream of the reference-pressurizing nitrous solenoid in the main nitrous supply line, the second nitrous regulator allows nitrous liquid to flow to an injection nozzle in the intake tract located 4–12 inches upstream of the throttle body.

If fuel pressure ever drops below a threshold of 50 psi, the NOS pressure switch will immediately cut off nitrous flow, preventing lean-mixture engine damage. What conditions could contribute to rail pressure drop? Start with the engine's normal fuel requirements at high rpm and loading. Add to this, say, air-density increases due to cold weather or lower altitude that add to the required pulse width, stressing fuel requirements to the maximum stock level. Now combine this with an armed and activated EFI nitrous system that suddenly amps up the fuel pressure. Fuel pump mass flow declines with pressure increases. Fuel pumps can lose efficiency due to aging, and this could be the month that pumping losses reach a critical threshold. Or there could be a minor—almost invisible—fuel leak that's the final factor that causes rail pressure to drop under a worst case set of circumstances.

Nitrous liquid injected into the intake boils almost immediately into a gas (simultaneously chilling the intake air and making additional "free" power available via a denser air charge, assuming there's enough fuel). Gaseous nitrous in the manifold increases the oxygen content of the intake charge by a few percent, and by the time nitrous reaches the intake valve, it has warmed up enough that there is little detrimental effect on gasoline vaporization. When nitrous is heated to 565 degrees Fahrenheit in the combustion chamber, the oxygen and nitrous molecules break apart and the oxygen becomes available for combustion.

How much additional power could a vintage CRX engine stand before destroying itself? A 30 to 50 percent power boost is about the limit unless you upgrade the engine's internals (particularly the pistons and rods). According to NOS, 50 horsepower is the maximum reliable increase you should use on a stock 1.6 Honda, though there were people driving time-bomb stock Hondas with 60- or 80-horse port-injection NOS systems that lived. For a while. These systems have larger nitrous jetting, recalibrated nitrous pressure to the Honda fuel pressure regulator for increased fueling, and *individual nitrous lines* running to each intake runner with separate nozzles installed for each cylinder.

The NOS EFI nitrous system was advertised to deliver 50 crankshaft horsepower. Testing on the Alamo Autosport Dynojet chassis dyno revealed a gain in peak power of 38 rear-wheel horsepower, increasing power from 96 to 134 horsepower with nitrous boost, a 40 percent power boost.

The great thing about nitrous injection is that when the system's armed the power boost is available instantly the moment you hit 100 percent throttle above 2,500 rpm (the lowest activation rpm recommended by NOS) and continues all the way to redline. Actually, when the nitrous hit, we were somewhat worried about clutch slip with the car strapped hard to the Dynojet where tire slip is virtually impossible no matter what the torque boost.

BOOSTED-ENGINE ANTI-KNOCK COUNTERMEASURES

At EFI NOS installation time, we added two devices to improve the safety of the system. One was a 550-horse NOS

Nitrous arming switch disables nitrous injection under all circumstances. When the arming switch is active, nitrous injection still cannot begin until the throttle is wide open.

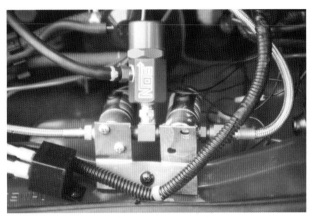

The next trick we tried was switching to an NOS "dry" nitrous kit, which introduces fuel during nitrous injection by jumping up the fuel pressure to the stock injectors. If fuel pressure ever drops off to the reference port on the blue fitting, it immediately chokes off the nitrous flow, saving the engine.

inline electric fuel pump, and the other was a J&S Safeguard individual-cylinder knock-retard computer/coil-driver. The Safeguard was introduced in 1991, and enhanced versions are still sold. The Safeguard is apparently still the only individual-cylinder knock-control system. The NOS inline fuel pump can be installed anywhere upstream of the fuel rail, but we installed it downstream of the fuel filter in the Honda's engine compartment and wired it to an automotive relay so that it only ran when the nitrous system was armed (by turning on the dash-mounted arming switch). We verified that the auxiliary fuel pump would not interfere with the pumping of the stock EFI fuel pump when the auxiliary pump was off.

We wired the Safeguard into the stock Honda ignition, and in this configuration the Safeguard could remove up to 20 degrees of timing in 2-degree increments from any or all individual cylinders found to be knocking via a crystal microphone (knock sensor) screwed into the block or intake manifold. NOS specified that the 50-horsepower Honda EFI nitrous system would work with stock timing and premium street fuel, but in case of additional heat and pressure from nitrous combustion or bad gasoline-induced detonation, the Safeguard would kill knock before it can damage the engine. A miniature dash-mounted display lit one or more LEDs according to how much timing was being removed from one or more cylinders. An adjustment screw

With nitrous testing completed, it was time for turbocharging. Here's the Turbonetics ceramic ball-bearing turbo with down pipe and CRX manifold, ready to rock 'n' roll.

permitted adjustment of the sensitivity of the Safeguard so that normal engine would not trigger spark retard. The J&S indicator display could also display air/fuel mixtures if you installed an auxiliary O_2 sensor.

The knock threshold for a particular cylinder depends on a lot of factors; rarely do all cylinders begin knocking at once, and the great thing about the J&S is that it listens for detonation, correlates the knock to a particular cylinder or cylinders, and retards ignition timing only on the slackers causing trouble rather than retarding all cylinders due to one or two problem areas. Individual-cylinder knock retard maintains higher power and lower coolant-jacket temperatures, while protecting the engine from knock-induced damage.

The J&S included an auxiliary wiring harness, processor module, indicator module, and the knock sensor, as well as power and ground leads. Tapping into the low-voltage ignition wiring located inside the CRX's integrated distributor/coil module is the best method to supply power to the module. Ideally, the knock sensor should be mounted at the top center of the block, but with no convenient threaded hole there we mounted it on the driver's side of the block, near the end of the block.

NITROUS FUEL THROUGH THE INJECTORS: NITROUS TIME VERSUS INJECTION PULSE WIDTH VERSUS RPM

Since nitrous injection occurs in a steady stream per time, the amount of nitrous that arrives in a particular cylinder is a function of the time it takes to complete each four-stroke cycle at the current engine speed. When activated, most nitrous systems

are delivering nitrous gas continuously at rate that is ideally constant. The result is that the slower the engine speed, the *more* the torque boost there is per individual combustion event (which is what it takes to constantly add a fixed-power boost). And since the delivery of nitrous is steady over time, increasing rpm will slice the amount of nitrous actually delivered to a cylinder into smaller and smaller amounts as engine speed increases.

By contrast, sequential electronic fuel injection delivers a single-injector squirt for a calculated length of time per power stroke, with injector size selected such that injection pulse width never exceeds about 80 percent of the available time per combustion cycle in a worst case in order to prevent injector overheating. The amount of fuel injected is thus unaffected by the combustion cycle at the current engine speed. Actual wide-open-throttle (WOT) fuel-injection pulse width will typically increase with rpm as the engine approaches peak-torque rpm, then decline somewhat as the torque curve noses over a bit as rpm approaches peak power.

Computer-controlled nitrous fuel enrichment logic takes into account the time available for constant nitrous injection in computing the required delta in injection pulse width needed to fuel the nitrous. If this is not done, the air/fuel mixture becomes increasingly rich as engine speed increases due to the fall off in time available for nitrous (oxygen) induction per power stroke.

Of course, EFI nitrous systems like the NOS dry system on the CRX would cost a lot more if they required a standalone aftermarket EMS to deliver sophisticated nitrous pulse width calculation. Fortunately, the spread between air/fuel ratios producing rich and lean best torque for gasoline is fairly wide. And the acceptable air/fuel ratio range gets even wider on the rich end if you're willing to tolerate suboptimal power increases. And suboptimal over-rich mixtures are actually a kind of cheap insurance against detonation and fuel starvation burn-downs, if you want to justify it that way. Most EFI nitrous kits that deliver nitrous fueling via a jump in fuel pressure live with increasingly suboptimal over-enrichment as rpm increases.

In the real world of street nitrous systems for street cars with stock engines and stock redlines in a price-elastic marketplace, increasingly rich air/fuel ratios are a fact of life on systems where the priority is to deliver a bunch of dirt-cheap power rather than wring out every last horsepower. For practical purposes, as a nitrous full-throttle roll-on proceeds, you *want* the air/fuel mixture to get increasingly rich for safety's sake, and if it gets a little richer than ideal, that's OK given the cost advantage of a simple mechanical system like the CRX's second nitrous kit.

For much more information about the incredibly interesting rocket science of nitrous, read my book *The Nitrous Oxide Performance Handbook*, available from Motorbooks.

CRX EFI DRY NITROUS BEFORE-BOOST CHECKLIST

- Verify the nitrous or fuel-jetting sizes (use the small nitrous-shot as a starting place).
- Change the fuel filter.
- Purge the nitrous line of any debris.
- Verify (nitrous-off) fuel-rail pressure (36 psi with vacuum reference hose disconnected and plugged).
- Attach a pressure gauge to verify fuel pressure rise during nitrous injection in the initial test run.
- Install new spark plugs, one to two heat ranges colder than stock.
- Ensure that the nitrous tank is oriented so G-forces don't interrupt the flow of liquid nitrous on hard acceleration (or cornering).
- Retard static spark timing 2 degrees.
- Consider optional low-rpm limit switch to prevent nitrous engagement at very low rpm. (Note: some Hondas may have trouble providing an adequate tach signal for the switch.)
- Perform a compression test/leakdown on the engine (before and after).
- Flow-test fuel injectors for uniformity and high-flow rate.
- Put unleaded race gas in fuel tank for initial testing (after that the best premium street gasoline).
- Inspect the stock ignition system (install new plugs, wires, distributor cap, and rotor).
- Upgrade coil, plugs, and wires (always a good idea on power-modified engines).
- What happens if the tank vents from over-pressure? Is the tank in the trunk or in the cockpit? Is the nitrous safety disk vented to the atmosphere, or will the car fill with nitrous-plus (nitrous oxide denatured with sulfur dioxide), possibly suffocating you, causing you to crash, or making you nauseated from sulfur dioxide inhalation?
- Are anti-knock countermeasures in place (i.e., boost timing retard device, J&S Safeguard knock-control system, and so on)?
- Does the fuel pump provide sufficient fuel mass under the most demanding conditions during nitrous boost?
- Is nitrous tank pressure OK?
- Is there a fire extinguisher on hand?

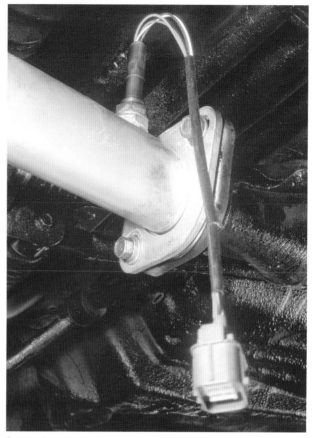

O_2 sensor keeps the Honda ECM happy at idle by enabling it to constantly seek the stoichiometric 14.7 air/fuel ratio.

- Is the nitrous system armed?
- Is there any chance nitrous has been released into the intake manifold while the engine was stopped? (This can cause explosion on startup.)
- Is the engine above 2,500 rpm?
- Is the clutch up to the job (depending on tires)?
- Is the nitrous nozzle aimed perpendicular to the throttle plate and centered in the air intake or throttle body?
- Is an extra car available, just in case you smoke the engine?
- Is a change of underwear available, in case you don't?

TURBO BOOST: 160.0 HORSEPOWER WORTH OF LOW-BUCK, LOW-BOOST, NON-INTERCOOLED TURBO POWER

At this point we put together a CRX turbo conversion system that retained the stock Honda EFI and stock engine management system and used a variable-rate-of-gain fuel pressure regulator to provide fuel enrichment under boost conditions in a way that was conceptually similar to the way we'd provided fuel enrichment for nitrous. Only in this case the fuel pressure increase would vary according to boost pressure rather than being an all-or-nothing fuel pressure increase like the EFI nitrous system. VRG regulators install inline in the fuel loop downstream of the stock regulator and increase fuel pressure as a multiple of boost pressure increases, producing more fuel per injector squirt during boost. Ideally you'll also have some kind of add-on electronic boost timing-retard device in place to prevent detonation. The alternative is retarding timing across of numbers corresponding to the correct injection pulse width for a representative list of engine speeds and manifold air density points. Although a stock naturally aspirated CRX would never see more than 1 bar of manifold absolute pressure, the stock Honda MAP sensor is actually capable of measuring up to 11-psi (0.75 bar) boost (though the ECM will hate you if you try it).

A stock CRX Si's static compression ratio is a bit over 9:1, which is enough to make the torque you'll need to have reasonable low-rpm torque at engine speeds below the threshold where there's sufficient exhaust energy to generate any turbo boost, that is, when the engine is still effectively naturally aspirated. Fortunately, with good engine management a 9:1 compression ratio should not constitute a serious pro-knock problem at higher levels of boost. The CRX engine block was quite robust at stock levels of power, but definitely not suitable for power levels hugely above stock. Most experts agreed that you could run up to 7-psi boost on a stock 1.6 CRX Si all day without problems, assumingly you had a well-designed basic turbo system and decent engine management, and that a more sophisticated turbo conversion that *never* permitted knock could probably survive 9 psi, maybe 10, using a good intercooler and great engine management air/fuel and spark calibrations—with race gas and the Safeguard knock-control system providing life insurance.

The consensus seemed to be that no matter what you did, with a stock-block Honda 1.6, you were living on borrowed time at boost levels *above* 9 or 10 psi, though some Honda engines just seemed more robust than others, living forever at 10-psi boost while others seemed to quickly go away at 8 or 9. The problem was that CRX rods, pistons, and block structures are toys compared to the super-duty components typically found on factory turbo engines, and they absolutely require upgrading or strengthening for more than 7-psi boost. But if you kept the CRX 1.6L's boost to the 7-psi range and didn't tempt yourself with a cockpit-adjustable boost controller you'd be fine. When you were ready for the really big power, unless you wanted to absolutely, definitely blow up the engine, you dismantled it and strengthened it internally and *then* you cranked up the boost. The good news is that 7-psi boost on a 1.6 CRX engine with stock internals makes a dramatic difference in power, and a really dramatic difference in the car's power-to-fun ratio.

We tested several turbo system configurations: Turbonetics ball-bearing and conventional T03 turbos, warm engine-compartment intake air versus cold-air intake, and stock exhaust with muffler and catalyst and straight-through exhaust. In general, turbo boost came on early, built quickly to 7 psi, produced greatly improved average torque, and made peak power and torque with the conventional Super-60 turbo delivering 148.2 wheel horsepower at 6,400, 128 lb-ft wheel torque at 5,000 rpm, and 160.0 wheel horsepower with the Turbonetics ball bearing turbo installed.

The turbo CRX was much stronger from just above idle all the way until the redline, and the rev-limiter hit at 6,500. Compared to the stock CRX's 92 to 96 horsepower, this is a gain of more than 66 percent power, more than we expected from a basic turbo kit without intercooling and significantly more power increase than what we'd obtained from the nitrous system. The thing is, turbos and nitrous make a different kind of power. Nitrous power comes in all at once, instantly, with the greatest impact at lower rpm, while the turbo power surges into action over a larger rpm range, continuously increasing engine power and torque as exhaust and intake gases feed back and boost increases with rpm to the max.

Initially, we provided boost fuel enrichment by installing this BEGi FMU downstream of the stock Honda fuel pressure regulator, to raise injection rail pressure as a multiple of boost pressure.

the board by re-clocking the distributor or other engine position sensor, but this will definitely hurt performance by providing insufficient spark advance during normally aspirated and low-boost operation.

A Bell Engineering fuel management unit (VRG regulator) provided fuel enrichment in place of the NOS fuel pressure jacking system, and the J&S Safeguard from earlier nitrous experiments was still in place to provide boost ignition retard on an individual-cylinder basis if required. We mounted a boost gauge on the A-pillar to provide the driver instant feedback on manifold pressure. The plan was to optimize power with the most basic non-intercooled turbo system at 6- to 7-psi boost, then add intercooling, programmable EFI, exhaust improvements, and so forth. The turbo kit had been designed to allow retention of the stock catalyst, muffler, and exhaust system, but there was plenty to be gained with exhaust-flow upgrades as the engine made more power.

Vintage stock Honda CRX are equipped with computer-controlled port-EFI of the speed-density variety. Rather than directly measuring engine airflow with a mass airflow (MAF) sensor, the CRX computer estimates airflow based on intake air temperature, manifold pressure, throttle angle (which correspond to engine loading), known engine displacement, and engine speed. These values are used to index into an internal calibration table

THE TURBO CONVERSION
Fuel Enrichment

Engines converted to turbocharging always need additional fuel under boost conditions merely to maintain stock wide-open-throttle (WOT) air/fuel ratios, and they virtually always need richer than stock air/fuel ratios to realize full power potential and fight detonation on a knock-limited engine running street gasoline.

The CRX turbo conversion initially received fuel enrichment during boost due to the effect of a Bell Engineering variable-rate-of-gain fuel pressure regulator (a.k.a., fuel management unit or FMU) installed downstream of the stock Honda fuel pressure regulator in the fuel return line. FMUs are normally adjusted to have null effect during naturally aspirated conditions at idle or light cruise and to increase fuel rail pressure during boost as an adjustable multiple of manifold pressure in the range of 4- to 7-psi increase in fuel pressure per pound of boost. As with the nitrous kit, increased fuel rail pressure causes the injectors to inject more fuel per timed squirt to maintain or enrich the air/fuel ratio.

The maximum boost of a turbo system with FMU fuel enrichment is ultimately limited by the inability of fuel injectors to function reliably at much more than 70-psi fuel pressure, which essentially limits maximum boost to the 5–10-psi range. Another constraint results from the reality that maximum fuel flow from a high-pressure centrifugal electric fuel pump is inversely proportional fuel pressure, and some fuel pumps are equipped with a high-pressure bypass valve that firmly limits maximum pressure. In many cases, even a low-boost turbo conversion will require an upgraded or auxiliary fuel pump.

Careful testing on the Alamo Dynojet revealed that the stock CRX fuel pump reached its volumetric limit (at the supernaturally high fuel pressure of the FMU) at roughly 135 driving-wheel horsepower. As discussed elsewhere in this book, the method for determining fuel pump capacity essentially involves energizing the fuel pump with the engine stopped and raising reference pressure at the regulator to manifold pressure a full boost with a hand-operated air pump. Measuring fuel flow per time from the regulator fuel return line equals the maximum amount of fuel that can be removed from the rail per time by the injectors before rail pressure begin to drop, which is unacceptable.

Obviously, FMU-fueled turbocharging is not going to work if an EFI nitrous kit needs the fuel pressure increase to fuel nitrous, but in this case a stock CRX engine block was not going to handle the combined power boost of both nitrous and turbocharging in any case. However, the next step in the project would be installing a DFI engine management system, at which point we'd remove the FMU and experiment with using *transient nitrous* at wide-open throttle to make instant torque and spank up turbine energy so the turbocharger would deliver full boost in record time. The plan was to switch off the nitrous as soon as turbo boost reached 3–5-psi boost to keep extreme combustion pressures from hurting the engine—with the side benefit that a tankful of N_2O lasts forever when used in this limited way.

Before turbocharging, the 550-horse NOS inline auxiliary fuel pump kicked in when the NOS kit began spewing nitrous. For the turbo conversion, we rewired the NOS pump so that a relay activated when the nitrous system was armed *or* when manifold pressure exceeded 2 psi.

Turbocharger: The Alamo Autosports turbo system on our project CRX was designed to use a T3-type turbocharger with a Turbonetics Super-60 compressor. The turbine section consisted of a 72-trim turbine wheel (standard T03 trim) and a 0.48 A/R

turbine housing (which is quite small) for improved low-end response on a 1.6-liter motor on the small end of the Super-60 envelope. Turbonetics marketed the Super-60 in both ceramic ball bearing and standard bushed designs and repeatedly demonstrated the ball bearing turbo's free-spinning advantages in increasing engine performance via faster spool-up and higher boost pressure per engine rpm. The Super-60 was designed to efficiently deliver 220–485 cfm for use on 150-335-horsepower engines.

We made Dynojet runs with both ball-bearing and standard turbos. Initial testing with the standard turbo delivered 14.6 horsepower, and subsequent intake, exhaust, fuel supply, and tuning mods brought power up by almost 25 to 148.2 wheel horsepower. Our experience with the Super-60 BB was that it was always the equivalent of a few hundred engine rpm ahead of the conventional Super-60, with the corresponding dyno power graphs almost parallel and the ball-bearing turbo's power and torque constantly ahead by several hundred rpm worth of power and torque all the way up to redline. Peak power near redline was up by 10 driving-wheel horsepower across the board with the ceramic ball-bearing turbo. The CRX was more fun to drive, accelerating harder and sooner, the car's gas pedal much more responsive. Performance on the street with 93-octane premium was subjectively equal to that with 100 octane, except on the few occasions when the J&S Safeguard pulled timing to kill detonation in 100-plus degree weather of south Texas.

Wastegate: We used a Turbonetics wastegate to limit maximum boost. The Deltagate was a dual-ported external wastegate that could limit boost in conventional mode by simply referencing manifold pressure to the exhaust-side diaphragm port of the wastegate actuator, which would overcome spring pressure when boost pressure climbed high enough and opened a poppet valve that diverted exhaust gases around the turbine, effectively reducing the power of the turbine and, therefore, the maximum cfm capacity of the compressor. The secondary Deltagate port, located on the other side of the diaphragm, can be used to exert an opposing force that tends to help the internal spring keep the wastegate closed. Standard practice in Deltagate mode was to feed full pressure from the compressor outlet to the primary Deltagate port and to feed manifold pressure—limited by a EMS-controlled PWM (boost-control) valve—to the Deltagate port, allowing maximum boost to be determined by the duty-cycle of the boost control valve.

The T-3 turbine housing is designed to allow installation of an internal wastegate. Although internal-type wastegates eliminate the need for wastegate plumbing fabrication work, the integrated turbo-wastegate concept increases the size of the turbocharger. Where space is a problem—as it was on the CRX—an external unit offers more options for packaging the turbo-wastegate system. We integrated a Deltagate mounting flange on the RD turbo exhaust header so the Deltagate bolted directly to exhaust header.

With the main turbo components in place, we reworked some RD intercooler tubing to route air from the turbo compressor to the CRX throttle body, installing an HKS pop-off valve to prevent compressor surge on sudden throttle closing.

Vintage CRX MAP sensors will measure almost 9-psi positive manifold pressure, but the Honda ECM will freak out if the stock MAP sensor reports higher-than-atmospheric manifold pressure, turning on the check engine light and switching to limp-home mode. To prevent this, we installed check valves that allowed accurate manifold pressure to reach the MAP sensor during vacuum conditions, but prevented boost pressure from entering the MAP reference hose when the turbo was making boost. How it works is this: When positive boost pressure moves toward the MAP sensor, several check valves that tee into the reference line open, bleeding off positive pressure before it can reach the sensor. Under vacuum conditions, the check valves close and the reference line provides accurate vacuum to the sensor.

The Bell Engineering FMU was installed in the fuel return hose downstream of the stock fuel pressure regulator, rate-of-gain set with a bleed valve, onset pressure (usually atmospheric pressure) adjusted with a bolt, and lock-nut diaphragm controlling internal spring pressure. In general, tightening the bleed increases the rate of gain. Start rich for safety, work lean for power.

We installed cold spark plugs to fight detonation, the coldest plugs that won't foul at idle.

If you are using a J&S Safeguard individual cylinder knock-retard device to control knock (as we were) the trick is to make sure ignition static timing is set at stock specs and let the Safeguard do the work. Follow instructions with other types of boost timing retard devices, but do not attempt to boost power without some electronic boost-timing retard device or you'll be forced to run super-high-octane race gas or retard static timing enough to severely reduce drivability under naturally aspirated conditions, or both. Safeguards are sensitive, with an adjustable knock-detection threshold, but keep in mind that it is harder to stop knock once started than it is to *prevent* it with timing retard. If the Safeguard is having to work a lot, you might do better to install an auxiliary boost-retard device that routinely removes a configurable amount of timing per-psi boost and leave the Safeguard in place as insurance that permits minimal routine boost retard, and still protecting the engine under rarely encountered worst-case pro-knock conditions.

We discovered that an isolated cold-air intake that ingested air exclusively from outside the engine compartment made five additional wheel horsepower on race gas and even more relative power on street gas by lowering combustion temperatures enough that the Safeguard did not need to pull timing as much on boost.

We began the CRX tuning process using race gasoline, in this case a blend of 108 unleaded and 93 octane Texas street premium. When you are looking for maximum power, start with lots of octane, find the limits, and then experiment with lower octane fuel combined with more aggressive timing retard and richer air/fuel ratios. Our highest priority was to makes sure the air/fuel ratio stayed rich and detonation never happened, and the way to do that is with a good, fast, accurate air/fuel-ratio meter that can be datalogged with engine rpm as it can on many chassis dynos. If you are using a tailpipe wideband sniffer, multiple feet of exhaust pipe will add a tiny delay and should ideally be configured away so the air/fuel ratio data matches engine rpm. Thinking ahead, we had installed an O_2 sensor bung for the wideband in the turbine discharge tube. You cannot optimize air/fuel ratio without a good wideband and you cannot optimize timing at all points without a load-holding dyno to optimize spark advance for peak torque.

GOING FOR BROKE: MAXIMUM STOCK-BLOCK TURBO POWER

Having made 134 horsepower with an EFI nitrous system and 160 wheel horsepower with a basic ball-bearing turbo system, a VRG regulator, a Safeguard knock-control system, and super-premium fuel, the phase-3 goal now was to extract every bit of power from our 1989 project CRX Turbo's 1.6-liter SOHC stock

block without killing the engine. Our strategy included adding the following major components: an Accel/DFI standalone aftermarket programmable EMS, intercooling, intermittent nitrous injection, electronic boost control, upgraded fuel supply, and a higher-flowing exhaust system.

The universal-type DFI EMS kit we installed on the Honda CRX included (1) an electronic control unit (ECU) equipped for reading inductive engine-position pickups, (2) a generic wiring harness adaptable to most vehicles, and (3) a basic set of GM-type engine sensors (with additional sensors available optionally). You need high-pressure fuel supply and return lines, a high-pressure fuel pump and regulator, injectors correctly sized for expected engine horsepower, a throttle body, and so forth, but all of this was already on the turbo EFI CRX, though we upgraded some components for the expected higher-horsepower.

Our DFI ECM had the standard bag of EMS tricks, including speed-density airflow estimation, idle speed stabilization anti-stall using a GM IAC throttle air-bypass stepper motor, idle/light-cruise air/fuel ratio control in closed-loop mode via exhaust gas oxygen sensor feedback, and the ability to improve idle quality with feedback-based micro changes in spark advance. The DFI was designed with a large variety of enrichment and enleanment offsets to base fuel and ignition computations to improve starting, warm-up, throttle transition, and more. The DFI was equipped with nitrous control logic that could provide up to three stages of nitrous delivery and matching fuel enrichment through the electronic injectors. When it came time,we'd be calibrating the DFI system the old-fashioned way (no auto-tune, no VE table) using a Windows laptop computer running CalMap graphical interface software, connected to the DFI ECM with a serial RS232 or USB interface cable. The DFI internal data structures included a 16x16 matrix to store injection pulse width for 256 combinations of engine loading and speed (no VE table), with a smaller matrix storing ignition advance in the same manner. Our DFI system measured engine speed and loading via a crank trigger and a MAP sensor, and used these values to look up injection time and spark advance in the internal tables on an ongoing basis.

Our DFI ECM was not designed for the harsh environment of an engine compartment, so we installed it below the dash, routing the wiring harness through the firewall into the engine compartment, where the DFI injector harness plugged seamlessly into a set of Honda-compatible 310-cc/min RC Engineering fuel injectors that upgrade fuel delivery potential 50 percent over the stock 220-cc injectors.

Next came the engine sensors, after drilling and tapping threaded bosses into the compressor-out air tube and the water jacket for installing GM coolant and intake air temperature sensors. We left the stock Honda sensors (not compatible with our version DFI) in place along with the stock Honda computer wiring harness. We mounted a 2-bar GM MAP sensor (accurate from high vacuum to 15-psi boost pressure on the firewall where the pressure port could be referenced to the intake manifold with a short length of vacuum hose). The CRX throttle position sensor (TPS) was a 0–5-volt linear potentiometer, which was usable after building a short adapter pigtail with a Honda-style connector for connection to the stock TPS on one end and the DFI TPS connector on the other. The final sensor was an optional three-wire GM-type heated exhaust gas oxygen sensor, used by the DFI ECM for closed-loop idle air/fuel trim. This O_2 sensor screwed into a K&N sensor boss we'd previously welded into the turbo downpipe like a spark plug. In the interests of

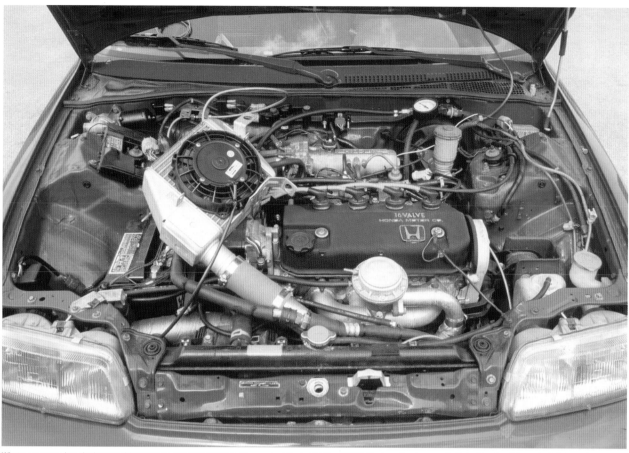

When we pumped up the boost to higher levels and added intercooling, we installed a DFI Gen 6 EMS. Back on the dyno, we tested with a fan-driven air-air-intercooler.

time, we did not make use of the DFI's optional IAC idle speed control though the DFI ECM could handle knock detection and retard with an optional GM knock-sensor module. We decided to retain the J&S Safeguard—with its individual-cylinder retard and sensitivity-adjustment capabilities—as a last line of defense against anti-knock detonation. At this point we connected the DFI harnesses 12-volt power line directly to the Honda battery, and wired the switched +12 volts line to the ignition switch where it would see 12 volts during starting *and* running modes.

In order for the DFI to control ignition functions, crank or cam trigger engine position information is mandatory in the form of a 180-degree inductive pickup/trigger. In fact, there are three inductive pickup or flying magnet triggers on the Honda distributor, indicating top dead center compression-stroke number one cylinder, 180-degree increments of crank rotation, and 120-degree increments of crank rotation.

All of these are essential to keep the Honda computer happy and functioning, which we would have preferred, since the Honda computer also controls air conditioning, alternator charging, fast-idle, tachometer, and other nice drivability features. Unfortunately—as is typical—the Honda inductive pickup circuitry was not powerful enough to drive the input sensor circuitry of two computers at once. Choices were (1) add amplification circuitry to the 180-degree trigger, (2) add another 180-degree trigger to the distributor or cam (four flying magnetic bolts required) or the crankshaft (two flying magnetic bolts required), or (3) make do without the Honda computer

online at all—which was what we did. This would require minor rewiring to the alternator and air conditioning control circuitry.

Following initial testing with the Honda computer handling timing and the DFI handling fueling, Alamo disconnected the Honda computer from the distributor and wired the distributor to the DFI so it could read the Honda's 180-degree cam-speed magnetic inductive pickup to determine engine position. In this mode, the DFI can provide timed low-voltage ignition pulses defining spark timing to an OEM ignition module or aftermarket coil-driver box (such as MSD 6-series, Accel 300+, etc.). For simplicity's sake, we continued using the J&S Safeguard module's coil-driver capability to drive the stock distributor-integral Honda coil.

For compatibility reasons associated with the GM's EST home-mode ignition-timing requirements, without correction, DFI-based timing would be retarded 10 degrees on a CRX. This required (1) that the distributor be rotated until the DFI's internal timing table entry corresponded precisely with actual engine position relative to the current compression-stroke cylinder location at the time of the spark event. With this accomplished, (2) the CRX distributor rotor could be re-clocked so the rotor was pointing at the correct plug-wire electrode in the distributor cap. We modified the plastic CRX rotor to this end, though it's possible to heat a vintage Honda distributor shaft with a torch until the pressed-on rotor-orienting stub shaft can be rotated 10 degrees.

To extract maximum performance and economy from the 1.6L Si engine, CRX alternator charging rate is partially controlled by the (stock) computer, which can reduce or eliminate charging at full throttle to reduce parasitic accessory power losses. The computer can also maximize charging during deceleration. Without the DFI computer online, the alternator would not charge at all. We connected two leads together with a jumper in the alternator-controller connector plug to provide conventional (non-EMS) charging.

The stock Honda computer also controlled A/C compressor clutch operation in order to disengage the clutch at wide-open throttle to further reduce accessory drag. The solution is to rewire the A/C control circuitry to eliminate the Honda ECM from the circuit and allow direct compressor control from the dash controls using a 30-amp relay with a nitrous-type full-throttle microswitch disable the relay at full throttle.

Upgrading the fuel supply is essential for any CRX engine making more than 135 horsepower. The stock Honda in-tank pump plumbed in series with an auxiliary NOS 550-horse inline unit provided more than enough fuel, and we stuck with the stock fuel supply and return lines. Like most ECMS, the DFI was set up to energize the fuel pump relay while starting and running and for a few seconds at key-on time to bring the fuel rail to full pressure. For safety reasons ECMs kill the fuel pump immediately if the engine stalls in case a crash ruptured the fuel supply line. With the NOS pump in place we had 300 horsepower worth of injector capacity and more than enough pumping capacity to fuel it at stock regulated fuel pressure.

Generally speaking, the cold plugs that won't load up at idle are the right way to go on a turbo conversion powerplant. Stock spark plugs may work OK with very low boost, and *hotter* plugs will resist fouling from rich idle mixtures, but when you begin pushing the limits of cylinder sealing, ring land integrity, and block and head structural strength, the overriding goal must be to avoid detonation at all costs. Two or more heat ranges colder than stock is a good place to start. Remember, however, that such plugs can easily foul if grossly rich mixtures accidentally occur during the calibration process. An engine begins running terribly, and the last thing you'll suspect is the plugs—because just a few minutes ago they were brand new. Suspect the plugs. Keep an extra set on hand. By the way, turbo engines require top-quality plug wires. It's normal for tuners who know what they're doing to set the plug gap at 0.029 instead of 0.039 or whatever it says in the manual for a stock NA powerplant. Plan on upgrading the plug wires, coil, and coil driver when you begin to pump up turbo boost. Even if the engine still sounds good, upgraded ignition can add 20 or 30 horsepower on a turbo-four.

Alamo Autosports knew from earlier experiments with CRX turbocharging that the stock Honda exhaust is a bad joke when you start to crank up the boost. In fact, we were amazed when the 1.6 engine made as much as 135 wheel horsepower with such a restrictive exhaust and cat installed, and we were not a bit surprised to make another 15 horsepower by disconnecting the exhaust and retuning. This time, to get the biggest power numbers, Alamo fabricated a custom 2.5-inch shorty high-flow exhaust system that bolted to the RD Racing turbo downpipe and included a 2.5-inch resonator with straight-down dump. It was illegal and really loud, but the plan was eventually to install a high-flow cat and a quiet—but high flow—muffler.

Meanwhile, to increase the area under the torque curve we needed electronic boost control. Some modern ECMs have built-in PWM boost-control capability, but we managed CRX boost with an HKS EVC (electronic valve controller) boost controller, an ingenious electromechanical device that manages manifold pressure seen by a wastegate—to raise average or peak boost, or both. The EVC uses fuzzy logic to determine how fast the turbo can build boost under maximum loading, how fast the wastegate opens, and how effective the wastegate is once open. Once the EVC understands a turbo system's capabilities, the EVC can keep the wastegate fully closed until an instant before full boost is achieved. It can then slam open the wastegate quickly and to the degree required to prevent over-boost, greatly increasing midrange torque compared to traditional mechanical wastegates, which begin to bleed off a certain amount of boost long before maximum boost has actually arrived, degrading potential midrange torque.

EVC kits include a dash-mounted controller with a harness that connects through the firewall to the HKS electro-pneumatic actuator unit and wires you connect to constant and switched 12-volt power and ground. Vacuum hoses connect the EVC to the intake manifold, compressor discharge (highest available boost pressure), and the standard wastegate port. Following installation and a learning procedure while driving, EVCs can be adjusted while you drive from the comfort of the cockpit. This can be deadly if you like to street race and have poor judgment about what level of overboost will kill your engine. Some people should not mount this device in the cockpit—you know who you are. In the end we used the EVC to crank up boost from the 5.5-psi boost pressure delivered by the Turbonetics Deltagate's nominal wastegate spring pressure of to 7.5 psi, and increase midrange boost and torque by 36 percent. As you'd expect, 36 percent more boost makes an amazing difference in performance.

But first it was tuning time.

With everything else in place, we connected a laptop serial cable to the interface connector on the DFI harness near the ECM, plugged the other end to a laptop, and fired up Calmap in Windows. The laptop was there to define global parameters in the computer (such as number of cylinders), and then to build fuel-injection pulse width and ignition timing tables. Internal DFI data structures included a 16x16 matrix to store injection pulse width for 256 combinations of engine loading and speed (no VE table), with a smaller matrix storing ignition advance in the same manner. The DFI system measured engine speed and loading via a crank trigger and a MAP sensor, and used these values to look up injection time and spark advance in the internal tables on an ongoing basis.

Actual calibration (mapping) of an engine management computer requires establishing a start-up map good enough to keep the engine running until it's warm, then tuning the engine at zero load across all speeds, setting injection pulse width at light load, then gradually loading the engine at various speeds while observing air/fuel ratios, exhaust gas temperatures, and dyno power and torque to get the perfect injection pulse width for lean best torque (richer if fuel cooling is required) at heavier loads. All elements of the DFI's 16x16 air/fuel matrix had to be set with the laptop PC, while avoiding dangerously lean mixtures at all cost. Optimized and safe ignition timing is vital but generally a little more predictable in advance.

Using extensive experience with hot-rod 1.6 Hondas, including various turbo CRXs, Alamo's Steve Webb got a head start building a custom air/fuel map project CRX Si by working with a map from a reasonably similar turbo CRX good diagnostic equipment. Period. Even with good equipment and experience, it typically takes at least one to four days to get a map that works well under normal conditions.

In the final dyno testing, we switched to air-water intercooling, which enabled us to achieve more than 100 percent cooling efficiency by cooling the charge-cooler with tap water. With a rigged air-water cooler and DFI engine controls, we more than doubled the stock 96 wheel horsepower to roughly 200.

With the DFI calibration shaping up well, we tested two different intercoolers that would lower combustion temperatures to control detonation and stuff the engine with denser, cooler air. Neither cooler was designed to fit the Honda engine compartment, but we kludged the coolers into place with temporary plumbing for Dynojet testing with the hood up and sorted things out later for street testing. The air-air unit was designed for a serious 2.2 Mitsubishi engine, while the air-water unit was a custom Norwood Autocraft design for the MR2 four-cylinder project in this book.

The air-water cooler was the more interesting, because it had the potential to achieve thermal efficiencies above 100 percent—meaning the compressed air from the turbocharger is cooled *below* ambient air temperatures—which is impossible with an air-cooled intercooler. We ran the air-water cooler on the project CRX on the Dynojet, using tap water from a hose for consistency and to maximize the results. For street driving with a water-cooled intercooler, you need an efficient heat exchanger with fan and bilge-pump-type circulation system to keep the intercooler nice and chilly, though it turns out that even if the water-cooler unit of an air-water intercooler is totally ineffective and water mass is acting as a *heat sink* cooled exclusively by intake air when the engine is *not* under boost, an air-water intercooler can cool compressed air during episodes of turbo boost with far less increase in water temperature that you'd think. For drag racing, you can circulate ice water from an onboard tank through the intercooler for even denser, colder intake air.

Other advantages of an air-water system include smaller intercooler size per BTUs of heat-removal capacity and the fact that separating the air-cooler unit from the water-cooling heat exchanger can add layout flexibility that makes custom installations much easier. On the other hand, air-water systems require electrical circulation pumps (with moving parts and electrical controls) and are more complex and prone to failure than simple rugged one-piece air-air intercoolers.

Our intercooler allowed us to safely run more boost (7.5 psi versus 5.5), and the denser, colder, higher-boost inlet air clearly contributed to the 45–55 additional wheel horsepower we made with the DFI in control. With 500-plus-wheel horses worth of intercooler cfm capability, we knew there'd be zero pressure drop at current power levels on the Honda. We also knew the cooler could keep intake air cold and safe and dense.

A nice feature of the DFI EMS was its ability to trigger nitrous solenoid activation, then provide precise fuel enrichment

through the port injectors by increasing base injection pulse width, with excellent fuel distribution to all cylinders guaranteed. The DFI could be programmed to provide default spark retard during nitrous injection by subtracting a configurable timing retard offset from calculated spark timing, (which could include a separate turbo boost-based timing offset).

Since the turbo system was capable of making as much power as the stock CRX engine could stand, we used *intermittent* nitrous to spank up the turbo quickly with a sudden blast of exhaust pressure and heat on full-throttle nitrous activation, at the same time radically and instantly increasing torque to full-boost-type levels. At which point 5-psi boost would kill the nitrous.

The way it worked was you configure the DFI system for nitrous by defined rules for nitrous activation (arming switch on, minimum engine rpm, 100 percent throttle position, and so on). You then define timing retard upon nitrous activation and fuel enrichment parameters (which must be properly synchronized with the numbered nitrous jet installed in the injection nozzle). You select a variable-length delay (if any) for nitrous activation after fuel enrichment begins in order to make sure nitrous never arrives in cylinders before fuel (to avoid incredibly destructive nitrous lean-out).

Alamo started with a 50-shot nitrous charge, and the stock clutch let go and the engine surged for the redline. A 30-shot yielded similar results. A 20-shot produced three nitrous-boosted dyno runs before the stock clutch gave out entirely. Since we wanted dyno results in a hurry, we installed a Stage IV Clutchmasters performance metal clutch system, capable of handling 375 to 400 wheel horsepower on the Honda with a reworked 1,400-pound clamping force pressure plate (double stock) and a spring-loaded, damped street-strip metal-puck clutch disc. This clutch was a mite touchier engaging from a full stop than a Stage III Clutchmasters system with the carbon-Kevlar disc, but the carbon clutch required 500 miles of break in, and we couldn't wait. Clutchmasters changed the geometry of the clutch fork to keep pedal engagement pressure down to near stock or even below stock level. The clutch system was extremely streetable.

RESULTS AND ANALYSIS

The CRX project produced some of the nicest dyno charts I've ever seen: smooth, linear, and predictable. With all the good stuff in place, we produced multiple runs that were very repeatable. Peak power with air-water intercooling and a nitrous shot between 2,500 and 3,500 rpm was in the high 190s at the wheels just above 6,000 rpm, with power on the way up when the run stopped near redline. Torque was nearly flat at 170 lb-ft from 2,500 to redline (nitrous armed), or from 3,500 to redline without nitrous.

It is interesting to compare the results of the turbo CRX, running sans intercooler at 5.5-psi boost, to an Eaton-supercharged Honda running 7-psi boost. The CRX made 10.7 more maximum horsepower and 12.0 lb-ft more peak torque, on less boost. The supercharger made more power and torque below 3,000—unless you armed the CRX's intermittent nitrous—in which case the CRX made a *ton* more torque everywhere above 2,000, and about 3 lb-ft less below 2,000. The graphs were otherwise similar until 4,500, at which point the turbo CRX began to pull ahead significantly. On less boost. At roughly equal levels of boost (7-psi blown, 7.5-psi turbo boost), the stock-block turbo CRX made 70–80 more peak horsepower! Which car do you think is faster? There is something to be said for efficient compressors and good intercooling.

Chapter 22
Project: Honda del Sol Si Turbo

The world changes. . . . When designing the Honda CRX turbo conversion project for this book, the choices were to retain the stock Honda engine-control system and add on electronic and mechanical aids to provide boost fuel enrichment and retard spark timing, or to junk the Honda EMS in favor of an aftermarket ECM. We did both.

When it came to the turbo Honda del Sol Si project in this chapter, there were new options. You could retain the stock Honda system but convert it to user-programmability for reconfiguration and recalibration. You could install a plug-and-play aftermarket EMS.

We decided to do both, contacting Hondata about using its programmability conversion for the factory Honda ECM and contacting AEM about using its replacement aftermarket ECM.

THE HONDATA TURBO DEL SOL

After reading several Hondata installation and user manuals, we peeled back the carpet on the passenger-side del Sol kick-panel,

unbolted and unplugged the del Sol's ECM, and shipped the 1.6-liter D-16Z SOHC VTEC engine's ECM to Hondata in California. Hondata socketed the main circuit board to permit installation of an aftermarket PROM chip, added some resistor-jumpers to the board that would enable the microprocessor to read from the new PROM, and installed a socket on the board suitable for connecting a communications cable to a Hondata user interface box.

Modern multivalve engines with port EFI are intentionally designed with very flat torque curves, and these engines typically use tricks like variable-length induction systems, variable valve timing (and lift, in the case of Honda's VTEC) to keep torque from falling off too fast in the upper rpm range. Flat torque curves make for simple, straightforward EMS calibrations (though VTEC engine management must deal with a transient dip in torque that tends to occur where the engine changes to the high-speed cam and charge velocity momentarily dips).

Since it would not be interesting to reprogram the del Sol ECM if the engine remained stock (it's already optimized for the

1995 Honda del Sol SOHC VTEC with turbo conversion and electronic intercooling.

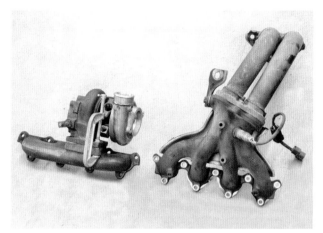

To make the del Sol recalibration project interesting, the highest priority was to get a turbocharger on the car. A special cast turbo exhaust manifold replaces the stock cast-iron header and downpipe, and tucks a T28 turbo close to the engine behind the radiator.

Turbocharged 1.6-liter Honda del Sol waiting for the next new Hondata PROM. Hondata mods made the stock Honda computer programmable and capable of datalogging. Hondata's "Hondalogger" box allowed a tuner to datalog the complement of stock Honda and modified sensors during test runs, including, optionally, wideband O_2 data.

job; there's nowhere to go), to make things more challenging and fun, I designed, built, and installed a custom turbo system. With excellent engine management, turbo-EFI engines are capable of producing extremely high levels of streetable specific power: Maximum-effort 1.8-liter Honda turbo engines running methanol were making 1,000 horsepower when the del Sol project went down. However, turbo engines—particularly ones with large, high-slow (and lazy) compressors—can be challenging to tune because they have more complex VE curves.

Turbo engines have trickier torque curves because turbo boost is never available immediately, especially in the lowest rpm range, but to some extent, the more boost they make, the more boost they *can* make. Centrifugal compressor airflow is essentially exponential with speed, so turbochargers need to accelerate into the 40,000–80,000 compressor rpm before they make much boost, which takes time. Meanwhile, at low engine speed and loading, the exhaust energy is simply not available to drive the turbine full-tilt. Once boost does take hold, more boost means more exhaust pressure and heat, which makes more boost, and so on and on and on. Small engines with big turbos lack low-end torque before the boost kicks in, but when it does, torque increases massively in a huge whoop of boost as the compressor comes up to speed. Not only does volumetric efficiency move around less predictably on turbo engines, but turbo engines are far more prone to detonation than normally aspirated powerplants and usually need at least some fuel-based combustion cooling and timing retard during boost. This means that finding the optimal air/fuel ratios is critical but also less predictable. Turbo engines make much more use of advanced features and high-resolution engine management system tables to keep air/fuel ratios and timing optimal and safe under all conditions and to retain excellent drivability while providing high specific power.

With a Majestic Turbo T3-T04 turbocharger installed on a stock Honda SOHC VTEC 1.6-liter engine, the del Sol's newly programmable Honda ECM arrived back in Texas from Hondata with the new socketing and jumpers on the circuit board, ready for building a turbo calibration on a Hondata-format aftermarket PROM.

Unfortunately, I'd built the turbo system at Bell Engineering near San Antonio, but planned to calibrate the Honda/Hondata

ECM at Alamo Autosports near Dallas, where a package of additional Hondata components awaited installation, including the new Hondata PROM, interface box, cabling, and so on. I needed a way to get the car to Dallas without a turbo calibration. The good news was that, if you interrupted one of the new Hondata jumpers on the main Honda circuit board, the ECM will run the engine from the stock Honda PROM, which remained in place. Unfortunately, a turbo conversion engine running a stock calibration could be expected to produce poor drivability and dangerous detonation without fuel enrichment under boost and perhaps a little timing retard under boost.

So I cut the J1 jumper and installed a microswitch between the leads inside the Honda ECM case and installed a BEGi fuel management unit to provide fuel enrichment under turbo boost by increasing fuel pressure as a multiple of boost pressure—and headed for Alamo Autosports near Dallas.

INSTALLING AND ACTIVATING HONDATA

At this point we installed the rest of the Hondata system by wiring in the small blue Hondata add-on auxiliary processor box to the main circuit board in the Honda ECM. The blue box contained circuitry and a nine-pin delta connector that enabled attachment of a laptop computer to the Honda ECM, which could then be used to datalog the EMS when the car is running. The Hondata box also contains an LED that glowed steadily or blinked to signify various types of internal events.

With the interface equipment in place, Hondata's ROMeditor laptop software can display Honda ECM fuel and timing tables for high-speed and low-speed cams with at least 20 predetermined rpm ranges and 13 load ranges, of which four represented 0.6, 3.9, 7.9, and 11.0-psi boost, respectively.

A stock del Sol MAP sensor is capable of measuring slightly more than 11 psi (0.75 bar) positive boost pressure, though the stock Honda ECM will freak and report an error at anything more than about 1-psi boost. The stock del Sol calibration provides fuel delivery and spark advance for the expected range of rpm and manifold pressure for a normally aspirated SOHC 1.6-liter Honda engine with stock Honda cam. For turbocharged operation, Hondata provided a calibration that specifies fuel delivery all the way to 11-psi boost (or up to 29-psi boost if

Optimizing the Hondata turbo calibration on the Dynojet.

you elect to take advantage of Hondata's ability to modify your Honda ECM to support a GM 3-bar MAP sensor).

Hondata had available a selection of turbo calibrations for the D-16Z powerplant. Alamo loaded a likely candidate believed to be safe into a rewritable PROM and installed it in the new socket installed by Hondata and drove the car onto the Dynojet.

DYNO-TUNING THE HONDATA-FIED HONDA EMS

Once the OEM Honda ECM has been socketed for an aftermarket (Hondata) PROM and the blue interface box installed, there were two methods of tuning:

1. If you had a PROM emulator available, you could remove the Hondata PROM, install an emulator cable in its place, and plug the Hondata PROM into the emulator, where the calibration could be modified on the fly while the engine was running and later dumped back to the PROM (see below).

2. If you did not have an emulator, the alternative was to use Hondata's ROMeditor to make changes to the calibration *offline* on a laptop (usually connected to the Hondata blue box so you could datalog dynoruns). Following evaluation and analysis of the most recent dynorun (ideally made by a dyno equipped with a wideband air/fuel ratio sensor) and the associated Hondata datalog. With the offline Honda calibration data corrected to reflect test results, you could burn a new PROM and install it into the Hondata Honda ECM socket for subsequent testing. There are two kinds of PROMs: those that can be written once and more expensive PROMs that can be rewritten many times.

An emulator is a fast microprocessor device that sucks in the data from a PROM device and stores it in a buffer in fast RAM where the data can be modified while performing its original function (running an engine, in this case) via the emulator. A short cable—short because even at the speed of light, long cables can negatively affect the timing of memory access—plugs into the PROM socket in the microcontroller (ECM, in this case), and the emulator responds to the multi-pin protocols an ECM uses to access PROM memory. Meanwhile, the PROM image in the emulator could be changed on the fly with a Windows

laptop PC—in the case of the del Sol while a Honda ECM was running an engine. When the Honda ECM executed a read operation to PROM memory, the emulator—as you'd expect—would faithfully emulate the electronic handshake signals of the Hondata PROM and supply PROM-image data in place of the data that would be supplied by the real PROM.

Hondata's ROMeditor PC software was equipped with commands that allowed it to read and write calibration data from the emulator, allowing the emulator to be used for dyno tuning, essentially achieving the on-the-fly programmability of a standalone programmable aftermarket EMS. Some emulators are fast enough that the PROM image calibration data can be changed while an engine is running without a hitch. However, more economical units might be slower to respond during a change, producing a noticeable hiccup that disturbs smooth engine operation. Unless you have a lightning-fast emulator, dynamic changes are not the best idea during high-load operation. The best compromise is to make dynoruns on a chassis dynamometer while running Hondata's HondaLogger datalogging software (or logging the air/fuel ratio with a wideband air/fuel ratio sensor connected to the dyno), and then make a change to the emulator between dynoruns.

When you are done modifying the PROM image to recalibrate the EMS, the revised calibration in the emulator can be offloaded from the laptop into a PROM burner where a new PROM can be blown (ROMeditor provides a burn PROM command).

DYNO-TUNING THE DEL SOL

In the case of the del Sol, we worked without an emulator (Alamo's was out for repair). We installed a Hondata PROM in a special carrier designed for easy R&R without damaging the delicate pins of the PROM.

One thing to keep in mind when tuning an engine using a wideband O_2 sensor is that the sensor is not located in the combustion chamber but is farther downstream in the exhaust header or exhaust system. There will always be at least a tiny delay between the parameters that generate a particular combustion event and the arrival of the exhaust gases at the wideband sensor where the exhaust gas oxygen can be converted into a voltage

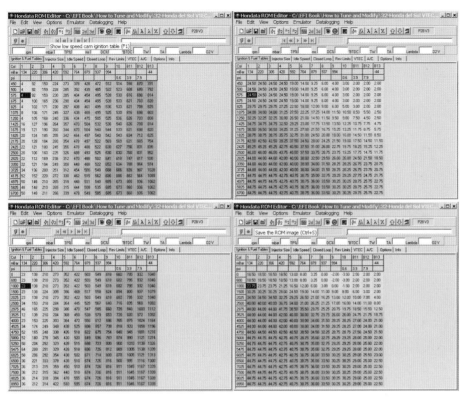

High- and low-speed Hondata calibrations for del Sol fuel and ignition.

for interpretation, say, as evidence of a particular air/fuel ratio in the intake.

If the engine is operating at steady state, at a particular speed and loading, there is no problem, and, in any case, exhaust gases travel fast in an engine under load at higher rpm. It is still useful to keep in mind that wideband O_2 data is actually past history on an engine accelerating hard at high rpm. Keep in mind also that engine conditions will have changed at least a little (and possibly more than a little on a really fast-revving engine) by the time you log exhaust gas oxygen data. Alamo owner Brice Yingling made the case that tailpipe wideband data on a Dynojet is 100 rpm or so old (some dynamometer systems enable you to program out delay in correlating wideband data with rpm or miles per hour, and some ECMs that read wideband sensor data can be configured to do the same thing).

Our base Hondata turbo calibration produced a spot on the dynorun air/fuel map at 6,500 rpm where the air/fuel ratio plunged deep into rich territory to such an extent that it was off the rich end of the scale below 10:1. We turned off closed-loop mode during the tuning process, though closed-loop was, in any case, configured only to operate below 790 millibars, about two-thirds of the way between high vacuum and zero vacuum. At that point we made a succession of about 12 dynoruns, working to smooth out the peaks and valleys in the air/fuel ratio graph by using ROMeditor to correct fuel cells in the immediate vicinity of the worst peaks and valleys, as well as selecting larger areas of the graph to modify using the *percentage change* function.

As it should, the Hondata turbo map we used started out extremely rich under most of the loading range, so tuning was mainly a matter of pulling fuel, though occasionally we added a bit back in selected areas. With no knock sensor capability on the car, we kept a sharp ear out for detonation (I find this is easier if you hold your hands over your ears to block out the main roar of the engine and exhaust). On the occasion or two where we heard a bit of knock at high rpm near redline, we immediately got out of the throttle and added fuel or pulled timing in that vicinity of the calibration.

Reviewing the dynoruns, it is clear that the default Hondata calibration was right enough that we didn't add a whole lot of power, but we certainly increased fuel efficiency and emissions by cleaning up the calibration.

In the end, the Hondata programming solution was easy. You need electronic technician's skills to socket the Honda ECM and install the jumpers, but once that's out of the way, a laptop and PROM burner—or maybe also an emulator—make turbocharging a Honda straightforward and rewarding. This is absolutely one of the best solutions for a street Honda turbo vehicle, and Hondata has some super-high-output race vehicles running on modified Honda factory ECMs.

ROMEDITOR

Our version of Hondata's ROMeditor calibration software provided a tuner with, first of all, the ability to modify the main high- and low-speed fuel and timing tables, each of which has 20 hard-coded rpm ranges and 13 loading ranges for a total of 260 speed-density breakpoints in each fuel table and 520 total. You could view fuel tables in normal mode as a spreadsheet-type matrix of integer fuel value numbers that were not pulse width but provided the magnitude relative to each other of how much fuel the EMS would deliver to the engine for the various possible combinations of speed and loading.

ROMeditor provided background shading for the table that bleeds from turquoise through green to red as fuel delivery increases in various segments of the table. You could also elect to view the fuel table as a set of injection duty-cycle (percentage on-time) numbers rather than the fuel values (anything over 100

The "sensitivity" of gasoline is fairly low until engine speed gets very high, so there is a fairly wide range of air/fuel ratios that produce peak or nearly peak power. Note how the air/fuel ratio in the bottom graph jumps richer simultaneously with the VTEC switch to the high-speed cam at 4,500 rpm.

percent indicated the injectors would be open constantly, which generally spells trouble). We could select the option of viewing or not viewing the four boost-table loading ranges starting at 0.6 psi and to view or not view the extended rpm above 9,000.

A tuner could alternatively view the fuel tables as a 2D graph, where the 13 load ranges were plotted as a line graph, each a function of rpm and fuel value, or as a single 3-D graph. You could also view a lambda (air/fuel ratio) table, a lambda differential table, and the target lambda table.

The high-speed and low-speed cam ignition tables are similar to the fuel tables, with the exception that they display degrees of spark advance before top dead center (BTDC).

ROMeditor also had a set of configuration parameters that provided the ability to

- Scale injector size for larger injectors (you specified the injector multiplier as a percentage of the stock injector flow rate, so 0.50 would automatically scale injection pulse width to 50 percent of normal to compensate for injectors with twice the fuel flow). ROMeditor also allowed special injector scaling for idle and acceleration conditions.
- Set idle target rpm by increasing or decreasing the idle air control (IAC) duty cycle.
- Choose to enable or disable closed-loop feedback mode (the Honda EMS targets the values in the target air/fuel ratio table) and to set the threshold loading above which the Honda EMS would switch to open-loop mode and disregard the O_2 sensor.
- Set a rev-limiter rpm and a boost fuel cut pressure in psi.
- Disable or enable VTEC cam-switching and specify the rpm and loading above which the Honda EMS will command a switch to the high-speed cam(s).
- Select the rpm and loading above which the EMS would turn off the air conditioning compressor.
- Select 3-bar MAP sensor mode, and disable or enable the knock sensor, ELD, injector error, barometric pressure sensing, and the O_2 sensor heater.

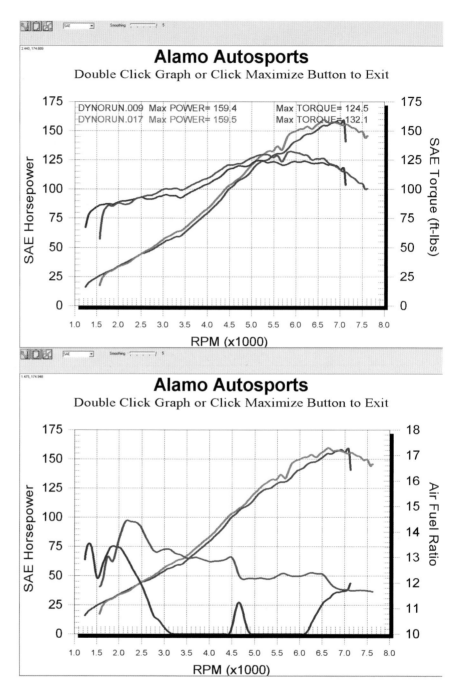

There were a rich set of editing commands for the tables, including undo, redo, undo history, cut, copy, paste, select all, increase selection, decrease selection, adjust selection, interpolate selection, and create boost tables.

Emulator commands included download table or entire ROM image to emulator, go to current cell, increase or decrease current cell, provide real time update, and reboot the ECM.

File commands included new, open, reopen, save, save as, protect ROM, close, print setup, print, import or export tables, convert ROM version, burn EPROM, settings, and exit.

Datalogging commands included connect, record, ECM information, beginning, rewind, play, fast forward, end, load recording, and save recording.

There were also several help commands.

In the final testing we installed an AEM plug-and-play EMS, which, sure enough, plugged straight into the del Sol's ECM harness. Note the start-up fuel map and engine data page on the laptop display.

Some of the most important pull-down commands were also available as buttons on one of two toolbars.

INSTALLING AEM'S PLUG-AND-PLAY SYSTEM

When it was time to try out the AEM system, it turned out installation was about as simple as installing a new printer on your Windows PC.

You open the passenger door of the del Sol and peel back the carpet that covers the stock Honda ECM located in the outside kick panel next to a passenger's right foot. You get out a 10-millimeter socket and loosen and remove the three bolts and nut that hold down the ECM. You pry off the sheet-metal cover that protects the connectors on the ECM from being damaged if your passenger kicks the kick panel. You'll see three connectors on the bottom of the ECM, each secured in place by a locking plastic tab. One at a time, squeezing on the plastic tab and connector (not the bundle of wires entering each connector), pull (don't force) each of the three connectors out of the ECM. The three connectors are not interchangeable. Now you remove the stock ECM. In some applications, you may need to cut one or two stock wires entering the ECM connectors, but normally you are immediately ready to install the AEM system. It may be easier to plug the AEM laptop serial cable into the ECM before you connect and secure the ECM.

The AEM unit actually had four connector sockets, but only three were needed for the Honda wiring (unless you wanted to use some of the myriad fancy programmable AEM features, such as nitrous control, boost control, and so forth—which was one huge advantage of the AEM over the Hondata solution). AEM provided a fourth plastic connector and pins that you could crimp to auxiliary wiring to control fancy performance equipment, but that was optional. The trick was to secure the AEM system to the kick panel using some sturdy cable ties, and route the serial cable under the carpeting to a convenient location to connect the laptop. Now push the carpeting back into place. Get out your laptop and plug in the AEM ECM to the serial/USB port. If you have not already done it, insert the AEM CD-ROM in your drive and follow the instruction for installing the EMS software and documentation (manuals).

Running a stock Honda engine, the first step is to select the correct start-up map and download it into the AEM ECM from the laptop, at which point you could load the calibration,

fire up the car, and drive away. If you are running a turbocharger as we were, AEM has a turbo calibration ready to install, but the plug-and-play calibration was designed to be a good starting point for a complete tune by someone who knew what they were doing on a chassis dynamometer with a wideband air/fuel ratio meter—or AEM's auxiliary wideband controller and UEGO sensor plugged into the AEM ECM. In our case, the Hondata ran the car smoothly enough to take the CRX on a spin around the parking lot and onto the Dynojet to polish the calibration. The AEM standalone programmable EMS could not make more power than the Hondata, but where the AEM system shone was its huge repertoire of optional tricks. If you were planning to run four—count them—stages of nitrous, you were good to go.

Chapter 23
Project: Turbo-EFI Jaguar XKE 4.2

The classis 4.2-liter Jaguar XKE featured in this project was born in 1969, fighting for breath through twin Stromberg emissions carbs. The Series 2 E-type was the slowest of the entire line, having lost its lovely triple SU carb induction system to the battle against smog in North American cities. Jaguar no longer advertised horsepower in 1969, but the car clearly had less than the Series 1 E-type's previously advertised 265 horsepower, which was known to be optimistic. Experts say a really "on" early three-carb E-type engine delivered 220 horsepower at the crankshaft, and the smogged-out engines used in later two-carb XKEs and the carbed or injected Jaguar sedans that used the 4.2-liter motor through 1987 had as little as 150 to 200 horsepower. By the early 1980s, Chevy and Ford V-8 conversion kits were popular for hot rodders who wanted to give an XKE a little more of an edge. People were attacking Jaguars with hacksaws and hammers. In the years since, many surviving E-types have been relegated to collector-car status, but people with street-driven XKE's know they can be a lot of fun to drive rather than just to have and appreciate for their timeless beauty. In any case, I was willing to give the Series 2 some help, but it had to stay Jaguar, engine and all.

This chapter describes the methods and equipment used to convert a 1969 E-type Jaguar to electronic engine management and turbocharging and to optimize the calibration on a Superflow engine dyno. The project continued for almost 10 years, and the earliest experiments took place at the dawn of EFI hot rodding in the days before the first aftermarket standalone engine management systems arrived with programmable digital controllers. In the course of the project I ran the engine on the road and dyno with several different engine management systems including:

- Vintage Bosch L-Jetronic EFI from a 1979 Jaguar XJ-6
- XJ-6 L-Jet hardware controlled by a fuel-only Haltech F3 standalone Programmable EMS
- Batch-fire Haltech E6 EMS with spark control and staged-injector capability
- Sequential EMS from EFI Technology

THE RAW MATERIAL

The 4.2L inline-six XK Jaguar engine was extremely advanced for its time. Like the Offenhauser four that dominated Indy 500 racing for many years, the twin-cam Jaguar six engine had decades of development behind it, with roots going back before World War II. The XK block was produced in 2.4, 3.4, 3.8, and 4.2 versions since the 1940s, and continued in production through 1987. The 4.2 used Weslake hemispherical combustion chambers in an aluminum head, twin overhead cams, large ports, multiple carbs, and a tough seven-bearing crankshaft with castle-nut rods above a 9-quart cast-aluminum oil pan.

With tremendous low-end torque off idle, the '69 4.2 XK engine seemed to beg for turbocharging to pump up the horsepower in the upper speed ranges where smogged versions of the E-type ran out of breath. The limited slip rear end could handle up to 600 horsepower, the crankshaft and bearings were strong and could easily handle large power increases, the hemispherical combustion chambers with centrally located spark plugs burned the charge quickly enough to effectively

A 1969 Jaguar E-type in full flight. The XKE weighs in at 2,550 pounds, including at least 600 pounds of engine and transmission.

EFI Turbo 4.2 Jaguar, Power and Torque				
Speed	Torque (1)	Torque (2)	Power (1)	Power (2)
1750	-	322	-	107
2000	285	311	108	118
2250	262	297	112	127
2500	268	303	128	144
2750	281	337	147	177
3000	289	418	165	239
3250	290	436	180	270
3500	313	440	209	293
3750	326	442	232	315
4000	352	438	268	334
4250	365	433	296	350
4500	380	415	326	356
4750	381	400	345	362
5000	238	369	227	351
5250	254	336	254	336

(1) 4.2L Six, 1 Rajay 300 series turbo, .6 A/R, 6 237cc/min Lucas disc fuel injectors, 1 Jaguar throttlebody, Turbonetics 5 psi Deltagate (actually allowed 12 psi boost!)
(2) 4.2L Six, 3 Airesearch T-2 turbos, 12 218cc/min Lucas disc fuel injectors, 6 TWM throttlebodies, no operative wastegates (12 psi boost)

The initial turbo conversion involved converting from the '69 Jag's twin-Stromberg emissions carbs to the older triple-SU set up, and Siamesing together a set of 4.2L cast-iron headers.

To provide boost retard, the initial turbo conversion used a primitive vacuum-advance, boost-retard distributor canister to pull timing under boost as an anti-detonation countermeasure. *MSD*

resist detonation, and the semi-restrained buildup of turbo boost would reasonably be forgiving on the clutch. But if you want turbocharging, you really need electronic fuel injection, a fact of life that was proven in the earliest turbocharged versions of this project, which were carbureted. The E-type's triple-SU carbureted induction system has its own kind of beauty, but by modern standards these old carbureted engines are inefficient, unreliable, and dirty, and ill-equipped to provide the kind of sophisticated engine management required to make high specific power with turbocharging.

For those who want the flexibility, reliability, power, low exhaust emissions, and straightforward on-the-fly laptop programmability of modern engine management, it turns out to be surprisingly easy to convert classis Jaguars to programmable fuel injection and spark controls without permanently modifying anything that detracts from collector value. What's more, for people who appreciate the XKE's race-bred performance capabilities and might even want to upgrade the car's performance, electronic engine management is fully compatible with headers, reground cams, high-compression pistons, ported and polished heads, turbochargers, superchargers, port nitrous injection, and other performance equipment.

When converting an old Jaguar XK engine to EFI, there are several ways to go:

1. Adapt a 1978–87 EFI manifold from an EFI 4.2 Jag sedan to the XKE engine, and along with the Bosch L-Jetronic sensors (including the Vane airflow meter), injectors, wiring harness, fuel pump, and ECM. Or discard the Bosch ECM and install and program an aftermarket computer, perhaps using larger fuel injectors for more horsepower potential. The L-Jet manifold bolts seamlessly to any 3.8 or 4.2 engine, but in the E-type engine compartment, the L-Jet manifold will require a 1-inch spacer-plate to move it outboard from the head plus minor modifications to fit within the E-type's front space frame.

2. Bolt on a Weber-type intake manifold in place of the stock SU or Stromberg manifold, and then, rather than installing the three dual-throat sidedraft Weber DCOE carbs typical of this conversion, install three TWM Weber-type throttle bodies, identical in overall size and bolt pattern, with each throat equipped to install one or two electronic injectors downstream of the butterfly in each throttle bore. Install high-pressure fuel supply and return lines and a standalone aftermarket EMS.

3. Mount three one-barrel throttle bodies directly on the XKE's tri-power intake manifold and drill the manifold runners for six weld-in to aluminum injector bosses.

4. Fabricate an aluminum "sheet-metal" manifold from scratch designed for a Ford or Chevy V-8 throttle body.

HOT ROD XKE

With the intention of building a hot rod E-type, I acquired a faded and tired but rust-free California Series 2 4.2 car, which is and was the lowest performing and least expensive of the XKE line. With the intention of turbocharging it, rather than the E-type's pop-up 9:1 pistons I rebuilt the engine with flat-top sedan-type 8:1 pistons to allow higher levels of boost without detonation. Keep in mind that 1978 Porsche 930 Turbos had *7:1* compression from the factory! In the original turbo version I Siamesed two cast-iron Jag headers together and constructed a collector with turbo flange and bolted on a .6 A/R Rajay 300E turbocharger. A Turbonetics Deltagate and mini-regulator allowed cockpit-adjustable maximum boost anywhere from 5 psi to the maximum-achievable boost of the Rajay compressor or blowup, whichever came first.

More complicated was how to route the boost air from the turbo's compressor around the cross-flow head to the carbs and

The Bosch L-Jetronic system's Vane Air Flow sensor measures intake air velocity against a spring-loaded air vane attached to a rotary potentiometer. Air velocity must be corrected for air temperature to equal air mass flow. Meter quickly runs out of authority and "pegs" with turbo conversion.

where to route the exhaust from the turbine, all in a very tight engine compartment—and what to do with all the extra heat.

As luck would have it, I was able to buy a nearly complete (fuel-only) 1979 Bosch L-Jet fuel-injection system from a California company that converted Jaguar sedans to American V-8 power. The only thing missing was the EFI wiring harness, a self-contained wiring loom that connects all the fuel-injection components to the computer and has only a handful of connections that must integrate into the car's electrical system: tach/coil, continuous power, switched power, starter voltage, and so on. Building a nice custom harness had its appeal, but in the end I bought a complete XJ-6 wiring harness from a Jaguar salvage yard, which cost nearly as much as the rest of the injection system.

When Jaguar converted the XJ-6 sedan to Bosch L-Jet injection in 1978, the resulting EFI version delivered 170 crankshaft bhp at 4,500 rpm and 232 lb-ft torque at 3,000. What was the upside fueling capacity of the L-Jet system in terms of horsepower? At the time I wasn't sure. A lot of the performance aftermarket still believed in four-barrel carbs, and EFI controllers were analog computers whose logic was hardwired into the circuitry, and other people who knew a lot more than I did then were struggling to get a handle on how to hot rod engines with electronic fuel injection. Who could you ask? Down the line it would turn out that the XJ-6's pintle-architecture Bosch injectors were capable of flowing 214 cc per minute of fuel. Convert this to horsepower potential (see the chapter of this book on actuators), was as simple as multiplying by 0.1902044 and multiplying the answer by the number of cylinders. If you were willing to run XJ-6 injectors wide-open at 100 percent duty cycle, they could fuel roughly 250 horsepower at standard pressure (2.5 bar), and 200 or so at the recommended 80 percent duty to prevent overheating the injectors (which Jaguar and Bosch would clearly have respected). A stock XJ-6 had 170 horsepower, which meant there was 30 horsepower of upside in the injectors, i.e., about a 20 percent power boost. But, again, this was an R&D project.

I removed the old Jaguar intake manifold and carb system and set about to install the XJ-6 EFI manifold. It quickly became clear there were problems. The L-Jet runners turned downward fairly steeply, unlike the XKE's stock carbureted manifold, which was horizontal, which meant the manifold plenum interfered with the E-type front space frame that surrounded the inline-six engine rather closely with longitudinal frame rails. You could relocate the manifold outward, but that caused the front of the plenum to interfere with a diagonal space frame rail. What's more, the rear of the plenum interfered slightly with the firewall above the passenger foot-well. In the end I built a 1-inch-thick spacer plate that located the L-Jet intake manifold directly outward,

which allowed the EFI runners to pass over the longitudinal frame rail and modified the passenger-side outboard diagonal frame rail to provide additional clearance. And I reworked the firewall sheet metal slightly to clear the rear of the plenum.

The manifold fit, but installing it was tricky. The geometry of the downward-curving intake runners and the thickness of the spacer plate would not allow bolts of sufficient length to clear the undersides of the intake runners at certain places, but tight space frame clearance prevented the manifold from sliding onto extended-length studs long enough to clear the spacer plate. The only solution was to (1) slide studs through the spacer and manifold flange from the engine side, (2) lower the whole intake manifold assembly into place from above, (3) screw in the studs finger-tight, (4) tighten the studs using two nuts jammed together at the outboard end of the studs, (5) unjam the outer nuts and remove, and (6) tighten the remaining nuts. Installing the L-Jet manifold on the XKE was not an operation you'd want to do often, though by the time I switched to a TWM manifold designed for triple Weber sidedraft DCOE carbs, I'd gotten pretty good at it.

With the turbo mounted on the modified exhaust header and the L-Jet intake manifold in place, I plumbed the compressor discharge to the throttle body on the opposite side of the cross-flow head by routing mandrel-bent mild-steel pipe bends between the rear of the cylinder head and the firewall.

Although mass airflow (MAF) sensors should be located downstream of a turbocharger to correctly measure air density after the effect of density changes, velocity airflow (VAF) sensors should be located upstream of a turbocharger to avoid damaging the air vane if the centrifugal compressor surges on sudden throttle closure. Unfortunately, relocating the Bosch L-Jet VAF from its the stock location above the intake plenum to the opposite side of the engine looked impossible, given the space constraints imposed by the turbocharger itself as well as the compressor and turbine induction and discharge plumbing and the oil supply and return lines in the vicinity of the turbocharger. Not to mention the XKE's heater and ventilation system. I went so far as to remove the heater-blower unit, but eventually figured out a way to relocate the VAF sensor in a place where you could duct inlet-air between it and the compressor inlet with flexible conduit as well as provide reasonably smooth airflow into the VAF from a remote air cleaner. By routing the stock L-Jet wiring harness carefully, it was possible to connect the harness to engine sensors and fuel injectors on the passenger side of the block and reach the air meter without extending the harness.

The stock L-Jet ECM is located in the trunk of XJ-6 sedans, out of the harsh engine environment far from EMI radio interference, so the harness was easily long enough to reach the XKE trunk once you cut holes in the firewall and rear trunk bulkhead with a drill-powered hole-saw.

The next task was to augment the stock XKE low-pressure in-tank electric fuel pump by installing the high-pressure inline Bosch L-Jet unit in the fuel line downstream of the stock pump and connecting the L-Jet pump to a relay controlled by the ECM's pump circuit. Like most EFI systems, the L-Jetronic system activates the pump for a few seconds when the key comes on and runs it while the engine is cranking or running. If the engine stops or if the multi-G crash-activated inertia switch is triggered, the ECM drops power to the pump regulator immediately to negate the possibility of spewing gasoline from a ruptured fuel line in case of a crash. I unbolted the metal access plate atop the XKE fuel tank containing the fuel tank gauge-sender and stock

No XKE Jaguar ever had electronic fuel injection, but the 4.2 engine outlived the XKE and acquired EFI in the late 1970s. The initial EFI Jaguar 4.2 used in this project was a fuel-only Bosch L-Jetronic system from a 1979 XJ-6 Jag sedan with the distributor-points ignition. The L-Jet system adapted nicely to the XKE engine, with the VAF air meter relocated across the engine to the exhaust side, upstream of the turbo's compressor inlet. Fuel enrichment came from the boost pressure reference to the stock L-Jet fuel pressure regulator—and twin auxiliary fuel injectors located about 9 inches upstream of the throttle body for better mixing under control of an AIC from Miller-Woods.

fuel pickup, and drilled and tapped it to accommodate a fuel return dump for excess fuel from the L-Jet fuel pressure regulator at the end of the injector rail.

The next thing was to install a O_2 sensor bung in the turbine discharge elbow downstream of the turbocharger. Very early Jag L-Jet systems were not equipped with O_2 sensors, and later systems will work without one, but the advantage of running an O_2 sensor is that it permits ECM's closed-loop algorithm to target the chemically perfect 14.7:1 air/fuel ratio by constantly correlating injection pulse width with exhaust-gas oxygen feedback from the O_2 sensor. Federal laws require a working O_2 sensor on an emissions-controlled vehicle if the original engine was so equipped.

The original XJ-6 L-Jet ECM received its engine-speed trigger signal from an electronic distributor, but connecting the ECM trigger input to the negative coil terminal on the XKE's breaker points ignition system worked fine.

I acquired a GM HEI vacuum-advance/boost-retard canister and modified it to fit the Jaguar points distributor in place of the stock vacuum advance canister, with a manifold pressure reference line running to the intake plenum. I installed stop-screws that could be adjusted to limit total advance or retard.

With all required L-Jet components installed on the XK engine, I grounded the ECM to the engine and battery and wired constant power connection to the battery and connected the ECM's switched power connection to the key switch.

When the engine cranked, there was a minor stumble. Followed by nothing. And more nothing. And still more nothing.

I checked all L-Jet electrical connections but everything seemed OK. I eventually pulled the hose-fed early EFI-style electronic injectors out of the manifold, plumbed everything back together and cranked the engine. Pffffuuuffff! All injectors batch-fired a massive burst of fuel twice each power stroke.

I began exhaustively testing the continuity of all L-Jet wiring. In the end it turned out that one of the pins in the six-wire VAF connector was pushed out of place, which caused

the sensor to report maximum airflow and trigger a maximum injection pulse, which flooded the engine almost immediately.

With the pin repaired, the engine fired up and ran great. I retarded static timing a little to protect against detonation and drove the car, at which point it turned out there was a big, ugly flat spot until the engine was fully warmed up. It turned out there were two problems: (1) The L-Jet coolant temperature sensor was defective, and (2) the XKE engine was equipped with a 160-degree thermostat, which prevented the engine from getting the coolant hot enough for the L-Jet ECM to fully disable warm-up enrichment. With a new ECT sensor and a 180-degree thermostat, all was well.

Until it was time to make boost at full throttle, at which point it became clear that the car was experiencing lean detonation above 5 psi. The engine needed fuel enrichment.

I wired the L-Jet cold-start valve to come on above 2-psi boost. The cold-start valve was a fuel injector of sorts consisting of a nonpulsed injection nozzle operated independently of the ECM by a thermo-time switch and a starter voltage that could squirt a continuous stream of fuel directly toward the throttle plate at cold temperatures to massively enrich that air/fuel ratio to get the engine started. I installed relays that allowed the original control circuit to activate the cold-start injector to perform its design function but allowed a secondary circuit under control of a pressure switch referenced to manifold pressure to turn on the injector when boost reached 2 psi. This crude, all-or-nothing fuel enrichment scheme stifled detonation enough to make some more boost and power but failed to prevent lean mixtures in one or two cylinders when boost began to get more serious.

I acquired an additional injector controller (AIC) kit built consisting of two additional PWM fuel injectors pulsed by a microcontroller with an internal MAP sensor referenced to the compressor discharge, with engine speed provided by the negative coil terminal. Installation instructions called for silver-soldering or MIG-welding twin injector bosses to the inlet air plumbing 9 to 12 inches upstream of the throttle body. Auxiliary injector fuel came from a tee installed in the high-pressure fuel supply line anywhere upstream of the main fuel rail. Two internal pots adjusted fuel enrichment independently for rpm and manifold pressure. With AIC dip switches set for a six-cylinder engine, the AIC pulsed the auxiliary injectors three times per engine revolution to enrich the air/fuel ratio to fight detonation and increase power. AIC installation instructions called for verifying that the fuel pump could maintain fuel rail pressure at higher levels of fuel flow and pressure. The trick was to plumb a mechanical gauge into the fuel line and tape it to the windshield where you could watch it while driving. What I saw was 38-psi fuel pressure at zero engine vacuum, with fuel pressure climbing to 45 psi at 7 psi, at which point pressure began to drop, indicating that the stock L-Jet pump had reached its limit and that the engine was not actually receiving the full benefit of the AIC at higher levels of boost. I installed a more powerful inline fuel pump and verified that fuel pressure now climbed in a one-to-one correspondence with boost pressure to 53 psi at 15-psi boost.

However, under some conditions there was still detonation above 12 psi.

I ordered a Spearco water injection system. Detonation occurs when combustion temperature and pressure get high enough as combustion proceeds that remaining charge gases explode all at once rather that burning smoothly like a fire through dry grass, and water's excellent heat of vaporization makes injecting water into the combustion chamber a powerful countermeasure against detonation as the energy required to boil water droplets steals large amounts of heat from burning charge in the combustion chamber. Water injection systems of the time were primitive compared to today's sophisticated systems. You got a plastic reservoir for storing distilled water or water with alcohol, an electric pump that attached to the reservoir, a metering orifice consisting of a hose barb with a very small metering orifice, an injection nozzle that installed in the air intake, a pressure switch and relay module to turn on the pump when boost got high enough, and a rubber hose to route water from the tank to the metering orifice to the injection nozzle.

With the AIC, water injection, and distributor boost-retard module installed, boost increased to 15 psi without detonation and there was a dramatic increase in performance. Out on the highway, power arrived on the turbo Jag with a bike-like rush.

After driving the L-Jet XKE for a time, Haltech introduced its fully programmable (fuel-only) Haltech F3 standalone aftermarket ECM, which meant it was no longer necessary to run an auxiliary injector controller. Now a single standalone programmable EMS could provide all required fuel enrichment through the primary port injectors rather than a single-point AIC, which could be expected to improve fuel distribution. I removed the L-Jet ECU and the AIC and installed an F3, wiring harness, and Haltech engine sensors on the XKE. With the ability to calibrate injection pulse width wherever you wanted it, it became possible to install larger fuel injectors or to increase fuel pressure through the existing injectors to increase the fuel flow of any length injector squirt and recalibrate the fuel table to put injection pulse width wherever you wanted it to achieve maximum performance. Performance of the turbo E-Type increased, with improved mixture distribution and additional fuel cooling, it became possible to increase overall ignition timing without detonation.

All was well in the world. For a while. And then it was time to move on. I decided to pull the Haltech F3 fuel-only ECU and install it on the Challenger project in this book and lean on the XKE a little harder.

STAGE 2

When it came time to consider additional modifications, I formulated the following goals:
1. More power
2. Reduced turbo lag
3. Electronic boost control
4. Electronic ignition with programmable spark advance
5. Eliminate water injection
6. Intercooling
7. Clean emissions
8. Eliminate intake restrictions from the L-Jet VAF and plumbing
9. Improve engine compartment layout to improve serviceability

Turbo lag can be reduced many ways, but one of the most interesting involves multiple low-inertia turbochargers of the right specification. Check.

On the other hand, turbo lag can be *killed* out of hand with nitrous injection. Check.

It so happened that NOS was testing a high-end ECM based on the EFI Technologies Competition ECM, a top-of-the-line system with twin-injector per cylinder capability designed for use on expensive tuner cars and cost-is-no-object Indy-500-type race cars, competition offshore boats, and other all-out vehicles where flexibility and reliability are vital. The Competition ECM

was equipped with mil-spec connectors and potted circuitry and a waterproof enclosure, and it was designed with the ability to control at least 15 classes of sensors and actuators. The system did not mess around with frivolous things like stabilizing idle via IAC, and it was did not support sissy knock sensors (in racing, the engine is expecting good race fuel, not 87-octane junk). However, it had some really nice features that are now standard on many ordinary engine management systems, but were not then, such as the ability the change the granularity of the fueling map in a nonlinear fashion, allowing rpm-based breakpoints to occur more frequently at some parts of the scale than others. This was a great feature for engines in which a linear interpolation between certain standard breakpoints of loading and rpm did not approximate an ideal fuel curve. You could change the granularity until linear interpolations *did* sufficiently approximate the ideal fuel curve. For the NOS version, EFI Technology had added logic to activate nitrous, to calculate a pulse width offset to provide nitrous fueling via ordinary port injectors, and to pulse a nitrous solenoid rapidly like an injector at an increasing rate of change to provide progressive nitrous flow that could arrive quickly, in a scorching sudden blast, or more gradually, depending on how it was configured. The Competition ECM could be programmed to control turbo boost by applying PWM techniques to control an electro-pneumatic valve that controlled the amount of manifold pressure seen at the control actuator of a wastegate. Like other EFI Competition systems, the NOS EMS could provide timed sequential fuel injection. By this time I was working as a car magazine writer-photographer and writing my first book about custom fuel injection, and NOS offered to send down one of the new ECMs. Check.

With nitrous injection and high-boost turbocharging, there was going to be a lot of dynamic range between the fuel required to idle and the fuel required at peak boost with nitrous blasting into the engine. This could be more of a problem before the advent of really large aftermarket peak-and-hold fuel injectors. Who ya gonna call?

Actually, Haltech. One of the earliest suppliers of standalone aftermarket engine management systems, Haltech had from the beginning provided the ability to stage fuel injectors in groups. Staged injection systems—where the primary fuel injectors operate under all conditions and secondary injectors join in at a configurable rpm and manifold pressure—can be sized to provide a lot of fuel for extreme boost and nitrous injection at the high end of the scale, but still idle well due to their ability to supply very small amounts of fuel very accurately compared to using a single set of very large injectors. The NOS ECM handled twin-injectors per cylinder but did not have the ability at that time to stage them. Haltech's E6 ECM could handle staging, but it did not yet handle sequential fuel injection or progressive nitrous or direct-fire ignition. Check—well, sort of.

I decided the thing to do was to test the turbo E-type with *both* the NOS/EFI Technology and a Haltech E6 engine management systems on a Superflow engine dyno and then on the road. At this point, the design goal became take it to the limit: *twin* turbos with liquid cooling. Hold on, let's say *three turbos*! Custom-fabricated turbo exhaust manifold . . . 12 injectors . . . one throttle per cylinder . . . port nitrous . . . speed-density injection with computer-controlled nitrous . . . crank-triggered ignition.

Meanwhile, to handle any injection scheme involving 12 injectors you'd need a method of mounting two injectors per cylinder. TWM was making DCOE Weber-type dual-throat

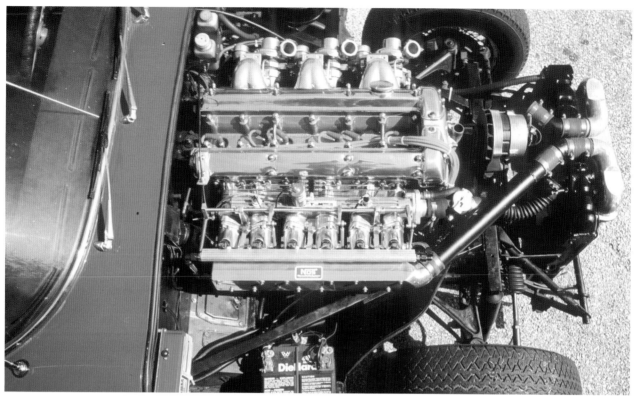

Following experiments with the L-Jet system managed by both an L-Jet ECM and then a Haltech F3 fuel-only ECM, we developed this triple-turbo 12-injector sequential EFI system with ignition control managed by a high-end NOS-brand EMS built by EFI Technologies. Note the port-nitrous system and single-stage nitrous solenoid designed to wake up the turbocharged at low rpm.

sidedraft throttle bodies with bosses that could be machined to accommodate twin injectors per intake runner. Check. Of course, that meant that you needed a Weber-type manifold. TWM, it turned out, could provide that too. Check.

BUILDING THE STAGE 2 TRIPLE TURBO SYSTEM

I acquired three of the smallest turbochargers you could find at the time, tiny Airesearch T-2 turbochargers of the type installed on late-'80s 2.0L Buick Skyhawk turbos and the JDM 1.5-liter Nissan 200SX Turbo. The T-2 was a compact turbocharger with integral wastegate and a relatively efficient compressor map. After fabricating front and rear three-cylinder Jaguar header flanges out of 1/2-inch-thick steel and acquiring Turbonetics inlet and outlet turbine flanges, I removed the original single-Rajay turbo exhaust manifold and spent some time playing with the three turbos, searching for the right design, the right geometry, the right materials to design a custom triple-turbo header that make everything work.

It turned out you could fit three turbos if you install them in a transverse position beside the inline engine. I mocked up the design and then turned it over to Austin race-car builder Jeff Latham, who implemented the design working with a band saw and a belt sander and a TIG welder and tight-radius black steel weld bends. The final product was beautiful, poetry in black steel, a triple-turbo exhaust system that bolted to the three T-2 turbine-inlet flanges.

My original concept was to have a water-cooled charge-cooler on the intake side of the engine that collected compressed air from the three turbos and cooled it with water chilled by a remote water-cooling heat exchanger in the nose of the car, but

forced-induction expert Corky Bell made the case for a custom air-cooled intercooler that mounted in front of the Jag radiator. We fabricated a three-into-one collector pipe that accumulated air from the three T-2 compressors and routed it toward the front of the car protected from the hot exhaust manifold by a sweet-looking aluminum heat shield that reflected exhaust heat away from the cold-side compressor discharge plumbing. Ivan Tull built twin 3-into-1 coolant manifolds to route engine coolant into and out of the liquid-cooled T-2 center sections. Meanwhile, Bell techs notched the top of the Jag radiator, lowered it about an inch, and constructed a gigantic intercooler from Thermal Transfer Systems core sections. The intercooler was set at an angle that provided room for air to rush around the sides to maintain reasonably good radiator efficiency. Bell techs fabricated an intake-side plenum outboard of the triple throttle bodies and plumbed it from the intercooler discharge.

We installed 12 288-cc/min Lucas injectors in the TWM throttle bodies and constructed injector fuel rails and plumbed the rails to the fuel supply system.

Upgrading to the Haltech E6 with ignition control was straightforward. Any changes in the engine's VE curve would result from the loss of the large-plenum L-Jet intake manifold and the change to the TWM individual-runner intake manifold and throttles and any resulting changes in intake runner inertia. But lacking a cam change, it seemed unlikely that the nonboosted portion of the XK engine's operating envelope would be greatly different, or that the low-boost operating envelope would suddenly be all wrong. The new turbochargers could be expected to make more boost more quickly at lower rpm, which would require calibrating the fuel table for higher boost at lower rpm

Engine dynos have a selection of common bell housing/flywheel/clutch adapters (i.e., Chevy small block, Ford Windsor, and Chevy BB)—but not Jaguar 4.2. I built this dyno adapter by cutting down an auto-trans Jag bell housing and welding on a rear plate designed to mate to a Chevy SB transmission.

than had previously been possible. In any case the pulse width entries in the fuel table from the Haltech F3 that had replaced the Bosch L-Jetronic ECM should be a reasonable facsimile of the VE curve in these areas. We copied down the F3 entries and entered them into the E6 fuel table. Then, using the Haltech Delta feature (which could be used to change entire map ranges or segments of ranges, or even all ranges by a mathematical function such as percentage), rescaled all fuel entries downward 35 percent to account for the increase in fuel flow resulting from upgrading 214 cc/min Bosch injectors to 288 cc/min Lucas injectors. We had a good timing table available from a Haltech E6 that had been calibrated on a load-holding dyno to manage a nonboosted 4.2 Jag engine, and we guesstimated conservative spark advance entries based on E6 timing tables from DOHC turbocharged engines with similar cam specs and combustion chamber size.

With the reconstructed XK map loaded in the Haltech E6, I turned the key on the XKE and the engine fired up immediately and idled nicely.

With Stage 2 fuel and turbo systems handled, I began building the parts needed to mount the XK engine on a Superflow engine dyno and looking for the best way to supply engine position for the NOS/EFI Technology ECM so the sequential system was ready to rock 'n' roll on the engine dyno when the Haltech E6 was finished doing its thing.

SEQUENTIAL INJECTION AND DIRECT IGNITION

Running an engine with sequential injection of direct-fire ignition, requires an accurate crank sensor, but you also need a cam trigger that allows the ECM to synchronize engine control with the correct phase of the four-stroke cycle, so you need a cam sync signal that occurs before the earliest possible ignition event on the compression stroke of the number one cylinder, that is, about 45 degrees before top dead center.

For a six-cylinder engine, six flying magnets will trigger a reference signal in the crank sensor 12 times per power stroke, which is plenty for controlling sequential injection and enough for controlling direct-fire ignition if the magnets and ref sensor are oriented right, though not enough for OBD-II misfire detection where exact timing of crank reference pulses can be used to detect micro-changes in crankshaft acceleration and deceleration that indicate misfires—which is why most late-model OEM crank triggers have 36-60 teeth on the crank trigger wheel.

I removed the XKE crank damper and had a good machinist drill and tap holes next to the pulley groove for installing six miniature magnetic bolts. In the meantime, I removed and set aside the stock XKE distributor and modified the rotor assembly of a failed XJ-6 electronic distributor to install a flying magnet and modified the distributor body to install a cam-speed sensor.

When using distributor and crank triggers to provide spark timing and sequential injection, it is necessary to coordinate (1) the position of the distributor body (which may or may not be adjustable), (2) the position of the sync trigger in the distributor body, (3) the clocking of the distributor rotor with flying magnet, (4) the position of the crank sensor, and (5) orientation of flying magnets on the crank.

It was a simple matter to offset the number-one cylinder crank magnet 15 degrees before TDC, separated from the other flying magnets in 60-degree intervals. This must be done by a competent machinist to high standards of precision to avoid spark scatter and other EMS problems.

To index the distributor, I positioned the crank pulley timing mark exactly over the timing pointer at TDC. The trick is machining a slot to hold the cam position sensor that permits at least 45 degrees of sensor movement. With engine reference position supplied by the crank sensor, rotating the distributor body will not directly change ignition timing, but the high-voltage rotor must be more or less centered on an electrode in the spark plug cap when spark occurs (always between, say, 0 degrees TDC and 40 degrees BTDC), so no plausible spark advance will result in excessive gap between the rotor electrode and the high-voltage distributor cap plug terminals.

Accel/DFI recommended the following procedure for indexing the distributor using a strobe light and a clear distributor cap:

1. Compute the midposition between least spark advance and most spark advance. Put the engine at this position on compression stroke no. 1 cylinder with a degree wheel, using degree markings already on the flywheel or damper, or by measuring the distance from TDC to some marked BTDC position. (Example: Suppose 10 degrees BTDC is 1 inch from TDC, and you are trying to locate 21 degrees BTDC. 21 ÷ 10 x 1 (inch) = 2.1 inches from TDC. Or suppose 10 degrees is 3/4 inch from TDC. 21 ÷ 10 x 0.75 = 1.575 inches.)

2. It is not critical to get the cam trigger perfect on systems with crank-triggered engine position sensors. The cam trigger is a reference indicating compression stroke, not a marker of engine position, but EFI Technologies specified the cam sync should be within 10 degrees of 45 degrees BTDC. (Obviously, it is truly critical to get a cam-speed trigger perfect if you are using it for engine position.)

3. With the engine at this position, point the rotor in a convenient direction for organizing plug wires and such (remove the distributor, if necessary, to index the distributor drive gear). The Jaguar distributor could only point in two directions since it engages a slot in a driven gear, not the crankshaft or camshaft itself. (Note: The distributor shaft drive gear can be set in various positions on the crankshaft drive gear from the bottom of the engine with the oil pan off.)

4. Install the distributor cap, place the no. 1 plug wire into an appropriate hole in the cap, and center it over the rotor.

5. Now move the engine to 45 degrees BTDC, observe the position of the flying magnet, and adjust the trigger so that it is exactly above the magnet. That's it.

ON THE DYNO

Somewhere in the midst of building and installing turbo and EFI parts and making guesses about how much power a 4.2L Turbo-EFI Jaguar could make, I decided the right thing to do was calibrate and test the engine on a Superflow engine dyno. Keep in mind, this was before there were affordable chassis dynos where you could drive on and rip off some power and torque numbers in about five minutes.

I acquired a 1982 Jaguar XJ-6 long block and rebuilt it to match the 1969 XK engine in the E-Type that had been converted to EFI and turbocharging and began making preparations to get it on the Superflow.

You are definitely not going to get an EFI turbo engine onto an engine dyno in anything like five minutes. Five hours is more like it. Five days, if you include some of the fabrication and prep work it takes to get less common or more complex engines to mate properly with an engine dyno. And once the engine is in place, a dyno R&D session can last many hours or days.

But a load-holding engine dyno is very flexible and powerful, and it has some huge advantages over inertial chassis dynos, or for that matter any type of chassis dyno. An engine dyno can be used to perform automated power pulls that last a matter of seconds and provide a readout of power and torque across the entire rpm range from as low as 1,750 rpm to redline and are comparable in some ways to a full-throttle roll-on on a Dynojet. This quick and simple measurement reveals your engine's capabilities and produces the chart of horsepower and torque versus rpm we've all seen but an engine dyno that's even more useful for tuning and computer calibration.

In manual mode, water-brake dynos like the Superflow will hold the engine at a specific rpm at any throttle position as long as you want it to in order to optimize the EMS for maximum torque or optimal air/fuel ratio or lowest fuel economy or lowest exhaust emissions. By varying the dyno load and engine speed and moving exhaustively through all the available breakpoints of the computer's internal air/fuel and spark timing tables, you can manually build raw fuel and spark tables, cell by cell. Where perfect tuning is important—especially on competition or emissions-controlled engines—tuners typically spend many hours on the engine dyno, working to squeeze every last pony, or every last mile-per-gallon, or the cleanest exhaust from the engine—fine-tuning every breakpoint.

There are other advantages to using an engine dyno for tuning EFI conversions or heavily modified EFI engines. An engine dyno can work an engine harder than it might ever be worked on the streets, torture-testing the powerplant by holding extremely high fixed levels of power over long periods when necessary. By carefully monitoring and datalogging exhaust gas temperatures, coolant temperature, and intercooler efficiency on the engine dyno, it is possible to develop an engine and EMS combination that is far more robust than what is possible on an inertial chassis dyno or safely achievable on the street or track. The engine dyno can load the powerplant to levels of torque and airflow that might be impossible to achieve on the street other than momentarily, due to tire spin or other factors—for perfect tuning of even what are otherwise the most transitory engine events.

On the dyno, you can scientifically test various engine modifications and get the real story about what works, when it works, and how well it works. The guesswork is gone. A driver can't accurately detect 8 horsepower, for example, by seat-of-the-pants testing, but the dyno can. Not only can one develop an exceptionally high state of tune, but any problems or weak points can be revealed in the strenuous environment of the dyno and fixed before the engine goes in the car.

In the dyno room itself, the engine sits on a stand with its clutch and bell housing connected to the water brake section of the dyno, with the engine mounted on a stand. The dyno environment provides a fuel supply, coolant to the engine's water pump, a flexible exhaust system routing gases to the outside atmosphere, and an oil cooler to keep oil temperature under control.

We tested and tuned Turbo-EFI 4.2 Jag engine at Kim Barr Racing's Superflow engine dyno in Dallas. Giant plastic tanks holding thousands of gallons of water waited to cool the engine and the water brake. A huge aircraft oil-cooler submerged in a barrel of water was available to cool a dyno engine's lubricant, with cold water flowing continuously through the barrel at a designated rate and draining into the dyno building's plumbing system. Enormous fans sucked ambient air through the dyno room from outdoors to keep things cool, and portable fans were available to blow directly on the intercooler, exhaust, and any other components that required special cooling. With the dyno fans off even momentarily, a high-output turbo motor like the 4.2L XK powerplant radiates heat at a furious rate. The headers rapidly glow red in a darkened room if the engine is running even briefly at high loading with the fans down.

In addition to the heat pumping out the exhaust and radiating from the surface of a dyno engine working as hard as it can, water moving through the water brake of a load-holding dyno in operation is heated furiously as it passes through what is essentially a 1,200-horsepower water pump. Kim Barr's Superflow had been upgraded to handle additional torque and equipped with twin 2,000-gallon backup water storage tanks that enabled it to measure up to 2,000 horsepower without turning the water into a boiling cauldron.

THE PLAN

We dyno tested a freshly rebuilt 1982 4.2-liter six-cylinder EFI Jaguar engine on Kim Barr Racing's Superflow engine dyno near Dallas, Texas. The long block had 0.030-over 8:1 compression forged pistons, chrome rings, an O-ringed block, and an annealed copper head gasket. The cylinder head was equipped with mild performance cams slightly hotter than stock with conservative overlap to be compatible with turbocharging. The engine had been garage-tested out of the car before arriving at the dyno, but it had never run under load.

The plan was to start by testing calibrating and testing the powerplant with the L-Jetronic EFI manifold equipped with six replacement high-flow injectors good for 300-plus horsepower worth of fuel. On the exhaust side, the plan was to install the Stage 1 turbocharging system based on stock XKE headers that fed into a custom two-into-one Y-pipe with flanges that mounted an external Turbonetics wastegate and a single Rajay turbocharger dumping into a single exhaust system.

Later, we'd test the engine with the TWM triple-Weber intake manifold with its triple DCOE-type dual-throat TWM throttle bodies with one throttle per cylinder and twin port-injectors firing directly at each intake valve. That system had the ability to deliver more than 500 horsepower worth of fuel and was equipped with a massive air-air intercooler for the turbocharger. On the exhaust side we'd test the intercooled turbocharging system with the three transverse Airesearch T-2s.

The plan was to build one or more calibrations that would work with the various intake and exhaust hardware under

Most engine dynos are designed to mate easily with a few common performance engines. An engine dyno typically presents a simulated transmission input shaft designed to mate to one of the above engine's clutch/pilot bushings, plus a plate that bolts to the rear of the equivalent bell housing and connects to the dyno's water-brake assembly with a semi-flexible coupling. The Kim Barr Superflow had adapters for the small-block Chevy V-8, the big-block Chevy V-8, and certain large Ford V-8s.

To get the 4.2 XK engine on the Superflow, I needed a bell housing that was "Jaguar" on the engine side and "small-block Chevy" on the transmission side. I found a damaged 4.2 Jag bell housing in a wrecking yard and discovered it was longer than the bell housing of a small-block Chevy. Knowing that, I had a machine shop saw off the rear to the length of a Chevy housing and weld on a thick aluminum plate machined to match the rear pattern of a Chevy housing—using a $25 junk Chevy three-speed manual transmission as a jig. By incredibly good luck, the 4.2 Jag's clutch disc used exactly the same 10-spline pattern as the small-block Chevy. If it hadn't, I would have used a Chevy disc and pressure plate or riveted a Chevy disc center section to a Jag disc outer section—or something. A Chevy SB pilot bushing is larger than what's on a Jaguar, but it was a simple matter to fabricate a bushing consisting of a Jaguar 4.2's outside diameter and a Chevy transmission input shaft's inside diameter.

It is definitely important to keep oil at safe temperatures below 220 on the long dyno sessions that may be needed for a from-scratch EFI calibration. Not all 4.2L Jaguar oil filter assemblies were equipped with an external oil cooler, but ours was. It was simple to divert engine oil to the dyno room's aircraft cooler.

In order to datalog an extremely accurate indication of combustion conditions and provide a good advance warning of impending trouble, I needed a way to mount Superflow EGT probes in the Jaguar exhaust ports. The trick was to drill and tap the cast-iron Jaguar turbo exhaust headers for brass 1/8-inch pipe to 1/8-inch compression fittings. These will hold EGT probes securely in place and prevent exhaust leaks that

would dissipate exhaust energy on a turbo motor likely to have significant exhaust back pressure during boost. At the same time I equipped each of the T-2 turbochargers with an exhaust gas oxygen sensor boss in the turbine discharge pipe that would allow installation of the UEGO probe of a Horiba fast wideband air/fuel ratio meter.

The Superflow dyno was set up to accommodate many different sizes and lengths of engines with adjustable motor mount connections. All I needed was a set of steel brackets that bolted to the Jag engine flanges at one end and the dyno brackets at the other. In fact, Kim Barr had a huge bucket of brackets, and we found two that worked without modification. With the engine of the dyno, we fabricated mandrel-bent tubing to interface the single and then the triple turbo exhausts to the 6-inch flex pipes the dyno uses to evacuate exhaust gases to the outside atmosphere.

I connected the dyno room oil cooler to fittings on the 4.2 jag oil filter housing engine using braided steel hose that added oil to the engine, and connected the Jag engine thermostat housing and water pump fitting to dyno cooling system. I connected the EMS wiring harness to the engine sensors and actuators and connected EMS ground and switched 12-volt to the DC power sources on the dyno, and then connected the dyno's fuel supply system to the engine and computer through the Superflow fuel-flow measurement equipment. To be on the safe side, we filled up the dyno tank with 107-octane Sunoco race fuel.

After that we installed the Superflow air-metering hat on the turbo inlet to datalog standard cubic feet per minute airflow and connected dyno oil pressure, EGT, and manifold pressure gauge probes to the engine. We connected the ECM and ignition to dyno electrical power, and connected the dyno's throttle actuator and starter wiring to the engine. We ran data-link connections from the ECM to a laptop PC in the dyno control room. We located the Horiba wideband meter in the dyno room window where it was facing the control room for easy air/fuel ratio viewing, and then got ready to fire up the engine.

controlled conditions where we could keep an eye on exhaust gas temperature (EGT) and air/fuel ratios as we loaded the engine to increasing levels of power.

This was a fairly complex engine. I wanted to get the engine running really right and preferred not to burn it down on the way. I also wanted to test the various EFI and turbo combinations and find out what really worked at medium to high levels of boost. I wanted to be scientific. If you're paying the bills the tuning process can be expensive in the case of an oddball turbo engine like the 4.2 Jag, which no one has ever seen before with high-boost turbos and electronic injection, and which probably no one knows the limits of. I wanted to get past the guesswork and get the system working perfectly before we turned the key with the engine in the car.

Bob Norwood operated the dyno in manual mode and calibrated the EMS. Kim Barr, who owned the dyno, had built the new XJ engine used for dyno testing, and Barr did the full-throttle dyno pulls when the calibrating was done and it was time to get the numbers.

CALIBRATING ON THE SUPERFLOW

Working with the 1979 L-Jet manifold and single-turbo exhaust, we got to work.

The engine cranked and started easily and ran decently while it warmed up and I dealt with some minor leaks and such. A minor problem showed up in the form of oil leaks from the cam covers and dipstick. For a while we fought high-voltage spark

problems. When the engine reached operating temperature, it was clear the base fuel map was rich.

Norwood worked on the idle maps with a laptop PC, lowering bar graphs with arrow keys to shorten injection pulse width at light loading manifold pressure.

With a good clean idle, he began the process of calibrating the engine on the dyno in full manual mode. The sequence was:
1. Establish a speed and loading via throttle and dyno load control, work the global mixture-trim function to hunt for the right air/fuel ratio, watching the UEGO and reading the dyno torque meter to find lean best torque (LBT).
2. Center the mixture trim dial and permanently change the appropriate element of the fuel map.
3. Move to another level of loading by raising the throttle and adding dyno load (an arrow on the laptop will point at the loading bar graph currently fueling the engine).
4. Adjust fuel for best torque, and move again—until all speed-loading breakpoints for this rpm range are adjusted.
5. When the fuel breakpoints look good, do a spark hook test to optimize timing for peak torque without detonation.
6. Raise engine speed 500 rpm to match the next defined Haltech rpm range.
7. Adjust the mixture for various engine loading bars in this rpm range.

The process is especially tough with turbos. Compressors make boost, feeding back horsepower, which supplies increased exhaust gases, which adds boost, which changes speed, which

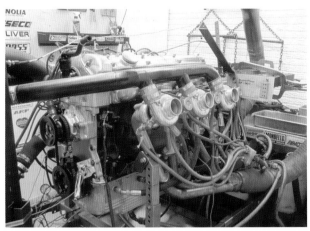

On the Kim Barr Superflow engine dyno, we tested the Jag 4.2 in single-turbo, L-Jet intake configuration, we installed the triple-turbo, individual-throttle intake. The engine made more than 300 lb-ft torque at 1,750 rpm, over 460 lb-ft at 4,750.

changes load, and so on. The process requires a deft hand and plenty of experience. Tuning a carb, you'd change idle mixture, main jets, emulsion tubes, and power valves, and so on, but with EFI, you play with arrow keys on a graph and a computer. Spark timing is adjusted similarly to fueling. Working this way, Norwood eventually completed calibrating the 4.2 Jaguar engine in its six-injector, one-turbo configuration.

Following calibration, Kim Barr ran several 1,750–5,500-rpm dyno runs in auto mode. We achieved more than 460 lb-ft of torque at 4,750, and as much as 345 horsepower at the same speed.

At this point, we let the engine cool and then converted to the 12-injector manifold with its three, dual-throat throttle bodies, each throat containing twin injectors of 218-cc/min capacity of the type used on Chevy 5.7-liter TPI motors. We also installed the second turbo system that supports three Turbo Power internal-wastegate Airesearch turbos. This configuration also included an intercooler. Each injector was capable of providing fuel for about 41 horsepower, for a total of roughly 500 horsepower with all 12 injectors in play. Using the Haltech E6 required an add-on driver box that allowed it to drive the additional six staged injectors.

With new injector sizes and changed volumetric efficiency, Bob Norwood began the meticulous, manual-mode recalibration of checking air/fuel ratios and spark timing, coordinating dyno load, throttle, fuel, and timing.

In this configuration, the motor made 322 lb-ft of torque at 1,750 rpm, peak torque of 442 lb-ft at 3,750 rpm, and 460 horsepower at 4,750 rpm, a 90 percent increase over stock. The big 4.2 six made it look and sound easy. Compared to the shattering roar of a wide-open V-8 often heard on the dyno, the unmuffled but turbocharged Jag had an eerily quiet, even-fire inline-six purr you could mistake for the purr of a big turbo-diesel generator, even at full throttle. Turbochargers muffle the exhaust note to the extent that the engine did not even require mufflers for street use. The three turbos maxed out at about 12-psi boost with the wastegates closed, indicating that there was probably a lot of backpressure at higher rpm and boost, limiting the total amount of horsepower.

WHEN JAG 4.2 TURBO ENGINES BREAK

The stock Jaguar 4.2-liter engine is a high-torque motor with long stroke and long rods, which is why these engines redline at only 5,500 rpm. High-rpm 4.2-six racing Jaguar engines require

strong aftermarket rods, special vibration dampers with the right balancing, and really good oil pressure. Turbo boost puts far less stress on rods than the momentum of the reciprocating piston/rod mass accelerating and decelerating, so I was not worried about killing rods from the turbocharged torque boost. It's rpm that breaks Jaguar engines, not boost.

However, boost can cause detonation, which can break a Jag 4.2 in a hurry. Knock under serious turbo boost will crack pistons, break rings, and melt or smash ring lands, which is why all knock-limited turbo engines running pump gasoline require serious anti-knock countermeasures. The turbo XK engine was built with 8:1 pistons that were selected to be compatible with a turbo system that might never have intercooling and a hardwired Bosch analog EMS that could not be tuned except using add-on external devices.

Higher compression pistons can work with modern programmable engine management systems as long as you give the engine plenty of fuel and as long as the turbo system has excellent intercooling or you're not running much boost, and as long as the EMS is set up with conservative boost-retard timing maps or equipped with a fast and effective knock-detection and control system. Some people say any turbo motor should have forged pistons, but a number of high-output Japanese factory turbo cars like the Turbo Supra and Turbo MR2 achieved good reliability using pressure-cast pistons. However, these cars do have sophisticated fail-safe anti-knock–control systems, including low-boost fuel and spark tables, and they have computer-controlled wastegates that allow the ECM to dial back maximum turbo boost when the engine is hot or under a lot of mechanical stress.

Given the radically long head studs on 4.2 Jags, cylinder head lifting under boost-enhanced combustion pressures can potentially result in loss of coolant or oil leaks and can also result in blown head gaskets. We began dyno-testing the Turbo EFI 4.2 Jag engine with wire O-rings installed in grooves machined in the cast-iron block that pressed against the fire rings of a stock composition head gasket. After blowing the composition head gasket once, we fabricated a custom copper head gasket, which caused no further problems.

Chapter 24
Project: Two-staged Forced Induction on the MR6

In this project I swapped a 1994 3.0L Toyota Camry 1MZ V6 into a 1991 mid-engine MR2 Turbo and installed Motec standalone programmable engine management and various power-adder systems. In the course of the project, power increased from 181 horsepower at the wheels to 537, a 3X increase.

In various Toyota and Lexus applications, the stock 1MZ motor had 185–225 advertised crankshaft horsepower. The wrecking-yard 1994 Lexus ES 300 powerplant used in this project was advertised to have 188 crankshaft horsepower. With a free-flow exhaust sans catalyst/muffler and a better fuel supply, we were able to make 181 wheel horsepower (whp) using a Motec M4-8 aftermarket EMS, which equates to 213 crankshaft horsepower, assuming 15 percent drivetrain and tire losses.

Following the V-6 engine swap, I and two Dallas-area tuning shops with Dynojet inertial chassis dynamometers tuned and tested the vehicle in various configurations, including the following:

1. Naturally aspirated 3.0L V-6 with no power-adders installed
2. Slightly modified TRD Eaton M62 blower kit designed for the 1994 and newer Toyota Camry
3. Custom Alamo Autosports/Majestic Turbo T04E-based turbocharging system
4. Twincharged, with both power-adders

In the most recent addendum to the project in preparation for the 2013 revision to this book, I pulled off the Motec M4-8 EMS and installed a MegaSquirt 3 system with Bosch LSU Wideband AFR—a highly flexible and economical do-it-yourself open-source EMS with all the modern features of a proprietary standalone aftermarket EMS. The MegaSquirt architecture allowed a knowledgeable enthusiast (or someone who had the time and motivation to *become* a knowledgeable enthusiast) to assemble the ECM motherboard (or not), and to customize the system to the application with a large variety of hardware options, and, if you choose, modifications to the operating software. This phase of the project is documented in a separate sidebar in this chapter.

Meanwhile, the modified TRD blower kit could be removed or replaced in less than an hour. The twin-entry turbocharger de-installed in about 90 minutes, with a "turbo-replacement pipe" connecting the engine exhaust to the 3-inch exhaust turbine-out downpipe and muffler. A Random Technology catalytic converter becomes an optional part of the exhaust upstream of the Borla muffler, installing or de-installing in less than five minutes.

The MR6 Project continued for many moons through seven main stages, five of which had occurred by the time the first version of this book was published in 2003. The fifth occurred shortly after, and the final stage occurred much more recently in preparation for the publication of the revised version of the book in 2013.

MR6 on the Alamo dyno at project end. Power increased from 181 rwhp to 537 rwhp.

1. 181 whp, Naturally Aspirated, Stock Engine Internals

At Alamo Autosports we replaced the stock 200-horsepower MR2 Turbo 2.0L four-banger with a 1MZ V-6 engine from a 1994 Lexus ES300/Toyota Camry. A 1994–2001+ 1MZ powerplant more or less bolts right up to a stock MR2 Turbo transaxle, which is very strong (see sidebar for details about the engine swap).

After playing around with the stock MAF-based Lexus engine management system, we installed a Motec M48 MAP-based programmable EMS at Norwood Autocraft in Dallas.

On the Norwood Dynojet, with free-flow exhaust, no catalytic converter, and a custom M4-8 dyno calibration, the car managed 181 whp.

2. 250-whp, 5-psi Supercharged, Stock Engine Internals

Toyota Racing Development (TRD) marketed a blower kit for several Camry, Solara, and Sienna van applications using the 1MZ V-6 based on the Eaton M62, a Gen-III Roots-type positive-displacement supercharger capable of delivering instant boost as soon as you hit the throttle. The pre-TVS M62 was a relatively efficient linear-flow positive-displacement supercharger with twisted-lobe rotors and a vacuum-controlled bypass valve to eliminate boost when the throttle was closed. Magnusen Products, which designed the TRD kit, developed a special casting that housed the Eaton rotor assembly in a replacement intake manifold. The blower manifold retained the stock throttle body in the original stock location. The TRD kit was set up with a drive-pulley assembly that delivered 5-psi maximum boost, creeping up from 3.5-psi available below 2,000 rpm.

Working at Norwood Autocraft, we easily adapted the kit to the 1MZ Lexus engine as installed in the MR2, mainly by raising the blower drive assembly slightly higher with respect to the engine timing cover in order to clear our special custom passenger-side engine-swap mount. The installation required making slight modifications to the MR2 shock tower to clear the serpentine belt in the vicinity of the supercharger drive pulley.

Running stock 288-cc/min fuel injectors on a stock 1MZ engine, the TRD supercharger kit was on the ragged edge of lean mixtures at 5-psi boost with the stock fuel injectors near 100 percent duty cycle, which was fine from an emissions point of view. The 1MZ is very resistant to knock, and if you bought the TRD kit through a Toyota dealer and had the dealer install it, Toyota would honor the factory new car warranty. The TRD kit worked for Toyota, but we wanted to maximize power, so we needed more fuel.

The quickest way to provide more fuel was to add a BEGI fuel management unit (FMU), which provides an adjustable variable-rate-of-gain (VRG) in fuel pressure as a multiple of increases in manifold boost, plus adjustable onset pressure (usually ambient pressure).

With the EMS calibration modified to work with the VRG regulator, the supercharged V-6 proved itself capable of delivering 250 to 260 wheel HP, depending on whether you were willing to go 250 or 750 rpm above the stock 6250 redline.

3. 320 whp, Twincharged, Stock Engine Internals

We built the first turbo system for the MR6 at Alamo Autosports. The Alamo turbo system mounted a single large T04R Majestic turbocharger on a bracket just above the rear of the transaxle to the left of the engine. The Majestic turbocharger was equipped with a 4-inch inlet and bullet-style aerodynamic compressor shaft nut.

The turbo conversion design added a collector to the original Alamo dual exhaust, combining both Vee banks into a single pipe behind the rear header, which routed exhaust gases to the rear, then to the left side of the car, and finally forward and upward between the main rear suspension cross-member and the anti-roll bar and into the turbine inlet.

We built a custom air-water intercooler and installed the air-cooler in the trunk of the car behind the rear engine firewall, routing the compressor discharge plumbing to the cooler through a hole sawed through the rear firewall to the bottom of the air-cooler unit. We routed air-cooler discharge back through a second port in the firewall directly to the throttle body.

The compound turbo-supercharging system now had the capability to deliver tremendous amounts of air to the cylinders, but the engine still sported stock internals.

Meanwhile, a set of 633-cc/min performance fuel injectors arrived from Bosch, theoretically good for 575 to 725 crankshaft horsepower, depending on brake-specific fuel consumption and maximum acceptable injector duty cycle.

Back on the Norwood Dynojet, with a new Norwood calibration, we worked our way up to 320 whp, at which point the engine was sneezing a bit of steam into the engine compartment under heavy boost from the rear Vee-bank head-block interface.

It was time for internal engine upgrades, including improved head fasteners.

4. 270 whp, Turbo-Only, 6-psi, Super-Duty Engine

The stock 1MZ was a strong aluminum engine with a steel crank supported by six-bolt main caps, structural upper oil pan, nine-bolt heads, steel cylinder sleeves, closed block deck, and other good features. But it was designed to handle 200 crankshaft horsepower.

This compound-supercharged 1MZ-FE V-6 runs a gigantic T76 turbocharger, intercooled, breathing down the neck of a TRD positive-displacement Eaton M62 supercharger. The combo makes immediate low-end boost, but when the turbo starts to wail, the two-stage boosting system generated 3 bar MAP.

Twin-entry 1MZ V-6 single-turbo exhaust system, designed to improve flow by preventing exhaust pulse collisions until exhaust is in the turbine.

Following engine disassembly and analysis, we ended up equipping the engine with Wiseco custom forged pistons, Crower forged steel rods, super-duty ARP main and head studs (with main cross-bolts), Kim Barr Racing block-deck cylinder O-rings, and Clark Copper head gaskets. GTP ported the heads to upgrade both exhaust and intake CFM, and Kim Barr Racing bored the cylinders for the new pistons.

Along with the stronger engine, we upgraded the ignition with six super-duty Ignition Solutions plasma-booster direct-fire coils. We installed a GMC Typhoon electronic boost controller—a pulsewidth-modulated (PWM) device designed to increase boost by feeding a programmable portion of manifold boost pressure to the Deltagate side of the Majestic wastegate under closed-loop Motec control. With 0 percent boost to the Deltagate port, the wastegate would provide 6-psi boost based solely on the nominal wastegate spring pressure. With 100 percent boost, it could rise until the engine blew up or the turbo ran out of breath (or blew up!), or until backpressure in the exhaust forced open the wastegate.

Majestic upgraded the thin-shaft turbocharger with a low-inertia nut and a .7 A/R turbine housing (versus the original .83 housing).

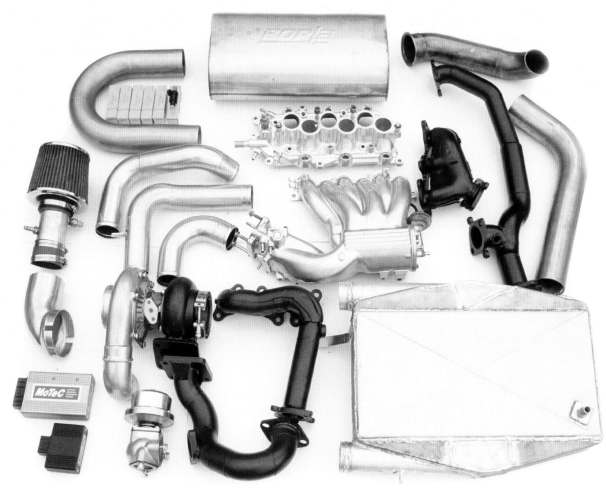

Here's the Alamo Autosports 1MZ intercooled turbo kit with Motec M48 EMS and big Bosch 630 cc/min peak-and-hold fuel injectors.

Back on the Dynojet, we tested the car turbo-only at 6-psi boost, whipping out 270 whp with electronic boost control deactivated and boost thus limited solely by standard wastegate spring pressure. We did some testing at higher boost with the addition of the electronic boost controller under Motec control, pushing power above 320 whp, but by this time we were intermittently fighting combustion gas leakage at the head gaskets. The best results would not happen without some additional engine work, turbo optimization, and a clutch refurbishing.

5. 503 whp, Turbo-Only (Twin-Entry), 24-psi, Super-Duty Engine

We yanked the powertrain to deal with head-gasket problems, but seized the opportunity to examine and optimize everything.

I began by redesigning the single-entry turbo system. A twin-entry turbo system can be very effective at improving low-rpm engine exhaust energy by minimizing collisions between the pressure waves of adjacent exhaust pulses, and Toyota saw enough valve in the scheme to equip the stock 2.0L MR2 with a twin-entry turbo system. In the case of the 1MZ's 1-2-3-4-5-6 firing order V-6, the trick was to isolate exhaust pulses 1-3-5 (front Vee-bank) from pulses 2-4-6 (rear Vee-bank). The new 1MZ system used a twin-entry turbine housing located directly behind the rear header and plumbing that kept the exhaust from the two Vee banks separate until the collector pipes entered the

twin-entry turbine flange. In order to extract exhaust from both Vee banks to a single wastegate while simultaneously preventing inglow-rpm exhaust pulses from colliding at the wastegate, I designed a steel barrier that maintained contact with the face of the wastegate poppet valve until it began to open (at which point maintaining maximum exhaust energy was irrelevant). I further optimized the turbo system by insulating all of the cold side to prevent heat-soak from the engine.

Meanwhile, we machined the engine for a larger-diameter set of cylinder O-rings and installed a stronger main studs: It developed that the head porting had enlarged the combustion chambers slightly, nullifying some of the clamping force of the original O-rings, and contributing to combustion leaks.

Back on the dyno, the turbo-only 1MZ engine managed 503 whp. Power was up at the top end, and torque was up in the lower and mid-rpm ranges. Who could ask for more?

We could. We did.

At this point the clutch let go. And we were again losing coolant. Time to pull the engine one more time.

6. The Final Frontier

We backed away from the copper head gaskets. With good combustion chambers, great intercooling, an efficient turbo, and race gasoline, we were not encountering gasket-killing knock problems but suffering from tenacious coolant leakages past the custom copper gaskets. After verifying that the block deck and head surfaces were dead flat, I installed stock Toyota composition head gaskets and removed the inner block wire O-rings. By themselves, the outer O-rings were just within the edge of the stock gasket's metal fire rings, which not only increased clamping force but helped prevent the head gasket's metal fire rings from being forced outward under extreme combustion pressures.

While the engine was apart, I had the crankshaft repolished and replaced the main and rod bearings and disassembled and serviced the oil pump.

Meanwhile, Clutchmasters changed the multi-disk clutch facing to a new experimental super-duty material in a quest for improved torque-holding capability combined with excellent streetability.

This was the time to install some additional sensors. In addition to the standard engine temp and air temp inputs, the Motec M4-8 ECU was equipped to accept input from an "aux temp" input, which, thus far, had not been used. I drilled and tapped the supercharger plenum downstream of the rotor assembly and installed a GM Delco 3,500-ohm air-temp sensor. Either could now be switched to the M4-8 aux temp input and datalogged. At this point it would be possible to calculate Eaton M62 charge heating by datalog the standard air temp sensor

located just upstream of the throttle body and compare it to data from the new blower plenum aux temp sensor. To evaluate intercooler effectiveness the same way, I installed an air temp sensor just downstream of the turbo compressor discharge.

It would be interesting as well to measure exhaust backpressure during turbo boost as well as intake pressure upstream of the throttle body on either end of the air-cooler when the supercharger was installed in order to determine the boost produced by the supercharger versus boost produced by the turbo. Up to this point, the M4-8 aux volt input had been dedicated to receiving data from a 1-bar MAP sensor open to the atmosphere to provide barometric pressure compensation. But if you weren't driving in the mountains and didn't care about ongoing barometric pressure compensation, you could potentially free up the aux volt port by configuring the ECM load calculation scheme to get ambient pressure from the 3-bar MAP sensor each time the key came on before the engine started. The freed-up aux volt input could be used to datalog compressor-discharge pressure via 3-bar MAP sensor or to datalog backpressure using a multibar pressure sensor referenced to turbine inlet pressure using a vacuum hose connected to a metal pipe long enough to cushion the sensor from destructive exhaust heat.

When it came time to make serious power, the stock 200-horse V-6 needed some super-duty parts, including Wiseco forged pistons, Crower forged rods, and a rebalanced 1MZ crankshaft.

I had acquired a Random Technology high-flow catalytic converter for testing and built a matching cat-eliminator pipe so the engine could easily be run with or without the cat. Installation would be a five-minute job once we had the final dynoruns sans catalyst. The plan was to produce peak power without the catalyst and then install it and see how much boost you could run without the cat hurting power.

Final Dynoruns

Working at Alamo Autosports with Brice Yingling and Bob Norwood, we decided to begin final dyno testing with a nice low-boost (10-psi) dynorun on 93-octane pump gasoline. The charge-cooler was plumbed to a faucet with a garden hose, with water draining from the charge-cooler into a second hose that dumped into the sewer. I connected the blower-discharge sensor to the aux temp port on the Motec and attached a pressure gauge to the front bank exhaust pipe just upstream of the twin-entry turbine flange.

I unscrewed the wastegate spring preload adjustment bolt nearly all the way. The Motec boost table was set to bring in full boost at 3,500 rpm.

On the dyno, Bob Norwood did a "soft" dynorun. Boost increased to 11 psi at 3,500 rpm, fibrillating between 12.5- and 15-psi in a run to 6,000 rpm. No one watched the new backpressure gauge on this run. Torque was fairly flat from 3,750 rpm at roughly 365 lb-ft before falling off gradually above 5,600 rpm. The engine made 394 peak whp at 5,900 rpm. Temperature in the blower discharge climbed from 108 to 124 degrees Fahrenheit. Intake air temp downstream of the intercooler stayed at 82 degrees Fahrenheit.

Second Dynorun

The next run was a "hard" dynorun, with power up by 20 whp over the same range, torque up approximately 15 lb-ft. Torque leveled off at 4,100 and stayed fairly flat to 5,600. Boost climbed to 16.5 psi at 4,100, fibrillated to 15.7 psi at 6,700. Peak power of 415 whp occurred at 6,200, with 390.3 lb-ft torque at 4,300—*still using 93-octane pump gas.*

This time we watched turbine-inlet exhaust backpressure, which was insignificant in the early run but climbed into the 15–20-psi range at peak power. It was difficult to tell exactly due to exhaust pulsations making the needle flutter.

The supercharger discharge plenum temperature sensor seemed to have heat-soaked to 118 degrees Fahrenheit at the beginning of the dynorun. Temperature climbed steadily to 126 by 5,750, increasing to 140 degrees Fahrenheit at 7,000.

Third Dynorun

With the MR6's fuel tank nearly empty, we added 5 gallons of 118-octane race gasoline.

We'd concluded that with wastegate spring preload adjusted to the minimal 6-psi setting, exhaust backpressure would force the wastegate poppet valve to crack open prematurely, preventing the turbocharger from making more than 22–24-psi boost. The obvious answer was to preload the wastegate spring more. We were about to discover that this solution produced blowback in the form of a new problem. I screwed in the wastegate adjustment bolt nearly all the way, which should increase nominal boost from 6 to maybe 9 psi. The Deltagate port was referenced to the compressor discharge by way of the Typhoon boost control valve, which was under Motec control. With the wastegate referenced to the compressor rather than the intake manifold, if the supercharger was installed you'd

expect minimum to be 9 psi *plus* the 3–5-psi output of the blower, for a total minimum boost in the 9–14-psi range.

Norwood hammered the throttle and ripped off a new dynorun. The boost controller and turbo combined to reach 19-psi boost at 4,150 rpm. MAP fibrillated—fairly flatly—until 5,450 rpm, at which point boost climbed inexorably from 20 psi at 5,750 to 28 psi at 6,500 with the boost controller at 100 percent duty cycle in a failed effort to limit boost.

It was clear in retrospect that clamping down on the wastegate adjustment bolt was causing the spring to bind, severely limiting the travel of the poppet valve; when exhaust volume became too high to flow through the partially closed valve, boost crept to 28 psi. The Catch-22: Too little wastegate adjustment pressure, you couldn't make boost above 24 psi due to backpressure forcing open the wastegate. Too much adjustment pressure and you couldn't stop creeping overboost due to severe limitations on the wastegate opening travel.

Power had peaked at 471.6 rwhp at 6,500. Torque remained flat from 4,000 to 6,100 rpm at a little more than 400 lb-ft. The gauge measuring backpressure had reached 35 psi. Supercharger discharge temperature—heat-soaked prior to the run—climbed from 126 to 137 degrees Fahrenheit. Air temp exiting the intercooler remained in the 82–86 degrees Fahrenheit range throughout the run even with the water turned off to the charge-cooler.

I backed out the wastegate spring a bit, and Norwood hit the start run button on the Dynojet and mashed the pedal to the metal. The dynorun proceeded normally until there was a sudden loud bang at 28-psi boost.

Forensic analysis subsequently revealed the turbo compressor had *exploded*. What was left when the compressor failed at 28-psi boost was the compressor hub, broken off where the shaft emerged through the compressor backplate and stripped completely of its blades, which were shrapnel in the bottom charger-cooler end-tank, which had trapped the metal and prevented it from entering the engine. The compressor backplate was hugely distorted and bulging outward toward the center section of the turbo. The turbine side appeared undamaged, the turbine wheel spinning freely as always on the hot-side shaft.

REGROUPING

At this point, we decided to fall back and regroup. I put the turbocharger on a Greyhound bus for Majestic Turbo in Waco, installed the turbo-eliminator pipe that enabled the MR6 to run without the turbocharger installed, and drove home to Austin where I pulled the wastegate the next day and installed a secondary inner spring to increase the nominal to 9 psi.

In Waco, confronted with a scored-up compressor housing, Majestic decided to machine the housing for a T-70 compressor wheel. I picked up the reconstructed turbocharger the next day and drove the MR6 to the Dynojet at Alamo. The plan now was to optimize power in turbo-only mode, and then reinstall the blower to see what that could do for low-end, whether top-end performance would be hurt by the blower manifold's relatively small runners and narrow compressor inlet.

Dallas, meanwhile, was experiencing some of the most dreadful early summer Texas weather imaginable, over 100-degrees with extremely high humidity.

On the Dynojet, the MR6 performed a series of runs to about 450 whp, at which point datalogs revealed significant compressor surging, with manifold pressure jumping around between 18 and 28 psi, and in one case momentarily crashing

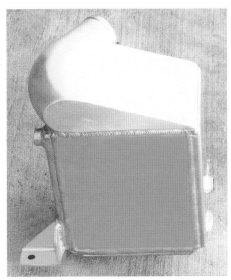

This large water-cooled charge-cooler sits in the engine compartment beside the throttlebody, and is capable of greater than 100-percent thermal efficiency with total-loss tap water or ice bath.

We wrestled with spark gap misfire problems under boost conditions until we junked the stock Toyota coils, installed these Ignition Solutions plasma booster coils, and reset dwell in the Motec ECM.

all the way down to atmospheric pressure before immediately building again into the 2- to 3-bar range.

All centrifugal compressors run the risk of surging if the compressor is pumping relatively little air mass at a high pressure ratio. Unlike a positive-displacement supercharger like the Eaton (where the architecture makes it physically impossible for air to move backward through the blower), turbos make boost by accelerating air to extremely high speed with a set of fan blades turning at up to 300,000 rpm or more at full howl in some cases. If a centrifugal compressor is making a lot of boost but not moving enough air mass, air can suddenly change direction and explode backward through the compressor, momentarily depleting the head of pressure in the diffuser section of the

compressor, typically with impressive noises that can sound like a coyote baying or a series of minor explosions and air disruptions.

Anything that lowers air pressure at the compressor inlet can intensify a tendency to surge by increasing the pressure ratio required to achieve a certain boost pressure. For example, an overly restrictive air-cleaner or intake tube. We clearly had bigger problems than an undersized air cleaner, but I took a look at the 5-inch-long-by-6-inch diameter conical K&N air cleaner that worked great at 250 horsepower and ordered the biggest one that would fit on the car.

GTP ported the 1MZ cylinders heads lightly for mild air flow increase.

Toyota 1MZ V-6, with new charge cooler installed in the engine compartment.

I wired in a boost controller using one of the digital pulse width–modulated (PWM) outputs. The controller delivers conditoned MAF ref at a specified pressure from the wastegate actuator diaphragm to increase maximum boost above nominal wastegate spring pressure.

FINAL TESTING

Before final testing I installed a Majestic T-61 turbocharger. With the T-70 operating within 5 percent of the surge line at high boost in the 5,000–6,000-rpm range, it was clear we needed a smaller turbo, and the obvious candidates were the T-66 and T-61. Assuming a minimal operating threshold of 65 percent thermal efficiency, the T-61 should be good for 640 flywheel horsepower, the T-66 680 horsepower. Limited to 60 percent efficiency, the T-61 could manage 670, the T-66 710. Whatever the charge heating, on the dyno there was little doubt that the hose-fed air-water intercooler would have no problem returning compressed charge to the temperature of the tap water. I decided to go with the T-61, which should provide excellent response and fast spooling.

Back at Alamo with 5 gallons of 118 octane in the tank, we hooked up to the Dynojet and got ready to rock 'n' roll, turbo-only. Once again, it was nearly 100 degrees in the dyno room in June in Texas.

In a little more than a day, we ran 46 dynoruns, with Alamo owner and chief tuner Brice Yingling calibrating the Motec this time in the final search for the optimal fuel and timing. With the boost-controller disabled and dual springs in the Majestic wastegate, the first run made 325 whp at 9-psi boost.

We methodically worked our way toward 22-psi boost, making changes to fuel, timing, and boost. Test equipment included the Dynojet inertial chassis dynamometer, the dyno's

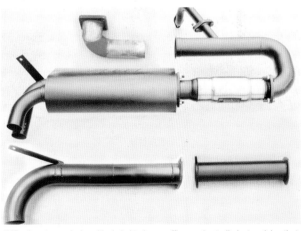

1MZ exhaust was designed included turbo-, muffler-, and cat-eliminator piping that enabled rapid transformation for testing of the same engine in naturally-aspirated, supercharged-only, turbocharged-only, and twin-charged configurations.

wideband air/fuel meter logging AFR with speed and power and torque, the Motec M48's internal logging capability, and temperature and pressure gauges.

At 22 psi, it became clear that we still did not have enough spring power to keep the wastegate closed against exhaust backpressure as boost increased, and I was forced again to begin

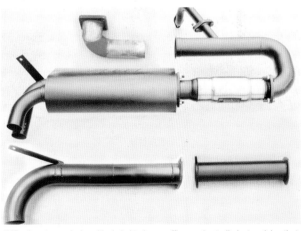

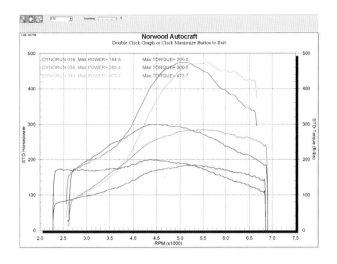

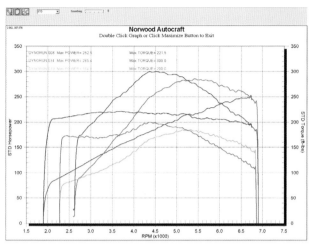

Stock 1MZ V-6, 6-psi boost, and 24 psi, turbo-only. Power rises from 185 to 285 to 475 rear-wheel horsepower.

Horsepower and torque for N.A., supercharged, and turbocharged configurations.

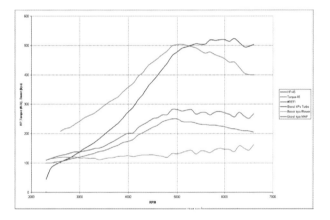

Dynorun 45 power and torque, with boost broken down by the contribution of the supercharger and turbocharger. Turbo was running out of breath as power approached 522 wheel horsepower.

adjusting the wastegate spring compressor bolt to clamp down harder on the spring, which, of course, simultaneously limited wastegate travel.

With Brice's tuning, the 1MZ managed 455 whp at 22 psi, which was still less than the peak output of the 2.0L 3S-GTE MR2 project, which had maxed out at roughly 470 whp.

Pushing on, the trick was to dive under the car on the dyno, adding additional turns to the wastegate adjustment bolt, then make a run with your fingers crossed, ready to get out of the throttle instantly if boost went wild.

But it never did. In fact, as we pushed on to 28-psi boost, the turbo ran out of breath. Progress stalled just below 500 whp; 500 was just a number, but it was a good number at the time. We scratched our heads and then I disconnected the air-intake and air-cleaner assembly from the compressor and aimed a powerful squirrel-cage fan toward the compressor air intake underneath the car. After a few more tuning runs, I clamped down on the wastegate bolt, and Brice hit the record button and mashed the gas pedal.

The car made a mighty groan as rpm pushed through 3,000, and suddenly the engine went nuclear. Torque increased 300 lb-ft in the next 2,000 rpm. When the run was over, the Dynojet monitor showed that the mighty 1MZ Turbo had managed 537 whp at 5,400 rpm on 28.5-psi boost.

Now it was time to see what the engine would do twincharged. As soon as the engine cooled a little I bolted on the TRD blower kit, and we got ready to roll once more with the wastegate clamped shut.

This time the engine was stronger than ever, ahead of the best turbo-only dynoruns by 20 to 40 whp through 4,500 rpm, at which point power surged upward through 500 whp. Brice aborted the run by 5,000. The engine was threatening to go nuts. Backing out on the wastegate bolt, we did several more runs, managing 524 horsepower across a broad range from 5,500 to nearly 7,000 rpm—on 23-psi boost.

At that point I installed the Random Tech cat and Borla muffler, and minutes later the car was back on the dyno for one last run. The power was down by 9 percent, from 525 to 478 whp, a loss of 47 whp. Most of the loss was due to the catalyst.

ANALYSIS AND SUMMARY: WHAT WE LEARNED ABOUT
Compound Turbo-Supercharging

- Turbocharging a Roots-equipped engine is like turbocharging a bigger NA motor with really good VE: The Eaton adds low-end grunt and provides an extra kick in midrange. With the MR6, as we began to run out of turbo capacity, the blower made a larger difference at the top-end. But the twincharged engine was making more boost than the turbo engine across the rpm range.

- The groaning "blower whine" noise of an Eaton supercharger disappears when force-fed by a large turbocharger because the blower is no longer having to work as hard. Some experts have claimed that once the turbo is howling, a force-fed Eaton blower is putting power back into the crank through the blower pulley, but that did not square with our experience. The net effect of the supercharger—which is sized and overdriven to have a greater pumping capacity than the engine itself—under all circumstances effectively increased the engine's displacement.

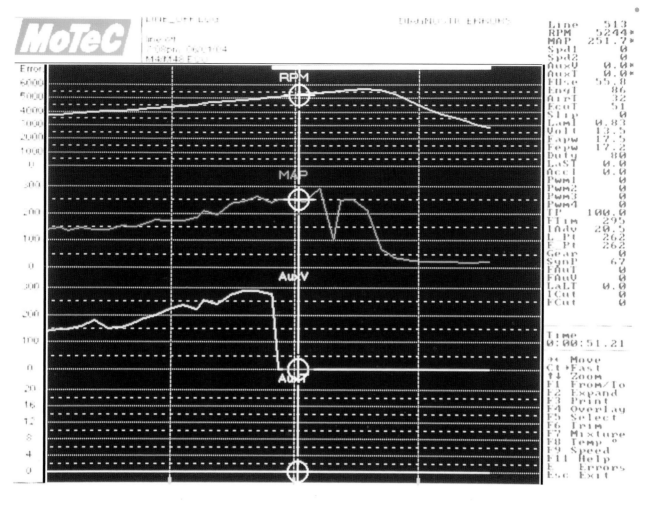

Motec M4-8 datalog showing boost surging as the wastegate and boost controller tried in vain to maintain steady manifold pressure.

When a turbo is making a lot of boost, with plenty of excess compressor capacity and a large surplus of exhaust energy, the displacement of the engine becomes less important, since the turbocharger can supply a large air surplus to a range of engine sizes. In the case of the MR6, the blower-only version delivered 3.5-5-psi boost to the engine, but when the turbo began to run out of steam in the twincharged version, the blower took up the slack, making up to 9-psi boost on top of what the turbo alone could achieve.

- Energy required to drive the blower can be deduced by considering the following: The turbo-only configuration made 537 whp at 5,400 on 26.5–29-psi boost. At the same rpm, the twincharged configuration made 505 whp on 24.5-psi boost, with the blower contributing 4- to 6-psi of the boost. If you subtract the horsepower produced by the 2- to 4.5-psi of additional turbo-only boost, the Eaton clearly was not consuming much power.

Eaton M62 Supercharger

- The instant the throttle was opened, the TRD bypass valve closed and the Eaton supercharger provided an instant jolt of 3-psi boost below 2,000 rpm and 5-psi boost at mid-to-high rpm. At high rpm the supercharger was actually adding up to 9 psi.

Increase in boost was linear and smooth with the Eaton, which flattened out the already flat torque curve of the stock variable-volume and length Toyota 1MZ intake system. The Eaton greatly extended the useful rpm range of an otherwise stock powerplant, providing almost 100 more horsepower at 6,500 to 7,000 rpm. The blower duplicated the effect of a bigger cam on a bigger motor, and this is equally true when you compound forced induction with a turbochargers.

Twin-Entry Majestic Turbo

- The twin-entry system proved the concept by increasing low-end boost and performance via increased exhaust energy, at no cost on the high end.
- Too much compressor can produce lazy response and surging or crashing boost pressure if too much boost builds at too low an airflow and compressor rpm. A street car will accelerate the best if you use the smallest turbo that will make the power you need. Keep in mind that a smaller turbo may require a *larger* wastegate in order to bypass sufficient exhaust gases efficiently.
- It is *very* important to get a handle on exhaust backpressure if you're developing a turbo system. Too

And then BANG! The turbocharger exploded, destroying the aluminum housing and stripping the blader from the compressor wheel. Fortunately, the intercooler prevented any shrapnel from entering the engine.

much backpressure on an engine with extremely large dynamic range can start to force open the wastegate at too low a boost, which can result in a torque-killing midrange situation where the wastegate cracks open, greatly depleting torque until the point at which the volume of exhaust gases increases enough to force boost to creep up to the maximum boost you really wanted—only at a higher rpm. If you're not datalogging boost pressure, you might never know you're a hundred horses down in the midrange, attributing it all to a lazy turbocharger.

- Acceptable street engine backpressure is usually 1.1–1.9 times manifold pressure. "Crossover" ratios less than 1.0 (backpressure *less* than boost pressure) can produce tremendous horsepower, but the turbocharger required to achieve crossover is likely to produce *very* lazy response for street use. At maximum performance, the MR6's T04R produced 35-psi gauge backpressure versus 28-psi boost, a 1.25 ratio. At lower boost, datalogging showed 24-psi backpressure versus 21-psi boost before the dynorun aborted, a 1.08 ratio. A 35-psi backpressure will certainly force open a 6-psi wastegate. The MR6 backpressure gauge showed no more than 15 to 20 psi developing before the wastegate began opening against a 6-psi wastegate spring with electronic boost control active and the engine below Motec target boost pressure. With the wastegate preload

adjustment bolt holding the wastegate closed, backpressure climbed to 35 psi. With dual wastegate springs delivering 9-psi nominal boost pressure, sufficient backpressure to begin forcing open the wastegate occurred by 22-psi boost, with a calculated 18+-psi threshold.

- Be careful when adjusting the wastegate spring preload bolt on an adjustable wastegate: On some designs, tightening the bolt increases spring pressure progressively and limits the amount the wastegate valve can open. If in doubt, bench test the wastegate with regulated pressure to verify full wastegate travel. Designs with deep actuator canisters are less likely to cause spring bind with a heavier preload.

- It would be nice to have a wastegate equipped with a position sensor that indicated the position of the poppet valve. We ended up trying to *deduce* what the wastegate was doing based on manifold pressure and the pulsewidth the electronic boost controller was sending boost to the Deltagate side of the wastegate actuator.

Air-Cooler

- With cooling provided by total-loss tap water, the MR6 charge-cooler maintained temperature within 5 degrees Fahrenheit during the hardest dyno pulls at nearly 30-psi boost. Worst-case air pressure drop through the cooler and throttle body was 2.0 psi at 3-bar boost.

- Plenty of air-water charge-cooler units heat-soak from the engine compartment when the engine is really cooking and become inter-*heaters*. One solution is insulating the charge-cooler unit from the engine compartment with foil-backed foam and fabric.

Engine Upgrades

- Porting a modern quad-cam engine without changing the cams is mostly a waste of time. Gallant Technical Performance increased the runner CFM at higher rpm, but the ported heads did not make more peak power: They made more power *above* peak power.

Cat and Muffler

- At 525 whp, installing the cat and muffler to the compound configuration eliminated 46 horsepower, about 8.8 percent.

- At 537 whp, adding only the catalyst eliminated 39 horsepower, a 7.2 percent reduction.

- At 440 to 455 whp, removing the muffler made virtually no difference.

Chapter 25
Project: Overboosted VW Golf 1.8T

If there were a 12-step program for people addicted to power, the owner of the 355-horse Golf 1.8T in this chapter could teach it—stand tall as a Bad Influence. Once you've had that high—once you've felt the thrill of hard acceleration squishing your face backward, sloshing the blood out of your frontal lobes and straight back into the darkest crevasses of the reptilian brain—there's no going back to your mom's goddamn Buick. You'll do anything for one more horsepower.

Two Kraut KKK turbos gave their lives to make it this far. But you have to break some eggs to make an omelet, right? In the case of the Golf 1.8T project, experience proved sometimes you have to trash some turbos to create a killer car capable of truly ugly deeds at the drags wars—all hotted up on 22-psi boost and cranking out 305 front-wheel horsepower on 110-octane unleaded Phillips race gas.

The engine was never out of this car—never even opened—but numbers from the Dynojet showed a measured 305-wheel horsepower on 1.4-bar boost, which arrived by 3,800 rpm. The 305 wheel horses translate to 355 at the flywheel, assuming 15 percent drivetrain and tire rolling losses. At the time of this writing, we did not know of a stronger streetable MK4 Golf 1.8T than this.

This Golf 1.8T rolled off the dealership as a silver GLS with 20-valve I4 turbo engine cranking out 150 advertised horsepower at the flywheel at 8-9-psi boost. A stock 1.8T was no slouch, decisively outrunning the six-cylinder 174-horse 2.8-liter Golf GLX VR6 from 30–50 by 1.6 seconds. The 1.8T made 142.4 BEFORE front-wheel horsepower on the Dynojet. The number 142.4 is awesome from a car with 150 advertised.

CHEAP TRICKS

The 1.8T project began in the usual way—with a software recalibration of the stock VW onboard computer via APR's K03 software (FedEx your onboard computer to APR overnight and they'll de-solder your stock PROM module and replace it with a proprietary daughter-board equipped with its own onboard microprocessor and multiple sockets for up to four PROM calibrations).

Modern naturally aspirated stock engines hardly ever benefit from chip tuning, but turbo engines are a different story because the horsepower output of a turbo engine system is not limited by the breathing capacity of the engine system as it is on an NA engine but instead by detonation and the ability of various highly stressed parts to survive under the harsh conditions of high boost. Automakers artificially de-rate power output to prevent warranty problems by limiting boost to conservative levels that protect the life of the engine in the hands of careless owners. Got 110-octane fuel for your turbo engine? Great: Turn up that boost. Willing to risk breaking the transaxle or CV joints? Pump up the volume some more. In this case, chip tuning unleashed a massive 1.1

A 2000 Golf 20-valve 1.8T, good for 150 stock crankshaft horsepower at 5,750 rpm, perhaps 130 at the wheels.

bar (16-psi) worth of midrange turbo boost in the Golf with a consequent massive increase in torque. The recalibration even unleashed a few extra clicks of turbo boost at peak power engine speeds, though 16-psi boost all the way through peak-power rpm was unavailable because it was beyond the capability of the stock fuel system.

APR's recalibration and a few tricks to improve engine breathing on the intake and exhaust side of the turbo powerplant allowed the project Golf to approach and then exceed 200 front-wheel horsepower on the Dynojet. Besides recalibration, Stage 1 hot rodding tricks included an Alamo custom 3-inch mandrel-bent cat-back exhaust, a Thermal R&D muffler, a K&N high-flow air filter element, and so forth.

The Stage 1 modifications altered maximum boost at peak torque and peak power, but left the factory VW ECM in charge of boost control via the stock electronic wastegate controller. Limiting maximum boost on a street turbo car is virtually always mandatory to prevent the effective compression ratio from rising to the point that the engine is destroyed by explosive detonation when the air/fuel mixture explodes rather than burning smoothly.

If you stick with the stock 1.8T ECM, it turns out that to achieve really high boost the engine must be run with the factory mass airflow (MAF) unit disconnected in order to prevent the computer from freaking at the excessive airflow—and countering by backing off the electronic throttle. If you remove the MAF, the check-engine light will come on, though special Golf PROMs have been created to fix that problem.

Hot rodding eventually killed the stock VW KKK-03 turbocharger, which simultaneously necessitated replacement and provided a pretty good excuse for getting a bigger turbo—especially since, at that time, it was tough to find rebuild parts and a new KKK-03 cost something like $1,400. The same forces that injured the original turbo also damaged the stock blow-off valve.

It is worth reiterating that the 1.8T was equipped with an electronic throttle, and hot rodders with drive-by-wire throttles need to beware of secret countermeasures against warranty-

Golf 1.8T engine cutaway, showing turbo system that would soon mutate to a whole other thing on the project car.

destroying levels of boost going on behind the scenes: You may only think you're at wide-open throttle when the pedal is down to the metal.

FULL-MONTY TRICKS

With the necessity of acquiring another turbocharger, the 1.8T project entered a new phase. External airflow modifications included:

1. Turbonetics T3-Super 60 turbocharger, good for at least 350 crankshaft horsepower worth of airflow at 22-psi boost-psi boost.
2. Greddy Type S blow-off valve, good for lots of blowing-off the drag strip if your cat somehow falls off on the way to the drag strip.
3. Turbonetics high-flow cast-iron exhaust header with T-3 bolt pattern at the turbine flange.
4. Tial competition-type wastegate, good—when fully open—for efficiently diverting massive quantities of exhaust around the turbine to control maximum boost without creeping as power goes wild.
5. Forced-performance high-flow, high-efficiency side-mount air-air intercooler, good for high airflow with low pressure drop.
6. Alamo-ported modified stock intake manifold with enlarged plenum, good for improved VE at high-rpm.
7. Alamo hand-ported throttle body assembly (everything helps).
8. Intake manifold modified to accept four additional 370-cc/min fuel injectors controlled by a Greddy Rebic IV additional injector controller unit—good to retain excellent stock drivability and emissions characteristics throughout startup, idle, low-speed, and cruise driving conditions (off-boost), while providing the high-end fuel needed to match the higher airflow capacities of the hot rod engine.
9. A one-way inline mechanical air-bleed device (technically a precisely controlled air leak) installed upstream of the

A Golf 1.8T with extensive external modifications.

stock manifold absolute pressure (MAP) sensor manifold pressure reference line—good for understating manifold pressure to the MAP sensor by 4 psi, thereby keeping the ECM blissfully unaware of the wild party going on in the intake manifold at high boost and preventing the ECM from initiating anti-horsepower countermeasures (pushing back the throttle).
10. Greddy Profec B boost controller, good to relieve the VW onboard computer of all boost-control responsibilities, enabling the driver to adjust boost anywhere between 0.65 bar (9.5-psi boost) on up to blowup.

GETTING FAST AND FURIOUS

How do you launch a FWD high-boost turbo mutant to extract the big performance numbers? Drive it like you're mad at it for any real performance; all the power's up near redline, right? In this case, no. Hotrod 1.8T torque exceeded the stock version's 150 lb-ft peak wheel torque across a broad swath of rpm from 3,000 through the stock 6,500 redline and beyond to 7,200

VW 20-valve engine, showing triple intake cam lobes. Note that the intake plenum has been amputated so a large intake chamber can be welded to the runners in an attempt to improve high-rpm air flow.

After the addition of lots of external bolt-on parts and some larger turbochargers, the car cranked out 335 rear-wheel horsepower on the Alamo Autosports Dynojet. With nitrous, the car later on managed more than 400 at the wheels.

The hot rod VW went through a succession of turbochargers as the owner became addicted to power increases.

VW Golf burning out with 335 rwhp.

rpm. Hot rod wheel torque was above 250 lb-ft from 4,000–6,000 rpm, reaching a peak nearly twice that of the stock Golf near 4,800 rpm.

A good limited slip differential was a necessity on the Golf 1.8T. Alamo Autosports installed a Peloquin billet LSD. Check. Good, soft, drag radial tires were essential to a decent launch. Check. (The project 1.8T ran 225/50/16 Nitto drag radials up front on custom alloy wheels for daily driving, 205/50/15 BFG drag radials on stock steelies for drag racing.) A clutch that will slip a bit without fading away completely in the heat when you ride it a bit was vital. Alamo installed a G60 flywheel and Clutchmasters Stage 1 Clutch G60 clutch.

DRIVING THE ALAMO GOLF

I jack with the seat until I like the driving position, floor the clutch, turn the key. The five-valve-per-cylinder 1.8 comes to life and settles quickly into a crisp idle. The engine's still being controlled by stock Motronic engine management algorithms, even if the MAP sensor does fib a bit to the computer under boost conditions. True, the PROM-based air/fuel and timing maps directing the Motronic system how to fuel this particular vehicle are bootlegged across the rpm range at positive manifold pressure for airflow numbers inconceivable on a stock Golf 1.8T.

Blip the throttle; transient response is nice. This engine likes the fuel, drinks down readily with the factory calibration. The Clutchmasters Stage 1 G60 feels light considering it's good for putting 400 horsepower to the road. I stab the throttle again for feel, and the engine responds smartly—just a tiny bit of that instant-on, instant-off feel you get when you twist the grip on a superbike. That's the Golf's 13-pound Alamo Autosports lightened and balanced flywheel, the lightweight Clutchmasters pressure plate and carbon disc setup, and the Unorthodox Racing lightweight underdrive pulleys.

I notch the shifter into gear and ease out the clutch and move rapidly through the darkened outskirts of Arlington. No traffic here, wider open now, OK to hammer it a bit, I figure. Did I mention this car has Alamo upgraded suspension (Koni coil-overs all around), tires, and wheels? OK, drop the clutch and push the Golf's five-speed slowly up through the gears. This is definitely not Grandma's Buick; subtle bumps are super-conducted directly through the seats in a way that lends a new meaning to the words *road feel*. But road feel through the steering wheel is also excellent, and the 17-inch tires feel like they're nailed to the asphalt with railroad spikes.

I urge the turbo Golf a little harder through the turns, seeing what it can do, feeling the tires grip the road, searching for any handling problems. No way: This thing is a control freak, German suspension at its best with good aftermarket upgrades, lightweight alloy block set down nice and low and tipped rearward, car's balanced beautifully, suspension tuned nicely, set on tall wide wheels with soft meaty tires.

Fifth gear, 20 miles per hour, plant the throttle firmly at wide open. I'm not sure how many-psi boost to claim for 3,000 rpm because the revs climb so fast. Max boost is easy to know, given the Greddy 60 millimeter digital 2-bar boost gauge with peak hold memory and matching Greddy air/fuel gauge. The tach streaks through 4,000, hell-bent for redline, the boost gauge maxed at 2.5 atmospheres absolute, and at this point the 1.8T's torque curve simply goes nuts, and the car is lunging forward like a set of planetary gears has locked up and someone is dumping nitrous oxide straight down the throttle body. The tach plunges through redline and buries itself deep in forbidden territory.

The hot rod 1.8T has already killed two turbos, a clutch, a stock differential, and a compressor-bypass valve on its way to glory, but this serial killer will surely kill a few unsuspecting Camaros or Mustangs at the drag wars or on the streets of Arlington, Texas.

Chapter 26
Project: Frank-M-Stein: M3 Turbo Cabriolet

Combining variable valve timing, several hundred cubic centimeter's worth of added bore and stroke with increased compression, intake and exhaust breathing tricks, appropriate engine management, super-duty parts from top to bottom, and a magnificently tuned suspension, BMW upgraded the 3-series coupe into the M3, one of the most exciting cars on earth—a no-compromise machine that could lick the likes of 300ZXs and Toyota Supra sports cars in all areas of performance and still carry four people to the 7-Eleven in comfort.

By contrast, the base 189-horse E36 325ic sold from 1991 to 2000 was a . . . nice car. Great for top-down days in the spring or fall when Dallas isn't hideously hot or uncomfortably cool—at the cost of a little additional weight over the 325i coupe that's needed to stiffen a flat chassis lacking the reinforcing triangulation of a steel roof. It's got the sex appeal of a genuine wind-in-your-face drop-top. It's a really nice car. It's just not an M3.

THE M3 SOLUTION

Project Frank-M-Stein began by testing the stock 325ic on the Alamo Autosports Dynojet chassis dyno. The 2.5-liter inline six delivered a maximum of just more than 150 lb-ft torque at 3,800 rpm and 151.4 rear-wheel horses at 6,000 rpm. Drivetrain and tire rolling resistance added up to a loss of roughly 21 percent from the advertised flywheel horsepower.

In Stage 1, Alamo techs installed a performance-calibration PROM and several enhancements designed to increase engine volumetric efficiency. The combination of B&B exhaust, RC Engineering big-bore throttle body, and custom high-flow cold-air intake was good for a torque increase between 4,000 to 6,500 rpm. Peak horsepower still occurred near 6,000 rpm, but the modifications delivered 20 additional wheel horsepower from 5,000 to 6,500 rpm. Such modifications open up the top half of the car's performance envelope.

But horsepower is addictive, and the car needed more midrange torque. In the second stage of Project Frank-M-Stein, Alamo lowered the engine's compression ratio with a thick steel head gasket and installed an Active Autowerke turbo kit. The result was nothing short of dramatic: a power boost of roughly 100 rear-wheel horsepower, a 66 percent increase.

In the third major stage of the project, Alamo acquired the parts to convert the car into a 1998 BMW M3 and installed all applicable items on the 325ic: 3.2-liter motor, transmission, driveshaft, limited slip differential, front and rear suspension components, and brake calipers. These items differed from stock 325ic equipment in the following way: Total displacement increased from 2,494 cubic centimeters to 3.2 liters, a gain of almost 30 percent. Thirty percent increase in displacement translated to massively increased low-end torque and improved power. It also translated to more high-energy exhaust gases to drive a turbocharger, which translated to increased responsiveness and reduced turbo lag.

While the 325ic's 2.5L powerplant made serious boost in the 3,500–3,700 range, the larger M3 engine produced significant turbo spooling at 2,500 rpm. Like all other M3 drivetrain components, the transmission had been strengthened to handle the increased torque and power of the M motor: The M3 driveshaft was beefier. The M3 limited slip differential—critical to getting to power to the ground without converting the tires directly from rubber to smoke—was stronger. Tuned suspension components from the M3 included the lower front A-arms, which were stiffened to handle the non-negligible possibility of an M3 driver initiating an exhaustive search for the car's limits. M3 brakes improved stopping distances, and fade was reduced

Alamo "M3 Cab" in action.

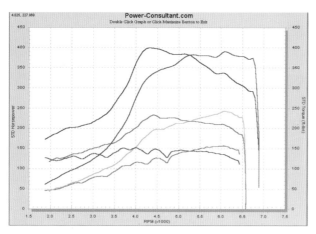

The bottom line: Stock 325-ci, turbo 325-ci, and turbo M3 dyno power. The combination of big-cube M3 torque and a big turbo quadrupled low-end and nearly tripled peak torque, pumping up peak horsepower from 160 to 385-plus at the wheels.

To cool down charge temperatures, Alamo added a giant air-air intercooler in front of the radiator and A/C condenser.

dramatically. Alamo substituted a set of drilled aftermarket brake rotors to further improve stopping performance.

Alamo designed a custom 3-inch turbo downpipe to remove exhaust gases from the turbine section of the turbocharger to reduce backpressure and further improve power and installed underdrive pulleys on the accessory-drive system to reduce accessory drive frictional losses. The car was set up to run 11–12-psi turbo boost around town on 93-octane Texas pump gas, and more on race gas. The cat was modified for easy removal if someone felt the need to go drag racing.

At this point, a super-duty clutch and lightweight flywheel seemed like a right-on idea.

MODIFYING MOTRONIC

Hot rodders with Porsches, BMWs, Volvos, and other vehicles with Bosch Motronic EFI have had several options when it comes to recalibrating fuel delivery and spark timing for turbo and blower conversions. The simplest is to use a variable-rate-of-gain (VRG) fuel pressure regulator to increase fuel pressure and fuel flow per injector squirt without modifying the EMS in any other way. This strategy can be effective up to about 7 psi, at which point you're running a lot of fuel pressure. Running really high pressures will eventually cause electronic ports injectors to malfunction, for example, refusing to close properly against the pressure, although many Bosch injectors have been run at 90 to 100 or more psi with no troubles. In any case, many BMW fuel pumps were equipped with bypass valves that kick in at around 80 psi to prevent over-pressurization. At the 4- to 7-psi boost range of a VRG fueling strategy, the stock knock sensor can usually retard timing quickly enough at the onset of trace detonation to protect the engine, negating the requirement to programmatically provide boost timing retard.

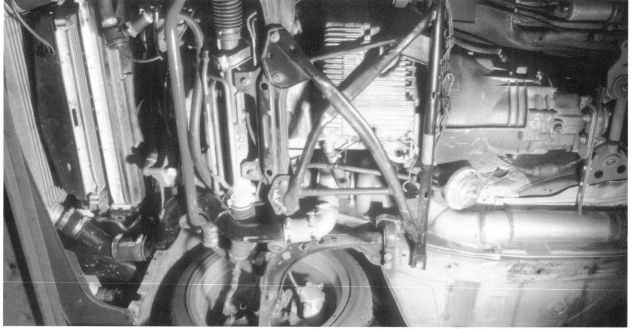

TurboM3 cab turbo plumbing connects the intercooler to the turbocharger in a route that takes it above the front anti-roll bar, under the steering rack, and beneath torque stays.

For higher levels of boost, many Euro-tuners have installed aftermarket engine management systems—Accel/DFI, Haltech, Electromotive, Motec, and others—that replace the stock ECM with one that is entirely programmable via laptop computer, building custom air/fuel and timing tables for any size injectors, no knock sensor required.

However, the increasing sophistication of late-model injection systems, and the integration of cruise control, transmission controls, or other functionality into the main onboard computer made the aftermarket solution increasingly problematic for people who want to retain all stock functionality. Yes, there are aftermarket systems capable of managing many auxiliary tasks only indirectly related to engine fuel and spark, but sophisticated and powerful aftermarket systems are expensive, and the programming effort can be difficult and expensive. What's more aftermarket programmable engine management systems are illegal for highway use in the U.S. on emissions-controlled vehicles. Tuners and enthusiasts have increasingly embraced a concept that could be summarized as, "Why throw the baby out with the bathwater?" Why junk the whole engine management system if all you need is some minor reprogramming of timing and injection pulse width in certain wide-open-throttle situations?

Tuners with Motronic engine management controls have several options when it comes to recalibration. Autothority and others have offered custom chips or PROM recalibrations for certain specific classes of engine modifications on frequently hot rodded engines, such as the Porsche 911 and some BMWs. Some late-model BMWs with OBD-II engine management can be reflashed with a new calibration if you have the tools and know-how (though BMW has fought back against owners who abused and damaged their engine with hot rod parts and then pulled the parts tried to get the engine repaired under warranty). Unfortunately, unless you have the Motronic calibration software and scan-tool interface yourself, you're here, with your car, and the custom chip programmer is not, so you may not get an optimal calibration for your specific engine—at least not without several iterations of custom chips followed by diagnostic testing and evaluation.

Since a stock M3 had totally different wiring from the 325i system, Alamo Autosports retained the stock 325ic ECM on Project Frank-M-Stein to control the new 3.2-liter M3 engine, but recalibrated the ECU in several iterations using files downloaded from Active Autowerke into the shop PROM-burner. The trick was, the EMS still thought it was running a 325 motor. Alamo's own Dynojet was an essential tool in optimizing the custom computer calibration. In the end, it would turn out that the M3 fuel injectors were a bottleneck, with the 440-cc/min injectors pushing 100 percent duty cycle.

TURBO M3

With the M3 engine and other equipment in place, Alamo reinstalled the turbo system that had recently been force-feeding just 2.5 liters of BMW inline-six. The turbo was a Mitsubishi TD06 with a 12-centimeter exhaust housing mated to a 3-inch custom downpipe with external wastegate. A complete package of external equipment was installed to deal with the M power: An Alamo Autosports custom cold-air intake with big mass airflow (MAF) meter and an RC Engineering high-flow throttle body eliminated the intake system as an airflow bottleneck. An Active Autowerke lightweight aluminum flywheel and high-performance racing clutch set were installed to improve engine responsiveness

Engine compartment stuffed full of "M-Power"—and turbo boost!

on sudden application of wide-open throttle and prevent clutch slip in a situation where you've got double the horsepower of the stock M3. Alamo added a stainless steel exhaust system to improve turbo spool-up response and improve peak power. Other parts included Eiback Pro-kit springs, front and rear anti-roll bars, and a front stress bar to increase chassis stiffness.

All forced-induction systems with more than 4-psi boost should ideally have intercooling to lower compressed charge air temperature to within 20 degrees Fahrenheit of ambient temperature to control combustion temperatures and prevent knock. This is particularly important on high-compression engines like the M3 with its 10.5:1 squeeze, though Alamo had installed a thicker steel head gasket to lower compression to 8.8:1. Alamo's M3 turbo system used a custom intercooler mounted in front of the radiator and air conditioning condenser, requiring removal of the front pusher radiator fan. This could mandate a rear fan upgrade for some climates and driving styles, but the stock rear fan seemed to get the job done in 95-plus-degree summer weather in Dallas. The intercooler was designed to handle the thermal loading of boost pressures as high as 15–20 psi (1.0–1.36 bar).

RESULT

The Alamo M3 Turbo-Cab was so rock-stable at three-digit speeds that swashbuckling through twisting turns felt easy, and mediocre drivers felt like great drivers. With Project Frank-M-Stein, when you wanted to go fast, you asked the car gently and it turned into a monster. Boost began at 2,500 rpm and reached 10 psi by 4,000 rpm. As the engine climbed to redline, you'd have almost 400 rear wheel horses that make going very fast look very easy—nearly 500 crankshaft horsepower. In race trim, the powerplant produces as much as 430 rear-wheel horsepower at boost levels over 15 psi. Project Frank-M-Stein was a testament to the truism that you can't be too rich, and you can't be too thin, and you can't have too much horsepower.

Appendix

Fuel Injector Specifications							
Manufacturer/ID	cc/min	lb/hr	Calculated HP per injector	kPa Test Pressure	Ohms	Vehicle Application	Engine Application
Bosch 0 280 150 208	133	13.0	26.6	300		BMW	323
Bosch 0 280 150 716	134	13.1	26.8	300			
Nippon Denso (light green)	145	14.2	29.0	255	2.4	Toyota	4KE
Nippon Denso (green)	145	14.2	29.0	255	2.4	Toyota	1GE
Bosch 0 280 150 211	146	14.3	29.2	300			
Lucas 5206003	147	14.4	29.4	300			Starlet
Lucas 5207007	147	14.4	29.4	270		Ford	1.6L
Bosch 0 280 150 715	149	14.6	29.8	300			
Nippon Denso (red/dark blue)	155	15.2	31.0	290	13.8	Toyota	
Nippon Denso (violet)	155	15.2	31.0	290	13.8	Toyota	3EE 2EE
Nippon Denso (sky-blue)	155	15.2	31.0	290	13.8	Toyota	1GFE
Nippon Denso (violet)	155	15.2	31.0	290	13.8	Toyota	4AFE
Lucas 5207003	164	16.1	32.8	300		Buick	
Lucas 5208006	164	16.1	32.8	250		Renault	
Bosch 0 280 150 704	170	16.7	34.0	300			
Bosch 0 280 150 209	176	17.3	35.2	300		Volvo	B200, B230
Nippon Denso (light green)	176	17.3	35.2	290	13.8	Toyota	4AFE
Nippon Denso (grey)	176	17.3	35.2	290	13.8	Toyota	4AFE
Bosch 0 280 150 121	178	17.5	35.6	300			
Nippon Denso (dark grey)	182	17.8	36.4	255	2	Toyota	4AGE
Nippon Denso (grey)	182	17.8	36.4	255	2.4	Toyota	4ME, 5ME, 5MGE
Bosch 0 280 150 100	185	18.1	37.0	300			
Bosch 0 280 150 114	185	18.1	37.0	300			
Bosch 0 280 150 116	185	18.1	37.0	300			
Bosch 0 280 150 203	185	18.1	37.0	300			
Bosch 0 280 50222	188	18.4	37.6	300		1985-6 GM	TPI 305 V8
AC 5235047	188	18.4	37.6	300		1985 GM	TPI 305 V8
AC 5235301	188	18.4	37.6	300		1987-8 GM	TPI 305 V8
AC 5235434	188	18.4	37.6	300		1989 GM	TPI 305 V8
AC 5235435	188	18.4	37.6	300		1989 GM	TPI 305 V8
Bosch 0 280 150 125	188	18.4	37.6	300			
Lucas 5202001	188	18.4	37.6	250		914	1.8L
Lucas 5204001	188	18.4	37.6	250		Fiat	
Lucas 5206002	188	18.4	37.6	250		Toyota	
Lucas 5207002	188	18.4	37.6	250		Chev	5.0L
Lucas 5208001	188	18.4	37.6	250		Nissan	280ZX
Lucas 5208003	188	18.4	37.6	250		Alfa	

Manufacturer/ID	cc/min	lb/hr	Calculated HP per injector	kPa Test Pressure	Ohms	Vehicle Application	Engine Application
Lucas 5208007	188	18.4	37.6	250		BMW	325E
Bosch 0 280 150 614	189	18.5	37.8	300			
Nippon Denso (dark grey)	200	19.6	40.0	290	1.7	Toyota	3SFE
Nippon Denso (beige)	200	19.6	40.0	290	1.7	Toyota	4YE
Nippon Denso (orange)	200	19.6	40.0	290	1.7	Toyota	22RE
Nippon Denso (brown)	200	19.6	40.0	290	1.7	Toyota	3VZE
Nippon Denso (pink)	200	19.6	40.0	290	2.7	Toyota	4AGE
Nippon Denso (dark blue)	200	19.6	40.0	290	13.8	Toyota	3SFE
Nippon Denso (orange/ blue)	200	19.6	40.0	290	13.8	Toyota	
Nippon Denso (brown)	200	19.6	40.0	290	13.8	Toyota	3VZFE
Nippon Denso (red)	200	19.6	40.0	290	13.8	Toyota	2VZFE
Lucas 5207013	201	19.7	40.2	270		Jeep	4.0L
Nippon Denso (blue)	210	20.6	42.0	255	2.4	Toyota	4AGE
Nippon Denso (sky blue)	213	20.9	42.6	290	13.8	Toyota	3FE
Nippon Denso (beige)	213	20.9	42.6	290	13.8	Toyota	4AGE
Nippon Denso (yellow)	213	20.9	42.6	290	13.8	Toyota	5SFE
Bosch 0 280 150 216	214	21.0	42.8			Buick	
Bosch 0 280 150 157	214	21.0	42.8	250		Jaguar	4.2L
Bosch 0 280 150 706	214	21.0	42.8	250			
Bosch 0 280 150 712	214	21.0	42.8	250		Saab	2.31 Turbo
Bosch 0 280 150 762	214	21.0	42.8	300		Volvo	B230F
AC 5235211	218	21.4	43.6	300		1986 GM	TPI 350 V8
AC 5235302	218	21.4	43.6	300		1987-8 GM	TPI 350 V8
AC 5235436	218	21.4	43.6	300		1989 GM	TPI 350 V8
AC 5235437	218	21.4	43.6	300		1989 GM	TPI 350 V8
Lucas 5207011	218	21.4	43.6	300		Chev	5.7L
Bosch 0 280 150 A9152	230	22.5	46.0	?		Alfa	Turbo
Bosch 0 280 150 201	236	23.1	47.2	300			
Lucas 5208004	237	23.1	47.2	250		Ford	
Lucas 5208005	237	23.1	47.2	250		Chrysler	BMW
Bosch 0 280 150 151	240	23.5	48.0			BMW	633
Nippon Denso(yellow/orange)	250	24.5	50.0	255	1.7	Toyota	
Nippon Denso (green)	250	24.5	50.0	290	13.8	Toyota	4AGE
Nippon Denso (violet)	250	24.5	50.0	290	13.8	Toyota	4AGE
Nippon Denso (brown)	250	24.5	50.0	255	13.8	Toyota	3SGE
Nippon Denso (violet)	251	24.5	50.2	290	13.8	Toyota	1UZFE
Bosch 0 280 150 001	265	26.0	53.0	300			
Bosch 0 280 150 002	265	26.0	53.0	300			
Bosch 0 280 150 009	265	26.0	53.0	300			
Bosch 0 280 150 218	275	27.0	55.0	300		Buick	

Manufacturer/ID	cc/min	lb/hr	Calculated HP per injector	kPa Test Pressure	Ohms	Vehicle Application	Engine Application
Nippon Denso (light green)	282	27.6	56.4	290	13.8	Toyota	2RZE
Nippon Denso (violet)	282	27.6	56.4	290	13.8	Toyota	2TZFE
Bosch 0 280 150 802	284	27.8	56.8	300		Volvo, Renault	B200Turbo
Nippon Denso (yellow)	295	28.9	59.0	255	2.7	Toyota	7MGE
Nippon Denso (pink)	295	28.9	59.0	255	1.6	Toyota	22RTE
Nippon Denso (green)	295	28.9	59.0	255	13.8	Toyota	3SGE
Bosch 0 280 150 811	298	29.2	59.6	350		Porsche	944 Turbo
Bosch 0 280 150 200	300	29.4	60.0	300		BMW	
Bosch 0 280 150 335	300	29.4	60.0	300		Volvo	B230 Turbo
Bosch 0 280 150 945	300	29.4	60.0			Ford Motorsport	
Nippon Denso (pink)	315	30.9	63.0	290	13.8	Toyota	3SGE
Nippon Denso (light green)	315	30.9	63.0	290	13.8	Toyota	7MGE
Bosch 0 280 150 804	337	33.0	67.4	300		Peugot	505 Turbo
Bosch 0 280 150 402	338	33.1	67.6	300		Ford	
Lucas 5207009	339	33.2	28.88				
Bosch 0 280 150 951	346	33.9	69.2	300		Porsche	
Bosch 0 280 155 009	346	33.9	69.2	300		Saab Turbo	
Nippon Denso (red/ orange)	346	33.9	73.0	255	2.9	Toyota	
Bosch 0 280 150 967	346	34.0					
Bosch 0 280 150 003	380	37.3	76.0	300			
Bosch 0 280 150 015	380	37.3	76.0	300			
Bosch 0 280 150 024	380	37.3	76.0	300		Volvo	B30E
Bosch 0 280 150 026	380	37.3	76.0	300			
Bosch 0 280 150 036	380	37.3	76.0	300		MB	4.51
Bosch 0 280 150 043	380	37.3	76.0	300		BMW	
Bosch 0 280 150 814	384	37.6	76.8	300			
Bosch 0 280 150 834	397	38.9	79.4	300			
Bosch 0 280 150 835	397	38.9	79.4	300		Chrysler	
Lucas 5207008	413	40.1	82.6				
Nippon Denso (black)	430	42.2	86.0	255	2.9	Toyota	7MGTE,3SGTE
Lucas 5208009	431	42.3	86.2				
Bosch R 280 410 144	434	42.5	86.8	300		Bosch R Sport	
Bosch 0 280 150 400	437	42.8	87.4	300		Ford	4.51
Bosch 0 280 150 401	437	42.8	87.4	300		Ford	
Bosch 0 280 150 041	480	47.1	96.0	300		MB	6.91
Bosch 0 280 150 403	503	49.3	100.6	300	0.5	Ford	
Lucas 5107010	530	52.0	106.1				

Index

993 Motronic ECU, 106

Accel DFI Gen 7 system, 130, 143, 179
Acceleration enrichment, 34, 218–219
Accelerator pedal position sensors (PPS), 40
Accelerometer performance meters, 223
Additional injector controller (AIC), 215–216
Aftermarket engine management system sources, 131
Aftermarket engine management systems, 129–146
Air cleaners, 78, 90
Air delivery, 69–71
Air meters, 76–77, 79
Air pressure, 192
Airflow bottlenecks, 76–81
Air/fuel ratios, 135–136, 180–181, 189–190, 194–195, 203, 213–215, 228–229
Air-metering sensors, 38
Alamo Autosports, 207, 282, 283, 284, 289, 292, 295, 298, 310, 311, 312, 314, 323, 324, 325, 327
APEXi Super Airflow Converter (SAFC), 121
Arithmetic-logic unit (ALU), 27
Auxiliary computer and interceptor sources, 128
Auxiliary injector controllers (AIC), 123

Barometric absolute pressure (BAP), 47
Bendix, 4, 57, 112
Bernoulli effect, 14, 21, 174
BMW M3, 148, 262, 325, 325–327
Boost controllers, 71–72, 86, 168
Bosch DI-Motronic fuel injection, 5
Bosch EMS, 112–113
Bosch engine management systems, 112–114
Bosch KE-Jetronic systems, 21, 112
Bosch K-Jetronic systems, 6, 21, 112, 159
Bosch L-Jetronic system, 161
Bosch L-Jetronic systems, 20, 45, 50, 104, 112, 161, 162, 279, 300, 301, 302, 303, 306, 307
Bosch pintle-type electronic fuel injector, 17, 57–58
Bosch rail components, 98

Cadillac, 6, 21, 60, 104, 108, 157, 272
Calibration, 100–101, 102–114, 136–137, 179–180, 184–186, 196–197, 200–203, 204–213
California Air Resources Board (CARB), 12, 124, 150, 241, 242, 243, 244, 253, 254, 257
Cam controls, 72, 80
Cam sensors, 17, 126, 167
Camaro SS, 256–260
Camaro-Firebird, 109, 155
Carabine ECU, 31
Carburetors, 5, 159–164, 184
Carmack, John, 83
Catalytic converters, 254
CB1 Cobra replica, 160
Chevrolet models, 6, 52, 109, 147, 155–156, 159, 194, 270, 272, 273
Chip installation, 107, 109, 110
CKP sensors, 39
Clean Air Act (1990), 10, 242–243, 244

Code access keys, 224
Cold-air intakes, 78
Cold-start enrichment, 33–34, 90, 217–218
Collins, Russ, 58, 195
Combustion chambers, 193–194
Combustion pressure sensors, 48
Compression ratios, 91
Control system bottlenecks, 83–88
Controller area network (CAN), 28, 30, 35, 74, 105–106, 107, 112, 143, 145, 146, 148, 149, 152, 155, 178, 227, 243, 245–246, 247, 248, 249–253, 262
Coolant temperature sensor (CTS), 232–233
Cooling system, 89
Corvettes, 6, 109, 155–156, 222
Crank sensors, 17, 67, 120, 167, 168, 225, 234, 306
Custom Porsche 968 turbo conversion, 78
Cylinder heads, 80

Data logging, 137
Design considerations, 88–91
Diagnostic algorithms, 224–225
Dial-back timing lights, 225
Diesel calibration, 100–101
Digital microprocessor, 26, 118, 121, 276
Digital multimeters, 225, 228, 229–230
Displacement, 80
Dodge Challenger, 276–281
Dual-plane manifolds, 171
Dual-resonance manifolds, 172
Dynamometers, 225–226
Dynojet, 185, 198, 207, 211, 213, 219, 225–226, 263, 267, 271, 274, 282–283, 285, 289, 293, 296, 297, 299, 307, 310, 311, 312, 314, 317, 318, 321, 323, 325, 327

ECU output modification devices, 118
ECU recalibration devices, 117–118
Edelbrock 3500, 15
EEC-IV, 36, 112–113
Electrical interference, 166
Electrical wiring installation, 165–166
Electrically erasable programmable read-only memory (EEPROM), 26–27, 30, 35, 105, 107, 109
Electrojector fuel injector, 4, 57, 112
Electronic control module (ECM), 178–179
Electronic control unit (ECU), 4, 28–31, 32, 37, 38–39, 45, 59, 62–63, 64, 68, 69–71, 74, 83–84, 86, 102, 104–105, 113–114, 115–116, 117–123, 124–125, 131, 132–133, 137, 138, 148, 149, 154, 155–156, 161, 162, 164, 165–166, 168, 170, 179, 180, 196–197, 200–201, 222, 223, 229–230
40, 40–41
Electronic diesel control (EDC), 97, 99, 100–101
Electronic diesel engines, 92–101
Electronic fuel injection (EFI), 4–8, 15–20, 21, 23–24, 28–31, 35, 56–65, 69–71, 75–91, 112, 116, 117–123, 133, 135–137, 138, 151–154, 155–156, 159, 161, 164, 169
Electronic fuel injectors, 56–63
Electronic stethoscopes, 226
Electronic throttle, 69–71

Emissions-control devices, 240–241, 254–255
EMS, 29–30, 32, 35, 36, 62, 64, 66
Engine control module (ECM), 166–167, 170, 222
Engine cycles, 21–23
Engine load sensors, 48
Engine swapping, 147–158, 159, 161, 242
Equations, 34–35
Exhaust, 80
Exhaust gas analyzers, 228–229
Exhaust gas sensors, 40–41
Exhaust gas temperature (EGT), 46–47, 99, 100–101, 184, 193, 215, 221, 226
Exhaust systems, 172–173
Extended ID, 247–248

Federal Test Procedure (FTP), 12, 150, 241, 242
Flame speed, 187–188
Ford, 52, 112–113, 239
Ford 460, 80, 159
Ford Focus, 135
Ford injectors, 159, 161
Frank-M-Stein, 325–327
Fuel bottlenecks, 81–83, 88
Fuel injectors, 56–63, 170
Fuel management units (FMU), 62, 83, 123
Fuel maps, 170, 194, 217
Fuel pressure detection, 135
Fuel pressure gauges, 226
Fuel pressure regulators, 82–83
Fuel pumps, 81–82
Fuel rail pressure (FRP), 47–48
Fuel requirements, 186–187

Gasoline-direct injection (G-DI), 262–263
General Motors, 52, 108–112, 155–156, 159, 161, 222, 239
Granularity, 134–135

Hacking software, 103–108
Hall effect, 38, 39, 40, 113, 231, 275
HKS, 77, 118, 121, 128, 143, 289, 292, 299
Hollow runners, 171
Honda CRX, 282–293
Honda Turbo del Sol, 294–299
Hondata, 294–299

Idle air control (AIC), 70, 71, 110, 180, 214, 218, 220, 239, 291, 298, 304
Idle speed control, 220
Ignition systems, 65–69, 167
Ignition tools, 226–227
Individual-cylinder direct injection, 8–9, 220
Individual-cylinder engine management, 220–221
Individual-port electronic fuel injection, 7–8
Individual-runner manifolds, 172
Information delivery, 74
Injector capacity, 81
Injector flow rate calculations, 60–61, 65
Injector tester, 227
Inline fuel pumps, 21, 61, 281, 285, 303
Input/output, 137–138, 247
Intake air temperature sensors (IAT), 45–46, 90, 165, 196, 217, 290

Intake manifolds, 16, 56–57, 63–64, 78–80, 164, 171–177
Intake port taper, 174
Intake ram pipes, 176
Intake ram tubes, 78
Intake runners, 174
Interceptors, 115–128, 123–128. <I>See also<m> piggybacks

Jaguars, 159, 161, 270–275, 300–309, 300–310
Japanese engines, 113–114

Karman-Vortex airflow sensors (K-V), 53
Knock controllers, 69
Knock sensors, 54–55, 84, 238
Kurzweil, Ray, 181

Laptops, 10, 12, 32, 35, 70, 74, 93, 103, 104, 105, 123, 133, 169, 179, 181, 224, 227–228, 250, 292, 295. <I>See also<m> hacking software
Lean best torque (LBT), 22, 46, 47, 117, 180, 193, 194, 213, 287, 292, 308
Lexus IS-F, 262–269
Limp-home strategies, 85–86
Lotus Europa, 158

Manifold air temperature (MAT), 230
Manifold pressure sensors (MAP), 49–50, 62, 77, 85, 86, 109, 120–121, 126, 133, 138, 149, 154, 156, 167, 168, 198, 203, 205, 206, 214, 228, 230–231, 237
Mass airflow sensors (MAF), 20–21, 31, 51–53, 76–77, 80–81, 83–84, 85, 86, 109, 110, 111, 120–121, 124, 126, 138, 154, 156, 203, 206, 213–214, 230, 238
Mazda RX7, 143, 176
Mechanical fuel injection, 4, 5–6, 112
Mitsubishi 3000GT VR4, 107
Mitsubishi ECM, 108, 110
Motec M800, 26
Motorola 6833x, 30, 37
Motorola 8061, 35
Motorola 68000, 30, 110–111
Motorola MC3484, 30
Motorola MPC500/5500, 25
Motorola PowerPC, 30, 112
MSD fuel pressure regulator, 18

Network management, 248
Network security, 248–249
Nitrous oxide injection, 73–74, 138, 168–169, 183, 284–288
Norwood, Bob, 46, 47, 83, 164, 170, 186, 194, 195, 214, 217, 262, 265, 267, 269, 270–271, 272, 274–275, 308–309, 314
Norwood Autocraft, 13, 162, 165, 266, 268, 272, 273, 274, 293, 310

Octane requirements, 192–193
OEM engine management systems, 30, 35, 36, 39, 44, 108–112, 238, 242, 243
Oil temperature sensors, 46
Onboard Diagnostics (OBD-I), 110, 111, 113, 233, 242, 243
Onboard Diagnostics (OBD-II), 9–12, 36, 41, 81, 97, 103, 104, 105–107, 108, 110, 112, 113, 114, 117, 120, 122, 185, 224, 227, 242–245, 246
Onboard Diagnostics (OBD-III), 114, 253–254

Oscilloscope, 227
Overboosting, 86, 96–97, 321–324
Oxygen sensors, 40–44, 167–168, 198–199, 202, 228, 229–230, 232

PDAs, 224
Perfect Power SMT8, 125, 128
Personal computers. <I>See<m> laptops
Piggybacks, 116, 117, 126–128
Plenum volume, 174–175
Pontiac models, 109
Porsche, 72, 73, 78, 85, 106, 112, 159, 301, 327
Port fuel injection, 57, 60, 63–64, 161, 164, 218, 220, 279–280
Position sensors, 38–39
Power draw, 166
Powerhaus 968 turbo, 85
Powertrain control module (PCM), 222
Pressure sensors, 47–55
Programmable engine management systems, 129–146, 163, 169, 178–179
Programmable read-only memory (PROM), 7, 9, 10, 13, 25–28, 32, 35–37, 84, 97, 99, 103–108, 109, 111, 112, 113, 117, 118, 154, 156, 161, 180, 226
Programmed fuel computer, 118
PROM tools, 227
Propane injection, 93, 96
Pulse width, 180–181, 194, 195–196

Rail components, 98
Random-access memory (RAM), 26, 28, 105, 227, 251
Reflashing, 258–260
Remote function actuation (RFA), 249
Resolution, 134–135
Resonation effects, 173–174
Rich best torque (RBT), 180
ROMeditor, 297–299
Running problems, 235–236

Scan tools, 227–228
Self-learning ECMs, 124–125, 128
Sensor-manipulation devices, 119–122
Sensors, installing, 167–168
Sequential injection, 30, 39, 132, 144, 145, 146, 167, 196, 213, 220, 221, 306
Sequential port injection of fuel (SPIF), 18–20, 21
Service manuals, 228
Services, 246–247
Shelby, Carroll, 160
Simulation, 252–253
Single overhead cam (SOHC), 107, 186, 282, 290, 294, 295, 299
Single-plane manifolds, 171–172
Spark advance, 188–189, 216–217
Spark timing, 88
Spark tools, 226–227
Spark trim, 220
Spark-ignition, diesel vs., 94–96
Specialty Equipment Marketing Association (SEMA), 243–244
Speed-density systems, 20–21, 31, 45, 46, 49, 52, 62, 77, 80, 81, 90, 102, 109, 121, 144, 149, 151, 154, 156, 164, 168, 189, 199, 200, 254
Spoofing, 252–253

Starting problems, 234–235
Startup maps, 194
Supercharging, 256–260
Superpumper-II, 123, 128

Tampering, 244
Techtom ROMboard (daughterboard), 109–110, 118
Temperature control, 74
Temperature sensors, 44–45, 167, 190–192, 228, 230, 232–233
Therminator, 99
Throttle body, 76
Throttle body injection (TBI), 147–148, 155–156, 159, 162–163, 276–278
Throttle position sensors (TPS), 40, 48–49, 69–70, 167, 168, 177, 223, 228, 231–232
Timing maps, 170, 194, 217
Titania O$_2$ sensors, 43
Torque sensors, 53
Toyota 1MZ, 79, 148, 316, 319
Toyota MR2, 73, 79, 86, 105, 118, 143, 147, 148, 151, 169, 293, 309, 310–312, 315, 318
Toyota MR6, 79, 167, 195, 310–320
TPS sensors, 18
Transmission control, 74
Tull, Ivan, 305
Tuned port injection (TPI), 36–37, 109, 113, 147–148, 155–156
Tunnel-ram manifolds, 172
Turbo conversion, 51, 78, 80, 81, 83, 85, 93, 101, 133, 148, 166, 167, 197, 262, 265, 282, 287, 288, 289–290, 292, 294, 295, 301, 302, 311
Turbo M3, 327
Turbodiesels, 92–101
Twin-turbo 351 Ford, 160
Twin-turbo Ferrari F50, 83

Universal exhaust gas oxygen (UEGO) sensors, 41–43, 202
User interface, 12, 31, 35, 74, 105, 107, 108, 111, 125, 133, 169, 179, 215, 224

Vacuum/boost source, 168
Vacuum/pressure pump, 228
Valve timing, 89–90
Vane airflow sensor (VAF). <I>See<m> velocity air meters (VAF)
Vane pressure convertor (VPC), 77, 121
Variable intake systems, 73
Varioram, 79, 172, 173
Vehicle speed sensors (VSS), 55, 152, 154, 238–239
Velocity air meters (VAF), 50–51, 120–121, 121, 237–238
VIN, 252
Volumetric efficiency (VE), 31–33, 37, 80, 81, 83, 135–136, 180–181, 182–183, 186–187, 199–213, 217
VOM meters, 228
Vortech blower, 77
VW Golf, 321–324

Water injection, 74
Western, Graham, 220–221
Wiring, 138, 165–166, 228

Yingling, Brice, 297, 314, 317–318

Notes

The Best Tools for the Job

High-Performance Handling for Street or Track
by Don Alexander
Paperback, 144 pages
149834 • 978-0760339947

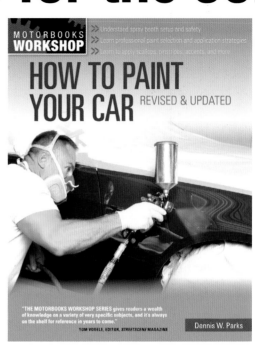

How to Paint Your Car: Revised & Updated
by Dennis Parks
Paperback, 192 pages
200273 • 978-0760343883

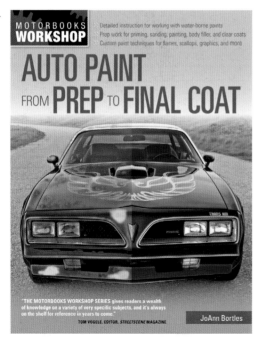

Auto Paint from Prep to Final Coat
by JoAnn Bortles
Paperback, 320 pages
194800 • 978-0760342787

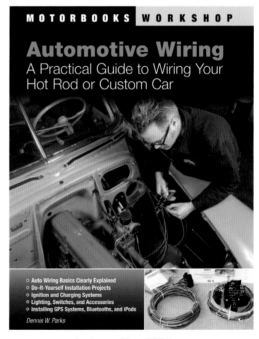

Automotive Wiring
by Dennis Parks
Paperback, 144 pages
149877 • 978-0760339923